ORGANIZATIONAL
BEHAVIOR

THIRD EDITION

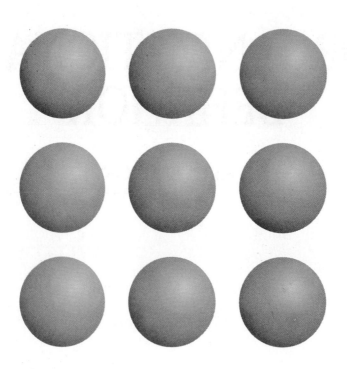

ORGANIZATIONAL BEHAVIOR

THIRD EDITION

ROBERT P. VECCHIO

Franklin D. Schurz Professor of Management
University of Notre Dame

The Dryden Press
Harcourt Brace College Publishers

Fort Worth   Philadelphia   San Diego   New York   Orlando   Austin   San Antonio
Toronto   Montreal   London   Sydney   Tokyo

Acquisitions Editor	Ruth Rominger
Developmental Editor	Dona Hightower
Project Editor	Matt Ball
Art Director	Jeanette Barber
Production Manager	Erin Gregg
Photo & Permissions Editor	Shirley Webster
Product Manager	Lisé Johnson
Marketing Assistant	Sam Stubblefield
Director of Editing, Design, and Production	Diane Southworth
Publisher	Elizabeth Widdicombe
Copy Editor	Carolyn Crabtree
Indexer	Leoni McVey
Composition	TSI Graphics
Text Type	10/12 Sabon

Requests for permission to make copies of any part of the work should be mailed to: Permissions Department, Harcourt Brace & Company, 6277 Sea Harbor Drive, Orlando, FL 32887–6777.

Address for Editorial Correspondence
The Dryden Press, 301 Commerce Street, Suite 3700, Fort Worth, TX 76102

Address for Orders
The Dryden Press, 6277 Sea Harbor Drive, Orlando, FL 32887
1-800-782-4479, or 1-800-433-0001 (in Florida)

ISBN: 0-03-098917-5

Library of Congress Catalog Card Number: 94-68483

Printed in the United States of America

4 5 6 7 8 9 0 1 2 3 039 9 8 7 6 5 4 3 2 1

The Dryden Press
Harcourt Brace College Publishers

To Betty, Julie, and Mark

The Dryden Press Series in Management

Holley and Jennings
The Labor Relations Process
Fifth Edition

Jauch and Coltrin
The Managerial Experience: Cases and Exercises
Sixth Edition

Kindler and Ginsburg
Strategic and Interpersonal Skill Building

Kirkpatrick and Lewis
Effective Supervision: Preparing for the 21st Century

Kuehl and Lambing
Small Business: Planning and Management
Third Edition

Kuratko and Hodgetts
Entrepreneurship: A Contemporary Approach
Third Edition

Kuratko and Welsch
Entrepreneurial Strategy: Text and Cases

Lee
Introduction to Management Science
Second Edition

Lengnick-Hall, Cynthia, and Hartman
Experiencing Quality

Lewis
Io Enterprises Simulation

Long and Arnold
The Power of Environmental Partnerships

McMullen and Long
Developing New Ventures: The Entrepreneurial Option

Matsuura
International Business: A New Era

Montanari, Morgan, and Bracker
Strategic Management: A Choice Approach

Morgan
Managing for Success

Northcraft and Neale
Organizational Behavior: A Management Challenge
Second Edition

Penderghast
Entrepreneurial Simulation Program

Sandburg
Career Design Software

Shipley and Ruthstrom
Cases in Operations Management

Sower, Motwani, and Savoie
Classic Readings in Operations Management

Van Matre
Foundations of TQM: A Readings Book

Vecchio
Organizational Behavior
Third Edition

Walton
Corporate Encounters: Law, Ethics, and the Business Environment

Zikmund
Business Research Methods
Fourth Edition

The Harcourt Brace College Outline Series

Pentico
Management Science

Pierson
Introduction to Business Information Systems

Sigband
Business Communication

Preface

It has been said that "if all the students who fell asleep in their Organizational Behavior classes were laid end to end, they'd be a lot more comfortable." One of my goals in preparing this textbook has been to present the substance of the field of organizational behavior in a manner that conveys the liveliness of the social dynamics of the work setting and, thereby, combats student drowsiness. I have been excited by this field since my first encounter with a course in organizational behavior, more than a few years ago as a student. The topic fascinated me because I had held a number of different jobs up to that point in my life, and I could see the relevance and value of understanding the interpersonal dynamics that exist in the workplace. I began to read more about human behavior in organizations and ultimately came to teach courses in organizational behavior. In writing this book, I have attempted to share some of my interest and enthusiasm for the field by taking the research-related foundations of organizational behavior and making them understandable and accessible to the nonresearcher.

ORGANIZATION OF THE TEXT

In preparing the third edition, I sought to maintain a balanced treatment of theory, research, and practice while presenting both the classic and current "cutting edge" theories. Important organizational behavior topics are covered, along with elements of human resources management, organizational development, and cross-cultural issues. In addition, I devote several chapters to organizational theory.

In Part I, the text begins with a consideration of how the field may be defined and a look at how it came into existence (Chapter 1). Next, the student is provided with an introductory treatment of how to understand the research base of the field of organizational behavior (Chapter 2). The substantive, topic-related chapters (Chapters 3 through 20) are organized and arranged so that the material progresses in traditional fashion from a micro (individual) to a more macro (group and organizational) focus. The later chapters are grouped into four major sections, reflecting this progression: Part II, Individual Processes; Part III, Interpersonal Processes; Part IV, Work Group Processes; and Part V, Organizational Structure and Processes. Under the heading of Individual Processes (Chapters 3 and 4 in Part II), topics in perception, personality, attitudes, and job satisfaction are explored. Interpersonal Processes (Chapters 5 through 8 in Part III) includes treatments of learning, motivation, job design, and performance appraisal; while Work Group Processes (Chapters 9 through 15 in Part IV) covers power, leadership, decision making, group dynamics, conflict, and stress. The final section, Organizational Structure and Processes (Chapters 16 through 20 in Part V), examines issues in communication, organizational design, environmental and cultural forces, and organizational change and development.

NEW TO THE THIRD EDITION

While accommodating the suggestions of reviewers and users of the book, my goal for the third edition was to maintain the book's clear coverage of important classical and contemporary concepts in organizational behavior. Over 50 new terms have been added. The structure of the text has been modified to provide five major chapter groupings. Also, after each chapter grouping, two in-depth cases have been added. All box items and opening vignettes have been updated or revised to tie them more closely to the chapter discussions. Some of the major new features of this edition follow:

- Leadership is now discussed in two chapters. Chapter 10 considers individual, trait, and behavioral approaches, while Chapter 11 considers situational approaches. Also, new and emerging topics in leadership, such as the triarchic intelligence view and charismatic leadership, are discussed.

- Employee empowerment is given extensive coverage in Chapter 7, one of three chapters devoted to motivation (Chapters 5, 6, and 7).

- Emotion in the work setting is examined in sections devoted to the topics of negative affectivity, organizational commitment, job involvement, emotional labor, and employee jealousy and envy.

- Ethics in decision making and ethics training programs are explored, along with the Code of Ethical Conduct of the Academy of Management.

- Other topics new to the third edition include the Culture-Quality Movement (Chapter 1), qualitative research (Chapter 2), self-serving biases (Chapter 3), self-efficacy (Chapter 5), distributive justice and flow (Chapter 6), greenfield sites (Chapter 7), managing diversity and organizational citizenship behaviors (Chapter 8), the foot-in-the-door principle (Chapter 9), motivation-to-manage and leadership succession (Chapter 10), judgmental biases, social loafing, and expert systems (Chapter 12), negotiation (Chapter 14), strategic alliances and conglomerates (Chapter 18), dominant culture, subcultures, socialization, and strong culture (Chapter 19).

PEDAGOGY

This textbook includes a number of pedagogical features designed to enhance student learning and comprehension.

LEARNING OBJECTIVES   Eight to ten learning objectives at the beginning of each chapter focus the reader's attention on the major issues within the chapter.

OPENING VIGNETTES   Short stories based on real organizations at the beginning of each chapter give a true-to-life flavor to chapter topics.

BOXED ITEMS   OB Focus and An Inside Look boxed features help illustrate the applications of organizational behavior principles. They provide current examples drawn from a variety of real corporations and businesses, and they emphasize aspects of ethics, diversity, and international issues as they apply to the field of organizational behavior.

SUMMARIES   At the end of each chapter, a summary recaps chapter learning objectives and highlights critical points.

KEY TERMS   Each chapter contains a list of key terms for the student to use in sorting out and reviewing important concepts.

QUESTIONS FOR DISCUSSION   At the end of each chapter, interesting questions help stimulate application of concepts and foster greater understanding of the material.

CRITICAL INCIDENTS AND EXPERIENTIAL EXERCISES   Each chapter is followed by a Critical Incident, a short case for discussion that applies chapter concepts. An Experiential Exercise is also included for each chapter. These exercises are a combination of classic favorites and all-new exercises; some are designed for individual use and some for group participation.

VIDEO CASES   Closely tied to the text, these end-of-part cases relate chapter topics to the real world. The videos that accompany these cases feature the *Challenger* disaster and Quad Graphics, Inc.

GLOSSARY   A glossary containing definitions of key terms appears at the end of the book. Key terms are set in boldfaced type where they first appear in the text.

SUPPLEMENTS

A comprehensive set of supplements accompanies the third edition of *Organizational Behavior*.

INSTRUCTOR'S MANUAL   This manual includes extensive chapter outlines; class openers; answers to discussion questions; additional experiential exercises; additional readings lists; examples from the popular press to help illustrate lectures; answers to in-text Critical Incidents and Experiential Exercises; additional cases; transparency masters; and teaching notes for the transparency acetates. The *Instructor's Manual* was prepared by Susan Stites-Doe, State University of New York at Brockport and Melissa Waite, State University of New York at Buffalo.

TEST BANK   Thoroughly revised and accuracy-tested, the *Test Bank* contains over 2,500 items to help gauge student comprehension. Its unique combination of question types includes true/false, multiple-choice, essay, and mini-case questions. Also, each question is classified according to level of difficulty. The revised *Test Bank* was prepared by William Bommer, Indiana University and Robert Vecchio, University of Notre Dame.

COMPUTERIZED TEST BANK   A computerized version of the printed test bank is available for IBM compatible computers.

TRANSPARENCY ACETATES   Color transparency acetates of key figures and concepts used in teaching organizational behavior and teaching notes for them are available. Teaching notes are included in the *Instructor's Manual*.

VIDEO PACKAGE   Five Videos, closely tied to the text, feature real-world organizations and events, including NASA's *Challenger* disaster and Quad Graphics, Inc. The videos focus on such topics as decision making, corporate culture, leadership, motivation, and enhancing employee performance. Please contact your Dryden Press sales representative for further information.

ACKNOWLEDGMENTS

The current and past editions of this book benefited from the efforts of many people. I must say a very special "thank you" to the following reviewers who made numerous suggestions on how to revise and improve the content of each chapter: Royce L. Abrahamson, Southwest Texas State University; Gail A. Ball, University of Nevada–Las Vegas; Richard R. Camp, Eastern Michigan University; Robert Cummins, University of Houston at Clear Lake; Arthur Darrow, Bowling Green State University; Allison Davis-Blake, University of Texas at Austin; William Hendrix, Clemson University; John Hollenbeck, Michigan State University; Charles Holloman, Augusta College; Bruce Kemelgor, University of Louisville; Wesley King, Jr., Miami University; Edward Miles, Georgia State University; Kevin Mossholder, Louisiana State University; Brian Niehoff, Kansas State University; Peter P. Poole, Lehigh University; Elizabeth Ravlin, University of South Carolina; Mark Sharfman, Pennsylvania State University; Sim Sitkin, University of Texas at Austin; Mark Turbin, University of Wyoming; David Vollrath, Indiana University at South Bend; and John Wissler, California State University at Fresno.

I am also indebted to the professionals at The Dryden Press who aided in the book's development, production, and design: Ruth Rominger, Dona Hightower, and Matt Ball, Jeanette Barber, Erin Gregg, and Shirley Webster. I am also grateful for the continued support of Jacqueline Marnocha who helped to prepare the final manuscript, and my wife, Betty, who critiqued much of the writing. Without their support, suggestions, patience, and encouragement, this edition would certainly not have been published. A final note of appreciation goes to my children, Julie and Mark, who helped by sharpening pencils and, mostly, by continuing to stay away from "Daddy's big mess in the dining room."

Robert P. Vecchio
October 1994

About the Author

Robert P. Vecchio, Ph.D. (University of Illinois, Champaign-Urbana) is Franklin D. Schurz Professor of Management and former chairman of the Department of Management and Administrativ₋ ₀ciences at the University of Notre Dame. Since joining Notre Dame in 1976, he has taught undergraduate and graduate courses in organizational behavior and human resources management. Professor Vecchio is a frequent contributor to academic journals, such as the *Journal of Applied Psychology, Organizational Behavior and Human Decision Processes,* the *Academy of Management Journal,* and the *Academy of Management Review.* Dr. Vecchio has served as a member of the editorial review boards of the *Academy of Management Review,* the *Journal of Management,* the *Journal of Managerial Issues,* the *International Journal of Organizational Analysis,* and the *Employee Responsibilities and Rights Journal.* His current research interests include employee motivation, employee jealousy and envy, job satisfaction, and leadership.

Contents in Brief

Contents

Individual Processes   69

Interpersonal Processes 155

Group Processes   295

Introduction to Organizational Behavior

Management is the art of getting other people to do all the work.

— Anonymous

Organizational behavior is the science of predicting how employees will behave, and then explaining why they don't.

— A Manager

After studying this chapter, you should be able to:

1. *Define the purpose and nature of the field of organizational behavior.*

2. *Tell why organizational behavior is an important field of study for managers.*

3. *Distinguish organizational behavior from organizational theory, human resources management, and organizational development.*

4. *Cite several significant applications of behavioral principles that occurred before 1900.*

5. *Outline the basic principles of scientific management and discuss the shortcomings of this approach to dealing with worker behavior.*

6. *Relate the findings of the Hawthorne Studies to the development of the human relations approach.*

7. *Explain why believers in the contingency approach rarely give a simple answer to a seemingly simple question.*

8. *Describe the currently dominant perspectives in the field of organizational behavior.*

9. *Respond to critics who contend that most principles of organizational behavior are obvious and based on common sense.*

An Introduction to Organizational Behavior
Overview and Origins

BUILDING A BETTER ORGANIZATION

What is the best way to manage an organization? Someone is always ready with an answer. In the early part of this century, it was popular to think of running a business more as a science than an art. Some managers adopted the principles of Frederick Winslow Taylor, who popularized time-and-motion studies. These people used observation, experimentation, and specific reasoning plus quantitative analysis to make their businesses more productive. Many of these managers also found themselves bogged down in the paperwork of this so-called "scientific management."

Then the pendulum began to swing. The 1960s saw the rise of people-oriented management theories. For example, trainers proposed to teach managers sensitivity and self-awareness by bringing together a group of people with no leader or agenda and waiting to see what would happen.

As a new, young manager for Pillsbury, John Clemens attended a T-Group (or training group) session with about 20 colleagues. Clemens recalls that their trainer, a psychiatrist, told them to sit on the floor and to remove their ties, shoes, and name tags. Then someone turned out the lights. Says Clemens, "We began crawling on the floor in the dark when I bumped into our president. It was atrocious. We would have done better by ourselves, figuring out how to sell more brownie mix."

Other theorists have attempted to help companies make the most of their human resources. Some executives have become concerned that employees keep fit in order to perform their best. For example, PA Executive Search Group tells potential clients that managers who smoke cost their companies $4,000 a year in higher absenteeism and lower productivity. In the face of such numbers, it is no wonder that companies have tried instituting wellness programs that encourage employees to eat right, exercise, and quit smoking. The question is whether the companies stay with these programs until they get results. Robert G. Cox, PA Executive Search's president, estimates that a wellness program "probably has a two-to-three-year life cycle."

A currently popular approach to running a company is to focus on its "organizational culture," that is, the values, goals, rituals, and heroes that characterize the company's style. Allan A. Kennedy, author of *Corporate Cultures*, tells of the enthusiasm his ideas have generated. He delivered a talk on organizational cultures to the top executives of an industrial-service corporation. At the dinner following the talk, the company chairman exclaimed, "This culture stuff is great!" Turning to the company president, the chairman added, "I want a culture by Monday."

Scientific management, T-Groups, wellness programs, and organizational culture are only a few of the many ways people have tried to understand and improve the workings of organizations. Where does a manager begin to sort out all these ideas? Perhaps the best place is with an understanding of the general principles of organizational behavior. This chapter will introduce you to what organizational behavior is all about and how it can help managers be more effective.

Source: John A. Byrne, "Business Fads: What's In—And Out," *Business Week,* January 20, 1986, 52–55, 58, 60, 61.

HAT IS ORGANIZATIONAL BEHAVIOR?

f us have wondered why some people succeed and others fail in the world
k. Most of us have also marveled at how some people seem to possess a
omless well of enthusiasm for their work, while others regard their work
as something slightly better than torture. Although most of us often do nothing more than speculate on the factors that affect our work lives, behavioral
scientists have established a relatively new field of inquiry concerned with the
scientific study of the behavioral processes that occur in work settings, the
field of *organizational behavior*. The content of this field is quite broad. It encompasses such topics as employee attitudes, motivation, and performance, to
name a few. And it extends to larger organizational and societal factors, such
as the structure of organizations and environmental pressures, that influence
an individual's behavior and attitudes.

The field of organizational behavior borrows many concepts and methods
from the behavioral and social sciences, such as psychology, sociology, political science, and anthropology, because all are relevant to understanding people's behavior in organizational settings. Consequently, issues and topics
touching on many academic disciplines may become the subject of study in the
field of organizational behavior. Thus, in the course of this book, we will examine sociological topics, such as the importance of organizational structure;
psychological questions, such as the importance of personality factors in explaining employee behavior; anthropological concerns with the meaning and
influence of culture; and political science topics, such as the distribution and
use of power in an organization. In general, however, organizational behavior
draws most heavily from the field of psychology. In fact, many of the major
theorists in the field are psychologists (for example, Maslow, Herzberg, Hackman, Lawler, and Skinner).

WHY BOTHER? OR, THREE REASONS FOR STUDYING ORGANIZATIONAL BEHAVIOR

PRACTICAL APPLICATIONS

There are important practical benefits to understanding the principles of organizational behavior. For example, the development of a personal style of leadership can be guided by knowledge of the results of studies that have attempted to relate leadership style to situational requirements (Chapters 10 and
11). The choice of a problem-solving strategy (Chapter 12) or the selection
of an appropriate employee appraisal format (Chapter 8) can be guided by
an understanding of the results of studies in the associated topic areas. Especially in the area of performance enhancement (Chapters 5 to 7), benefits
can be gained by applying the knowledge that has been gathered in the field
of organizational behavior. Additionally, because the environment in which
organizations operate is increasing in complexity (Chapter 18), one must understand how to design effective organization structures (Chapter 17) and

how to relate to individuals from diverse, and often international, backgrounds (Chapter 19).

It is difficult to overstate the practical importance of being able to deal effectively with others in organizational settings. Attracting and developing talented individuals are two issues critically important to the survival and prosperity of an organization. Emphasis on the *human element* (instead of on technical, financial, and other tangible resources) often separates competing organizations when it comes to organizational performance. This occurs because all serious competitors in a given industry are likely to have attained nearly the same level of technical sophistication. Thus, other things being equal, organizations that have talented and dedicated employees are likely to be more effective. Furthermore, within a given industry, the variability on human dimensions across organizations is likely to be greater than the variability on technical dimensions. Consequently, we can argue that the element that is most important to an organization's welfare—and the one that may be most neglected because of its less tangible nature—is the behavioral element.

As an illustration of how crucial the human element is to organizational excellence, consider professional football teams. All have much the same equipment and facilities. For example, each team has a stadium, a staff of trainers, practice facilities, state-of-the-art equipment, and the like. In addition, each team has the same number of members and essentially the same structure. Therefore, what distinguishes one team from another in the eyes of sports enthusiasts and on the field is largely traceable to the human element: the talent of the players and coaches, the ability of coaches to develop their players' talents, and the ability of the coaches and players to motivate themselves to high levels of accomplishment.

A similar illustration can be made for the reputations of universities and colleges. Generally speaking, colleges that seek to have prestigious reputations have much the same facilities (for example, classrooms, dormitories, and attractive landscaping). However, those institutions having faculty members who possess strong reputations in their fields and students who are more competitively admitted have more solid reputations. The separation of institutions on the dimension of reputation is based largely on the human element.

PERSONAL GROWTH

The second reason for studying organizational behavior is the personal fulfillment we gain from understanding our fellow humans. Understanding others may also lead to greater self-knowledge and self-insight. Such personal growth is an aspect of education that is often cited as the greatest benefit of studying the liberal arts and sciences. Some may question the practical value of this feature in the business world. But it can, in fact, make a difference when it comes to advancing beyond an entry-level position. Entry-level hirings are based largely on technical competency, such as certification in a specialized area by a BBA, a CPA, or an MBA. Promotions, however, are often based on more than mere technical competency. They are often based on demonstrated abilities to understand and work effectively with superiors, peers, and subordinates. In short, an understanding of organizational behavior may not be a "union card" that helps you get your first job in any obvious way, but it will be invaluable to you once you have that first job and seek to distinguish yourself.

Students who are taking an introductory organizational behavior (OB) course should understand that the purpose of such a course is to provide a framework into which later personal organizational experiences can be integrated. The course material, therefore, forms a foundation for increasing the extent to which they can learn from experience. In short, *what* one learns in an OB course is not as critical as *how* the course prepares one to learn (and thereby to grow) in an organization. The material in an OB course is relevant to personal growth whether one works for a large, established corporation (such as a General Motors, an IBM, or a Du Pont) or a relatively small, fledgling organization. In other instances, innovations are made initially within organizations. Later, researchers develop and test explanations as to why the innovations are effective, and under what circumstances these innovations are likely to be particularly effective. A good illustration of how innovation preceded our theoretical understanding is given by "mutual goal-setting" that involves a supervisor and an individual subordinate (see Chapter 7).

As a field, organizational behavior is constantly opening new frontiers of knowledge. Most of the researchers in the field are young and recently trained. In fact, it is a fairly safe bet that the vast majority of professionals who have ever claimed an affiliation with the field of organizational behavior are still alive today. Many of the journals that publish the findings of OB research are relatively new. As you will notice in reading this text, the studies cited are all fairly recent, covering only the past few decades. Yet the widespread acceptance of organizational behavior as an important subject for future managers is evidenced by the fact that an OB course is included in the curriculum of virtually every business school.

INCREASED KNOWLEDGE

The third goal of organizational behavior is to gather knowledge about people in work settings. At a minimum, the field seeks to gather knowledge for its own sake. As evidenced by the progress of many "pure science" fields, such as physics, space research, and chemistry, the practical use of certain findings may not be apparent for years.

A similar process occurs in the field of organizational behavior. For example, early research on leadership processes identified two major dimensions of leadership (to be discussed fully in Chapter 10). Training specialists who followed this research came to apply the findings in the design of the leadership training programs that are now offered to organizations. Additionally, the study of OB can help one think in a critical fashion about matters that relate to the experience of working. Such critical thinking ability can be useful in analyzing both employee and personal problems.

ORGANIZATIONAL BEHAVIOR AND ITS RELATED FIELDS

Organizational behavior is the systematic study of the behavior and attitudes of both individuals and groups within organizations.[1] This may be termed a micro-level perspective. At the micro level, an organization's organizationwide attributes, such as size and structure, are usually taken as givens that have uniform effects on behavior in a particular situation. The focus or unit of analysis for the micro perspective is primarily the individual.

Organizational theory focuses on the organization as the unit of analysis. Organizational attributes, such as goals, technology, and culture, are the objects of study. Organizational theory often uses an across-organizations approach, or macro-level perspective, in gathering new knowledge. Organizational behavior and organizational theory use distinctly different research methods. Organizational behavior usually relies on laboratory and field experimentation for gathering information, while organizational theory tends to rely more on surveys and case studies. Nonetheless, it would be an oversimplification to assume that organizational behavior is oriented solely to understanding individual behavior, just as it would be a mistake to conclude that organizational theory is concerned exclusively with theory.

The field of **human resources management** (or personnel management) attempts to apply the principles of the behavioral sciences in the workplace. While organizational behavior is somewhat more concept oriented, human resources management is more concerned with applied techniques and behavioral technology. Human resources management tries to provide a link between the individual and the organization by designing and implementing systems to attract, develop, and motivate individuals within an organization.

Organizational development is concerned with the introduction of successful changes in organizations. Organizational development specialists sometimes approach the task of change from a macro perspective focusing on the structure and values of the organization. Ultimately, these efforts are intended to enhance organizational effectiveness.

One can distinguish organizational behavior from other closely related fields by its emphasis on the scientific study of behavioral phenomena at the individual and group levels. Organizational theory focuses largely on organizational and environmental phenomena; human resources management focuses on the application of behavioral knowledge in selecting, placing, and training personnel; and organizational development focuses on enhancing organizational performance. A useful but perhaps somewhat oversimplified way of understanding these four fields is to distinguish among them on two dimensions: the micro versus macro level of analysis, and theory versus application. A consideration of the combinations that result from crossing these two dimensions suggests that organizational behavior is a micro/theory-oriented field, human resources management is a micro/application-oriented field, organizational theory is a macro/theory-oriented field, and organizational development is a macro/application-oriented field. (Figure 1.1 summarizes the results of a crossing of these two dimensions.) In this text, you will notice that

FIGURE 1.1

FOUR FIELDS IN THE ORGANIZATIONAL SCIENCES

the related fields of organizational theory, human resources management, and organizational development will also be discussed occasionally.

In summary, the field of organizational behavior is characterized by *diversity,* as a consequence of drawing from many different disciplines; *newness,* as evidenced by its relatively recent emergence on the scientific scene; and *vitality,* as demonstrated by the growing number of members in the field, the growth of new publications, and the intensity of scientific debate within the field.

STUDYING THE BEHAVIOR OF PEOPLE AT WORK: PAST AND PRESENT

Today, organizational behavior is a growing field, rich in its variety of approaches. It is interesting to examine the various ways of viewing worker behavior that have emerged over the years (Figure 1.2). Taking a historical perspective on attitudes toward worker behavior helps us to both understand where organizational behavior stands today and visualize the directions it may take in the future.

PRE–SCIENTIFIC MANAGEMENT PERIOD (BEFORE 1900)

Perhaps the earliest application of a behavioral principle occurred during prehistoric times, when the principle of division of labor was probably applied for the first time. Anthropologists suggest that one of the simplest devices for improving a family unit's chances of survival lies in assigning specialized roles to individuals who are best able to perform them. Consequently, it is likely that sex-typed behaviors emerged during the prehistoric era in response to certain biological necessities. While the women stayed back to guard the campsite and children, the men took the role of chasing game.*

---

*With a high rate of infant mortality and little or no knowledge of contraception, a state of virtual perpetual pregnancy also probably hindered female mobility.

FIGURE 1.2
MAJOR PERIODS IN THE DEVELOPMENT OF THE FIELD OF ORGANIZATIONAL BEHAVIOR

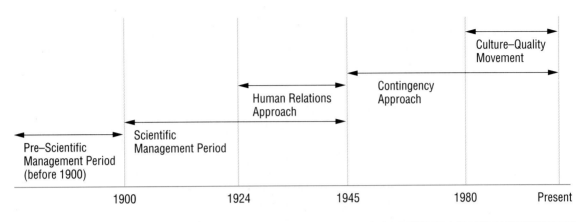

The earliest written evidence of a deliberate concern about managing workers' behavior appears in accounts provided by the Chinese and Mesopotamians between 3000 and 4000 B.C., relating to the importance of the specialization of labor and hierarchy of authority. Unfortunately, these writings do not provide a cumulative body of knowledge that would benefit today's managers.[2] Similarly, the ancient Romans wrote about the results of their efforts to reorganize the lines of communication in the legions and to decentralize decision making in an empire of over 50 million people.[3] These reports suggest that the problems of effectively managing people are perennial and that humans have long felt the need to develop a systemized body of knowledge about such issues.[†] Table 1.1 lists some important contributions to management during the pre-scientific era.

Historical documents do not provide much further insight on managing others until the time of Niccolò Machiavelli, a sixteenth-century Italian philosopher and politician. Machiavelli is probably best known for his suggestions of extreme political pragmatism. He endorsed such ethically questionable principles as the "ends justify the means." Machiavelli's place in history is nonetheless secure in that he called attention to the use of deception in manipulating others for one's own purposes. In Chapter 9, we will examine more closely some of Machiavelli's notions.

At much the same time that Machiavelli was writing his treatises on political realism, an important event took place in Venice. The then-powerful city-state created a shipyard for building and refitting its naval war fleet. The

[†]It is interesting to note that the earliest recorded labor dispute concerned monotony of diet and working conditions in ancient Egypt (1153 B.C.), while the earliest recorded strike, which concerned meal breaks, was led by an orchestra leader named Aristos in ancient Rome (309 B.C.).[4]

TABLE 1.1

SOME IMPORTANT EVENTS DURING THE PRE–SCIENTIFIC MANAGEMENT PERIOD

Approximate Year	Individual or Group	Major Managerial Contributions
5000 B.C.	Sumerians	Record keeping
4000 B.C.	Egyptians	Recognition of need for fair play in management; allowing workers to vent complaints
1800 B.C.	Hammurabi	Establishment of minimum wage
400 B.C.	Cyrus	Use of motion study, layout, materials handling
A.D. 30	Jesus Christ	Golden Rule, human relations perspective
late 1400s	Venetians	Numbering of inventoried parts, interchangeability of parts, assembly-line technique, inventory control
1776	Adam Smith	Application of principle of specialization to manufacturing workers
1832	Charles Babbage	Time-and-motion study, division of labor, effects of colors on employee efficiency
1881	Joseph Wharton	Established college course in business management

Source: Claude S. George, *The History of Management Thought,* Englewood Cliffs, N.J., Prentice-Hall, 1972.

arsenal at Venice became one of the largest industrial plants of the time (see Figure 1.3). Due to its size, its managers developed a focus on efficiency; in fact, many of their methods would be familiar to modern businesspeople. For example, the Venetians devised an assembly-line system that is roughly similar to modern assembly lines. Galleys were sailed up canals, which were bordered by warehouses stocked with the necessary equipment for refitting a damaged galley or building a new one. As a galley was sailed past each warehouse, the appropriate fittings were brought out and immediately attached. In addition to devising an early form of assembly line, the Venetians introduced routine beverage breaks for their personnel: wine was provided six times a day.[‡] They used a merit-rating plan to review employees' contributions and to assign pay raises based on performance. Employees who produced items that could be counted (such as oars) were paid on a piece-rate basis. They also invented new accounting systems to keep track of all expenditures and systems for controlling inventory. Unfortunately, many of the Venetians' innovations were not widely adopted at the time (except for their advances in accounting, which spread throughout Europe). The notion of a *formal* beverage break for workers was not reintroduced until the twentieth century.

Early military commanders (for example, von Clausewitz and Napoleon) also recorded their experiences with managing others. For example, these indi-

[‡]Because of this frequent use of wine, it is likely that the quality of work done on ships toward the end of the day was less than the quality of work done earlier in the day.

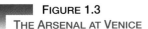
FIGURE 1.3
THE ARSENAL AT VENICE

From a watercolor plan by Antonio di Natale. The largest industrial complex in Europe at the time, the arsenal employed 5,000 workers and sheltered 150 galleys.

Source: Pegli Museo Navale.

viduals wrote of the practical value of various organizing principles (such as the number of subordinates that an administrator can effectively handle).[5]

SCIENTIFIC MANAGEMENT (1900–1945)

The Industrial Revolution of the nineteenth century brought about many radical changes in the management of workers. In contrast to the work of craftspeople of earlier times, work became centrally located in factories. Also, jobs required less skill because machines controlled production processes. Though production increased dramatically, other results of these sweeping changes were not all positive. Some writers, most notably Adam Smith and Karl Marx, pointed out that simplification of work processes beyond a certain point could have diminishing returns and produce feelings of alienation in workers.

Although we recognize the significance of these criticisms of work simplification today, the industrialists of the early twentieth century were not yet ready to do so. They preferred an engineering approach to managing worker behavior called **scientific management.** Scientific management, developed by Frederick Taylor, called for the careful analysis of tasks and time-and-motion studies in conjunction with piece-rate pay schemes in order to improve productivity.[§] Believers in scientific management searched for the "one best way" to perform a task. They introduced standard parts and procedures. In the extreme, the scientific management approach subscribes to the belief that one single best solution exists for a given situation.

The scientific management approach to dealing with worker behavior has been criticized on a number of counts. A major shortcoming is that much time and effort must be devoted to establishing work standards, closely monitoring many aspects of the work process, and calculating rates of pay. The cost of these activities may offset the expected benefits. A further problem lies in worker resistance to attempts to measure effort and productivity. This resistance may be manifested in slowdowns when workers are aware that they are being observed.

Workers also oppose changes in pay schemes because they suspect that the new rates may be designed to speed up production. For example, Taylor advocated pay schemes that only gave workers a maximum wage increase of roughly 60 percent regardless of how much worker productivity increased. Taylor's 1911 description of his handling of a worker at the Bethlehem Steel Works provides an illustration of the inequity that can result from such a pay scheme.[6] The job of Schmidt, a pig-iron handler, was to move large, 100-pound slabs ("pigs") of iron from a loading dock onto a railroad car (Figure 1.4). While employed by Bethlehem Steel as a consultant, Taylor designed an incentive pay scheme (coupled with rest periods) that encouraged Schmidt to haul substantially more iron in a given day. Schmidt responded to the incentive plan by raising his efforts so that his wages increased from $1.15 per day to $1.85 per day. In order to obtain this higher wage, Schmidt hauled $47\frac{1}{2}$ tons of iron per day, whereas he had previously hauled only $12\frac{1}{2}$ tons of iron per day. The inequity that exists in this situation can be understood by calculating and comparing the relative percentage increases in pay and productivity. Schmidt's pay increased 61 percent while his productivity increased 280 percent. Clearly, the company was benefiting more from Schmidt's increased productivity than was Schmidt himself. Taylor's belief that workers should be limited to a 60 percent increase in wages was based on his assumption that greater rewards would make workers more defiant and difficult to manage. This conclusion was based not on scientifically gathered evidence but on untested personal assumptions about human nature. Furthermore, Taylor believed that management was entitled to substantial profits because management bore the responsibility and costs of designing new production techniques.

Taylor's concepts of time-and-motion studies, elemental analysis of tasks, and standards for productivity were partly a reflection of his training as an engineer. A legacy of these concepts is that many jobs are still designed with the goal of maximizing short-run efficiency. The negative implications of workers

[§]In addition to his contributions to time-and-motion study, Fred Taylor was also the U.S. tennis doubles champion in 1881.

FIGURE 1.4
BETHLEHEM STEEL PIG-IRON HANDLERS

Source: Courtesy of Bethlehem Steel.

performing simplified, repetitive tasks did not concern the advocates of scientific management.**

Among Taylor's more famous disciples were the husband-and-wife consulting team of Frank and Lillian Gilbreth. Devotees of time-and-motion study, the Gilbreths developed a highly ordered family life that received notoriety in the book *Cheaper by the Dozen.* Following time-and-motion principles, Frank Gilbreth redesigned the manner in which bricklaying was performed so as to greatly improve productivity. The Gilbreths also developed an elaborate system for redesigning jobs based on the notion of an irreducible time-and-motion unit of a work task, termed a *therblig* (Gilbreth roughly spelled backward). Along with Taylor, the Gilbreths founded an association to promote scientific management.††

**As a counterpoint to these criticisms, some recent writers have argued that Taylor has been much maligned and that his techniques of time study, standardization, goal setting, and monetary incentives may have been based on fundamentally correct concepts for dealing with numerous situations.[7] The validity of one of Taylor's more novel suggestions, that supervisors should learn how to swear in order to motivate others, has not as yet been demonstrated. Scientific management ran into early opposition from labor organizers when it was proposed as an approach to improve efficiency at U.S. military arsenals. A resulting Congressional investigation, held in 1912, ruled against the use of scientific management in arsenals and naval shipyards. Labor opponents also claimed that Schmidt, the pig-iron hauler, had actually died from being overworked. With the aide of a detective, Taylor was able to locate Schmidt (whose real name was Henry Knolle), who was alive and well.[8]

††Although Taylor and the Gilbreths initially admired each other's work, they eventually had a falling out. Taylor sought to discredit the Gilbreths, and they criticized his views as well. The Gilbreths had the last word, as Taylor died in 1915.

HUMAN RELATIONS APPROACH (1924–1945): THE HAWTHORNE STUDIES

During the same period in which scientific management was popular, another school of thought emerged, the **human relations approach.** The human relations approach, which partially grew out of the field of psychology, emphasized the importance of motivation and attitudes in explaining worker behavior. The approach drew much of its strength and following from the results of a series of studies conducted at the Hawthorne plant of the Western Electric Company, located in the western suburbs of Chicago. The **Hawthorne Studies** were begun in 1924 and spanned 10 years.[9] The Hawthorne experiments were important because they demonstrated that in addition to the job itself certain factors can influence workers' behavior. Informal social groups, management-employee relations, and the interrelatedness among the many facets of work settings were found to be quite influential.

The Hawthorne Studies represented a major step forward in the attempt to systematically study worker behavior. Although the studies can be grouped into at least five major efforts or divisions, three are of particular interest: the Illumination Experiments, the Relay Assembly Room Study, and the Bank Wiring Room Study.

THE ILLUMINATION EXPERIMENTS   In the **Illumination Experiments,** the researchers investigated the effects of increased illumination on worker productivity. At the time, electric lighting was becoming more widely available in factories, and a scientifically based demonstration of the beneficial effects of lighting was desired by both managers and researchers. In one illumination experiment, one group of workers was selected to work under a constant intensity of light while three other groups worked under varying intensities of light. The results were surprising in that both the group under a uniform intensity and the test groups showed appreciable gains in productivity. In one extreme condition, the illumination intensity was reduced to the equivalent of working by moonlight. Despite this apparent handicap, the workers maintained production levels and reported no eyestrain and less fatigue than they had when working in a more illuminated condition.

Because these results defied reason, the researchers considered the possibility that something besides light intensity had affected the workers' reactions. To find out what other factors could have influenced the outcomes, the researchers designed a yet more elaborate series of studies.

THE RELAY ASSEMBLY ROOM STUDY   In the **Relay Assembly Room Study,** a small group of female employees was taken from its regular workplace and assigned to assemble small telephone relays in an arrangement that was very similar to that of the actual Relay Assembly Department. The decision to separate the women from the remainder of the work force was based on the researchers' desire to maintain total control over the experimental working environment. Of special interest to the investigators was whether changes in the work setting would influence the women's productivity. Among the changes that the investigators tried were the introduction of rest periods, a free mid-morning lunch, a workday that was a half-hour shorter, a five-day workweek (a novel idea at that time), and variations in methods of payment.

The researchers hoped that their studies would show that the introduction of 10-minute rest periods produced a 12 percent increase in productivity, while a five-day workweek decreased productivity by 16 percent, and so on. But once again, the results were perplexing. Instead of finding that some conditions increased productivity while others decreased it, the researchers found that productivity followed a gradual upward trend over the course of the entire study, regardless of the condition instituted. In addition, when the women were in the test room, their rate of absenteeism was lower than in their original job setting.

These results, as well as results of the illumination studies, led the Hawthorne researchers to consider the psychological aspects of the work setting in addition to its more objective features. Careful analysis suggested that the positive outcomes were partially attributable to the fact that the workers enjoyed the attention and recognition that the researchers had been showing them. For example, during the illumination studies, the workers commented favorably on all the changes that were made in the lighting. And in the relay assembly test room, the workers displayed positive attitudes toward the entire research enterprise. In response to the favorable treatment that they received in the test situations, compared to the usual treatment of workers in that era,[‡‡] the workers reciprocated by providing the results that they thought the researchers wanted. This phenomenon, in which the alteration of social and psychological aspects of a work setting results in enhanced performance largely because the employees realize they are being observed, has been termed the **Hawthorne effect.** The Hawthorne effect often explains many instances in which the mere study of people at work, in and of itself, can be responsible for an observed set of results.[§§]

THE BANK WIRING ROOM STUDY   Another important Hawthorne study, the **Bank Wiring Room Study,** sought to gather more information about the social nature of work groups. For this study, a group of 14 men who wired telephone banks was observed in a standard shop condition (Figure 1.5). An observer

---

[‡‡]In a follow-up interview conducted in the 1970s with one of the women who actually participated in the study, it was reported that it was not uncommon at that time for supervisors to punish a group of operators who failed to meet their assigned standard. One form of this punishment consisted of not permitting the operators to use the elevators.

[§§]Recently, there has been much debate over whether the actual results of the Hawthorne Studies in fact showed substantial and incontrovertible evidence of improved performance due to the workers' being observed.[10] The criticisms stem partly from the lack of extremely tight controls in the study (e.g., some of the workers who were studied initially were replaced by other workers for various reasons during the long course of the study). Nonetheless, the vast majority of scholars who study organizational behavior accept the general conclusions of the Hawthorne researchers and acknowledge the likely existence of such a phenomenon as the Hawthorne effect.

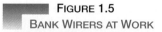

FIGURE 1.5
BANK WIRERS AT WORK

Source: Reprinted by permission of Pitman Publishing Ltd., London.

was stationed in the room with instructions to take continuous notes on the workers' actions. The observer was not allowed to give orders or become involved in conversations with the workers. Although the workers were initially very apprehensive about the observer, they settled into more natural and relaxed behavior after roughly three weeks. Because the foreman for the work group also supervised other workers in another room, and because the observer was deliberately unobtrusive, the workers were relatively free from constant supervision.

Although the workers were paid according to their output, the observer soon noted that the workers had established an informal daily norm of 6,600 units per person. Typically, the men would pace their work so that they reached the norm near the end of the day. Of course, some of the men could do more than 6,600 units. But if they indicated that they would prefer to be more productive, they risked becoming the victims of various schemes for controlling production.

The two most frequent schemes consisted of minor verbal and physical harassment. Verbal harassment took the form of name calling. More productive individuals were labeled "speed king," "company man," and "Phar Lap" (a prize-winning racehorse of the time).

Physical harassment sometimes took the form of a game called "binging." A "bing" was a sharp blow to the muscle of the upper arm. The game of binging would be played in rounds. At first, one worker would hit a very productive individual on the arm. As the fellow who was struck was obligated to defend his manhood, he would hit the aggressor back in a like manner. The aggressor would then strike the victim on the same arm as before, and so on. After several rounds of exchanging blows ... each other's arms, the two would eventually stop from exhaustion or pain. The game was always carried off in a good-natured fashion. And after it was finished, the two participants would usually laugh and make friendly remarks about the power of each other's punches.

Binging served several purposes for those who wished to see production restricted in the work unit. First, the game interrupted the production routine within the group at the same time that it disrupted the routine of the highly productive individual in that he had to finish the rest of the workday with a sore arm. The alleged good humor of the game was also an important element. The aggressor always offered his friendship at the conclusion of the contest. This friendship could then be used as the basis for further attempts to influence the ambitious worker to restrict his efforts. If the contest ended on a bitter note, the door would be closed to future attempts to dissuade the worker via verbal or physical methods.

In other observations, the Hawthorne researchers noted that a social order existed within the work unit that was based on clique membership rather than job function. Cliques could be identified by their membership criteria: One should not be a rate buster (someone who produces too much), a chiseler (someone who produces below the unit's informal work norm), or a squealer (someone who passes to a supervisor information that could harm a coworker). In short, an intricate social arrangement was identified within the work unit that maintained its existence through such mechanisms as ridicule, sarcasm, and binging.

Many scholars believe that the Hawthorne Studies show the importance of the social nature of workers. This would seem to contradict the economic or rational approach to worker behavior that is implicit in the principles of scientific management. But just as the scientific management approach possesses problems of application, so does the human relations approach. The greatest difficulties stem from an unproven assumption that is the cornerstone of the human relations approach: the belief that workers who are satisfied with their jobs will feel indebted to their employers and will show their appreciation by being more productive. This suggests a reciprocal relationship between management and labor—that greater concern for improving the condition of workers will pay dividends to employers through greater productivity from happier and more appreciative workers.

Unfortunately, this simple *quid pro quo* relationship has not been firmly established. Studies have not found clear evidence of a relationship between worker satisfaction and productivity.*** Due to this lack of evidence, it is

---

***As we shall see in Chapter 4, the entire issue of the relationship between worker satisfaction and worker productivity is a complex one.

difficult to endorse the position that managers should worry about their workers' level of contentment in the hope that workers will return the favor. Nonetheless, managers cannot ignore the issue of worker well-being for other solid, defensible reasons, as we shall demonstrate in Chapter 4.

CONTINGENCY APPROACH (1945–PRESENT)

Following World War II, a new perspective on organizational behavior began to develop. Called the **contingency approach,** it acknowledged the difficulty of offering simple general principles to explain or predict behavior in organizational settings. Nonetheless, the contingency approach did not abandon the search for principles, but instead sought to specify the conditions under which we can expect to find certain relationships. As such, it represented a search for the factors that would aid in predicting and explaining behavior. Organizational behavior researchers who subscribe to the contingency approach believe that employee behavior is too complex to be explained by only a few simple and straightforward principles. Instead, they seek to identify the factors that are jointly necessary for a given principle to hold. Contingency researchers recognize the *interdependency* of personal and situational factors in the determination of employee behavior.

If you ask a contingency researcher for a simple answer to a seemingly simple question, you should expect to be given a fairly complex and highly qualified answer. Because human behavior is itself complex, a statement of behavioral principles must also be complex.

For example, consider this seemingly simple question: Which is the better way to behave as a manager, autocratically or democratically? Contingency researchers would not simply pick one alternative over the other, but would try to identify a set of conditions in which one style of supervision could be expected to yield superior results compared to the other style. They would consider such issues as subordinates' expectations and preferences for different styles of leadership. To be sure, if you are in charge of a band of fascists, your subordinates might well expect and desire that you rule with an iron fist.

Cultural differences would also be taken into account in choosing a style of supervision. For example, in the United States, democratic and participative supervision is endorsed, while an autocratic supervisory style is generally frowned on. But in other countries, a leader who shows empathy and is willing to be influenced by subordinates might be viewed as being weak. In addition, the leader's ability to enact a particular supervisory style would be an important consideration, as would the nature of the task to be performed.

Finally, a contingency researcher would want to know what criteria will be used to measure the success of a leadership style. Will the leader be judged according to subordinates' satisfaction, quantity or quality of unit performance, the leader's satisfaction, organizational survival, or some other criterion?

In most cases, a contingency researcher's answer can be summarized in two words: "It depends." But this two-word answer is not meant to be eva-

An Inside Look
The Power of Empowerment

All across the United States, the command and control style of management that has served America for the last generation is giving way to the newer management techniques of empowerment and teamwork. But there's often a major roadblock standing in the way: old-style, fist-shaking managers who aren't ready to relinquish the power they've spent entire careers accumulating.

What modern managers need to understand is that employee empowerment doesn't mean giving up total control. On the contrary, managers often accept greater responsibility in team environments or in organizations that have recently downsized. Flattened organizations and leaner work forces present a number of challenges to middle managers: handling heavier work loads, overseeing larger staff, having a greater number of direct reports, and delegating work to teams. Thus, it's important for managers to realize that empowering employees is a means to sharing power, not transferring it altogether.

Managers may experience a sort of withdrawal from the old ways of doing things. Fearful of losing control as the number of people they work with increases, managers may initially resist changes. Eventually, tentative acceptance sets in, as they begin sharing small doses of power with employees. Fortunately, perceptive managers ultimately realize that empowered employees with a stake in the process are more committed to success and make better decisions. The synergies of teamwork surface as employee teams begin to spread throughout the organization, and the efficiencies of teamwork begin to pay off. To transform stodgy attitudes about teamwork, more and more companies are enrolling employee teams in structured Outward Bound–type experiences that involve activities such as rope-climbing and mountain-scaling expeditions. The goals of these programs are to build trust and group cohesion.

Of course, employees empowered to run operations must also be empowered to make their own mistakes. Experience is often the best teacher, and although painful, managers must be willing to let staffers temporarily drift in the wrong direction with a project.

Evidence of the benefits of empowerment and teamwork is beginning to emerge. A direct marketing arm of Hewlett-Packard Co. has found empowerment to be a powerful motivator: In just one year, employee morale has skyrocketed and productivity is up 40 percent. With results like that, managers can't afford to dismiss the power of empowerment.

Source: Joseph Weber, "Letting Go Is Hard To Do," *Business Week,* Special Enterprise Issue, 1993, 218–219.

sive, as a contingency researcher will then attempt to identify precisely what the important dependencies are. Contingency researchers assume that the number of important dependencies can be specified. On the basis of this, they then search for a valid representation of worker behavior. Today, most specialists in the field of organizational behavior subscribe to the contingency approach. The need to establish the validity of behavioral principles by using a truly scientific approach is also widely accepted. The questions surrounding how one can forcefully make such demonstrations will be the focus of Chapter 2.

CULTURE-QUALITY MOVEMENT (1980–PRESENT)

The last two decades of the twentieth century witnessed the rise of two related themes. The themes grew out of the work of organizational consultants and applied researchers that tied the ascent of Japan's industrial power to corporate ability to inspire commitment, while simultaneously maintaining flexibility.[11] Two terms that gained quick interest among managers and organizational researchers were *corporate culture* and *quality improvement*. The authors of several popular books in the early 1980s—Peters and Waterman, *In Search of Excellence;* Deal and Kennedy, *Corporate Culture*; and Ouchi, *Theory Z*—focused on how to build a strong set of shared positive values and norms within a corporation (that is, a strong corporate culture) while emphasizing quality, service, high performance, and flexibility.[12] Simultaneously, Western industry developed an interest in designing an effective response to growing global competition. High quality was seen to be the result of high employee commitment and loyalty. High levels of employee commitment and loyalty were believed to result, partially, from greater employee involvement in decision making. In order to establish new mechanisms for employment involvement, changes were seen as being necessary in existing corporate cultures, and the establishment and maintenance of new cultures became the goal. In some organizations, a deliberate focus can be identified that seeks to have employees openly discuss aspects of corporate culture, and suggest techiques for achieving a culture that emphasizes greater teamwork and cooperation.

Advocates of the **culture-quality movement** claim that productivity and financial returns can be significantly enhanced by developing cultures that emphasize key values. Presently, the evidence suggests that, properly introduced, there are economic advantages to following principles of the culture-quality movement. However, for every success story there may be at least as many failed attempts. The case for the culture-quality movement will be discussed in further detail in chapters devoted to the enhancement of employee motivation (Chapter 7) and cultural influences (Chapter 19).

It should be noted that the two current views (that is, the contingency approach and the culture-quality movement) did not integrate the previous approaches of scientific management and human relations, but instead replaced them as the clearly dominant perspectives for the study of organizational behavior. The two earlier approaches have not gone the way of the dinosaurs, however. Although the fervor that surrounded them has clearly waned, they still have some advocates. The human relations adherents tend to be associated with a humanistically oriented, altruistic philosophical camp, while the latter-day scientific management advocates are often found in close association with schools of engineering. The smart money is betting on the eventual replacement of the culture-quality movement by a future, as yet unforeseeable, perspective, while the contingency approach, because of its broadness, will likely be a part of the field as long as it retains an empirical basis.

CRITICISMS OF THE FIELD

Although the field of organizational behavior is relatively new, it has created quite a bit of controversy, drawing criticism from scholars in the field itself, as well as from students and managers. The fact that organizational behavior generates such debate is evidence that the field is truly alive and developing.

The two most frequent criticisms of organizational behavior as a field of study are raised by students in introductory courses. They often say that much of what they learned in their organizational behavior course is fairly obvious

OB Focus
The Importance of Implementation

Total Quality Management. Worker empowerment. Process re-engineering. Benchmarking. American businesses are constantly trying on the latest in management fashion, but the key to lasting results, in the form of a motivated and productive work force, is implementation. Without customizing generic management practices to the needs and idiosyncracies of individual companies, and anticipating the program's ramifications, full satisfaction with these new management techniques is an impossible dream. According to a recent survey by the Electronic Power Research Institute of more than 300 large companies, satisfaction with popular management techniques among executives who had implemented them ranged from 35 to 60 percent. However, employees and customers rated the effectiveness of these same practices at between 10 and 20 percent. Clearly, there is ample room for improvement, and some companies are quick to realize this.

American Express' international division recently experienced an unpleasant side effect of re-engineering, the practice of reorganizing work processes to more ef-fectively provide service to customers. With re-engineering, organizational hierarchies often become flatter, allowing greater flexibility and improved communications. However, by making American Express leaner, layers of jobs AmEx managers had looked to for their next promotions were eliminated. To keep employee morale from falling, American Express works with employees to identify skills in need of refinement and development and encourages managers to consider lateral moves as career-enhancing opportunities.

Employees at Ocean Showboat, an Atlantic City, N.J., casino company, became so concerned that their suggestions to reduce bureaucracy would backfire that Ocean Showboat management decided to take a different approach. The company had previously adopted a philosophy of Total Quality Management (TQM), one in which employees, individually and in teams, learn and apply new skills to foster reliable products and services. But when employees became reluctant to make additional suggestions the organization shelved TQM. The company now characterizes itself as a "learning organization," one in which employees learn new skills in an effort to promote company growth and job security. Whether this reorientation in philosophy will produce the intended results remains to be seen.

When Pacific Gas & Electric adopted benchmarking a few years ago, employees toured other organizations to learn how business problems, ranging from data processing to inventory control, were handled. What PG&E management had failed to do, however, was to give these nomadic employees a mission. Only when specific parameters regarding what data to collect were understood by the employees touring these facilities did the company begin reaping the benefits of benchmarking.

As these examples illustrate, to keep morale and productivity sufficiently high, companies need to tinker with and customize their programs. Too often, management practices fail to deliver promised results because of inadequate preparation. It's not enough to simply adopt a new program; managers must plan for its implementation and guide the process along the way.

Source: Fred R. Bleakley, "The Best Laid Plans: Many Companies Try Management Fads, Only to See Them Flop," *The Wall Street Journal,* July 6, 1993, A1.

and that most of it could be derived from common sense. We will consider each of these comments in turn.

IT'S SO OBVIOUS

The observation that most of the content of organizational behavior is obvious usually arises in response to reading the results of studies that have been conducted in the field. For example, consider the following behavioral principles that have frequently been demonstrated in behavioral studies: "Rewarding workers on the basis of their past performance is likely to improve their subsequent performance," or "An employee will tend to like a coworker who has indicated a liking for her or him."††† Some people may think that these statements are ridiculously self-evident and that anyone could make these observations without going through the trouble of scientific studies. And since any one of us could predict such principles, why bother to develop a field around such clichés?

To examine the criticism that organizational researchers do little more than restate the obvious, consider the following case. As part of the effort to win World War II, the U.S. Army set up a research branch of the War Department. During the course of the war, the research branch conducted several hundred studies on such issues as soldiers' attitudes, morale, and feelings of frustration. In the process, over 600,000 soldiers were interviewed. The results of these studies were so extensive that their final summary required four volumes. When these volumes were finally published in 1949, they were widely criticized in the popular press. One criticism was that many of the findings were terribly obvious. For example, a major conclusion of the report was that many soldiers were unhappy during the war. This conclusion seemed so self-evident that it raised questions about the legitimacy of investing energy and time in attitude surveys that generate such obvious findings.

In a review of the four-volume work, Paul Lazarsfeld, a sociologist, provided a brief list of typical findings.[13] How would you rate the novelty of each of the following statements taken from his review?

1. As long as the war continued, enlisted men were more desirous of returning home to the United States than they were after the collapse of the Nazi regime. (Would anyone be surprised to find that soldiers do not want to be killed?)

2. Soldiers from the southern states were better able to tolerate the tropical climate in the South Pacific than were soldiers from the northern states. (Given differences in upbringing and adjustment to climate, this too could be easily predicted.)

3. White enlisted men were more desirous of promotions than were black enlisted men. (Given the lack of real opportunities for blacks in the U.S. military at that time, this is not unexpected.)

4. Highly educated men had more difficulty adjusting to army life, especially as manifested by minor psychological disorders, than did men who were less well educated. (The highly cerebral individual might easily be expected to have difficulty adjusting to a situation requiring obedience and unquestioning acceptance of a difficult daily regimen.)

5. Blacks from the southern states preferred to serve under white officers who were also from the southern states, versus officers from the northern states. (Similarity in backgrounds and values could easily explain this result.)

6. Soldiers who had grown up in rural areas were better able to adjust to army life than were soldiers from urban areas. (Sleeping under the stars might be

†††These statements are variations on the "law of effect" and "the reciprocity principle of interpersonal attraction."

a difficult adjustment for someone who had rarely, if ever, stepped off a slab of concrete.)

If we acknowledge the obvious nature of these findings, we must question the entire enterprise of research on people in organizational setting. If these are the basic data that serve to develop principles in the field, then the average person is already fairly sophisticated about organizational behavior.

These statements would be true except for one important fact. The previous list presents the exact *opposite* of the actual findings. In truth, soldiers preferred to remain overseas until the war was concluded and wanted to return home afterwards. Southerners had no greater tolerance for the heat of the South Pacific, blacks were more desirous of promotion, poorly educated men had more difficulties in adjusting to army life, and so forth. In each instance, we can now generate an explanation that once again is seemingly obvious. For example, the soldier's desire to remain overseas could be explained by their commitment to completing the war effort and by their patriotism, while homesickness became strong after their mission was complete; blacks were more desirous of promotion because they were relatively deprived of opportunities as a group; and so on. Had the true findings been presented initially, our reaction would be that they too were obvious.

The notion that behavioral phenomena are obvious is therefore something of a delusion. It may well be that when we are presented with a statement concerning human behavior, we engage in a defensive reaction in which we state, "Oh sure, I would have guessed it." This tendency to claim that we would have foreseen the relative inevitability of an outcome is termed **hindsight bias.** This reaction may be very self-satisfying (after all, it suggests we are well in control of our surroundings), but clearly it also can be very much in error. As every manner of human behavior is at least conceivable, we must not fall into the trap of self-deception by relying on intuition and armchair theorizing in place of an empirical search for evidence. Also, we must search for the joint factors, both personal and situational, that are responsible for a particular regularity in human behavior. Healthy skepticism is necessary because nearly every explanation of human behavior, regardless of its truth or falsity, can be dismissed as obvious after we have heard it.

IT'S ONLY COMMON SENSE

The criticism that much of organizational behavior is deducible from common sense is also without foundation. Consider that common sense, when you cite examples, is reducible to a series of widely accepted truisms. If you follow the tenets of common sense, you presumably will make judgments based on the collected wisdom of past generations. But, over the years, this collected wisdom has generated a truism for every conceivable situation, so that common sense can be cited as the basis for following contradictory courses of action.

For example, consider a hiring decision involving several competing applicants. Common sense would advise that you thoroughly investigate the credentials of all candidates: "Look before you leap." Therefore, let us assume that you prolong your search until you have more data on the candidates. In the meantime, your two best candidates take offers from other companies. Your taking time to gather more information can then be criticized for violating another commonsense truism: "He who hesitates is lost." Since common sense places its bets on both sides of an issue, it can be easily cited, *after* the fact, to explain any success or failure. Consequently, common sense has no value as a means of predicting future events because it never backs one outcome over another.‡‡‡

As further evidence of this point, consider the following pairs of common-sense truisms:

1a. If at first you don't succeed, try, try again.

 b. Don't beat your head against a brick wall.

2a. You're never too old to learn.

 b. You can't teach an old dog new tricks.

3a. Nothing ventured, nothing gained.

 b. It's better to be safe than sorry.

4a. Nice guys finish last.

 b. Do unto others as you would have others do unto you.

5a. Haste makes waste.

 b. Time waits for no one.

6a. Out of sight, out of mind.

 b. Absence makes the heart grow fonder.

7a. Two heads are better than one.

 b. Too many cooks spoil the broth.§§§

A FRAMEWORK FOR STUDYING ORGANIZATIONAL BEHAVIOR

In practice, managers and researchers who are interested in organizational behavior tend to group issues and topics within a number of more or less common categories, such as performance appraisal, communication, attitudes, leadership, and the like. These commonly used categories form the basis for the chapter topics of this book. The order of the chapters follows a logical flow from within-individual issues to between-individual issues, and ultimately to individual–organizational issues. Thus, the chapters flow from micro (smaller) to macro (larger) levels of analysis and discussion.

---

‡‡‡For a more esoteric examination of the relationships between the behavioral sciences and common sense, see Note 14.

§§§Psychologist Karl Halvor Teigen created a clever experiment wherein he converted 24 proverbs into their opposites. For example, "Fear is stronger than love" became "Love is stronger than fear," and "Truth needs no colors" became "Truth needs colors." Students given lists containing some authentic proverbs and some reversed proverbs judged both sets to be equally true.[15]

FIGURE 1.6

A FRAMEWORK FOR STUDYING ORGANIZATIONAL BEHAVIOR

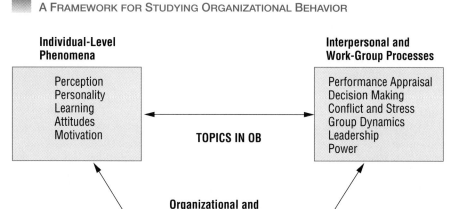

Individual-Level Phenomena

Perception
Personality
Learning
Attitudes
Motivation

TOPICS IN OB

Interpersonal and Work-Group Processes

Performance Appraisal
Decision Making
Conflict and Stress
Group Dynamics
Leadership
Power

Organizational and Environmental Dynamics

Communication
Organizational Structure
Cultural Influences
Organizational Development
Organizational Change

Figure 1.6 summarizes the organization of these topics by grouping many of the chapter headings within three larger categories. Initially, we will consider individual-level topics, such as perception, personality, learning, and attitudes. Afterwards, we will examine interpersonal and work-group processes, such as leadership and group dynamics. Last, we will consider organizational and environmental forces, such as structural and cultural influences.

In essence, we will start with the upper-left cluster of topics in Figure 1.6 and proceed clockwise through the framework. An important feature of the framework is the interconnectedness of the clusters (as noted by the use of the ever-popular two-headed arrow). These interconnections denote the interplay, or mutual influence, that exists among the topics. That is to say, interpersonal processes are influenced by both individual and organizational factors, and vice versa. For example, the actual design of a performance appraisal system will be partly a product of individual and organizational forces. The appraisal system, in turn, will influence both individual-level and organizationwide activities. Behavioral processes do not occur in a vacuum. Instead, they should be thought of as potential causes and consequences of other processes.

SUMMARY

1. Define the purpose and nature of the field of organizational behavior.
Organizational behavior (OB) is a relatively new field of inquiry concerned with the scientific study of the behavioral processes that occur in work settings. Borrowing many of its concepts and methods from the behavioral and

social sciences, OB explores a wide range of subjects that span (1) individually based phenomena, such as perception and personality, (2) interpersonal and work-group processes, such as motivation and leadership, and (3) organizational and environmental forces, such as structural and cultural influences. Due to its newness, OB is a dynamic and promising field characterized by diversity and vitality.

2. Tell why organizational behavior is an important field of study for managers.

Understanding OB will help managers in at least three ways. First, through OB, managers can learn to better understand and enhance their subordinates', their superiors', and their own performance. Second, managers will find that studying OB can lead to personal growth. Better understanding of others can be highly fulfilling and contribute to greater self-knowledge and self-insight. Third, OB offers managers knowledge for its own sake. Although some OB findings may not yet have practical applications, they are nonetheless valuable additions to the cumulative store of human knowledge.

3. Distinguish organizational behavior from organizational theory, human resources management, and organizational development.

Strictly speaking, organizational behavior is the systematic study of the behavior of individuals and groups within organizations. In contrast, organizational theory focuses on the organization as the unit of analysis, and organizational attributes such as goals, technology, and culture are the objects of study. The field of human resources management attempts to apply the principles of the behavioral sciences in the workplace by designing and implementing systems for attracting, developing, and motivating individuals within an organization. Finally, organizational development seeks to enhance organizational performance through instituting systematic changes in the structure and values of an organization.

4. Cite several significant applications of behavioral principles that occurred before 1900.

Prehistoric humans were probably the first to recognize the benefits of division of labor. To increase their chances of survival, family units assigned specialized roles to the individuals who were best able to perform them. As far back as 4000 B.C., the Chinese and Mesopotamians wrote about the importance of specialized labor and hierarchy of authority, while somewhat later the ancient Romans wrote about their efforts to reorganize the lines of communication in the legions and decentralize decision making throughout their empire. In the sixteenth century, the Italian philosopher and politician Machiavelli provided insights into managing others, contending that in any situation the ends justify the means and advocating the use of deception and manipulation to further one's own purposes. At much the same time, the city-state of Venice developed a sophisticated and efficient assembly-line system of repairing damaged ships and building new ones. The Venetians were also the first to allow their workers to take regular beverage breaks. In addition, they used a merit-rating plan to assign pay raises and devised sophisticated accounting systems to track expenditures and control inventory. The written accounts of the experience of military commanders have also suggested insights on how to effectively manage others.

5. Outline the basic principles of scientific management and discuss the shortcomings of this approach to dealing with worker behavior.

Essentially an approach to controlling worker behavior developed by Frederick Taylor, an engineer, scientific management used detailed task analysis and time-and-motion studies in conjunction with piece-rate pay schemes to increase productivity. In their search for the single best way to perform a given task, the proponents of scientific management imposed standard parts and standard procedures on manufacturing processes. This approach had many critics. Among its shortcomings was the huge amount of time and effort required to establish work standards, monitor the work process, and calculate rates of pay. Fearing that the new pay rates were an attempt to speed up production, many workers used deliberate slowdowns to resist attempts to measure their effort and productivity. In fact, the pay schemes recommended by Taylor could lead to dramatic inequities in pay.

6. Relate the findings of the Hawthorne Studies to the development of the human relations approach.

The human relations approach, which partially grew out of the field of psychology, emphasized the importance of motivation and attitudes in explaining worker behavior. This philosophy drew many of its beliefs from the findings of the Hawthorne Studies, a series of studies conducted at a single manufacturing plant over the course of ten years. Three of the studies yielded especially compelling results. The Illumination Experiments first signaled the possibility that factors other than the job itself can influence workers' behavior. The Relay Assembly Room Study, in turn, led researchers to recognize the Hawthorne effect, while the Bank Wiring Room Study showed how peer pressure could affect individual productivity. The Hawthorne Studies represented a major step forward in the attempt to systematically study worker behavior and demonstrated that informal social groups, management–employee relations, and the interrelatedness of many other factors all contribute to on-the-job performance.

7. Explain why believers in the contingency approach rarely give a simple answer to a seemingly simple question.

Proponents of the contingency approach contend that the complexity of worker behavior defies simple explanations. They seek to identify the many personal and situational factors that are jointly necessary to explain and predict behavior. Today, most specialists in the field of OB subscribe to the contingency approach.

8. Describe the currently dominant perspectives in the field of organizational behavior.

There are presently two dominant perspectives in the field of organizational behavior: the contingency approach and the culture-quality movement. The contingency approach attempts to explain and predict behavior from an analysis of the interdependencies of personal and situational forces. The culture-quality movement focuses on the role of corporate culture in influencing employee performance. Important aspects of corporate culture, such as employee participation in decision making, are seen as underlying employee commitment and loyalty, which in turn affect the quality of employee output.

9. Respond to critics who contend that most principles of organizational behavior are obvious and based on common sense.

Because every manner of human behavior is at least conceivable, we have a tendency to believe that many OB findings appear to be obvious. Such a reaction could lead to a reliance on intuition and armchair theorizing in place of empirical research. No matter how obvious a statement about behavior may be, OB researchers do not accept it as fact until it is scientifically proven. We might also assume that much of OB is deducible from common sense. Since common sense often backs both sides of an issue, it can easily be cited after the fact to explain any success or failure and has no value in predicting future events.

KEY TERMS

Organizational behavior
Organizational theory
Human resources management
Organizational development
Scientific management
Human relations approach
Hawthorne Studies

Illumination Experiments
Relay Assembly Room Study
Hawthorne effect
Bank Wiring Room Study
Contingency approach
Culture-quality movement
Hindsight bias

REVIEW AND DISCUSSION QUESTIONS

1. Organizational behavior is a relatively young field of study that borrows many concepts and methods from the behavioral and social sciences. What advantages and disadvantages can you see in such youth and diversity?

2. Having graduated from college with a degree in organizational behavior, you are now seeking your first full-time job. The recruiter for Harold Guaranty Trust, where you'd like to work, tells you that only accounting majors are accepted into their management training program. What would you say to persuade the recruiter that your studies should qualify you for management training as well.

3. You are an assembly-line worker at a small auto parts manufacturer in Michigan that has called in four consultants who each specialize in a different field—organizational behavior, organizational theory, human resources management, and organizational development. Which consultant's efforts will probably affect you most? Which will most affect your supervisor? Which will most affect the president of the company? Explain your responses.

4. Although we have written records of ancient Chinese and Mesopotamian thoughts on the importance of specialized labor and the hierarchy of au-

thority, modern managers may not find these accounts very helpful. Why not?

5. How would you explain the former popularity of scientific management? Why do you think this movement eventually lost its following? What aspects of scientific management would account for this approach's enduring popularity in certain schools of engineering?

6. After reading about the Relay Assembly Room Study, the supervisor of a typing pool decides that her subordinates will perform better if they know that she is observing them. Therefore, every day at 10 A.M. and 2 P.M. she walks up and down the rows of desks, pausing to watch each typist. Is this situation likely to produce the Hawthorne effect? What other effects are possible? How would you explain these outcomes to the supervisor?

7. To earn extra money, you and three friends organize a free-lance yard crew to sell lawn mowing, leaf raking, and similar household services to the homeowners near your campus. Although you only work after school and on weekends, there is immediately great demand for your services because you are so conscientious, courteous, and efficient. After a few weeks, however, one of your partners starts arriving late every day, another rarely comes to work at all, and the third sits and watches while you do all the mowing and raking. How would you use the contingency approach to explain your partners' behavior? What factors would you consider? What conclusions would you draw?

8. The recruiter from Harold Guaranty Trust (see Question 2) remains unconvinced of the value of your degree in organizational behavior. "After all," he says, "most findings in OB are obvious and the rest are common sense." What would you say to change his mind?

CRITICAL INCIDENT

You Just Can't Get Good Help Anymore

The Greenley Corporation's profit over the last five years had increased at an annual rate of 13.5 percent. Most of this increase was a direct result of subcontracts the firm had secured from other companies.

Six months ago, to deal with its 90-day backlog of orders, Greenley introduced an incentive plan to increase output. There were several versions of the plan, each tailored to specific jobs. The one for assemblers and packers offered a bonus of 25 percent for all work over standard. The average assembler-packer was making $5.75 an hour and was expected to assemble and pack 10 units within this period. With time allowed for lunch and rest breaks, people put in seven hours of work and were expected to produce 70 units, resulting in a base of 57.5¢ per unit.

If the assembler-packer chose to work on Saturday, the rate was time and a half, and management also promised to pay the 25 percent bonus for output over standard. One of the assembler-packers who turned out 82 units a day received a weekly gross pay of $317.70. The calculations were as follows:

Average weekly pay
(7 hours × $5.75 per hour × 5 days) $201.25

Bonus for 12 extra units per day
(57.5¢ per unit × 1.25 percent bonus
× 12 extra units × 5 days)   43.13

Saturday overtime
(7 hours × $8.625 [$5.75 per hour × 1.5
for overtime])   60.38

Saturday bonus for 12 extra units
(57.5¢ per unit × 1.5 for overtime × 1.25
percent for incentive × 12 units)   <u> 12.94</u>
                                                      $317.70

Last week the production department reported that there was a 100-day backlog of orders. The vice president in charge of production told the president that he would like to start finding subcontractors for some of these orders. The president gave his consent but urged the manager to try to get as much of the work as possible done in-house. "If necessary," he said, "raise the incentive to 35 percent of base pay." The vice president agreed to do so, but pointed out to the president that only 6 percent of the total plant work force was willing to work on Saturday. "I don't think we're having much success with our incentive program. If you ask me, you just can't get good help anymore."

QUESTIONS

1. Does the Greenley management think that money motivates people? Explain.
2. Why is the incentive plan not proving effective?
3. Based on the vice president's last comment, how would you characterize his view of human nature?

J. Altman, E. Valenzi, and R. Hodgetts, *Organizational Behavior* (New York: Academic Press, 1985), p. 29.

EXPERIENTIAL EXERCISE

What Do You "Know" about Human Behavior?

Chapter 1 discusses various approaches to the study of organizational behavior. Implicit in the discussion is the point that organizational behavior is an empirically based social science. As such, behavioral researchers must rely on various methods to collect data. Yet much of what we "know" about interacting with others is not derived from data gathering. We develop opinions, hunches, and so forth in our daily lives that help us decide what to do.

The following exercise is designed to give you some feedback about what you think you may "know" about human behavior.

Mark T (true) or F (false) next to each statement to indicate your agreement with it. The correct answers are provided at the end.

_____ 1. People are inherently social.

_____ 2. People who are often silent are usually deep thinkers.

_____ 3. On average, men are better drivers than women.

_____ 4. Most managers prefer to use written communication (for example, memos).

_____ 5. There are certain aspects of personality that are common to all people.

_____ 6. More people who are high achievers come from an upper-middle-class background.

_____ 7. Women apparently have more intuition than men.

_____ 8. Introverts are more sensitive to abstract ideas and feelings than are extroverts.

_____ 9. Most people who are highly intelligent seem to be physically weak.

_____ 10. High-risk takers also seem to be high achievers.

_____ 11. People are more likely to attribute success to luck or "breaks."

_____ 12. Those who smoke appear to take more sick days off from work than nonsmokers.

_____ 13. An appreciation for art or music appears to be inherited.

_____ 14. It appears that most people primarily work for money.

_____ 15. It seems that most great athletes are of below-average intelligence.

_____ 16. Very religious people seem to come mostly from poor backgrounds.

_____ 17. Seventy-five percent of the U.S. population apparently prefers to gather information through intuition.

_____ 18. It appears that most blind people possess excellent hearing.

_____ 19. Most people who go to work for the government are low-risk takers.

_____ 20. University professors have higher self-esteem than do members of any other occupational group.

_____ 21. The best workers in an organization often produce two or three times as much work as the poorest workers.

_____ 22. In social interactions, women look more at the other person than do men.

_____ 23. In the United States, there seems to be a greater emphasis on "fitting in" rather than on "standing out" in social situations.

_____ 24. Good leaders have become quite common in most organizations.

_____ 25. Attempting to influence the behavior of others is a natural human tendency.

_____ 26. Top-level executives appear to have a greater need for money than for power.

_____ 27. History suggests that most famous people were born of poor, hard-working parents.

_____ 28. One's experiences as an infant and child tend to determine behavior in later life.

_____ 29. Work stress is undesirable and should be avoided whenever possible.

_____ 30. Most successful relationships support the notion that opposites attract.

Below are the answers to the statements. Check your answers to see how well you "know" human behavior. Most students get between 16 and 22 right; how did you do?

You may recall that, in introducing this exercise, the point was made that much of what you "know" about human behavior is not based on research. As such, it tends to be in error.

Organizational behavior, however, is based on more than opinion and intuition. It is a science. Therefore, as you begin reading and studying the following chapters, remember that the information is empirically based.

1. T	11. F	21. T
2. F	12. T	22. T
3. F	13. F	23. F
4. F	14. F	24. F
5. T	15. F	25. T
6. T	16. F	26. F
7. F	17. F	27. F
8. T	18. F	28. T
9. F	19. F	29. F
10. F	20. T	30. F

Source: Written by Bruce Kemelgor, University of Louisville; used by permission.

NOTES

1. L.L. Cummings, "Toward Organizational Behavior," *Academy of Management Review* 3 (1978): 90–98.

2. D.A. Wren, *The Evolution of Management Thought* (New York: Wiley, 1979).

3. C. George, *The History of Management Thought* (Englewood Cliffs, N.J.: Prentice-Hall, 1972); S.A. Cook, F.E. Adcock, and M.P. Charlesworth, eds.,

The Cambridge Ancient History (Cambridge: The University Press, 1966).

4. A. Russell, ed., *Guinness Book of World Records* (New York: Bantam Books, 1988), p. 403.

5. F.L. Lane, *Venetian Ships and Shipbuilders of the Renaissance* (Baltimore: Johns Hopkins Press, 1934); E.H. Altham, *The Principles of War* (London: Macmillan, 1914); C. von

Clausewitz, *On War,* translated by J. Graham (New York: Barnes and Noble, 1968); A.L. Wagner, *Organization and Tactics* (New York: B. Westmann, 1985).

6. F.W. Taylor, *The Principles of Scientific Management* (New York: Norton, 1911); J. Gies, "Automating the Worker," *Invention and Technology* (Winter, 1991): 56–63; F.J. Lundy, "Hugo Münsterberg: Victim or Visionary?" *Journal of Applied Psychology* 77 (1992): 787–802.

7. L.W. Fry, "The Maligned F.W. Taylor: A Reply to His Many Critics," *Academy of Management Review* 30 (1976): 124–139; E.A. Locke "The Ideas of Frederick W. Taylor: An Evaluation," *Academy of Management Review* 7 (1982): 14–24.

8. C.D. Wrege and R.G. Greenwood, *Frederick Taylor: The Father of Scientific Management: Myth and Reality* (Homewood, Ill.: Irwin, 1991); J.M. Gotcher, "Assisting the Handicapped: The Pioneering Efforts of Frank and Lillian Gilbreth," *Journal of Management* 18 (1992): 5–13.

9. F.J. Roethlisberger and W.J. Dickson, *Management and the Worker: An Account of a Research Program Conducted by the Western Electric Company, Hawthorne Works, Chicago* (Cambridge, Mass.: Harvard University Press, 1939); "Hawthorne Revisited: The Legend and the Legacy," *Organizational Dynamics* 3 (1975): 67–68; A.H. Schulman, J.W. Gibson, and R.G. Greenwood, "The Hawthorne Studies: What Are We Teaching? What Should We Be Teaching?" (Paper presented at the National Meeting of the Academy of Management, 1991); E. Mayo, *The Human Problems of an Industrial Civilization* (New York: Viking, 1933).

10. D. Bramel and R. Friend, "Hawthorne, the Myth of the Docile Worker, and Class Bias in Psychology," *American Psychologist* 36 (1981): 867–878; E.A. Locke, "Critique of Bramel and Friend," *American Psychologist* 37 (1982): 858–859; H.M. Parsons, "What Caused the Hawthorne Effect? A Scientific Detective Story," *Administration and Society* 10 (1978): 259–283; J. Feldman, "Ideology Without Data," *American Psychologist* 37 (1982): 857–858; R. Stagner, "The Importance of Historical Context," *American Psychologist* 37 (1982): 856; R.H. Franke, "The Hawthorne Experiments: Empirical Findings and Implications for Management," (Paper presented at the National Meeting of the Academy of Management, 1987); R.H. Franke and R.P. Urian, "Illumination and Productivity at Hawthorne," (Paper presented at the National Meeting of the Academy of Management, 1991).

11. S.R. Barley and G. Kunda, "Design and Devotion: Surges of Rational and Normative Ideologies of Control in Managerial Discourse," *Administrative Science Quarterly,* 37 (1992): 363–399.

12. T.J. Peters and R.H. Waterman, Jr., *In Search of Excellence* (New York: Harper and Row, 1982); T.E. Deal and A.A. Kennedy, *Corporate Cultures* (Reading, Mass.: Addison-Wesley, 1982); W.G. Ouchi, *Theory Z: How American Business Can Meet the Japanese Challenge* (Reading, Mass.: Addison-Wesley, 1981).

13. P.F. Lazarsfeld, "The American Soldier— An Expository Review," *Public Opinion Quarterly* 13 (1949): 377–404; P. Slovic and B. Fischhoff, "On the Psychology of Experimental Surprises," *Journal of Experimental Psychology: Human Perception and Performance* 3 (1977): 544–551; J.J. Christensen-Szalanski and C. Fabian-Willham, "The Hindsight Bias: A Meta-Analysis," *Organizational Behavior and Human Decision Processes* 48 (1991): 147–168.

14. G.J. Fletcher, "Psychology and Common Sense," *American Psychologist* 39 (1984): 203–213; R.P. Vecchio, "Some Popular (But Misguided) Criticisms of the Organizational Sciences," *Organizational Behavior Teaching Review* 11 (1987): 28–34.

15. A. Kohn, "You Know What They Say . . . ," *Psychology Today* 22 (1988): 36–41.

If all the behavioral
scientists in the world were
laid end to end, it would be
a good thing.

— Anonymous

Science is a means whereby
noncreative people can
create.

— Abe Maslow

LEARNING OBJECTIVES

*After studying this chapter, you
should be able to:*

1. *Summarize the starting
   assumptions that enable
   organizational behavior
   researchers to systematize
   their studies.*

2. *Define the essential steps in
   the scientific research process.*

3. *Enumerate the fundamental
   goals of OB research.*

4. *Distinguish an independent
   variable from a dependent
   variable, an intervening
   variable, and a moderating
   variable.*

5. *Differentiate the correlational
   method of research from the
   experimental method and
   assess the strengths and
   weaknesses of each approach.*

6. *Identify the most frequently
   used strategies and settings of
   OB research.*

7. *Discuss why the design of
   research studies requires a
   trade-off between internal and
   external validity.*

8. *Cite the most important
   ethical issues that OB
   researchers must bear in mind.*

9. *Outline the basic format of a
   typical OB research report.*

Approaches to Studying Organizational Behavior

A NEW METHOD OF ASSESSING MANAGERIAL EFFECTIVENESS

One of the newest tools designed to foster open communication and trust in today's organizations is *upward feedback,* a process whereby supervisors receive constructive feedback about their performance from their subordinates. Not only is this a revolutionary approach to fostering feedback and communication between a manager and employees, it also represents a new way to collect information about a manager's performance. Previously, when management wanted feedback from staffers, confidential surveys were completed by employees, analyzed, and fed back to management in an aggregate, anonymous form. Today's upward feedback systems are more interactive and results-oriented, often involving one-on-one communication between managers and employees.

Understandably, most managers are not thrilled with the prospect of receiving negative feedback, and many employees are reluctant to provide frank evaluations of their supervisor's performance. The key to making upward feedback work is to create an environment of shared leadership, where both parties recognize the benefits of honest communication. By providing a framework for discussing every-

one's responsibility to the corporate vision, managers and their workers can identify ways to jointly pursue corporate goals.

BP Exploration, a division of British Petroleum, provides trained feedback consultants to mitigate feelings of discomfort and hostility a supervisor might have toward employees. In the first step of the upward feedback process, direct reports by employees rate managers on 23 management practices (such as frequency of meeting with individual employees to review performance). Originally, the questionnaires were returned to a consultant who analyzed and summarized the data. Now employees anonymously complete the questionnaires on an on-line computer system that compiles the data and sends a summary report directly to the supervisor via electronic mail. At the manager's discretion, the feedback consultant will discuss the report with the manager, which helps prepare the supervisor for the next step of the process: meeting with employees. A staff meeting is held to help the manager comprehend and accept the survey results. To facilitate an honest and objective discussion of the manager's performance, the feedback consultant may be present at the meeting. While not revealing

their individual responses, employees are encouraged to be candid about the manager's performance. To get discussion going, managers may pose open-ended questions to employees such as, "Here's an area where my feedback indicates I need improvement. Whether you agree with this assessment or not, tell me what specific things I might or might not be doing." Eventually, BP Exploration hopes to foster enough trust between managers and their employees that employee anonymity will be unnecessary, and feedback consultants will no longer need to facilitate these meetings.

Two elements are crucial to the success of upward feedback programs. First, both employees and managers must be willing and able to communicate constructively and honestly. Second, employee feedback should be translated into developmental plans to ensure managers work on their weaknesses. If behavioral changes don't follow open discussions of performance, upward feedback systems may backfire, creating deep resentments that will be difficult to overturn.

Organizations that are dismantling bureaucracies and other barriers to communications are

(continued on following page)

(continued from previous page)

ideal candidates for upward feedback systems. They also work well in organizations that support learning and change, and where employees feel free to offer their ideas without fear of reprisal. Upward feedback systems will undoubtedly become more popular as the need for flexibility in organizations continues. Properly implemented, upward feedback systems can provide organizations with new opportunities for constructive communication and change.

Collecting and analyzing data about employee behavior is at the heart of research in Organizational Behavior. To understand the dynamics of organizations we must study and assess the effectiveness of organizational practices and processes such as upward feedback systems. This chapter introduces you to the principles and methods of research in OB, allowing you to appreciate the complexities of studying employee behavior.

Source: Milan Moravec, Herman Gyr, and Lisa Friedman, "A 21st Century Communication Tool," *HRMagazine,* July 1993, 77–81.

In the previous chapter, we defined organizational behavior (OB) as the systematic study of human behavior within organizational settings. The actual approach by which we study employees in work settings constitutes a behavioral science. As such, it stresses the importance of careful logic, attention to measurement, and reliance on empirical evidence. Evidence that is empirical is based on observation and is, therefore, verifiable. By limiting OB studies to empirical evidence, we eliminate potentially fruitless debates on the nature of behavior and focus instead on hard evidence obtained from research studies. The final words for an empiricist who is engaged in a philosophical debate are, "Show me your data."

Before we can examine the information that the field of OB has to offer, we need to consider the ways in which such information is gathered and interpreted. Consequently, this chapter presents the purposes, rationale, and methods of organizational behavior research—that is, the "how" of OB research. It is not the goal of this chapter to train researchers; rather, the information in the chapter is intended to aid readers in becoming enlightened consumers of management literature.[*]

STARTING ASSUMPTIONS

Behavioral phenomena are unlike many phenomena we might study in that they influence, and are influenced by, many processes. As a result, OB researchers accept several starting assumptions that enable them to systematize their research efforts. These assumptions are summarized in Table 2.1.

BEHAVIOR IS PREDICTABLE

First, OB researchers assume that behavior is predictable. In essence, they assume that the entire effort to study employee behavior will be successful. The

---

[*]For those readers who are considering becoming academic researchers, I recommend learning a good deal more about research methods, plus obtaining a copy of *The Compleat Academic,* edited by Mark Zanna and John Darley (Hillsdale, N.J.: Lawrence Erlbaum, 1987). The text provides a practical overview of how to break into academic publishing and how to manage an academic career.

■ **TABLE 2.1**
FOUR ASSUMPTIONS OF OB RESEARCH

1. Behavior can be predicted.
2. Behavior is caused.
3. Behavior has a finite number of causes.
4. Generalities can be reasonably drawn.

reverse of this assumption—that is, that behavior is unpredictable—would negate the value of systematically studying employee behavior. Our own day-to-day experience, however, suggests that behavior is often predictable due to certain regularities that we observe in our own and others' behavior. For example, you may have noticed that unhappy workers are more likely to quit their jobs in favor of employment elsewhere. Or you may have noticed that new employees tend to cling together as a group until they feel that they are assimilated into the workplace. If human behavior were random or capricious, the conduct of our daily affairs would be virtually impossible. Therefore, the assumption of predictability appears reasonable.

BEHAVIOR IS CAUSED

A second assumption is that behavior is caused. This assumption is crucial to the study of behavior because otherwise we could not draw connections between behavior and the observable influences that affect it. Almost everyone would agree that there are causes for much of human behavior. The simplest example is a reflex response, such as pulling your hand away from an overheated piece of machinery. For more sophisticated behaviors, the causes are more complex. Sophisticated behaviors should, nonetheless, be subject to causal influences.[†]

BEHAVIOR HAS MANY CAUSES

In the study of organizational behavior, we must further assume that behavior has multiple but limited causes. Simply stated, this means that human action is typically the result of a set of forces, the total number of which is finite. Given the assumption of multiple but limited causality, we approach the study of employee behavior with a recognition that our explanations will need to be complex in order to represent the complexity of the causal processes. But we can also be reassured that the number of important causal factors will probably not be endless.

GENERALITIES CAN BE DRAWN

Finally, researchers assume that despite the fundamental uniqueness of every situation, generalities can nonetheless be drawn. For example, all employees

---

[†]As Voltaire wrote, "It would be very singular that all nature, all the planets, should obey eternal laws, and that there should be a little animal, five feet high, who, in contempt of these laws, could act as he pleased."[1]

are different, and all have basically different job experiences, but they can be expected to react similarly to certain situations. Thus, when faced with the prospect of a pay cut or give-back of benefits, most employees will react similarly, regardless of their position within the company.

THE SCIENTIFIC METHOD IN OB RESEARCH

Scientific research follows a particular process, as shown in Figure 2.1. The process consists of three essential steps: induction, deduction, and verification.

INDUCTION

In the first step, **induction,** we start with a set of observations or facts and generate a theoretical statement that can explain them. In this way, we move from a set of very specific observations to a general explanatory principle, or theory. A theory is a statement of interrelated principles, assumptions, and definitions that is generated by a researcher in an attempt to explain a set of observations.[‡] As you might suspect, many possible theories can be constructed to explain a set of observations. Some, of course, will be better than others. Demonstrating which theories are better is an important part of the scientific approach.

DEDUCTION

Deduction, the second step, is part of the process for determining whether a particular theory is a good representation. The use of logic guides us in deducing (from a theory) a prediction of what to expect under specified circumstances.

VERIFICATION

In the final step in the process, **verification,** we attempt to determine the truth or falsehood of a prediction—and by inference, the adequacy of the underly-

FIGURE 2.1
THE SCIENTIFIC METHOD

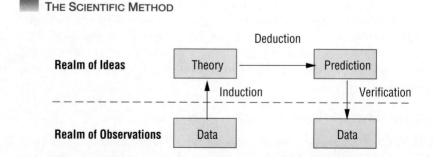

[‡]Without theory, we have little more than a collection of unordered observations. As noted by Henri Poincaré, "Science is built of facts, the way a house is built of bricks; but an accumulation of facts is no more a science than a pile of bricks is a house."

ing theory—by gathering new data and checking to see if they support or refute the deduced predictions. Support for a prediction suggests that our theoretical constructions are on the right track. A failure to find support for a prediction, assuming that our research methods and deductive logic are sound, suggests that the theoretical basis of the prediction is in need of revision.

THE SCIENTIFIC METHOD IN PRACTICE

As an illustration, consider the question of how workers respond to unfair or inequitable situations. Many observers have commented on the importance of feelings of justice or fairness in determining workers' performance and satisfaction. From these observations J. Stacy Adams generated a set of propositions to explain the major issues on which individuals focus when judging their relative state of equity.[2] The theory that Adams generated is, in fact, quite elaborate, but one facet of it concerns the quality and quantity of output that an individual can be expected to produce under a piece-rate pay scheme. Specifically, Adams predicted that an individual who feels overpaid on such a pay scheme will increase the quality of each unit of production but decrease the quantity of units produced. This prediction is based on the principle that people will try to maximize equity by adjusting their efforts and also attempting to control their rewards. Clearly, this prediction is somewhat counterintuitive in that most of us would predict that people who feel overpaid would probably be very productive.

In a study designed to test this prediction, two groups of workers were paid on a piece-rate basis to conduct interviews.[3] One group was paid a reasonable rate per interview, while the other group was paid a much higher rate. As Adams predicted, the highly paid group actually conducted fewer interviews than did the more reasonably paid workers. However, the quality of the interviews, as measured by the number of words recorded by each interviewer, was greater for the workers who were overpaid. Because these results support Adams's predictions for worker performance in an overpaid setting, by inference they suggest that his theoretical formulations are correct.

In this example, we see the major steps of the research process:

1. Adams made a number of observations about inequity: He collected anecdotal and research-based accounts of worker behavior in inequitable settings. From his observations, he induced (developed) a fairly detailed and complete set of theoretical propositions about people's psychological and behavioral reactions to inequity.

2. From his propositions, Adams deduced the "if–then" prediction that the maximization of equity is more important to most people than is the raw maximization of pay, so that if workers feel overpaid, then certain changes in performance will occur.

3. As part of the verification process, the "if" aspects of Adams's prediction were set up in a controlled situation that satisfied the logical requirements for testing them. The results of the study, therefore, corroborated the theoretically based expectation—that is, the "then" part of the "if–then" statement.

This illustration helps to show the importance of theory in OB research. If Adams had not carefully formulated and articulated his theory, we might have simply followed our intuitive impulses regarding the likely behavior of employees who are overcompensated. The results indicate that our impulses would have misguided us to believe that quantity would be higher and quality would be lower, when actually the opposite is true. As noted in Chapter 1, all varieties of human behavior are conceivable. Therefore, we use theory to guide our study of employee behavior and data to guide our further refinement of our theoretical constructions.

REFINING THEORIES

At this point, you may be thinking that it is still likely that overcompensated employees will increase their quantity of output and sacrifice the quality. It is difficult to give up the notion that people act primarily out of self-interest. Therefore, you may argue that only under certain conditions and with certain types of people would we be more likely to find an altruistic response to over-compensation. Through this thought process, you generate further refinements and qualifications of the theoretical propositions in light of your own personal experience and observation. They, in turn, suggest the need for further research. If you wished to test your refinements, you would carefully lay out the logic and the associated predictions. Next, you would design and conduct an experiment to see if your hunches are correct. If they are, the original theoretical propositions would require revision. If they are not, you would have to consider why your predictions were not supported. Were there errors in your initial observations of behavior? Were there errors in logic? Errors in designing the study? Errors in analyzing the data from your study? In large part, the refinement process consists of identifying and testing plausible rival explanations for obtained results. If these alternative, rival explanations can be eliminated, then we can have greater confidence in the accuracy of our explanations.

Theories are set forth to be revised or refuted. Although a theory may be supported time and again, if it is static or self-contained, it is of little value in obtaining new knowledge. In other words, a theory should suggest and direct further research. Other things being equal, a theory that suggests new ideas (or new "rocks to be looked under") is preferable to a theory that is stated in a very complete or closed fashion.

THE NECESSITY OF TESTABILITY

A scientific theory must be testable. A set of propositions, however logical and appealing, that does not generate a specific prediction that can be tested for truth or falsehood is of no real value to the search for new knowledge. For example, an organizational consultant whose training program I once attended professed to believe a set of theoretical propositions that included the notion that all people are born with the knowledge of what life is like on other planets in the galaxy. Over time, so the thesis went, people lose this knowledge. When challenged by his audience to show evidence of his claims, the speaker stated that proof could not be provided because, as children learn to speak, the very process of learning a language conflicts with and eliminates their prior knowledge of other planets.

In analyzing this proposal carefully, you will note that it is stated in an untestable fashion. It is evident that one can make any outlandish claim if it is defined in a way that renders it untestable. Thus, the requirement that propositions be testable is absolutely essential for separating pipe dreams from real processes.

THE GOALS OF RESEARCH

In organizational behavior, as in other fields, the research process has four major goals. The first goal is *description*. Describing behavior or events leads to a classification system that paves the way for attaining the other three goals. The second goal is simple *prediction* of behavior or events. Prediction may consist of nothing more than an extrapolation from past events. *Explanation*, the third goal, involves the statement of the underlying processes that produce or are responsible for events or behaviors. Lastly, *control* of some behaviors or events is desirable as the ultimate goal of research.

As an example of how these four goals are pursued, consider how OB has approached the subject of employee turnover. Early on, researchers recognized the need to classify turnover into at least two major divisions: voluntary (or quitting based on personal choice) and involuntary (or forced termination). Researchers then turned their attention to predicting the different kinds of turnover from a knowledge of employee attributes, such as sex, expressed dissatisfaction, number of children, and so on. After these findings were established, researchers focused on developing theoretical models to explain the antecedents and consequences of turnover. Still more recently, research has been directed toward controlling or managing turnover so that poor performers are encouraged to leave while superior performers are discouraged from leaving.

RESEARCH TERMINOLOGY

Researchers in OB, as well as in other fields, employ a common set of terms to describe their work. To fully understand their writings, one must be familiar with the most commonly used terms, such as hypotheses and four types of variables (summarized in Table 2.2).

TABLE 2.2
FOUR TYPES OF VARIABLES IN OB RESEARCH

Type	Definition
Independent Variable	A suspected cause of or influence on another variable
Dependent Variable	An outcome or consequence that is attributable to the independent variable
Intervening Variable	A useful concept for explaining the link between the independent variable and the dependent variable
Moderating Variable	A factor influencing the form of the relationship between the independent variable and the dependent variable

INDEPENDENT AND DEPENDENT VARIABLES

An **independent variable** is a set of values (measurements) that is believed to cause changes in another set of values. For example, the different values obtained by employees on an intelligence test can serve as an index of an important influence on employee learning in a training program. In this instance, intelligence would be an independent variable if one chose to study its influence. A value that is affected by the independent variable is a **dependent variable.** The specific values of this second set are "dependent" on the specific values of the independent variable.

As an illustration, consider a study on the effects of seating arrangements on feelings of success in two-person negotiations. A researcher might set up several different seating arrangements around a table of a given size. For instance, the researcher might first place two seats side-by-side, then arrange them kitty-corner, and finally put them on opposite sides of the table. The researcher chooses these seating arrangements because they are suspected to cause or contribute to feelings of success in negotiations. Thus, the seating arrangement is the independent variable.

After groups of two are given an exercise in negotiating a difficult confrontational issue, they are asked to complete a questionnaire that indicates the extent to which they feel satisfied that they reached a mutually acceptable resolution. The researcher suspects that the responses will be influenced by the seating arrangement to which the people were assigned. Because the responses are assumed to depend on the seating arrangements, they are the dependent variable.

HYPOTHESES

A **hypothesis** is a prediction or hunch. It is a statement of how the independent and dependent variables are related. A researcher tests whether a hypothesis should be accepted or rejected by examining the results of a study. In the seating example, one hypothesis might be that the arrangement in which the negotiators sit across from each other at the table leads to the lowest degree of reported satisfaction, while the side-by-side arrangement leads to the highest. The data gathered would dictate whether to accept or reject the hypothesis that seating arrangement affects feelings of satisfaction.

INTERVENING VARIABLES

Sometimes researchers find it useful to propose **intervening variables** in their theories. An intervening variable is an unobservable state or process that helps to explain the link between an independent variable and a dependent variable. An example of an intervening variable in OB theorizing would be "attitudes." Attitudes are not directly observable but must be inferred from measurements of other variables that are assumed to be closely related to them. In the seating arrangement example, a theorist might propose that any relationship between seating and feelings of success in negotiation occurs because seating arrangements arouse attitudes of cooperation or competition in participants. These attitudes in turn might influence reactions to the experience of negotiation.

OB Focus
Discrimination Goes Global

In many multinational corporations there is a disparity in the number of women versus men placed on overseas assignments. To better understand this phenomenon, McGill University researchers have tested three primary hypotheses: (1) women are not interested in pursuing international careers, (2) companies are hesitant to send women abroad, and (3) the prejudicial feelings of foreigners prevent women from doing their jobs.

To investigate the merit of the first hypothesis, more than 1,000 graduating MBA students were surveyed to determine if women were less interested than men in international careers. The results indicated that men were "not significantly" more interested than women in international careers. About 80 percent of both men and women desire international assignments at some point in their careers.

To test the second hypothesis, interviews were conducted with human resource vice presidents and managers from a sample of large North American organizations. More than half the

companies admitted their reluctance to send women managers abroad, confirming the second hypothesis. The reasons given for their hesitation were numerous: concern that foreigners would be prejudiced against women managers, formidable dual-career issues, concerns about physical safety, and the strain of traveling in underdeveloped countries.

The third hypothesis was tested by surveying women managers of American organizations currently on international assignments. The researchers found that 97 percent of women expatriates were successful in their assignments, and that in many cases, being a woman has helped, not hindered, the manager abroad. Rather than being the receptor of prejudicial attacks by foreigners, women are often at an advantage in foreign countries simply because they stand out. Because female managers are so uncommon in some foreign environs, they may receive different treatment than men. Foreign managers often find women more interesting and easy to talk to, and women are more likely to be remembered

after the first meeting with foreigners. Thus, the notion that foreigners are prejudiced against women expatriates is simply a myth. It seems that even in cultures where women are not as prominent in the business community, cultural roles reserved for local women are not applied to foreigners.

It appears that the insular attitudes about women managers abroad are held by managers in the United States, and not by foreigners. Managers in host countries place greater saliency on nationality over gender—women expatriates are seen as foreigners who are women, not women who happen to be foreigners. The distinction is important because it indicates that American managers falsely assume foreign perceptions of women will be insurmountable roadblocks for American female managers. As businesses become more global and more women are called upon for higher level duties, shortsighted attitudes like these may prevent American organizations from efficiently utilizing their increasingly diverse work forces.

Sources: Nancy J. Adler, "Woman Managers in a Global Economy," *HRMagazine*, September 1993, 52–55; Nancy J. Adler, "Competitive Frontiers: Women Managing Across Borders," in Nancy J. Adler and Dafna N. Izraeli, eds., *Competitive Frontiers: Women Managers in a Global Economy*, (Colchester, Vt.: Blackwell Publishers, 1993).

MODERATING VARIABLES

Another notion sometimes used in OB research is that of moderating variables. A **moderating variable** is one that is responsible for a change in the relationship between an independent and a dependent variable.[4] That is to say, the relationship between the independent and dependent variables varies in association with the values of a third variable, the moderating variable. If you recall the discussion of the contingency approach in Chapter 1, you will recognize that a moderating variable represents a dependency, in that the nature of the relationship between two variables depends on the status of a third dimension.

In a sense, the contingency approach centers on identifying important moderating variables.

Organizational researchers generally believe that moderators, or interdependencies, are very important for describing and explaining behavioral phenomena. As an illustration, consider the proposal that gender may moderate the relationship between seating arrangement and feelings of success in negotiations. Stated as a hypothesis, one might predict that males are likely to respond that they experienced lower feelings of success than did females when placed in a confrontational seating arrangement (for example, on opposite sides of a table).

Another example would be the proposal that the relationship between employee intelligence and job satisfaction might be moderated by the level of a job, so that the relationship is positive for high-level jobs but negative (or inverse) for low-level jobs. This example suggests that more intelligent employees respond favorably to challenging and responsible jobs, but respond negatively to jobs that do not tap their abilities. Less intelligent employees might be frustrated by highly challenging jobs, yet find jobs requiring less mental exercise to be more satisfying.

TWO MAJOR RESEARCH METHODS

OB research may employ either a correlational or an experimental method.

THE CORRELATIONAL METHOD

The **correlational method** of research is concerned with the relationship between two variables, particularly whether changes in one variable are associated with changes in another variable. As variable *A* increases, does variable *B* also increase? If so, a positive association or correlation would be indicated. Or, as variable *A* increases, does variable *B* decrease? In such cases, a negative, or inverse, correlation is implied.

Although the results of correlational studies may tell us whether and how two variables are associated, they can provide no more than a descriptive summary of a relationship. In a sense, the results of correlational research provide a snapshot of a relationship and do not really tell why or how the relationship was produced.

A study reported by Kasl and French employed the correlational method.[5] Their results identified a positive correlation between the occupational status of industrial workers and measures of physical and emotional health. In their study, the researchers did not manipulate occupational status or degree of health.[§] They merely correlated values of these two measures in their search for an association. If we attempt to find a causal relationship between the two variables, one shortcoming of the correlational method becomes apparent: Does health influence attainment of a high- or low-status job? Or does attain-

---

[§]In fact, one cannot conceive of an ethical study in which either status or health would be manipulated in order to study their effects.

ment of a particular kind of job influence health? Does another factor vary in association with both status and health (for instance, prior education), so that this third variable is in fact responsible for the observed correlation? These three alternative explanations—(1) that variable *A* causes *B*, (2) that variable *B* causes *A*, and (3) that a third variable causes changes in both variables *A* and *B*—are all possible interpretations for an observed correlation. No firm conclusions about causality can be drawn from purely correlational evidence.

As a further illustration, consider a hypothetical positive correlation between daily ice cream sales and the number of daily drownings that occur at seaside resorts. Three causal explanations are possible here: (1) ice cream consumption could lead to drownings (in accordance with our grandmothers' warnings about the danger of getting cramps if we eat before we swim); (2) drownings could lead to increased ice cream consumption (crowds might gather to watch rescue efforts and subsequently frequent ice cream stands); and (3) daily temperature could influence both ice cream consumption and drownings (when the temperature rises, people tend to eat more ice cream and venture more often into the water).

In addition to these three causal explanations for an observed correlation, there is also a fourth: *spuriousness*. Spuriousness occurs when an apparently nontrivial correlation is due to chance alone. This fourth explanation is always a possibility. However, researchers attempt to reduce the likelihood of spuriousness by gathering a large number of observations.

A well-known example of a correlation that is probably spurious is the correlation between the overall yearly performance of the Dow Jones Industrial Average and the league affiliation of the winning football team in the Super Bowl. Throughout the first 27 Super Bowls, the league affiliation of the winning team has been an excellent predictor of whether the Dow Jones Average would rise or fall during the coming year. If the winning team was a member of the National Football League, the Dow Jones Average would generally rise; if the winning team was a member of the American Football League, the average would fall. Therefore, in years when the Packers, Redskins, Colts, and Forty-Niners were winners, the economy improved. In the years when the Dolphins and Chiefs won, the economy suffered. It is difficult to offer a causal explanation for this strong correlation. Yet the correlation cannot be completely dismissed by saying that it is the likely result of chance.[**] It is likely that in additional years we will see a breakdown in this pattern of prediction. That is to say, the use of a large number of observations helps to ensure that correlational results are not due to spuriousness.[††]

Despite its shortcoming, correlational research can be valuable. In fact, certain questions can be addressed only through the use of a correlational

---

[**]Based on statistical probability, the probability of this association occurring in 24 of 27 instances (assuming chance is the only factor operating) is less than one in ten million!

[††]It is possible that in the future some people who are aware that the league affiliation of the Super Bowl winner is a predictor of economic activity may consciously use the outcome of the game as a forecast of future economic prosperity. If they do, they may conduct their financial affairs in ways that bring about fulfillment of their own prophecy.

method. For example, the relationship between economic depressions and employee attitudes can only be studied correlationally, since it is not feasible to create an economic depression for research purposes. Also, correlational studies may be a productive first step in analyzing certain events, as a prelude to more controlled studies. It is important to remember, however, that it is impossible to infer causality from correlational evidence with a high degree of confidence.

THE EXPERIMENTAL METHOD

When feasible, the experimental method is the preferred method for studying cause-and-effect relationships. In the **experimental method,** a researcher manipulates a particular variable (the independent variable) in the hope of observing corresponding changes in another measure (the dependent variable). Other variables that might also influence the results but that are not of immediate interest to the researcher are controlled or eliminated through the careful design of the study.

The experimental method was used in the seating arrangement study discussed earlier. In the example, seating arrangements were deliberately manipulated in order to study their effects. The researcher attributed differences in the measures (that is, the reported emotional reactions) to the only major manipulated difference that existed across the conditions (that is, the different seating arrangements).

Researchers must make certain assumptions in order to draw causal inferences from studies based on the experimental method. For example, researchers infer that an independent variable produced changes in a dependent variable because they assume that if one event precedes another, the only accepted order of causality is that the earlier event caused the later event. Similarly, there is no substitute for a personal understanding of the phenomenon under investigation. Without this understanding, an investigator could seem to follow the experimental method closely and yet reach ridiculous conclusions.‡‡

RESEARCH STRATEGIES AND SETTINGS

A variety of strategies and settings are used in carrying out the two major methods of OB research. Among the most frequently employed are case studies, surveys, field experiments, laboratory experiments, and archival research, as well as unobtrusive measures. The advantages and disadvantages of each strategy and setting are summarized in Table 2.3.

---

‡‡ As an example, you may recall the story about the scientist who cut off the hind legs of a trained jumping frog. After removing the legs, he commanded the frog to jump. Since the frog now failed to jump on command, the scientist recorded in his log, "Removal of a frog's hind legs induces deafness." This story is actually an illustration of the danger of making inferences that are beyond the available data (in that the scientist did not actually measure deafness).

TABLE 2.3
RESEARCH STRATEGIES AND SETTINGS: ADVANTAGES AND DISADVANTAGES

	Advantages	Disadvantages
Case Study	Provides insights Suggests hypotheses	Little rigor or control Simplistic
Survey	Informative Best for studying attitudes Fairly quick and inexpensive	Response tendencies Correlational evidence
Field Experiment	Permits causal inferences Easier to generalize results Greater realism Can arouse less employee suspicion	Limited degree of control Employees are not randomly selected
Laboratory Experiment	High degree of control and precision Permits strong causal inferences Random assignment is possible	Often artificial and unrealistic Limited generalizability of results Arouses subject suspicion
Archival Research	Unobtrusive Relevant to the topic of interest	Limited to using available data Correlational evidence

CASE STUDIES

The least rigorous approach to studying organizational behavior is to gather information informally. In a **case study,** an investigator closely examines the goings-on in an organization but makes no effort to control or eliminate alternative causal explanations for what is observed. The observations gathered for a case study can also vary, ranging from casual personal recollections of the researcher's own experience to more elaborate routines that involve interviewing others or making daily entries in a diary. Case studies are typically based on the intense study of only one organization, although several organizations are sometimes examined. In an illustration of the case-study approach, Witte examined the introduction of industrial democracy in a company manufacturing stereo equipment on the West Coast.[6]§§ The industrial-democracy project involved the creation of autonomous, or self-regulating, work groups; the frequent use of voting to decide issues; worker representation on high-level decision-making committees; and so on. To assess the effects of these efforts, Witte gathered data from tape recordings of committee meetings, the outcomes of votes, a personal diary, several sets of interviews, and casual remarks from employees. Witte's role in the situation was that of a participant-observer, in that he was employed by the firm to administer some of these radical changes.

The results that Witte reported are difficult to interpret in terms of the effectiveness of introducing industrial democracy. Because a formal comparison group was not available and because he did not obtain hard data on such questions as whether changes in productivity were due to the democratic experiment, one cannot reach solid conclusions on the likely effects of introducing

§§Industrial democracy is a system of administration that attempts to institute political equality for all members of a firm by the use of certain decision-making mechanisms such as referenda, mass assemblies, and election of representatives to councils and committees.

industrial democracy. Also, Witte's role as a participant-observer who had a personal interest in the success or failure of industrial democracy could lead to questions about his objectivity. Case studies do possess several important positive features. Their results can be useful in generating hypotheses for further testing in more controlled studies. Also, case studies can provide insights that aid in theorizing. Finally, the results of case studies may suggest causal variables that help to explain a process.

SURVEYS

Researchers often use surveys to gather data about organizational behavior. A **survey** is a set of questions, either oral or written, designed to collect people's personal responses to a subject of interest to a researcher. Some phenomena, such as workers' attitudes toward their supervisor, are especially well suited to survey studies. But other phenomena, such as worker effort, may be better studied through observation or experimentation. Researchers must decide on a case-by-case basis whether a survey will serve their purposes.

When constructing a survey, the researcher must consider a number of potential problems, most of them related to respondents' reactions. For example, the questions must be designed so that respondents can answer easily and accurately, even if their responses are unlikely or rare. Otherwise, the collected data may be unreliable. Questions must also be worded in such a way that they do not bias the respondents' answers. Respondents may also react to the personal attributes of an interviewer or the general appearance of a questionnaire and, as a result, offer answers that they might not otherwise endorse. Respondents may also show response tendencies, or biases. Several common forms of bias are (1) *social desirability,* the tendency to give the answers that are believed to be most socially acceptable, (2) *acquiescence/defiance,* the tendency to agree or disagree with whatever question is posed, regardless of its content, and (3) *extremism,* the tendency to either rely on or avoid extreme options when responding to a question.

In a study of the relationship between race and job satisfaction, data were gathered from a national sample of 2,600 full-time workers.[7] The data were gathered through interviews over a period of several years by the National Opinion Research Center of the University of Chicago. Among the many questions put to the respondents were items about level of satisfaction with present employment, job title, years of education, and self-classification of race. The results indicated that job satisfaction was higher for people who had more education and were in higher-status jobs, regardless of race. Education and job status were closely related, as one might readily predict. On the average, blacks were significantly less satisfied with their work than were whites. However, most of the black workers also occupied jobs of lesser status and had less formal education. These results, of course, are descriptive and do not tell whether blacks and whites differ in job satisfaction independently of education and job status. Although we implicitly assume that education leads to higher job status, we do not know from these results whether race in itself influences satisfaction, job status, and education. This illustration is fairly typical of the advantages as well as the limitations associated with survey research. Although the results of survey research tell us something we may not have known, the results may be of somewhat limited value because we cannot easily draw firm causal inferences.

FIELD EXPERIMENTS

Another strategy for studying organizational behavior topics is the field experiment. It permits cause-and-effect inferences if several reasonable assumptions can be made. A **field experiment** is a study in which a variable is manipulated in one setting while the same variable remains unchanged in another, similar setting. If we can assume that the two settings were identical on all potentially important dimensions and that no other changes were introduced in the two settings during the course of the study, then any differences in a dependent variable that may be observed between the two settings can be *at least partially* attributed to the one variable that was deliberately manipulated, the independent variable.

It is necessary to be very cautious in making causal inferences based on field experiments because many *seemingly* trivial variables may not be controlled. Thus, when we say that differences are *at least partially due* to the one variable that was changed, we acknowledge that other influences may also be operating to produce the obtained results.

As an example of a field experiment, consider a study by Muczyk on the effects of a management-by-objectives (MBO) program in a multibranch bank.[8]*** In order to test for the influence of MBO on bank-branch performance, Muczyk introduced the program in 13 branches (the treatment group), but did not introduce it in a small group of comparable branches (the comparison group). Because the branches were geographically separated, Muczyk could reasonably assume that employees would not be overly conscious of their different working conditions.

After monitoring branch performance for a one-year period, Muczyk observed an increase in performance at the branches that had been given the MBO program. If this were the only evidence available, we would probably conclude that the MBO program was highly effective. But performance results for the comparison group led to a very different conclusion. Over the course of the year-long study, the comparison group also showed a gain in performance. Because both the treatment and the comparison groups manifested the same pattern of results, we must conclude that the MBO program did not have an appreciable impact.

The ability to reach firmer conclusions about the impact of variables is a major advantage of a field experiment. Another advantage is that such a

*** Management by objectives (MBO) is an organizational program wherein a supervisor and subordinate meet on a regular basis to engage in setting specific, measurable performance goals. It is a relatively popular management technique that is designed to improve employee motivation and performance. MBO is discussed in greater detail in Chapter 7.

study's results can easily be generalized to the population of interest. For example, if you want to study the hiring-decision process in large accounting firms, you can do a field experiment using a sample of personnel specialists from the appropriate firms and, based on the results, draw conclusions about the entire population with relative ease. A field experiment may also create less suspicion among participants than would a survey because a field experiment can often be more subtly integrated into the ongoing activities of an organization. Finally, through field experiments, situations can be studied in the real world that, for ethical reasons, could not be created in a laboratory environment. For example, the behavior of people in such interesting situations as exit interviews (after they have given notice that they are quitting), hospital emergency rooms, and military crises can only be reasonably studied in their actual settings.

Field experiments also have several disadvantages. Perhaps the most notable is the researcher's lack of control over all potentially important variables. Because we cannot be certain which factors in a situation need to be controlled in order to draw strong inferences and because we face real-world constraints on our control of some factors, we cannot have complete confidence in the causal inferences we may draw from field experiments.

A further obstacle to drawing causal inferences arises because the employees we study in organizations are, in a sense, "contaminated" by their roles or positions. Organizational members are typically selected for specific reasons, have been through some form of training, and have consciously chosen to remain with the organization rather than seek employment elsewhere. Consequently, the members of an organization may have unique perspectives and abilities that could interact with other variables we may choose to experiment with, and, in the process, enhance or diminish their effects.

LABORATORY EXPERIMENTS

The epitome of scientific inquiry is the laboratory experiment. In such a study, the researcher has total control over the design of the study and the selection of variables to be manipulated and measured. A **laboratory experiment** involves the careful creation of conditions in which only the factors of interest to the researcher are permitted to vary. Even the selection of the types of individuals to be studied is controlled by the researcher.

As an illustration, imagine an investigation into the effects of different pay schemes on goal setting. In an experimental laboratory study, the researcher would decide on the various pay schemes to be contrasted, such as piece rate, hourly rate, and salary. Then he or she would choose the exact rates, after careful consideration of regional differences in pay and the subjects' expectations based on the task to be performed. Next, the researcher would select the precise task to be performed, for example, assembly work, paper handling, or problem solving, as well as the kind of individual to be studied, such as college students, housewives, or the hardcore unemployed.

Each participant would then be assigned to one of the pay schemes and asked to set a target number of units to be produced in a given period of time.

This target number would serve as the primary measure of the effect of the incentive pay scheme. With all possible extraneous factors controlled, the investigator could reasonably conclude that differences in goal setting across the various pay schemes were due to differing incentive qualities of the pay schemes.

The powerful advantage of control, or precision, that is afforded by the laboratory experiment is offset by several potential disadvantages. An important one is that the results are obtained in a fairly unrealistic setting; that is, people do not typically report to laboratory settings to engage in brief exercises. Also, the people who are readily available to participate in laboratory experiments are not often the people to whom the investigator wishes to generalize the conclusions of a study. For example, many studies are conducted with samples of undergraduate or MBA students, while the population of ultimate interest may actually be executives, campus recruiters, or first-level supervisors.[9] The students may not be directly comparable to the group of interest because their responses to experimental procedures and their prior work experience may predispose them to act in ways that are not typical of people in the workaday world. The nonrepresentative nature of both the setting and the sample in most laboratory experiments, therefore, limits the ability to generalize the results that are obtained.

A further problem is that the laboratory setting may encourage subjects to behave in a particular, unrealistic fashion. The cues and signals of an experimental setting that indicate to the subject how to respond are called **demand characteristics**. One need only recall the behavior of the relay assembly workers in the Hawthorne Studies (Chapter 1) to recognize the potentially disruptive influence of a subject's awareness that he or she is being studied. In that study, the workers' awareness of their being studied led them to behave as they thought they were expected to behave, rather than as they might have behaved if the changes in their work setting had occurred more naturally. This example underscores one of the perplexing problems of studying behavior in a laboratory: Humans react to the knowledge that they are under scrutiny. This does not negate the value of lab studies for examining phenomena that are not likely to be affected by subject awareness—for example, studies that involve highly absorbing and personally motivating tasks, or studies crafted so that the subjects are not aware of being studied. But studies that do not or cannot reduce subjects' awareness of being monitored must be carefully examined to determine if that awareness in any way affected the results.[†††]

[†††]The entire problem of the object of study responding to the process of being studied is not unique to the behavioral sciences; it is a potential problem in all sciences. The problem lies in the issue of the degree to which the measurement process alters the thing being measured. To some degree, the measurement process will always have some effect, however trivial or irrelevant. For example, if we measure the width of a table with a yardstick, we will alter (to a trivial degree) the top of the table. The surface of the table will be changed because a portion of it will be shaded by the ruler (and, therefore, the temperature of the surface will be changed slightly). While these changes in temperature (and therefore molecular motion) and weight are assumed to be irrelevant to the constancy of the table's width, the table has nonetheless been affected by the measurement process. In brief, the very act of measuring an object can—to some small degree, it is hoped—influence the object. This is a potential problem for all forms of measurement.

In defense of laboratory experiments, two points need to be highlighted. First, behavior in the lab is still behavior. It is no less human than behavior in organizational settings. Although the conditions created in a lab may never occur in precisely the same way in an organization, the predisposition to behave in a certain way remains a potentiality for organizational settings. As a potentiality, the response must be considered in any full explanation of what occurs in an organizational setting.

Second, laboratory experiments provide the opportunity to assign subjects randomly to experimental conditions. This feature is especially important for the study of human behavior because all humans possess attitudes and acquired habits that can have unpredictable effects on the results of an experiment. **Random assignment,** in which individuals have an equal likelihood of being placed in an experimental group or a comparison group, overcomes the problem of these potentially confounding (that is, extraneous but important) factors. By randomly assigning people to experimental conditions, we can be certain that equal proportions of confounding influences will be present in each group. This will ensure that the effects of such influences will also be equal from group to group. Therefore, there should be no expected difference between groups other than that which is due to the experimental manipulation.

Laboratory research and field research are not mutually exclusive alternatives. A researcher is not restricted to studying a form of behavior in either one or the other setting. Rather, the approaches are complementary. A program of research may begin with the uncovering of a behavioral process in a field setting. Because this original evidence is from an uncontrolled setting, a laboratory study may be conducted in order to minimize extraneous influences. The results of the lab study may then suggest other directions for research that can only be studied in field settings. In short, the research process requires moving from one setting to the other, with each setting offering answers that can only be obtained in that particular setting.

ARCHIVAL RESEARCH

Archival research uses already existing information to study behavioral processes. The sources of data for archival research are endlessly diverse, ranging from scholarly books and journals to newspaper and magazine articles, stock market quotations, and personal correspondence. One outstanding example of archival research is provided by David McClelland's work on achievement motivation.[10] McClelland hypothesized that a strong emphasis on achievement in the upbringing of children would be predictive of a nation's economic growth. In order to measure the variable of emphasis on achievement in childhood, McClelland examined the achievement imagery presented in grade-school readers (reading textbooks) from 23 countries. He assigned scores to the readers according to a previously defined set of rules that counted references to standards of excellence and the importance of hard work. To measure economic growth, McClelland looked at the increase in the amount of electricity that was produced per capita in each country during the two following decades. Intriguingly, McClelland identified a significant positive correlation between the level of prior achievement emphasis and the per capita growth in electrical production in subsequent decades.

Unobtrusive Measures

As we have already noted, humans tend to change their behavior when they know they are being observed. Thus, using an **unobtrusive measure,** a research approach that does not interfere with employees' usual behavior, is highly desirable.

In addition to using high technology to unobtrusively measure employee behavior (for example, the ethically debatable use of hidden cameras and tape recorders), one can also employ an unobtrusive approach by looking for evidence of past behavior. For example, the degree of selective wear or use of some item or the deposit of materials can provide evidence of past behavior.[11] An automobile dealer, Z-Frank Chevrolet of Chicago, has used the technique of having mechanics record the position of radio dials when cars are brought in for service. From this evidence, the dealer was able to estimate the popularity of various radio stations and thereby decide which stations to use for advertising.

The directors of the Chicago Museum of Science and Industry wanted to determine which of their exhibits were the most popular. Many of the exhibits are fascinating because they employ lights, motion, and models that illustrate various principles. But many of the exhibits illustrate principles that museum visitors do not understand. Therefore, you can foresee the potential problems of simply stopping visitors as they leave the museum to ask them which exhibit they enjoyed the most. Because of a desire not to reveal their lack of understanding, respondents might answer that the "nuclear fission exhibit" was most enjoyable, when in fact the "captured Nazi U-boat" was their favorite exhibit. To avoid the potential problems of identifying how visitors felt about the exhibits, investigators checked the frequency with which floor tiles had to be replaced around the various exhibits. This selective wear was taken as a measure of the relative popularity of exhibits. Results revealed that while most exhibits only required tile replacement after a period of years, a chick-hatching incubator exhibit required tile replacement every six weeks.

As these examples show, unobtrusive measures have the distinctive feature of not requiring the cooperation of the respondent, while simultaneously reducing the possible contamination of the measurement process itself. Also, the design of unobtrusive measures requires a good deal of creativity and ingenuity.

In addition to such actuarial records as voting patterns, budgets, and judicial records, various organizational records are often possible sources of data (for example, records of sales, absenteeism, and productivity). It has been proposed that unobtrusive measures of job satisfaction might even be possible. For example, one might monitor trips to the water cooler and the number of toilet flushes as indices of employee dissatisfaction across departments, in the

An Inside Look
High-Tech Observation or an Invasion of Privacy?

Technology is enabling today's managers to collect more information about employee behavior. Besides such standard devices as bugs and wiretaps, bosses now can use special chairs to measure how much the person in the chair is wiggling—the assumption being that someone who is wiggling isn't working. General Electric Company has installed tiny fish-eye lenses behind pinholes in walls and ceilings to watch employees suspected of crimes. At Du Pont, hidden long-distance cameras monitor the loading docks.

A modern technique for monitoring work is to have computers keep track of the performance of the employees using them. For example, at many airlines, computers measure the number of reservations written by each employee. Managers at Chicago-based Management Recruiters Inc. surreptitiously monitor computerized schedules that indicate which recruiters interview the most job candidates. Safeway Stores Inc. in Oakland, California, has installed dash-

board computers on its trucks. The computers record driving speed, oil pressure, engine RPMs, idling time, and the number and length of times the truck is stopped. If the record for a driver is abnormal, the company's management investigates, thereby saving money spent on maintenance and fuel and encouraging drivers to be more careful.

Not surprisingly, employees tend to object to such monitoring when they learn about it. According to George Sveum, secretary of Teamsters Local 350 in Martinez, California, the union has filed a number of grievances when Safeway has used its computer data as the basis for suspending or discharging drivers. Says Sveum, "If a trucker is just two minutes late, he can be brought up on charges." Office workers who are subjected to computerized monitoring complain that it creates a sweatshop environment and invades their privacy.

Despite the complaints, the law has generally tended to give employers wide latitude in monitoring worker activities. Employ-

ers may eavesdrop on office telephone conversations, observe employees through cameras, and go through employees' offices, desks, lockers, and mail. In 1987, in fact, approximately 14,000 employers listened in on the telephone conversations of almost 1.5 million workers, most of whom were not told they were being monitored. To win a lawsuit for invasion of privacy, workers must prove that their "reasonable expectations of privacy" outweigh a company's reasons for eavesdropping. Even then, the company can justify its actions if it has informed its employees of its surveillance policies.

As technology strengthens management's hand, Congress may give a boost to privacy advocates. The legislature is considering bills that would require more notification when a person is being monitored. Such attention is making workplace privacy, in the words of corporate lawyer Eric H. Joss, "the hottest employment law topic of the 1990s."

Source: Jeffrey Rothfeder and Michele Galen, "Is Your Boss Spying on You?" *Business Week*, January 15, 1990, 74–75.

perhaps reasonable assumption that unhappy employees spend relatively more time away from their jobs and proportionately more time around the water cooler or in the restrooms.

INTERNAL AND EXTERNAL VALIDITY

Now that we have reviewed a number of research strategies and settings, it is useful to consider two larger questions. The first question concerns whether the treatment variable had the hypothesized or predicted effect. This is a question of whether a study possesses **internal validity.** The second question concerns whether the results of a study can be generalized beyond the immediate sample, measures, and situation. The extent to which a study's results can be generalized is termed **external validity.**

One might reason that an ideal study would be both highly internally valid (that is, so tightly and rigorously controlled that one could easily make inferences about the independent variable's effects) and highly externally valid (designed so that one could easily generalize the results to settings and samples of interest). Unfortunately, the design of studies usually involves a trade-off between these two features: The more internally valid a study is, the less externally valid it is likely to be, and vice versa. A study that is designed to be internally valid usually involves creating a very artificial and unrealistic situation such that one has difficulty in drawing inferences for naturally occurring situations. On the other hand, if we study samples and settings of primary interest to us, we are likely to be examining conditions that lack the control necessary to draw causal inferences about the independent variable. Therefore, as we attempt to maximize the internal validity of a study, we sacrifice generalizability. If we strive to maximize external validity, we sacrifice control over important variables. This trade-off is partly due to the inclusion of certain features in studies, such as random assignment, which have mutually exclusive implications. Although the control feature of random assignment leads to the internal validity of a study, it creates an unrealistic circumstance. Without random assignment, we may enhance external validity, but we would reduce internal validity.

The research strategies that have been considered can be judged in terms of how each contributes to enhancing internal and external validity. The least internally valid research approach is the case study, while the most internally valid is the laboratory experiment. Conversely, the least externally valid approach is the laboratory experiment, while one has difficulty attributing any internal validity to the results of a case study. This last statement suggests an important point: If a study is not at least internally valid to a minimal level (such that one cannot comfortably draw any inferences about an independent variable), then a discussion of external validity is moot. Internal validity may, therefore, be considered a more critical concern than external validity. Perhaps the best one can hope to achieve for a single study in the way of a compromise between the goals of internal and external validity is represented by a field experiment. A field experiment involves conditions of primary interest to the researcher (as evidenced by the selection of a particular site), while also striving for a degree of control over major variables.

It can be said that case studies, archival research, and unobtrusive measures comprise a more **qualitative approach** to studying organizational behavior, while surveys, field experiments, and lab experiments comprise a comparatively more traditional approach. Both approaches endorse the view that behavior is "caused" and does not occur randomly. However, the qualitative approach tends to regard social phenomena as being partially created by the process of observers who try to understand it. The more traditional approach tends to view social phenomena as existing concretely and separately from the observer. Qualitative research often relies on participative involvement by researchers in observing social events, while traditional research tries to distance the researcher from social events. Also, the goal of qualitative research is more typically to gain insight or a more elementary understanding, while the goal of traditional research is to develop causal models.[12]

ETHICS IN RESEARCH

The study of employee behavior in organizational settings sometimes raises ethical questions. Although most studies in organizational behavior are relatively innocuous (compared, say, to medical research), the possibility of ethical violations nonetheless exists.[13]

Researchers in organizational behavior need to be aware of potential ethical problems. For instance, they should respect an individual's freedom to choose whether to participate in a study. They should also respect an individual's right to be fully informed about a study when deciding whether to participate. It is highly unethical to place people in a situation where they could be psychologically harmed without giving them a full explanation of any potential danger and assuring them that they can withdraw from participation at their discretion.[14]

Another ethical issue is the participant's right to privacy. A researcher may violate this right in different ways. For example, people may be observed without their knowledge. Also, highly personal questions may be posed on questionnaires or asked of friends and coworkers without the participant's knowledge. Another potential form of invasion of privacy is the use of a participant-observer in a study. In such an instance, the observer may be pretending to be essentially a coworker while hiding his or her true identity and goals from colleagues.

A researcher who fails to treat data (especially personal-opinion data) confidentially may be accused of unethical behavior. One way to avoid this is to provide participants with an option to answer questions anonymously. A researcher must also be careful not to injure the reputation of individuals or organizations when reporting results from a study. One ethical question should guide researchers' behavior: Does a proposed study raise even a slight possibility that individual rights could be violated? If the answer is yes, the study should not be conducted. If there is any doubt about the reasonableness of conducting a study, the codes of ethics of the Academy of Management, the American Psychological Association, or the American Sociological Association should be consulted.[15‡‡‡]

HOW TO READ AN OB RESEARCH REPORT

Since much information about organizational behavior is presented in journal articles and technical reports, it is useful to understand the format in which reports are presented. The typical research report contains five major sections: abstract, introduction, method, results, and discussion.

---

‡‡‡ A summary of the Academy of Management's Code of Ethical Conduct is contained in Appendix A.

ABSTRACT

An *abstract* is a summary that appears at the beginning of a report. It gives a brief, one-paragraph overview of the major features of the study. It provides a descriptive outline of the study's purpose, methods, results, and conclusions.

INTRODUCTION

The first major portion of the report is the *introduction,* which explains the rationale or purpose of the study. It usually begins with a review of past research on the topic and justifies the need for the present study. The hypotheses to be tested and the logic by which the hypotheses were deduced are presented in the introduction.

METHOD

The *method* section describes the sample, measuring instruments, setting, and procedures used in conducting the study. These features are extremely important because they often contain points that would limit the study's generalizability or raise questions about its internal validity.

RESULTS

Analyses of the data, especially statistical tests and graphs, are presented in the *results* section. The results are usually presented in highly technical terms that presuppose a substantial familiarity with statistical techniques. For most readers, the results are the most difficult part of the report to read and understand.

DISCUSSION

The last section of a research report, the *discussion,* reviews the major points of the study and draws conclusions from the results. It usually includes a statement about the limitations of the study and other qualifying aspects, and presents insights and suggestions about how future research in the topic should be conducted. Finally, the discussion examines the possible importance of the study for a given area of research and the implications of the results in light of past research.

At first, you may find OB research reports difficult to understand because they are often written in highly technical terms. Although you may need some persistence to develop the ability to read such reports, the rewards for your effort will be a fuller understanding of employee behavior.

Figure 2.2 lists the major journals and magazines devoted to topics in the field of organizational behavior. The journals tend to be more technical in nature, while the magazines are more comprehensible to the layperson.

FIGURE 2.2

MAJOR JOURNALS AND MAGAZINES DEVOTED TO TOPICS IN THE FIELD OF
ORGANIZATIONAL BEHAVIOR

Journals	Magazines
Academy of Management Journal	Business Horizons
Academy of Management Review	California Management Review
Administrative Science Quarterly	Harvard Business Review
Human Relations	Human Resources Management
Journal of Applied Psychology	Management Review
Journal of Management	Organizational Dynamics
Journal of Organizational Behavior	Personnel Journal
Journal of Vocational Behavior	Supervisory Management
Organizational Behavior and Human Decision Processes	Training and Development Journal
Personnel Psychology	

SUMMARY

1. Summarize the starting assumptions that enable organizational behavior researchers to systematize their studies.
Behavioral phenomena are complex in that they influence, and are influenced by, many processes. Thus, to systematize their studies, OB researchers accept four key assumptions: (1) behavior is predictable, (2) behavior is caused, (3) behavior has many causes but the total number of possible causes is limited, and (4) it is possible to draw generalities about behavior.

2. Define the essential steps in the scientific research process.
In the first step, induction, the researcher starts with a set of observations or facts and generates a theory that explains them. In the second step, deduction, the researcher makes logical predictions of what to expect under specified circumstances in an effort to determine whether the theory is a good representation of the behavior it seeks to explain. In the third step, verification, the researcher checks the truth or falsehood of a prediction by gathering new data to see if they refute or support prior assumptions.

3. Enumerate the fundamental goals of OB research.
In OB, as in other fields, the research process has four main goals: (1) description of behavior and events in order to create a classification system that paves the way for attaining the other three goals, (2) prediction of behavior and events, (3) explanation of the underlying processes that produce behavior and events, and (4) control of some behavior and events.

4. Distinguish an independent variable from a dependent variable, an intervening variable, and a moderating variable.
To understand a specific behavior or event, researchers must study the relationships among its basic elements, or variables. Thus, they start with a hypothesis, or prediction, about how a change in one variable will affect another variable. The factor or event that they believe will cause a change is

called the independent variable, while the factor or event that is expected to be affected is called the dependent variable. The dependent variable is the phenomenon that the researchers seek to explain.

The relationship between an independent and a dependent variable is not always simple and direct. Consequently, researchers may include some intervening variables in their explanations. An intervening variable is an unobservable state or process that helps to explain the link between an independent and a dependent variable. In addition, the relationship between two variables may be influenced by a third variable, called a moderating variable.

5. Differentiate the correlational method of research from the experimental method and assess the strengths and weaknesses of each approach.
An OB study may employ either a correlational or an experimental method. The correlational method focuses on the relationship between two variables, seeking to determine if changes in one variable will produce changes in another. Although the results of correlational studies may tell whether and how two variables are related, they will not indicate why or how the relationship was produced. Despite this limitation, correlational research can be a productive first step in analyzing certain events and may be the only appropriate technique in some cases.

When researchers want to study cause-and-effect relationships, they usually prefer to use the experimental method. In this approach, a researcher manipulates an independent variable in the hope of observing corresponding changes in a dependent variable. Through careful design, other variables that might influence the results but are not of interest are controlled or eliminated. Despite the greater rigor of the experimental method, researchers must keep in mind two limitations of the experimental approach. First, they can only *infer* that an independent variable caused changes in a dependent variable because the independent event preceded the dependent event—they cannot *prove* that it did. Second, in order to avoid reaching distorted conclusions, the researchers must have an adequate understanding of the phenomenon under investigation.

6. Identify the most frequently used strategies and settings of OB research.
Five basic strategies and settings are used in OB research. In a case study, an investigator closely examines the goings-on in an organization through, for example, personal recollections, interviews with others, and daily diary entries. The researcher makes no attempt to control variables or eliminate alternative causal explanations for what is observed. Although case studies rarely produce hard data, they can be useful in generating hypotheses, providing insights that aid theorizing, and suggesting causal variables that help explain a process.

A survey is a set of questions, either oral or written, designed to collect personal responses to a topic of research. A survey must be carefully designed so that it will be easy to answer accurately and will compensate for or avoid respondents' biases. Although survey research may uncover new information, it rarely offers insights into cause-and-effect relationships.

When researchers want to make inferences about causes and effects, they may prefer to use field experiments. In this approach, an independent variable is manipulated in one setting while the same variable remains unchanged in another, similar setting. Assuming that the two settings are identical and that no other changes are introduced, the researcher should be able to assume that any changes in the dependent variable are at least partially attributable to manipulation of the independent variable. However, some variables may be beyond the researcher's control. In addition, participants in the experiment are not necessarily representative and may have unique perspectives that could influence the results.

Researchers can often avoid the pitfalls of field experiments through the use of laboratory experiments, in which the researcher carefully creates conditions in which only the factors of interest are permitted to vary. Such vastly increased control is highly desirable, but it is offset by a number of disadvantages. Because the laboratory conditions are artificially created, both the setting and the participants may bear little resemblance to the real-world situation of interest. Moreover, the specialized laboratory setting may encourage subjects to behave unrealistically.

Finally, researchers may do archival research, using already existing information in scholarly books and journals, newspapers, popular magazines, government documents, and the like to study a behavioral phenomenon of interest. Researchers may also employ unobtrusive measures to gather desired information. Because unobtrusive measures do not interfere with subjects' usual behavior, they often provide evidence that is insightful.

7. Discuss why the design of research studies requires a trade-off between internal and external validity.

In interpreting any study, we must evaluate both its internal and its external validity. Internal validity is concerned with whether one can draw inferences about the effect of the independent variable, while external validity is gauged by the extent to which the study's results can be generalized beyond the immediate research setting. In reality, the more internally valid a study is, the less externally valid it is likely to be, and vice versa. This occurs because a study designed to be internally valid (for example, a laboratory experiment) usually requires the creation of an artificial setting that may not have many parallels to naturally occurring situations. On the other hand, when researchers study a phenomenon in its natural environment (for example, a case study), they often lack the control necessary to draw causal inferences about the independent variable. Given this double bind, a trade-off between internal and external validity is unavoidable.

8. Cite the most important ethical issues that OB researchers must bear in mind.

Because OB research focuses on human beings, investigators must be highly ethical in their choice of methods and treatment of participants. For example, a researcher should always respect an individual's right to privacy and rights to be physically and psychologically safe, fully informed, and free to choose whether to take part in a study. A researcher should treat all information confidentially and meticulously avoid injuring the reputation of any individual or organization when reporting the results of a study. The overriding question for every researcher should be: Does a proposed study raise even the remote possibility that individual rights could be violated? If there is any doubt, the study should not be conducted.

9. Outline the basic format of a typical OB research report.

The typical research report contains five key sections. The abstract is a brief overview of the study's significant features. The introduction explains the purpose of the study, reviews the relevant past research, justifies the need for the current study, and presents and explains the hypotheses to be tested. The method section describes the sample, measuring instruments, setting, and procedures used, while the results section presents analyses of the data, especially statistical tests and graphs. Finally, the discussion section reviews the main points of the study and draws conclusions from the results.

KEY TERMS

Induction	Survey
Deduction	Field experiment
Verification	Laboratory experiment
Independent variable	Demand characteristics
Dependent variable	Random assignment
Hypothesis	Archival research
Intervening variable	Unobtrusive measure
Moderating variable	Internal validity
Correlational method	External validity
Experimental method	Qualitative approach
Case study	

REVIEW AND DISCUSSION QUESTIONS

1. In your opinion, how reasonable are the four starting assumptions of OB research? Do they cover every eventuality? Should some of the assumptions be eliminated? Should other assumptions be added? Be specific in your criticisms and suggestions.

2. Explain in your own words the scientific method as depicted in Figure 2.1. How does each element of the model fit into the total process?

3. The research goals of OB are the same as the research goals of any other scientific field. Should they be? Why or why not?

4. Two OB students, Archie Stack and Val Marion, plan to investigate the relationship between the number of hours their fellow OB students study and the final grades they receive. Their prediction is that students who spend more time studying will receive higher grades. What are the independent and dependent variables in this situation? What intervening and moderating variables should Archie and Val anticipate?

5. Should the student researchers in Question 4 use a correlational or an experimental method of investigation? What elements of the situation should

influence their decision? What advantages and disadvantages should they expect from the method they choose?

6. What research strategy or setting would you recommend for each of the following situations? Why? (You may suggest more than one approach if you think that a combination would yield better results.)
   a. The human resources department at a large manufacturing firm wants to know how assembly-line employees feel about a newly instituted piece-rate scheme.
   b. A nationwide hospital chain asks a consultant in organizational behavior to determine if providing on-site day-care facilities at each of its 30 branches will reduce absenteeism among employees who are parents of preschoolers.
   c. An OB researcher hopes to prove that there is a definite link between workers' productivity and the amount of encouragement they receive from their supervisor.
   d. A consultant who specializes in organizational behavior is hired by a fast-food chain to discover why a competitor's employees seem to be more productive than the client's employees.
   e. The president of an American auto manufacturer is considering a joint venture with a Japanese firm. If the plan goes through, a new plant will be built in the United States, with day-to-day operations managed by the Japanese. The president wants to know what adjustments such a system would demand of American workers.

7. Discuss the trade-off between internal and external validity that Archie and Val will have to make in conducting the study described in Question 4. Will their results ultimately have greater internal validity or greater external validity? Why?

8. What ethical issues should Archie and Val keep in mind as they plan and conduct their research? What ethical objections might their subjects raise? Might the two be forced to abandon their project for ethical reasons?

9. Assume that Archie and Val have completed their research and are ready to present their findings. What format should they use? What information should they include in each section?

CRITICAL INCIDENT

A Way to Manage Demand?

At Southeastern State University, the Principles of Management course has always been taught in small lecture-discussion classes of approximately 40 students each. Because of the very high demand for this course, and the fact that resources for hiring additional faculty to teach more sections were not available, the departmental faculty suggested that some alternative teaching methods be explored.

Three alternative methods of presenting the course were proposed. One method was to retain the traditional lecture-discussion format with 40 students per class. A second approach was to combine several sections into a large lecture format. Approximately 160 students would attend this lecture twice a week, followed by a question-and-answer lab session with a graduate teaching assistant. The third approach involved the use of videotape. The students assigned to this approach would attend the videotaped lectures and, if they had questions, they could direct them to a graduate assistant who would meet with them once per week for a lab session.

Each student was to be randomly assigned to one of the three conditions. At the end of the semester, the results of student performance were to be evaluated. Average scores on a multiple-choice exam were to be used as the measure of each approach's effectiveness.

As Dean of the Business School, you have several questions to ask of the departmental faculty before giving your consent.

1. Should the students be randomly assigned to the various conditions or should they be allowed to choose their own sections?

2. Is the proposed measure of effectiveness a reasonable way of deciding which approach is best? What other ways could be used to determine which teaching format is most effective?

3. Explain the type of research design that is being proposed.

EXPERIENTIAL EXERCISE

Approaches to Studying Organizational Behavior

Step 1   Please read the following case and respond to the questions that follow.

Step 2   Form small groups of four to seven members to discuss the questions and formulate one cohesive plan of action based on the consensus.

BROCKPORT FOUNDRY INC.

Brockport Foundry has been in operation for 75 years. It is a family-owned business operated by President and Chief Executive Officer Peter O'Shay. Peter took the helm as CEO following the sudden death of his father last year. The elder Mr. O'Shay was 85 at the time of his death. Mr. O'Shay had built the company up from nothing over the course of 55 years.

Today the company employs 150 people. A handful of them have worked for Brockport Foundry for their entire adult lives. Most of them have been with the foundry for five years or more. The majority work as laborers on the foundry floor, pouring molten metal into molds in the manufacture of cast products. An insurance salesperson was shocked recently to learn that some of the employees are functionally illiterate. They could not complete application forms, nor could they sign their names to essential documents. The foundry has never been unionized.

The company is now in a dramatic stage of transition. Even though Peter, aged 48, is well known to foundry employees (he was chief operating officer at the time of his father's death), his style of management is different from that of his father. He is beginning to make changes that he deems to be essential to the long-term viability of the company, and not everyone agrees with those changes.

The 1980s and 1990s were not kind to U.S. foundries. Competition from foreign automakers and an overall recessionary business climate proved to be fatal to many foundries whose crafted works simply couldn't measure up against the products of some foreign competitors. The Japanese, for example, used robotics and advanced technologies to produce very high quality products at prices much lower than those offered by U.S. foundries whose equipment dated back to the early 1900s. At one point during the 1980s, U.S. foundries were closing at the rate of one per week.

Peter knew that changes had to be made to ensure that the Brockport Foundry would not be added to the list of casualties. He immediately set out to streamline the production process to allow for cost savings and production efficiencies. He joined a national trade association that provided a wealth of market research to the company. He even laid off 25 workers with the promise of rehiring them should business improve.

Yesterday, Greg Barnhardt, the plant manager, approached Peter. He reported that employees seem to be exhibiting signs of work-related stress and are anxious about their futures with the company. One man even admitted that a union representative has asked if he could meet with employees, and they have consented. Greg adds that employees are not fully participating in weekly problem-solving meetings, that they appear to be showing up just because they have to.

Peter wants to find out what's going on and he has hired you, an employee of a consulting firm that specializes in OB research, to get to the bottom of the problem.

QUESTIONS

1. In light of the issues discussed in the chapter, what research strategy would you use? Why?
2. Explain exactly how you would work with this strategy.

GROUP ASSIGNMENT

Reach a consensus regarding the appropriate research strategy to use, and develop it as fully as you can in the time given.

OPTIONAL GROUP ASSIGNMENT

Greg thinks he can do a better job of researching this situation than you can. He has developed a survey that he administered to employees and is working on gathering the results. Neither you nor Peter knew anything of the survey before it was administered.

Greg handed the survey exactly as it appears below to employees as they stood in line to punch the time clock at the close of a business day (the easiest place to gain access to them all at once). They were not told anything about its purpose, nor were they offered any information about how the results would be used. They were simply asked to fill it out and bring it in to work the next day. An empty box was set up to receive surveys.

Survey for All Employees

1. How long have you worked at Brockport Foundry? (check one answer)

    _____ less than 1 year   _____ 1 to 3 years   _____ 3 to 5 years

    _____ 5 to 10 years   _____ 10 to 15 years   _____ over 15 years

2. On a scale of one to ten, with one being the lowest and ten being the highest, please tell me how satisfied you are with your job. _____

3. Why do you feel this way?

    _____

    _____

    _____

4. Do your feelings of satisfaction relate to any of the following factors? (Please check all that apply.)

    _____ work hours   _____ your workstation   _____ supervision

    _____ goal clarity   _____ top management   _____ your pay

    _____ your coworkers   _____ your work quota

Other comments:

_____

_____

_____

_____

_____

Source: Written by Susan Stites Doe, State University of New York College at Buffalo.

QUESTIONS

1. What do you think of Greg's idea of administering a survey?
2. What objectives does the survey serve?
3. How could you improve the survey?
4. What impact might the administration of a survey have on the situation?

NOTES

1. W.C. Dampier, *A History of Science and Its Relations with Philosophy and Religion* (London: Cambridge University Press, 1949), 197.

2. J.S. Adams, "Toward an Understanding of Inequity," *Journal of Abnormal and Social Psychology* 67 (1963): 422–436.

3. R.P. Vecchio, "An Individual-Differences Interpretation of the Conflicting Predictions Generated by Equity Theory and Expectancy Theory," *Journal of Applied Psychology* 66 (1981): 470–481.

4. L.H. Peters, E.J. O'Connor, and S.L. Wise, "The Specification and Testing of Useful Moderator Variable Hypotheses," in *Method and Analysis in Organizational Research,* ed. T.S. Bateman and G.R. Ferris (Reston, Va.: Reston, 1984).

5. S.V. Kasl and J.R.P. French, Jr., "The Effects of Occupational Status on Physical and Mental Health," *Journal of Social Issues* 18 (1962): 67–89.

6. J.F. Witte, *Democracy, Authority, and Alienation in Work: Worker Participation in an American Corporation* (University of Chicago Press, 1980).

7. R.P. Vecchio, "Worker Alienation as a Moderator of the Job Quality–Job Satisfaction Relationship: The Case of Racial Differences," *Academy of Management Journal* 23 (1980): 479–486.

8. J.P. Muczyk, "A Controlled Field Experiment Measuring the Impact of MBO on Performance Data" (Unpublished paper, Cleveland State University, 1976).

9. M.E. Gordon, L.A. Slade, and N. Schmitt, "The Science of the Sophomore Revisited: From Conjecture to Empiricism," *Academy of Management Review* 11 (1986): 191–207; J. Greenberg, "The College Sophomore as Guinea Pig," *Academy of Management Review* 12 (1987): 157–159.

10. D.C. McClelland, *The Achieving Society* (Princeton, N.J.: Van Nostrand, 1961).

11. E.J. Webb, D.T. Campbell, R.D. Schwartz, and L. Sechrest, *Unobtrusive Measures: Nonreactive Research in the Social Sciences* (Chicago: Rand-McNally, 1966); E.J. Webb and K.E. Weick, "Unobtrusive Measures in Organizational Theory: A Reminder," *Administrative Science Quarterly* 24 (1979): 650–659.

12. G. Morgan and L. Smircich, "The Case for Qualitative Research," *Academy of Management Review* 5 (1980): 491–500; J. Van Maanen, "Reclaiming Qualitative Methods for Organizational Research: A Preface," *Administrative Science Quarterly* 24 (1979): 520–526.

13. P. H. Mirris and S. E. Seashore "Being Ethical in Organizational Research," *American Psychologist* 34 (1979): 766–780.

14. P.J. Runkel and J.E. McGrath, *Research on Human Behavior* (New York: Holt, Rinehart and Winston, 1972).

15. *Ethical Principles in the Conduct of Research with Human Participants* (Washington D.C.: APA, 1973); American Sociological Association, *Code of Ethics* (Washington, D.C.: ASA, 1971); "The Academy of Management Code of Ethical Conduct," *Academy of Management Journal* 35 (1992): 1135–1142.

CHAPTER 2 APPENDIX

The Academy of Management Code of Ethical Conduct*
(Approved August 1990)

CREDO

We believe in discovering, sharing, and applying managerial knowledge.

PREAMBLE

Our professional goals are to enhance the learning of students, colleagues, and others and to improve the effectiveness of organizations through our teaching, research, and practice of management. We have five major responsibilities:

- To our students: Relationships with students require respect, fairness, and caring, along with recognition of our commitment to the subject matter and to teaching excellence.
- To managerial knowledge: Prudence in research design, human subject use, confidentiality, result reporting, and proper attribution of work is a necessity.
- To the Academy of Management and the larger professional environment: Support of the Academy's mission and objectives, service to the Academy and our institutions, and the recognition of the dignity and personal worth of colleagues is required.
- To both managers and the practice of management: Exchange of ideas and information between the academic and organizational communities is essential.
- To all people with whom we live and work in the world community: Sensitivity to other people, to diverse cultures, to the needs of the poor and disadvantaged, to ethical issues, and to newly emerging ethical dilemmas is required.

STUDENT RELATIONSHIPS

In our roles as educators, the central principles that underlie appropriate student-educator relationships are professionalism, respect, fairness, and concern.

ADVANCEMENT OF MANAGERIAL KNOWLEDGE

Academy member research should be done honestly, have a clear purpose, show respect for the rights of all individuals and organizations, efficiently use resources, and advance knowledge in the field.

---

*This is a summary. This code has been reprinted in its entirety in the appendix of this book on pp. 681–686. The entire code appears in the *Academy of Management Journal* 36, no. 6 (December 1993), 1694–1698.

THE ACADEMY OF MANAGEMENT AND THE LARGER PROFESSIONAL ENVIRONMENT

The Mission Statement of the Academy describes member benefits and professional opportunities which impose corresponding duties and service responsibilities.[**]

MANAGERS AND THE PRACTICE OF MANAGEMENT

Consulting with client organizations ("clients") has the potential for enriching the teaching and practice of management, for translating theory into practice, and for furthering research and community service. To maximize such potential benefits, it is essential that members who consult be guided by the ideals of competence, integrity, and objectivity.

THE WORLD COMMUNITY

As citizens of the world community, Academy members may have much to contribute in shaping global consciousness by their teaching, research, and service.

[**]The Mission of the Academy is stated in Article II of the Constitution of the Academy of Management that appears in the *Academy of Management Handbook* (April 1989), p. 28.
Source: Used with permission from the Academy of Management Journal, 1993, Vol. 36 No. 6 pp. 1694–1898.

Individual Processes

If I hadn't believed it, I
wouldn't have seen it.
— Anonymous

Success is simply a
matter of luck. Ask any
failure.
— Earl Wilson

Yon Cassius has a lean and
hungry look;
He thinks too much;
Such men are dangerous.
— William Shakespeare

LEARNING OBJECTIVES

*After studying this chapter,
you should be able to:*

1. *Defend the notion that
   perception is a complex
   and active process.*
2. *Explain how facial
   expressions and other
   nonverbal cues affect the
   accuracy of our
   perceptions.*
3. *Identify the most common
   obstacles to accurate
   perception.*
4. *Outline the basic principles
   of attribution theory.*
5. *Discuss the concept of
   personality and the factors
   that affect its development.*
6. *Describe the most commonly used techniques for
   measuring personality
   attributes.*
7. *Specify and define several
   dimensions of personality
   that are especially relevant
   to organizational behavior.*

Perception and Personality

INTIMIDATING EXECUTIVES

Think your boss is an ogre? Difficult to please? Too demanding? You might want to think again (and count your blessings) after considering the behavior of the following executives. These anecdotes were highlighted in *Fortune,* and are presented here as food for thought regarding the role of a leader's perceptions and personality in managing an organization.

- CEO Linda Wachner of Warnaco, a large clothing manufacturer, rules with an iron fist. She once warned a new executive that he better start firing people if he wanted to be taken seriously. Her meetings often start at 5 P.M. and run throughout the night. The "Do It Now" logo emblazoned on top executives' notebooks is meant to be taken seriously: She once called an executive 31 times over Thanksgiving weekend. (He had quit by the following Monday.) Regarding her style of management, she has been quoted as saying, "If you don't like it, leave. It's not a prison."

- Steve Jobs, founder of Apple Computer and CEO of NeXT Computer, has a penchant for perfection. Employees who fail to meet his extraordinary expectations are known to receive public verbal attacks, complete with expletives and derisive comments. Two victims were NeXT engineers who had toiled nights and weekends for 15 months to meet an impossible deadline for a groundbreaking chip. Following a public castigation in front of their peers, they finished the project, and one swiftly left the company.

- Cypress Semiconductor chief executive T. J. Rogers admits his management style can be abrasive. His regular seat at meetings is not at the head of the table, but rather a corner chair to allow him greater visual access to employees seated around the table. He uses this position strategically, often firing off difficult, technical questions to unsuspecting employees. Some employees cram for these meetings, like a student studying for an exam, while others arrive early for meetings in the hopes of getting a seat out of the line of Rogers's fire.

- According to some of his employees, Jack Connors, CEO of advertising firm Hill Holliday, has a dual personality. Jack is the caring, engaging salesman who has been known to dip into his own pocket to help out employees: He's loaned employ-ees money and even paid for private school for the child of one employee who got in trouble with the law. But the counter-personality that seeps out of Jack's persona on a periodic basis is the antithesis of Jack. Jack is sometimes prone to explosive outbursts (Jack Attacks as they're known around the office) that can leave employees shaking. Once, in objection to some unsavory sales projections, Jack started kicking the chair of the executive who was presenting the projections—with the executive still in it. So loud are some Jack Attacks that Jack's voice can often be heard reverberating throughout headquarters.

And then there are the bosses who were nominated by their employees in a national competition to find the most intimidating boss. The winner described a boss who threatened immediate dismissal for anyone who adjusted the office thermostat. Another boss who finished in the top made employees bark like dogs to receive a paycheck. Not to be forgotten was the boss who liked to "playfully" choke and bite employees.

Just what is it about these individuals that incites such bizarre

(continued on following page)

(continued from previous page)

behaviors? Experts agree that such bosses have an unhealthy desire for perfection. To them, winning is everything. They often set impossible goals and are unrelenting in their desire for the company to achieve them. Being only human, employees fall short of their lofty expectations and these bosses can't handle what they perceive to be failure.

Although these examples may represent extremes in eccentric personalities and distorted perceptions, perception and personality play an important role in organizational behavior. This chapter provides a foundation for understanding the influences of perception and personality on organizations and employee behavior.

Source: Brian Dumaine, "America's Toughest Bosses," *Fortune,* October 18, 1993, 38–50.

Being able to accurately perceive and understand others is an important ability for any manager. How we come to know others and understand their behavior are related to perception and personality, two topics that we will consider in this chapter.

The Perception of Others

Although our experience of those around us seems very direct and immediate, careful analysis of what is involved in perceiving others indicates that the process of recognizing and understanding others (that is, person **perception**) is quite complex. For example, imagine that you are looking at a person seated at another desk (in a work or school setting). You will likely notice that the individual is of a certain sex and age, with a particular hair color, and so forth. These attributes all seem to be quite clear and inherent in the person being viewed. But a careful analysis of this hypothetical episode reveals that much more is involved. In actuality, cells in the retina of your eyes were activated by light waves reflected off the person. These retinal cells triggered neural impulses that traveled via the optic nerve to various locations in the brain. The impulses that reached the higher centers of the brain were then constructed into the experience of viewing the person at the next desk. In considering the chain of events involved in perception, we recognize that we do not have direct and immediate experience with the object, but instead rely on neural transmissions and electrochemical translations of stimuli. As perception researchers prefer to say, we are only dealing with our own neural activities, not with the actual person.

Most people also erroneously assume that the perceptual process is a largely passive, or totally receptive, process dictated by attributes of the observed object. Yet the process of viewing a person involves an active, directed focus on the part of the perceiver. For example, when you are viewing another person you are simultaneously being bombarded with other stimuli. The sounds in the room, the weight of your clothes, and the pressure of the chair in which you may be seated are all competing for your attention. However, you actively select and process specific information from your environment. Thus, it is clear that the perceiver is actively involved in the construction of his or her experiences. Alluding to this active involvement in selecting, structuring, and interpreting experiences, perception researchers are fond of saying, "There's more to the issue of perception than actually meets the eye."

In a well-known demonstration of the active role of the perceiver in the perceptual process, Leeper devised a clever means for displaying this natural predisposition.[1] As stimuli, Leeper prepared three drawings of a woman (Figure 3.1). One version of the drawing clearly shows a young woman looking over her shoulder, while a second depicts a much older woman. The third version of the drawing was created to be fairly ambiguous—that is, either the old woman or the young woman could be seen, depending on the observer's point of view. In his study, Leeper presented the picture of either the young woman or the old woman to two groups of subjects. Following this initial exposure, he presented the subjects with the ambiguous drawing. All the subjects who were initially exposed to the old woman reported seeing her when they first viewed the ambiguous picture. Meanwhile, the vast majority (95 percent) of subjects who had initially viewed the drawing of the young woman thought that the ambiguous drawing was a likeness of a young woman.

In this illustrative study, the subjects processed the information in accordance with a prepared mental set. In essence, the subjects structured the information to be consistent with their previous experience. Clearly, perception is not a passive or simple process. It is influenced by individual dispositions and prior experience.

ACCURACY IN PERCEIVING OTHERS

There is great value in being able to accurately assess the emotions and personality characteristics of others. Being able to tell whether others are experiencing a particular emotion enables us to gauge the effects of our words and actions. Knowing something about an individual's personality traits can be highly useful in interpersonal relations. All of us, to some extent, engage in "reading" the emotional styles and personality traits of others. When we approach a new coworker, we are likely to try to accurately assess that person's

 FIGURE 3.1

The interpretation of the picture in A depends on whether one has been previously exposed to the picture in B or C.

feelings and traits. The success of salespeople, among others, depends in large part on their ability to accurately assess others.

FACIAL EXPRESSIONS   Research findings suggest that most of us are able to identify certain emotional states from facial expressions. Several of these facial expressions are universally recognized. For example, smiles and frowns convey the same meaning regardless of an individual's culture.[2]*

Although much research has shown that we can generally read facial expressions in research settings where participants are likely to be fairly honest in their behavior, the "real world" presents many more problems. As anyone who has dealt with a used car salesperson or a politician knows, facial expressions can be very deceiving. Some people are masters of deception, skilled not only in concealing their feelings but also in falsifying their facial expressions.

But such behavior is not foolproof. Based on their research, Ekman and Friesen identified several clues that can help a viewer determine the sincerity of someone's facial expressions.[4] The researchers found that if the time between an emotionally arousing event and a person's facial reaction is too great, the reaction is probably dishonest. Also, if all aspects of a person's facial expression do not agree, deceit may be involved. For example, consider a facial reaction in which a person's eyebrows are raised as if in amazement, but her mouth is closed. A perceptive viewer might suspect the sincerity of the expression, because in a genuinely amazed reaction, a person's mouth is likely to be open. A third clue is provided by very brief facial expressions that appear on a person's face for a fraction of a second. These microexpressions are likely to convey genuine emotions that emerge just before the person exercises facial control.

Another indication of deception is a subtle shift in the tone or pitch of a person's speaking voice.[5] When someone is lying, there is often a detectable rise in the pitch of his or her voice. **Nonverbal cues,** such as posture shifts, scratching, and frequent licking of the lips, can provide subtle indications of nervousness and, by inference, of possible deceit.[6] Also, increased eye blinking is associated with psychological stress in that people blink more often when excited or angry.

OTHER NONVERBAL CUES   Nonverbal cues are important in situations in which people are formally evaluated. For example, employment interviews are one important arena in which people attempt to control the impressions they transmit to each other. In a study of the impact of nonverbal cues, Imada and Hakel[7] hired undergraduates to conduct employment interviews with a stranger. The interviewee, in fact, was a trained accomplice (confederate) of

---

*Charles Darwin was one of the first researchers to study the judgment of emotional states seriously.[3] He contended that the facial expressions associated with emotions were remnants of muscular movements that had functional value in our species' history. As an illustration, consider that the facial posture for displaying disgust is quite similar to the facial expression that occurs during regurgitation. He further argued that certain facial expressions are invariably correlated with specific emotional reactions. For example, a smile would indicate that a person is experiencing a pleasant or happy reaction.

the researchers, who behaved in one of two possible nonverbal styles. In one condition, the confederate behaved in a style intended to evoke a positive evaluation. Specifically, the interviewee maintained substantial eye contact with the interviewer, sat up straight, smiled a good deal, and frequently leaned toward the interviewer. In the other condition, the confederate's behavior involved slouching in the chair, having little eye contact, smiling not at all, and leaning away from the interviewer. The interviewers' ratings differed significantly as a function of the confederate's nonverbal cues. In particular, they gave the interviewee higher ratings for competence, motivation, and recommendation for hiring when they experienced the nonverbal cues that were deliberately designed to evoke a positive reaction.

A primary implication of these results is that nonverbal cues have powerful effects on our appraisals of each other. Job interviewers are likely to be swayed by such cues when other facets of competing individuals, such as educational qualifications and experience, are equal. Partly because nonverbal cues can be confusing, the actual success rate for interviewers in predicting performance has been fairly poor.[8]

Of all the nonverbal cues used in perceiving and judging others, eye contact is among the most important. Generally, the more eye contact that occurs between two people, the more favorably the relationship is likely to be judged by others.[9] People typically conclude that when others avoid eye contact, it is due to a negative state, such as guilt or depression.[10]

Eye contact that is carried to extremes, however, such as staring, is socially arousing but disruptive. In instances of such staring, the nonverbal message is typically inferred to be that of hatred and potential aggression.[11] Most often, staring has the effect of driving others away (that is, people normally leave a situation when they have been stared at). In organizational settings, staring is sometimes used as a device for extracting compliance from a coworker. For example, if a coworker is having trouble unloading a heavy parcel, he or she may stare at you in order to induce a sense of guilt, which in turn might motivate you to offer your assistance. Given that overt aggression is not socially acceptable in organizations, staring is one of the more powerful social devices for communicating hostility.

PERCEPTION OF PERSONALITY TRAITS

Although much research has been conducted to determine whether some individuals excel in judging others, the efforts have been hampered by several problems. The most notable problem has been the difficulty of determining a specific, unquestionable criterion against which to compare an evaluator's judgment. Many criteria have been proposed (for example, test scores, self-assessments, and peer assessments), but all can be criticized for having possible flaws. For example, test scores do not capture actual behavior, while self-assessments of personality traits may be biased in a favorable direction. Other problems for studying accuracy in personality assessment have arisen from methodological shortcomings in the definition of accuracy.[12]

An Inside Look
Overcoming Perceptions of Career Plateau

To breathe new life into plateaued employees, many companies are offering a variety of opportunities to make career plateaus more invigorating. Among them are additional training, lateral moves, short sabbaticals, and new methods of determining compensation. Some companies, restricted by delayering and less cash flow, are even using such techniques in lieu of raises and promotions. From the employee's perspective, the key to combating the 'Is this all there is?' syndrome is to perceive the current state of affairs not as a crisis but as an opportunity for personal growth and development, as the following examples illustrate.

Tired of pushing papers for 13 years, an equal employment opportunity officer at an Alabama utility company decided he needed a change. For six months, he traded his office attire for a hardhat and overalls, repairing gas lines and digging ditches with the company's construction crew. Coming home filthy every day and digging trenches in the Alabama heat gave him a fresh perspective on his desk job.

To broaden her opportunities, a 43-year-old General Motors supervisor decided to return to school to become a truck designer. After two years' additional schooling and one more to go, she's confident she made the right move: "The more you learn, the more salable you are."

Being repeatedly passed over for a promotion allowed an AT&T industrial psychologist to reframe his goals. Rather than change employers, a move he perceived as risky, he became more involved in his family, coaching his son and daughter in Little League and basketball.

Clearly, it is in a company's best interests to help employees cope with career plateau. According to Beverly Kaye, an in-placement consultant, "What you want is for employees to be *productively* plateaued. They may not be moving up in an organization, but if they feel stuck, productivity suffers and absenteeism soars."

Sources: Jaclyn Fierman, "Beating the Midlife Career Crisis," *Fortune*, September 6, 1993, 52–62; Joann S. Lublin, "Strategic Sidling: Lateral Moves Aren't Always a Mistake," *The Wall Street Journal*, August 4, 1993, B1.

Despite these research problems, it is nonetheless possible to draw several guarded conclusions about the characteristics of people who are good judges of others. According to one researcher, they typically possess high intelligence, esthetic and dramatic interests, good emotional adjustment, and a specialization in the physical sciences rather than in the social sciences.[13] These findings generally make sense, except that we would probably expect specialists in the social sciences to be good judges of personality. One reasonable explanation for the reverse finding is the possible tendency for people who are interested in social relations to be overly sensitive to small differences among people. Sensitivity can lead to overdifferentiation in a judgment task (that is, the tendency to overestimate the importance of small differences). Given that most human attributes (for example, height, weight, and so on as well as personality traits) follow a bell-shaped, normal distribution, one can be accurate a large percentage of the time when judging others by simply sticking close to the center (or average) of the distribution. Using extreme assessments of others to make judgments can lead to a larger number of errors.

When people try to predict others' behavior from subjective assessments of personality, they are not particularly successful. This has far-reaching ramifications in the workplace, because such predictions are made many times a day by people who are responsible for hiring employees. When other, more objective qualifications, such as experience and education, are equal, assessors often make subjective personality judgments in predicting performance.

MECHANISTIC VERSUS IMPRESSIONISTIC PREDICTION

Evidence on the ability of human judges to make use of personality assessments in forecasting the behavior of others shows that people generally are not adept at the task. Something of a debate has been waged for several decades over whether the task of predicting behavior from personality indices is better done with a **mechanistic** combination of the data or an **impressionistic** (human judge) approach. In a thorough literature review, Jerry Wiggins has summarized much of the debate.[14] According to Wiggins, the impressionistic approach relies on an intuitive, or subjective, combination of information about an individual when attempting to predict behavior (for example, worker performance, absenteeism, or sales). The mechanistic, or statistical, approach involves combining information mathematically in an optimal manner. The typical statistical device is regression analysis, which uses a mathematical technique to optimally weight data to minimize the magnitude of error in prediction. When the two approaches to predicting behavior have been applied to the same set of data, the mechanistic approach has been found to be equal or superior to the impressionistic approach. The mechanistic approach has been found to be superior whether the judges are students, managers, or social scientists.

Although these results suggest that statistical manipulations of data produce more accurate predictions of human behavior, it would be erroneous to conclude that there is no place for humans in the field. Instead, the role of humans should be viewed as one of devising and validating statistical prediction systems. Once a statistical prediction system is devised and validated, it is perhaps best for the humans to be removed from the prediction process. The superiority of the mechanical process is largely due to the fact that a mathematically optimal combination of data cannot easily be beaten by an error-prone and inconsistent judge (that is, a human).

In addition to being the creative force behind a statistical prediction scheme, humans have one other advantage over the mechanistic approach. Because the mechanistic approach requires large sets of data (that is, a large sample size, to generate the optimal weights under the mathematical assumptions of statistical devices), there are many situations in which the statistical approach cannot be used—for example, in unique or one-of-a-kind situations in which no data are available for generating a regression analysis, or where only a single prediction is to be made for one individual (and/or the cost does not warrant the development of a regression analysis). In such circumstances, the impressionistic approach is the only recourse.

OBSTACLES TO ACCURATE PERCEPTION

There are many barriers to the precise perception of others' behavior. Each barrier is a possible source of misleading or distorted information. Table 3.1 summarizes these barriers.

■ **TABLE 3.1**
COMMON OBSTACLES TO PERCEPTION

Stereotyping
Halo Effect
Projection
Perceptual Distortion
Subliminal Influences
Selective Perception

STEREOTYPING   **Stereotypes** are judgments of others that are based on group membership. Such attributes as sex, race, ethnic group, and age are the basis of commonly held stereotypes. For example, the beliefs that older workers are not capable of being trained for new tasks and that younger workers cannot handle responsibility are commonly held stereotypes. Occupational groupings also frequently serve as the basis for stereotypes. For example, consider your own views of, say, police officers, top-level corporate executives, and union officials. Even relatively superficial attributes can be the basis of stereotypes, as evidenced by such clichés as "redheads are short-tempered."

This is not to say that stereotypes are totally worthless and inaccurate. In some instances, stereotypes can provide a useful shortcut for quick evaluation. But the potential costs of erroneous evaluations must always be considered.

In the aggregate, stereotypes may, in fact, be based on group characteristics; this is the "kernel of truth" notion of stereotypes.[15] The proposal argues that some stereotypical beliefs are based on an element of truth, in that the beliefs are derived from observations that hold for an entire group but that do not hold with much accuracy for given individuals in the group. While the popular stereotype of, say, police officers may have some accuracy, the variability of the traits of individual police officers is so great that it is extremely difficult to classify an individual officer accurately from the stereotypical information alone.

THE HALO EFFECT   The **halo effect** occurs when a perceiver uses a general impression of favorableness or unfavorableness as the basis for judgments about more specific traits. In essence, the perceiver's evaluation is influenced by an overall impression. The halo effect explains why a subordinate who is liked by a superior can do no wrong in the superior's eyes, while a subordinate who is disliked may have difficulty obtaining a favorable review from the same superior.

Most students have witnessed the phenomenon in classroom settings, where an instructor might rate a student highly on participation because of a prior favorable impression of that student, when an actual tally of participation in the class might reveal that the favored student spoke no more frequently than other less highly rated students. One study revealed that U.S. Army officers who were liked were judged to be more intelligent than officers

OB Focus
Busters vs. Boomers: A Tale of Competing Perceptions

Call them Busters, Xers, the twentysomething generation. A new cohort of Americans is moving into the workplace, creating a generational fault line and raising tensions between those who remember President Kennedy's assassination and those who don't. The problem is simple: Busters are entering the work force at a time when corporate ranks are already overfilled with boomer-aged managers in a hurry to go nowhere. The result is that busters are often either unemployed or underemployed in McJobs, the term given to subservient types of jobs that offer a minimal paycheck and little or no opportunities for career advancement. Busters employed in McJobs are often frustrated because they perceive themselves as having more energy and technological savvy to offer organizations than many baby boomers who coasted into jobs on the crest of the 1980s' employment wave. Boomers, on the other hand, perceive busters as whiny and naive, unwilling to start at entry-level jobs and work their way up in the organization as generations before them have. But as companies continue to downsize and de-

layer, the vertical pyramids of advancement become flatter. The younger generation believes they won't get the same opportunities as the generation that preceded them.

They're right. The numbers are bleak. Average annual job growth in managerial and technical fields has been about 310,000 in the 1990s, compared to 1.8 million jobs each year during the 1980s. The Bureau of Labor Statistics predicts nearly one-third of the graduating classes of 1990 through 2005 will be employed in jobs that don't require a college degree, compared to 19 percent in 1980. And if that weren't enough bad news, real income is also falling. The median income for households headed by adults under 30 was $24,500 in 1993, a 21 percent drop in constant dollars from 1973.

Ironically, many organizations could use the infusion of new talent that busters have to offer. In general, their technological skills are superior to their older cohort's, and busters are often willing to work for less pay. Managers need to be sensitive to both groups to ensure workplace har-

mony and mitigate the potential tension and resentment between the two cohorts. Boomers may feel threatened by these young whippersnappers, and busters just want the opportunity to show their stuff. Organizations should harness the creativity and energy of newly minted graduates by using their skills to create competitive advantage. Consultant David Cannon says, "The fact is that Generation X [the generation of busters] is very well built for the organization of today. A company that gets into new products and does things differently is exhilarating to younger people."

Companies that fail to acknowledge the competing perceptions of the two cohorts may be hurt in the long run. The tensions between the groups are real and deep-rooted. Much of the disharmony between the groups can be reduced by implementing programs that put teeth into such buzzwords as *empowerment, teamwork, communication, feedback,* and *recognition.* These practices can go a long way in allowing employees to overcome their differences and work in harmony toward a common goal.

Sources: Suneel Ratan, "Generational Tension in the Office: Why Busters Hate Boomers," *Fortune,* October 4, 1993, 56–70; Laura Zinn, Christopher Power, Dori Jones Yang, Alice Z. Cuneo, and David Ross, "Move Over, Boomers: The Busters Are Here—And They're Angry," *Business Week,* December 14, 1992, 74–82.

who were disliked, while an examination of scores on intelligence tests revealed no differences between the two groups of officers.[16]

It has also been observed that judges tend to link certain traits. For example, when a person is judged to be aggressive, he or she is also likely to be seen as highly energetic. The trait of industriousness tends to be linked to that of honesty. Someone who is a churchgoer is likely to be viewed as clean or neat. This phenomenon has come to be termed **implicit personality theory.** Simply stated, it is the tendency to perceive trait X in an individual given that trait Y exists. Because the consistency of correlations or clusterings of traits is not that substantial, assessments of others that are grounded in an implicit personality approach are likely to be in error.

A somewhat related concept is the notion of **central traits.** In a now famous study, Solomon Asch observed that certain specific traits of a person being judged were particularly powerful in influencing the judgment of other traits.[17] Asch presented two groups of students with differing lists of character traits. One group heard a stimulus person described as intelligent, skillful, industrious, warm, determined, practical, and cautious, while a second group heard the same list with the simple substitution of the word *cold* for *warm*. When the students were asked to rate the stimulus person on other traits (such as generous, wise, happy, reliable), the two groups of raters provided very different assessments. From these results, Asch concluded that warm and cold acted as central traits that had substantial responsibility for organizing the development of impressions. Other traits that Asch studied, such as polite and blunt, did not appear to influence impression formation to nearly the same extent. Asch's results suggest that if one wanted to slant another's impressions of, for example, a coworker, this could easily be done by describing the coworker as an essentially warm (or cold) person.

These studies also suggest that our impressions of others are often based on very skimpy information. Our readiness to "fill in the gaps" is partly a matter of expediency and convenience, and partly due to learned associations of traits such as stereotyping and the halo effect.

PROJECTION   We have a tendency to ascribe our own feelings and attributes to others. This is known as **projection.** It is a defense mechanism that helps us to protect ourselves from unpleasant or unacceptable truths. An individual's emotional state has been shown to influence his or her perception of that emotional state in others. In one study, fear was aroused in a group of subjects by telling them that they would later receive an electric shock.[18] Before any shock was administered, members of the group were asked to evaluate the fearfulness of other subjects. Compared to a control group, which had not been threatened with electric shock, the shock-threatened subjects tended to describe others as more fearful and aggressive.

In another study, individuals who were rated high on such unattractive traits as obstinacy, stinginess, and disorderliness tended to rate others as being higher on these same traits.[19] These results suggest the possibility of projecting one's own undesirable traits onto others. Consequently, it is easy to imagine a situation in which a manager who is fearful of organizational change and distrustful of others would project these attributes onto his coworkers, believing that they are fearful of change and cannot be trusted.

PERCEPTUAL DISTORTION   In addition to defending our ego by projecting feelings and attributes onto others, we may simply deny that something occurred or that we witnessed something. Similarly, we may modify or distort what we report in an attempt to avoid an unpleasant reality. Or we may deliberately pay attention only to what we want to see. These acts are forms of **perceptual distortion.**[†]

Illusions are another form of perceptual distortion. We are all familiar with the notion of an illusion, in which our perception of something does not reflect its reality. Consider, for example, the well-known illusion of perceptual contrast shown in Figure 3.2. The grey area is of uniform color, yet when judged within a context, the grey ring appears to have differing tones. The context influences our perception and creates an illusion of difference that does not exist. So too in social relations, an individual may give a particular impression due to the context in which he or she is being judged. For example, an individual of moderate intelligence might be judged as being of substantially higher intelligence because of a prior belief that workers in his job classification are not typically very intelligent. This social misperception is based on an illusion influenced by context.

SUBLIMINAL INFLUENCES   Our perception of others may be affected by factors that we are not fully aware of. Influences that are below our threshold of awareness are called **subliminal influences.** Studies have shown that some degree of perceptual detection can occur even when people are unaware of having

FIGURE 3.2

Notice that the grey circle or ring is uniform in brightness. Now, place a pencil along the vertical line that is the border between the light and dark sections of the square. Has the apparent brightness of each half of the circle changed?

[†]An interesting example of perceptual distortion is given by *occupational centrism,* the tendency to see one's own profession or work as more important than that of others. The concept is illustrated by a story attributed to Knute Rockne of Notre Dame. After a particularly successful season, the question was asked as to who was responsible for the victories, the line or the backfield. After being put to a vote, the line won, not surprisingly, seven to four.[20]

seen anything.[21] However, the effectiveness of attempts at deliberately designed subliminal influence appears to be overrated. Generally, stimuli of greater intensity have greater influence.

The existence of subliminal influences can be demonstrated by the successful use of posthypnotic suggestions. In such cases, a person is hypnotized and told that when she awakes, she will respond in a specific way to a specific cue, such as whistling when she hears the word *bird*. The individual later responds to the cue when not hypnotized, but cannot recall the origin of the suggestion or the motive for her action. Also, if two sharp pins are placed very near each other on the skin of a person's back, most individuals cannot consciously distinguish whether there are two pins or only one. Yet, when forced to guess, most subjects correctly guess the number of pins.

As another illustration, consider that a configuration of people or objects can create a sense of uneasiness in a perceiver even though the perceiver may be unaware of the origin of the feelings. For example, Figure 3.3 might create a feeling of dread in viewers without their being able to articulate exactly what they find upsetting. However, further examination of the picture (held either

 FIGURE 3.3

close up or at a distance) reveals that a disturbing image is embedded in the scene. Such influences in social perception and in day-to-day life are likely to be very subtle.

SELECTIVE PERCEPTION   Yet another obstacle to accurate perception arises from the tendency to be influenced by our own interests. As it is not possible to take in all stimuli we receive, we tend to select out certain elements. As an illustration of this, consider the experience that follows the purchase of a car. Suddenly you begin to notice that type of car on the street much more frequently. **Selective perception** occurs in organizations when managers tend to interpret problem situations in light of their own background and interest. For example, given an ambiguous problematic situation, a sales manager will be inclined to see sales issues as the underlying cause while a production manager will be inclined to see manufacturing-related issues.

THE STUDY OF ATTRIBUTIONS

Within the area of perceptual research, one of the more widely studied topics is the process of attribution. The term *attribution* is used to describe the process people go through to explain the causes of the behavior of others. Initially popularized by Fritz Heider, **attribution theory** focuses on the inference process that is used to deduce others' dispositions or traits from observations of their behavior.[22] Central to Heider's theory is the proposal that people perceive behavior as being caused, either by the individual in question or by the environment. This is a distinction between internal causality and external causality—that is, whether people initiate actions or merely react to their environment. In addition, Heider proposed that the outcome of a particular action is perceived to be the result of environmental and personal forces as well as the influences of personal power (ability) and effort (trying).

Consider the demolition of a building. Either an earthquake or a person with a wrecking ball could achieve the same result. The environmental force (the earthquake) could aid the personal force (the person with a wrecking ball), or either force could produce the same result with the other force absent. Personal and environmental forces conceivably can also work against each other and thereby cancel out one another.

The theory's components of personal power and effort are also important. If either of these components is absent, the strength of the personal force is reduced to zero. An observer of a set of actions must be able to take these various factors into account in order to make a correct attribution about a person.

Another variable of importance in the attribution process is the notion of noncommon effects. A given action may reflect several dispositions. Therefore, in order to sort out the underlying dispositions, it is necessary for the observer to have evidence that clearly points to a particular disposition. For example, someone may run several personal errands for his boss, who is ill, and also make an anonymous contribution to a charity. Running errands could be motivated both by altruism and by a desire for approval. The charitable donation could by motivated by altruism, but also by a desire to have a larger tax deduction on income taxes. The common effect is the aid of another, while approval and a tax deduction are noncommon effects. The conclusion to be reached is that the person under observation is altruistic.

Social status is often viewed as determining the extent to which an individual acts freely versus being controlled by the environment. In a study by Thibaut and Riecken, student subjects were assigned the task of convincing either a high-status individual or a low-status individual that a choice of materials for a project was a good one.[23] The high- and low-status individuals were confederates of the investigators who accepted the subjects' attempts at influence and conceded the wisdom of each subject's choice of materials. When the subjects were later asked to rate the extent to which the compliance they received from their listeners was freely given, differences were observed that favored the high-status individual (that is, the compliance of the high-status individual was seen as more internally caused or freely given, relative to that of the low-status individual). Subjects also reported a greater amount of attraction for the high-status individual. High-status individuals, therefore, are viewed as acting more freely and, perhaps as a consequence, are more subject to praise as well as censure.

A related argument can be made that the perception of being externally controlled is partly a function of the perceived strength of environmental forces. In a study by Strickland, two subjects served as subordinates for a supervisor-subject.[24] The two subordinates performed a task for ten trials. The supervisor-subject was permitted to monitor the performance of subordinate A for nine trials and subordinate B for two trials. Although the investigator arranged the situation so that both subordinates had nearly identical performance records, the supervisor-subject indicated that he trusted subordinate B (the less-supervised worker) more than subordinate A. Subordinate A's performance was also viewed as being more externally controlled than subordinate B's. Since the supervisors saw their monitoring of A as relatively high, A's behavior was viewed as being more externally controlled.

Attribution research has also studied tendencies to systematically distort one's view of behavior. One illustration is termed the **fundamental attribution error,** wherein we attribute the behaviors of others to internal factors. For example, you might conclude that another employee is doing poorly in meeting a sales quota because of a lack of ambition, when it may be that the other employee's sales territory does not provide much opportunity. The fundamental attribution error leads people to blame the victims of misfortune. For example, unemployed workers are viewed as lazy, and the homeless are seen as irresponsible. Women who are the victims of sexual harassment at work may be accused of being seductive.

The attributions that people make concerning the causes of their own behavior tend to be influenced by whether the outcome is positive or negative. This tendency to take credit for success (attributing it to personal traits or personal effort) and to blame failure on external, environmental causes is termed the **self-serving bias.** Students sometimes manifest the self-serving bias when they attribute their success on tests to their intellectual prowess or having studied hard, and attribute their poor test performance to unfair test construction by the teacher. Self-serving bias is also manifest when people compare themselves to others on subjective and socially desirable dimensions. For example, most business managers view themselves as being more ethical than the average manager, and superior on perform ...ce dimensions.[25] Also, most managers see themselves as more open to innovation than do their subordinates or outside observers.[‡]

PERSONALITY

Thus far in this chapter, we have considered the difficulties of accurately perceiving others. Let us now turn our attention to how individuals differ. Such differences are what make social life stimulating and sometimes frustrating. First, we will consider the nature of personality and the determinants of personality. Next, we will examine the techniques used to measure differences in personality. And last, we will look at several important dimensions of individual differences

Personality is defined here as the relatively enduring individual traits and dispositions that form a pattern distinguishing one person from all others. This is by no means a universally accepted definition. In fact, there are nearly as many definitions of personality as there are theories of personality. Nonetheless, for our purposes, this definition will suffice.[§]

The concept of personality represents stylistic differences in the behavior of people. Let us suppose, for example, that you have closely observed the behavior of one of your coworkers. This person rarely speaks in group meetings, has virtually no friends at work, and seems to prefer to be alone most of the time. From these observations, you would likely infer that this individual is introverted. This would help to explain the individual's past and present behavior and predict his behavior in future situations. Our definition of personality includes the notion that the traits are relatively enduring, which implies consistency of behavior across situations and over time. To be sure, people do change over time, but the rate of such change is typically very gradual. Normal maturation processes are sufficiently slow that we can usefully assess individual traits with a fair degree of certainty as to their stability.

THE DETERMINANTS OF PERSONALITY

There has been considerable debate about the origins of an individual's personality. One point of view argues that personality is largely determined at

---

[‡]As most academic administrators are aware, university faculty members are not exempt from the self-serving bias. One study found that 94 percent of the faculty at one institution, and 90 percent of the faculty members in a survey of 24 institutions, judged themselves to be superior to their average colleague.[26]

[§]It should be noted that some writers have questioned whether the notion of personality is even necessary. They contend that individual attributes can be easily explained by reducing the observations of an individual's "personality" to more basic concepts, such as habits, conditioned reflexes, attitudes, and so on. In other words, "personality" is something akin to the canals on Mars: It may be more in the eye of the beholder (as part of the observer's structuring of what is being observed) than it is an actual feature. There may be some truth to this criticism of the entire enterprise of studying personality. However, the *consistency* that we find within an individual's behavior suggests that it may well be worthwhile to infer the existence of traits and dispositions that can partially account for and thereby help explain employee behavior.

conception by each individual's unique complement of genes. In essence, this perspective holds that personality traits, such as temperament and sociability, are determined in much the same way as hair color and facial features.

The counterpoint to the heredity position is an environmental argument. Environmentalists contend that the results of experience can shape and alter an individual's personality. For example, whether an individual is lethargic or industrious would be determined by whether she was rewarded or punished by parents, teachers, and friends for displaying related behaviors in the past. If the notion of the work ethic was ingrained in an individual at an early age and she repeatedly encountered situations in which hard work paid off, she would be inclined to espouse values that support the work ethic.

Some evidence shows that heredity can determine personality. Perhaps the most intriguing indication of the importance of genetic predisposition comes from studies of identical twins who have been separated at birth and raised apart. Even though many of the twins were raised by families from different social classes, and sometimes in different countries, each set shared many common traits. For example, food and clothing preferences and such personal habits as smoking, fingernail biting, and the sporting of moustaches were often shared by the separately raised pairs.[27]

A considerable amount of evidence also suggests that the situations to which a person is exposed influence personality traits. The most striking illustration arises from cross-cultural comparisons. As many people have noted, the personality traits of Westerners are often distinct from traits of people raised in other cultures, such as Orientals and Asian Indians. Also, people who are raised in a new culture from an early age often reflect the influence of their experiences within that new culture.

One can also find evidence of a link between personality and more immediate environmental influences. For example, research on the relationship of birth order to personality has revealed some interesting findings. Firstborn children are more dependent, more influenced by social pressure, and more prone to schizophrenia than are later-born children.[28] Compared to later-borns, firstborns view the world as more predictable, rational, and orderly. In addition, firstborns are less likely to defy authority, and are more ambitious, more cooperative, and more concerned with being socially accepted. A disproportionate number of firstborns are listed in *Who's Who*. In one interesting study, it was found that the U.S. voting population has tended to elect firstborns to the presidency during years of relative crisis, for example, in an election year before the outbreak of a war.[29]

The personality differences that have been identified between firstborn and later-born children are believed to result from the differing experiences to which the children are exposed. Firstborns are generally treated differently by parents. Compared to later-borns, they tend to receive more attention at first but are then expected to behave more responsibly in looking after younger children.

For most students of the topic, the heredity–environment debate is resolved by recognizing the importance of *both* heredity and environment as determinants of personality. Heredity may predispose an individual to certain patterns of behavior, while environmental forces may precipitate more specific patterns of action. Both sets of factors are necessary for a fuller accounting of individual behavior.

One of the more perplexing aspects of personality is its general resistance to modification. Studies of attempts to change an individual's personality typically show that it is very difficult, if not impossible, to do so for many individuals. This difficulty does not negate the possibility of personality change via environmental forces, but instead argues that the magnitude of such forces for change and the inclination of individuals to change are typically not sufficient. This resistance to change is significant because it suggests that managers must learn to deal with people's personality traits in the work setting. In short, a manager's hope of dramatically altering a worker's personality traits is not great. It may be more realistic to try to accept people as they are or to try for only modest accommodations between personality features and job requirements.

ASSESSING PERSONALITY TRAITS

There are many different techniques for measuring personality attributes. Among them are personality ratings, situational tests, inventories, and projective techniques.**

PERSONALITY RATINGS   A well-known device for assessing personality is the use of ratings. The most frequently used formats of such **personality ratings** are five-point and seven-point scales, with adjectives as endpoints, or anchors, for the scales (see Chapter 4 for examples of rating scales). Such rating scales may not yield reliable assessments because the meanings associated with the endpoints and midpoints are not clearly defined. Thus, different raters may interpret the same scale differently.

This approach can be improved upon by using rating scales whose scale points are clearly defined by specific behavioral indicators. For example, consider the following example of a scale for measuring the trait of competitiveness.[31]

> 1 = *Sensitive to the presence of competitive situations but becomes disorganized, let down, or unproductive, or flees from them. Discouraged about own abilities or appears to seek defeat compulsively.*
> 2 = *No real competitive interest; enjoys games for the fun of playing them but relatively unimportant who wins.*
> 3 = *Is stimulated by competitive situations and enjoys excelling, but can accept defeat without much strain. Periodic competitive sprees but not persistent and pervasive.*
> 4 = *Enjoys excelling competitors to the point of being upset when faced with a loss, takes failure very hard, or can't restrain an overt expression of satisfaction after winning. Competitive drive is very pronounced in several fields or has one field in which it is terribly important to excel.*

**What follows is a review of the major techniques used for assessing traits. Omitted from discussion is the technique of graphology, or handwriting analysis. Oddly, and sadly, the technique is used by a sizable number of firms in the United States, Canada, and Western Europe. Although reliable scoring schemes have been developed for features of slant and height, there is no evidence of the validity of these measurements for predicting job performance or individual standing on more widely accepted measures of personality.[30]

5 = *Extreme drive to excel competitors, won't play if can't win, always picks inferior opponents, or cheats to win. Beating competitors is primary or only satisfaction in work or play situations. Competitive drives extend to many situations that most individuals would not define as competitive.*

As this example implies, it is important that a rater be in a position to observe the traits in question. The rater must also be unbiased and frank.[††] Typically, evaluators are reluctant to use the extreme negative positions on rating scales. As a consequence, ratings are often clustered toward the positive end of the scale, with the result that ratings do not discriminate among individuals and are, therefore, not informative.

SITUATIONAL TESTS   **Situational tests** (or behavioral tests) involve the direct observation of an individual's behavior in a setting that is designed to provide information about personality. The earliest situational tests were used to assess personality in children. For example, to assess the trait of honesty, students were asked to grade their own papers. A later check of the papers indicated how honest each student was. In an assessment of charitableness, children were invited to anonymously donate small gifts, such as school supplies, to less fortunate children. Because the individual items were surreptitiously marked, it was possible to identify how much each child donated.

As part of a situational test of honesty in adults, conducted by the military during World War II, soldiers were placed in isolation in a test situation in which a series of numerical problems were to be solved. The answer book was available in the room, but each individual was instructed to not open the book. By secretly observing the individual from behind a screen, the assessors were able to determine the individual's level of honesty.[32]

Another illustration of situational testing is provided by Toyota's screening program at its Georgetown, Kentucky, auto-assembly plant. As part of this program, the problem-solving ability of applicants is tested by putting them through a flawed mock-up of an assembly line and asking them to suggest improvements in the line's procedures.[33]

Situational tests offer many advantages. They are less subjective than rating scales, and the trait in question can sometimes be assessed in a fairly natural setting. This suggests that the results of the assessment will be more valid. Unfortunately, situational tests are very expensive to create and administer. Additionally, certain traits, such as self-esteem, do not readily lend themselves to situational assessment.

PERSONALITY INVENTORIES   **Personality inventories** are perhaps the most widely used method of assessing personality characteristics. Typically, inventories ask the respondent to indicate whether a statement pertains to or is true of himself or herself. A typical inventory question would be, " Do you find it easy

---

[††]Unfortunately, raters are sometimes asked to perform evaluations without having an opportunity to observe the necessary traits. For example, university professors are often asked to provide evaluations of students who apply to MBA programs or law school. Many times these evaluations include ratings of such personality traits as maturity, social ascendency, and dependability. Most faculty members, however, have only superficial contact with the students that they are asked to evaluate and oftentimes are very generous in their ratings.

to make friends?" The first concerted effort to use a personality inventory occurred during World War I when the U.S. Army attempted to identify men who were likely to have severe adverse emotional reactions to the rigors of trench warfare. Rather than screen the men with interviews, Woodworth devised a lengthy questionnaire, called the Personal Data Sheet, in which an individual would essentially interview himself.[34] Among the 116 items in the Personal Data Sheet were:

1. Have you ever had a vision?
2. Do you sometimes feel that you are being watched?
3. Have you ever had dizzy spells?
4. Do you feel that you have hurt yourself by taking drugs?
5. Did you have a happy childhood?

Individuals were screened out if they answered a specified number of questions in the "neurotic" direction.

Today, many devices are used to assess literally hundreds of personality characteristics. As aids in determining whether a suitable inventory is available and whether the device has acceptable measurement characteristics, the researcher can consult such reference sources as *Mental Measurements Yearbook* and *Tests in Print*.[35]

Although inventories have the clear advantage of ease of administration, there remains the problem of the possible "faking" of answers and the related issue of the "approval motive"—the respondent's tendency to answer in a socially desirable fashion.[36] Some of the more sophisticated inventories, however, provide checks for faking. Items are included in the inventory that do not measure personality traits per se but instead act as "flags" that a respondent is answering dishonestly.[‡‡]

PROJECTIVE TECHNIQUES   **Projective techniques** are designed to probe the more subtle aspects of an individual's personality. The most commonly used forms of projectives are inkblot tests, storytelling devices, and sentence completions.

The Rorschach Test   Projective techniques are based on the belief that a person will provide a highly individualistic interpretation of an ambiguous stimulus (Figure 3.4).[§§] This notion was used by Hermann Rorschach, a Swiss psychiatrist, when he created his well-known inkblot test called the **Rorschach test**. Individuals are scored as much on *why* they report seeing something as they are on *what* they report seeing. Responses are typically scored in

---

[‡‡]Faking scales are typically devised by paying people to fake their answers deliberately in a specific direction (either "fake good" or "fake bad"). Their responses to the questions are then analyzed to identify the items that discriminate between intentional fakers and others who are paid to answer honestly.

[§§]This tendency to interpret ambiguous stimuli in a unique, personalized manner was first noted by Leonardo da Vinci. As the story goes, one day during a playful moment, da Vinci threw a paint-soaked sponge at an apprentice. The apprentice ducked and the sponge struck a wall, leaving a smudge. Da Vinci noticed that the smudge, on various occasions, reminded him of different objects. More interesting was his observation that when visitors to his workshop were asked what they saw in the smudge, they reported seeing things that made sense in light of their occupations or past experiences.[37]

FIGURE 3.4
AN INKBLOT OF THE TYPE USED IN THE RORSCHACH TECHNIQUE

accordance with one of several schemes. However, the interpretation of the scoring is far less standard.

Another drawback of the Rorschach is the lack of evidence about its reliability and validity. Nonetheless, it is one of the most widely used devices in personality assessment. Its popularity stems from its frequent use as a probe into personality rather than as a definitive assessment.

Storytelling   **Storytelling** devices have a better track record than the Rorschach test in terms of standardized interpretation, reliability, and usefulness as a predictor of behavior. The most widely used storytelling technique is the **Thematic Apperception Test, or TAT.**[38] The TAT is composed of 20 pictures, each of which portrays a social setting of ambiguous meaning. For example, one picture shows a boy staring wistfully at a violin. For each picture, the respondent is asked to provide a story that contains the following elements: a description of the characters in the story, a statement about what is presently going on in the picture, and explanations of what led up to the current situation as well as how the story is likely to conclude. The 20 stories are then analyzed for recurring themes. Assuming that people identify with the protagonist of their stories, it is possible to draw inferences about a respondent's attitudes, needs, aspirations, and self-perception. Figure 3.5 presents a picture of the type used in the TAT.

Sentence Completions   **Sentence completions** are a third popular variety of projective technique in which respondents are asked to supply the endings for a series of partial sentences. The format of sentence completions is fairly straightforward. For example,

1. I wish my boss would _____.
2. I feel good about myself when _____.
3. The trouble with my coworkers is _____.

FIGURE 3.5
A PICTURE OF THE TYPE USED IN THE THEMATIC APPERCEPTION TEST

In some instances, standardized scoring schemes have been developed to aid in interpreting the responses. Because the intent of sentence completions is relatively transparent and respondents are usually given unlimited time to answer, this test format is best used when respondents have little to gain by faking their answers. Appropriate situations might include sensitivity-training sessions and team-building exercises. When people answer honestly, their responses to incomplete sentences can be very enlightening.

IMPORTANT DIMENSIONS OF PERSONALITY

There is an enormous number of human traits. It has been estimated that there may be as many as 5,000 adjectives that could be used to describe personality traits. In terms of relevance to organizational behavior, however, the number of important personality traits is much smaller. Consequently, for now we will limit our discussion to five dimensions of personality: locus of control, authoritarianism, the work ethic, cognitive style, and moral maturity. In organizational behavior research, these five dimensions have received much more attention than others. Throughout this text, however, we will consider other personality dimensions as they pertain to behavior in the workplace.

LOCUS OF CONTROL   Psychologist Julian Rotter proposed that the likelihood of an individual's engaging in a particular act is a function of (1) the person's expectancy that the act will yield rewards and (2) the personal value of those rewards to the individual.[39] In essence, Rotter's proposal rests on the notion of locus of control. **Locus of control** is the extent to which individuals believe that control over their lives lies within their own control or in environmental forces beyond their control. Someone who strongly believes that she controls events has a high *internal locus of control*, while someone who feels that she is at the mercy of fate has a high *external locus of control.*

Rotter developed a scale for measuring the extent to which an individual is internally or externally oriented. The Internal-External Control Scale asks the respondent to choose one of two possible interpretations as the cause of an event. The alternatives reflect internal versus external control. The following are sample items from the scale.[40]

1a. In the long run, people get the respect they deserve in this world.
 b. Unfortunately, an individual's worth often passes unrecognized, no matter how hard he tries.

2a. In my case, getting what I want has little or nothing to do with luck.
 b. Many times, we might just as well decide what to do by flipping a coin.

3a. By taking an active part in political and social affairs, people can control world events.
 b. Many times, I feel that I have little influence over the things that happen to me.

As you can see from these items, choice "a" in these examples indicates an internal response, while choice "b" exemplifies an external response.

Research based on the locus-of-control concept has yielded interesting results. It has been found, for example, that internally oriented individuals are less likely to respond to group pressures or persuasive communications.[41] Furthermore, a number of studies have observed that internal orientation is associated with success in school. For black students in particular, locus of control was a better predictor of academic achievement than was any other variable studied, including school location and quality.[42]

Social class and racial differences in locus of control have also been reported, in that upper-class individuals and whites tend to score as more internally oriented relative to lower-class individuals and blacks.[43] Because social class is correlated with race, it is difficult to say whether poverty or discrimination is a more important cause of an external locus of control. To be sure, the experience of powerlessness and the lack of personal evidence that hard work leads to success contribute to the external orientation that is found in certain segments of society.[44]

It is perhaps not surprising that compared to externally oriented individuals, internally oriented individuals have higher incomes, hold jobs of higher status, and advance more rapidly in their careers.[45] What perhaps is surprising is that scores on Rotter's scale have been shifting over the years with test scores revealing that Americans appear to be becoming more externally oriented.[46]

Finally, it should be noted that internally and externally oriented individuals differ in the kinds of rewards they prefer. Externally oriented individuals, who believe that forces beyond their control are responsible for success, tend to prefer such extrinsic rewards as increased pay and job security. In contrast, internally oriented individuals usually prefer intrinsic (self-supplied) rewards such as a feeling of accomplishment and sense of achievement.[47] Internally oriented individuals, however, are not completely exempt from difficulties. It has been found that extreme internals may be maladjusted "controllers" who strive to have total control over their own and others' outcomes by being aggressive, intrusive, and domineering. For such individuals, frustration and anxiety are likely when they are in a subservient role or a setting where goal attainment is beyond their control.[48] The implication is fairly clear: Managers who understand their subordinates' loci of control can better tailor their reward systems to reflect individual needs.

AUTHORITARIANISM   Another well-researched personality dimension is **authoritarianism** (that is, a blind acceptance of authority). Given the importance of power relations in organizational settings, the topic of authoritarianism is clearly a pertinent one.

The study of authoritarianism was begun during World War II by a group of researchers who fled Hitler's campaign of antisemitism. These researchers, who collaborated throughout the 1940s, conducted a program of research culminating in the publication of the book *The Authoritarian Personality.*[49] As part of their research efforts, they produced scales for measuring four facets of authoritarianism: fascism, ethnocentrism, antisemitism, and political-economic conservatism. Sample items from each of the four scales follow:

- Obedience and respect for authority are the most important virtues children should learn (fascism scale).

- There will always be wars because, for one thing, there will always be races who ruthlessly try to grab more than their share (ethnocentrism scale).

- Jews tend to remain a foreign element in American society, to preserve their old social standards, and to resist the American way of life (antisemitism scale).

- A political candidate, to be worth voting for, must first and foremost have a good character, one that will fight inefficiency, graft, and vice (political-economic conservatism scale).

Researchers have found that highly authoritarian individuals tend to reject minority group members;[50] view others in relatively simplistic terms;[51] vote for conservative political candidates;[52] endorse strong parental control as a way of making family decisions;[53] and are less well educated.[54] In addition, it has been found that workers who are rated as highly authoritarian are more productive under authoritarian supervision.[55]

Early research on the authoritarian personality has been criticized for being a liberal polemic against political conservatism in the guise of a politically neutral analysis of personality. In order to correct this point, Rokeach proposed the more general but related construct of dogmatism.[56] **Dogmatism** is defined as a system of beliefs that is organized around an acceptance of absolute authority and intolerance toward others. By this definition, a left-wing radical, such as an extreme Marxist-communist, could be judged to be as dogmatic as a right-wing radical, such as a follower of Nazism.

Dogmatic individuals tend to be closed-minded and inflexible. Highly dogmatic managers are likely to reach decisions in relatively little time, after a limited search for data. They are also likely to be extremely confident about the quality of their decisions.[57] In addition, highly dogmatic employees report substantial differences between how they spend their time on the job and how they would prefer to spend their time.[58]

THE WORK ETHIC   The **work ethic** embodies a cluster of beliefs, including a belief in the dignity of all work, contempt for idleness and self-indulgence, and a belief that if you work hard, you will be rewarded. Personality research seems to indicate that a stable predisposition toward the work ethic can be identified. The measurement of this predisposition is typically done through inventories asking respondents to describe their own beliefs and behaviors. Individuals who subscribe to the work ethic have been found to be more accepting of authoritarian leadership.[59] They also tend to have an interest in jobs that can be characterized as concrete as opposed to abstract; for example, they may prefer carpentry to journalism. When asked to perform simple, dull, and repetitive tasks without financial incentive, endorsers of the work ethic are more persistent and productive.[60] When told that they are doing poorly on a boring task in comparison to other performers, endorsers of the work ethic respond by increasing their efforts, while others reduce their efforts.[61] In response to positive feedback, both endorsers and nonendorsers of the work ethic increase their effort.

Recent evidence suggests that the work ethic may be waning in the United States. For example, Cherrington reported that older workers are more prone to endorse the work ethic than are younger workers.[62] If we assume that the work ethic's belief system is learned early in life, this finding suggests the work ethic may be eroding. In a study of workers' desire to continue working even if they no longer had the financial need to do so, it was found that the number of people who would choose early retirement increased in the past decades.[63] In 1955, only 20 percent of the respondents indicated that they would quit working if they did not need the money. But by the late 1970s, this percentage had increased to 28 percent. From such evidence, we may conclude that adherence to the work ethic may be diminishing and that it may be gradually being replaced by a leisure ethic. The unprecedented current affluence of the United States in comparison to all other countries and all other times is a likely contributing factor to this attitudinal shift. It should be noted, however, that such cultural value shifts are not new and that the present shift may reflect a more fundamental process of gradual cultural maturation.[64]

COGNITIVE STYLE   Carl Gustav Jung, a famous European psychoanalyst, proposed a model of **cognitive styles,** or modes of problem solving. He suggested four dimensions of psychological functioning: Introverted versus Extroverted, Thinking versus Feeling, Sensing versus Intuiting, and Judging versus Perceiving. Introverts are oriented toward the inner world of ideas and feelings, while extroverts are oriented toward the outer world of people and objects. Thinkers desire to make decisions logically, while feelers base decisions on subjective grounds. Sensing individuals prefer to focus on details, while intuitive individuals prefer to focus on broad issues. Judging types desire to resolve issues, while perceiving types are comparatively flexible and seek additional information. By crossing the various types, 16 distinct personality types can be identified.

The measurement of these types has relied heavily on a paper-and-pencil test known as the Myers-Briggs Type Indicator, developed by the mother-daughter team of Katherine Briggs and Isabel Briggs-Myers. Table 3.2 summarizes some of the characteristics found to be associated with these different cognitive styles. The Myers-Briggs Type Indicator has become one of the more widely used personality tests in the United States, within the nominally normal

TABLE 3.2

THE 16 COGNITIVE STYLES OF THE MYERS-BRIGGS TYPOLOGY

		Sensing Types (S)		Intuitive Types (N)	
		Thinking (T)	Feeling (F)	Feeling (F)	Thinking (T)
Introverts (I)	Judging (J)	ISTJ: Serious, quiet, practical, logical, dependable	ISFJ: Quiet, friendly, thorough, considerate	INFJ: Quietly forceful, succeeds by perseverance, conscientious	INTJ: Skeptical, critical, independent, determined, original
	Perceiving (P)	ISTP: Cool onlookers, quiet, reserved and analytical, flashes of original humor	ISFP: Retiring, sensitive, kind, modest, relaxed about getting things done	INFP: Cares about learning, ideas, and independent projects; undertakes too much, but gets it done	INTP: Quiet, reserved, impersonal, enjoys scientific subjects, little liking for parties or small talk
Extroverts (E)	Perceiving (P)	ESTP: Matter-of-fact, doesn't worry, may be blunt or insensitive	ESFP: Easy-going, accepting, friendly, likes sports and making things	ENFP: Warmly enthusiastic, high-spirited, imaginative, quick with solutions and help with problems	ENTP: Quick, ingenious, will argue either side of issue for fun, may neglect routine assignments
	Judging (J)	ESTJ: Practical, realistic, has a natural head for business or mechanics, likes to organize and run activities	ESFJ: Warm-hearted, talkative, popular, born cooperator, desires harmony, little interest in abstract subjects	ENFJ: Responsive and responsible, feels real concern for what others think or want, sociable, sensitive to praise and criticism	ENTJ: Hearty, frank, decisive, a leader, may be more positive than own experience in area warrants

Source: I. B. Myers and K. C. Briggs, *Myers-Briggs Type Indicator* (Princeton, N.J.: Educational Testing Service, 1962). Modified and reproduced by special permission of the publisher, Consulting Psychologists Press, Inc., Palo Alto, CA 94303 from *Myers-Briggs Type Indicator* by Katharine C. Briggs and Isabel Briggs Myers. Copyright 1983 by Consulting Psychologists Press, Inc. All rights reserved.

population. Typically, the test is given as part of management development programs to aid executives in understanding how they appear to others. Companies that have relied on the Myers-Briggs Type Indicator include Allied-Signal, Apple, AT&T, Citicorp, Exxon, General Electric, Honeywell, and 3M.

Research using the Myers-Briggs Type Indicator has generally supported the typology and shown that people of different cognitive styles prefer different occupations. For example, the ENTP individual is termed the "conceptualizer." This person loves new possibilities and hates routines. They are more likely to be an entrepreneur than a corporate executive. The ISTJ person is termed the "traditionalist," and often may be found in accounting and financial positions. The INTJ person is labeled the "visionary." Such individuals, although only a small proportion of the population, have a disproportionate representation among chief executives. One of the most common types in the general population, as well as among managers, is the ESTJ, termed the "organizer."[65]

Sometimes the test is used as an aid for improving work-team functioning. Following feedback and discussion, team members can gain insights to the orientations of coworkers and themselves, as well as to how their different orientations may help or hinder team dynamics. Skeptics might argue that it is the greater communication and discussion that generates positive results, rather than the feedback provided by the Myers-Briggs test per se.

MORAL MATURITY   The topic of ethical decision making in organizations has received increasing attention in recent years. Surveys of managers who are lower in an organization's structure report more pressure to compromise their personal values in order to achieve company goals.[66] One *Wall Street Journal* survey revealed that 4 out of 20 executives reported having been asked to behave unethically.[67]

A popular model of moral judgment was developed and tested by Lawrence Kohlberg, a psychologist.[68] His **moral maturity** model emphasizes the cognitive, or reasoning, processes that can be used to characterize individuals when making ethical decisions. Kohlberg's research identified six stages of moral development. Moral development is reflected in movement from stage to stage in a fixed, or invariant, and irreversible sequence. Any individual's reasoning can be said to be operating in a manner characteristic of one of these stages. Table 3.3 outlines the six stages of Kohlberg's model. At stages one and two (termed the preconventional level), a person is focused on such concrete consequences as rewards and punishments, and personal interest. At stages three and four (the conventional level), correct behavior and judgment are defined by the expectations of good behavior of one's family and society. At stages five and six (the principled level), correct behavior or judgment is defined in terms of universal values and principles.

Kohlberg and his research associates have developed several tests for measuring a person's stage of moral maturity. Studies of behavior and decision making reveal that individuals of higher moral maturity are less likely to cheat in laboratory experiments and less likely to follow the orders of an authority figure if the directives are likely to injure another individual. Highly moral individuals are more likely to help another individual who is in need of assis-

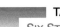

TABLE 3.3

SIX STAGES OF MORAL DEVELOPMENT

Stage	What is considered to be proper
Preconventional Level	
Stage One: Obedience and punishment orientation	Sticking to rules to avoid punishment. Obedience for its own sake.
Stage Two: Instrumental purpose and exchange	Following rules only when it is in one's immediate interest. Right is an equal exchange, a fair deal.
Conventional Level	
Stage Three: Interpersonal accord, conformity, mutual expectations	Stereotypical "good" behavior. Living up to what is expected by people close to you.
Stage Four: Social accord and system maintenance	Fulfilling duties and obligations to which one has agreed. Upholding laws except in extreme cases where they conflict with fixed social duties. Contributing to the society, group.
Principled Level	
Stage Five: Social contract and individual rights	Being aware that people hold a variety of values, that rules are relative to the group. Upholding rules because they are the social contract. Upholding nonrelative values and rights regardless of majority opinion.
Stage Six: Universal ethical principles	Following self-chosen ethical principles. When laws violate these principles, act in accord with principles.

Adapted from L. Kohlberg, "Moral Stages and Moralizations: The Cognitive-Developmental Approach," in *Moral Development and Behavior: Theory, Research, and Social Issues,* ed. T. Lickona (New York: Holt, Rinehart and Winston, 1969): 34–35.

tance.[69] More highly morally mature individuals also are less likely to engage in padding an expense account.[70] Kohlberg's model of the stages of moral development has been found to be a reasonable representation of people in non-Western cultures as well.[71] However, Carol Gilligan has challenged Kohlberg's views as reflecting an abstract, impersonal concept of justice that is more characteristic of male than female moral judgment. Gilligan's research suggests that males may focus more on issues of justice, while females may emphasize caring and the fulfillment of human needs.[72]

Although an individual may be inclined to behave morally as a function of an important predisposition, the context in which an individual is operating can also have a powerful influence on ethical conduct. As noted by Linda Trevino of Penn State University, ethical decision making and behavior can be better explained and predicted by the interaction of both individual and situational factors.[73]

OTHER DIMENSIONS OF PERSONALITY   Five other personality dimensions are also relevant to behavior in the workplace. Because they are frequently studied in connection with other topics, we will consider them later in the text. Specifically, need motivation will be considered in the chapter on motivation (Chapter 6), Machiavellianism will be examined in the chapter on power and influence (Chapter 9), cognitive complexity will be related to the topic of leadership (Chapters 10 and 11), and risk taking and creativity will be discussed in the chapter on decision making (Chapter 12).

THE PREDICTIVE UTILITY OF PERSONALITY MEASURES

A number of studies have been conducted that use personality data to predict employees' performance. The results of these studies typically are modest.[74] Usually, the correlation between a personality trait and performance is low, but positive. Given our daily observations of the strong presence of personality and its role in daily interpersonal behavior, the lack of a stronger relationship between personality and performance may seem surprising. But there are several reasons for this occurrence. First, personality measurement usually involves only a few aspects of an individual's makeup. Also, the measured dimensions may not be particularly relevant to the specific work situation. Thus, when researchers know more about the specific requirements of a given job, they are able to demonstrate the role of specific personality dimensions more convincingly. For example, it has been found that extroversion is a valid predictor for occupations involving social interaction (for example, sales and management). Also, both extroversion and openness to experience have been found to predict training proficiency.[75]

Furthermore, the measurement of performance itself is not simple. Often, performance measures address only part of the total picture, omitting qualitative features of performance in favor of more easily quantified features. For example, customer satisfaction with bank tellers is likely to be influenced by the teller's personality traits. However, banks typically assess tellers on the single dimension of whether their cash drawers balance at the end of the day. Also, customers are not surveyed about their impressions of the teller following a transaction. As salespeople will testify, the impressions they make on customers are important to their performance. However, this critical qualitative element of sales is not often measured; instead, sales volume, a quantitative element, is the standard. It is interesting to note that in a study of sales performance that examined personality traits as predictors, it was found that a composite of such personality traits as social dominance, gregariousness, and altruistic interest in serving others was a useful predictor of sales success.[76]

Also, it should be noted that single studies attempting to predict performance from personality measures are often limited by a number of research design problems, such as restriction of possible ranges on predictors and criteria, and unreliability of measures. These problems, however, can be overcome by cumulating results across studies and applying statistical corrections in what is termed a *meta-analysis*.[77] It must be noted that none of the difficulties associated with measuring and attempting to use personality dimensions as predictors lead one to conclude that personality is an unimportant topic.

Finally, it has been demonstrated that if the results are sufficiently vague and general, people will readily accept the results of personality testing, even when the assessment is completely fabricated.[78] Termed the **Barnum effect***** (based on circus-owner P. T. Barnum's observation on universal gullibility),

---

***The Barnum effect is strongest with statements that are vague (for example, "You enjoy a certain amount of change and variety in your work"), double-ended (for example, "You are generally cheerful and optimistic, but can get depressed at times"), typical for a person's group (for example, "You find that your job is not always easy"), and favorable (for example, "You are forceful and well-liked by others").

this phenomenon argues for the need to validate test results against stronger criteria than simple endorsement or believability by the test-taker.

SUMMARY

1. Defend the notion that perception is a complex and active process.

Perception is the process by which an individual selects, organizes, and interprets information about the environment and thus gives it personal meaning. Because the environment and the individual's physiological and psychological systems are so complicated, perception is an extremely complex process. The individual takes an active role in screening out irrelevant stimuli and carefully structuring the relevant stimuli into meaningful messages that apply to the immediate situation. This is done in accordance with a prepared mental set based on previous experiences. In this way, the perceiver actually constructs his or her own version of the environment.

2. Explain how facial expressions and other nonverbal cues affect the accuracy of our perceptions.

People's facial expressions and other nonverbal cues help us gauge the effects of our words and actions. When a person's words, facial expression, and nonverbal cues are all in agreement, they reinforce our perceptions. However, because people are masters at disguising their true intentions and feelings, it is important to watch for discrepancies between verbal and nonverbal cues. Nonverbal cues, such as amount of eye contact, frequency of smiling, and posture, can influence our perceptions of others.

3. Identify the most common obstacles to accurate perception.

There are many barriers to precise perception, each a possible source of misleading or distorted information. Among the most common are stereotyping, the halo effect, projection, perceptual distortion, and subliminal influences. A stereotype is a judgment of an individual based on certain characteristics attributed to a specific group. A person who has been thus categorized is expected to behave in fixed, preconceived ways, without regard to individual differences. The halo effect occurs when a perceiver's evaluation of specific traits is influenced by an overall impression, either favorable or unfavorable. Projection is the tendency to ascribe our own feelings and traits to others in order to protect ourselves from unpleasant or unacceptable truths. A related defense mechanism is perceptual distortion, the altering of a perception in order to avoid an unpleasant reality. Another obstacle arises from selective perception, or the tendency to be influenced by our own interests. Finally, our perception may be misled by subliminal influences, factors that are below our threshold of awareness. In such cases, an individual reacts without realizing the source of influence.

4. Outline the basic principles of attribution theory.

According to attribution theory, when we observe an event, we try to understand its cause, assess responsibility for its outcome, and evaluate the personal qualities of the people involved. A key factor in attribution is whether the observer believes that the event is caused by an individual (internal causality) or by the environment (external causality). For example, a supervisor may attribute an employee's poor performance either to the worker's own laziness or to substandard working conditions. The cause that the supervisor infers will greatly influence his or her perception of the individual, the traits he or she attributes to the employee, and the steps taken to deal with the situation.

5. Discuss the concept of personality and the factors that affect its development.

Personality is the relatively enduring pattern of individual traits and dispositions that distinguishes one person from all others. The origin of individual personality is the subject of considerable debate, with one point of view contending that personality is largely determined by heredity, and another holding that personality is primarily the product of environment. In fact, both heredity and environment are important determinants of personality. Heredity may predispose an individual to certain patterns of behavior, while environmental forces may cause more specific patterns of behavior.

6. Describe the most commonly used techniques for measuring personality attributes.

Although there are many different techniques for measuring personality attributes, the most frequently used are ratings, situational tests, inventories, and projective techniques. Ratings usually take the form of five- or seven-point scales with adjectives describing personality traits as endpoints, or anchors. Some ratings include specific definitions for each point on the scale. In situational tests, an individual's behavior is directly observed in a setting that is specifically designed to reveal personality. Although they are expensive to create and administer, the results of situational tests are less subjective and therefore more valid than the results of ratings. Personality inventories, widely used to measure personality traits, ask individuals to respond to a series of statements by indicating whether the statements describe themselves. Projective techniques are designed to probe the more subtle aspects of personality by asking the individual to respond to deliberately ambiguous stimuli. Included in this category are inkblot tests, storytelling, and sentence completions.

7. Specify and define several dimensions of personality that are especially relevant to organizational behavior.

Five dimensions of personality have received substantial attention in OB research: locus of control, authoritarianism, the work ethic, cognitive style, and moral maturity. Locus of control identifies where individuals feel that control over their life lies: within their own control or in environmental forces beyond their control. Internally oriented persons differ from externally oriented individuals in terms of responsiveness to group pressures, success in school, income, job status, speed of career advancement, and preference for specific kinds of rewards. Authoritarianism is the extent to which an individual favors blind submission to authority and believes that power should be concentrated in a leader or an elite class. This dimension has far-ranging implications for an individual's behavior as both a leader and a group member. The work ethic embodies a cluster of beliefs, including respect for the dignity of all work, contempt for idleness and self-indulgence, and faith that hard work will be rewarded. Recent evidence suggests that the work ethic may be waning in the

United States. Cognitive style refers to four modes of gathering and evaluating information: introversion-extroversion, thinking-feeling, sensing-intuiting, and judging-perceiving. Moral maturity refers to one's stage of ethical judgment.

KEY TERMS

Perception	Personality ratings
Nonverbal cues	Situational tests
Mechanistic or statistical prediction	Personality inventories
Impressionistic prediction	Projective techniques
Stereotypes	Rorschach test
Halo effect	Storytelling
Implicit personality theory	Thematic Apperception
Central traits	Test (TAT)
Projection	Sentence completion
Perceptual distortion	Locus of control
Subliminal influences	Authoritarianism
Selective perception	Dogmatism
Attribution theory	Work ethic
Fundamental attribution error	Cognitive style
Self-serving bias	Moral maturity
Personality	Barnum effect

REVIEW AND DISCUSSION QUESTIONS

1. Hal, Sara, and Mike all attended the same sales meeting at which a new breakfast cereal—Nummy Flakes—was introduced. Afterwards, they discussed their reactions. "What a drag!" said Hal. "Meetings are such a waste of time. That new product manager is really ignorant. And 'Nummy Flakes'? What a dumb name!" "Wait a minute," replied Mike. "I thought the new manager was really dynamic—and cute, too. With her masterminding the marketing campaign, I bet Nummy Flakes will be a terrific success." "All right, you guys," chimed in Sara. "Rather than jumping to conclusions, why don't you give both the new product manager and Nummy Flakes time to rise or fall on their own merits?" How does the complexity of the perceptual process help to explain these three persons' different reactions to the same event?

2. If you were interviewing candidates for a job, what verbal and nonverbal cues would most likely leave you with a positive impression of an individual? Which cues would most likely leave you with a negative impression? Would the cues and their interpretations change if you were the interviewee instead of the interviewer? How and why?

3. In the sales meeting situation presented in Question 1, how are stereotyping, the halo effect, projection, perceptual distortion, selective perception, and subliminal influences reflected in Hal's, Mike's, and Sara's reactions?

4. How would attribution theory account for Hal's, Mike's, and Sara's responses to the new product manager?

5. "All this psychology stuff just makes excuses for people's weaknesses," observed Mr. Tuggle, the supervisor of the customer service department. "I say that if workers can do their jobs, then fine—keep them. And if they can't do their jobs, then it's their problem—fire them. What does some academic notion like personality and its development have to do with the real world of work?" Answer Mr. Tuggle's question, helping him to see how an understanding of individual personality differences can improve both his own effectiveness and that of his subordinates.

6. The personnel director of Graycote, Inc., a medium-sized paint manufacturer where you are serving a summer internship, thinks it might be a good idea to use some form of personality assessment when screening job applicants. Since Graycote is too small to have a psychologist on staff, the director asks you to look into the available possibilities. Prepare a report that summarizes the characteristics of the most commonly used personality measures, reviews their pros and cons, and recommends a course of action based on Graycote's limited financial and personnel resources.

7. Define each of the following dimensions of personality and explain why it is especially important for managers to understand. Based on your personal experience, either at work or at school, cite examples of behavior that strike you as typifying the extremes as well as the midpoint of each dimension.

   - locus of control
   - authoritarianism
   - the work ethic
   - cognitive style
   - moral maturity

CRITICAL INCIDENT

A Questionable "Fit"

Irene Long was recently promoted to department manger of accounting for the Badger Manufacturing Company. Badger produces metal toolboxes and related items under its own brand and for private labels. Irene has worked in the finance area and in accounting with Badger for twelve years. When the previous manager retired, she was asked to fill the position.

Several problems have arisen over the past two months between Irene and her manager Wayne, the vice president of finance and accounting. Wayne wants Irene to "run" the accounting department. This involves handling all the day-to-day issues, staying on top of what needs to be done, and so on. When you, the consultant, met with Wayne, he described Irene as too laid-back and not assertive enough in assuming her new responsibilities. Wayne provided you with some examples of Irene's failing to get things done on time, not following up on other people's duties to provide her with information, and always waiting to be told what to do instead of initiating action.

In meeting with Irene, you find that she feels that Wayne does not appreciate her and her abilities. She claims that she is willing to do whatever needs to be done but Wayne does not provide good direction. Irene says she wants to do a good job, but that she is not going to be a dictator. When you ask if she likes her new job, Irene replies that she thinks so, but she's not sure.

You decide that it would be helpful to assess Irene's personality type and you administer the Myers-Briggs Type Indicator. Irene's score indicates that she is more of a Sensing/Thinking type (ST). Giving Wayne the same test, you discover that he is an Intuiting/Thinking type (NT).

Using the type information, and what you know about the working relationship between Wayne and Irene, address each of the following questions:

1. What are the major difficulties Irene and Wayne have in trying to develop a working relationship?

2. What should be the major issues each must consider in trying to work together?

3. Using the Myers-Briggs information, what strategy would you propose for resolving the difficulties between Irene and Wayne?

EXPERIENTIAL EXERCISE

A Study in Attribution

Step 1   Read the following news article.

Hours Before Blasts, Workers Fought to Contain Hexane
(Courier-Journal, *February 16*)

Hours before Louisville's sewers exploded Friday, six workers at the Ralston Purina plant used a five-gallon pail on a rope to try to scoop up excess amounts of the toxic chemical hexane that had begun to back up into the plant.

In interviews, Ralston employees described struggles to contain the volatile chemical.

The workers shut down the plant about 11 P.M. when they discovered a backup of hexane from the sewer.

The efforts failed: A few hours later miles of the city's sewer began to explode.

The preliminary findings of the state fire marshal's office are that the explosive solvent hexane escaped from the Ralston Purina plant and that it overwhelmed the containment basin, the plant's final line of defense to keep any hexane from going in the city's sewers.

While all of the problems may not be known, in interviews with Ralston employees and some government officials, The Courier-Journal has pieced together a version of last week's difficulties at the plant leading up to the sewer blasts that did at least $42 million in damage to public property.

Their version suggests that mechanical failure, rather than human error, may have been principally at fault in the incident.

About 8 A.M. Wednesday, a stirring arm broke in a vat filled with soybean meal. Before repairs could be made and production resumed, a surge of near-zero weather swept into the Louisville area, freezing pipes in the plant's solvent building.

Not until 5 or 5:30 P.M. Thursday was an attempt made to resume the plant's operation.

About 8 P.M., employees noticed that more than the normal amount of hexane was being used by the processing system. Some company officials have said that when the plant is starting up after a shut-down, more hexane is needed—but employees who knew that expressed concern nevertheless.

The employees also noticed that a wastewater evaporator, through which small amounts of hexane flow to be vaporized for recovery, was not heating close to its normal temperature of 180 to 200 degrees.

The employees tried to correct that problem by using an extra steam hose to heat the evaporator. But for some reason, that didn't work.

The employees called a supervisor at his home about 9:15, and he told them that if they could not increase the temperature in the evaporator, they should call him back.

About 11 P.M., it was discovered that hexane and water were backing up from the containment basin to the solvent building. The liquid mixture at that point was visible through an open sewer grating.

Almost simultaneously, the employees shut down the system and tried to call the supervisor. His line was busy and another supervisor was called.

After a series of calls, two supervisors came to the plant and notified the Metropolitan Sewer District (MSD) of a possible hexane spill.

By employees' accounts, that call was made about midnight. That contradicts the MSD version, which put the call at about 1 A.M.

It was discovered that excessive amounts of hexane were in the containment basin—the last line of defense designed to hold any excess hexane and keep it from getting into the sewer.

When workers discovered how much hexane was in the basin, they bailed it out of the basin with a five-gallon drum on a rope.

Between about midnight and 2 A.M. the workers filled six or seven 55-gallon drums with the chemical. They quit when they ran out of empty drums.

The two operators on duty in the six-story solvent building had been told to fine-tune the complex system of pipes, heaters, pumps, and condensers to bring the system into balance. But it became clear that something was seriously wrong.

Jim Reed, the company spokesman, said last night that "cold temperatures may have led to a malfunction of certain operating equipment."

Reed said that company investigators suspect that is the case but that it hasn't been determined.

Apparently, the answer is locked inside the now-idle equipment in the solvent building.

Investigators apparently have not found any simple explanation, such as a broken pipe producing an obvious spill, although that possibility has not been ruled out.

Reed, the company spokesman, said last night that the company was operated safely and in accordance with regulations.

Some employees say that, because of the cold weather, or because of freeze-damage to some equipment, the recovery process may have failed—flooding the system with liquid hexane.

Investigators say they have turned up nothing yet to substantiate that theory.

Step 2   Either individually or in small groups, as directed by your instructor, answer the following question: According to the article, who or what was responsible for the explosion?

Step 3   Now read the following article about the sewer explosion.

Fire Officials Say They Had a Way to Prevent Blasts
(Louisville Times, *February 17*)

The explosions that wracked Old Louisville early Friday might have been defused if the extent of a chemical leak had been discovered during the night, fire officials say.

The established procedure whenever potentially explosive or flammable chemicals spill into the sewers is to open fire hydrants along the line, flooding the sewers with water to dilute the chemical.

And that's what the fire department would have done along the sewer line from the Ralston Purina Co. plant of Floyd Street if fire officials had been notified of the extent of the leak that they suspect fueled the explosions.

Instead, several hundred—or maybe as much as thousands of— gallons of hexane flowed through the line during the night until a spark ignited the chemical vapors. The chain of explosions that followed tore up streets and caused up to $42 million in damage.

The key to whether the explosions could have been prevented is that the MSD (Metropolitan Sewer District) inspector, who responded to a call from the Ralston Purina plant at approximately 1:30 A.M., didn't find any signs of explosive fumes in the sewers when he checked them.

His findings have puzzled investigators and some Ralston Purina workers have said the MSD inspector conducted only a cursory investigation of the leak when he came to the plant.

However, MSD officials have refused to allow the inspector, Jim Surace, to respond to those allegations or say publicly what testing he did at the plant.

Ralston Purina officials called MSD—as the law requires—because they suspected that some hexane had leaked into the sewers because of a malfunction in their equipment.

Initially, company officials told MSD that up to 500 gallons of hexane may have spilled into the sewers. Since the explosions, investigators have speculated that the force of the blasts indicates that much more of the chemical—perhaps thousands of gallons—had to have been in the sewers.

Ralston Purina officials continued yesterday to assert that no definite link has been established between their plant and the explosions.

Ralston Purina's statement yesterday also seemed to be aimed at countering statements from some workers at the plant that officials hesitated—

perhaps dangerously long—before they shut the plant because they didn't want to lose production time.

Charles Chapman, business representative for Local 604 of the Chemical Workers Union, said some of his union members who worked at the plant that night told him workers realized the hexane back-up was serious as early as 6 P.M., but supervisors didn't want to shut down.

The plant had been shut down the day before because of problems caused by cold weather. Workers were attempting to start it up again Thursday night when the hexane problem arose.

Company spokesmen have declined to comment on why MSD was not called earlier than 1 A.M., at least an hour and a half after the first leak was apparently suspected.

State fire marshals suspect that the hexane from the first leak may have already passed through the sewers before the MSD inspector left around 3 A.M. That leak eventually produced the explosion, according to the fire marshal's scenario.

Judging from water marks on the basin from which the hexane flowed into the sewers, one specialist in hazardous materials now believes that as many as 8,000 gallons of the highly explosive chemical may have leaked into the sewers last Thursday night and Friday morning.

That conflicts with the 500 gallons initially reported to the Metropolitan Sewer District by the company.

The specialist said he believes workers pumped as much hexane into the plant's system that night as it ordinarily uses in 10 to 20 days—possibly as many as 20,000 gallons.

"Once they used that much, they should have known something was screwy," he said. "Everybody there was well aware it was going in the sewer system."

A federal investigator added, "They were very fortunate the plant didn't blow up."

Two sources—one an MSD official and the other a local investigator—said Surace's report on that night indicates that plant officials did not tell him hexane was flooding the basin that feeds into the sewers.

"As I understand it, if it was in the basin, theoretically it was contained. He wouldn't look in the basin," the MSD official said. "Normally, if it's in the basin, it meant they had a handle on it."

A local investigator said Surace would have realized a dangerous spill was imminent if the company had told him it had lost seven or eight thousand gallons. But, he said, "It should indicate from Jim's report that they did not."

The same source said even if plant officials didn't realize the seriousness of the leak when they first called MSD—or while Surace was there—they should have called back as soon as they did.

Even immediately after the explosions, another investigator said, "The easy thing would have been to call the fire department and MSD and say, 'We've got a problem.'"

"The fire department would have come and pumped more water in [the basin] or put dirt down the sewer to block it or something. But they [Ralston Purina] did not do that."

Step 4   Either individually or in small groups, as directed by your instructor, answer the following question: Based on this story, who or what was responsible for the sewer explosion?

Step 5   In small groups or with the entire class, answer the following questions:

1. How do the two accounts of the sewer explosion differ?
2. Who is responsible for this accident?
3. How does our knowledge of attributional biases allow us to predict the differences between the two versions?
4. What do you believe is the most likely cause of the accident?
5. How could we and those involved in the situation more accurately attribute the cause of the explosion?

NOTES

1. R. Leeper, "The Role of Motivation in Learning: A study of the Phenomenon of Differential Motivation Control of the Utilization of Habits," *Journal of Genetic Psychology* 46 (1935): 3–40.

2. R. Buck, *Nonverbal Behavior and the Communication of Effect* (New York: Guilford Press, 1983); P. Ekman, "Cross-cultural Studies of Facial Expression," in *Darwin and Facial Expression*, ed. P. Ekman (New York: Academic Press, 1973).

3. C. Darwin, *The Expression of the Emotions in Man and Animals* (London: Murray, 1872).

4. P. Ekman and W.V. Friesen, *Unmasking the Face* (Englewood Cliffs, N.J.: Prentice-Hall, 1975).

5. L.A. Streeter, R.M. Krauss, V. Galler, C. Olson, and W. Apple, "Pitch Changes During Attempted Deception," *Journal of Personality and Social Psychology* 35 (1977): 345–350.

6. R.E. Kraut, "Verbal and Nonverbal Cues in the Perception of Lying," *Journal of Personality and Social Psychology* 36 (1978): 388–391; S. Chollar, "In the Blink of an Eye," *Psychology Today* 22 (1988): 8–10.

7. A.S. Imada and M.D. Hakel, "Influence of Nonverbal Communication and Rater Proximity on Impressions and Decisions in Simulated Employment Interviews," *Journal of Applied Psychology* 62 (1977): 295–300.

8. L. Ulrich and D. Trumbo, "The Selection Interview Since 1949," *Psychological Bulletin* 63 (1965): 100–116.

9. C.L. Kleinke, F.B. Meeker, and C. LaFong, "Effects of Gaze, Touch, and Use of Name on Evaluation of 'Engaged' Couples," *Journal of Research in Personality* 1 (1974): 368–373.

10. M.L. Knapp, *Nonverbal Communication in Human Interaction*, 2d ed. (New York: Holt, Rinehart and Winston, 1978).

11. P.C. Ellsworth and J.M. Carlsmith, "Eye Contact and Gaze Aversion in an Aggressive Encounter," *Journal of Personality and Social Psychology* 28 (1973): 280–292; P.C. Ellsworth and E.J. Langer, "Staring and Approach: An Interpretation of the Stare as a Nonspecific Activator," *Journal of Personality and Social Psychology* 33 (1976): 117–122.

12. L.J. Cronbach, "Processes Affecting Scores on 'understanding of others' and 'assumed similarity,'" *Psychological Bulletin* 52 (1955): 177–193.

13. R. Taft, "The Ability to Judge People," *Psychological Bulletin* 52 (1955): 1–23.

14. J.S. Wiggins, *Personality and Prediction: Principles of Personality Assessment*

(Reading, Mass.: Addison-Wesley, 1973);
B. Kleinmuntz, "Why We Still Use Our
Heads Instead of Formulas: Toward an
Integrative Approach," *Psychological
Bulletin* (1990): 296–310.

15. H.C. Triandis and V. Vassiliou,
"Frequency of Contact and
Stereotyping," *Journal of Personality and
Social Psychology* 7 (1967): 316–328.

16. S.S. Zalkind and T.W. Costello,
"Perception: Some Recent Research and
Implications for Administration,"
Administrative Science Quarterly 7
(1962): 218–235.

17. S.E. Asch, "Forming Impressions of
Personality," *Journal of Abnormal and
Social Psychology* 41 (1946): 258–290.

18. S. Feshback and R.D. Singer, "The
Effects of Fear Arousal upon Social
Perception," *Journal of Abnormal and
Social Psychology* 55 (1957): 283–288.

19. S.S. Sears, "Experimental Studies of
Perception, I. Attribution of Traits,"
Journal of Social Psychology 7 (1936):
151–163.

20. R. Jacobs and J. Farr, "Industrial and
Organizational Psychology at the
Pennsylvania State University," *The
Industrial-Organizational Psychologist*
30 (1993): 75–79.

21. J.V. McConnell, R.L. Cutler, and E.B.
McNeil, "Subliminal Stimulation: An
Overview," *American Psychologist* 13
(1958): 229–242; J.V. McConnell,
"Reinvention of Subliminal Perception,"
Skeptical Inquirer 13 (1989): 427–429;
A.G. Greenwald, E.R. Spangenberg, A.R.
Pratkanis, and J. Eskenazi, "Double-
blind Tests of Subliminal Self-Help
Audiotapes," *Psychological Science* 2
(1991): 119–122; B.C. Audley,
"Subliminal Tapes: Controlled Tapes,"
Skeptical Inquirer 16 (1992): 349–350;
P.M. Merikle and H.E. Skanes,
"Subliminal Self-Help Audiotapes: A
Search for Placebo Effects," *Journal of
Applied Psychology* 77 (1992): 772–776.

22. F. Heider, "Social Perception and
Phenomenal Causality," *Psychological
Review* 51 (1944): 358–374; F. Heider,
*The Psychology of Interpersonal
Relations* (New York: Wiley, 1958);
W. Ryan, *Blaming the Victim* (New York:
Vintage Books, 1977); Y. Trope, "The
Multiple Roles of Context in
Dispositional Judgment," in *On-Line
Cognition in Person Cognition,* ed. J.N.
Bassil (Hillsdale, N.J.: Lawrence Erlbaum

Assoc. 1989); R.S. Wyer, G.V.
Bodenhausen, and R.W. Gorman,
"Cognitive Mediators to Rape," *Journal
of Personality and Social Psychology* 48
(1985): 324–338; J. M. Crant and T.S.
Bateman, "Assignment of Credit and
Blame for Performance Outcomes,"
Academy of Management Journal 36
(1993): 7–27.

23. J.W. Thibaut and H.W. Riecken, "Some
Determinants and Consequences of the
Perception of Social Causality," *Journal
of Personality* 24 (1955): 113–133.

24. L.H. Strickland, "Surveillance and
Trust," *Journal of Personality* 26 (1958):
200–215.

25. R. Baumhart, *An Honest Profit* (New
York: Holt, Rinehart and Winston,
1968); S.N. Brenner and E.A. Molander,
"Is the Ethics of Business Changing?"
Harvard Business Review (1977): 57–71;
J.S. French, "The Conceptualization and
the Measurement of Mental Health in
Terms of Self-Identity Theory," in *The
Definition and Measurement of Mental
Health,* ed. S.B. Sells (Washington, D.C.:
Dept. of Health, Education, and Welfare,
1968); E.P. Hollander, "Leadership and
Power," in *The Handbook of Social
Psychology,* 3rd ed., ed. G. Lindzey and
E. Aronson (New York: Random House,
1985).

26. P. Cross, "Not *Can* but *Will* College
Teaching Be Improved?" *New Directions
for Higher Education* (Spring 1977):
1–15; R.T. Blackburn, G.R. Pellino, A.
Boberg, and C. O'Connell, "Are
Instructional Improvement Programs Off
Target?" *Current Issues in Higher
Education* 1 (1980): 31–48.

27. C. Holden, "Identical Twins Reared
Apart," *Science* (March 1980):
1323–1324.

28. J.R. Warren, "Birth Order and Social
Behavior," *Psychological Bulletin* 65
(1966): 38–49.

29. L.H. Stewart, "Birth Order and Political
Leadership: I. The American Presidents"
(Paper presented at the annual meeting of
the American Psychological Association,
1970).

30. A. Rafaeli and R.J. Klimoski, "Predicting
Sales Success Through Handwriting
Analysis: An Evaluation of the Effects of
Training and Handwriting Sample
Content," *Journal of Applied Psychology*
68 (1983): 212–217; G. Ben-Shakkar, M.
Bar-Hillel, Y. Bilu, E. Ben-Abba, and

A. Flug, "Can Graphology Predict Occupational Success: Two Empirical Studies and Some Methodological Ruminations," *Journal of Applied Psychology* 71 (1986): 645–653.

31. J.W. Macfarlane, L. Allen, and M.P. Honzik, "A Developmental Study of the Behavior Problems of Normal Children Between 21 Months and 14 Years," *University of California Publications in Child Development* 2 (1954): 483.

32. D.W. Mackinnon, "Violation of Prohibitions," in *Explorations in Personality,* ed. H. Murray (New York: Oxford University Press, 1938).

33. R. Koenig, "Toyota Takes Pains, and Time, Filling Jobs at Its Kentucky Plant," *The Wall Street Journal,* December 1, 1987, 1.

34. R.S. Woodworth, *Personal Data Sheet* (Chicago: Stoelting, 1918).

35. J.C. Nunnally, *Psychometric Theory* (New York: McGraw-Hill, 1994); O.K. Buros, ed., *Tests in Print III* (University of Nebraska, 1983); O.K. Buros, ed., *Mental Measurements Yearbook* (University of Nebraska, 1941–).

36. D.P. Crowne and D. Marlowe, *The Approval Motive: Studies in Evaluative Dependence* (New York: Wiley, 1964).

37. A.I. Rabin, "Projective Methods: An Historical Introduction," in *Projective Techniques in Personality Assessment,* ed. A. Rabin (New York: Springer, 1958), 3.

38. C.D. Morgan and H.A. Murray, "A Method of Investigating Fantasies: The Thematic Apperception Test," *Archives of Neurological Psychiatry* 34 (1935): 289–306; W.D. Spangler, "Validity of Questionnaire and TAT Measures of Need for Achievement: Two Meta-analyses," *Psychological Bulletin* 112 (1992): 140–154.

39. J.B. Rotter, "Level of Aspiration as a Method of Studying Personality, III. Group Validity Studies," *Character and Personality* 11 (1943): 254–274; J.B. Rotter, "Generalized Expectancies for Internal versus External Control of Reinforcement," *Psychological Monographs* 80, no. 609 (1966).

40. Rotter, "Generalized Expectancies," 11–12.

41. H.M. Lefcourt, "Recent Developments in the Study of Locus of Control," in *Progress in Experimental Personality Research,* ed. B. Maher (New York: Academic Press, 1972), 1–39; R.W. Renn and R.J. Vandenberg, "Differences in Employee Attitudes and Behaviors Based on Rotter's (1966) Internal-External Locus of Control," *Human Relations* 44 (1991): 1161–1178.

42. J.S. Coleman, E.Q. Campbell, L.J. Hobson, J. McPartland, A.M. Mood, F.D. Weinfeld, and R.L. York, *Equality of Educational Opportunity* (Washington, D.C.: Government Printing Office, 1966).

43. R.P. Vecchio, "Workers' Belief in Internal versus External Determinants of Success," *Journal of Social Psychology* 114 (1981): 199–207.

44. M. Seeman, "On the Meaning of Alienation," *American Sociological Review* 24 (1959): 782–791; M. Seeman, "Alienation and Social Learning in a Reformatory," *American Sociological Review* 69 (1963): 270–284.

45. P.J. Andrisani and C. Nestel, "Internal-External Control as a Contributor to and Outcome of Work Experience," *Journal of Applied Psychology* 61 (1976): 156–165.

46. J.B. Rotter, "Some Problems and Misconceptions Related to the Construct of Internal versus External Control of Reinforcement," *Journal of Consulting and Clinical Psychology* 43 (1975): 56–67.

47. R.M. Baron and R.L. Ganz, "Effects of Locus of Control and Type of Feedback on the Task Performance of Lower-Class Black Children," *Journal of Personality and Social Psychology* 21 (1972): 124–130.

48 P.T. Wong and C.F. Sproule, "An Attribution Analysis of the Locus of Control Construct and the Trent Attribution Profile," in *Research with the Locus of Control Construct: Vol. 3, Extensions and Limitations,* ed. H.M. Lefcourt (New York: Academic Press, 1984): 309–360.

49. T. Adorno, E. Frenkel-Brunswik, D. Levinson, and N. Sanford, *The Authoritarian Personality* (New York: Harper and Row, 1950).

50. J.G. Martin and F.R. Westie, "The Tolerant Personality," *American Sociological Review* 24 (1959): 521–528.

51. I. Steiner and H. Johnson, "Authoritarianism and 'tolerance of trait inconsistency,'" *Journal of Abnormal and*

Social Psychology 67 (1963): 388–391; D. Narby, B. Cutler, and G. Moran, "A Meta-analysis of the Association Between Authoritarianism and Jurors' Perceptions of Defendant Culpability," *Journal of Applied Psychology* 78 (1992): 34–42.

52. O. Milton, "Presidential Choice and Performance on a Scale of Authoritarianism," *American Psychologist* 7 (1952): 597–598; L. S. Wrightsman, "Attitudinal and Personality Correlates of Presidential Voting Preferences" (Paper presented at the annual meeting of the American Psychological Association, 1965).

53. D.J. Levinson and P.E. Huffman, "Traditional Family Ideology and Its Relation to Personality," *Journal of Personality* 23 (1955): 251–273.

54. L.S. Wrightsman, *Social Psychology in the Seventies* (Belmont, Calif.: Wadsworth, 1972).

55. V.H. Vroom, "Some Personality Determinants of the Effects of Participation," *Journal of Abnormal and Social Psychology* 59 (1959): 322–327.

56. M. Rokeach, *The Open and Closed Mind* (New York: Basic Books, 1960).

57. R.N. Taylor and M.D. Dunnette, "Influence of Dogmatism, Risk-taking Propensity, and Intelligence on Decision-making Strategies for a Sample of Industrial Managers," *Journal of Applied Psychology* 59 (1974): 420–423.

58. J.P. Esposito and H.C. Richards, "Dogmatism and the Congruence between Self-reported Job Preference and Performance among School Supervisors," *Journal of Applied Psychology* 59 (1974): 389–391.

59. J.M. Minelo and J. Garrett, "The Protestant Ethic as a Personality Variable," *Journal of Counseling and Clinical Psychology* 36 (1971): 40–44.

60. M. Merrens and J. Garrett, "The Protestant Ethic Scale as a Predictor of Effective Work Performance," *Journal of Applied Psychology* 60 (1975): 125–127.

61. J. Greenberg, "The Protestant Work Ethic and Reactions to Negative Performance Evaluation on a Laboratory Task," *Journal of Applied Psychology* 62 (1977): 682–690.

62. O. Cherrington, "The Values of Younger Workers." *Business Horizons* 20 (1977): 18–20; R. Eisenberger, *Blue Monday: The Loss of the Work Ethic in America* (New York: Paragon House, 1989).

63. R.P. Vecchio, "The Function and Meaning of Work and the Job: Morse and Weiss (1955) Revisited," *Academy of Management Journal* 23 (1980): 361–367.

64. P.A. Sorokin, *The Crisis of Our Age: The Social and Cultural Outlook* (New York: Dutton, 1941).

65. I.B. Myers and K.C. Briggs, *Myers-Briggs Type Indicator* (Princeton, N.J.: Educational Testing Service, 1962); W. Taggert and D. Robey, "Minds and Managers: On the Dual Nature of Human Information Processing and Mangement," *Academy of Management Review* 6 (1981): 187–195; J.W. Slocum and D. Hellriegel, "A Look at How Managers' Minds Work," *Business Horizons* 26 (1983): 58–68; W. Woods, "Personality Tests Are Back," *Fortune,* March 30, 1987, 74–82.

66. A.B. Carroll, "Linking Business Ethics to Behavior in Organizations," *SAM Advanced Management Journal* 43 (1978): 4–11

67. R. Ricklees, "Ethics in America," *The Wall Street Journal,* October 31, 1983, 33.

68. L. Kohlberg, "Stage and Sequence: The Cognitive-Developmental Approach to Socialization," in *Handbook of Socialization Theory and Research,* ed. D.A. Goslin (Chicago: Rand-McNally, 1969), 347–400.

69. L. Kohlberg and D. Candee, "The Relationship of Moral Judgment to Moral Action," in *Morality, Moral Behavior and Moral Development,* ed. W. Kurtines and J. Gerwitz (New York: Wiley, 1984), 52–73.

70. W.E. Stratton, W. Flynn, and G. Johnson, "Moral Development and Decision Making: A Study of Student Ethics," *Journal of Enterprise Management* 3 (1981): 35–41.

71. J.R. Snarey, "Cross-cultural Universality of Social-Moral Development: A Critical Review of Kohlbergian Research," *Psychological Bulletin* 97 (1985): 202–232.

72. C. Gilligan, *In a Different Voice: Psychological Theory and Women's Development* (Cambridge, Mass.: Howard University Press, 1982); C. Gilligan and G. Wiggins, "The Origins of Morality in Early Childhood Relationships," in *The Emergence of*

Morality, ed. J. Kagan and S. Lamb (Chicago, Ill.: University of Chicago Press, 1987).

73. L.K. Trevino, "Ethical Decision Making in Organizations: A Person-Situation Interactionist Model," *Academy of Management Review* 11 (1986): 601–617; J. George, "The Role of Personality in Organizational Life: Issues and Evidence," *Journal of Management* 18 (1992): 185–213; R. Tett, D. Jackson, and M. Rothstein, "Personality Measures vs. Predictors of Job Performance: A Meta-analytic Review," *Personnel Psychology* 44 (1991): 703–742.

74. E.E. Ghiselli, "The Validity of Aptitude Tests in Personnel Selection," *Personnel Psychology* 26 (1973): 461–477.

75. M.R. Barrick and M.K. Mount, "The Big Five Personality Dimensions and Job Performance: A Meta-analysis," *Personnel Psychology* 44 (1991): 1–26.

76. J.L. Hughes, "Expressed Personality Needs as Predictors of Sales Success," *Personnel Psychology* 9 (1956): 347–357.

77. F.L. Schmidt and J.E. Hunter, "Development of a General Solution to the Problem of Validity Generalization," *Journal of Applied Psychology* 62 (1977): 529–540; J.E. Hunter, F.L. Schmidt, and K. Pearlman, "History and Accuracy of Validity Generalization Equations: A Response to the Callender and Osburn Reply," *Journal of Applied Psychology* 67 (1982): 853–858.

78. D.H. Dickson and I.W. Kelly, "The 'Barnum Effect' in Personality Assessment: A Review of the Literature," *Psychological Reports* 57 (1985): 367–382; A. Furnham and S. Schofield, "Accepting Personality Test Feedback: A Review of the Barnum Effect," *Current Psychological Research and Reviews* 6 (1987): 162–178.

Working 9 to 5,
What a way to make a living,
Barely getting by,
It's all taking and no giving.
— **Dolly Parton**

Work is a four-letter word.
— **Abbie Hoffman**

Job satisfaction? I didn't
know the two words went
together!

— **A steelworker**

LEARNING OBJECTIVES

*After studying this chapter,
you should be able to:*

1. *Explain the nature of attitudes and their essential
   components.*
2. *Outline the most widely
   used methods of measuring
   attitudes.*
3. *Identify the means through
   which attitudes are formed.*
4. *Specify the components of
   attitude change and trace
   the steps in the change
   process.*
5. *Tell why management
   should take an interest in
   workers' job satisfaction.*
6. *Note the principal methods
   of measuring job satisfaction.*
7. *Cite the most frequent
   sources of job satisfaction.*
8. *Describe some typical employee responses to low job
   satisfaction.*

Attitudes and Job Satisfaction

HOW SATISFIED ARE EXECUTIVE-LEVEL MANAGERS?

Surveys of employee attitudes have become commonplace in many organizations. Interested in taking the pulse of the organization, companies often solicit feedback in the form of satisfaction surveys to determine if employees are happy with their working conditions, pay and benefits, and other company policies. Rarely, however, is the magnifying glass pointed in the other direction. Surveying executives about their levels of job satisfaction is far less common. Perhaps it should be done more frequently, as a 1992 study by Paul Ray Berndtson at Cornell University revealed executive-level managers often have ambiguous feelings regarding satisfaction with their jobs.

More than 3,500 executives were surveyed, and respondents were primarily white (94 percent), male (93 percent) and middle-aged (average age of 46). On average, they had one dependent child, and 43 percent had spouses working outside the home. Although the survey covered top-level managers and executives, the typical respondent was a senior executive, two levels below the chief execu-

tive. Respondents worked an average of 56 hours per week, seven more hours than they preferred. Regarding the most important areas in their lives, 38 percent ranked work first, while 34 percent ranked family first.

Executives listed several stressors in their jobs: Over 40 percent were dissatisfied by the degree to which politics, not performance, affects organizational decisions; over a quarter of the respondents were concerned about job security; and more than 20 percent were unhappy with the amount of red tape involved in doing their jobs.

Work and family issues also cropped up in the survey results, particularly at the chief executive level. Younger chief executives, in particular, were more likely to have working spouses and thus feel the pressures of work and family conflict to which executives even ten years ago were immune. Nearly half the respondents reported that work interferes with their personal time and 44 percent indicated they were too tired to pursue other interests after work. Interestingly, senior executives,

those below the chief executive, did not have the same concerns about leading balanced lives.

Despite 60 percent of the sample responding they were happy with their jobs, three-quarters of chief executives indicated they were looking for new jobs, and half had received job offers in the past year. One of the survey's sponsors interprets this finding cautiously. He says that just because managers are investigating alternative employment opportunities doesn't mean they're actively moving from organization to organization. Rather, executives test the waters to get more career leverage with their current employers. By scouting the external market for their skills, executives are positioning themselves to create opportunities internally.

This chapter describes why companies should be concerned about the attitudes and job satisfaction of all employees. It begins by exploring the nature and formation of attitudes in general, then turns to the more specific issue of job satisfaction.

Source: Barbara Presley Noble, "Job Hunting Isn't Always Goodbye," *New York Times,* December 5, 1993, F25.

Much of the excitement and fascination of organizational life stems from differences of opinion. One member of a work group may feel that the supervisor is overbearing, while another may find the same supervisor highly likable. People also have different attitudes toward the quality of their jobs, the adequacy of their pay, and so on. These attitudes help to explain a good deal of the behavior that occurs in organizational settings. For example, attitudes toward supervisors and company policies predict workers' endorsement of unionization. Also, attitudinal differences can explain why people have different reactions to essentially the same work experiences.

THE NATURE OF ATTITUDES

When we use the term *attitude* in daily speech, such as when we speak of our attitude toward the space program or our attitude toward social welfare, we are usually referring to our feelings about something. But organizational behavior researchers prefer a more precise definition. In organizational behavior, an **attitude** is an idea charged with emotion that predisposes a set of actions to a specific group of stimuli.[1] This definition covers the three essential components of an attitude: the cognitive, the affective, and the behavioral.

The **cognitive**, or knowing, **component** of an attitude is represented in our definition by the word "idea." By an idea, we mean that some category we use in our thinking is an essential feature of an attitude. For example, we would infer the category "authority figures" from observing the responses of a friend to teachers, police officers, parents, and supervisors. The **affective**, or emotional, **component** of an attitude is noted in the phrase "charged with emotion." The emotional component of an attitude is its most critical feature and is reflected in such comments as "I like . . . ," "I dislike . . . ," and "I hope. . . ."

The **behavioral component** of an attitude refers to a predisposition to act in a particular way. In our definition of an attitude, the behavioral component is represented by the phrase "predisposes a set of actions to a specific group of stimuli." The behavioral component is demonstrated by such actions as seeking or avoiding certain people and situations, purchasing a particular product, and so on.

It is important to note that the behavioral predisposition is determined to some extent by the cognitive and the affective components.* Consider, for example, someone who believes that her job offers no opportunity for advancement (the cognitive aspect). She states that being in a dead-end job is very distasteful to her (the emotional component). Consequently, she says that she is going to begin searching for another job (the behavioral predisposition).

---

* Imagine a South Sea Islander who is seeing a helicopter for the first time in his life. Since he does not have the category "helicopter" in his mental repertoire, he may possibly categorize the stimulus as a monster. Given the emotion associated with the category "monster," he will likely throw rocks at the helicopter or flee from it. Upon learning that the object is not threatening and given encouragement to approach, he will come to develop a new category for the object. It would be erroneous to infer that the islander had an initially unfavorable attitude toward helicopters, because he did not truly possess the category of helicopter.

MEASURING ATTITUDES

Attitudes are not directly observable. Their existence and nature must be inferred. Thus, people who study attitudes (such as organizational behavior researchers, social psychologists, marketing researchers, political scientists, communication researchers, and pollsters) cannot examine attitudes directly, but must instead consider the three aspects of attitudes.

Attempts to study attitudes focus most frequently on the affective component. Measures of the affective component can be physiological (heart rate, blood pressure, and pupil dilation, for example) or verbal (as in the use of survey questions). The cognitive component can be measured through verbal statements of belief (such as personal estimates that an outcome will follow an event) or reports of categorizations and attributes (for example, whether a person classifies others directly as liberals or conservatives, versus recognizing the existence of many gradations of political beliefs). The behavioral component can be measured by studying actual behavior (whether employees request job transfers, or how they vote in an election) or by studying statements of intention to act in a particular way.

GRAPHIC SCALES   The most commonly used device for studying attitudes is the **graphic scale.** Since researcher Rensis Likert first advocated such scales, they have become exceedingly popular.[2] A graphic, or Likert, scale asks a person to indicate his or her degree of agreement with a statement by checking one of five possible positions: strongly agree, agree, undecided, disagree, or strongly disagree. A sample Likert scale item would be:

Trade unions have too great an effect on the economy.

Strongly :____ :____ :____ :____ :____: Strongly
Disagree   1   2   3   4   5   Agree

It is not absolutely necessary to have five possible positions for responding. The simplest response format would consist of only two options:

Agree ____   Disagree ____

But research indicates that the reliability of rating scales increases with the number of steps in the scale.[†]

SEMANTIC DIFFERENTIAL SCALES   **Semantic differential scales** are another useful attitude measure. These scales ask for ratings based on a pair of adjectives that are opposite in meaning.[4] The following semantic differential scale items could be used to assess an employee's feelings toward an immediate supervisor.

[†]The increase in reliability is fairly rapid as we move from 2 to 20 steps, with the gain in reliability leveling off at 7 steps. After 11 steps, there is fairly little gain in reliability for the additional refinement.[3] As a result, many attitude researchers prefer to use scales with 7 or 11 steps.

My Immediate Supervisor

| Ineffective | :___ :___ :___ :___ :___ :___ :___: | Effective |
| | 1   2   3   4   5   6   7 | |

| Foolish | :___ :___ :___ :___ :___ :___ :___: | Wise |
| | 1   2   3   4   5   6   7 | |

| Weak | :___ :___ :___ :___ :___ :___ :___: | Strong |
| | 1   2   3   4   5   6   7 | |

| Impolite | :___ :___ :___ :___ :___ :___ :___: | Polite |
| | 1   2   3   4   5   6   7 | |

| Bad | :___ :___ :___ :___ :___ :___ :___: | Good |
| | 1   2   3   4   5   6   7 | |

ATTITUDE FORMATION

Attitudes are acquired through learning.[‡] Their sources can be divided into three categories: direct experience, social communication, and emotional conditioning.

DIRECT EXPERIENCE   Our direct and personal involvement with the objects in our environment create our attitudes, both positive and negative. It is difficult to like someone who ignores you or is overbearing, and it is difficult to dislike someone who is warm and responsive to you or who pays you compliments. On the other hand, lack of contact can facilitate the development of negative attitudes. This principle is suggested by the sometimes deliberate maintenance of distance between soldiers and their enemies in order to reduce the possibility of interpersonal liking.

Interestingly, simple exposure to an object can lead to positive evaluations.[5] Repeated exposure to an object having no strong prior emotional value attached to it is sufficient to enhance one's attitude toward the object. These findings suggest that "familiarity breeds attraction." Based on these findings, Milgram proposed the notion of the "familiar stranger"—that is, a person you see with some regularity, but never interact with socially.[6] Examples of familiar strangers are people with whom you wait each morning to catch a bus, fellow students in a classroom with whom you do not speak, and office workers with whom you share an elevator each day. If by chance you meet one of these people outside of their typical setting, you are likely to develop a positive interpersonal relationship quickly.

SOCIAL COMMUNICATION   We also develop attitudes from social communication. Few of us have ever actually met the president of a *Fortune* 500 com-

---

[‡]Alternative explanations for the origin of attitudes (for example, inborn or genetic explanations) are difficult to defend. However, it is not inconceivable that there may be genetic differences in individual susceptibility to persuasion.

OB Focus
Attitudes about AIDS in the Workplace

A 1993 study by the National Leadership Coalition on AIDS regarding employees' perceptions of AIDS revealed some troubling attitudes: When working Americans were asked how HIV-positive people would be treated at their place of employment, 89 percent responded the individual *should* be treated like any other employee with a serious disability or illness, and 78 percent said they *would* be treated like any other employee. However, when these same respondents were asked if they would feel comfortable working with someone who is HIV-positive, two-thirds said they *would not*, and just over one-quarter said they *should not* feel comfortable. Over 30 percent felt an HIV-positive employee *would* be dismissed or put on disability at the first sign of illness, while one-quarter said he or she *should* be immediately dismissed or placed on disability.

These conflicting responses indicate people are torn between giving socially desirable answers and expressing their real attitudes and fears about AIDS. The Centers for Disease Control predicts that 1 in every 250 Americans has been infected by HIV, the virus that causes AIDS, and most of them are in the 25-to-44 age bracket, the core age group of the American work force. Fear and misunderstanding about the disease can wreak havoc in any organization. When an employee in a suburban Atlanta Toys 'R' Us store developed AIDS and died, employee morale and performance plunged. Even six months after the death of their coworker, employees still would not use the water fountain or bathroom. Unlike other terminal illnesses, the virus provokes prejudice and irrational behaviors among otherwise rational individuals. Managers, in particular, must be sensitive yet protective about managing employees with the virus. Communication and education are crucial, as standardized company AIDS policies are often unable to anticipate the complexities of managing the virus. Lee Smith, a former Levi Strauss and Co. executive and current chairman of the National Leadership Coalition on AIDS, says, "I was not trained to manage fear, discrimination, and dying in the workplace."

The results of a quality-of-work-life survey, presented in 1993 by the National Gay and Lesbian Task Force Policy Institute, shed new light on the steps companies are taking toward managing AIDS in the workplace. The survey was completed by only 98 of the *Fortune* 1000 companies and outright refusals were received by 145 companies. Of those that responded, three-quarters stated they had nondiscrimination policies that include sexual orientation, and more than two-thirds offer AIDS education programs and support for people with HIV or AIDS. This is a step in the right direction, but workplace education for all employees is regarded as the best offense to lessen anxiety and misperceptions about the virus.

Sources: Ron Stodghill II, "Managing AIDS: How One Boss Struggled to Cope," *Business Week,* February 1, 1993, 48–52; Ron Stodghill II, Russell Mitchell, Karen Thurston, Christina Del Valle, "Why AIDS Policy Must Be a Special Policy," *Business Week,* February 1, 1993, 53–54; Barbara Presley Noble, "Attitudes Clash on Jobs and AIDS," *New York Times,* November 7, 1993, F25.

pany or a union official. Yet all of us have attitudes toward such individuals that are based on messages transmitted to us by others. For example, parents influence their children's attitudes toward people of other races and ethnic origins. Politicians and the managers of the mass media can also control the information we receive, which in turn influences attitudes. Coworkers can also greatly influence an employee's attitudes toward a job. This process occurs when employees attempt to influence a coworker to share their view (positive, negative, or indifferent) of many of the features of their work setting.[7]

EMOTIONAL CONDITIONING   Attitudes also can be formed via emotional conditioning. As will be discussed in Chapter 5, physiological reactions can be aroused by pairing a neutral stimulus with a positive or negative event. This process suggests that attitudes are sometimes formed for reasons not always rational. For example, we may come to endorse a particular point of view in part because the source of the message is highly attractive or entertaining.

Because we encounter objects and persons in contexts that have their own rewarding or punishing features, our attitudes toward them are susceptible to a wide variety of contaminating influences. Janis, Kay, and Kirschner reported an intriguing study that demonstrated the influence of context in shaping attitudes.[8] As part of a study of the effects of persuasive communication, they provided soft drinks for some subjects to enjoy while reading specific material. The results showed that the individuals who had been provided soft drinks were persuaded by what they had read to a greater degree than individuals who had not been given soft drinks. This set of results suggests that seemingly trivial factors within a given setting can have discernible effects. Other research indicates that people form a positive attitude toward a product when it is paired with soothing colors or enjoyable music.

ATTITUDE CHANGE

People are constantly trying to change each other's attitudes. Advertisers want to change the public's attitudes toward their clients' products. Union leaders, managers, and employees attempt to influence others' attitudes in favor of their points of view. Over the years, a good deal of research has been conducted on the topic of attitude change by people in the fields of marketing, communications, social psychology, and political science as well as in the field of organizational behavior. Despite the diversity of the approaches of these researchers, the research findings are generally accepted by most students of the topic, regardless of their discipline.

THE COMPONENTS OF ATTITUDE CHANGE   Four factors are involved in attitude change: the source, the message, the medium, and the audience. The process of attitude change follows five steps: attention, comprehension, yielding, retention, and action (Table 4.1).

Source factors refer to aspects of the presenter of an attitude change attempt (intent to persuade, attractiveness, and so forth). **Message factors** are the

TABLE 4.1

INFLUENCES AND STEPS IN ATTITUDE CHANGE

Factors That Influence Attitude Change (Independent Variables)	Steps in the Attitude Change Process (Dependent Variables)
Source	Attention
Message	Comprehension
Medium	Yielding
Audience	Retention
	Action

specific structure and content of what is transmitted in a persuasive appeal (for example, whether one or two sides of an issue are presented). **Medium factors** involve the effects of the channel that is employed (printed material, a face-to-face appeal, and so on). **Audience factors** deal with the influence of individual characteristics (for example, aspects of the personality of the target person).

The five steps in the process of attitude change focus on the target person's attention (whether the person is attentive to and receiving the persuasive appeal), comprehension (whether the appeal is understood as it was intended to be), yielding (whether the individual truly surrenders to the persuasion), retention (whether the individual's attitude change is more than merely transitory), and action (whether the attitude change attempt alters subsequent behavior).

Most researchers believe that an individual must go through all five steps in the process of attitude change. But researchers who believe in the possibility of subliminal influences contend that messages that are not attended to or comprehended can still influence attitudes and later behavior. Subliminal messages that are sometimes embedded in background music in department stores in an effort to discourage shoplifting are based on this premise.

The most prevalent approach to studying attitudes labels the four sets of factors (source, message, medium, and audience) as *independent variables*—factors to be manipulated by researchers in order to study their influence—and views the five steps in the process as *dependent variables*—outcomes or measures of the effects of changes in the independent variable. As an introductory overview of the topic of attitude change, some of the major findings associated with each of the four factors will be discussed.

Source Factors   The source of an attempt at attitude change can have a significant influence on the magnitude and direction of the change. Research shows that people are more likely to be influenced by sources that seem more expert and attractive. People also respond better to sources who are similar to themselves. That is why politicians often try to emphasize the traits and experiences that they have in common with their audience.

The initial degree of liking that an audience feels for the source is also important. Generally, the more a person likes the source of a persuasive appeal, the greater the likelihood of attitude change in the hoped-for direction. This can be explained from the perspective of **balance theory**.[9] Balance theory proposes that we try to maintain a fair degree of order or consistency among our beliefs. We can portray many simple situations involving attitude change attempts using a triangular model (Figure 4.1).

Imagine a source whose opinion you highly value (for example, your secretary) tells you he or she strongly dislikes another secretary whom you like somewhat. This places you in a socially difficult situation. Such a situation is unbalanced in that you probably feel a psychological tension or strain (see Figure 4.1a). Balance theory predicts you will probably attempt to restore harmony or balance by altering your feelings on the weakest of three links. In our example, your attraction to the source is likely to be the strongest link. Assuming that the source's dislike for the other secretary is substantial (and not likely

REPRESENTATIONS OF UNBALANCED AND BALANCED SITUATIONS

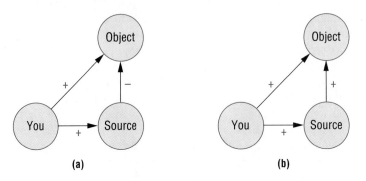

(a)   (b)

Positive and negative signs represent comfortable and uncomfortable psychological states.

to be changed by simple persuasion), it is likely your favorable evaluation of the other secretary will be diminished. However, if your evaluation of the other secretary is extremely positive, you may exert substantial effort to change your secretary's attitude.

An ideal balanced situation, of course, is one where all three links are positive (see Figure 4.1b). Situations in which any two links are negative—such as hearing a person you dislike making a statement that you find distasteful—are also balanced or consistent. When diagramming social situations, an odd number of negative signs is an indication of unbalance, while an even number signifies balance.

The use of highly attractive sources for endorsing products is based on the same logic that underlies balance theory. Advertisers hope that the linkage between the target person and the initially neutral object will produce a positive response by virtue of the other linkages being positive. In interpersonal relations, we sometimes rely on a similar ploy by telling others that a prestigious or attractive individual has endorsed some object or course of action. This tactic is occasionally used to steer the target person away from a course of action or an object by citing a disliked person's endorsement.

Message Factors   The influence of both the content and the structure of messages has been heavily researched. One content factor that has been intensely studied is the power of playing on people's fears. Portraying fearful situations is a potent means of inducing attitude change. For example, attempts to sell life insurance via the media typically rely on fear appeals, as do attempts to sell such products as radial tires and motor oil. By increasing the level of the threat, one could expect to encourage individuals to surrender to an endorsed position. However, one can also imagine appeals to fear having an opposite effect, in which people respond by becoming more resistant to the persuasive appeal (for example, by putting up blinders). Research on the topic, which has examined the influence of fear appeals in many diverse contexts, has uncovered evidence of the existence of both attitude change and audience resistance (although most studies have reported a positive association between increasing levels of fear and the amount of attitude change[10]). For purposes of attitude change, it is likely that there is an optimal level of fear arousal, beyond which the appeal can have an adverse effect. This optimal level, however, may be difficult to pinpoint without conducting an empirical search, since the level is likely to vary across individuals and topic areas.

Another message factor that has received considerable study is whether conclusions in an appeal are more persuasive when explicit (stated for the audience) or implicit (unstated but derivable from the arguments made in the appeal). One can argue for the greater effectiveness of either explicit conclusions or implicit conclusions. For example, an explicit conclusion would aid in audience comprehension. On the other hand, an implicit conclusion would allow people to discover the main point by themselves, with greater acceptance of the conclusion possibly resulting. The results of research on the topic suggest that the explicit approach is generally more effective than the implicit approach, perhaps because the explicit approach improves message receptivity (that is, audience comprehension). However, the implicit approach may be more effective in producing attitude change if the topic is one that is highly ego-involving. Since most of the topics studied have not been ego-involving (as is also true of most media advertising), it is possible that the potential usefulness of the implicit approach has been understated.

Considerable research has also been conducted on the effectiveness of presenting both sides of an argument as opposed to presenting a one-sided argument that ignores the opposing point of view. Controlled studies contrasting two-sided and one-sided presentations suggest that success of either appeal depends on other factors. Ignoring the opposing point of view tends to be more effective with individuals who initially favor the presenter's conclusion (it appears that they do not wish to have any doubts raised). Those initially opposed to the presenter's conclusion are more likely to be persuaded by a presentation showing both sides of an issue. The intelligence of the audience is an additional consideration, in that individuals who are more intelligent are likely to expect an even-handed (two-sided) presentation of an issue before they will form an opinion. The level of familiarity or controversy surrounding an issue is also important; topics that are relatively unknown to an audience can be more easily handled by merely ignoring the unpublicized or unfamiliar point of view, since the audience may be unaware of opposing arguments.

Medium Factors   During the 1960s and early 1970s, attitude researchers were greatly interested in the ways that media affected people's attitudes.[11] More recently, researchers have become more skeptical about the once-popular notion that the medium has greater impact on an audience than has the message itself. Research suggests that people find spoken appeals more influential than written appeals, even though they comprehend written appeals better, and they are more likely to be persuaded by face-to-face appeals. The greater effectiveness of face-to-face appeals may be due to the social pressure that a listener feels to avoid being rude and to comply with a speaker's explicit or implied request.

In comparison to other channels of communication, the mass media appear to be relatively ineffective in significantly altering attitudes. The mass media can, however, instruct and inform the public about the existence and the availability of objects and issues. The public's resistance to the influence of mass media appears to stem from a lack of strong involvement in media presentations. Generally speaking, the more immediate and personalized the attitude change attempt, the greater the degree of audience compliance.

Audience Factors   Individual differences have been examined in connection with the magnitude of attitude change. The more commonly studied audience factors include age (both chronological age and mental age), sex, self-esteem, and prior beliefs.

There is a fairly consistent relationship between chronological age and persuasibility. Suggestibility peaks at about age 8 or 9 and then decreases.§ The decline in suggestibility with age may be steeper, however, for males than females. Mental age (that is, intelligence) bears a far less consistent relationship with susceptibility to persuasion. It appears that intelligence is also generally related to a greater degree of attention and comprehension, but inversely related to degree of yielding.

Sex and persuasibility have long been assumed to be related; females are generally regarded as being more easily influenced by attitude change attempts. Evidence of sex effects has been reported in many different studies.[12] Typically, this effect has been attributed to greater cultural pressure on females to be conforming and compliant. More recently, a review of the sex effect literature has called into question the accuracy of the simple statement concerning female compliance.[13] The sex of the influencer and influencee may affect the level of influence. Also, female compliance with attitude change attempts may be diminishing as the societal norm of accepting and encouraging female noncompliance becomes more widely endorsed.

Intuitively, we would expect that self-esteem would be related to an individual's susceptibility to persuasion, with high self-esteem individuals less easily persuasible than low self-esteem individuals. However, the relation of self-esteem and ease of persuasibility may be different for males and females. Low self-esteem females appear to be alienated from and rejecting of attempts to influence their attitudes, while an inverse relationship exists for males.[14]

A person's prior beliefs play an important role in determining his or her response to an attitude change attempt. As mentioned earlier in our discussion of balance theory, people desire to have consistency among their beliefs. Inconsistency, or dissonance (to borrow the musical analogy of a dissonant chord), is stressful.

---

§ It was probably more than coincidence that Hitler's Youth Corps was directed toward young people in this age range.

One of the interesting aspects of dissonance is the influence it can have on altering our attitudes. Leon Festinger has argued that when individuals behave in ways that run counter to their private beliefs, and little external justification exists to explain or rationalize away their behavior in light of their original beliefs, then their attitudes are likely to be altered in order to bring about consistency between their beliefs and behavior.[15]

As a test of the principle of **cognitive** (or mental) **dissonance,** Festinger and Carlsmith conducted a now well-known experiment.[16] College students were asked to perform a boring task (repeatedly turning wooden pegs). After two hours of tedium, the subject was asked to tell the next subject that the experiment was fun and exciting (clearly, a request to make a statement that the subject did not believe in). Ostensibly, the subject was being asked to help create a mental set in the mind of the next subject in order to study the performance effects of being given a positive expectation about a task. Each subject was offered either $1.00 or $20.00 for serving as an assistant to the researcher by lying to the next subject. After attempting to deceive the next subject during a brief conversation in a waiting room, each subject was then asked to complete a lengthy questionnaire.

Of interest to the researchers was the evaluation of the boring task by the subjects who were paid to say something that they did not believe. The results showed that those subjects who were offered $20.00 for advocating something they did not initially believe in continued to hold a low opinion of the attractiveness of the task (that is, they had an external justification for having lied—they did it for the money). As predicted by Festinger's theory of cognitive dissonance, those subjects who were offered only $1.00 rated the task as being enjoyable. This attitude change resulted from the subjects' felt need to justify the inconsistency of their earlier actions and their prior beliefs. Since the subjects offered $1.00 could not explain away their behavior by attributing it to a financial incentive (and since they could not change the historical fact that they had endorsed a statement they did not believe was truthful), they were under a degree of psychological pressure to alter their attitude toward the task (that is, they actually came to view it as enjoyable).

This finding, and other related dissonance study findings, are all the more intriguing because of the counterintuitive nature of the dissonance reduction process. The principles of learning theory, a view to be discussed in Chapter 5, would predict that the subjects who received the larger reward ($20.00) would be more likely to change their attitude in a favorable direction.

In a related study of the dissonance phenomenon, Aronson and Mills studied the evaluations of social groups after a price had been paid to gain membership to the group.[17] Specifically, they required college women to undergo the equivalent of initiation rites in order to gain admission to a highly desirable social group. The results suggested that the greater the cost to the individual (the more severe the price of initiation), the more dissonance the individual experienced when she later learned that the group was, objectively, quite uninteresting and socially unattractive. The reduction of dissonance was manifested by the initiates who paid the "higher price" for admission to the group by their providing more favorable evaluations of the social group. A clear implication of this finding is that the more that people can be made to "pay" for admission to a group (be it membership in a fraternity or a corporation), the more likely they are to value eventual acceptance into that group.

ATTITUDES AND ACTIONS

The link between verbal statements and behaviors is not simple, or always direct. In some situations you may notice a good deal of inconsistency between what people say and what they do.

Mental states and behaviors may be controlled by different mechanisms.[18] Verbal statements are often made in response to very different constraints and pressures than are behavioral expressions. Actions are influenced by such additional forces as norms, changes in group affiliation and salience, and the opportunity to engage in specific behaviors. Research conducted by Martin Fishbein of the University of Illinois suggests that when the strength of a group's norms and the strength of an individual's desire to comply with such influences are taken into account, attitudes can be used to predict actions with surprising accuracy.[19] The degree of accuracy is especially great if the time horizon for the prediction is not extremely distant.

The need for individuals to have specific knowledge about how to comply with an attempt to change their attitudes is also important for explaining subsequent behavior. In a study of the effectiveness of an attempt to persuade college students to get tetanus shots, one group of subjects merely received information on the importance of obtaining the shot, while another group received the same appeal plus specific information on how to reach the campus infirmary, whom to see, the best hours to visit the infirmary, a campus map, and so on. Although students in both groups were apparently favorably influenced by the persuasive appeal, the percentage of students in each group who actually obtained the shot differed, with the students who had gotten the specific information about how to obtain the shot being far more likely to receive it.

Generally, it can be stated that attitudes often do affect behavior. Available evidence suggests that attitudes that are very specific in nature and that are developed from direct experience with a person or an object do affect many forms of behavior.[20]

JOB SATISFACTION

Emotional reactions to work experiences are inevitable. One's thinking, feeling, and action tendencies (that is, one's attitude) toward work is termed **job satisfaction.** As is true of all attitudes, a person's level of job satisfaction is influenced by experience. Although a worker's attitudes are formed by the job itself, communications from others can also play an important role. Furthermore, a worker's expectations about a job can greatly influence his or her interpretation and evaluation of work-related experiences.[21]

THE IMPORTANCE OF JOB SATISFACTION

Modern managers recognize that an organization's performance should be measured in human dimensions as well as in terms of return on investment, market share, profit after taxes, and the like. A variety of reasons support the desirability of attending to workers' satisfaction. Perhaps the foremost reason is a moral one. Consider that working is a requirement for most people. The alternative, a subsistence-level existence based on government and charitable support, is unacceptable to most people. Given that most people must work, and that most people will spend the majority of their adult lives at work, it can be argued that employers have a *moral obligation* to make the experience personally rewarding (or, at a minimum, not painful or dehumanizing).**

Workers' *physical and mental well-being* appear to be correlated with job satisfaction in that more highly satisfied workers have better physical and mental health records.[22] This evidence, however, is strictly correlational in nature. As a consequence, it is difficult to say in what direction the "causal arrow" is pointing. It is also conceivable that other factors that may come into play (for example, educational level and income) could be largely responsible for the observed correlations. Nonetheless, serious job dissatisfaction, as manifested by stress, can lead to a variety of physiological disorders, including ulcers and arterial disease.

Job satisfaction can also play an important role in a company's *ability to attract and retain qualified workers.* An organization's very survival rests heavily on this ability, and a company that is known to mistreat its personnel will have difficulty in drawing the best people to staff its positions.

Low levels of job satisfaction have been related to such problems as *turnover,*[23] *absenteeism,*[24] *union-organizing activity,*[25] and the *filing of grievances.*[26] Because such problems can be costly and disruptive to an organization, they cannot be lightly dismissed. Thus, job satisfaction is exceedingly important for the well-being of the organization as well as for the individual.

MEASURING JOB SATISFACTION

In recognition of the importance of job satisfaction, many organizations monitor employee attitudes. Though many large organizations, such as General Electric, Hewlett-Packard, and Sears, routinely conduct their own surveys of employee satisfaction, others, such as Wells Fargo and Leaseway Transportation, hire consulting firms to handle the task of assessing employee attitudes.[27]

Although in-depth interviews and questionnaires are sometimes used to measure job satisfaction, the most commonly used method is the anonymous survey. The variety of attitude scales that are employed in surveys reflects the diversity of approaches to conceptualizing job satisfaction (Figure 4.2). The

**It is an interesting exercise to calculate the proportion of one's life that is spent at work. Consider that the average adult will live to a predicted actuarial age. The number of years, in fact hours, of life that a person has left can then be determined. This finite number of hours can be further divided into unconscious time (spent sleeping), conscious but uninteresting and nonproductive time (when engaging in routine activities such as brushing teeth, dressing, and commuting), and conscious productive time. As a percentage, the majority of conscious productive time will be spent working.

earliest approaches characterized job satisfaction in global terms—that is, satisfaction was viewed as an overall reaction to one's job in its entirety.[††] Scales such as the GM Faces Scale[28] and the Brayfield-Rothe Job Satisfaction Questionnaire[29] exemplify the **global approach.** More recently a faceted approach to studying employee satisfaction has emerged. The **faceted approach** attempts to study employee reactions to each of several aspects, or facets, of the job (for example, one's supervisor, pay, or coworkers). Two outstanding examples of the faceted approach are the Job Descriptive Index[30] and the Minnesota Satisfaction Questionnaire.[31]

Global or facet-free scales offer the advantages of being relatively brief and easy to administer. In fact, if a set of simple instructions is read to the participants, the GM Faces Scale can be administered to employees who are illiterate. The faceted scales tend to be more lengthy; the Minnesota Satisfaction Questionnaire, or MSQ, has 100 items covering a total of 20 different facets. The Job Descriptive Index, or JDI, offers something of a compromise between length, ease of administration, required level of education of the respondent, and number of job facets (that is, pay, coworkers, supervision, opportunities for promotion, and the work itself). For these reasons (along with evidence of its reliability and validity), the JDI is one of the most widely known and commonly used devices for measuring job satisfaction.

The faceted approach is logically superior to the global approach, in that one can easily imagine instances in which an employee might be dissatisfied with his or her coworkers but extremely satisfied with the work itself. As previously mentioned, such scales as the JDI and the MSQ permit the independent assessment of attitudes on a number of distinct dimensions. In practice, the responses of people to these different facets tend to be positively correlated, so that people who are satisfied with their supervisor also tend to be satisfied with their coworkers, and so on. This evidence suggests that it may be reasonable to conclude that a general or global factor underlies the responses. In summary, most researchers acknowledge the need to use faceted scales, since they yield more specific information. However, most respondents in satisfaction surveys do not appear to compartmentalize their feelings.

SOURCES OF JOB SATISFACTION

Over 3,000 studies have been conducted on the topic of job satisfaction, or morale as it was more frequently termed in previous years.[‡‡] Their results tend to point to much the same conclusions. For example, certain variables are consistently correlated with job satisfaction (Table 4.2). One of the most important variables is job level. Satisfaction is higher among workers in higher-level

---

[††] Perhaps the earliest report of a study of job satisfaction was a treatise by Rammizzini in Modeno, Italy, in the early 1600s. Having noted a look of disgust on the faces of cesspool cleaners, he decided to question them on their feelings about their work. In the mid-1800s, Karl Marx developed a satisfaction questionnaire. However, the early forms of surveys more often asked *supervisors* to state what they believed workers felt about their jobs, rather than asking the workers themselves.

[‡‡] Blum and Naylor, however, maintain that the terms *satisfaction* and *morale* should not be used interchangeably, since satisfaction is an individual phenomenon, while morale is a by-product of personal experiences in a group setting.[32]

FIGURE 4.2

SAMPLE ITEMS FROM VARIOUS JOB SATISFACTION SCALES

Brayfield-Rothe Job Satisfaction Scale

My job is like a hobby to me.

Strongly Agree   Agree   Undecided   Disagree   Strongly Disagree

I enjoy my work more than my leisure time.

Strongly Agree   Agree   Undecided   Disagree   Strongly Disagree

---

Job Descriptive Index

How well does each word describe your pay? Circle Y if it does describe your pay, N if it does not describe your pay, or ? if you cannot decide.

Less than I deserve   Y N ?   Insecure   Y N ?   Highly paid   Y N ?

GM Faces Scale

Consider all aspects of your job. Circle the face which best describes your feelings about your job in general.

  7   6   5   4   3   2   1

Minnesota Satisfaction Questionnaire

On my present job, this is how I feel about . . .

1. Being able to keep busy all the time.

Very Dissatisfied   Dissatisfied   Neutral   Satisfied   Very Satisfied

2. The praise I get for doing a good job.

Very Dissatisfied   Dissatisfied   Neutral   Satisfied   Very Satisfied

---

positions, while satisfaction tends to be lowest among holders of jobs that can be characterized as hot, heavy, or dangerous, such as work in steel mills and unskilled jobs.

Length of service and race are also frequently correlated with job satisfaction. Individuals with less time on the job and black workers are, in the aggregate, somewhat more dissatisfied than "long-termers" and white workers. Of course, it is difficult to draw any firm conclusions from such correlational evidence because job level is also associated with length of service and race. Long-termers tend to be in higher-level jobs, and black workers tend to be less educated and are more likely to hold unskilled positions.[33]

Females are also more likely to be found in lower-level jobs. Historically, lower female expectations for employment opportunities have been fairly consistent with the lack of opportunities for women. Evidence of sex differences in job satisfaction levels has been mixed. It is likely, however, that rising expectations of women in the labor force will produce differences in job satisfaction between the sexes. It is also likely that differences in job satisfaction between younger and older women will become more evident as a result of the growing disparity in expectations between generations.

Finally, organizational size has been identified as a correlate of job satisfaction. Employees in smaller organizations tend to be more satisfied than employees in larger organizations.[34] The size of an organization may not in and of itself affect job satisfaction, but size is associated with more specific sources of satisfaction.

INTRINSIC VERSUS EXTRINSIC SOURCES OF SATISFACTION   All sources of job satisfaction fall into two categories: intrinsic and extrinsic. Intrinsic sources originate from within the individual and have psychological value. Such satisfactions are essentially self-administered. Autonomy (that is, independence, such as the ability to choose one's own work pace) is one source of intrinsic satisfaction.

Extrinsic sources of satisfaction originate from outside the individual; they come from his or her environment. Forces beyond the individual's control determine the frequency and magnitude of extrinsic sources of satisfaction. Working conditions and opportunities to interact with coworkers are sources of extrinsic satisfaction, as are job security and fringe benefits.

In addition, some sources of satisfaction serve a dual purpose in that they can be extrinsic, or tangible, in nature while having intrinsic, or psychological, value because of what they symbolize. Both a high salary and rapid career progress would offer dual sources of satisfaction.

EXPECTATIONS   Satisfaction is a very personal experience that depends heavily on an individual's expectations. For example, imagine that you have just been offered an executive position that pays $150,000 a year. It sounds attractive, of course. In the abstract, it's difficult to conceive of how someone could be dissatisfied with such a salary. Suppose, however, that you discover that

---

TABLE 4.2

CAUSES AND CONSEQUENCES OF JOB SATISFACTION

Causes		Consequences	
Pay and benefits	Autonomy	Absenteeism	Mental well-being
Coworkers	Job challenge	Tardiness	Grievances
Supervisors	Working conditions	Turnover	Sabotage
Opportunities for promotion	Job security	Early retirement	
	Sense of recognition	Union activity	
Job level	Initial expectations	Physical well-being	

An Inside Look
How to Keep American Employees Abroad Satisfied

According to the Society for Human Resources Management, a professional society of human resources practitioners and researchers, about 250,000 American employees work abroad, and thousands more are in the midst of returning from or planning an overseas assignment. As companies become more global it is likely that the number of American expatriates will continue to increase. For this reason, many companies may need to reconsider the unique circumstances—professional, cultural, and personal—of Americans abroad. Americans in foreign lands can face a variety of problems, ranging from inadequate pensions to substandard health care. Although many companies pat themselves on the back for preparing their employees for overseas assignments, expatriate employees are often dissatisfied with their company's programs.

A 1992 survey of 209 workers in 66 companies found sizable gaps between what companies provide to expatriates and what expatriate employees want. Employees felt companies provided inadequate assistance in career planning, culture training, and opportunities to return home, and were dissatisfied with the levels of quality of health care and cost of living adjustments provided in the foreign country. In all cases, the disparities between employees' desires and what the company provided ranged from 35 percent to 75 percent.

Overseas assignments provoke additional stressors for many managers. Trying to assimilate back into domestic operations after returning from abroad can be extremely difficult. Other employees may lose touch with their home office—the "out of country, out of mind" syndrome. Family life may also be strained, as the novelty of a new environment wears off and families grow restless.

A company that has thought through the implications of sending managers abroad and prepared an expatriate policy manual that spells out the terms and conditions of the assignment stands the best chance of keeping Americans abroad satisfied. Providing a well-planned assignment, keeping track of the employee's progress, and preparing in advance for repatriation help ensure that overseas assignments are win-win situations for employees and their companies.

Sources: Mary Rowland, "Thriving in a Foreign Environment," *New York Times,* December 5, 1993, F17; Stephanie Overman, "You Don't Have to Be a Big Fish to Swim in International Waters," *HRMagazine,* September 1993, 47–51.

---

other people who have much the same job are receiving $500,000 to $900,000 per year. What formerly seemed to be an attractive salary would suddenly become unsatisfactory.

Expectations can have a powerful influence on a person's level of satisfaction. For example, new employees often have unrealistically high expectations. In the time between being offered a job and the first day of work, new employees may fantasize about how rapidly they will rise in the new organization, what immediate working conditions will be like, and so on. Once on the job, however, they may experience a shock when confronted with a number of harsh realities. They may discover that no promotion ladder extends from their current position, that their coworkers are not very pleasant, or that the lunch room and restrooms are dilapidated. The unrealistic expectations of new employees may be generated partly by personal fantasy and by the media. But company recruiters may also play a role by deceiving prospective employees about the nature of their future employment.

Companies can counter the potential problem of unrealistic expectations by providing job-orientation programs that present a more realistic point of view. The effects of realistic job previews on individual's reactions to their work have been extensively studied. With minor exceptions,[35] the results have generally shown that individuals who are told both the bad and the good features of their new jobs before they begin working have higher levels of job satisfaction, lower initial expectations about the job, and a lower rate of early turnover.[36][§§] Some organizations (for example, Nissan Motor Manufacturing at its Smyrna, Tennessee, facility) modify the concept of providing realistic previews by having prospective employees participate in "preemployment" programs that are essentially "job tryouts." During a job tryout, an applicant completes a variety of exercises that simulate job-related tasks. Although the tryout is of value to the employer as it serves as both a screening and an indoctrination experience, the employee also gains an appreciation of what the actual job is likely to entail.[37]

DISPOSITIONAL INFLUENCES   Although much work in the area of job satisfaction indicates that external influences, such as job design, affect employee attitudes, some recent research suggests that individual job attitudes may be fairly consistent over time and jobs. In a nationwide longitudinal study of the job satisfaction of 5,000 middle-aged men, Staw and Ross found significant stability over a 5-year period. Even when individuals changed employers and/or occupations, prior attitudes continued to be a strong predictor of later job satisfaction. These findings suggest that individuals may be predisposed to feel good or bad about their employment situation, regardless of the actual specifics of the situation. These results help to explain why some people seem to be perpetually unhappy with their work or life, and others appear generally content and good-natured regardless of changes in their surroundings. In short, people may carry with them, across jobs, predispositions to feel good or bad about work. Researchers have coined the term **negative affectivity** to describe this predisposition to feel dissatisfied with one's job or life in general. People who are relatively high on negative affectivity are comparatively introspective and tend to dwell on the negative side of themselves and the world. Such individuals tend to interpret ambiguous information more negatively and to provide negative evaluations of predominantly neutral or innocuous objects common to everyday life (for example, one's telephone number, one's first name, or 8 1/2-by-11 inch paper). More recent research by Tim Judge, Ed Locke, and Charles Hulin suggests that such thought processes as perfectionistic tendencies and dependence on others, which are related to clinical depression, may adversely influence feelings of well-being and job satisfaction.[38]

A perhaps even more surprising finding in this area comes from research on the possible influence of genetics on job satisfaction. Specifically, researchers at the University of Minnesota studied the reported job satisfaction of identical twins who had been reared apart. These researchers found that a significant proportion of the variance in the job satisfaction responses could be

---

[§§] The importance of creating realistic expectations is increasingly being recognized. In addition to profit-oriented organizations, nonprofit organizations such as religious orders are using realistic job previews. One group of religious women provides a realistic preview to young women who are considering joining their convent. The preview is designed to show the drabness of the individual rooms and the hardships of daily chores. It is hoped that such previews will diminish attrition in the order by reducing the occasional expectation that life in the order will be a *Sound of Music*–type experience.

attributed to genetics. Similarities across pairs of twins existed despite differences in jobs.[39] These findings suggest that organizations may have less control over employee satisfaction than previously thought. However, the likelihood that genetics is a contributing factor to job satisfaction does not mean that job satisfaction is not influenced by environmental factors.[40]

THE SEARCH FOR TRENDS IN JOB SATISFACTION

Based on magazine articles, television, and movies, we might be tempted to conclude that most workers are dissatisfied with their jobs. However, available evidence indicates that such a conclusion would be in error. Surveys of workers in the United States show that the vast majority are fairly satisfied with their jobs. One set of surveys that spanned a 20-year period revealed that satisfied workers comprised 80 to 90 percent of the labor force in a given year.[41] Other representative samplings reveal much the same pattern.[42]

Despite this reassuring evidence, some alarmists argue that worker satisfaction is declining and that the resulting rise in worker alienation could lead to worker revolt. It is perhaps the implicit threat of a worker revolution that makes the prospect of declining satisfaction a topic of widespread concern.[***]

Due to increasing levels of education, expectations in the work force are rising. If better educated workers do not obtain better jobs, it is conceivable that job satisfaction could decline over the coming years. The unprecedented affluence of recent decades may also contribute to the creation of a more defiant work force that is less concerned with traditional extrinsic rewards and incentives, such as job security, and more concerned with intrinsic rewards, such as having a challenging and interesting job.

Studies over the years that have asked employees to rank the features of employment they most prefer suggest that such a change has already taken place.[43] Other evidence indicates that interest in work itself may be diminishing. Based on a study that they conducted in 1954, Morse and Weiss reported that 80 percent of the work force said that they would prefer to continue working even if they did not have a financial need to do so.[44] In a similar survey conducted during the 1970s, it was reported that only 72 percent of the work force would continue to work if they did not have the financial need to do so.[45] This and other evidence suggest that the work ethic may be giving way to a leisure ethic in the United States. In the future, managers may well face the added challenge of directing a work force that may be more demanding, more highly educated, and less interested in work as an end in itself. Surprisingly, these changes will take place at a time when the quality of working and living conditions has never been better.

[***] The evidence of fairly high general job satisfaction should not be interpreted as indicating that working conditions (in factories, for example) are not in need of improvement. Such problems are overlooked when one examines aggregate data for the entire work force. Also, people are remarkably adaptive to many unpleasant situations, and they often find alternative sources of satisfaction in otherwise adverse conditions. For example, social relations can be a major source of satisfaction in a dull and repetitive job. As evidence that many workers desire better positions, consider that only 24 percent of blue-collar employees report that they would choose the same type of work again. For white-collar employees, the figure only rises to 41 percent. Therefore, many people probably aspire to better conditions, although they are reasonably content with their present situation.

CONSEQUENCES OF JOB DISSATISFACTION

WITHDRAWAL BEHAVIORS   Individuals are usually drawn to situations that are rewarding, while they tend to withdraw from situations that are unrewarding or painful. This principle of reward and punishment appears to underlie much of the evidence on the relationship between job satisfaction and employee behavior.

Absenteeism   Each year, more work time is lost due to absenteeism than to strikes and lockouts. Absenteeism's direct costs to business are estimated at up to $30 billion. Studies of absenteeism have often found that less satisfied employees are more likely to miss work.[46] When studying absenteeism, it is important to distinguish between avoidable (or voluntary) absenteeism and unavoidable (or involuntary) absenteeism. Unavoidable absenteeism—for example, that due to illness or family emergency—is largely unrelated to level of job satisfaction.

To examine the relationship between satisfaction and absenteeism, Frank Smith studied the attendance rate of office employees at the Chicago headquarters of Sears, Roebuck on the day of a severe blizzard.[47] As a comparison group, Smith examined the attendance rate of employees in a New York City office, where, on the same day, the weather was pleasant. By relating absenteeism to individual job satisfaction data, Smith found that absenteeism in Chicago was more variable—that is, highly satisfied employees were far more likely to make the extra effort to report to work despite the blizzard, while dissatisfied employees were more likely to remain home.

Tardiness   It is also generally believed that chronic tardiness tends to reflect employee dissatisfaction.[48] Of course, it cannot be assumed that chronic tardiness is invariably due to dissatisfaction, because intervening factors, such as car pooling or preparing a large family for school each morning, often play a role. Nonetheless, certain forms of employee tardiness, such as that caused by lingering in the parking lot or restroom, may be attributed to such attitudinal factors as dissatisfaction, low job involvement, or low professional commitment. Over and above attitudinal factors, the existence of formal organizational penalties and incentives related to tardiness, as well as social pressures, can play a role in an individual's decision to be tardy.[49]

Turnover   Studies have shown, with a fair degree of consistency, that dissatisfied employees are more likely to quit. The specific influence of dissatisfaction on the decision to quit may be only moderate, however, because a variety of other factors are also involved. Perhaps of greatest influence is the availability of alternative employment opportunities. For example, general economic conditions and an employee's sense of confidence in the marketability of personal skills probably play major roles in the decision to seek a new job.[50] Fluctuations in quit rates, for example, are strongly associated with changes in job opportunities (as during periods of rising employment). In fact, the majority of the variation in quit rates may be explained by the simple factor of the business cycle.[51]

Although we might be tempted to think that managers should try to reduce employee turnover, it has been suggested that turnover may not be inherently undesirable. In fact, the desirability of turnover depends on who is leaving. If the people who are quitting are generally superior performers, turnover needs to be reduced or eliminated. But if turnover is great among poor performers, the change is actually in the best interests of the organization. The notion that high turnover among poor performers can benefit an organization is termed **functional turnover.**[52] Attempts to document the prevalence of functional turnover, in which quit rates are analyzed separately for high and low performers, are fairly new. Thus, it is difficult to say as yet how prevalent functional turnover may be or to identify the precise mechanisms through which organizations can foster functional turnover.

Early Retirement   Another topic of recent interest is the relationship between job satisfaction and the decision to take early retirement. One might expect that the choice of whether to take early retirement would be influenced by level of job satisfaction. In a study of state civil servants, Schmitt and McLane found supportive evidence that employees who chose early retirement held less positive attitudes toward their positions than did those who chose to remain working.[53] Job level was also associated with early retirement in that individuals in lower-level jobs were more likely to take advantage of the opportunity to retire than were individuals in higher-level positions.

Union Activity   Increased interest in union activity has long been accepted as a consequence of employee dissatisfaction,[54] but empirical evidence in support of this notion has been obtained only recently. In an attitude survey of over 62,000 employees, Clay Hamner and Frank Smith observed that roughly one-third of the variance in union activity could be predicted from job-satisfaction information.[55] The single most important predictor of union activity was dissatisfaction with supervision. Although dissatisfaction with other facets of the job contributed to the level of union activity, dissatisfaction with pay had no significant relationship.

Studies by Getman, Goldberg, and Herman and by Schriesheim have provided evidence that attitudes regarding job satisfaction and toward unions in general can predict voting behavior in union elections.[56] Pro-union voting was associated with concern for economic issues (such as security and working conditions) rather than noneconomic issues (such as the desire for creativity and independence). In the Getman, Goldberg, and Herman study, information on job satisfaction permitted the prediction of employee voting with an accuracy rate of 75 percent. In addition to voting behavior, other forms of union activity (such as the frequency of strikes and grievance rates within departments) have been found to be correlated with job dissatisfaction.[57] Therefore, some organizations, such as Sears, Roebuck, deliberately use periodic attitude surveys as an early-warning system to spot problems that may lead to union organizing activity.[58]

Hostile Actions   There is good reason to believe that extremely dissatisfied employees occasionally engage in hostile actions directed against their employers or coworkers. Hostile actions include sabotaging machinery or production, employee theft, vandalizing company property, unfairly criticizing the employer to customers or the public, and physical violence directed at coworkers and superiors. Other, more specific examples of hostile actions include deliberately destroying databases, placing work gloves into gears in order to halt assembly lines, tampering with company records, and overfilling or underfilling customer orders.[59]

To date, there has been little empirical research on the relationship between dissatisfaction and hostile actions. As noted by Giacolone and Rosenfeld, such behavior is difficult to study because employees as well as employers are reluctant to discuss the topic with either insiders or outsiders.[60] Also, such actions do not commonly produce a discernible pattern for study, nor are such actions often easily attributable to a specific saboteur.[†††] Employees who engage in sabotage may, understandably, not be easily identifiable as they ordinarily appear content and compliant.[61] One confidential survey, however, did find that self-reports of hostile actions (theft, vandalism, deliberate destruction of work projects, and so on) were significantly correlated with employee dissatisfaction.[62] From a theoretical basis, it may be that some employees engage in violent acts because of a desire to feel a sense of mastery or control over their work environment, which is not attainable through nonviolent means. In short, sabotage may represent an attempt to create the feeling that one is not at the mercy of one's employer.[63]

JOB SATISFACTION AND PRODUCTIVITY

Most people believe that satisfied workers are more productive workers. They reason that satisfied employees are inclined to be more involved with their work and, therefore, are more productive. Empirical research, however, has not identified much support for this proposal. In fact, the available evidence suggests that the relationship between job satisfaction and productivity is a very weak one. In an early review of a large variety of job satisfaction–productivity studies, Vroom concluded that the median correlation between satisfaction and productivity is 0.14 (that is, very low, but positive).[64] More recent literature reviews found that the correlation between satisfaction and performance is about 0.17.[65] These correlations suggest that very little variance in performance can be attributed to job satisfaction.

Because people tend to overestimate the influence of job satisfaction, they underestimate other factors that contribute to productivity. Among these other factors are informal work norms, task interdependence, and machine pacing of productivity. These forces often restrict the range of individual productivity. For example, coworkers usually will not allow an individual to work too fast or too slow (since a worker who is too productive will create a logjam at the next workstation, and one who is not productive enough will create a bottle-

---

[†††]Our word *sabotage* is derived from the French word *sabot,* a hollowed-out wooden shoe worn by European peasants. During the Industrial Revolution, disgruntled factory workers were said to "sabotage" the production process by tossing their wooden shoes into the machinery.

neck for other workers who supply materials to the individual). Furthermore, machine pacing and production planning are designed to reduce uncertainty and maintain strong control over the production process. These factors serve to limit employees' freedom to vary their performance to match their personal desires.

Although these factors help explain the lack of strong empirical support for a relationship between performance and satisfaction, they do not refute the proposition that such a relationship exists. The belief that these variables are related, or at least influence each other, is still widely held by the business community and debated by researchers. Some researchers have suggested that the two dimensions will be correlated only when satisfaction can have a direct impact on performance.[66] For example, in situations in which there is little pressure to be productive, the two dimensions are more likely to be correlated. In situations with high pressure to produce (perhaps the majority of situations), employees will be fairly productive by necessity, and the two variables are unlikely to be correlated.

Other researchers have argued that satisfaction and performance are potentially correlated as a consequence of their being causally related. Three variations on this argument have been raised. The first viewpoint contends that *satisfaction causes performance.* This proposal was the underlying premise for the human relations approach, which assumes that if you make workers happy, they will reciprocate by being more productive. To date, no evidence clearly demonstrates that workers feel a strong urge to reciprocate with high performance in exchange for a felt concern for their feelings.

The second viewpoint holds that *performance causes satisfaction.* That is, high performers tend to be more satisfied than low performers. It is usually suggested that performance influences satisfaction via the receipt of *equitable rewards.* In other words, satisfaction can be viewed as a reaction to rewards rather than simply a reaction to job performance in itself.

Figure 4.3 summarizes the view of those who believe that performance causes satisfaction. Job satisfaction is seen as a reaction to the rewards generated

■ **FIGURE 4.3**
THE "PERFORMANCE CAUSES SATISFACTION" VIEW

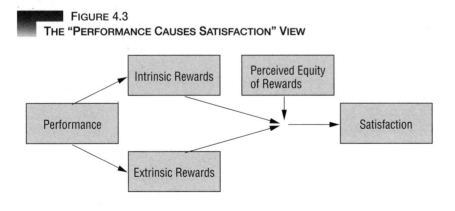

Source: E.E. Lawler and L.W. Porter, "The Effect of Performance on Job Satisfaction," *Industrial Relations*, (1967): 20–28.

by performance. Whether the rewards are perceived as equitable is also a consideration. The definition of equitable rewards, in turn, is partially influenced by perception of one's own performance and resulting deservedness. According to this point of view, the failure to find a stronger association between satisfaction and productivity lies partly in the failure of many organizations to tie rewards to performance. As we will see in Chapter 5, wages and salaries are often not clearly based on performance.

A third viewpoint contends that *satisfaction and performance influence each other.*[67] According to this viewpoint, the impact of job satisfaction on performance is probably very indirect. For example, satisfaction may indirectly influence performance through the belief that performance will be rewarded equitably. The impact of performance on satisfaction is perhaps greater than the impact of satisfaction on performance because, as noted earlier, there are potentially more intervening factors between the experience of satisfaction and later performance than there are between performance and later satisfaction.

THE IMPORTANCE OF A POSITIVE CORRELATION BETWEEN JOB SATISFACTION AND PRODUCTIVITY   If superior performers are receiving greater rewards than poor performers, satisfaction levels should be higher among superior performers. The consequence of such a state of affairs is that satisfaction and performance will be positively correlated. Therefore, the extent to which satisfaction and performance are positively correlated within an organization is a partial indication of the extent to which an organization is "healthy." Consider the converse situation of an organization in which satisfaction and performance are inversely related. Such a situation would be one in which poorer performers are more satisfied than higher performers and in which functional turnover is probably low. Clearly, this situation, as well as a situation in which satisfaction and performance are totally uncorrelated, is not in the best long-term interest of the organization. Managers should therefore strive to create linkages between performance and satisfaction by offering highly attractive, equitable rewards that are tied to performance.

A FRAMEWORK FOR UNDERSTANDING EMPLOYEE RESPONSES TO DISSATISFACTION

As the preceding sections suggest, employees can respond to the experience of dissatisfaction in a variety of ways. For example, they may withdraw (i.e., be absent or late more often), file grievances, withhold effort, or engage in sabotage. Also, they may simply tolerate a dissatisfying situation out of a sense of loyalty to the organization, or in the hope that the situation will improve. The responses that employees make to the experience of dissatisfaction can be conceptualized along two dimensions: active-passive and constructive-destructive (Figure 4.4).

Exit behaviors, such as quitting or frequent absenteeism, reflect an active but destructive response; voice behaviors, such as filing a formal complaint with supervisors, reflect an active but constructive response; loyalty behaviors, such as waiting for one's employer to remedy poor conditions or not express-

FIGURE 4.4

A FRAMEWORK FOR VIEWING EMPLOYEE RESPONSES TO JOB DISSATISFACTION

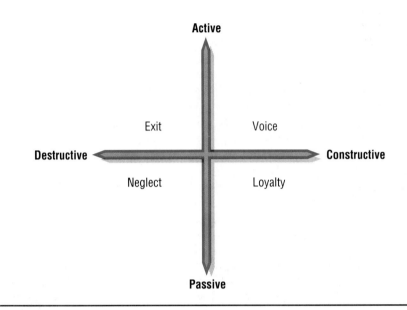

ing disfavor during a time of layoffs and budget cutbacks, reflect a more passive but constructive response; and neglect behaviors, such as failing to correct easily detected work errors, reflect a passive but destructive response. Active forms of hostile action, such as deliberate sabotage that destroys property or injures another, do not readily fit under the exit heading. However, such actions can be interpreted as opening oneself to the risk of being terminated if detected. Research on the Exit-Voice-Neglect-Loyalty framework suggests that employees do recognize these options. However, the precise prediction of which alternative an employee may select, as well as the sequence or ordering of alternative actions an employee may pursue, has proven problematic.[68]

OTHER WORK-RELATED ATTITUDES

In addition to employee job satisfaction, two attitudes that receive a fair amount of attention in the organizational literature are organizational commitment and job involvement. Although these two attitudes have not been studied for nearly as long as job satisfaction, they are the focus of a great deal of recent interest.

Organizational commitment refers to an employee's degree of identification with an organization and its goals, as well as the employee's desire to maintain membership in the organization. From this definition, we should expect to find that organizational commitment is a fairly useful predictor of employee turnover, as well as a predictor of performance, absenteeism, and tardiness. Thus far, the evidence indicates that organizational commitment does predict turnover, exceeding the predictive power of job satisfaction. However, the relationship of organizational commitment to other variables is not nearly as strong.[69] Like job satisfaction, a variety of additional influences probably interact with organizational commitment in determining its level of impact. Many employers recognize the potential utility offered by a high level of employee commitment and, therefore, desire to raise the existing level of commitment in their work forces. Efforts to enhance commitment range from offering significant opportunities for employees to participate in decision making (which will be discussed in Chapter 7) to the more mundane use of logos and slogans to convey corporate symbolism and values. Although there is a popular perception that organizational commitment is stronger in Far Eastern companies than in U.S. firms, available evidence indicates that the level of employee commitment in the United States exceeds that found in both Japan and Korea.[70]

Job involvement refers to the extent to which an employee identifies with his or her job and relies on evidence of job performance as an indication of personal self-worth. As this definition suggests, the construct of job involvement is somewhat similar to organizational commitment in that they both are concerned with an employee's identification with the work experience. However, the constructs differ in that job involvement is more closely associated with identification with one's immediate work activities rather than identification with organizational goals. Also, job involvement includes a concern with maintaining one's work-related self-esteem. That is, for people who are highly involved in their jobs, whether or not one feels good about oneself is closely related to how one performs one's job. Individuals who are characteristically high on job involvement can be said to "eat, breathe, and sleep" their jobs. Research on job involvement has found that employees who are highly involved in their work have lower absence rates, lower quit rates, and higher job satisfaction.[71] Also, job involvement has been found to be related to low dogmatism and an internal orientation on the dimension of locus of control (see Chapter 3).[72] How to deliberately raise the level of employee job involvement is not clear. Offering more psychologically enriching work (a topic that will be discussed in Chapter 7) may be effective only for certain individuals. Also, the tendency to define one's own sense of personal worth based on work performance may be fairly well established by the time an individual is old enough to enter the work force. Therefore, the individual difference variable of job involvement is somewhat akin to the personality construct of the work ethic (discussed in the previous chapter) in that both propensities may be a function of earlier pre-work experiences that include the transmission of values by primary caretakers and the influence of role models.[73]

SUMMARY

1. Explain the nature of attitudes and their essential components.
An attitude is an idea charged with emotion that predisposes an individual to react in a particular way when confronted with a specific situation. Thus, an

attitude has three basic components: (1) the cognitive component, (2) the affective component, and (3) the behavioral component. It is important to note that the behavioral predisposition is determined to some extent by the cognitive and the affective components.

2. Outline the most widely used methods of measuring attitudes.

Because attitudes are not directly observable, they cannot be directly studied. Consequently, in their attempts at greater understanding, researchers examine the three basic components. The affective component is measured with physiological and verbal tests, the cognitive component is measured through statements of belief or reports of categorizations or beliefs, and the behavioral component is measured through observations of actual behavior. The two most common written tests of attitudes are graphic scales, which ask an individual to indicate his or her degree of agreement with a series of statements, and semantic differential scales, which ask for ratings based on pairs of adjectives that are opposite in meaning.

3. Identify the means through which attitudes are formed.

We acquire our attitudes through three kinds of learning. We may develop either positive or negative attitudes through direct experience—our own personal involvement with people and things in our environment. Our attitudes may also grow out of our social communication with others—we will be influenced by the information we receive from parents, friends, coworkers, managers, and personal acquaintances as well as by information culled from public figures and mass media. And we form attitudes through emotional conditioning—a process that suggests our attitudes are not always based on rational grounds.

4. Specify the components of attitude change and trace the steps in the change process.

Four factors are involved in attitude change: (1) source factors are the characteristics of the originator of an attempted attitude change, (2) message factors are the specific structure and content of the persuasive appeal, (3) medium factors are the characteristics and effects of the channel of communication, and (4) audience factors are the characteristics of the target of the attitude change. These are the four key influences on an individual's process of changing attitudes. To achieve a lasting change in attitude, most researchers believe that an individual must go through five required phases: (1) attention to the attempt to persuade, (2) comprehension of the persuasive appeal, (3) yielding to persuasion, (4) retention of the new attitude, and (5) action in keeping with the new attitude.

5. Tell why management should take an interest in workers' job satisfaction.

Job satisfaction is the product of an individual's thoughts, feelings, and attitudes toward work. Because organizational performance should be measured in human as well as financial terms, management cannot ignore the significance of job satisfaction. Some might argue that because most people must work and consequently spend much of their adult lives doing so, companies have a moral obligation to make work rewarding. The company also benefits, however, because studies show that satisfied workers enjoy better physical and mental health and that job satisfaction plays a significant role in a firm's ability to attract and retain qualified workers. Furthermore, low levels of job satisfaction have been related to such problems as turnover, absenteeism, union organizing, and the filing of grievances. Thus, job satisfaction is a crucial issue for both individuals and organizations.

6. Note the principal methods of measuring job satisfaction.

In-depth interviews and questionnaires are sometimes used to measure job satisfaction, but the most common method uses anonymous surveys employing attitude scales. Global, or facet-free, scales look at satisfaction in terms of a worker's overall reaction to his or her job. They are relatively brief and easy to administer. More recently, faceted scales that examine employees' reactions to specific aspects of a job have gained popularity. Although such scales yield more detailed information than do global scales, they are also more lengthy and complicated to administer.

7. Cite the most frequent sources of job satisfaction.

The results of numerous studies indicate that certain variables are consistently correlated with job satisfaction, among them job level, length of service, and size of organization. In addition, satisfaction strongly depends on the individual's expectations and personal disposition. Although surveys of the U.S. work force indicate that the vast majority of workers are fairly satisfied with their jobs, recent trends indicate that, in the future, managers may well be challenged by a work force that is more demanding, more educated, and less interested in work as an end in itself.

8. Describe some typical employee responses to low job satisfaction.

Among the most common reactions to low job satisfaction are withdrawal behaviors, such as absenteeism, tardiness, turnover, and early retirement. Employees may also express their dissatisfaction through increased union activity and hostile actions. Although numerous studies have investigated the relationship between job satisfaction and productivity, there is little empirical evidence to support the pervasive notion that satisfied workers are more productive.

KEY TERMS

Attitude	Balance theory
Cognitive component	Cognitive dissonance
Affective component	Job satisfaction
Behavioral component	Global approach
Graphic scale	Faceted approach
Semantic differential scale	Negative affectivity
Source factors	Functional turnover
Message factors	Organizational commitment
Medium factors	Job involvement
Audience factors	

REVIEW AND DISCUSSION QUESTIONS

1. Ralph, one of your subordinates, took an instant dislike to Myra, a new coworker, because he thinks that her clothes are too informal and her hair is too long. "You know," he complains to you, "her work is just as sloppy as her appearance." In fact, you know that Myra's work is excellent, so you reply, "Ralph, I think your attitude toward Myra is clouding your judgment." "Attitude?" he asks. "What do you mean by attitude?" Explain exactly what you mean.

2. You have been called in as a consultant by the operations department of a mail order company that wants to measure order takers' attitudes toward their jobs. Explain why attitudes cannot be directly measured, review the alternatives, and describe some likely test formats.

3. As a result of your explanation in response to Question 1, your subordinate Ralph is growing increasingly interested in the subject of attitudes. "Where do you think I got this attitude?" he asks. Tell him how attitudes are formed.

4. Having won Ralph's confidence with your explanations of attitudes and their formation, you think you may be able to persuade him to change his attitude toward Myra. How would you accomplish this goal? What source, message, medium, and audience factors would you have to consider? What specific steps would you lead Ralph through? How successful do you think you would be?

5. Both in the past and in many other countries today, employers have paid little attention to their employees' job satisfaction. Why should employers be interested in job satisfaction? In your opinion, why is job satisfaction primarily a modern and Western concern?

6. What approach would you use to measure the job satisfaction of each of the following groups? Why?

   a. coal miners   c. dentists
   b. computer programmers   d. migrant farmworkers

7. Were you surprised to learn that 80 to 90 percent of workers in the United States are satisfied with their jobs? Why or why not? How would you account for this high level of job satisfaction? Would you expect this trend to continue?

8. If you were a manager, what clues would help you identify employees who were dissatisfied with their jobs? As long as your workers were productive, could you assume that they were satisfied? Could you assume that greater satisfaction would lead to greater productivity? Why or why not?

CRITICAL INCIDENT

When the Shoe Is on the Other Foot

Underhill Packing Co. is a meat-processing firm that has been growing over the past 10 years. Phil had worked on the processing line for almost 8 years.

During that time, the union had gone on strike three times, with each incident lasting 4 to 6 weeks.

Approximately 6 months ago, Phil was promoted to a supervisor's position. The job offered several thousand dollars more in salary and the opportunity was too good to pass up. Phil had always supported the union but now he was part of the management group.

Over the past couple of months, two incidents have occurred that have Phil thinking. One concerned a disagreement he had with a union steward who accused Phil of harassing a worker. Phil maintained that he had to tell the worker several times one day to keep busy and get back to work. Nevertheless, a grievance was filed and later withdrawn only after Phil was asked to apologize.

The second incident involved a worker who was repeatedly late to work. Phil documented each occurrence and, after the third time in two weeks, he sent the worker home without pay as stipulated in the labor–management contract. Again, a grievance was filed claiming that Phil was overstepping his authority and harassing the worker. The time card indicated that the worker had clocked-in on time, but Phil insisted that he was 10 to 15 minutes late each time.

Phil has become upset and angry over these situations and believes that the union is trying to discredit him. He likes his job as supervisor, but wishes someone had told him more about union–management relations and how to deal with them.

Questions

1. How would you characterize Phil's attitude toward the union when he first became a supervisor?

2. Do you believe his attitude has changed? To what do you attribute this change?

3. What factors are likely to affect the attitudes of those who move from being a worker to being a supervisor?

Experiential Exercise

Assessing Your Job Satisfaction

As discussed in this chapter, job satisfaction is an extremely important factor for the well-being of both the individual and the organization. In this exercise, you are asked to assess your feelings of job satisfaction in terms of your present job or in the kind of job you think you will have when you complete this aspect of your education.

If you are currently employed, either part-time or full-time, respond in terms of your current job. If you are not currently employed, describe your last job. If you have never worked, respond in terms of the kind of job you realistically think you will have when you start working.

Step 1 Below are 20 statements concerning characteristics or attributes of your job. For each statement, provide two ratings:

a. How much of the characteristic *is there now* associated with your job?

b. How much of the characteristic *should there be* associated with your job?

Circle the number on the scale that represents the amount of the characteristic being rated. That is, low numbers represent minimum amounts and high numbers represent maximum amounts. Thus, if you think there is very little of the characteristic associated with your job, circle 1. If you think there's a little, circle 2. If you think there is a lot of the characteristic, circle 4, and so on. For each scale, circle only one number. Please do all the scales.

1. The extent to which my job is challenging:
   a. How much is there now?   (min) 1 2 3 4 5   (max)
   b. How much should there be?   1 2 3 4 5

2. The feeling of personal accomplishment one gets from being in my job position:
   a. How much is there now?   (min) 1 2 3 4 5   (max)
   b. How much should there be?   1 2 3 4 5

3. The extent to which the pay associated with my job is appropriate:
   a. How much is there now?   (min) 1 2 3 4 5   (max)
   b. How much should there be?   1 2 3 4 5

4. The feeling of security one has in my job:
   a. How much is there now?   (min) 1 2 3 4 5   (max)
   b. How much should there be?   1 2 3 4 5

5. The opportunity one has to work closely with others and develop close friendships:
   a. How much is there now?   (min) 1 2 3 4 5   (max)
   b. How much should there be?   1 2 3 4 5

6. The extent to which one is recognized for achievements in performing my job:
   a. How much is there now?   (min) 1 2 3 4 5   (max)
   b. How much should there be?   1 2 3 4 5

7. The extent to which my job gives me prestige and status within the organization:
   a. How much is there now?   (min) 1 2 3 4 5   (max)
   b. How much should there be?   1 2 3 4 5

8. The opportunity my job provides for developing a sense of responsibility:
   a. How much is there now?   (min) 1 2 3 4 5   (max)
   b. How much should there be?   1 2 3 4 5

9. The extent to which my job provides an appropriate set of fringe benefits:
   a. How much is there now?   (min) 1 2 3 4 5   (max)
   b. How much should there be?   1 2 3 4 5

10. The opportunity my job provides for being involved in making decisions:
    a. How much is there now?   (min) 1 2 3 4 5 (max)
    b. How much should there be?   1 2 3 4 5

11. The extent to which my job provides appropriate working conditions:
    a. How much is there now?   (min) 1 2 3 4 5 (max)
    b. How much should there be?   1 2 3 4 5

12. The opportunity for autonomy (that is, independent thought and action) in my job:
    a. How much is there now?   (min) 1 2 3 4 5 (max)
    b. How much should there be?   1 2 3 4 5

13. The feeling of being "in the know"—that is, having access to important or useful information in my job:
    a. How much is there now?   (min) 1 2 3 4 5 (max)
    b. How much should there be?   1 2 3 4 5

14. The opportunity for participating in establishing goals and objectives for my job:
    a. How much is there now?   (min) 1 2 3 4 5 (max)
    b. How much should there be?   1 2 3 4 5

15. The extent to which my job is governed by appropriate rules and procedures:
    a. How much is there now?   (min) 1 2 3 4 5 (max)
    b. How much should there be?   1 2 3 4 5

16. The opportunity my job provides for meeting challenges and solving problems:
    a. How much is there now?   (min) 1 2 3 4 5 (max)
    b. How much should there be?   1 2 3 4 5

17. The opportunity to earn additional income (for example, bonus, overtime) in my job beyond the normal wages:
    a. How much is there now?   (min) 1 2 3 4 5 (max)
    b. How much should there be?   1 2 3 4 5

18. The feeling of being able to use my unique abilities in performing my job:
    a. How much is there now?   (min) 1 2 3 4 5 (max)
    b. How much should there be?   1 2 3 4 5

19. The extent to which policies and procedures governing advancement are appropriate in my job:
    a. How much is there now?   (min) 1 2 3 4 5 (max)
    b. How much should there be?   1 2 3 4 5

20. The extent to which my supervisor sees to it that every person does a fair day's work:
    a. How much is there now?   (min) 1 2 3 4 5 (max)
    b. How much should there be?   1 2 3 4 5

Step 2   Compute your satisfaction/dissatisfaction score for each of the items using the table below. The extent of your satisfaction/dissatisfaction with each job characteristic is scored as the rating for (b) minus the rating for (a); that is, "how much should there be" minus "how much is there now."

1. For each question, subtract part (a)'s rating from part (b)'s rating—that is, (b) − (a).

2. Enter the (b) − (a) value for each question in the space next to the number of that question in the following columns. If (a) is greater than (b), be sure to retain the minus sign for the difference.

3. Next, add the numbers in each column to obtain a total for each category. Again, be sure to retain any minus signs.

4. Divide this total by the number of questions used to measure each category.

Remember, this adjusted score is a measure of dissatisfaction. The lower it is, the more satisfied you are. The higher it is, the more dissatisfied you are.

Intrinsic Factors	Extrinsic Factors
1b − 1a = _____	3b − 3a = _____
2b − 2a = _____	4b − 4a = _____
6b − 6a = _____	5b − 5a = _____
7b − 7a = _____	9b − 9a = _____
8b − 8a = _____	11b - 11a = _____
10b − 10a = _____	15b - 15a = _____
12b − 12a = _____	17b - 17a = _____
13b − 13a = _____	19b - 19a = _____
14b − 14a = _____	20b - 20a = _____
16b − 16a = _____	
18b − 18a = _____	
Total: _____	Total: _____
Divide by: 11	Divide by: 9
Adjusted Score: _____	Adjusted Score: _____

Step 3 Your instructor will ask you to form groups of three to five people. Each group should discuss the members' satisfaction scores in terms of:

1. The features of the job that could be viewed as responsible for each person's high and low satisfaction scores.

2. What might be done to change each job so as to lessen the dissatisfaction.

3. What type of job, for each individual, might lead to improved job satisfaction.

Step 4 Be prepared to share your responses to the previous questions with the entire class. In addition, you could discuss the implications of these findings for career planning. That is, what attributes of your job are significant in terms of satisfaction/dissatisfaction? How can such information assist you in making career decisions?

NOTES

1. H.C. Triandis, "A Critique and Experimental Design for the Study of the Relationship Between Productivity and Job Satisfaction," *Psychological Bulletin* 56 (1959): 309–316; A.H. Eagly, "Uneven Progress: Social Psychology and the Study of Attitudes," *Journal of Personality and Social Psychology* 63 (1992): 693–710.

2. R.A. Likert, "A Technique for the Measurement of Attitudes," *Archives of Psychology* 140 (1932): 44–53.

3. J.C. Nunnally, *Psychometric Theory* (New York: McGraw-Hill, 1994).

4. C.E. Osgood, G.J. Suci, and P.H. Tannenbaum, *The Measurement of Meaning* (Urbana, Ill.: University of Illinois Press, 1957).

5. R.B. Zajonc, "Attitudinal Effects of Mere Exposure," *Journal of Personality and Social Psychology Monograph Supplement* 9 (1968): 1–27.

6. S. Milgram, "The Experience of Living in Cities," *Science* 167 (1970): 1461–1468.

7. G.J. Blau and R.D. Katerberg, "Toward Enhancing Research with the Social Information Processing Approach to Job Design," *Academy of Management Journal* 7 (1982): 543–550.

8. I. Janis, D. Kaye, and P. Kirschner, "Facilitating Effects of 'Eating-While-Reading' on Responsiveness to Persuasive Communications," *Journal of Personality and Social Psychology* 1 (1965): 181–186; S.E. Middlestadt, "The Effect of Background and Ambient Color on Product Attitudes and Beliefs," *Advances in Consumer Research* 17 (1990): 244–249; G.J. Gorn, "The Effects of Music in Advertising on Choice Behavior: A Classical Conditioning Approach," *Journal of Marketing* 46 (1982): 94–101.

9. F. Heider, *The Psychology of Interpersonal Relations* (New York: Wiley, 1958).

10. H. Leventhal, "Fear—for Your Health," in *Readings in Psychology Today,* 2d ed. (Del Mar, Calif.: CRM Books, 1972), 627–631.

11. M. McLuhan, *Understanding Media* (New York: McGraw-Hill, 1964).

12. K. Gergen and D. Marlowe, eds., *Personality and Social Psychology* (Reading, Mass.: Addison-Wesley, 1969).

13. A.H. Eagley and L.L. Carli, "Sex of Researchers and Sex-typed Communications as Determinants of Sex Differences in Influenceability: A Meta-analysis of Social Influence Studies," *Psychological Bulletin* 90 (1981): 1–20.

14. K. Gergen and R. Bauer, "The Interactive Effects of Self-esteem and Task Difficulty in Social Conformity," *Journal of Personality and Social Psychology* 6 (1967): 16–22; R.A. Josephs, H.R. Markus, R.W. Tafarodi, "Gender and Self-esteem," *Journal of Personality and Social Psychology* 63 (1992): 391–402; N. Rhodes and W. Wood, "Self-esteem and Intelligence Affect Influenceability: The Mediating Role of Message Reception," *Psychological Bulletin* 111 (1992): 156–171.

15. L. Festinger, *A Theory of Cognitive Dissonance* (Stanford, Calif.: Stanford University Press, 1957).

16. L. Festinger and J.M. Carlsmith, "Cognitive Consequences of Forced Compliance," *Journal of Abnormal and Social Psychology* 58 (1959): 203–210.

17. E. Aronson and J. Mills, "The Effect of Severity of Initiation on Liking for a Group," *Journal of Abnormal and Social Psychology* 59 (1959): 177–181.

18. R.P. Abelson, "Are Attitudes Necessary?" in *Attitudes, Conflict, and Social Change,* ed. B.T. King and E. McGinnis (New York: Academic Press, 1972), 19–32.

19. M. Fishbein, "Attitude and the Prediction of Behavior," in *Readings in Attitude Theory and Measurement,* ed. M. Fishbein (New York: Wiley, 1967), 477–492.

20. R.H. Fazio and M.P. Zanna, "Direct Experience and Attitude-Behavior Consistency," in *Advances in Experimental Social Psychology,* vol. 14, ed. L. Berkowitz (New York: Academic Press, 1981).

21. Blau and Katerberg, "Toward Enhancing Research with the Social Information Processing Approach."

22. E. Palmore, "Predicting Longevity: A Follow-up Controlling for Age," *Gerontology* (Winter 1969); A.W. Kornhauser, *Mental Health of the Industrial Worker: A Detroit Study* (New York: Wiley, 1965).

23. H.J. Arnold and D.C. Feldman, "A Multivariate Model of Job Turnover,"

Journal of Applied Psychology 67 (1981): 350–360.

24. J.A. Breaugh, "Predicting Absenteeism from Prior Absenteeism and Work Attitudes," *Journal of Applied Psychology* 66 (1981): 555–560.

25. J.M. Brett, "Why Employees Want Unions," *Organizational Dynamics* (Spring 1980): 847–859.

26. R.B. Dunham and F.J. Smith, *Organizational Surveys* (Glenview, Ill.: Scott, Foresman, 1979).

27. "A Finger on the Pulse: Companies Expand Use of Employee Surveys," *The Wall Street Journal*, October 27, 1986, 23.

28. F.J. Landy, "The Early Years of I/O: J.D. Houser and J.D.I.," *Industrial Psychologist* 26 (1989): 63–64; T. Kunin, "The Construction of a New Type of Attitude Measure," *Personnel Psychology* 8 (1955): 65–78.

29. A.H. Brayfield and H.F. Rothe, "An Index of Job Satisfaction," *Journal of Applied Psychology* 35 (1951): 307–311.

30. P.C. Smith, L.N. Kendall, and C.L. Hulin, *The Measurement of Satisfaction in Work and Retirement* (Chicago: Rand-McNally, 1969).

31. D.J. Weiss, R.V. David, G.W. England, and L.H. Lofquist, *Manual for the Minnesota Satisfaction Questionnaire*, Minnesota Studies in Vocational Rehabilitation: 22 (Minneapolis: University of Minnesota Industrial Relations Center, 1967); R.W. Rice, D.A. Gentile, and D.B. McFarlin, "Facet Importance and Job Satisfaction," *Journal of Applied Psychology* 76 (1991): 31–39.

32. M.L. Blum and J.C. Naylor, *Industrial Psychology* (New York: Harper and Row, 1968).

33. R.P. Vecchio, "Worker Alienation as a Moderator of the Job Quality–Job Satisfaction Relationship: The Case of Racial Differences," *Academy of Management Journal* 23 (1980): 479–486; A. Dalessio, W.H. Silverman, and J.R. Schuck, "Paths to Turnover: A Reanalysis and Review of Existing Data on the Mobley, Horner, and Hollingsworth Turnover Model," *Human Relations* 39 (1986): 245–263; M.F. Ket de Vries, D. Miller, J.M. Toulouse, P. Friesen, M. Boivert, and R. Theriault, "Using the Life Cycle to Anticipate Satisfaction at Work," *Journal of Forecasting* 3 (1984): 161–172.

34. L.W. Porter and E.E. Lawler, "Properties of Organization Structure in Relation to Job Attitudes and Job Behavior," *Psychological Bulletin* 64 (1965): 23–51.

35. R. Katerberg, "A Study of Met Expectations in an Organization" (Master's thesis, University of Illinois–Urbana, 1976).

36. S.M. Colarelli, "Methods of Communication and Mediating Processes in Realistic Job Previews," *Journal of Applied Psychology* 69 (1984): 633–642; J.P. Wanous, "Tell It Like It Is at Realistic Job Previews," *Personnel* 52 (1975): 50–60; J. Wanous, T. Poland, S. Premack, and K. Shannon-Davis, "The Effects of Met Expectations on Newcomer Attitudes and Behaviors: A Review and Meta-analysis," *Journal of Applied Psychology* 76 (1991): 288–297.

37. S.L. Premack and J.P. Wanous, "A Meta-analysis of Realistic Job Preview Experiments," *Journal of Applied Psychology* 69 (1985): 706–719; J.P. Wanous, *Organizational Entry: Recruitment, Selection, Orientation, and Socialization of Newcomers* (Reading, Mass.: Addison-Wesley, 1992); J.P. Wanous and A. Colella, "Organizational Entry Research: Current Status and Future Directions," in *Research in Personnel and Human Resources Management* vol. 7, ed. K. Rowland and G. Ferris (Greenwich, Conn.: JAI Press, 1989), 59–120; P.W. Hom, R.W. Griffeth, L.E. Palich, and J.S. Bracher, "Realistic Job Previews for New Professionals: A Two-Occupation Test of Mediating Processes" (Working paper, Arizona State University, 1993); R.J. Vandenberg and V. Scarpello, "The Matching Model: An Examination of the Processes Underlying Realistic Job Previews," *Journal of Applied Psychology* 75 (1990): 60–67.

38. B.M. Staw and J. Ross, "Stability in the Midst of Change: A Dispositional Approach to Job Attitudes," *Journal of Applied Psychology* 70 (1985): 469–480; B.M. Staw, N.E. Bell, and J.A. Clausen, "The Dispositional Approach to Job Attitudes: A Lifetime Longitudinal Test," *Administrative Science Quarterly* 31 (1986): 56–77; T.A. Judge and E.A. Locke, "Effect of Dysfunctional Thought Processes on Subjective Well-being and Job Satisfaction," *Journal of Applied Psychology* 78 (1993): in press; T.A. Judge, "The Dispositional Perspective in Human Resources Research," in *Research in Personnel and Human*

Resources Management, 10th ed., ed.
G.R. Ferris and K.M. Rowland
(Greenwich, Conn.: JAI Press, 1992):
31–72; T.A. Judge and C.L. Hulin, "Job
Satisfaction as a Reflection of
Disposition: A Multiple Source Causal
Analysis," *Organizational Behavior and
Human Decision Processes* (in press);
A.P. Brief, M.J. George, B.S. Robinson,
and J. Webster, "Should Negative
Affectivity Remain an Unmeasured
Variable in the Study of Job Stress?"
Journal of Applied Psychology 73
(1988): 193–198; I. Levin and J.P. Stokes,
"Dispositional Approach to Job
Satisfaction: Role of Negative Affectivity,
Journal of Applied Psychology 74
(1989): 752–758; K.R. Parkes, "Coping,
Negative Affectivity, and the Work
Environment: Additive and Interactive
Predictors of Mental Health," *Journal of
Applied Psychology* 75 (1990): 399–409;
P.Y. Chen and P.E. Spector, "Negative
Affectivity as the Underlying Cause of
Correlations Between Stressors and
Strains," *Journal of Applied Psychology*
76 (1991): 398–407; D. Watson and L.
Clark, "Negative Affectivity: The
Disposition to Experience Aversive
Psychological States," *Psychological
Bulletin* 96 (1984): 465–490; T. Judge,
"Does Affective Disposition Moderate
the Relationship Between Job Satisfaction
and Voluntary Turnover?" *Journal of
Applied Psychology* 78 (1993): 395–401;
J. George and A. Brief, "Feeling Good—
Doing Good: A Conceptual Analysis of
the Mood at Work–Organizational
Spontaneity Relationship," *Psychological
Bulletin* 132 (1992): 310–329.

39. R.D. Arvey, T.J. Bouchard, H.L. Segal,
and L.M. Abraham, "Job Satisfaction:
Environmental and Genetic
Components," *Journal of Applied
Psychology* 74 (1989): 187–192.

40. A. Davis-Blake and J. Pfeffer, "Just a
Mirage: The Search for Dispositional
Effects in Organizational Research,"
Academy of Management Review 14
(1989): 385–400; I. Levin and J. Stokes,
"Dispositional Approach to Job
Satisfaction," *Journal of Applied
Psychology* 74 (1989): 752–758; T.J.
Bouchard, R.D. Arvey, L. Keller, and N.
Segal, "Genetic Influences on Job
Satisfaction: A Reply to Cropanzano and
James," *Journal of Applied Psychology*
76 (1991): 89–93.

41. R.P. Quinn and G.L. Staines, *The 1977
Quality of Employment Survey* (Ann

Arbor: Institute for Social Research,
University of Michigan, 1979).

42. C.N. Weaver, "Job Satisfaction in the
United States in the 1970s," *Journal of
Applied Psychology* 65 (1980): 364–367.

43. H.L. Sheppard and N. Herrick, *Where
Have All the Robots Gone?* New York:
Free Press, 1972).

44. M.C. Morse and R.S. Weiss, "The
Function and Meaning of Work and the
Job," *American Sociological Review* 20
(1955): 191–198.

45. R.P. Vecchio, "The Function and
Meaning of Work and the Job: Morse
and Weiss (1955) Revisited," *Academy of
Management Journal* 23 (1980):
361–367.

46. G. Johns, "The Great Escape,"
Psychology Today, October 1987, 30–33;
L.R. Waters and D. Roach, "Relationship
Between Job Attitudes and Two Forms of
Withdrawal from the Work Situation,"
Journal of Applied Psychology 55
(1971): 92–94; R. Hackett and R.M.
Guion, "A Reevaluation of the
Absenteeism–Job Satisfaction
Relationship," *Organizational Behavior
and Human Decision Processes* (1985):
340–381; K.D. Scott and G.S. Taylor,
"An Examination of Conflicting Findings
on the Relationship Between Job
Satisfaction and Absenteeism: A Meta-
analysis," *Academy of Management
Journal* 28 (1985): 588–612.

47. F.J. Smith, "Work Attitudes as Predictors
of Attendance on a Specific Day," *Journal
of Applied Psychology* 62 (1977): 16–19.

48. L.W. Porter and R.M. Steers,
"Organizational, Work, and Personal
Factors in Employee Turnover and
Absenteeism," *Psychological Bulletin* 80
(1973): 151–176; S. Adler and J. Golan,
"Lateness as a Withdrawal Behavior,"
Journal of Applied Psychology 66
(1981): 544–554.

49. R.M. Steers and S.R. Rhodes, "Major
Influences on Employee Attendance: A
Process Model," *Journal of Applied
Psychology* 63 (1978): 391–407.

50. R.P. Vecchio, "Workers' Perceptions of
Job Market Favorability and Job
Insecurity," *Mid-Atlantic Journal of
Business* 21 (1983): 9–16; J.M. Carsten
and P.E. Spector, "Unemployment, Job
Satisfaction, and Employee Turnover: A
Meta-analytic Test of the Muchinsky
Model, *Journal of Applied Psychology* 72
(1987): 374–381.

51. H. Wool, "What's Wrong with Work in America?: A Review Essay," *Monthly Labor Review* 96 (1973): 38–44.

52. D.R. Dalton and W.D. Todor, "Turnover Turned Over: An Expanded and Positive Perspective," *Academy of Management Review* 4 (1979): 225–236; D.R. Dalton, W.D. Todor, and D.M. Krachhardt, "Turnover Overstated: The Functional Taxonomy," *Academy of Management Review* 7 (1982): 117–123; M.B. Staw, "The Consequences of Turnover," *Journal of Occupational Behavior* (1980): 253–273.

53. N. Schmitt and J.T. McLane, "The Relationship Between Job Attitudes and the Decision to Retire," *Academy of Management Journal* 24 (1981): 795–802; D. Hanisch and C.L. Hulin, "Job Attitudes and Organizational Withdrawal: An Examination of Retirement and Other Voluntary Withdrawal Behaviors," *Journal of Vocational Behavior* 37 (1990): 60–78; N. Schmitt and J.T. McLane, "The Relationship Between Job Attitudes and the Decision to Retire," *Academy of Management Journal* 24 (1981): 795–802.

54. R. Stagner and H. Rosen, *Psychology of Union-Management Relations* (Monterey, Calif.: Brooks-Cole, 1965).

55. W.C. Hamner and F.J. Smith, "Work Attitudes as Predictors of Unionization Activity," *Journal of Applied Psychology* 63 (1978): 415–421.

56. J.G. Getman, S.B. Goldberg, and J.B. Herman, *Union Representation Elections: Law and Reality* (New York: Russell Sage Foundation, 1976); C.A. Schriesheim, "Job Satisfaction, Attitudes Toward Unions, and Voting in a Union Representation Election," *Journal of Applied Psychology* 63 (1978): 548–552; M.D. Zalesny, "Comparison of Economic and Noneconomic Factors in Predicting Faculty Vote Preference in a Union Representation Election," *Journal of Applied Psychology* 70 (1985): 243–256.

57. E.A. Fleishman and E. F. Harris, "Patterns of Leadership Behavior Related to Employee Grievances and Turnover," *Personnel Psychology* 15 (1962): 54–56; E.A. Fleishman, E.F. Harris, and H.E. Burtt, *Leadership and Supervision in Individuals* (Columbus: Ohio State University Personnel Research Board, 1955).

58. D. Buss, "Job Tryouts Without Pay Get More Testing in U.S. Auto Plants," *The Wall Street Journal*, January 10, 1985, 31.

59. M. Sprouse, *Sabotage in the American Workplace: Anecdotes of Dissatisfaction, Mischief and Revenge* (San Francisco: Pressure Drop Press, 1992).

60. R.A. Giacolone and P. Rosenfeld, "Reasons for Employee Sabotage in the Workplace," *Journal of Business and Psychology* 1 (1987): 367–378.

61. M.D. Crino and T.L. Leap, "What HR Managers Must Know about Employee Sabotage," *Personnel* (1989): 31–37.

62. C.M. Staehle, *Job Dissatisfaction and Action Alternatives: A Study of the Relationship Between Dissatisfaction and Behaviors in Work Organizations* (Honors thesis, College of Business and Management, University of Maryland, 1985).

63. V.L. Allen and D.B. Greenberger, "Destruction and Perceived Control," in *Advances in Experimental Psychology,* 2d ed., ed. A. Baum and J.E. Singer (N.J.: Erlbaum, 1980).

64. V.H. Vroom, *Work and Motivation* (New York: Purley, 1964).

65. M.T. Iaffaldana and P.M. Muchinsky, "Job Satisfaction and Job Performance: A Meta-analysis," *Psychological Bulletin* 97 (1985): 251–273; P.M. Podsakoff and L. Williams, "The Relationship Between Job Performance and Job Satisfaction," in *Generalizing from Laboratory to Field Settings,* ed. E.A. Locke (Lexington, Mass.: Lexington Books, 1986), 207–253.

66. R.B. Ewen, "Pressure for Production, Task Difficulty, and the Correlation Between Job Satisfaction and Job Performance," *Journal of Applied Psychology* 58 (1973): 378–380; R.S. Bhagat, "Conditions Under Which Stronger Job Performance–Job Satisfaction Relationships May Be Observed: A Closer Look at Two Situational Contingencies," *Academy of Management Journal* 25 (1982): 772–789; Triandis, "A Critique and Experimental Design."

67. E.E. Lawler and L.W. Porter, "The Effect of Performance on Job Satisfaction," *Industrial Relations* 7 (1967): 20–28.

68. D. Farrell, "Exit, Voice, Loyalty, and Neglect as Responses to Job Dissatisfaction: A Multidimensional Scaling Study," *Academy of Management*

Journal 26 (1983): 596–606; M.J. Withey and W.H. Cooper, "Predicting Exit, Voice, Loyalty, and Neglect," *Administrative Science Quarterly* 34 (1989): 521–539.

69. T.S. Bateman and S. Strasser, "A Longitudinal Analysis of the Antecedents of Organizational Commitment," *Academy of Management Journal* 27 (1984): 95–112; S. Parasuraman and J.A. Alutto, "Sources and Outcomes of Stress in Organizational Settings: Toward the Development of a Structural Model," *Academy of Management Journal* 27 (1984): 330–350; A.E. Reichers, "A Review and Reconceptualization of Organizational Commitment," *Academy of Management Review* 10 (1985): 465–476; R.C. Mayer and F.D. Schoorman, "Predicting Participation and Production Outcomes Through a Two-Dimensional Model of Organizational Commitment," *Academy of Management Journal* 35 (1992): 671–684; J.P. Meyer, D. Bobocel, and N. Allen, "Development of Organizational Commitment During the First Year of Employment: A Longitudinal Study of Pre- and Post-Entry Influences," *Journal of Management* 17 (1991): 717–734; R.J. Vandenberg and C.E. Lance, "Examining the Causal Order of Job Satisfaction and Organizational Commitment," *Journal of Management* 18 (1992): 153–168; R. Tett and J. Meyer, "Job Satisfaction, Organizational Commitment, Turnover Intention, and Turnover: Path Analyses Based on Meta-analytic Findings," *Personnel Psychology* 46 (1993): 259–294.

70. F. Luthans, H.S. McCaul, and N.G. Dodd, "Organizational Commitment: A Comparison of American, Japanese, and Korean Employees," *Academy of Management Journal* 28 (1985): 213–219.

71. G.J. Blau and K.R. Boal, "Conceptualizing How Job Involvement and Organizational Commitment Affect Turnover and Absenteeism," *Academy of Management Review* 12 (1987): 288–300; S. Rabinowitz and D.T. Hall, "Organizational Research in Job Involvement," *Psychological Bulletin* 84 (1977): 265–288; T.M. Lodahl and M. Kejner, "The Definition and Measurement of Job Involvement," *Journal of Applied Psychology* 49 (1965): 24–33; P. Weissenberg and L.W. Gruenfeld, "Relationship Between Job Satisfaction and Job Involvement," *Journal of Applied Psychology* 52 (1968): 469–473; R. Kanungo, *Work Orientation: An Integrative Approach* (New York: Praeger, 1982).

72. M. Evans, cited in D.T. Hall and R. Mansfield, "Relationships of Age and Seniority with Career Variables of Engineers and Scientists," *Journal of Applied Psychology* 60 (1975): 201–210; K.E. Runyon, "Some Interactions Between Personality Variables and Management Styles," *Journal of Applied Psychology* 57 (1973): 288–294.

73. R. Dubin, "Industrial Workers' Worlds: A Study of the 'Central Life Interests' of Industrial Workers," *Social Problems* 3 (1956): 131–142; T.M. Lodahl, "Patterns of Job Attitudes in Two Assembly Technologies," *Administrative Science Quarterly* 8 (1964): 482–519; A.L. Siegal, *Industrial Psychology* (Homewood, Ill.: Irwin, 1969); S. Rabinowitz, "An Examination of the Influence of Individual Difference Variables and Perceived Job Stimulation on Job Involvement" (Master's thesis, Michigan State University, 1975).

VIDEO CASE   QUAD GRAPHICS, INC.

Harry Quadracci's daydreams about his career after law school probably didn't include a vision of himself on stage leading amateur performers in songs from *Pirates of Penzance*. He found himself performing as part of his role as the C.E.O. of Quad Graphics, the full-color printing company he started in 1970 when he quit his position as a labor negotiator for a large Wisconsin printing company owned by his father. The annual stage performance is an integral part of the company's spirited, team-oriented culture. Quad Graphics had grown to employ approximately 3,300 people and generated annual sales of one-half billion dollars. Its clients included *Newsweek, Time, U.S. News & World Report, Playboy, Lillian Vernon,* and *James River Traders.*

Quadracci had always resisted hard-nosed, antilabor management tactics. In starting his own firm, he was anxious to employ an entirely new strategy for human resource management.

He built his organization based firmly on trust. The book *The 100 Best Companies to Work for in America* (Doubleday, 1992) honors Quad Graphics, highlighting the ways it implements trust to form the backbone of its culture:

- Trust in teamwork. Employees trust that together they will accomplish more than they would individually.

- Trust in responsibility. Employers trust that each worker will carry his/her fair share of the load.

- Trust in productivity. Customers trust that Quad Graphics' work will represent the most competitive levels of pricing, quality, and innovation available.

- Trust in management. Shareholders, customers, and employees trust that the company will make decisive judgments for long-term success rather than focus only on short-term goals like today's profit.

- Trust in thinking small. Quad Graphics peo-

ple all trust in each other: They regard each other as persons of equal value; they respect the dignity of individuals by recognizing individual accomplishments, as well as the feelings and needs of individuals and their families; they all share the same goals and purposes in life.

These principles illustrate that, at Quad Graphics, trust is more than an empty promise.

Quad Graphics has far fewer rules and regulations than most companies of its size, and that's no accident. It's the way the founder likes to run the show. Quadracci calls his personal and direct style of management, expressly avoiding formalized rules and regulations, "Theory Q." As opposed to the traditional American top-down "Theory X" style or the Japanese participatory "Theory Z," Quadracci maintains the attitude that communications should be personal, vocal, and spontaneous, and that one should avoid the shelter of more formal, traditional limits such as job descriptions, time clocks, policies, and procedures.

Quadracci works to ensure that employees are happy and satisfied in their work, and also that they are challenged. Most of Quad's employees have completed high school educations at most. Quadracci believes that the key to corporate growth is these individuals' growth via on-going training and development. The burden of this training and development falls mostly on peers. Employees train one another.

Nearly 1,000 people complete the various training courses that Quad Graphics sponsors each week in a remodeled former elementary school building. With the exception of new recruits, who are paid to attend what amounts to basic training, the vast majority attend classes on their own time. Graduates of previous Quad classes teach their peers.

After completing basic training, part of an employee's job is to begin learning other jobs. This way all employees can contribute to improving the firm's management and productivity. This sense of shared purpose driven by individual responsibility nurtures a vital, creative work environment. Passing knowledge among fellow workers makes everyone's job easier and stimulates employees' growth in new directions. As many decisions are made on the plant floor as possible in the belief that the best ideas come from the people doing the work.

Each division operates as a separate company. Most divisions hire their own workers to suit their own needs, and most newly hired employees are referred by current employees. The in-house newspaper once reported that 39.5 percent of all employees were somehow related to other employees. This was called the "ouchi rating," taken from a Japanese term that translates roughly as "part of the family." At the time of the in-house article, the median age of Quad Graphics employees was 27.

The sharing of authority that brings decision making to the ground floor of the organization attracts and holds these employees, as do the foundation of trust and the focus on education. A number of other conditions keep employment at Quad Graphics attractive. For one, employees own approximately 40 percent of the company. They share in its profits via a plan that links take-home pay to efficiency.

Quad Graphics' unusual shift schedule is attractive as well. Each employee works three 12-hour shifts a week and every other Sunday (at double salary). This amounts to pay for 48 hours per week while working 42 hours.

The culture of equality among peers also helps individuals flourish. Plant managers wear the same uniforms everyone else does. Every employee gets a clean, dark-blue uniform daily.

The company welcomes individual advice and input, encouraging employees to "get big by thinking small." Quad employees have developed improvements in production equipment and generated new business ideas as well. Employees have even initiated entire new operating units like ink manufacturing, equipment repair, and Quad Tech, a high-tech division that devel-

ops new printing technologies for sale to other printers.

The company allows all managers to use its 57th Street apartment in Manhattan for visits to New York City. The company even picks up the air fare for two. This exposes young managers from Wisconsin to the home turf and daily operations of most of their clients.

Harry Quadracci pays close attention to the physical environment of the company, believing that it can be an important tool to promote employee creativity and voluntarism. These attitudes can deteriorate when employees run machines that run machines. Most Quad Graphics employees monitor computers that take over many of the mechanical tasks once performed by people. To combat boredom this separation from the work might cause and to promote a joyful workplace, a popcorn machine on the shop floor is available to anyone at any time. Overhead pipes and machines throughout the factory are painted in a rainbow of colors.

The company supports workers' interests outside the narrow limits of their jobs as well. Employees have set up child-care facilities and food service facilities at Quad. They built up physical fitness programs that encourage teamwork and comradeship along with better health. Also, Quad pays employees $30 to attend a seminar to help them quit smoking. Those who quit for a year receive a bonus of $200.

A symbol of the firm's convivial team atmosphere, the stage show led by Quadracci has become a traditional part of the annual Christmas party. All managers participate, and the performers rehearse on their own time. The affairs have centered on a number of themes. Once, the party took the form of a sit-down dinner for 2,200 employees and their guests at the firm's new Sussex, Wisconsin plant. The show that year followed a circus parade theme, with all managers dressed as clowns and Quadracci, dressed as a ringmaster, riding in on an elephant.

Quad Graphics' state-of-the-art printing plants, phenomenal growth, and unique philosophy of management promote employees' sense of shared purpose. Besides churning out the product, technology helps the firm create a better, happier, more satisfying work environment for its workers. This combination of personal vision and technical development has made Quad Graphics a very successful company, and one employees like to work for.

QUESTIONS

1. What medium factors does Quadracci consider appropriate? Does he favor any particular medium factor over others? Why?

2. Quad Graphics promotes employee job satisfaction in many ways. What benefits does this create?

3. To what factors do you attribute the company's high degree of job satisfaction?

4. Do you foresee any potential problems related to the high ouchi factor at Quad? (Hint: Might this create barriers to effective perception?)

5. Could Harry Quadracci's personality be described in terms of the Myers-Briggs typology?

Source: Written by Susan Stites Doe, State University of New York College at Brockport.

Interpersonal Processes

5

Experience is what enables
you to recognize a mistake
when you make it again.
— Earl Wilson

Around here we use the
"carrot-and-stick"
approach—you know what
the "stick" is, the "carrot"
means that we won't use
the "stick."

— A foreman

LEARNING OBJECTIVES

*After studying this chapter,
you should be able to:*

1. *Explain what learning is
   and why managers need to
   understand the learning
   process.*
2. *Describe the process of
   classical conditioning and
   cite several examples of this
   form of learning in the
   workplace.*
3. *Tell what observational
   learning is and how it occurs in the workplace.*
4. *Discuss the nature of operant conditioning and cite
   four rules for applying operant conditioning principles to enhance employee
   performance.*
5. *Summarize the advantages
   and disadvantages of OB
   Mod.*
6. *Analyze the role of punishment in shaping employee
   behavior.*

Changing Employee Behavior through Consequences
Learning and Punishment

CHANGING BEHAVIOR FROM THE TOP DOWN

At Thermwood Corporation, Ken Susnjara, the chairman, president, and chief executive officer, knew that something had to change. The small manufacturer of robots and automation equipment, which Susnjara had founded in 1969, was losing money fast. Susnjara decided that he needed to learn a new way of operating.

He temporarily turned over leadership of Thermwood to the company's sales manager and became a salesman for Thermwood's products. Listening to customers quickly taught Susnjara what was wrong.

About 60 percent of Thermwood's sales are to small and medium-sized companies, for which the equipment is often the biggest purchase they ever make. Therefore, the customers want reliability more than anything else. And because small companies often cannot afford employees with sophisticated technical skills, the customers are also looking for equipment that is easy to use.

However, Thermwood, like its competitors, was focused in-stead on developing the leading technology. Says Susnjara, "We had gotten caught up in the industry hype. We were very engineering- and R&D-oriented. We were developing all sorts of fancy systems that nobody really had any use for." He concluded that the company must begin to focus more on reliability.

Back at the helm, Susnjara restructured the company along product lines, then set out to find a way of leading his managers to change their behavior so that they focused more on the customer. He cut the top executives' salaries by two-thirds to three-fourths, which would be supplemented by a bonus plan based on each division's profits. Says Susnjara, "The formula was such that, if you were even marginally successful, you could make a fortune."

With rewards like that dangled in front of them, the managers came around quickly. According to Susnjara, the company regained popularity after only about two weeks under this new arrangement. "It is almost unbe-lievable," he says, "when people are handling their own money, how well they do with it. Instantly, it was as though a fog lifted." The top managers began restructuring and cutting out unneeded expenses.

To keep management focused on the customer, the company has begun requiring that every officer of Thermwood meet with customers at least four times a month. Explains Susnjara, "We need to make sure that we don't lose sight of the fundamental values that got us back to where we are today."

At Thermwood, Ken Susnjara changed his behavior by learning ways to satisfy customers. In turn, he used a system of rewards to change the behavior of his managers. This chapter introduces the process of learning, examining what learning is and the ways in which it takes place. The chapter explores how learning occurs in the workplace and how managers use various learning techniques to shape employee behavior.

Source: John H. Sheridan, "Out of the Isolation Booth," *Industry Week,* June 19, 1989, 18–19.

Learning, one of the most fundamental behavioral processes, involves both the development and the modification of thoughts and behaviors. Other concepts and aspects of organizational behavior (for example, motivation and supervision) that we will discuss in later chapters can be more fully explained with the use of learning principles.

New employees bring with them a set of previously learned ways of behaving. They are then expected to learn additional information that applies to their jobs. Established employees continue to develop their job-related skills and abilities. Therefore, learning is a never-ending process for all employees. The process is also very complex. For example, an employee who has already learned one way to perform a job may have trouble learning a second, albeit better, way.

An employee's motivation to perform is closely linked to learning. Therefore, a manager who understands the learning process can use the principles of learning to guide employee behavior and performance. To be successful, employee training and development programs must be based on sound learning principles.

THE NATURE OF LEARNING

Learning is a fairly permanent change in behavior that occurs as a result of experience.[1] A distinctive feature of this definition is the term *change*. In order to say that learning has occurred, a change, or modification, of behavior must be evident. The change in behavior must also be more than temporary. It should also be possible to attribute this change to the occurrence of an event. Thus, while learning is a process that we cannot observe directly, we can infer that learning has occurred when we observe a fairly permanent change in behavior.

Only in this century have researchers begun to systematically study the learning process. Their efforts have produced three approaches to the explanation of learning: classical conditioning; observational, or vicarious, learning; and operant, or instrumental, conditioning.

CLASSICAL CONDITIONING

Early in the twentieth century, Ivan Pavlov, a Russian physiologist, conducted research on digestive glands. In the course of his research, Pavlov discovered that a laboratory dog's secretions of saliva were controlled by both learning processes and direct physiological stimulation. He noted that the sound of approaching footsteps, as well as the simple sight of food, would cause a dog to salivate.

In later research, Pavlov focused even more closely on how various stimuli could be used to produce a desired response. Specifically, he paired the ringing of a bell with the presentation of food to a dog. After a number of pairings, the sound of the bell alone (that is, without the food) was sufficient to produce salivation. Based on his experiments, Pavlov developed the notion of classical conditioning.

In **classical conditioning**, an **unconditioned stimulus (UCS)**—or stimulus that has the capacity to reliably evoke a naturally occurring reflexive or **unconditioned response (UR)**—is paired with the occurrence of a neutral stimu-

Figure 5.1

A Summary of Classical Conditioning

Initially:

UCS ————————————————➤ UCR
(e.g., Food)   (Salivation)

After pairing a bell's tone with food:

UCS + CS ————————————➤ UCR
(Food)(Bell)   (Salivation)

The bell alone can evoke a reflex-like response:

CS ————————————————➤ CR
(Bell)   (Salivation)

lus, one that does not have an initial capacity to evoke the response of interest. Following a number of simultaneous presentations of the unconditioned stimulus and the neutral stimulus, the mere presence of the neutral stimulus will evoke a reflexive response. This reflex-like response is termed the **conditioned response (CR)**. When a neutral stimulus attains this capacity, it is termed a **conditioned stimulus (CS)**. In Pavlov's experiments, the sight of food was the unconditioned stimulus that evoked the unconditioned response of salivation. The sound of the bell was the neutral stimulus that attained the power of a conditioned stimulus; that is, the bell gained power to evoke the conditioned, or learned, response of salivation. In classical conditioning, the initial relationship of UCS → UR is replaced by CS → CR (Figure 5.1).*

Many jobs require conditioned responses. For example, driving a 40-foot tractor trailer or a forklift calls for reflexive behaviors. The driver's ability to apply the brakes quickly and firmly or otherwise react appropriately depends on conditioned responses to previously neutral stimuli, such as warning lights.† A manager's goal of training personnel to the point where they do not require continual monitoring and feedback also calls for classical conditioning.

*In an early demonstration of the power of classical conditioning, John Watson used Pavlovian techniques with an 11-month-old boy to condition a phobic (fear) reaction to white furry objects.[2] The conditioning sequence consisted of pairing the presence of a white lab rat with a loud noise. After a number of pairings, the mere presence of white furry objects (such as a man's white beard) was sufficient to produce a fearful reaction in the boy. In a sense, the boy had developed a seemingly irrational fear of white furry objects. Before Watson could desensitize the boy (for instance, by pairing white furry objects with the presence of food), the boy's mother left town, taking the boy along. Whether the boy may have overcome the phobic reaction on his own is debatable. This case represents one of the first ethically questionable uses of conditioning techniques. After this experience, Watson abandoned research along these lines and went into advertising.

†If you normally drive a car with a manual transmission but later switch to a car with an automatic transmission, you may notice your left foot reflexively stomping on a nonexistent clutch pedal. This is an example of a conditioned response encountered in everyday life.

OBSERVATIONAL LEARNING

Much of the learning that occurs in organizations is based on observation. For example, a new employee may observe a skilled employee performing a task. After simply observing the activities, the new employee is able to model her behavior after her observations. **Observational learning** occurs when a person witnesses the behavior of another and vicariously experiences the consequences of the other person's actions.[3] When tasks are fairly simple, observational learning can be immediate and complete; numerous trials and rehearsals are unnecessary. Furthermore, no apparent reward is administered in observational learning. Quick mastery of behavior and the lack of a visible reward for correct responses are unique to observational learning.

Some contend that the reward in observational learning is purely psychological. In essence, the individual engages in *self-rewarding,* perhaps by congratulating himself or herself each time a correct action occurs. If we accept this suggestion, then we must consider the existence of a competency motive—that is, the desire to feel in control of one's surroundings and, therefore, self-sufficient.[4] Feelings of competency, or **self-efficacy,** can be said to derive from a sense of being able to master a task. In contrast to classical conditioning, in which the learner is totally dependent on someone else to set up the scheme for learning, observational learning is largely self-regulated. The choice of what to attend to, as well as how, when, and where to respond, is a matter of personal choice.

As previously noted, much of the learning that takes place in organizational settings is observational. In addition to informal observational learning, employees sometimes undergo formal training programs that rely on the same process. For example, the use of training films presumes that the observers will imitate the desirable forms of conduct portrayed on the screen. Training manuals and lectures are based on the premise that trainees will absorb, retain, and enact the preferred forms of conduct in their jobs. At Xerox, for example, managerial training seminars often involve learning by watching films or videotapes of desired activities, as well as by role playing. These seminars cover such topics as interviewing, selling, listening, and reading effectively.[5] At a minimum, such training experiences can increase employee awareness of the existence of alternative ways of responding to problem situations.

Many advocates of observational learning contend that it is most successful when external rewards are provided.[6] Thus, they join observational learning principles with conditioning principles and recognize the importance of both individual cognition (that is, mental events) and external rewards.

INSTRUMENTAL, OR OPERANT, CONDITIONING

Much of human behavior in organizations is instrumental, in the sense that people act on their surroundings as well as deliberately move into and out of different situations. In other words, the behavior of employees is often instrumental in bringing about a desired outcome. When a desired outcome is obtained, the likelihood of that behavior recurring is enhanced. These principles are summarized in Thorndike's **Law of Effect,** which states that responses that are followed by a desirable experience will be more likely to occur in the future, while responses that are followed by undesirable experiences will be less likely to occur.[7] More loosely stated, the law proposes that behavior that produces pleasant outcomes is more likely to recur, while behavior that produces unpleasant outcomes is less likely to recur.

In **operant conditioning,** reinforcement is used in conjunction with a response. There are two kinds of reinforcements: positive and negative. **Positive reinforcement** is any event used to increase the frequency of a response (for example, praise from a supervisor for the successful completion of a task). **Negative reinforcement** is any event that, when removed, increases the frequency of a response (for example, a loud buzzer that sounds when a worker fails to monitor a machine's operation and that shuts off only when the worker responds appropriately, or the criticism of a supervisor, which the worker can learn to avoid by performing a task correctly).

Both positive and negative reinforcement can increase the strength and frequency of the behaviors they follow. However, these two types of reinforcement will create work environments with very different characteristics and behavioral dynamics. Positive reinforcement will lead to people performing in order to seek positive outcomes, while negative reinforcement will lead to people responding out of fear and anxiety.

CLASSICAL CONDITIONING VERSUS OPERANT CONDITIONING   Classical conditioning and operant conditioning possess some interesting similarities and differences. The similarities stem from the shared perspective that performance is enhanced by pairing desirable outcomes with behavior and diminished with the removal of such associated outcomes. One major difference between the two types of learning lies in classical conditioning's focus on relatively reflexive and simple responses. By contrast, operant conditioning focuses on voluntary and fairly complex responses. In essence, classical conditioning is concerned with training a person to produce a particular response (that is, a reflexive action), while operant conditioning is concerned with eliciting the response from a person (that is, a voluntary action).

It was once widely believed that the two types of conditioning represented two separate learning processes, with operant conditioning under the control of the central nervous system (that is, primarily the brain itself), and classical conditioning under the control of the other parts of the nervous system (primarily the chains of nerves running along the sides of the spinal cord that influence glandular activity). The correctness of this distinction, however, has been seriously questioned in light of studies suggesting that certain reflexive responses (for example, one's own blood pressure and heart rate) can be brought under voluntary control. Also, many apparently voluntary responses can be classically conditioned.[8] Such evidence suggests that learning may be fundamentally a single process. The two types of conditioning should perhaps be viewed as different manifestations of a more basic phenomenon. It would therefore be inappropriate to state that one type of conditioning provides a superior understanding of learning relative to the other.

USING OPERANT CONDITIONING PRINCIPLES IN ORGANIZATIONAL SETTINGS

B. F. Skinner and his associates have elaborated on the principles of operant conditioning to the point where a systematic approach to the modification of human behavior has now been developed.[9] Although Skinner has not dealt with the topic of organizational behavior in his research, a number of OB researchers have adapted his principles to the field. The application of Skinner's principles to organizational settings is called organizational behavior modification, or **OB Mod.**

ACQUIRING COMPLEX BEHAVIORS: SHAPING

One particularly powerful technique used to modify behavior is termed *shaping*. **Shaping** involves reinforcing small approximations of the final desired behavior. As shaping progresses, the reward is gradually withheld until larger portions of the complete task are performed. Many times, the desired worker behavior involves a set of responses so complex that the complete pattern of correct behavior is not likely to occur all at once. When shaping is used the individual receives reinforcement for small, successive approximations of the desired behavior. For example, learning to operate a complex piece of machinery is likely to take a long period of time. In applying the principle of shaping, a trainer would praise a worker for each gradual improvement in operating the machine. Praise would then be withheld until more complex patterns of behavior were successfully performed.

MAINTAINING DESIRED BEHAVIOR

Because a manager cannot always be available to administer reinforcement, it is highly desirable that subordinates learn to perform at high levels without continual reward. To achieve this, the manager must increase the strength of the desired response to the point where it will not disappear if reinforcement is not provided. The elimination of a response due to the discontinuation of reinforcement is called **extinction.** For desired behaviors, extinction should be avoided, while for inappropriate behaviors, such as tardiness and insubordination, extinction may be actively sought.

A manager wants to increase a desired behavior's **resistance to extinction;** that is, he or she wants to ensure the response's persistence in the absence of reinforcement. Increased resistance to extinction can be achieved through **partial reinforcement.** When partial, or intermittent, reinforcement is used, a response is rewarded in a noncontinuous, or variable, manner. An alternative approach would be to praise a subordinate for every correct response, an approach termed **continuous reinforcement.** Behavior learned under a partial reinforcement scheme is more resistant to extinction than behavior learned under a continuous reinforcement scheme.

OB Focus
Pass GO! and Collect 200 Points

Continental Cablevision, a Pompano Beach, Florida, cable TV operator, has devised a novel management incentive program called Conopoly, a business-related game based on the popular Monopoly board game. Every three months supervisors, managers, and directors receive 200 "Conopoly Reserve Notes," in 5-, 10-, and 20-point denominations, similar to Monopoly money. What's different is that in Conopoly the holders of the financial notes must award them to *other* supervisors and managers in the company. To be awarded these notes, supervisors and managers must exhibit behaviors that support quality business practices, such as enhancing interdepartmental relations and providing superior external and internal customer service. Each note is then inscribed with the names of the persons awarding and receiving the notes. Once a month, supervisors and managers can exchange the notes awarded to them for bogus properties that bear the names of local Continental Cablevision franchises, such as Leisureville or Deerfield Beach. Once they own the property, noteholders can upgrade the property by purchasing pay channels, additional outlets, and digital cable radio service.

To ensure all participants actively recognize and reward good behaviors, any participant who has not awarded 80 percent of the allotted points by the end of each quarter cannot purchase or upgrade any properties without incurring a 50-point fine. Once a month, supervisors and managers can purchase "chance" cards, ranging from a half-day off with pay to a half-day in another department to foster interdepartmental learning.

At year's end, all properties are appraised by a team of Continental Cablevision directors, and the participant with the highest net worth in property and upgrades wins an all-expense-paid four-night trip to Treasure Bay in the Bahamas. Runners-up receive a weekend at a local resort and dinner for two.

So far, the game has been a great success. Participants like it because it fosters positive managerial behaviors and broadens their understanding of the business. Managers contemplate the properties they want to buy and the appropriate upgrades to purchase, given the property demographics. Even more important, managers are more aware of the behaviors they and others exhibit, and positive behaviors receive immediate reinforcement.

Source: Karen L. Webb and Sandra L. O'Neil, "Creative Game Rewards Managers," *HRMagazine,* November 1993, 55–56.

SCHEDULES OF REINFORCEMENT   The scheduling of reinforcement is a particularly important aspect of OB Mod. There are four major kinds of partial reinforcement schedules: (1) fixed interval, (2) variable interval, (3) fixed ratio, and (4) variable ratio. **Interval schedules** reinforce behavior on the basis of time elapsed, while **ratio schedules** are based on the number of times the behavior is performed. In a **fixed schedule,** the amount of time or number of behaviors is specified in advance, while in a **variable schedule,** the amount of time or number of behaviors varies.

Fixed Interval Schedule   A **fixed interval schedule** reinforces individuals for their response after a predetermined period of time has elapsed. Although the response must meet minimal standards, performance beyond the minimum does not lead to greater rewards. Performance under a fixed interval schedule of reinforcement tends to be poor. As one might expect, the lack of a direct relationship between rewards and level of performance leads to only the minimal amount of effort necessary to meet the standard. In essence, a fixed interval scheme offers workers little incentive. Nonetheless, most organizations rely on such a schedule when they compensate employees on a weekly or hourly basis and ignore performance as long as it meets minimal standards.

Research with both animal and human subjects indicates that responses learned under fixed interval schedules of reinforcement diminish or extinguish very rapidly when rewards are withheld.

Variable Interval Schedule   With a **variable interval schedule,** reinforcement is administered after varying periods of time have elapsed. Although the average period of time may be calculated, an individual cannot predict in advance how much time will elapse between reinforcements. (Recall that in a fixed interval scheme, the time period can be predicted precisely.)

As an example of such a scheme, consider a top-level manager's unannounced but fairly regular twice-monthly visits to a loading dock. Although the employees cannot say precisely when the manager will visit, they can nonetheless assume that *on the average* the manager will make an inspection every two weeks or so. Because of the controlling influence of the evaluative experience, it is possible that performance will drop somewhat after reinforcement is administered.

Fixed Ratio Schedule   In a **fixed ratio schedule,** reinforcement is given in exchange for a predetermined number of responses. The most common business use of a fixed ratio schedule is the piece-rate pay scheme. Under such a scheme, fruit pickers might be paid a set amount of money for every 10 pounds of fruit that they harvest. Performance tends to be higher under fixed ratio schedules than it is under interval schedules, but performance is likely to drop temporarily immediately after reinforcement. Thus, on the average, performance is high, but it tends to be variable. In such a scheme, employees are likely to exert effort in spurts in order to attain a given specified level of output.

Variable Ratio Schedule   Under a **variable ratio schedule,** reinforcement is provided after an individual has produced a number of desired responses. The desired number of responses, or standard, however, is not precisely stated, but instead varies around an average number. To receive reinforcement, an individual might have to correctly perform a behavior 18 times in one instance, 8 times the next, 15 times the next, and so on, with the average number being perhaps 12.

Although very few, if any, companies use a variable ratio schedule as their primary wage-payment method, many organizations use the scheme in other ways. For example, managers commonly praise employees via a variable ratio schedule. Thus, employees can rarely be certain beforehand that their actions will be rewarded. Other examples include the intermittent use of cash bonuses, public recognition, and other awards for good performance.

COMPARING SCHEDULES OF REINFORCEMENT   When these methods of reinforcement are compared (Table 5.1), the variable ratio schedule is clearly the most effective in producing a consistently high level of performance. Behaviors rewarded under a variable ratio schedule are also the most resistant to extinction. As two illustrations, consider gambling and intimidating behavior. In gambling (say, playing slot machines or betting on horse races), one is rewarded on a variable ratio schedule in that one only wins occasionally. Despite

■ **TABLE 5.1**
A COMPARISON OF SCHEDULES OF PARTIAL REINFORCEMENT

	Fixed Interval	**Variable Interval**	**Fixed Ratio**	**Variable Ratio**
Form of Reward	Reward after a specific time period	Reward after a varying time period	Reward after a specific number of responses	Reward after an average number of responses
Influence on Behavior	Mediocre performance	Fairly high, somewhat unstable performance	Fairly high and stable performance	Very high performance
Influence on Extinction	Little resistance to extinction	Somewhat resistant to extinction	Little resistance to extinction	Very resistant to extinction
Organizational Examples	Hourly and weekly pay schemes	Unannounced inspections, informal appraisals of performance	Piece-rate pay schemes, bonuses	Awards, praise, bonuses tied to variable standard of output

Source: Adapted from *Introduction to Organizational Behavior* by R. M. Steers, p. 137. Copyright © 1981 by Scott, Foresman and Company. Reprinted by permission of HarperCollins College Publishers.

the fact that in the long run gambling does not pay, the activity has an addictive quality in that it is always possible that the next play will be the lucky one that pays off.

An example of a negative behavior that is rewarded on a variable ratio schedule is a senior employee's threats and intimidating behavior. As most young managers find, it is difficult to ignore such posturing. By *occasionally* giving in to the angry senior employee, however, a manager is rewarding the employee on a variable ratio schedule. A likely consequence of such intermittent rewarding is that the employee will persist in his intimidating behaviors, given that he cannot be certain beforehand whether a particular instance will be the "lucky one" that pays off (in an analogous fashion to gambling). In general, a variable ratio reward schedule will enhance a response's resistance to extinction.

By contrast, the fixed interval schedule is the least effective scheme when judged against the criteria of performance enhancement and resistance to extinction. Perhaps because of their ease of administration, fixed interval schedules of reinforcement are the most commonly used in organizations. Relative to the fixed interval and variable ratio schedules, the two other schedules (fixed ratio and variable interval) can be judged as intermediate in effectiveness.

RULES FOR APPLYING OPERANT CONDITIONING PRINCIPLES

Hamner and Hamner have outlined a number of rules for application of the principles of operant conditioning.[10] If a manager follows these rules in dealing with subordinates, their performance should be enhanced. With some modification, the rules offered by Hamner and Hamner can be summarized as follows:

1. *Use differential rewarding.* Many managers try to treat all subordinates alike. Although this sounds noble, it tends to encourage mediocrity. When all employees receive equal rewards, superior performers begin to feel that their efforts are unappreciated, while poorer performers recognize that they will not be penalized for minimal effort. In response, over time, most above-average performers will drop their performance to the minimal level. A few superior performers may, of course, persist, but most will lower their efforts to the level that they feel equals their rewards.

   When rewards are commensurate with performance, however, subordinates receive a quite different message. Superior performers get the signal that their efforts are valued, and potentially high performers are encouraged to try harder.

2. *Identify valued rewards for individuals.* If a manager hopes to influence an employee's behavior through the use of rewards, the rewards must have value to the employee. One of the best ways to obtain such information is simply to ask employees what rewards they would like to receive. Younger workers may prefer more paid vacation days or greater involvement in decision making, while older workers may choose better medical insurance or a larger contribution to their pension plan.

3. *Instruct subordinates on how rewards are tied to performance.* In order for operant conditioning principles to be maximally effective, employees must clearly understand how rewards and performance are connected. When specific information is lacking, subordinates may try to second-guess their manager's intentions by constructing their own imagined system of rewards. Thus, much confusion and counterproductivity can be avoided if a manager clearly states goals for performance and explains how rewards will be related to performance.

4. *Provide informative feedback on performance.* In order to meet their manager's standards of performance, employees must have instructive feedback. Their manager must evaluate and interpret their performance for them, indicating how well or how poorly they are doing and suggesting specific ways to improve. In addition to providing guidance, feedback can also serve as an additional form of reinforcement.

SETTING UP AN OB MOD PROGRAM

Advocates of OB Mod principles have laid out five basic steps necessary to establish on OB Mod program (Figure 5.2).[11] First, performance must be defined in purely behavioral terms. This means that performance must be reducible to observable and measurable events. Second, an estimate of typical or baseline performance is taken by conducting an assessment of performance by a simple tallying. The goal of this tallying is to obtain an objective measure of the current level of performance. The third step involves the establishment of specific, reasonable performance goals for each employee and communicating these goals to the employee. The fourth step consists of each employee performing his or her job while keeping personal records of performance. The

FIGURE 5.2
ESSENTIAL STEPS IN SETTING UP AN OB MOD PROGRAM

1. Define Target Behavior
2. Measure Frequency of Behavior
3. Establish and Communicate Behavior Goals
4. Monitor Behavior
5. Administer Rewards

employees' maintenance of their own performance records provides constant self-feedback. Finally, the fifth step, the administration of rewards (such as praise, recognition, or bonuses), is considered the key element in OB Mod. Positive reinforcement from the supervisor is intended to strengthen the desired actions, while withholding reinforcement is intended to extinguish undesirable action.

DOES OB MOD WORK?

Studies of the effectiveness of OB Mod programs have generally indicated that they constitute a useful approach to improving employee performance. In a review of research on OB Mod programs, Hamner and Hamner identified ten organizations that had experimented with OB Mod.[12] In nine of the ten cases, the introduction of OB Mod was judged as having had a positive effect. Many other recent examples (some involving control or comparison groups) also point to the success of OB Mod. Most instances in which OB Mod was applied shared several common characteristics. The typical OB Mod program attempts to improve either the performance or the attendance of blue-collar workers by providing immediate feedback about behavior and using praise or recognition from superiors as reinforcers. Interestingly, the programs do not commonly use money as a reinforcer of superior performance. More typically, such social rewards as praise and recognition are used. The use of these less costly rewards may be partially responsible for the appeal of OB Mod to many managers.

CONTROVERSIES SURROUNDING OB MOD

Although much of the available evidence suggests that many OB Mod programs have been successful, there is a good deal of controversy surrounding the application of operant principles in organizations.[13]

Opponents of OB Mod accuse it of being manipulative, charging that OB Mod programs suggest a deliberate and calculated effort to control the behavior of others, sometimes at the cost of the individuals who are being controlled. Opponents argue that OB Mod smacks of a "Big Brother" approach to management, in which an all-knowing, all-powerful overseer attempts to maintain control and forced dependency by unilaterally defining the rules of the game.

Advocates of OB Mod acknowledge that the potential for misuse does exist, but they contend that good judgment is likely to prevail because deception and exploitation are apt to meet with worker resistance. Advocates of operant conditioning point out that, although the term *manipulation* may have negative connotations, it is ultimately a manager's responsibility to ensure that employee behavior contributes to the larger mission of an enterprise. Thus, managers must be aware of the factors that influence employee behavior and use them to fulfill their responsibilities to the company.

Another criticism of OB Mod is that it is not an original technique for managing employees. In some respects, OB Mod has much in common with Frederick W. Taylor's principles of scientific management (see Chapter 1). For example, OB Mod programs require closer supervision of employees, more specific definitions of job activities, frequent evaluation and feedback, and the distribution of rewards based on output. The reliance of OB Mod on such rewards as praise and recognition can also be viewed as merely taking a page out of the human relations approach to management. At the least, it is fair to say that the OB Mod approach does borrow from other traditions in the field of organizational behavior.

An added criticism of OB Mod surrounds the faithfulness of OB Mod programs to operant principles. Many programs employ only a watered-down version of the principles of operant conditioning. For example, in programs relying heavily on self-feedback (in which employees maintain their own performance records), an alternative explanation of positive performance results—one based on the notion of self-reinforcement—can be posited.[14]

Conversely, in programs that are in closer conformity with operant conditioning principles, unpleasant questions arise as to whether an organization should be condoning such programs. For example, the following OB Mod program was designed to reduce high absenteeism in a manufacturing facility.[15] On every day an employee attended work, he or she drew a card from a deck of playing cards. After a week's time, each employee would have drawn five cards, a poker hand. The employee with the best hand received, say, a $40 bonus. This program employs the principle of intermittent rewards using a variable ratio schedule. The reward is both externally administered and contingent on behavior. In fact, such programs do reduce absenteeism rates. Unfortunately, they also raise two questions: (1) should an organization endorse a form of gambling, the aim of which is to develop an addictive behavior in employees? and (2) should employees be enticed to work at a presumably distasteful job that most likely is responsible for the high absenteeism? In short, it might be more appropriate and more compassionate to first investigate the *causes* of high absenteeism and then remedy the causes by modifying the job, rather than focusing on the superficial manifestation of an underlying problem.

Operant conditioning has also been criticized for ignoring the importance of internally mediated rewards, for example, the motivation that results from the inherent enjoyment of performing certain attractive tasks. Deci suggests that the emphasis of OB Mod on externally administered, contingent rewards focuses attention on only one of the important features of motivation.[16] Furthermore, he argues that the use of such rewards for performing tasks that are intrinsically rewarding can undercut the motivation that a task may offer.

A final criticism of OB Mod is its lack of concern for mental processes. Because operant conditioning grew out of early work with animals and partly because of a reaction against early research attempts to study mental events, advocates of OB Mod have downplayed the importance of dealing with thought processes. To be sure, cognitive experiences are an important aspect of being human that cannot be totally ignored in any complete explanation of employee behavior.

THE ROLE OF PUNISHMENT

So far, we have focused primarily on the use of reward as a means of altering behavior, but the use of punishment must also be considered (Table 5.2). For purposes of discussion, we will define **punishment** as an undesirable event that follows a behavior it intends to eliminate. Punishment's role in shaping employee behavior is quite complex. Often, in response to its administration, an employee will not eliminate the undesirable behavior, but instead will seek other ways of engaging in the behavior as well as ways of getting even with the punisher. In most cases, punishment leads to only a temporary suppression of the punished behavior. Consequently, any proposal to use punishment must be carefully thought out.

TABLE 5.2
FREQUENTLY USED REWARDS AND PUNISHMENTS

Rewards	Punishments
Bonuses	Reprimands
Promotions	Oral warnings
Pay increases	Ostracism
Vacation time	Probation
Time off	Criticism from superiors
Use of company car	Suspension
Awards	Citations
Praise and recognition	Disciplinary hearing
Increase in formal responsibility	Written warning
Increase in department budget	Pay cut
	Demotion
Sense of accomplishment	Reduced authority
Self-recognition	Undesired transfer
	Termination

ALTERNATIVES TO PUNISHMENT

Before using punishment to eliminate undesired behavior, managers should consider several other strategies. One alternative is to rearrange the work setting so that the undesired response cannot occur. For example, if unauthorized individuals are using a copying machine, the installation of a lock and a meter will prevent further misuse.

A second strategy is extinction. As noted earlier, a response can be extinguished if the reward with which it is usually paired is eliminated. Identifying the reward that undesired behavior generates for an employee is often not too difficult. In some instances, the reward may actually be the satisfaction of knowing that a peer or supervisor has been annoyed. Extinction in such cases might consist of ignoring the irksome behavior, thereby reducing the probability that it will recur.

To be sure, ignoring undesirable behaviors is a form of inaction. However, many managers will attest that doing nothing about certain minor problem situations can sometimes be the best way to deal with them. For example, a problem may arise that seems to demand that some form of elaborate and detailed managerial action be taken (for example, an employee may frequently complain that a company policy is unfair). Sometimes, merely postponing discussion of the problem will coincide with the elimination of the origin of the problem (for instance, a problem employee may quit) or the diminution of its importance over time.

EFFECTIVE PUNISHMENT

In some instances, none of these alternatives may be feasible. It may be too costly or physically impossible to change a situation to prevent the undesired behavior. Possibly the undesired behavior may provide its own reward and thus resist extinction. Or the undesired behavior may be so serious that it warrants some form of punishment. Advocates of the *reasoned* use of punishment contend that punishment can work under very specific conditions.[17] The features of effective punishment in the workplace are similar to those we have all encountered in daily life. For example, we have all learned to be careful in dealing with electricity and fire without personally resenting them. We accept the punishing aspects of natural forces due to certain common features: The punishment is impersonal, fairly immediate and strong, reliable over time, uniform from person to person, and specifically produced in response to an individual's own actions. Figure 5.3 lists the features of effective punishment.

Effective punishment in an organizational setting should possess the same attributes. The recipient should recognize that the punishment is not directed toward his or her character or sense of self-worth. The punishment should be given as soon as possible after the undesired behavior. It should be sufficiently severe that it cannot be ignored. It should be administered with consistency across instances and across people. Finally, it should be extremely clear that the punishment was caused by the specific actions of the transgressor. As a result, the punishment is informative in that the recipient can see the connection between behavior and punishment.

FIGURE 5.3
FEATURES OF EFFECTIVE PUNISHMENT

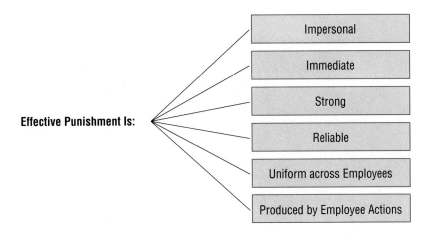

In organizations, many factors undermine these principles and thereby reduce the effectiveness of punishment. For example, some managers may ignore an occasional transgression in the hopes of extinguishing it. But as a result, they may seem inconsistent in dealing with the undesired behavior, and the occasional attention that they do give may seem capricious. Some managers may delay administering punishment due to indecision. Others may feel guilty after punishing an employee. If a manager then responds to his or her guilt feelings by showering the employee with positive attention, the intended effects of the punishment may be greatly diluted.

GUIDELINES FOR ADMINISTERING DISCIPLINE

Given that some situations require the use of discipline, the question is how to deliver it and in what form. The answer depends on several major considerations. An important one is a supervisor's personal style of leadership. Leadership style (see Chapter 10) influences both the preferred method of discipline and the practicality of other methods. For example, a manager who subscribes to the human relations approach may prefer to avoid punishment and in fact may be unable to enforce a strict approach.

Employees' backgrounds also determine which approaches to punishment will be most effective. Highly educated employees or professionals may object to a strict approach, while blue-collar workers might readily accept the same approach. The size of an organization is another influence on the nature of discipline. Larger organizations have more formal systems of discipline. Given the difficulties inherent in coordinating larger enterprises, employees are often willing to accept a more formal system of discipline.

An Inside Look
An Effective Punishment Strategy for Spa Mechanics

The inspiration for Barry Fribush's business, Bubbling Bath Spa and Tub Works, Inc.—and for its style of managing workers—came from his experience as a customer. In the late 1970s, Fribush, who was then running a printing business and advertising agency, bought a hot tub. "It was terrible," he reports. "It kept breaking down, and there was no easy way to get it repaired. I figured I could do a better job selling and servicing them."

When Fribush founded Bubbling Bath, he set out to make sure that his customers wouldn't have to share his negative experiences. Besides stocking top-quality spas and hiring experienced mechanics, Fribush had to consider how to ensure that the mechanics were providing the best possible service.

A key part of his approach was a rational punishment for doing poor work: If a mechanic has to go back to a customer to redo a job, the mechanic doesn't get paid for second call. Instead of earning a generous $25 an hour, he or she earns nothing. Mechanics are aware of this policy in advance, so they can control the consequences of their behavior. The policy also means that the consequences of poor work are immediate and consistent among mechanics.

Perhaps it is because this policy meets the criteria of effective punishment that it has worked so well. According to Fribush, when he started Bubbling Bath, an average of 30 percent of all repair jobs were callbacks. Since the company instituted the policy of no pay for redoing a job, callbacks have almost been eliminated. Furthermore, customer referrals helped place Bubbling Bath on *Inc.* magazine's listing of the fastest-growing small private companies in 1989.

Source: Paul B. Brown, "For You, Our Valued Customer," *Inc.,* January 1990, 108–109.

PROGRESSIVE DISCIPLINE

Discipline should ultimately be a tool to improve performance. Its foremost goal should be to *change* behavior rather than simply to punish it. One very popular approach is **progressive discipline,** a system in which penalties are increased according to the frequency and severity of infractions. The rules are known in advance and are imposed objectively. Repeated transgressions ultimately lead to an employee's termination. A positive feature of progressive discipline is that it provides individuals with the opportunity to alter their own behavior; that is, it gives a person another chance if the infraction is not severe. Punishment is designed to be informative and to lead to a modification of the undesired behavior.

Progressive discipline programs consist of a series of steps that gradually impose increasingly severe penalties. For example, consider an employee who is repeatedly late to work by one or two hours. With a progressive discipline scheme, the employee would receive an informal verbal warning from the supervisor for the first offense. A second offense within a specified period of time would result in a meeting between the employee, the immediate supervisor, and a shift supervisor at which the employee would receive a formal oral warning. If the employee violated the same rule again, she would receive a formal written warning that would become part of her permanent record. A fourth infraction would lead to the employee being suspended without pay for the remainder of the workday. This fourth step might be coupled with the technique of mailing a letter to the employee's spouse. The letter would describe the seriousness of the situation (that is, the danger of the employee being ultimately terminated) and seek to enlist the spouse's cooperation in "turning around" the employee. If after all this, the employee was late to work on a fifth occasion, she would be terminated.

It should be noted that at every step in this process the employee is aware that a company policy is being enforced and that the superior's actions are not based on personal malice. Another benefit of such a program is that it provides guidance to supervisors about how to deal with infractions of company rules. A supervisor need not debate whether or how to discipline employees because the course of action is clearly spelled out. Unions are also more likely to accept the outcome of progressive discipline because union stewards often attend disciplinary meetings and are kept informed of the disciplinary actions.

Most progressive discipline programs can be tailored to the severity of the offense. For such serious offenses as gambling in the locker room or fighting, the discipline might begin at step four (suspension). For an unconscionable offense, such as theft of a large sum of money from the organization, discipline might skip to step five (termination).

Many companies post a list of how various infractions will be treated within a progressive discipline scheme (Table 5.3). For example, category A offenses might consist of such minor infractions as tardiness, category B offenses might cover such actions as sleeping on the job, and category C offenses might include major transgressions. All employees would understand that each category is associated with a different step in the progressive discipline program.

CONDUCTING A DISCIPLINARY MEETING

One of the most distasteful tasks a supervisor can face is conducting a meeting devoted to disciplining a subordinate. Given the emotions involved, and win/lose implications for both parties, it is easy to understand why some supervisors are reluctant to administer punishment.

From the reports of actual experiences of supervisors, there are certain ground rules that can make disciplinary meetings more effective.

1. *Have a private meeting with the offender.* There's an old saying of managers, "Praise in public, punish in private." In the interests of protecting the individual's dignity, it is necessary that criticism and punishment be administered behind closed doors.

2. *Don't lose your cool.* Of course, this is more easily said than done. If it becomes impossible for the supervisor to control rage during a disciplinary meeting, it is perhaps best to break it off and set another time to complete the meeting. Words that are exchanged in anger are invariably regretted later on. If a subordinate displays anger, it is important not to respond in kind, but instead to remain calm.

3. *Be certain of your facts.* Some supervisors jump the gun when disciplining subordinates in that they are prepared to discipline an individual (for a variety of reasons) but do not have the facts to back up their charges. For example, imagine a supervisor who starts disciplinary action against an employee who is late returning from lunch. A subsequent investigation might

■ **TABLE 5.3**
SUGGESTED STEPS FOR DISCIPLINARY ACTION

A. *Offenses resulting in first, oral warning; second, written warning; and third, immediate discharge*

    1. Uncivil conduct

    2. Tardiness

    3. Failure to punch the time clock

    4. Foul language

    5. Incompetence or inefficiency in performing job

    6. Unauthorized absence

B. *Offenses resulting in first, written warning; then, immediate discharge*

    1. Sleeping on the job

    2. Gambling

    3. Negligent use of property

    4. Failure to comply with published rules, regulations, or executive order

    5. Failing to report to work without notification for one or two days

C. *Offenses resulting in immediate discharge*

    1. Theft

    2. Destruction of property

    3. Fighting

    4. Use of drugs

    5. Gross insubordination

    6. Conduct unbecoming an employee

    7. Falsifying time cards

    8. Falsification of information in applying for position

    9. Failing to report to work without notification for three or more days

    10. Failure to maintain current license or certification

    11. Refusal to work

    12. Actions that endanger the safety, health, or well-being of others

Source: R. L. Oberle, "Administering Disciplinary Actions," *Personnel Journal,* 1978, 30.

reveal that the employee was late to work because she had to take her sick child to the hospital.

4. *Select an appropriate punishment.* The severity of the punishment should match the severity of the offense. It is perhaps best if a progressive discipline system has been previously worked out. Such a system can then be consulted when deciding on the most appropriate action.

5. *Accomplish the following three objectives: (a) state what is wrong, (b) state what you expect, and (c) state what happens if you don't get what you expect.* When stating the problem, your expectations, and the possible consequences, it is important to be very clear and specific. It is likely to be a mistake to diminish the seriousness of a problem in the mere hope of social harmony. During the course of the meeting, the employee should be asked to indicate that he or she understands your expectations and the possible consequences of further infractions.

6. *Keep records.* It is almost a cliché to say that employees are becoming more litigious. Because you may be required to present evidence in court or at a grievance hearing, it is essential that records be maintained on the nature and content of all disciplinary meetings. One advantage to keeping records is that it will add strength to your case if your actions are ever contested. When keeping records, it is best to follow the rules of journalism: Answer the questions of who, what, when, where, and how as they pertain to a behavioral incident.

TERMINATION

CONDUCTING A TERMINATION MEETING

Managers rarely discharge an employee, primarily because they find the psychological pressures of doing so too unpleasant. Some managers will try to delegate the responsibility to someone else in the organization, such as a personnel officer. However, it is more professionally correct for the immediate supervisor to conduct the termination meeting. If the discharge does not need to occur immediately, it is recommended that the meeting be scheduled for the end of the workday or at the end of the week.[18] Because these are times when other employees are usually gone, it saves the parties involved from possible embarrassment. It also avoids the potential problems that can arise when a disgruntled employee remains on the premises with a long workday left to be completed.

The reasons for the discharge should be laid out within the first few minutes of the meeting. This is not a time to get involved in an argument over details. The finality of the decision must be conveyed. It is also not a good time to lecture the employee on his or her character flaws or to attempt to play psychotherapist. The session need not last longer than 10 minutes—in fact, the longer the meeting continues, the more likely the parties are to say something they may later regret.

Following a discharge meeting, it is recommended that the matter not be discussed with employees who are not in a "need to know" position. This may seem counterproductive—after all, if the discharge were just, wouldn't it be best to emphasize that the person had been terminated and that justice had prevailed? But given the litigious nature of employer–employee relations, it is best that nothing be said that could be construed as criticism or defamation of the discharged employee's character.

Consider the following case of the manager of a Sears, Roebuck auto-repair department who resigned after being charged with stealing parts and money from his employer. He gave his resignation in exchange for the employer's promise not to take the case to court. (It's a fairly common practice in such instances to offer employees a choice between resignation and prosecution.) When the discharged employee's subordinates demanded to know why he had been terminated, the employer revealed that the supervisor had resigned rather than be prosecuted and further implied that he was guilty of various criminal acts. When the former supervisor learned that he had been labeled a thief by his former employer, he sued for slander (recall that he resigned but did not sign a confession or admit any wrongdoing) and won.[19]‡ In hindsight, it would have been wiser for the employer not to have discussed the reason for the termination with the remaining employees. One disadvantage of refusing to discuss termination, however, is that damage can be done to morale if employees suspect that their employer dismisses workers arbitrarily.

INDIRECT APPROACHES

A fair number of organizations rely on indirect approaches to termination. One such approach is the indefinite layoff, in which a worker is told that he or she will be recalled when business picks up. While the worker is laid off, however, the employer redefines the job by changing the work process in some manner. This redefinition is intended to disqualify the former jobholder from reapplying for the new job. Because the process of indefinite layoff is done in slow steps, it minimizes worker awareness and possible protest.

Another indirect (and likewise questionable) approach to termination is to force an employee to resign by reducing his or her responsibilities. This approach is more commonly taken with management-level employees. Being reassigned to a job in the corporation's equivalent of Siberia or having various perquisites taken away are fairly clear signs that a resignation is expected.

Another example of an indirect approach taken with management-level employees is to ask a manager to prepare a letter of resignation, ostensibly as a show of good faith and in the hopes of extracting a quicker decision from superiors on a promotion or reappointment. The employer then turns around and actually accepts the resignation even though it was previously implied that the offer to resign would be rejected at a higher level.

Ideally, an organization should rely less on external devices for disciplining its employees and more on an employee's own self-discipline. Developing the desire for self-discipline and the identification of individuals who possess this desire will be topics of discussion throughout the remaining chapters.

SUMMARY

1. Explain what learning is and why managers need to understand the learning process.

Learning is a fairly permanent change in behavior that occurs as a result of experience. It is a complex and never-ending process for all employees that can greatly affect both performance and motivation. Consequently, a manager who understands the learning process can use its principles to guide employee behavior and achieve organizational goals.

2. Describe the process of classical conditioning and cite several examples of this form of learning in the workplace.

In classical conditioning, an unconditioned stimulus is repeatedly paired with a neutral stimulus until the neutral stimulus alone can elicit the same response

‡ The settlement was for $50,000.

that was evoked by the unconditioned stimulus. When this occurs, the neutral stimulus is termed a conditioned stimulus and the response, a conditioned response. Many jobs require conditioned responses. For example, a truck driver's ability to apply the brakes quickly and firmly depends on a conditioned response to a conditioned stimulus, such as a warning light. A manager's attempt to train personnel to the point where they no longer require continual monitoring may also involve classical conditioning.

3. Tell what observational learning is and how it occurs in the workplace.

Observational learning occurs when a person witnesses the behavior of another and vicariously experiences the consequence of that person's behavior. This form of learning is very common in organizations. For example, a new employee may observe an experienced employee performing a task and then model her own behavior on the observations. Employees who attend training programs also learn from observation by viewing films, reading manuals, and attending lectures.

4. Discuss the nature of operant conditioning and cite four rules for applying operant conditioning principles to enhance employee performance.

Operant conditioning is based on the notion that behavior is a function of its outcomes. Thus, behavior that produces a pleasant outcome is more likely to be repeated, while behavior that produces an unpleasant outcome is likely not to recur. To use the principles of operant conditioning to encourage desired behavior in the workplace, managers should follow four basic rules: (1) Match the reward to the performance, so that superior performers receive greater rewards. (2) Match the reward to the individual's preferences. (3) Be sure that subordinates understand how rewards are tied to performance. (4) Give employees informative feedback about their performance.

5. Summarize the advantages and disadvantages of OB Mod.

Organizational behavior modification, or OB Mod, is the application of the principles of operant conditioning to organizational settings in the attempt to alter employee behavior. The typical OB Mod intervention seeks to improve either the performance or the attendance of blue-collar workers by providing immediate feedback about behavior and by employing praise or recognition as reinforcers. Studies have indicated that such programs are generally quite effective. Nonetheless, OB Mod has many critics who contend that it is manipulative, unoriginal, and of questionable faithfulness to true operant conditioning principles, and that it ignores the role of mental processes in behavior.

6. Analyze the role of punishment in shaping employee behavior.

Punishment is an undesirable event that follows a behavior it intends to eliminate. Its role in shaping employee behavior is quite complex and its administration often does not eliminate the undesirable behavior. Consequently, any proposal to use punishment should be carefully thought out in light of the available alternatives. For punishment to be effective, (1) the recipient must recognize that it is not directed at his or her character or self-worth, (2) it should be given as soon as possible after the undesired behavior, (3) it should be sufficiently severe that it cannot be ignored, (4) it should be administered consistently across instances and people, and (5) it should be extremely clear that the punishment was caused by the specific actions of the transgressor. Ultimately, punishment should be used as a tool to change behavior and improve performance rather than as an end in itself. A well-planned progressive discipline program, consisting of a series of steps imposing increasingly severe penalties, can often accomplish this purpose.

KEY TERMS

Learning	Extinction
Classical conditioning	Resistance to extinction
Unconditioned stimulus	Partial reinforcement
Unconditioned response	Continuous reinforcement
Conditioned response	Interval schedule
Conditioned stimulus	Ratio schedule
Observational learning	Fixed schedule
Self-efficacy	Variable schedule
Law of Effect	Fixed interval schedule
Operant conditioning	Variable interval schedule
Positive reinforcement	Fixed ratio schedule
Negative reinforcement	Variable ratio schedule
OB Mod	Punishment
Shaping	Progressive discipline

REVIEW AND DISCUSSION QUESTIONS

1. American corporations spend an estimated $60 billion annually on employee training. In your opinion, why are businesses willing to spend so much money on educating workers?

2. Some people contend that the principles of classical conditioning are more applicable to animals in laboratories than to humans in the workplace. Do you agree or disagree? Why?

3. Describe a situation in which you learned a new skill through observation. In what other ways might you have picked up the same skill? Compare the strengths and weaknesses of each approach, select the most effective one, and defend your choice.

4. In your opinion, is the assigning of grades at the end of each school term a form of operant conditioning? Why or why not?

5. Imagine that your school is planning to institute an OB Mod program to reduce tardiness for early morning classes. How would you recommend that such a program be set up? What reinforcers would you suggest? Do you think that such a program would be effective in reducing tardiness? Would you participate in it yourself? Explain your responses.

6. Some people contend that because its negative side effects may outweigh its potential benefits, punishment should not be used in the modern workplace. Furthermore, they claim that a manager who is truly on top of things

need not fall back on punishment in order to guide subordinates. Do you agree with this position? Why or why not?

CRITICAL INCIDENT

The Wrong Reinforcement?

Royal Coach Corporation is a large manufacturer of school buses and related small vehicles that are used by tour groups, airport shuttle services, and so forth. A large warehouse operation is crucial to the success of the production process as many different parts are stored and then moved to the line as needed.

Charles Hodges has worked for Royal for almost four years. He is 26, single, and lives at home with his parents. His job in the warehouse involves moving raw materials to various assembly lines as they are needed. His work is steady and he uses both a forklift and motorized hand truck to transport parts.

Charles has had a history of sporadic absences from work over the past few years. These absences usually last two or three days at a time. Charles has also been late to work many times.

It is after 7:00 A.M. and Charles has not shown up for work. The warehouse crew is shorthanded once again. Charles's supervisor pulls his file while trying to decide what to do. This is the fourth supervisor for whom Charles has worked while at Royal. Each of the previous supervisors had placed written comments about Charles in the folder. Each had noted that after several periods of being absent, Charles would be called in for a meeting and promise to improve his attendance. Thereafter, he usually did.

Charles was generally a good worker. He did his job, but was not exceptional. He earned good wages and always seemed to have plenty of spending money. Two of his previous supervisors were fairly laid-back and permitted their employees to do their jobs with a minimum of supervision. A third was more autocratic and provided close supervision. He was the type who offered both help and criticism, and monitored everyone. According to the attendance record, Charles had missed more days under this supervisor than under any of the others.

It appeared to the present supervisor that Charles might be starting another period of absenteeism. He had already missed one day that week. The supervisor decided that something had to be done.

QUESTIONS

1. What principles of reinforcement have Charles's previous supervisors used? Why hasn't this reinforcement been effective?

2. What type of behavior modification program might the present supervisor try to use?

3. If a behavior modification approach does not seem to work, what should the supervisor do?

EXPERIENTIAL EXERCISE

Handling Discipline—A Role Play

I. Introduction   The text discussion focused on the importance of reinforcing appropriate behavior and recognizing the need to confront actions that are ill-suited to the workplace. It is often easier for a manager to reinforce or reward positive actions than it is to discipline or punish negative ones. This activity provides you with an opportunity to apply some of these concepts in a no-risk situation. What you learn from the experience will enable you to be more skillful when you must handle a real situation.

II. Procedure

1. Your instructor may assign individuals or ask for volunteers to play the three roles in this situation. All others in the class may function as observers.

2. Everyone should read the following description of the situation:

    Jim Turner and Bill Evans, mechanics in the service department, had been told to clean some large service equipment in the rear of the garage. When their supervisor checked on them, they were tossing pennies at a line they had drawn on the floor, clearly gambling. This is the second problem this week with Turner, a new employee who has been with the company only eight months. On the other occasion, he was found sitting in the restroom looking at a comic book when he should have been putting away his tools and reading a manual he was asked to look over. Bill Evans has been with the company for seven years and is considered one of the most reliable and hard-working employees. He has never given any trouble.

3. The two persons playing the roles of Jim and Bill can begin to enact their parts (tossing pennies at a line, and so on). The individual who is playing the part of their supervisor should think of responses to the following questions. The supervisor should then begin the role play at the point of walking in and discovering the gambling. The supervisor's role play should demonstrate how he or she chose to answer these questions.

    a. How would you handle this situation?

    b. What penalties would you impose?

    c. Would you impose the same penalty for each employee?

4. Continue the role play until everyone understands what is going to occur in terms of any sanctions. When that point is reached, the activity can be terminated.

III. Discussion

1. How do the observers feel about the way the situation was handled?

2. Do the observers feel that a reasonable conclusion was reached?

3. Analyze any face-saving behaviors that were evidenced.

4. How did the supervisor feel in dealing with the situation? How did Jim and Bill feel?

5. Did the supervisor attempt to apply progressive discipline concepts in this situation? What were they?

6. Is a disciplinary meeting warranted? With whom and why? How should it be handled?

Source: Written by Bruce Kemelgor, University of Louisville; used by permission.

NOTES

1. G.H. Bower and E.R. Hilgard, *Theories of Learning* (Englewood Cliffs, N.J.: Prentice-Hall, 1981).

2. J.B. Watson and R. Rayner, "Conditioned Emotional Reactions," *Journal of Experimental Psychology* 3 (1920): 1–14.

3. A. Bandura, *Social Learning Theory* (Englewood Cliffs, N.J.: Prentice-Hall, 1977).

4. R.W. White, "Motivation Reconsidered: The Concept of Competence," *Psychological Review* 66 (1959): 297–333.

5. T.J. Peters and R.H. Waterman, Jr., *In Search of Excellence: Lessons from America's Best-Run Companies* (New York: Harper and Row, 1982).

6. A.P. Goldstein and M. Sorcher, *Changing Supervisor Behavior* (New York: Pergamon, 1974).

7. E.L. Thorndike, *Animal Intelligence* (New York: Macmillan, 1911).

8. N.E. Miller and B.R. Dvorkin, "Visceral Learning," in *Contemporary Trends in Cardiovascular Psychophysiology,* ed. P.A. Obrist et al. (Chicago: Aldine, 1973); B.T. Engel, "Operant Conditioning of Cardiac Function: A Status Report," *Psychophysiology* 9 (1972): 161–177.

9. B.F. Skinner, *The Behavior of Organisms* (New York: Appleton, 1938); L.W. Fredericksen, *Handbook of Organizational Behavior Management* (New York: Wiley, 1982); J.L. Komaki, "Applied Behavior Analysis and Organizational Behavior: Reciprocal Influence of the Two Fields," in *Research in Organizational Behavior,* vol. 8, ed. B.M. Staw and L.L. Cummings (Greenwich, Conn.: JAI, 1986).

10. W.C. Hamner and E.P. Hamner, "Behavior Modification on the Bottom Line," *Organizational Dynamics* 4 (1976): 3–21.

11. W.C. Hamner, "Worker Motivation Programs: The Importance of Climate, Structure, and Performance Consequences," in *Contemporary Problems in Personnel,* ed. W.C. Hamner and F.L. Schmidt (Chicago: St. Clair Press, 1977); F. Luthans and R. Kreitner, *Organizational Behavior Modification* (Glenview, Ill.: Scott, Foresman, 1975).

12. Hamner and Hamner, "Behavior Modification on the Bottom Line."

13. E.A. Locke, "The Myths of Behavior Mod in Organizations," *Academy of Management Review* 2 (1977): 543–553.

14. F.H. Kanfer and P. Karoly, "Self-control: A Behavioristic Excursion into the Lion's Den," *Behavior Therapy* 3 (1972): 398–416.

15. E. Pedalino and V. Gamboa, "Behavior Modification and Absenteeism: Intervention in One Industrial Setting," *Journal of Applied Psychology* 59 (1974): 694–698.

16. E.L. Deci, "The Effects of Contingent and Noncontingent Rewards and Controls on Intrinsic Motivation," *Organizational Behavior and Human Performance* 8 (1972): 217–229; P.C. Jordan, "Effects of Extrinsic Reward on Intrinsic Motivation: A Field Experiment," *Academy of Management Journal* 29 (1986): 405–411; U.J. Wiersma, "The Effects of Extrinsic Rewards in Intrinsic Motivation: A Meta-analysis," *Journal of Occupational and Organizational Psychology* 65 (1992): 101–114; W.E. Scott, J.L. Farh, and P.M. Podsakoff, "The Effects of 'Intrinsic' and 'Extrinsic' Reinforcement Contingencies on Task Behavior," *Organizational Behavior and Human Decision Processes* 41 (1988): 405–425.

17. R.L. Solomon, "Punishment," *American Psychologist* 19 (1964): 239–253.

18. R.D. Buchanan, "How to Apply Constructive Discipline," *Food Service Marketing* 40 (October 1978): 63–67.

19. *Haddad v. Sears, Roebuck and Co.,* 526 F.2d 83 (6th Cir. 1975).

6

Work is the price you pay
for money.
— **Anonymous**

If hard work were such a
wonderful thing, surely the
rich would have kept it all to
themselves.
— **Lane Kirkland,
AFL-CIO President**

*After studying this chapter, you
should be able to:*

1. *Describe how hedonism explains behavior and state limitations of this explanation.*

2. *Summarize the impact of instinctual theories on the understanding of motivation.*

3. *Describe a technique for uncovering a person's dominant needs.*

4. *Describe Maslow's hierarchy of needs.*

5. *Compare the ways motivator factors and hygiene factors may influence employees.*

6. *Describe how expectations can influence an employee's efforts.*

7. *Explain how behavior modification affects behavior in organizations.*

8. *Explain how employees' sense of equity affects their motivation.*

9. *Describe how social learning influences behavior.*

10. *Identify steps managers can take to motivate employees.*

Motivation

GETTING THE WORKERS INVOLVED

A decade ago, there was plenty of room for improvement at A. O. Smith Corporation's automotive works in Milwaukee. Workers were bored with jobs that required them to perform routine tasks in which they welded and riveted car and truck frames, repeating the same task every 20 seconds. Workers' pay was based partly on the number of pieces produced, so they hurried to move parts through without regard to quality. As a result, quality was so poor that the company stationed workers at the end of the assembly lines to repair frames that were built improperly the first time. In 1981, 20 percent of the frames produced on a Ford Ranger line had to be repaired before they could be shipped out. Furthermore, absenteeism some days was as high as 20 percent.

To motivate the workers to do better, A. O. Smith sought to get them more involved in running the company. However, the various committees and discussion groups Smith formed, with and without union involvement, just didn't seem to make much of a difference. Finally, in 1987, Smith decided it would have to make a radical change.

The company decided to involve workers in decision making in a more significant way. Smith reorganized them into production teams that effectively were to manage themselves. Each team comprises five to seven workers, who rotate from one job to another. The team members elect team leaders, who take on many managerial duties, including scheduling production and overtime, ordering maintenance work, and stopping the assembly line to correct defects. The company also eliminated the piecework pay system, initially freezing employees' wages (rather than simply effectively cutting compensation by eliminating the piecework incentives).

Although the additional responsibilities might seem to be simply an added burden for workers, A. O. Smith hoped that the changes would make jobs more interesting, thereby motivating employees to do better. Some evidence suggests that the plan may be working. By 1988, the rate of productivity growth had doubled, and defects on the Ranger line had fallen to 3 percent. Shop steward Charles Perkins is an enthusiastic convert to the new program. "They just turned control of the shops over to us," he explains. "Our destiny is in our own hands. I love it!"

Involving workers in managing and decision making is just one of many approaches to motivating an organization's employees. This chapter explores the concepts behind such efforts. It begins by discussing basic knowledge of how people are motivated, then goes on to describe ways these principles apply to the organization. The chapter closes with some ideas managers can use in creating an environment that motivates.

Source: John Hoerr, "The Cultural Revolution at A. O. Smith," *Business Week*, May 29, 1989, 66, 68.

Recently, I took a tour of a large manufacturing plant on the East Coast. My guide, a first-level supervisor, highlighted the size and capabilities of the facility. Since I was very much impressed by the large number of people who were employed in the plant, I asked my guide, "How many people work here?" Not knowing the intent of my question, he answered, "About half!"

This experience underscores one of the major concerns of all managers: How to motivate others to higher levels of performance. In one survey of over 4,000 adults, 57 percent reported that they could easily be more productive in their jobs if they wanted to.[1] As this evidence suggests, there is an untapped potential for greater productivity. The key to motivating others lies in somehow arousing and channeling their desire to produce.

THE NATURE OF MOTIVATION

Exactly how to motivate others is difficult to determine because motivation itself is such a complex phenomenon. For example, specific behavior may be the result of several motives, rather than a single motive. Furthermore, people who express essentially the same motive may engage in very different behaviors, while people who express very different motives may engage in very similar behavior.

Motives cannot be directly observed; they can only be inferred from the behavior of others. This difficulty can easily lead to errors in interpretation. In addition, motives are dynamic, or constantly changing. The changes result from the rise and fall of a motive's importance as it is variously satisfied or unsatisfied. To complicate things further, some motives do not decrease in importance when a desired goal is attained. Perhaps the best example of this is the reaction that may accompany a pay raise. Often, the raise increases, rather than decreases, an employee's desire for more money.

The complexity of motivational processes is perhaps matched by the complexity and variety of approaches that have been offered to explain motivation. In this chapter, we will review the major approaches to explaining worker behavior and consider a possible integration of these views.

HEDONISM

One of the earliest attempts to explain individual motivation occurs in the writings of utilitarian, or hedonistic, philosophers. In the 1800s, philosophers such as Jeremy Bentham and John Stuart Mill proposed that most, if not all, individual behavior could be explained by the principle of **hedonism.**[2] This principle holds that people will seek pleasure and avoid pain. According to Bentham and Mill, people are fairly rational when choosing between alternative courses of action, and their decisions reflect a careful weighing of costs and benefits.[*]

---

[*]As an explanatory framework, hedonism is actually a very old approach. Epicurus, an early Greek philosopher, proposed essentially the same viewpoint many centuries before Bentham and Mill. The real legacy of Bentham and Mill has been the subsequent generation of more specific explanations of human behavior that were laid on the foundations of hedonistic principles.

The principle of hedonism tends to be too vague and general to be of much use in explaining worker behavior. The hedonistic perspective is most accurate in explaining behavior *after the fact*. That is, after a person engages in a behavior, we can say that he or she acted in order to attain pleasure and/or to avoid pain. All actions, however, can be described as hedonistic. Even such altruistic behavior as sacrificing your life to save the lives of others in a combat situation can be viewed as selfishly motivated. One can reason, after the event, that the apparently altruistic act was performed in order to avoid a later sense of guilt. Because hedonistic explanations work best in explaining actions after they occur, they are not useful in predicting behavior.

INSTINCTUAL THEORIES

From about 1890 to 1920, instinctual views of motivation were popular. The writings of William James and Sigmund Freud endorsed the view that **instincts** (that is, inborn or innate predispositions) largely determine an individual's interpretation of and response to situations.[3] One of Freud's major contributions to this discussion was his emphasis on the role of unconscious motives (motives of which an individual is unaware). Although unconscious motives may play a role in behavior (the existence of unconscious motives can be demonstrated by verbal "slips," dream symbolism, and hypnotic suggestions), the impact of unconscious motives is probably not great.

Instinctual views continued to gain acceptance until the number of proposed instincts reached approximately 6,000! Included among them were the needs for autonomy, deference, dominance, exhibitionism, harm avoidance, order, play, and sex. The large number of identified instincts reflected the wide variety of possible human behaviors. But, like hedonism, instincts can be proposed, after the fact, to explain any act. Because of its own enormity and lack of a practical framework for deciphering the growing list of instincts, the instinctual approach lost its following.

ACHIEVEMENT MOTIVATION THEORY

THE THEMATIC APPERCEPTION TEST   One legacy of the instinctual approach is the use of story-telling techniques to uncover dominant needs (that is, recurring concerns for goal attainment). While devising his own lengthy instinct-related list, Henry A. Murray created a test for establishing the presence and strength of various needs.[4] Specifically, Murray compiled a set of drawings cut out of stories in magazines. Even without their associated stories, the drawings were intriguing and provocative. For example, one drawing showed a man who was apparently outraged and about to run out of a room, while a woman attempted to restrain him from committing what might be a rash act.

Murray used a set of 20 drawings as a projective story-telling device (see Figure 3.6 for an example). In administering his test, called the Thematic Apperception Test, or TAT, Murray would ask the respondent to look at each drawing and offer a story to explain it.[5] Each story was to include a description of the main characters as well as summaries of what led up to the situation, what was currently going on, and what was a likely outcome. Murray observed that people's stories tended to reflect their dominant needs. For example, the stories that people create when they are placed in need-heightening situations (such as when they are deprived of food, sleep, or social contact) typically contain themes devoted to the heightened need. Thus, in a food deprivation study, the stories may involve people going to a banquet or returning from a hamburger stand.

THE MCCLELLAND STUDIES   David McClelland, a successor of Murray, continued to use story-telling techniques to understand dominant needs.[6] McClelland, however, focused on a more limited set of needs: the **need for achievement,** the **need for affiliation,** and the **need for power.**[7]

McClelland's research on the need for achievement has received the greatest attention in organizational behavior literature. In his studies, McClelland sought first to identify persons with a high need to achieve. He interpreted recurring themes of hard work and success in their stories as signs of a high need to achieve. He then studied these high-achievement individuals in a variety of natural and laboratory settings.

Based on these studies, McClelland and his colleagues were able to identify some factors that indicated a predisposition to strive for success.[8] In general, high performance levels and executive success appear to be correlated with a high need for achievement. Individuals with a relatively high need for achievement tend to prefer situations that involve moderate risk and personal responsibility for success rather than luck, and they desire specific feedback on their performance.

The need for achievement partly determines how employees will respond to challenging job assignments, because task persistence and the acceptance of challenge are closely related to this need. High achievers are driven by the prospect of performance-based satisfaction rather than by monetary gain. For these individuals, money is primarily a source of feedback on personal performance rather than an end in itself. Other evidence suggests that high-achievement individuals are more likely to set clocks and watches ahead by 10 or more minutes to avoid being late for appointments and that they doodle in a distinctive style (making clear symbols and filling up the bottom of a page, seldom retracing a line).

The need for achievement is an important explanation of individual success and failure, but it can be overemphasized. Though having the drive to succeed is desirable in many situations, it is not always appropriate to every job in every organization. Furthermore, individuals who are dominated by the need for achievement may have difficulties in getting along with coworkers.

In fact, a manager's effectiveness depends not on a single dimension but on a pattern of needs and the appropriateness of the pattern for a given work setting (for example, manufacturing versus social service). Managers should have a reasonably high need for power in order to function effectively as leaders.[9] A moderate level of need for affiliation can also be useful in many settings. In one study of the promotion histories of 237 managers at AT&T, McClelland and Boyatzis found that a moderate-to-high need for power and a low need for affiliation were associated with managerial success for nontechnical (nonengineering) managers.[10] Also, high need for achievement was associated with career advancement, but only at lower-level positions, where individual contributions may be more important than the ability to influence others. The career success of technical managers with engineering responsibilities, however, could not be predicted from the same measures.

Individuals who have a high need for affiliation tend to be warm and friendly in their relationships. But unless their affiliation needs are balanced by the needs for achievement and power, they are likely to be seen as relatively ineffective in many settings.[11] Their ineffectiveness may stem from the fear of disrupting social relations by being direct and confrontational, even though a forthright approach may be the most appropriate.

McClelland's research on the need for achievement has moved into two further directions: the origins and the economic consequences of achievement motivation. The origin of achievement motivation appears to lie in one's socialization during childhood. Parents who encourage early self-reliance in their children (for example, by training a child to cross the street alone at a relatively early age) produce children who are more achievement-oriented later in life. However, early independence training must also be coupled with supportiveness. Warmth or supportiveness is crucial in that the self-reliant child must not feel that he or she has been abandoned.

Religious differences in emphasis on personal achievement have also been identified.[12] These differences may largely be due to parental emphasis on personal striving versus obedience to authority. Research suggests that Protestant and Jewish parents generally emphasize striving and independence, whereas Catholic parents are more likely to emphasize obedience.[13] These differences are reflected in later life. For example, a comparison of the average level of educational attainment for the three major religious groups in the United States revealed that Jews attain higher than average educational levels.[14] The same study notes that Jews and Protestants, as compared to Catholics, also respond to job challenge and responsibility in more positive ways by displaying higher levels of job satisfaction in higher-quality jobs. These differences, of course, are based on aggregate, or large-sample, findings. Therefore, a specific individual's religion is not necessarily an accurate predictor, given the wide variability that occurs for all three major religious groups. The continuing assimilation of religious groups into the mainstream culture is also believed to be diminishing differences among the groups.

McClelland proposed that a culture's growth is due to the level of need for achievement inherent in its population.[15] His research indicates that increases in the level of need for achievement precede increases in economic activity. An analysis of the literature of various cultures (including an analysis of popular themes in children's readers and the folklore of preliterate tribes) suggests that an increase in achievement themes may precede an increase in economic growth.

McClelland also proposed that achievement motivation can be enhanced in adults who otherwise lack a high level.[16] Training programs have been designed to heighten achievement motivation by having participants focus on goal setting and on thinking and acting in a high-achievement manner. The results of such programs have reportedly been successful; participants are likely to have greater subsequent success in their careers, as measured by rates of promotion, salary progress, and business expansion. One program, run by the Metropolitan Economic Development Association in Minneapolis-St. Paul for small-business owners and potential entrepreneurs, required participants to complete and interpret their responses to the Thematic Apperception Test as well as to engage in goal setting. Follow-up data revealed that participants experienced significant increases in personal income and expanded business activity.[17] However, because many participants in such training programs are selected for their entrepreneurial predisposition, it is difficult to say with certainty that the training program in itself was responsible for their later success. It is altogether possible that a placebo, or guinea pig, effect accounts for the reported enhancement in personal performance. More carefully controlled studies are needed in this area before we can firmly conclude that an individual's need for achievement can be substantially modified by training programs.

Maslow's Hierarchy of Needs

At much the same time that Murray and McClelland were formulating their views of motivation, Abraham Maslow was developing a more complete view of individual motivation.[18] From his work as a clinical psychologist, Maslow devised a model for explaining the essential needs for healthy psychological development. Maslow incorporated McClelland's emphasis on the importance of social acceptance, personal control, recognition, and achievement, but he went several steps further by proposing additional sets of needs and suggesting a rational order for them.

According to Maslow, needs can be classified into a hierarchy, with the needs that are lower in the hierarchy being more essential to survival. Maslow's **hierarchy of needs** is illustrated in Figure 6.1. Lower-order needs, called **deficiency needs,** must be satisfied to ensure an individual's very existence and security. Higher-order needs, or **growth needs,** are concerned with personal development and realization of one's potential. The specific needs under each general category are then arranged into a five-step hierarchy reflecting the increasingly psychological nature of each set.

Deficiency Needs

1. *Physiological needs.* This most basic level of Maslow's hierarchy includes the needs for food, water, sleep, oxygen, warmth, and freedom from pain. If these needs are unsatisfied, an individual's actions will be dominated by attempts to fulfill them. If these needs are sufficiently met, the second set of needs will emerge.

2. *Safety needs.* These needs relate to obtaining a secure environment in which an individual is free from threats. Society provides many devices for meeting these needs: insurance policies, job-tenure arrangements, savings ac-

FIGURE 6.1

MASLOW'S HIERARCHY OF NEEDS

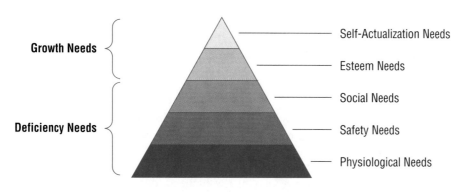

counts, and police and fire departments. If a person is reasonably safe and secure, a third set of needs will probably emerge.

3. *Social needs.* The third set includes the needs for affection, love, and sexual expression. The absence of friends or loved ones can lead to serious psychological maladjustment.

GROWTH NEEDS

4. *Esteem needs.* If the deficiency needs are reasonably satisfied, a concern for self-respect and the esteem of others may arise. Esteem needs include the desires for achievement, prestige, and recognition as well as appreciation and attention from others.

5. *Self-actualization needs.* This category includes the desire for self-fulfillment. Personal development may be expressed in many different ways—for example, maternally, athletically, artistically, or occupationally. Some individuals may never experience the desire to develop their own potential. An individual who attains self-actualization will occasionally have peak experiences. A **peak experience** can best be described as a sense of euphoria that is not chemically induced.[†] It can be felt as a sense of completeness or of oneness with the universe.

One of Maslow's basic premises was that the five categories of needs followed a hierarchical ordering in terms of potency. By this he meant that if a deficiency arises, a lower-order need can supersede a higher-order need to demand its fulfillment. For instance, imagine that you are engaged in a pleasant conversation with a group of coworkers (you are satisfying your social needs)

[†]Drugs, however, do appear to be used to trigger peak experiences by some college students. In one survey, drug use ranked fourth in occurrence, behind "looking at the beauties of nature," "moments of quiet reflection," and "listening to music," and ahead of "physical exercise," "watching little children," "reading a novel," and "prayer."[19]

when suddenly your oxygen is cut off. It would, of course, be very difficult to think of anything else at that time except the restoration of oxygen, a lower-level need. This capacity of lower-order needs to assert themselves is termed **prepotency.**[‡]

More typically, needs emerge gradually rather than suddenly. These unsatisfied needs produce an internal tension that must be reduced. Generally, needs are not 100 percent satisfied; partial satisfaction is more common. For example, physiological needs may be 95 percent satisfied, safety needs 65 percent, social 45 percent, and so on.[20]

Most organizations probably do a fairly good job of satisfying employees' lower-order needs either directly (by opportunities to feel warm, safe, and part of a work group) or indirectly (by wages that can be used to purchase goods that will satisfy various needs). But organizations are not nearly so successful at providing opportunities to satisfy the higher-order needs for esteem and self-actualization. Research by Lyman Porter suggested that upper-level employees are often concerned with esteem and self-actualization needs that may go unmet.[21]

Maslow believed that managers should strive to create the climate necessary to develop employees' potentials to their fullest. Ideal organizational climates would provide opportunities for independence, recognition, and responsibility. Poor work climates, Maslow contended, lead to high levels of employee frustration, low job satisfaction, and high rates of turnover. Maslow's theory, therefore, is of greatest importance in establishing organizational policies.

Research findings on the validity of Maslow's hierarchy of needs have not always been supportive. For example, the proposed notion of prepotency has been difficult to verify. The measurement of various features of the model has also been problematic.[22] Because certain concepts that Maslow proposed (such as self-actualization) were derived from his work with neurotic clients in his practice as a psychologist, we cannot be certain to what extent the various principles can be generalized to the normal adult work force. Although the notion of self-actualization may be important to a person who is struggling with his or her self-identity, it may have little meaning or importance to an unskilled laborer who has made a personal accommodation to the limits of his or her current position. As is generally true of the humanistic perspective, much of Maslow's writing also suffers from a degree of imprecision and fuzziness in terminology and conceptualization.[§] Despite these problems, Maslow nonetheless deserves credit for being one of the first to espouse a humanistic approach to the treatment of employees.

[‡]An illustration of the dynamic and hierarchical nature of motives is given by the following anecdote. Going to work, I saw a sad, unkempt man holding a sign—"Will work for food." The man was picked up by another driver. Later, I saw the same man, now looking healthy and full, holding a new sign—"Will work for clothes." Again, he got into another car and was driven off. At the end of the day, on my way home, I saw the same man again, now wearing a new suit of clothes and holding yet another sign—"Will work for sex."

[§]The number of needs that Maslow proposed (five sets) may be an over-refinement. Alderfer has proposed a three-step hierarchical theory: ERG theory.[23] Alderfer's view argues for the three broad need categories of Existence, Relatedness, and Growth. ERG theory also allows for the simultaneous importance of various needs (as does Maslow's view) and attempts to explain movement down (as well as up) the hierarchy by factors related to frustration and psychological regression.

More recently, Mihaly Csikszentmihalyi, a professor at the University of Chicago, has proposed the notion of **flow**.[24] This concept refers to optimal experiences of joy and creativity in which an individual is so totally absorbed in an activity that little else seems to matter. The idea of flow is similar to Maslow's notion of peak experience, wherein there is a loss of self-consciousness. To be attained, flow experiences require great discipline, such as that required of a piano virtuoso, an experienced rock climber, or a craftsperson. To improve the quality of life through work, Csikszentmihalyi argues that jobs should be redesigned so that they resemble flow-producing activities by matching job challenges to individual skill level. Both Maslow and Csikszentmihalyi agree that certain childhood experiences and family life are required for a person to later experience personal fulfillment. Specifically, they argue that parents should provide a safe, nonthreatening, communicative environment that encourages, but does not push, children to try new and challenging activities. Additionally, parents should display trust toward children and encourage personal growth, rather than impose their own definitions of success on their children.

TWO-FACTOR THEORY

One of the most widely known and influential views of work motivation is Fred Herzberg's **two-factor theory**.[25] As part of a study of job satisfaction, Herzberg and his colleagues conducted in-depth interviews with 203 engineers and accountants in the Pittsburgh area. The researchers asked respondents to recall two separate job-related events in which their work satisfaction had improved or declined. The responses suggested that the work-related factors that led to feelings of satisfaction were different from those factors that led to dissatisfaction. The satisfiers usually pertained to the content of the job and included such factors as career advancement, recognition, sense of responsibility, and feelings of achievement. Herzberg called these **motivator factors**. The dissatisfiers more often stemmed from the context in which the job was performed. They related to job security, company policies, interpersonal relations, and working conditions. Herzberg called these **hygiene factors**.

Herzberg reasoned that motivator factors had the potential to motivate workers to higher levels of performance because they provided opportunities for personal satisfaction. Although the absence of these factors would not make employees *unhappy*, it would leave them feeling somewhat neutral toward their jobs.

Although they could not induce a worker to higher levels of performance, hygiene factors could create great dissatisfaction if they were not attended to. Hygiene factors could make a worker very unhappy, but they could not create more than a neutral feeling toward the job even if they were ideally modified.

Herzberg's argument is unique in that it differentiates the factors that motivate employees from those that lead to dissatisfaction. Furthermore, two-factor theory (or motivator–hygiene theory, as it is sometimes called) contends that improving physical working conditions may help to reduce worker discontent, but will not provide sufficient incentive for most workers to strive for superior performance. As a hypothetical illustration, consider the removal of your garbage from the front of your home every week. This issue is a hygiene factor in that it has the capacity to make one very unhappy if it is not attended to (imagine your unhappiness if the trash were not removed for a period of several weeks). Alternatively, if your trash is removed with complete regularity, you are not likely to turn cartwheels upon seeing that the garbage has been taken away sometime during the day. Trash removal, like poor working conditions, is something that we expect to have taken care of, but take little interest in once it is remedied. Motivator (or psychological) aspects of many jobs, in turn, tend to be neglected.

In essence, Herzberg contends that attraction toward work and dissatisfaction leading to the avoidance of work are not opposite ends of a single bipolar continuum. Instead, two separate, unipolar continua should be used to represent the independent influences of the motivator and hygiene factors. Graphically, the influence of motivator factors can range from neutral to positive,

while the influence of hygiene factors can range from neutral to negative.

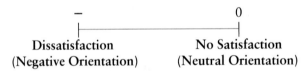

Another way of expressing two-factor theory is to graph the relationships between increasing levels of job factors (motivators and hygienes) and orientation toward work satisfaction. As Figure 6.2 shows, inattention to hygiene factors can lead to serious dissatisfaction, while beyond a moderate level, increased attention to hygiene factors brings no further increase in satisfaction. Conversely, low levels of motivator factors can at worst only lead to neutrality. But high levels of motivator factors can yield significant gains in satisfaction.

The extremes on each factor and the combination of these extremes are worth considering. A job that combines high levels of motivator and hygiene factors would be ideal, while the combination of low levels on both would be undesirable. The combination of a high level of motivator factors with a very low level of hygiene factors yields the situation like that of the "starving artist," that is, a person who greatly enjoys working but is unhappy with poor working conditions, wages, and the like. According to Herzberg, the opposite situation—a combination of a high level of hygiene factors with a low level of motivator factors—would produce a state of total neutrality.

If two-factor theory is valid, we can expect to find evidence for the curvilinear relations presented in Figure 6.2. In fact, a number of studies have provided evidence of these relationships. Unfortunately, another set of studies has

FIGURE 6.2

PREDICTED RELATIONSHIPS BETWEEN LEVEL OF JOB FACTORS AND WORKER
ORIENTATION/SATISFACTION

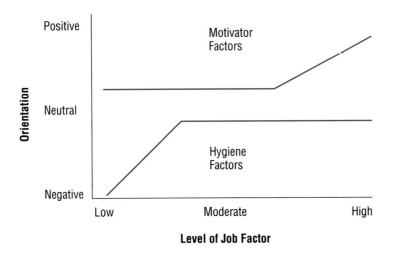

not found similar support. The nonsupportive studies typically report a linear
(or straight-line) relationship between the level of a factor and worker satisfaction. Figure 6.3 summarizes these linear associations, in which the motivator
or psychological factors appear to be more important in determining worker

FIGURE 6.3

FREQUENTLY OBSERVED RELATIONSHIPS BETWEEN LEVEL OF JOB FACTORS
AND WORKER ORIENTATION/SATISFACTION

OB Focus
Mary Kay Motivates

In 30 years, sales of Mary Kay Cosmetics have grown from $198,000 to over $613 million in 1993, primarily due to the motivating power of its founder, Mary Kay Ash. Mary Kay's sales force numbers 300,000, of whom 6,500 drive complimentary pink Mary Kay Cadillacs, and 74 have earned commissions in excess of $1 million over the course of their Mary Kay careers. But it's the recognition that Mary Kay lavishes on her employees—as much as or perhaps more than the money—that propels her sales force to produce.

For an annual three-day sales rally, Mary Kay "daughters," as they're known, embark on a pilgrimage to Dallas to give and receive recognition for their sales efforts. Each year May Kay crowns four Queens—women who have excelled at sales or recruiting—complete with tiaras and roses. Minks and diamonds are doled out generously to those who have met targeted sales goals. Recogni-

tion comes not only from Mary Kay herself, but from everyone else at the rally. Color-coded suits, sashes, badges, and jewelry symbolize each woman's achievements: Pink suits are worn by regional sales directors and white suits by national sales directors. One sales director had a gold bracelet with 32 diamonds in the shape of "$1,000,000," representing the amount she and her sales force had sold the previous year. Special pins and badges are worn by women with lesser sales volumes. This type of straightforward pronouncement of the rewards to be earned for hard work motivates other women to produce. It's called Mary Kay enthusiasm, and it runs rampant at the sales rally.

Although the annual rally is the motivational pinnacle for many beauty consultants, Mary Kay bestows recognition year-round. She regularly invites star sales performers to accompany her on ex-

clusive, five-star trips to such destinations as London and Acapulco. And she maintains a personal interest in her "daughters," sending greeting cards and offering comforting touches during family illnesses.

The motivating potential of Mary Kay enthusiasm has attracted people with diverse backgrounds. Mary Kay beauty consultants are no longer bored housewives. Today's "daughters" include lawyers, pediatricians, and MBAs. Two-thirds of the sales force sells Mary Kay cosmetics in addition to holding down a full-time job. In some cases, husbands have quit their jobs to become office managers for their spouses.

Clearly, Mary Kay Cosmetics has championed the motivating potential of compensation—both financial and emotional—and although Mary Kay, at age 75, has handed major responsibility for company operations over to her son, Mary Kay enthusiasm lives on.

Source: Alan Farnham, "Mary Kay's Lessons in Leadership," *Fortune,* September 20, 1993, 68–77.

response than the hygiene or environmental factors (this is indicated by the line for motivator factors being above the line for hygiene factors). Most studies of two-factor theory reveal the relatively greater importance of psychological factors versus environmental factors.

A comparison of conflicting studies suggests that the method used to study the theory is related to the degree of support that the theory receives. Typically, studies using the interview method (which Herzberg employed in his original study) have obtained evidence that the theory is valid, whereas studies employing other methods (such as questionnaires) have failed to find support for the theory's principles. This suggests that the theory may be **method-bound,** that is, the theory can only be supported by a particular method.[26]**

**Method-bound theories represent interesting traps for scientists. A couple of centuries ago, researchers suggested the notion of "phylgistin" to explain why things burned as long as they did. So the reasoning went, paper had a lot of phylgistin, water had none, and some rocks (coal) amazingly contained phylgistin. The way to measure the amount of this strange substance was simply to burn the object. The longer it burned, the more phylgistin it contained. Phylgistin was conveniently defined as being odorless, colorless, tasteless, and weightless, so that the only method for measuring its volume was to time how long an object burned. Clearly, our ancestors were deceiving themselves (with a forerunner of the concept of oxygen) by constructing a theory that could be tested with only a single method.

Critics of the two-factor theory argue that respondents in an interview setting may be providing answers in an ego-defensive manner. According to this argument, respondents are inclined to report that the good things that happen to them at work are related to their own efforts, while the bad things are due to external or environmental forces. It is easier to blame coworkers and company policy when things go poorly than it is to blame oneself. In addition, critics point out that many of the job factors that are rather neatly compartmentalized as motivators or hygienes within the theory are not exclusively members of one set or the other. For example, salary is certainly a potential source of dissatisfaction, and salary is externally administered (a hygiene factor). However, salary can be a source of personal pride and, therefore, serves as a source of psychological reward (a motivator factor).

Despite these shortcomings, two-factor theory has had a substantial influence on the thinking of managers and researchers. It is probably safe to say that two-factor theory is one of the most widely known theories of motivation (rightly or wrongly) in managerial circles. The theory's influence continues through its prescriptions for job redesign.

Two-factor theory can be seen as building on the work of Maslow. Table 6.1 compares the factors from the two theories. As the table shows, both theories focus on much the same facets of work life. Herzberg's contribution has been to refine and extend the work of Maslow by (1) suggesting different dynamics and interplay among the facets, and (2) underscoring the significance of higher-order factors in the determination of worker motivation.

EXPECTANCY THEORY

Expectancy theory (or perhaps more properly, theories, since a variety of expectancy approaches have emerged during recent decades) represents an attempt

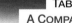

TABLE 6.1
A COMPARISON OF FACTORS IN MASLOW'S HIERARCHY OF NEEDS AND HERZBERG'S TWO-FACTOR THEORY

Hierarchy of Needs	Two-Factor Theory
Growth Needs	*Motivators (Satisfiers)*
Self-actualization	Responsibility Work itself Achievement Advancement
Esteem	Recognition Advancement opportunities
Deficiency Needs	*Hygienes (Dissatisfiers)*
Social	Supervision Interpersonal relations Status Salary
Safety	Company policy Job security
Physiological	Working conditions

to explain worker motivation in terms of anticipated rewards. These theoretical models assume that people make rational decisions based on economic realities. Many researchers are attracted to expectancy theory because it tries to bring together both personal and situational influences.

Although many variations of expectancy theory have been proposed, the most widely cited version was proposed by Victor Vroom of Yale University.[27] Vroom's model argues that the psychological force on an employee to exert effort is a function of his or her expectancies about the future and the valence (or attractiveness) of specific future outcomes. Two kinds of expectations are important in the model: the expectation that effort will lead to performance and the expectation that performance will lead to rewards.[††]

EFFORT–PERFORMANCE EXPECTANCY (E→P)   In deciding on a course of action, employees will consider whether their effort will translate into a desired accomplishment. If the obstacles are such that they cannot reasonably expect their effort to lead to an acceptable level of performance, their motivation to perform will be diminished.

PERFORMANCE–OUTCOME EXPECTANCY (P→O)   Another consideration is whether a given level of performance will result in the obtainment of a particular outcome. The more strongly a person believes that performance will lead to a positive outcome (or the avoidance of a negative outcome), the more likely it is that he or she will be motivated to higher levels of performance.

VALENCE (V)   The outcomes that an employee receives can be evaluated in terms of their value or attractiveness. Expectancy theorists, however, prefer to use the special term **valence** to denote this attractiveness. The valence that an individual attaches to an outcome is a very personal matter that cannot be accurately predicted by other people. Thus, it is essential to ask an individual about the valences that he or she attaches to anticipated outcomes. The valence of a given outcome may also vary in relation to how recently the individual has been rewarded.

The linkages of effort–performance expectancy and performance–outcome expectancy can be measured by questioning individuals on the subjective probabilities that they believe characterize the linkages. **Subjective probabilities** are estimates of the likelihood that one event will follow another. In this case, respondents would be asked to report their personal probability estimates that effort will lead to performance and that performance will lead to a given outcome. These probabilities can range from 0, indicating a belief that one event will definitely *not* follow the other, to 1.0, indicating complete confidence that one event *will* follow the other. The valence of an outcome is assessed by having respondents provide an associated value that can range from –1.0 (highly unattractive) to +1.0 (highly attractive).

[††]What follows is essentially a "bare-bones" or introductory-level discussion of expectancy theory.

The probability estimates can be multiplied together to yield an overall expectancy value. This value can then be multiplied by the associated valence to yield a summary index of the psychological force on an individual to exert effort. In summary, the mathematics involved are:

$$(E{\to}P) \times (P{\to}O) \times (V) = \text{Motivational Force}$$

As an example, consider a salesperson who is deciding whether to make additional sales calls. She believes that the additional calls (effort) will lead to additional sales (performance) and that the additional sales will lead to a bonus (outcome). The size, or magnitude, of the bonus (valence) must also be considered. For illustrative purposes, imagine that the salesperson's probability estimate of E→P is .8, and the estimate of P→O is .7. Also, the anticipated bonus has a valence of +.6. The motivational force that is exerted on the salesperson is given by (.8) × (.7) × (.6) = .34. If she had valued the bonus more highly, so that its valence were +.9, the motivational force would have been (.8) × (.7) × (.9) = .50. If she felt that the bonus was trivial, the valence portion of the equation would significantly reduce her motivational force.

Several clear implications for motivating others can be derived from expectancy theory. First, it is important for employees to recognize that effort and performance are closely related. A manager's job should include the establishment of conditions that help to translate effort into performance. This may involve the removal of obstacles and the creation of production systems that help employees see the link between effort and performance.

Managers also need to create linkages between rewards and performance. To establish this connection, the creation and maintenance of reward systems are necessary. Furthermore, the rewards that are offered should be tailored to the values of the individual employee. This may require surveying employees in order to determine individual preferences among reward options. Lastly, conflicting expectancies and rewards need to be eliminated. Conflicting influences may arise when coworkers attempt to restrict another's performance or when conflicting demands are made by different supervisors.

Research on the principles of expectancy theory has generally been supportive.[28] However, expectancy theory has become exceedingly complex. Careful readings of Vroom's work have also led many researchers in quite different research directions.[29] A true test of the complete expectancy model would require an enormous effort on the part of participants to answer a very large number of questions. The resulting information would also have to be combined in a matrix-algebra format in order to include the many combinations of *multiple* levels of effort, performance, and reward that could be anticipated.[30] In addition, expectancy theory's relevance is limited to settings where a conscious, reward-maximization decision-making process is operating. For individuals who do not follow such a process (or in settings that induce different decision-making processes), an expectancy theory view may not be appropriate. Yet, despite its esoteric character and the doubtfulness of the proposition that employees actually engage in a cognitive calculus before making decisions, expectancy theory remains a popular framework for explaining employee motivation.[31]

REINFORCEMENT THEORY

The principles of operant conditioning, presented in Chapter 5, can also be used to explain work motivation. The allocation of rewards in exchange for specific behaviors can have a powerful effect on subsequent behavior. The design of specific reward systems will be considered further in Chapter 7.

Operant conditioning, or **behavior modification** as its applied version is termed, is particularly influential in directing behavior if rewards are (1) substantial and highly desired, (2) administered intermittently, and (3) differentially distributed so that higher levels of performance lead to proportionally larger increases in reward.[32]

Proponents of organizational behavior modification (OB Mod) prefer to diagnose situations in terms of an "antecedent–behavior–consequence" or A–B–C framework.[33] Antecedents are stimuli that precede behaviors. Consequences are the outcomes, or rewards and punishments, that follow from behaviors. These consequences, in turn, serve as antecedents for subsequent behavior. By managing the consequences of behavior, OB Mod specialists seek to modify later behavior.

Reinforcement theory and expectancy theory have a similar conceptual foundation. Both approaches derive from a simple hedonistic base. However, **reinforcement theory** focuses on the influence of past rewards in shaping present behavior, while expectancy theory focuses on the influence of anticipated rewards on present behavior. Reinforcement theory has been characterized as *hedonism of the past,* whereas expectancy theory has been described as *hedonism of the future.*[34] The historical emphasis of reinforcement theory partly stems from the approach's initial focus on studying nonverbal animals of limited mental ability (such as rats and pigeons). In contrast, expectancy theory research has been devoted to studying the behavior of humans. Despite their differing origins, both expectancy and reinforcement theories generate essentially identical predictions for behavior in a variety of settings.

The two approaches do differ, however, in their predictions of what effects will result from a change in the scheduling of rewards. If a person is rewarded continuously (that is, with an expectancy of 1.0) and then rewards are shifted so that they are administered less often (that is, on an intermittent schedule), expectancy theory predicts a decline in motivation, while reinforcement theory predicts that motivation will persist. Although a formal competitive test of these differing predictions has not been reported as yet for employee samples, persistence in the absence of rewards could reasonably be expected (based on day-to-day observations of employees). Because of its relative simplicity and ease of application, reinforcement theory appears to have more followers within the field of applied work motivation than expectancy theory.

EQUITY THEORY

Feelings of fairness, or equity, can serve as a powerful stimulus to increase or decrease effort. J. Stacy Adams has proposed a theory that attempts to explain the influence of such feelings on employee behavior.[35] Adams' **equity theory**

An Inside Look
Reinforcing the Use of New Technology

When Sandoz Pharmaceuticals set out to introduce its salespeople to using computers, the company made sure that the employees would feel well rewarded for learning the new system, which uses laptop computers to link sales reps with headquarters. The positive reinforcement took the form of ease of use, company approval, and more free time for salespeople.

First, the company made sure that the system would fit the needs of the salespeople and that they would benefit from any information they entered into the system. The system's designers gave the sales reps access to the information they entered. The designers also sent teams to meet with sales reps and regional managers, studying their routines and requirements to ensure that the system would be easy to use in the field.

After developing the system, the company initiated an internal promotional campaign, which included a humorous videotape showing how the system would help a salesperson on a typical day. This program taught the sales reps to use the system and also showed that doing so was important to the company, meaning that employees who learned the system would meet with company approval.

The company instituted a pilot program to test the new system, and the sales reps began reaping the major reward: the savings in time that resulted from not doing as much paperwork as they had been. The sales reps who tried the new system began to have time to call on one addi-

tional physician every two days. Also, said one salesperson, "The weekends are now my own. On Friday evening, I used to begin writing my weekly report. Now, by just entering a comment on my day's activities, my report is prepared each week for me."

Thus, Sandoz used a form of OB Mod to motivate its salespeople to use the company's new technology. The promotional campaign, company approval, and training program served as antecedents stimulating the behavior of using the laptop computers. A variety of rewards ensued, including ease of use, access to information, and time freed from paperwork. These consequences subsequently served as antecedents for future behavior involving use of the computer system.

Source: Sharon Faber, "When Employees Ask: 'What's in It for Me?'" *Business Month*, September 1989, 79.

assumes that people will strive to restore equity if they feel an imbalance exists.

Basic to equity theory is the belief that employees continuously monitor the degree of equity or inequity that exists in their working relations by comparing their own outcomes and inputs with those of another highly similar person. In the context of equity theory, *outcomes* are anything that employees view as being provided by their jobs or the organization. Outcomes include pay, an office with a window, access to the executive washroom, the size of one's ashtrays, use of a company car, and so on. *Inputs* include all the contributions that a person makes to the employment relationship. Examples of inputs include personal effort, years and kind of education, prior work experience, training, and the like. Generally speaking, an input is anything that a person believes he or she should be compensated for. Table 6.2 provides a list of inputs and outcomes that employees typically consider important.

The inputs and outputs that a person views as relevant are very personal choices. According to equity theory, it is essential to ask individuals their reactions to possible outcomes and inputs when attempting to assess the degree of equity or inequity that they feel exists.

TABLE 6.2
EXAMPLES OF INPUTS AND OUTCOMES IN ADAM'S THEORY OF EQUITY

Inputs	Outcomes
Effort	Salary
Education	Fringe benefits
Training	Travel allowance
Experience	Number of subordinates
Loyalty	Autonomy
Age	Titles
	Status symbols
	Job assignments
	Time off
	Opportunities for overtime

Adams contends that an individual will estimate the ratio of outcomes to inputs, but this ratio is of only partial importance. Each person also calculates a similar ratio for a person whom he or she judges to be in a similar position. This second person is called the *comparison other*. Adams predicts that an employee will be relatively satisfied if his or her own ratio of outcomes to inputs is equivalent to the ratio for the comparison other. This condition may be summarized as follows:

$$\frac{\text{Outcomes A}}{\text{Inputs A}} = \frac{\text{Outcomes B}}{\text{Inputs B}} \tag{1}$$

If person A feels that his ratio is either higher or lower than person B's, he should experience a sense of inequity. The magnitude of this feeling will be proportional to the size of the gap between the ratios. Feelings of inequity produce a psychological tension that requires reduction.

$$\frac{\text{Outcomes A}}{\text{Inputs A}} < \frac{\text{Outcomes B}}{\text{Inputs B}} \tag{2}$$

If person A is undercompensated in comparison to person B (equation 2), he may attempt to restore equity by working on one of the four components in the two ratios:

1. He may increase his own outcomes by asking for a raise.

2. He may decrease his own inputs by being less productive.

3. He may decrease person B's outcomes by persuading his boss to alter B's pay.

4. He may increase B's inputs by pressuring her to work harder.

If person B is undercompensated in comparison to person A (equation 3), equity theory predicts that person A will experience guilt and will attempt to restore equity by altering one or more of the four components of the two ratios. For example, person A may attempt to reduce his own outcomes or increase person B's outcomes by appealing to his boss for an adjustment. Also, person A may increase his inputs by exerting greater effort on the job. Lastly, person A may help person B to decrease her input, perhaps by coaching her in how to work more efficiently.

$$\frac{\text{Outcomes A}}{\text{Inputs A}} > \frac{\text{Outcomes B}}{\text{Inputs B}} \tag{3}$$

If the four components of the ratios cannot be altered and if the magnitude of inequity is substantial, person A would be forced to choose another course of action. He might:

1. Alter his perceptions of the situation so that the inequity no longer seems unjustified, saying, for example, "I deserve to earn more money because I work harder than most people."
2. Leave the field by quitting or obtaining a transfer.
3. Choose a different comparison other, someone whose ratio provides a less uncomfortable contrast.

In essence, equity theory focuses on the issue of **distributive justice.** Distributive justice may be defined as the fairness of the amount of a reward as perceived by the reward's recipient, and as compared against the amount of a reward given to another. Another aspect of perceived fairness that is actually not part of equity theory per se is the notion of **procedural justice.** This type of justice may be defined as the fairness of the manner (or method) by which rewards are allocated, again as perceived by the recipient of the reward. Procedural justice, a somewhat independent issue from distributive justice, focuses on the way in which allocation decisions are made, rather than the result of the decisions.

Much of the initial research on equity theory focused on demonstrating that the desire to restore equity would occur in work settings. Generally, the results supported the theory.[36] One of the more frequently used research designs for studying equity processes has been to create a short-term work situation for college students wherein their rate of pay (hourly versus piece-rate) is fixed. A comparison other is created in the mind of the employee, and a belief that one is equitably paid, overpaid, or underpaid is then induced. By virtue of controlling the design of these situations, the only readily available avenue for restoring equity is to alter effort (that is, the employee cannot alter the inputs or outcomes of the comparison other, and so on).

The theory's specific predictions for such highly controlled conditions are very clear. Figure 6.4 displays the predicted changes in quantity and quality of performance (compared to an equitable condition) in relative overcompensation and undercompensation, under hourly and piece-rate pay conditions. The predictions also reflect the interdependency of effort, quantity, and outcomes in piece-rate schemes. For example, increases in quantity in a piece-rate scheme lead to greater rewards—an undesirable situation for someone who already feels overcompensated.

Figure 6.4 also summarizes the predictions that expectancy theory would generate for the various conditions. In certain conditions, equity theory and expectancy clearly disagree. For example, one of the most interesting aspects of equity theory is its prediction for worker performance in a condition of overcompensation on a piece-rate pay scheme (as when someone is paid 40 cents per unit of output, while the comparison other receives only 20 cents per unit). In such a situation, the more units that the overcompensated employee produces, the more inequity he or she will generate. Therefore, to restore equity, the overcompensated individual should produce relatively fewer units of output. However, the quality of each unit should increase as a result of the individual's desire to exert greater effort and thereby restore equity by increasing the inputs portion of his or her ratio. This prediction is quite different from what would be predicted from an expectancy theory perspective. Expectancy theory, of course, is grounded in the philosophy of hedonism, while equity theory is founded on the principle of equity maximization, which takes a more altruistic view of human nature.

FIGURE 6.4

PREDICTED CHANGES IN QUANTITY AND QUALITY OF PERFORMANCE AS A FUNCTION OF INEQUITY CONDITION AND RATE OF PAY FOR EXPECTANCY THEORY AND EQUITY THEORY

[a]Expectancy theory does not make rigid predictions for these settings in that effort and performance may not be correlated in some situations.

[b]These predictions may also be inversely stated depending on whether quality and quantity are inversely related for a given task.

Evidence from studies of the condition of overcompensation on a piece-rate scheme has demonstrated that workers will, in fact, decrease the quantity of their output and increase the quality of their output relative to more equitably paid workers. This phenomenon is somewhat transitory, however, and diminishes over a period of several days.[37] The inability of expectancy theory or reinforcement theory to readily predict this result largely stems from the absence of employee comparison processes in these theories as originally formulated. Clearly, a consideration of employee comparison processes adds something to our ability to predict employee behavior accurately.

Intuitively, it is difficult to accept the notion that people who are overpaid will not attempt to maximize quantity. In a study that sought to identify individual differences in the desire to restore equity versus maximization of reward, the performance of overpaid individuals and that of equitably paid individuals were compared under a piece-rate scheme.[38] Results suggested that actions of individuals who were measured as being more altruistic (that is, more morally mature) were more likely to follow the predictions of equity theory (decreasing quantity of output and increasing quality) than actions of individuals who were measured as being less altruistic. Therefore, equity theory may provide a better description of the behavior of less principled individuals.

Although equity theory has been criticized for not explicitly predicting which method an employee will select in order to restore equity,[39] the theory presents a unique perspective on a major facet of work motivation. The perception of fairness is an important determinant of the impact of any reward system. Furthermore, the equity theory perspective continues to generate additional research initiatives. For example, alternative versions of Adams' original ratios and the process that underlies the selection of a comparison other are currently being investigated.[40]

SOCIAL LEARNING THEORY

Social learning theory is another approach to motivation.[41] The desire to imitate models can be very powerful. Modeling first manifests itself in childhood, when children imitate adults and other siblings. In organizations, a desire to imitate superior performers or supervisors may be strong in some individuals. Certainly, the taking of roles and the imitation of previously witnessed behavior illustrate the subtle influences of social learning.

Social learning theory contends that people develop expectancies about their capacity to behave in certain ways and the probability that such behavior will result in rewards. The first of these expectancies relates to how they perceive their own competence, while the second pertains to outcomes and is analogous to the concepts of expectancy theory. Therefore, organizational training programs that rely on films, lectures, and role-playing techniques (that is, the vast majority of organization-sponsored training programs) are using an approach based on social learning theory principles. The self-administration of rewards is also an important part of social learning theory. Modeling, or imitative behavior, serves as a standard for administering self-reinforcement in the form of increased personal satisfaction and enhanced self-image. The direct instruction of employees by peers, supervisors, or trainers on how to set personal standards for performance can also be used, but whether employees accept such direct instruction probably depends on such factors as the power and attractiveness of the instructors.[42] The use of social learning theory principles in conjunction with extrinsic rewards for performance may provide a most effective combination of motivational approaches.

A COMPREHENSIVE MODEL OF MOTIVATION

So far we have examined a number of different perspectives on work motivation. Although each perspective takes a somewhat different approach to motivation, it is possible to identify similarities among them and to integrate them into a larger conceptual framework.

Each approach falls into one of two categories: content theories or process theories. **Content theories** focus on *what* motivates people to perform. They are concerned with identifying the different rewards that people seek in their work. The theories of Maslow, Herzberg, and McClelland are essentially content theories. The other theories that we have examined are more concerned with *how* rewards control behavior. These theories focus on the dynamics, or process aspects, of work motivation. Expectancy, equity, reinforcement, and social learning theories are examples of **process theories**.

The content and process theories can be integrated into a still broader conceptual framework. Figure 6.5 presents a well-known and accepted framework proposed by Lyman Porter and Edward E. Lawler.[43] In essence, they outlined a dynamic model of motivation—the **Porter-Lawler model**—that includes many of the aforementioned theories as components of a larger process.

Beginning on the left-hand side of the model, the expected value of a reward combines with the expectation that effort will result in a reward. These two influences determine the level of effort that an employee exerts. Effort, however, does not simply or easily convert into performance (or accomplishment). The employee's abilities and role perceptions interact in determining the level of accomplishment. Unless a person has a minimum level of ability and the correct understanding of just how to perform a job, his or her effort will not yield an acceptable level of performance.

Performance may or may not be linked to rewards in a given situation; hence, the wavy lines between rewards and performance. The employee's expectations of what is equitable in the way of rewards is influenced by the awareness of his or her own performance. Perceptions of equity or inequity interact with the rewards actually received to determine the level of satisfaction.

The model includes two feedback loops. The first links satisfaction to subsequent estimates of the value of rewards. If an employee feels that rewards received for past performance are not particularly satisfying, he or she will diminish future efforts. The second feedback loop runs from the performance–rewards linkages to the expectation that future effort will result in rewards. Here again, the employee's future effort will be influenced by his or her past experiences.

FIGURE 6.5
THE PORTER-LAWLER MODEL OF MOTIVATION

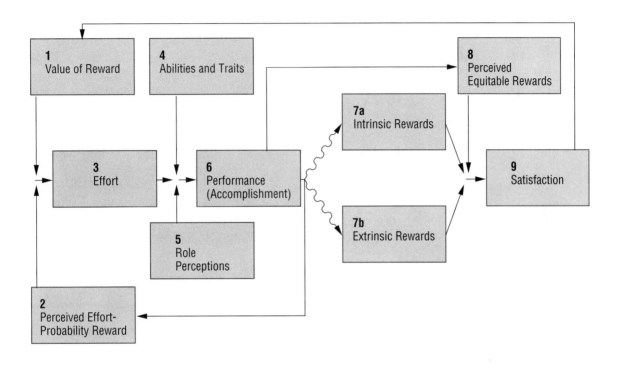

If we consider the various theories of motivation in light of the Porter-Lawler model, we see that each can be incorporated within this larger framework. Maslow's distinction between higher- and lower-order needs, as well as Herzberg's distinction between motivator factors (intrinsic factors) and hygiene factors (extrinsic factors), are represented by boxes 7a and 7b in the model. McClelland's principles regarding needs for achievement, affiliation, and power are contained in the intrinsic reward aspect of the model. Expectancy theory's principles are incorporated in the valence and expectancy features of the model, boxes 1 and 2. The concepts of equity theory are contained in box 8. Their influence is reflected in the interaction of equity perceptions and rewards in determining satisfaction.

The linkage between rewards and performance is a primary theme in reinforcement theory. The conversion of the wavy lines that connect rewards to performance into straight lines is a goal of OB Mod advocates. The feedback loop from the performance–reward linkage to the expectancy estimate of box 2 incorporates a major operant conditioning principle (the importance of consequences for future behavior). Imitation and proper role conduct, important features of social learning theory, are implicit in box 5, role perceptions.

Several of the boxes in the model were not discussed in this chapter. However, job satisfaction (box 9) was considered in Chapter 4. Abilities and traits (box 4) are in the province of human resources (or personnel) specialists, who attempt to select individuals who possess the requisite abilities and traits for successful job performance. Effort (box 3) is a topic that is typically considered by students of human factors engineering or work design.

The Porter-Lawler model does a good job of summarizing the major approaches to studying work behavior. From the perspective of the model, it is clear that the field of organizational behavior, which might appear fragmented because of the diversity of the topics it investigates, is not in disarray or segmented in its efforts to understand work behavior. Each of the various investigative lines of research can be viewed as examining different pieces of a larger puzzle. Although the Porter-Lawler model may not be the final word in describing work behavior, it nicely summarizes and integrates a good deal of what is already known about individual behavior in work settings.

The importance of the Porter-Lawler model for managers is substantial. The model underscores the many facets of the motivational process, each of which must be understood and attended to if a manager wishes to be successful in motivating subordinates. The complexity of the model also emphasizes the fact that many things can go wrong and thereby undermine a manager's efforts. The following checklist, derived from the model, suggests that to be successful managers should:

1. Offer valued rewards

2. Create perceptions that effort will lead to rewards

3. Design jobs so that effort leads to high performance

4. Hire qualified employees

5. Train employees in the correct manner for performing their tasks

6. Design tasks so that performance is measurable

7. Design reward systems so that rewards are tied to performance

8. Ensure that rewards are viewed as fair and equitable

SUMMARY

1. Describe how hedonism explains behavior and state limitations of this explanation.
The principle of hedonism states that people will seek pleasure and avoid pain. They make rational choices based on a careful weighing of costs and benefits. In explaining motivation, hedonism tends to be vague and is most accurate in explaining behavior after the fact. Thus, it is not often useful for predicting behavior.

2. Summarize the impact of instinctual theories on the understanding of motivation.

Freud and others focused on the role of unconscious motivations for human behavior. Use of the instinctual theory grew, along with the number of instincts proposed. Ultimately, the theory was difficult to apply.

3. Describe a technique for uncovering a person's dominant needs.

The Thematic Apperception Test uses drawings to uncover an individual's dominant needs. When a person tells stories about the drawings, he or she is likely to refer to a heightened need. Other researchers have used similar techniques to focus on specific needs.

4. Describe Maslow's hierarchy of needs.

Maslow grouped needs into deficiency (lower-order) and growth (higher-order) needs. From lowest to highest, deficiency needs are physiological needs, safety needs, and social needs; growth needs are esteem needs and self-actualization needs.

5. Compare the ways motivator factors and hygiene factors may influence employees.

Motivator factors lead to feelings of satisfaction. These factors include career advancement, recognition, a sense of responsibility, and a feeling of achievement. The absence of hygiene factors leads to dissatisfaction. These factors involve job security, company policies, interpersonal relations, and working conditions. In theory, the absence of motivator factors does not make employees dissatisfied, nor do high levels of hygiene factors serve to increase employee satisfaction.

6. Describe how expectations can influence an employee's efforts.

Employees consider whether their effort will translate into a desired accomplishment (effort–performance expectancy) and whether a given level of performance will result in obtaining a particular outcome (performance–outcome expectancy). Employees are predicted to make the greatest effort when these expectancies are high.

7. Explain how behavior modification affects behavior in organizations.

Behavior modification interprets actions in terms of antecedents, behaviors, and consequences. Antecedents are stimuli that precede behaviors. Consequences are the rewards or punishments that follow from behaviors and become antecedents for subsequent behavior. Behavior modification involves managing the consequences of behavior, which can influence future behavior.

8. Explain how employees' sense of equity affects their motivation.

Employees continuously monitor the degree of equity in their working relations. An employee will be relatively satisfied if his or her own ratio of outcomes to inputs is equivalent to the ratio for a comparison employee. Employees will strive to restore equity if they feel an imbalance exists.

9. Describe how social learning influences behavior.

People develop expectations about their capacity to behave in certain ways and the probability that their behavior will result in rewards. When a person meets a standard of behavior, that person rewards himself or herself with increased personal satisfaction and enhanced self-image.

10. Identify steps managers can take to motivate employees.

To motivate employees, managers should offer valued rewards, create perceptions that effort will lead to rewards, design jobs so that effort leads to high performance, hire qualified employees, train employees to do their tasks correctly, design tasks so that performance is measurable, design reward systems that tie rewards to performance, and ensure that rewards are seen as fair and equitable.

KEY TERMS

Hedonism	Method-bound
Instincts	Expectancy theory
Need for achievement	Valence
Need for affiliation	Subjective probabilities
Need for power	Behavior modification
Hierarchy of needs	Reinforcement theory
Deficiency needs	Equity theory
Growth needs	Distributive justice
Peak experience	Procedural justice
Prepotency	Social learning theory
Flow	Content theories
Two-factor theory	Process theories
Motivator factors	Porter-Lawler model
Hygiene factors	

REVIEW AND DISCUSSION QUESTIONS

1. Why is it difficult to determine how to motivate other people?

2. The Thematic Apperception Test grew out of instinctual theories. What do these two notions have in common?

3. Al Ambitious has interviewed the applicants for a management trainee position and narrowed them down to five. He just read about a new psychological test that measures individual need for achievement, and he wonders whether it would be a good way to decide which of the five candidates to hire. Would this test alone be a good basis for Al's hiring decision? Why or why not?

4. From lowest to highest, what are the categories of needs in Maslow's hierarchy? Might a person strive to fulfill a higher need before all the lower ones are totally met?

5. What are motivator factors and hygiene factors? How might workers likely feel about jobs that lacked motivator factors but provided hygiene factors? Based on two-factor theory, would enhancing job security make workers satisfied?

6. Which factors in two-factor theory correspond to Maslow's deficiency needs? Which factors correspond to growth needs? Give some examples of job attributes that could fulfill what Maslow calls the need for self-actualization.

7. Eva Adams has just been assigned to the sales territory for Montana, Washington, and Alaska. Sales for this territory have tended to lag behind the rest of the nation, and Eva's manager has promised her a bonus if she can increase sales by 15 percent for this year. Much as Eva wants the bonus, she believes her territory is just a bad one. What can Eva's manager do to motivate her?

8. Adam Evers, MBA, has spent 20 years with Advanced Extrusion, remaining loyal even through the cutbacks of the last recession. Because the workload has grown in recent years, Advanced Extrusion hired Ned New, a recent college graduate, to assist Adam in the finance department. Adam is shocked to learn that Ned will have the same title as he does and that they will be sharing the office Adam formerly had to himself. According to equity theory, what responses might Adam make to this situation?

9. What are content theories and process theories? Give examples of each.

10. In what ways can managers create a work environment that motivates employees? Do these actions constitute exploitation of employees or are they justified? Explain your answer.

CRITICAL INCIDENT

Salary versus Commission

Jerry Palmer was not an outstanding marketing student in college and felt very fortunate to have secured a sales position with a pharmaceutical firm. The pay appeared to be competitive and, best of all, he was going to be working with a fixed salary rather than on commission.

During the first year, Jerry had a hard time making sales. But as he kept working at improving his sales techniques, his sales began to rise. By the end of his third year, and based on discussions with other salespeople, Jerry believed he had become one of the top sales representatives in the company. However, since the company never revealed how its salespeople performed (no sales data, and so forth), Jerry never knew if he was a top seller or not.

Last year was an excellent one for Jerry. His manager called him in for a brief meeting in October and praised him for his efforts. He was even told that if the company had ten more people like him they would probably be number one in the industry. Jerry took these comments to mean he was an excellent sales representative. He had exceeded his sales goals by over 20 percent and was looking forward to another great year.

This year he is off to a good start and appears well on his way to exceeding the sales goal once again. However, Jerry has begun having some motivational problems. He has heard that competitors annually have sales contests and that they recognize top performers as salesperson of the month. He knows that they also give out awards and hold banquets. Jerry has begun to get upset with his company. He asked his manager about considering such incentives or even having a salary plus commission program. He was told "that's not how this company does things" and that he "shouldn't worry about it."

Jerry is starting to look around for another position with a competitor. He is convinced that pay should be tied to performance.

QUESTIONS

1. Why do you believe Jerry came to be dissatisfied with his company's fixed-salary payment policy?

2. In light of McClelland's notion of need for achievement, how would you characterize Jerry?

3. What is now motivating Jerry? What type of incentive program would probably be attractive to him?

EXPERIENTIAL EXERCISE

What Do Employees Want from Their Jobs?

This activity is designed to help you think about the above question and to help you better understand the factors that influence an employee to perform. Because it can be difficult to motivate, it is vital to recognize and understand the factors that employees seek on the job. By providing opportunities to have various needs satisfied, one can provide employees with a motivating environment.

1. Examine the following list of factors and think of how employees (that is, people you've worked with or supervised) would rank them. Remember, you are looking at this list from the employee's perspective. Your ranking should reflect what you think they would say they wanted from their jobs. Place a 1 after the factor you believe they would want most from their job, a 2 after the next most wanted factor, and so on.

Factors	Ranking	Supervisors' Rankings[*]	Employees' Rankings[*]
a. Interesting, challenging work			
b. A feeling of being "in" on things			
c. Job security			
d. Competent supervisor			
e. Good working conditions			
f. Tactful discipline			
g. Promotion and growth in organization			
h. Appreciation of work well done			
i. Sympathetic understanding of personal problems			
j. Good wages			
k. Involvement in plans or decisions			
l. Loyalty and support from management			
m. Relevant and timely feedback on performance			
n. Clear goals and objectives			

[*]Will be provided by your instructor.

2. After you have completed ranking these factors, your instructor will provide you with the supervisors' rankings from a study. Record these rankings in the appropriate column.

3. Looking at the supervisors' rankings compared to yours:
   a. Are you and the supervisors making similar assumptions about the workers' job satisfaction?
   b. Do you notice any areas or clusters of work factors to which there are similar rankings?
   c. (If asked to do by your instructor) Was the average class ranking on selected factors similar to that of the supervisors? How do you account for the differences?

4. Your instructor will now provide you with the employees' rankings. Given this information, the following discussion questions are of interest:
   a. Is there generally good agreement between the employees' rankings and those of their supervisors? And your ranking?
   b. On what factors or clusters of factors is there general agreement or disagreement?
   c. If there are some large differences, to what do you attribute them? What role might perception play?

5. Your instructor will ask you to form groups of four to six people. As a group, discuss the following questions:
   a. Why do you believe the supervisors and employees ranked the factors as they did?
   b. What are some implications of the data for managers?
   c. What should managers do to create motivating environments?

Source: Written by Bruce Kemelgor, University of Louisville; used by permission.

NOTES

1. "America's Growing Anti-business Mood," *Business Week,* June 17, 1972, 101.

2. J.S. Mill, *Utilitarianism* (New York: Liberal Arts Press, 1949).

3. W. James, *The Principles of Psychology* (New York: Holt, 1890); S. Freud, *Civilization and Its Discontents* (London: Hogarth Press, 1930).

4. H.A. Murray, *Explorations in Personality* (New York: Oxford University Press, 1938).

5. H.A. Murray, *Thematic Apperception Test Manual* (Cambridge, Mass: Harvard University Press, 1943).

6. D.C. McClelland, *The Achieving Society* (Princeton: Van Nostrand, 1961); D.C. McClelland, "Toward a Theory of Motive Acquisition," *American Psychologist* 23 (1965): 321–333.

7. D.C. McClelland, J.W. Atkinson, R.A. Clark, and E.L. Lowell, *The Achievement Motive* (New York: Appleton-Century-Crofts, 1953).

8. D.C. McClelland and D.G. Winter, *Motivating Economic Achievement* (New York: Free Press, 1969);G.A. Steiner and J.B. Miner, *Management Policy and Strategy* (New York: Macmillan, 1977).

9. H.A. Wainer and I.M. Rubin, "Motivation of Research and Development Entrepreneurs: Determinants of Company Success," *Journal of Applied Psychology* 53 (1969): 178–184.

10. D.C. McClelland and R.E. Boyatzis,

"Leadership Motive Pattern and Long-term Success in Management," *Journal of Applied Psychology* 67 (1967): 737–743.

11. D.A. Kolb and R. Boyatzis, "On the Dynamics of the Helping Relationship," *Journal of Applied Behavioral Science* 6 (1970): 230–237.

12. R.F. Berdie, *After High School—What?* (Minneapolis: University of Minnesota, 1954).

13. G.H. Elder, Jr., "Structural Variations in the Child Rearing Relationship," *Sociometry* 25 (1962): 241–262.

14. R.P. Vecchio, "A Test of a Moderator of the Job Satisfaction–Job Quality Relationship: The Case of Religious Affiliation," *Journal of Applied Psychology* 65 (1980): 195–201.

15. McClelland, *The Achieving Society*.

16. McClelland, "Toward a Theory of Motive Acquisition"; R.L. Helmreich, L.L. Sawin, and A.L. Carsrud, "The Honeymoon Effect in Job Performance: Temporal Increases in Predictive Power of Achievement Motivation," *Journal of Applied Psychology* 71 (1986): 185–188.

17. D.E. Durand, "Effects of Achievement Motivation and Skill Training on the Entrepreneurial Behavior of Black Businessmen," *Organizational Behavior and Human Performance* 14 (1975): 76–90; J.A. Timmons, "Black Is Beautiful—Is It Bountiful?" *Harvard Business Review* 49 (1971): 81–94; Metropolitan Economic Development Association, "Business Leadership Training—What's Happening," *MEDA Reports 5*, no. 1 (1977): 1–7.

18. A.H. Maslow, *Motivation and Personality* (New York: Harper, 1954); A.H. Maslow, *Toward a Psychology of Being* (New York: Van Nostrand, 1968).

19. C. Keutzer, "Whatever Turns You On: Triggers to Transcendent Experiences," *Journal of Humanistic Psychology* 8 (1978): 68–72.

20. A.H. Maslow, "A Theory of Human Motivation," *Psychological Review* 50 (1943): 370–396.

21. L.W. Porter, "A Study of Perceived Need Satisfaction in Bottom and Middle Management Jobs," *Journal of Applied Psychology* 45 (1961): 1–10.

22. M.A. Wahba and L.G. Bridwell, "Maslow Reconsidered: A Review of Research on the Need Hierarchy Theory," *Organizational Behavior and Human Performance* 15 (1976): 212–240; E.E. Lawler and J.L. Suttle, "A Causal Correlational Test of the Need Hierarchy Concept," *Organizational Behavior and Human Performance* 7 (1972): 265–287; D.T. Hall and K.E. Nougaim, "An Examination of Maslow's Need Hierarchy in an Organizational Setting," *Organizational Behavior and Human Performance* 3 (1968): 12–35.

23. C.P. Alderfer, *Existence, Relatedness, and Growth* (New York: Free Press, 1972).

24. M. Csikszentmihalyi, *Flow: The Psychology of Optimal Experience* (New York: Harper and Row, 1990).

25. F. Herzberg, B. Mausner, and B. Synderman, *The Motivation to Work* (New York: Wiley, 1959).

26. H.M. Soliman, "Motivation–Hygiene Theory of Job Attitudes," *Journal of Applied Psychology* 55 (1970): 452–461; J. Schneider and E.A. Locke, "A Critique of Herzberg's Classification System and a Suggested Revision," *Organizational Behavior and Human Performance* 12 (1971): 441–458.

27. J. Galbraith and L.L. Cummings, "An Empirical Investigation of the Motivational Determinants of Task Performance: Interactive Effects Between Valence–Instrumentality and Motivation–Ability," *Organizational Behavior and Human Performance* 2 (1967): 237–258; L.W. Porter and E.E. Lawler, *Managerial Attitudes and Performance* (Homewood, Ill.: Irwin, 1968); J.P. Campbell, M.D. Dunnette, E.E. Lawler, and K.E. Weick, *Managerial Behavior, Performance, and Effectiveness* (New York: McGraw-Hill, 1970); M. Sussmann and R.P. Vecchio, "Conceptualizations of Valence and Instrumentality: A Fourfold Model," *Organizational Behavior and Human Performance* 36 (1985): 96–112; V.H. Vroom, *Work and Motivation* (New York: Wiley, 1964).

28. T.R. Mitchell, "Expectancy Models of Job Satisfaction, Occupational Preference and Effort: A Theoretical, Methodological, and Empirical Appraisal," *Psychological Bulletin* 81 (1974): 1096–1112; J.P. Campbell and R.D. Pritchard, "Motivation Theory in Industrial and Organizational Psychology," in *Handbook of Industrial and Organizational Psychology*, ed. M. Dunnette (Chicago:Rand McNally, 1976), 63–130.

29. Sussmann and Vecchio, "Conceptualizations of Valence and Instrumentality."

30. J. Hollenback, "A Matrix Method for Expectancy Research," *Academy of Management Review* 4 (1979): 579–587.

31. B.M. Staw and G.R. Salancik, eds., *New Directions in Organizational Behavior* (Chicago: St. Clair Press, 1976), 77.

32. B.F. Skinner and W.F. Dowling, "Conversation with B.F. Skinner," *Organizational Dynamics* 1 (1973): 31–40.

33. F. Luthans and R. Kreitner, *Organizational Behavior Modification* (Glenview, Ill.: Scott, Foresman, 1975); F. Luthans, *Organizational Behavior* (New York: McGraw-Hill, 1977).

34. Vroom, *Work and Motivation.*

35. J.S. Adams, "Injustice in Social Exchange," in *Advances in Experimental Social Psychology,* vol. 2, ed. L. Berkowitz (New York: Academic Press, 1965).

36. P.S. Goodman and A. Friedman, "An Examination of Adams' Theory of Inequity," *Administrative Science Quarterly* 16 (1971): 271–288; J.S. Adams and S. Freedman, "Equity Theory Revisited: Comments and Annotated Bibliography," in *Advances in Experimental Social Psychology,* vol. 9, ed. L. Berkowitz and E. Walster (New York: Academic Press, 1976); Campbell and Pritchard, "Motivation Theory in Industrial and Organizational Psychology."

37. E.E. Lawler, C.A. Koplin, T.E. Young, and J.A. Faden, "Inequity Reduction Over Time in an Induced Overpayment Situation," *Organizational Behavior and Human Performance* 3 (1968): 253–268; J.W. Harder, "Equity Theory versus Expectancy Theory: The Case of Major League Baseball Free Agents," *Journal of Applied Psychology* 76 (1991): 458–464;

C. Kulik and M. Ambrose, "Personal and Situational Determinants of Referent Choice," *Academy of Management Review* 17 (1992): 212–237.

38. R.P. Vecchio, "An Individual Differences Interpretation of the Conflicting Predictions Generated by Equity Theory and Expectancy Theory," *Journal of Applied Psychology* 66 (1981): 470–481.

39. R. Mowday, "Equity Theory Predictions of Behavior in Organizations," in *Motivation and Work Behavior,* 2d ed., ed. R.M. Steers and L.W. Porter (New York: McGraw-Hill, 1979); M.R. Carrell and J.E. Dittrich, "Equity Theory: The Recent Literature, Methodological Considerations and New Directions," *Academy of Management Review* 3 (1978): 202–210; R.W. Griffeth, R.P. Vecchio, and J.W. Logan, "Equity Theory and Interpersonal Attraction," *Journal of Applied Psychology* 74 (1989): 394–401; R. Huseman, J. Hatfield, and E. Miles, "A New Perspective on Equity Theory," *Academy of Management Review* 12 (1987): 222–234.

40. P.S. Goodman, "Social Comparison Processes in Organizations," in *New Directions in Organizational Behavior,* ed. B.M. Staw and G.R. Salancik (Chicago: St. Clair Press, 1976); R.P. Vecchio, "Predicting Worker Performance in Inequitable Settings," *Academy of Management Review* 7 (1982): 103–110; R.P. Vecchio, "Models of Psychological Inequity," *Organizational Behavior and Human Performance* 34 (1984): 266–282.

41. A. Bandura, *Social Learning Theory* (Englewood Cliffs, N.J.: Prentice-Hall, 1977).

42. A.P. Goldstein and M. Sorcher, *Changing Supervisor Behavior* (New York: Pergamon, 1974).

43. Porter and Lawler, *Managerial Attitudes and Performance.*

CHAPTER

7

Choose a job you love, and you will never have to work a day in your life.
— Confucius

People think we make $3 million and $4 million a year. They don't realize that most of us only make $500,000.
— Pete Incaviglia, Texas Ranger baseball player

Constant labor of one uniform kind destroys the intensity and flow of [a person's] spirits.
— Karl Marx

LEARNING OBJECTIVES

After studying this chapter, you should be able to:

1. *Distinguish between extrinsic and intrinsic rewards.*
2. *Compare various types of rewards on the dimensions of average importance, flexibility, frequency, and visibility.*
3. *Evaluate the merits of different pay-for-performance schemes.*
4. *Explain why incentive plans have lost popularity.*
5. *Describe three attributes of goals that are important for improving performance.*
6. *Describe management by objectives and some of its advantages and possible problems.*
7. *Give some examples of the power of self-fulfilling prophecies.*
8. *Describe some ways of constructively managing self-fulfilling prophecies.*
9. *Describe methods of job redesign used to reduce worker discontent.*
10. *List the job characteristics that enhance a sense of the meaningfulness of one's work, a sense of responsibility, and knowledge of the results of one's work.*
11. *Discuss some obstacles to job redesign.*
12. *Describe the essential elements of quality circles.*
13. *Explain how self-directed work teams operate, and identify major consequences and problems of such teams.*

Enhancing Employee Motivation
Rewards, Goals, Expectations, and Empowerment

NO MISTAKES ALLOWED

In the early 1980s, Motorola was struggling to keep up with stiff competition. The company had already lost out to Japanese companies, notably Toshiba and NEC, in the global competition for color television and car radios. It seemed that an important problem was that Japan was winning the quality war, using an emphasis on producing goods with zero defects. At the same time, observed Arthur Sundry, whose two-way radio division was then the best at Motorola, "Our quality levels really stink."

To reverse this decline, Motorola's top management decided to boost quality. Chairman Bob Galvin began by asking managers in the Communications Sector to seek a tenfold improvement in quality. The managers replied with an even more ambitious proposal: zero defects.

The managers called their plan Six Sigma, with sigma referring to the common symbol for standard deviation in statistics. The idea was that if all of production were described by a normal distribution curve, the defect-free products should fall within six standard deviations, which would include almost all of the products. In other words, products would be perfect 99.9999998 percent of the time.

Impressed, Chairman Galvin charged the Communications Sector with achieving this objective within six years. He then began expanding the program to the rest of the company. In 1989, Motorola began linking most performance review and bonus incentives to the Six Sigma requirements.

As sales and profits shot up and employees began earning quality-related bonuses, Motorolans began to credit the Six Sigma program with the company's and their better fortunes. At the Communications Sector, a 27-person unit recently celebrated its 255th straight week without a defect. An enthusiastic proponent of Six Sigma in the Communications Sector is Kim Fudge, the sector's manager of operations. "We have some large data-communications systems with tens of thousands of parts," he explains, "so you can see how reckless it is to operate at three sigma [99.7 percent error-free performance]." His remark refers to the fact that if just 0.3 percent of 10,000 parts contain errors, the system has 30 defects.

While zero-defects management is becoming a buzzword in American business, what makes Motorola's program unusual is that it extends to white-collar workers, such as sales and staff positions. For example, to moti-

vate quality order taking, Motorola inserts cards with its products that customers are to fill out if they receive an incorrect order. To make a quarterly bonus, a phone salesperson must have no more than one card returned per 2,000 orders.

In the marketing services department, where brochures and manuals are prepared, Six Sigma poses challenges in developing measurable standards. The department measures whatever it can: errors in photography, pricing, and grammar, for example. Enthusiasm for Six Sigma has led management to seek other measures as well, such as whether publications contain too much jargon.

Motorola's ultimate objective? "We will continue to improve quality," says Richard Buetow, vice president and director of quality, "till we become the perfect company."

Establishing goals such as zero defects is one way to motivate employees to do better. This chapter discusses ways to motivate employees through such techniques as offering rewards, setting goals, managing expectations, and redesigning jobs.

Source: Mark Stuart Gill, "Stalking Six Sigma," *Business Month*, January 1990, 42–46.

In Chapter 6, we considered a variety of perspectives on the topic of work motivation. As shown by the Porter-Lawler model at the conclusion of the chapter, each of these perspectives offers insights into the process by which employees are motivated to perform. In this chapter, we will examine four ways to apply our knowledge of the motivational process in order to enhance employee performance: through reward systems, goal setting, management of expectations, and employee empowerment.

REWARD SYSTEMS

Motivational theorists often distinguish between extrinsic and intrinsic rewards. **Extrinsic rewards** come from sources that are outside of, or external to, the individual, while **intrinsic rewards** may be more accurately characterized as self-administered. Examples of extrinsic rewards include pay, fringe benefits, promotions, and perquisites. Examples of intrinsic rewards are feelings of competence, accomplishment, responsibility, and personal growth. Although we typically think of extrinsic rewards as the primary means by which managers attempt to influence subordinates to perform well, intrinsics can also be used. In particular, the design of a job plays an important role in creating opportunities for intrinsic rewards. We will consider the redesign of work later in this chapter and, for the moment, will focus only on extrinsic reward systems.

THE ROLE OF COMPENSATION

Edward E. Lawler III is one of the strongest advocates of tying rewards to performance. Although Lawler has studied the use of a number of different types of rewards, he is perhaps best known for his writings on how to use pay as a means of motivating employees.[1] Although organizations can use a variety of rewards, they tend to rely on only a few. Pay is used most frequently because it possesses certain optimal characteristics.

First, a good reward should be valued by its recipient—and there is no question that pay is highly important to most people. Second, the size of a reward should be flexible. Some rewards, such as promotions, cannot be divided into various-sized portions, but the size of a pay raise can be easily manipulated. Third, the value of a reward should remain relatively constant. Some rewards, such as verbal praise, may lose their value if used repeatedly, but pay can be given frequently without diminishing its worth. Finally, for a reward to be effective (as noted in our discussion of expectancy theory in Chapter 6), the relationship of a reward to performance must be obvious. Because pay is so visible, employees can easily see the relationship between it and their performance. Thus, if we compare pay with other major organizational rewards on the dimensions of importance, flexibility, frequency, and visibility, pay is clearly one of the strongest resources available for improving performance (Table 7.1).

As has been noted several times in this text, the linking of rewards to performance is critical. Many managers think that performance and pay are closely linked in the units that they administer. However, in one survey, Lawler found that only 22 percent of workers in the United States believe that there is

TABLE 7.1

A COMPARISON OF FIVE MAJOR ORGANIZATIONAL REWARDS

	Average Importance	Flexibility in Amount	Frequency	Visibility
Pay	High	High	High	Potentially high
Promotion	High	Low	Low	High
Fringe Benefits	High	Moderate	Low	Moderate
Status Symbols	Moderate	High	Low	High
Awards and Certificates	Low	High	Low	High

Source: Adapted from E.E. Lawler III, "Reward Systems," in J.R. Hackman and J.L. Suttle (eds.) *Improving Life at Work*. Glenview, Ill.: Scott, Foresman, 1977.

a direct link between how hard they work and how much they are paid.[2] There are a number of reasons for this disturbing perception. How hard one works, of course, may not be related to one's level of accomplishment. Intervening forces, such as uncooperative coworkers, unanticipated interruptions, and faulty equipment, can all conspire to undercut an employee's best intentions. Determining an employee's level of accomplishment is also an imprecise technology. Performance appraisal systems (a topic to be considered more fully in Chapter 8) need to be designed to foster the perception that the measurement of performance is both objective and fair.

Attempts to relate pay and performance vary widely across organizations. These pay-for-performance schemes differ on three major dimensions: (1) the organizational unit, (2) the method of measuring performance, and (3) the form of monetary reward. One of three organizational units usually serves as the basis for comparing performance: the individual, the work group, or the total organization. The methods of measuring performance are more diverse and vary in terms of subjectivity. Ratings by supervisors are clearly the most widely used but most subjective device. Hard productivity data, such as sales figures and the number of units a person produces, are very objective. Other indexes of cost effectiveness and profitability (for example, number of errors and wastage) are also sometimes used. The two most common forms of monetary rewards are the bonus, which is a one-time, lump-sum reward, and the salary increment, which is a cumulative reward. Some organizations, for example Lincoln Electric, pay employees on a piecework system with an annual bonus based on the quality of output.[3]

Lawler has examined the combinations of the three dimensions of unit, performance, and pay, and offered an assessment of the effectiveness of each.[4] Table 7.2 summarizes his ratings of the pay-for-performance schemes. Note that the ratings reveal several patterns. The perception that pay is tied to performance is enhanced when rewards are administered on the basis of individual performance. Bonus schemes receive higher ratings on this dimension than do salary schemes. Objective measures of performance (productivity, cost

■ TABLE 7.2
RATINGS OF PAY-FOR-PERFORMANCE SCHEMES*

	Method of Measuring Performance	Ties Pay to Performance	Reduces Negative Side Effects	Encourages Cooperation	Employee Acceptance
Salary Reward					
Individual	Productivity	4	1	1	4
	Cost Effectiveness	3	1	1	4
	Supervisor Rating	3	1	1	3
Group	Productivity	3	1	2	4
	Cost Effectiveness	3	1	2	4
	Supervisor Rating	2	1	2	3
Organizationwide	Productivity	2	1	3	4
	Cost Effectiveness	2	1	2	4
Bonus					
Individual	Productivity	5	3	1	2
	Cost Effectiveness	4	2	1	2
	Supervisor Rating	4	2	1	2
Group	Productivity	4	1	3	3
	Cost Effectiveness	3	1	3	3
	Supervisor Rating	3	1	3	3
Organizationwide	Productivity	3	1	3	4
	Cost Effectiveness	3	1	3	4
	Profit	2	1	3	3

*Ratings can range from 1 to 5, with 5 denoting a scheme is higher on that dimension.
Source: Adapted from E.E. Lawler III, "Reward Systems," in J.R. Hackman and J.L. Suttle (eds.) *Improving Life at Work*. Glenview, Ill.: Scott, Foresman, 1977.

effectiveness) also elicit higher ratings. The most successful pay schemes are, therefore, likely to be individually based bonus plans that rely on objective measures of performance. Such schemes do have some negative side effects, according to Lawler; for example, social ostracism of superior performers and falsification of performance reports are more likely to occur with individually based bonus schemes.

Cooperation among group members tends to be greater with group and organizationwide pay plans. Such schemes foster the desire to help coworkers because of the perception that success is mutually beneficial. Individual schemes, on the other hand, encourage a greater sense of competitiveness.

On the dimension of employee acceptance, most of the pay plans rated moderately well. Individually based bonus plans, however, received a somewhat lower rating, possibly because the increased competition and the potential for falsification of performance reports produce the belief that the scheme is unfair.

In general, Lawler's analysis suggests that there is no single best pay incentive plan. Instead, each situation must be examined in terms of its unique characteristics. It is also important to note that these pay plans are not mutually exclusive. It is entirely possible to set up multiple or overlapping pay plans.

HOW EFFECTIVE ARE INCENTIVE PLANS?   Although available research indicates that incentive pay plans can increase productivity by 15 to 35 percent, the popularity of such plans has declined in recent decades.[5] Piece-rate schemes in particular have lost their appeal. Incentive plans have run into problems because of a variety of factors, including adversarial relationships, class consciousness, and societal changes.

Adversarial Relationships   When faced with incentive pay schemes, employees may use a number of ploys to lower production rates. When being observed, workers may produce at a very slow rate in order to deceive time-study consultants. And they may be reluctant to suggest improved methods for performing a task. Furthermore, informal norms will sometimes overpower individual initiative (see, for example, the Bank Wiring Room Study in Chapter 1). As an additional tactic for dealing with the establishment of incentive schemes, employees may turn to collective bargaining by electing a union to negotiate on their behalf.

Class Consciousness   Because the tasks involved in higher-level jobs (such as administrative and supervisory positions) do not lend themselves to easy quantification, incentive schemes are used more often for workers than for managers. This distinction can lead to a sense of "us versus them" within an organization's work force. The sense of being discriminated against can, in turn, feed otherwise latent hostilities. The consciousness of class differences coupled with the adversarial tactics mentioned above may produce protectionism, little sharing of information, a narrow definition of loyalty, and little trust. In general, an unhealthy organizational culture can be expected to emerge.

Societal Changes   The nature of work has changed significantly since the beginning of this century. At present, many jobs involve service or information delivery. High technology has gained increasing importance in many otherwise simple jobs. The stand-alone jobs that involved simple manufacturing are being replaced by interdependent jobs that require the use of more complex equipment in more continuous process-type operations.

In addition, there has been a movement in some settings to redesign work to make it less simple and repetitive, and thus to increase worker satisfaction, reduce turnover, and improve the quality of output. These attempts to enrich the nature of the work experience by offering more meaningful, complex, and interdependent tasks often create situations in which it is extremely difficult to measure performance in a simple, accurate, and fair manner.

THE FUTURE   Lawler foresees no major social changes that might increase the popularity of incentive pay.[6] Our country's recent poor growth in national productivity and its competitive disadvantage as a manufacturer in international circles suggest, however, that incentive pay as a means of improving performance should not be abandoned. Interestingly, a majority of workers (61 percent) express a desire for their pay to be tied to performance.

As a strategy for the future, Lawler suggests some combination of profit sharing, stock ownership, and gain sharing. At present, the use of all three

OB Focus
An Alternative Perspective on Rewards

An interesting and controversial perspective on the effects of incentive pay plans is provided by Alfie Kohn, the leading opponent of incentive pay. According to Kohn, such reward systems are akin to bribes, or dangling pieces of meat in front of a hungry dog. Incentives produce only temporary compliance, he argues, and are terribly ineffective at producing long-term changes in attitudes or behavior. Rewards merely motivate people to get more rewards.

Kohn provides six compelling arguments against the use of incentives:

1. *Pay is not a motivator.* Many studies have shown that employees rank pay fifth or sixth on a list of motivators, behind a sense of accomplishment in performing the work, recognition from peers and management, career advancement, and management support. Moreover, Kohn argues that, just because cutting an employee's paycheck in half might devastate morale and productivity, it doesn't necessarily follow that doubling a person's pay would result in better work.

2. *Rewards punish.* Not receiving an expected reward has the same effect as being punished. Rewards are manipulated by those who give them, and the more desirable the reward, the more morale suffers by not receiving it.

3. *Rewards rupture relationships.* Incentive pay plans, argues Kohn, are antithetical to teamwork and open, productive supervisor–worker relationships. When pay is contingent on performance, an employee is less likely to ask a supervisor for help. Consequently, problems are kept hidden from supervisors in order to maintain an illusion of competence, and employee performance ultimately suffers.

4. *Rewards ignore reasons.* Incentive plans designed to make employees more productive disguise underlying problems. Managers will never understand the root cause of these problems and optimal performance can never be achieved.

5. *Rewards discourage risk-taking.* When pay is contingent, workers are less willing to take risks, explore hunches, or search for alternative solutions. Originality, creativity, and risk-taking wane.

6. *Rewards undermine interest.* Having a sincere love for what you do is far more motivating than any financial reward. The more rewards are associated with an employee doing good work, the less interested that employee will be in doing the work. Rewards come to be seen as a means to an end, and the employee loses intrinsic interest in the end itself.

It is important to realize, however, that Kohn's beliefs are not uniformly accepted. Numerous opponents of Kohn's view point out that extrinsic motivators, such as pay, can enhance a worker's intrinsic motivation to work; that rewards do not necessarily control or manipulate behavior, but, rather, provide focus and reinforce good performance; and that mounting evidence shows that profit-sharing and Employee Stock Ownership Plans facilitate employee co-operation. Although managers and researchers acknowledge that incentive pay can have its drawbacks, they contend that Kohn has not provided any legitimate alternatives to traditional reward systems. At a time when organizations are demanding more work out of fewer people, and flexibility and teamwork are becoming prerequisites to staying in business, properly crafted incentive plans provide one means for joining employers and workers in the risks and successes of the organization.

Sources: Alfie Kohn, "For Best Results, Forget the Bonus," *New York Times*, October 17, 1993, F11; Alfie Kohn, "Why Incentive Plans Cannot Work," *Harvard Business Review* (September–October, 1993): 54–63; "Rethinking Rewards," *Harvard Business Review* (November–December, 1993): 37–49.

types of plans appears to be increasing. Profit sharing and stock ownership are more commonly used than gain sharing. As a motivator, the link between reward and performance may be too weak to be effective, since one's on-the-job efforts are not immediately and visibly tied to the organization's performance. However, profit sharing and stock ownership emphasize the long-term benefits of joint efforts, and therefore may be ideal for directing the behavior of higher-level employees in ways that are beneficial to the entire organization. These

21

two incentive schemes also can have significant symbolic value for employees in that they may develop a greater sense of identification with the organization.

The earliest **gain-sharing** plans were devised by union leader Joseph Scanlon over 30 years ago, but this approach is still considered relatively new. Essentially, gain sharing ties an individual's bonuses to the performance of a business unit. Specifically, such a plan might provide monthly bonuses to all members of a department or plant if a predetermined formula indicates that there has been a measurable decrease in the cost of materials, supplies, operations, or labor, For example, Herman Miller, a furniture manufacturer with a long involvement in gain sharing, offers a bonus system plus opportunities for employees to participate in decision making.[7] Similarly, such diverse organizations as Cummins Engine Company, TWA, and ROLM have gain-sharing plans.

The growing popularity of gain sharing appears to be due to several factors. Gain sharing is often introduced in a participative fashion, with employees being given a say in the design of the plan. Also, all employees—both managers and workers—are likely to be covered in the plan. In addition, because the setting of individual work standards and the calculation of individual compensation are not necessary in a gain-sharing plan, workers perceive the system as fairer.

Although Lawler foresees an increase in the use of gain-sharing plans, there may be limits to their use. For example, their implementation in such nonmanufacturing settings as hospitals may prove problematic because of the difficulty of establishing and measuring costs. As a recommendation, Lawler advocates the implementation of *multiple* pay systems in order to improve productivity and profitability. He further suggests that motivation will be at its maximum when employees have both a psychological stake and a financial stake in unit success.[8]

One of the more recent innovations in the area of compensation management is a variable pay-for-performance plan that typically starts with a reduced base wage or salary, but offers attractive bonuses to employees for attaining specific performance targets or other goals. Although bonus plans are not a new concept, the new plans attempt to tie risk and reward closer together. As a result, employee pay may be reduced during lean times. Experience with these plans (at such firms as Corning, Du Pont, Monsanto, and Valvoline) shows that employees can earn as much as 120 percent of the average wages of comparable jobs—or as little as 90 percent. One survey revealed that 35 percent of the *Fortune* 500 companies are experimenting with some form of pay-for-performance plan. Generally, such variable-pay plans seem to fare better in service industries where employees are more accustomed to commissions or other forms of non-fixed compensation.[9]

GOAL SETTING

Managers and employees need to understand each other's goals. In addition, managers are responsible for helping employees in setting goals or objectives. With a clear understanding of explicit goals or objectives, managers and employees can work together to achieve specific outcomes. Research on employee goals for performing a task suggests that several attributes of goals are especially important for improving performance: goal specificity, goal difficulty, and goal acceptance.[10]

SPECIFICITY

Goal specificity refers to the preciseness with which a goal or objective is stated. Increases in goal specificity are positively related to increases in performance. Very specific goals that are quantifiable reduce ambiguity and thereby help to focus employees' efforts.[11] Therefore, it is generally a good idea to avoid developing or stating goals in very broad or ambiguous terms.

DIFFICULTY

Increasing **goal difficulty** can also result in superior performance. The more difficult the goal is, so the research results suggest, the more challenging the task is perceived as being. Greater task challenge, in turn, results in greater effort being put forth by an employee. One major limitation to this argument, however, is that the goals must be feasible. Setting outlandish goals or goals that are unquestionably out of the reach of the employee will more likely lead to frustration and rejection of the goal.

ACCEPTANCE

Employees must also accept the goals that are set. **Goal acceptance** is most likely to occur when assigned goals correspond with personal aspirations. Difficult, specific goals that are accepted by an employee will therefore result in superior performance. This line of reasoning suggests that managers must encourage employees to focus on measurable and challenging goals while trying to elicit employee commitment to the goals.

MANAGEMENT BY OBJECTIVES

Management-by-objectives (MBO) is a practical application of the reasoning behind the notion of goal-setting theory. MBO is a process in which employees participate with management in the setting of goals, or objectives.[12] An essential feature of an MBO program is that it involves a one-on-one negotiation session between a supervisor and a subordinate in order to set concrete, objective goals for the employee's performance. During the session, a deadline is set for the measurement of accomplishment, and the paths to the desired goals and the removal of possible obstacles are discussed. After an established period of time has elapsed (typically six months or a year), the supervisor and subordinate meet again to review the subordinate's performance using the agreed-upon goals as a measuring stick. Figure 7.1 summarizes the essential steps in the MBO process.

A positive feature of an MBO system lies in its emphasis on establishing specific, measurable goals. In fact, a goal is unacceptable or inadmissible in an MBO system unless it is measurable. You may think that this is impossible for

FIGURE 7.1

AN OUTLINE OF THE STEPS IN THE MBO PROCESS

all goals, especially those of top-level executives. Although it is difficult to set measurable goals at the higher levels of an organization, it is nonetheless possible. For example, one such quantifiable goal might be that an institution will be ranked in the top ten by an annual polling of executives in the same industry. Or, the head coach of a college football team may set a goal of making the top 20 in the Associated Press's coaches' poll within the next five years. Some more typical goals would be to increase market share from 45 to 55 percent by the end of the next fiscal year, to increase annual production by 10 percent, or to increase profits after taxes by 3 percent. Some goals can be measured in simple yes or no fashion. For example, the goal of establishing a training program for sales personnel or completing a feasibility study by a certain date can be judged in a simple success or failure fashion when the deadline arises. Either such a project has been completed or it has not.

Advocates of MBO believe that everyone in an organization could and should be involved in goal setting. This includes all personnel, from the chief executive officer (who may set goals in consultation with the board of directors) to the newest member of the clean-up crew. In practice, however, middle-level managers and first-line supervisors are more commonly involved in such goal-setting systems.

Proponents of MBO systems also believe that supervisors must play a special role in the goal-setting process. Supervisors should view themselves as coaches or counselors whose role is to aid their subordinates in goal attainment. This role of coach/counselor extends beyond merely helping to identify and remove obstacles to goal attainment (for example, using personal influence to expedite shipments from another department). It also implies that the supervisor will serve as a mentor—someone to whom subordinates can go with their work-related problems and assume that they will be treated with respect and support.

DO MBO SYSTEMS WORK?   Research at such organizations as Black and Decker, Wells Fargo, and General Electric has shown that, on the whole, MBO programs can succeed.[13] Because MBO relies on the established principles of goal setting, it has great potential for improving performance. Real-world constraints, however, can sometimes reduce the positive impact of a goal-setting system.

One major obstacle to the success of an MBO program can be lack of support from top-level executives. If key people in the organization—especially the president and vice presidents—do not fully endorse MBO, their lack of support will likely be felt and responded to at lower levels. The net effect will be a decided lack of enthusiasm for the program.

Problems may also arise if managers are not interested in having subordinates participate in the goal-setting process. Some managers prefer to retain an evaluative and superior posture and are uncomfortable with the notion of being a coach or counselor to their subordinates.

Personality conflicts between superiors and subordinates are another potential problem for goal-setting systems, as is competitiveness. A superior who feels threatened by talented subordinates may do little to help them be more successful and, consequently, more visible. In addition, subordinates may hesitate to set challenging goals for fear of failure and its consequences.

MBO systems also tend to emphasize the quantifiable aspects of performance while ignoring the more qualitative aspects. This is an understandable tendency, since participants in MBO systems are encouraged to focus on measurable dimensions of performance. Qualitative aspects of performance, which are often more difficult to identify and measure, are likely to be overlooked or de-emphasized. For example, how can the quality of service that an organization provides or an organization's image in the local community be defined and measured?

Because the success of an MBO system rests heavily on the quality of the relationship between supervisor and subordinates, the degree of trust and supportiveness that exists in a work unit is a central concern. For an MBO system to be highly successful, these elements are critical prerequisites. The absence of trust and supportiveness severely restricts the system's effectiveness.*

Despite these many potential obstacles, the track record of MBO has been fairly good. In a recent review of the research literature devoted to MBO, Robert Rodgers and John E. Hunter examined 70 reports that included quantitative evaluations of MBO programs. Their findings showed productivity gains in 68 of 70 evaluation studies. The average productivity increase was 47

---

*This point prompts the paradoxical observation that MBO systems work best in situations where they may be needed the least (that is, where good supervisor–subordinate relations already exist), and MBO systems work least well in situations where they are needed most desperately (where divisiveness and conflict exist)!

percent, while cost data showed an average savings of 26 percent. Employee attendance was also shown to improve by 24 percent. Follow-up surveys of the level of top-management support for the programs revealed that productivity increased by 57 percent when top-management commitment was high, 33 percent when commitment was average, and only 6 percent when commitment was low.[14]

MBO has passed through several phases since its introduction in the 1950s. Initially, MBO was greeted with much enthusiasm by managers and management scholars. During the late 1960s and early 1970s, MBO appeared to be "sweeping the nation." Presently, MBO is viewed more objectively by scholars and practitioners as a tool that (like any tool) can be most effective under specific favorable conditions. It is now becoming passé even to invoke the initials MBO. In fact, the principles and philosophies of MBO have become so emotion-laden in the minds of managers that an organization will often introduce an MBO system under a different label. For example, an organization may establish a program called START (an acronym for Set Targets and Review Them) or GAP (Goal Acceptance Program). The mechanics of such programs are likely to borrow heavily, if not totally, from the MBO approach. In short, the trend is toward putting old wine into new bottles, with a recognition that mutual goal setting is not a panacea for all organizational problems under all possible circumstances.

EXPECTATIONS

One of the more subtle approaches to influencing employee performance is through expectations.[15] People communicate their performance expectations both verbally and nonverbally. Often, we send cues revealing that we either approve or disapprove of another's conduct. This approach to influencing employee performance is often employed without deliberate intent in that few of us consciously try to influence others by our transmitted expectations. The use of expectations to change performance, however, is receiving increasing recognition in the field of organizational behavior as a powerful force in influencing employee effort and performance.

THE POWER OF SELF-FULFILLING PROPHECIES

Perhaps the clearest examples of the power of expectations can be seen in the responsiveness of children to the expectations of parents and teachers. All of us have seen children who are labeled as "little devils" or "star pupils" respond exactly as expected. It can be said more generally that an individual often responds to expectations in a manner that supports the beliefs of the person who transmits the cues.

Robert Rosenthal of Harvard University is the foremost researcher of the power of expectations. In one investigation, Rosenthal and Jacobson studied the influence of elementary school teachers' expectations on their pupils.[16] At the start of the school year, pupils were given an academic aptitude test. The investigators then provided false feedback to the teachers, identifying 20 percent of the children as likely to bloom academically during the coming school year. In fact, the likely "bloomers" had been selected by a random process. At the end of the school year, all pupils were again tested. The results showed that the so-called bloomers did in fact bloom, as evidenced by significant gains in IQ in comparison to their classmates. Because the teachers' expectations were the only deliberately manipulated aspect in this study, the investigators concluded that the changes in student performance were largely due to qualitative differences in how the teachers related to individual students.

In their report of this study, entitled *Pygmalion in the Classroom*, Rosenthal and Jacobson argued that the teachers probably conveyed messages of expected success and failure to individual students.[†] The students, in turn, responded by living up to the teachers' expectations. In essence, each teacher held a prophecy, or expectation, for each student, and each student then behaved to fulfill the expectation. This process is called a **self-fulfilling prophecy (SFP)**.

The relevance of the SFP phenomenon for organizations is straightforward. Employees, like all people, desire approval from their superiors. To some degree, supervisors transmit cues, or expectations, that an individual has the potential to succeed or, alternatively, will never succeed. Employees then typically respond by conforming to the communicated prophecy. An employee who receives positive cues can seemingly do no wrong, while an employee who receives negative cues can rarely do anything right. When faced with negative expectations, part of an employee's failure stems from the fear of being evaluated harshly by a supervisor. This obsession distracts the individual from performing well and encourages him or her to interpret ambiguous situations in a more negative light.

In a study that paralleled that of Rosenthal and Jacobson, King studied the performance of a group of hard-core unemployed men who were enrolled in a welding course.[17] Initially, King gave the men a test of mechanical aptitude. The classroom supervisors were then given false feedback about the students' test performances, with some of the men arbitrarily labeled as "high-aptitude" students. As in the Pygmalion study, the only real difference lay in the minds of the observers. At the end of the course, the men were given a comprehensive test of welding knowledge. The so-called high-aptitude individuals did in fact do better on the test than their classmates. In addition, these same individuals were absent fewer times during the course and completed many of the exercises ahead of their peers. A confidential poll of the men regarding the popularity of their classmates revealed that the "high-aptitude" men were the most popular members of the class (that is, they were rated "most preferred to be with" by their classmates).

A more controlled study of the SFP phenomenon was reported by Eden and Shani in a study entitled "Pygmalion Goes to Boot Camp."[18] In their

---

[†]Pygmalion, a character in Greek mythology, is said to have sculpted a stone statue of a lovely maiden. Because he fell in love with the statue and wished strongly for it to be a living person, the gods took pity on him and brought the statue to life, hence fulfilling his aspirations.

study, Eden and Shani randomly labeled soldiers in the Israeli army as having "high command potential." These soldiers were then assigned to various instructors who were familiar with their alleged potential. Although the soldiers had different instructors, the results were much the same: Soldiers who had been randomly labeled as having high potential displayed superior performance during their training experience when compared to other trainees.[‡]

From these examples, it is clear that the SFP phenomenon is not limited to young children or animals.[§] Other examples of the SFP effect can also be cited. A bank run, in which the depositors flock to a bank and demand their money, is a classic illustration of a self-fulfilling prophecy. In a bank run, the depositors act collectively on a rumor of insolvency and thereby convert the rumor into reality. To some extent, the rate of inflation is partially due to an SFP. Consider a situation in which union bargaining representatives expect that inflation in the coming year will be around 3 percent. With this expectation, they will feel obligated to demand at least a 3 percent increase in wages in order to keep up with inflation. Manufacturing firms will, in turn, see their labor costs rising by at least 3 percent because of the workers' demands and will raise their prices accordingly. Thus, the expectation that the cost of everything will go up at least 3 percent in the coming year helps to create a situation in which the prophecy is fulfilled.[**]

THE CONSTRUCTIVE MANAGEMENT OF SELF-FULFILLING PROPHECIES

All too often we are unwitting participants in self-fulfilling prophecies, either as the perpetrator (cue sender) or benefactor/victim (cue receiver). In organizations, the effects of this influence process can be substantial. Rather than lament the traps of SFPs, it is perhaps best to think about how we can control this process to positive ends. Since we cannot avoid influencing one another's actions, it is important to consider how we can use SFP to encourage optimal performance from all organizational members.

A primary consideration in using SFP for benevolent purposes is to be more sensitive to how others perceive us. That is to say, we should strive to be more aware of how subtle aspects of our own behavior and speech communicate our thoughts to others. Small factors, such as amount of eye contact, tone of voice, phrasing of sentences, and so on, can speak volumes about how we

[‡]The statistical magnitude of the SFP effects was also substantial: The percentage of variability in subsequent performance that could be accounted for or explained by the SFP phenomenon was 73 percent, while 66 percent of the variability in attitudinal data could be attributed to the phenomenon.

[§]As an example of how humans and animals communicate expectations, consider how a dog typically reacts when we convey cues of fear versus confidence: Fear typically evokes an aggressive response, while confidence and relaxation elicit acceptance. In a dramatic illustration of the potential for subtle communication between humans and animals, Rosenthal and Fode told college students that individual lab rats they were asked to train in a maze were "bright" (allegedly based on past maze performance) or "dull."[19] The bright rats in fact outperformed the dull rats when the college students actually trained them to run a maze. Without knowing it, the college students had related to the rats in ways that conveyed positive or negative performance expectations. The rats were able to sense and respond to the students' cues.

[**]It should be apparent that inflation is not solely attributable to an SFP process. Other factors (such as changes in oil prices, oil shortages, and the size of the money supply) can also play a role.

truly feel. Thus, we must pay greater attention to controlling our own actions in order to communicate positive expectations to all individuals.

Many times, managers honestly feel that they treat all subordinates equally, but they communicate personal biases nonetheless. Workers rarely feel that their supervisors treat all subordinates alike. Most commonly, they claim that some subordinates are members of the boss's inner circle, while other are viewed as outsiders.

Managers can also use SFP to foster motivation. One technique for doing so is to display enthusiasm for the work unit's mission. Such enthusiasm will usually be contagious and spread to subordinates. A contagious enthusiasm that focuses on task accomplishment also draws attention away from interpersonal concerns of relative likes and dislikes.

SFPs may also play a role when performance appraisal schemes rely too heavily on subjective appraisals. In such cases, personal bias can be introduced. One common safeguard against this potential problem is the use of more objective indexes of performance. Sales figures or widgets produced per day should provide less biased measures of performance. Yet, even the perception of seemingly simple objective indexes such as these can be influenced by prior expectations.

To illustrate the point that even the perception of simple objective events can be biased by prior expectations, consider a study done in the area of extrasensory perception (ESP) research.[20] Researchers surveyed a group of college students on the extent to which they believed in ESP and related phenomena (for example, psychokinesis). Based on their responses, the students were sorted into two groups: "believers" and "skeptics." Members of the two groups were then invited to participate in a study that was purportedly being made of the ability of a well-known psychic who tried to influence a set of over 50 dice to turn up a large number of 6s. In truth, no one directly handled the dice spilling—it was done by machine, and a camera was positioned over the table to film the outcomes of 20 spillings of the dice. Also, no psychic was involved in the study. Upon viewing the film, the students were asked to record the number of times that they saw the number 6 appear on the screen. A third group of observers (a control group that was not asked any questions about belief in ESP) was later asked to view the same film without being given any cover story concerning a well-known psychic (that is, they were simply asked to count the number of 6s on the dice after each of the 20 tosses onto the table).

The average results for the three groups revealed that the believers counted a large number of 6s (significantly more than statistical theory would predict), the skeptics counted very few 6s (significantly less than would be predicted statistically), and the control group reported an intermediate number of 6s (within a predicted range derived from statistical theory). Thus, the believers reported evidence of psychokinesis, while the skeptics found evidence of a reverse psychokinesis! Clearly, prior expectations do influence the perception of seemingly simple objective events. The arousal of prior expectations, therefore, can be a powerful distorter of one's perception. This example should not

An Inside Look
Benefits, Empowerment, and Concern: A Winning Combination

Jack Rennie, founder of Pacer Systems in Billerica, Massachusetts, knows his competitors pay better, but he has been able to foster a loyal work force by providing benefits, empowerment, and concern. The company employs 340 people and sells design and engineering services as well as testing equipment and controls. A full range of benefits is offered to employees: health and life insurance, allowances for athletic equipment and career-related education, an employee credit union, and stock options for managers. Profit sharing is under consideration, and most employees participate in annual bonus pools that provide spot bonuses based on work unit and company profitability.

Just as important in motivating employees is Pacer System's culture of participative decision making. Participation is the norm at all levels of the organization and Rennie believes that it helps keep employees involved and motivated. A few years ago Pacer considered acquiring a nearby manufacturing concern. Groups of employees from engineering, accounting, and human resources spent half a year assessing the feasibility of a successful acquisition and presented their findings to the executive committee. From their recommendations the committee voted to acquire the company, and Rennie readily admits it was a sound decision.

The other ingredient to keep-

ing good employees, says Rennie, is conveying to them that you care about their well-being. Several years ago a long-term, loyal employee suffered a heart attack. He was worried that his sick leave would expire, and that he would have to get by on lower-level, short-term disability benefits. Rennie continued the disabled worker's salary beyond the insurance payout period. Throughout the organization, workers' commitment was visibly elevated, confirming that intangible rewards bear important long-lasting benefits.

Source: Charles Burck, "The Real World of the Entrepreneur," *Fortune*, April 5, 1993, 65–66.

lead one to despair of the possibility of accurate perception, but instead should caution one as to the power and prevalence of expectation.

In summary, our expectations influence both our perception of others and the behavior of others. In order to optimize the performance of every subordinate, it is essential that managers pay great attention to their prior expectations and the transmission of those expectations. This is not to advocate the manipulation of others by conveying deceptive cues. Rather, it is to advocate bringing out the best in others by treating them supportively and optimistically. The principle of using expectations to maximize performance may be summarized as follows: "Do not treat others as you may believe they are—treat them as if they are already what you hope they will become."

EMPLOYEE EMPOWERMENT

In addition to reward systems, goal setting, and the management of expectations, employee motivation can be enhanced by increasing an individual's sense of self-control at work. This notion of increasing employee self-determination is sometimes termed *employee involvement* or *employee participation*. However, a broader term that encompasses a number of specific techniques is **employee empowerment.** Employee empowerment refers to a set of motivational techniques that are designed to improve employee performance through increased levels of employee participation and self-determination. A major feature of employee empowerment is the deliberate merging of organizational and individual goals. In this section we will examine three specific techniques: job redesign, quality circles, and self-directed work teams. Job redesign has traditionally focused on improved individual productivity, while quality circles and self-directed work teams are more group focused.

JOB REDESIGN

A portion of the material wealth of our culture stems from the application of the principle of division of labor. The division of labor was recognized as an important factor in increasing productivity during the Industrial Revolution, when mechanization and job fragmentation began to emerge most strongly. Although Adam Smith, in his book *An Inquiry into the Nature and Causes of the Wealth of Nations,* identified division of labor as an important factor in improving productivity, he also suggested it had the potential to "corrupt" the worker through repetition and drudgery.[21] Karl Marx also observed that the trend toward industrialization in the West was creating a less than ideal set of circumstances for workers. As a solution, Marx advocated the overthrow of the capitalist system and the creation of a state in which factories and products were owned collectively by the workers.[††]

Despite these concerns, job specialization and greater division of labor continued. The productivity gains of job specialization resulted from decreased time spent changing tasks, decreased training time for employees, and increased skill due to repetition. Labor was also less able to claim that important skills were involved in the tasks and, therefore, was less able to demand higher wages. The early decades of this century witnessed a continuing drive toward job simplification, with the principles of scientific management (Chapter 1) helping to spur on the trend.[‡‡]

More recently, management scholars have recognized that job simplification can improve productivity *up to a point.* Beyond that point, worker dissatisfaction can set in (Figure 7.2). Workers then become hostile toward the task and the employer, and consequently reduce their efforts or increase labor costs through absenteeism or turnover. The challenge, as many managers see it, is to find the ideal level of simplification that maximizes productivity without risking worker discontent. In practice, most managers have been more likely to focus on increasing productivity at some cost to worker satisfaction. To be sure, a level of worker discontent that risks causing a wildcat strike or serious insubordination is to be avoided. But levels short of that extreme may be incurred in order to increase short-run production.

[††]Another solution was offered by an eccentric, Ned Lud, who feared that the Industrial Revolution would eliminate the means of livelihood of many peasants. Lud and his later followers, called Luddites, deliberately destroyed spinning and farming machinery in the early 1800s, not realizing that the Industrial Revolution actually helped to create many new jobs.

[‡‡]One of the dullest and most repetitious jobs with which I am familiar is that of bottle capper in a perfume factory. The job entails screwing on small perfume bottle caps for eight hours a day. These workers cannot leave their workstation unless a relief person is present. Also, if a worker is running out of caps, it is a different person's sole responsibility to see that the bin of bottle caps is replenished. For the record, the longest substantiated industrial career in a single job was that of Polly Gadsby, who began working at the age of 9 and wrapped elastic for the same company until her death at the age of 95.

FIGURE 7.2
RELATIONSHIP OF JOB SIMPLIFICATION TO PRODUCTIVITY

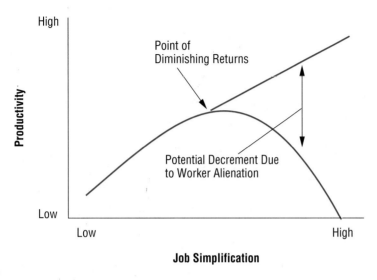

For numerous reasons, working conditions continue to improve. Since the emergence of the organized labor movement in the 1930s, management has rarely used work speed-ups—a tactic in which the pace of an assembly line is drastically increased for a short period of time. Workers (especially younger, better educated workers) are also more likely to express a desire for more challenging work. And due to larger societal trends respecting individual rights and liberties, a movement toward the enrichment, or humanization, of work is gaining strength. In the opinion of Filley, House, and Kerr, this movement represents something akin to the return swing of the pendulum.[22] For many centuries, craftsperson-type jobs (where job simplification is low) were prevalent. In the nineteenth century, the trend moved toward more simplified work, and now the trend appears to be heading back toward jobs with less simplification (although the era of the craftsperson may not fully return). In a sense, the world of work has been passing through a period of relative dehumanization. More recently, the trend is toward the rehumanization of work.

METHODS OF JOB REDESIGN   The first serious attempt to break from the principles of job simplification occurred during the 1940s and 1950s. This approach, called **job enlargement,** involves an increase in the variety of an employee's activities. In essence, a job is extended to include additional elements without really altering its content. For example, a worker may solder the red wires as well as the black wires. On the whole, job enlargement tends to improve worker satisfaction and the quality of production. The quantity of production, however, does not appear to be clearly or directly affected.

Job rotation is a related notion in the area of job redesign. In job rotation, the task stays the same, but the personnel who perform the task are systematically changed. Many organizations use job rotation as a training device to improve workers' flexibility. But the available evidence suggests that it does not aid either worker satisfaction or performance. Nonetheless, job rotation may be the only available means for introducing variety into jobs that cannot be redesigned to make them more meaningful or challenging.

Fred Herzberg was one of the first people to make an important observation about job-redesign efforts.[23] He noted that many redesign efforts focused on changing the *variety* of activities without changing their content. Also, the new designs did not give workers control over their jobs. Often, workers' efforts were paced by the rate of an assembly-line process instead of being self-paced. Herzberg proposed that autonomy and self-regulation are important causes of positive changes in worker behavior. He also felt that job-redesign efforts should focus on giving more decision-making responsibility to workers, rather than merely expanding the number of tasks performed. A distinction can thus be made between vertical and horizontal expansions of a job. Vertical expansion represents **job enrichment,** while horizontal expansion represents job enlargement. The specific job factors that have the potential to enrich work are drawn from the list of motivators that Herzberg proposed in his two-factor theory of work motivation (see Chapter 6).

Studies of job enrichment processes have tended to be success stories.[24] One of the more widely known examples of job enrichment programs is provided by Volvo's experiences at the Kalmar and Uddevalla plants in Sweden. The program changed the conventional assembly-line method of manufacturing to a more employee-centered system of controlling the assembly process. The assembly system relied on computer-controlled trolleys that carried partially assembled automobiles through the plant. However, reports of this experience and other job enrichment programs (such as those at Texas Instruments, General Foods, and Polaroid) have tended to be informal and lacking in rigor, so drawing a conclusive assessment of the value of job enrichment efforts is difficult.[25] Also, the Volvo plants at Kalmar and Uddevalla were eventually closed because of high absenteeism and low productivity (despite high employee satisfaction and high quality of output).

In what may be viewed as something of a backlash to the job enrichment movement, it has been argued that not everyone is interested in an enriched job. This position has been presented with several variations. The most extreme statement is that people are very adaptable and will adjust to most situations. Taking what may seem to be a callous perspective, the head of a human resources division of one large firm recently stated that it was not important to worry about the pay level of the organization's lower-level employees because the people are "accustomed to managing financial hardship."

A more moderate view is that only certain people desire enriched work, while others actually prefer the freedom from hassles resulting from an unchallenging job. Similarly, some claim that the high walls created by being "in a rut" offer a certain degree of insulation and security from potentially threatening surroundings.

Charles Hulin and Milton Blood have best expressed the moderate position on the need to consider individual differences.[26] They contend that a further important consideration is whether workers are from urban or rural areas. Rural workers may be more likely to subscribe to middle-class work norms, such as a belief in the Protestant work ethic and a positive view of achievement. In contrast, urban workers are more likely to be alienated from the work norms of the middle class and instead subscribe to the norms of a more heterogeneous urban subculture.

In analyzing data from over 1,300 blue-collar workers in 21 plants in the eastern United States, Blood and Hulin found that a worker's degree of urbanization tended to influence the relationship between job level and job satisfaction.[27] Specifically, they reported that employees in more urbanized settings responded with less job satisfaction to jobs of greater responsibility, whereas employees in less urbanized communities responded with increasing levels of job satisfaction to jobs of greater responsibility.

Although the consideration of individual differences seems to be intuitively reasonable, and one can easily imagine situations in which specific individuals may prefer nonchallenging work, more recent evidence from a national sample suggests that the magnitude of the differences among workers is not that great.[28] These data suggest that the vast majority of people respond positively to jobs of increasing quality (that is, greater challenge, autonomy, and responsibility), but that the strength of this desire is greater in some segments of the population. Blood and Hulin's study notwithstanding, it appears that workers rarely report negative reactions to increases in job quality.[29]

JOB CHARACTERISTICS THEORY   J. Richard Hackman and Greg Oldham have proposed a comprehensive theory of job enrichment that attempts to explain how various job dimensions affect worker behavior.[30] Their job **characteristics theory** also accounts for the possible influence of individual differences on the desire for enriched work. To their credit, Hackman and Oldham have tried to establish empirically the accuracy of their model and have designed measures of key variables.

The main components of their model and the links among them are portrayed in Figure 7.3. According to the model, a number of work outcomes, such as desire to perform well (that is, high internal work motivation) and satisfaction, are influenced by the experience of three critical psychological states. These three states—the meaningfulness of work, felt responsibility, and knowledge of results of job—are all "critical" in the sense that the absence of any one of them will not foster the desired outcomes. Each of the three states is influenced in turn by the various core job characteristics. Specifically, a sense of the meaningfulness of work is enhanced by the presence of

1. *Skill variety*, or the extent to which a job requires that different duties be performed involving a number of different skills,

2. *Task identity*, or the extent to which a person is permitted to complete a "whole" or identifiable piece of work from start to finish, and

FIGURE 7.3

THE JOB CHARACTERISTICS MODEL OF JOB ENRICHMENT

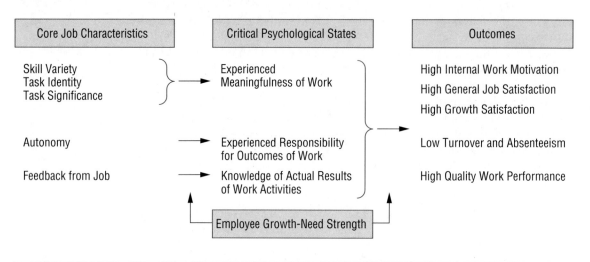

Source: Adapted from J.R. Hackman and G.R. Oldham, *Work Redesign* (Reading, Mass.: Addison-Wesley, 1980), 77.

3. *Task significance,* or the extent to which a job affects the lives of others (that is, is the job of some value to others in the organization or the world?).

Responsibility is enhanced by the presence of

4. *Autonomy,* or the extent to which a job offers independence and self-determination for the scheduling of work and the performance of associated tasks.

And knowledge of results is determined by

5. *Feedback from the job,* or the extent to which the conduct of the job provides clear and direct information on the effectiveness of the worker's performance.

   To assess the degree to which a job is enriched, Hackman and Oldham developed a series of questions that determine the extent to which a worker views his or her job as possessing each of the five job characteristics. Responses to the **job diagnostic survey** can then be combined in accordance with a formula for assessing a job's overall potential for motivating an individual. The Motivating Potential Score, or MPS, is given by:

$$\text{Motivating Potential Score (MPS)} = \left(\frac{\text{Skill Variety} + \text{Task Identity} + \text{Task Significance}}{3} \right) \times \text{Autonomy} \times \text{Feedback}$$

Because the formula involves the multiplication of terms, it suggests that a low or near-zero value on the job characteristics that define a critical psychological state will also lead to a total MPS value of near zero. The MPS formula is particularly useful for comparing different jobs and for assessing the same job over time (as might be done in a study of the effects of a job enrichment effort).

To illustrate the importance of the core job characteristics, consider almost any recreational activity in which people engage. The game of golf provides a particularly useful example. Golf involves a variety of skills and requires the use of personal judgment, as in deciding which club to use. A player completes the entire course, as opposed to only a portion. The game also possesses a form of significance, in that players keep a tally of the number of strokes they take to move the ball from the tee to the cup. This tally permits players to compare their performance against several standards: their own past performance on the hole, the par (or standard) for the hole, and the performance of their competitors. Autonomy is involved in that players are personally responsible for their performance. They are in charge of their own conduct and, consequently, their own success or failure. Finally, feedback is immediate. A player learns instantly if his or her shot hooks, slices, or lands in the sand. Clearly, the game of golf is highly "enriched," which explains why many people spend much of their spare time on the links.

It is interesting to consider what the game of golf would be like with any of the core characteristics removed. Suppose that feedback were eliminated, so that a player could not watch the flight of the ball to see how far it went or where it landed. Or imagine that autonomy were removed, so that a player had to follow someone else's directions on how to play each shot. In both cases, a great deal of the game's interest would be lost. If we failed to keep a tally of strokes (or a score of performance) and simply hit the ball around the course, we would also make the game less meaningful. In short, the removal of any of the critical psychological states would diminish the experience of enrichment or fulfillment and tend to make the activities seem more like "work" (in the most negative sense of the word).[§§]

To complete our discussion of the job characteristics model, we need to consider one additional component: the strength of an employee's desire for personal growth experiences in the work setting. Clearly, not everyone responds positively to challenging work. Some individuals prefer to be given assignments that are very clear-cut and offer little challenge. An attempt to enrich such people's jobs may be futile. In recognition of this fact, Hackman and Oldham have incorporated the notion of an individual differences moderator variable into their model (see Chapter 2 for a discussion of the concept of moderator variables). **Employee growth-need strength** enters the enrichment experience in two places: (1) it moderates the experience of psychological states in reaction to job characteristics (that is, individuals who are higher on growth-need strength tend to experience the states more fully), and (2) it moderates the relationship between the psychological states and worker outcomes

---

[§§]Another good illustration is given by video games. Objectively, the activity involved in playing video games is often highly repetitive. However, the sense of feedback, personal autonomy, and meaningfulness produced by a form of scoring provide a strong intrinsic appeal that can lead to an almost addictive involvement.

(that is, individuals who are higher on growth-need strength tend to have more positive outcomes in response to the psychological states). In short, the job characteristics model holds that the enrichment process will succeed only with individuals who are predisposed to benefit from the enrichment experience.

Evidence on the Validity of the Job Characteristics Model   The job characteristics model has been tested extensively in recent years. By and large, the results support the model's predictions.[31] The model appears to predict internal work motivation and job satisfaction quite well, and absenteeism less well. Predicting performance has proven to be more problematic. Quality enhancement is somewhat more certain, while quantity enhancement is not very reliable. It seems that the further one moves from psychological variables to job behaviors, the less successful the model is as a predictor. Moreover, the multiplicative scheme for combining the five job characteristics to determine a job's Motivating Potential Score may be an overrefinement in that a simple additive combination of values for the five characteristics predicts nearly as well.

OTHER JOB REDESIGN APPROACHES   In addition to job enrichment, three other work redesign techniques are also growing in popularity: flextime, the modified workweek, and telecommuting.

Flextime refers to a work schedule that gives employees some discretion in arranging their working hours. Most frequently, the employer specifies a period of time during the day when all employees must be present—the core time. Employees may then schedule the rest of their work hours according to their own preferences. In most cases, the earliest starting time and latest stopping time are prescribed, as is the total number of hours that an employee must complete every week. Many flextime plans also hold an employee to a two-hour maximum time limit for lunch. But within these constraints, employees are free to select starting and finishing times each day. To be sure, flextime does not redesign the actual tasks that workers perform, but it does offer each employee a means of balancing work and home life.

Research on flextime has yielded generally positive results. For example, Cohen and Gadon reported that absenteeism and turnover were lowered, while performance increased following the introduction of flextime.[32] Significant increases in productivity were also reported in a study by Schein, Maurer, and Novak.[33] Other experiments have also tended to find positive effects, especially in reduced absenteeism and turnover.[34]

Modified workweek plans attempt to design alternatives for the currently prevalent 8-hour day, 5-day workweek. The most commonly adopted design is the 4-day, 10 hours per day workweek, or 4-40 scheme. Because the rest of the business world still follows a 5-day workweek (and therefore expects to communicate and send goods on a 5-day schedule), many experimenting organizations have had to stagger their 4-day plans so that part of the company will be open on any given workday.

The impact of the 4-40 schedule has been mixed. Although employees can enjoy longer stretches of uninterrupted leisure time and less commuting, they are more likely to be fatigued from working longer shifts. Absenteeism, however, is often reduced due to the potentially greater cost that a lost workday has for the individual employee. Informal evidence of the productivity gains of 4-40 programs, such as surveys based on managers' impressions, has tended to be positive.[35] But other evidence tends to be mixed. Ivancevich and Lyon found that while performance and satisfaction increased following the introduction of a 4-40 scheme, both outcomes returned to original levels after about two years.[36] A survey by Cohen and Gadon suggests that some companies that have experimented with 4-40 schemes are returning to a traditional workweek.[37] Despite such mixed findings, most social forecasters predict that a 4-40 workweek lies in our future.[38] Most of these predictions, which were made during the late 1970s and early 1980s, assumed a continuing, long-term energy crisis. So the reasoning goes, substantial start-up and heating/cooling costs for manufacturing and office facilities, as well as reduced commuting costs, could be realized by the nationwide adoption of a 4-40 workweek.

Telecommuting refers to the use of computer links with one's employer that permit the completion of all or part of one's job at home. Several million employees in North America are currently involved in telecommuting, and projections indicate that this number will increase in the coming years. Telecommuting tends to be used most in information-intensive and information-processing industries, such as insurance, banking, financial services, and market research. Firms with successful telecommuting experiences include American Express, Mountain Bell, Hanover Trust, J.C. Penney, Beneficial Finance Corporation, Apple Computer, and Travelers Insurance.

Telecommuting offers some clear advantages to both the employer and employee. For example, there is a reduced need for work space at the employer's site, and the employee is spared the cost and time of commuting. In addition to being free from distractions at the workplace, employees are able to spend more time with family members. This can be of great importance to employees who must provide care for the young or elderly. Research on the impact of telecommuting on employee productivity suggests that gains of 15 to 30 percent are not uncommon, most probably as a result of employees being free from workplace interruptions.[39] Also, telecommuters report higher job satisfaction levels, perhaps because of fewer work-related frustrations.

On the downside, telecommuters are "out of the loop" in terms of being part of the workplace political network. Because of such isolation, they may be bypassed for promotions or receive smaller raises. Also, they may feel a greater sense of social isolation than other employees. These potential drawbacks suggest that employers should screen individuals who are interested in telecommuting. Such screening would identify those who can handle the negative aspects of telecommuting and who can be productive without immediate supervision. Also, telecommuters might be required to come to the office site periodically to talk with their supervisor and specific individuals, as well as to socialize with other employees.

OBSTACLES TO JOB REDESIGN   The introduction of a job redesign program, like any change effort, is seldom a simple task. Numerous obstacles are likely to arise, and some of the greatest resistance is likely to come from the employees themselves. Frequently, employees as well as managers are comfortable with the informal power systems that already exist. They thus view job redesign as an intrusion on the existing social order. Unions also tend to oppose job redesign, perceiving such efforts as schemes for extracting greater work from employees without providing hard compensation in exchange. As one union member once said, "If you want to make me feel proud or tell me I'm doing a good job, say it with money!"

Supervisors often fear job redesign efforts as well. Their fears are grounded in the belief that an increase in employee self-control or self-monitoring will result in a need for fewer supervisors. This fear is valid in that a successful job enrichment program will reduce the need to monitor employee performance closely.***

Further problems may arise if employees are not personally involved in the job redesign effort. Including employees in the redesign process can be a powerful means of gaining their commitment to the program's success.

A final, and less easily remedied, limitation of job redesign involves the diminishment of the impact of redesign programs on successive "generations" of employees. Due to naturally occurring turnover, the employees who witnessed a work redesign change will eventually be replaced by employees who did not experience the change. These newer employees may take their now-enriched jobs for granted because they lack the perspective of long-time employees, who clearly recognize the before–after contrast. Merely telling a recently hired employee that his job is much better than it used to be, thanks to a redesign program, is unlikely to have much real impact on his feelings and behavior. Thus, job redesign efforts may have their strongest positive effects on employees who experience the change personally and are therefore sensitive to the changes. The natural attrition and replacement of workers may tend to diminish the positive impact of redesign efforts over time. As yet, this suspected process of diminished impact has received only informal consideration by job redesign specialists. The magnitude of this potential limitation and the possible remedies remain to be explored.

QUALITY CIRCLES

In recent years, quality circles have begun to appear in a growing number of firms in the United States. **Quality circles** are employee committees of six to ten workers who meet once or twice a week (usually on company time) to discuss production and problems with product quality. Although the notion of quality circles originated in the United States, it took root in Japan after World War II (after being introduced in Japan by American consultants). The use of quality circles was reintroduced to the United States, partly due to a fascination with Japan's business success.

In a quality circle program (1) membership is voluntary (employees must not be coerced into participating), (2) circle members are trained in problem-

---

***One consultant who specializes in the introduction of job enrichment programs told me that the greatest initial protest to such proposed programs is likely to come from first-level supervisors, who typically argue that *their employees* will not like the new situation.

solving techniques, (3) members develop solutions to problems that they submit to management through formal presentations, and (4) members monitor the outcome of their solutions. Figure 7.4 presents a model of the quality circle process.

It has been estimated that from 12 to 25 percent of the Japanese work force participates in quality circles.[40] Although the proportion of the United States work force that participates in quality circles is still relatively small, it has been growing rapidly since the early 1980s. Most of this growth has been in the manufacturing sector, and the firms that have implemented quality circles have experienced impressive success. For example, at Honeywell, a high-technology electronics firm, several hundred quality circles are in use; in addition to improving productivity, they have reduced absenteeism. Other large U.S. companies that have successfully introduced quality circles include American Airlines, General Motors, Ford Motor Company, Hughes Aircraft, International Harvester, Texas Instruments, Westinghouse, and Northop. Many smaller firms have experimented with quality circles, too, as have such service-oriented institutions as hospitals and YMCAs.

Although all quality circles share certain common elements, programs may vary on a number of features. While there is very little hard evidence to indicate exactly which details are critical to a quality circle's effectiveness, Blair, Cohen, and Hurwitz have suggested that certain traits are characteristic of successful programs.[41] Chief among these is *commitment by top-level management* to the program. If top management does not fully endorse and support a circle program, the lack of enthusiasm will be detected and duplicated by others. As a result, the circle program will probably not receive the serious support it needs from lower-level supervisors. Second, successful programs are

FIGURE 7.4
A MODEL OF THE QUALITY CIRCLE PROCESS

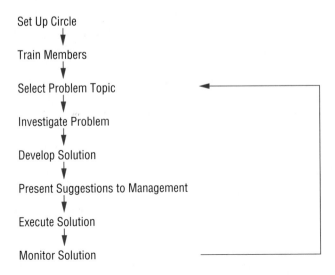

more likely to have *group facilitators*—usually senior workers rather than supervisors—*who have been specially trained* in both group relations and problem-solving strategies. Third, members of circles must be assured that they *will not lose their jobs or have their responsibilities reduced as a result of their suggestions.* Fourth, *recognition must be given* to individuals and circles for suggesting workable solutions to operational problems. At Northop, for example, a quality circle is awarded 10 percent of any dollar savings that result from its suggestions. Such monetary rewards are uncommon, however, as most organizations prefer to rely on psychological rewards to motivate participation.

Advocates of quality circles are quick to point out the approach's relatively low cost and logical reliance on front-line workers to suggest improvements in operations. When employees are the source of suggested improvements, they are more likely to accept changes because they feel a sense of ownership and responsibility. In addition, workers, managers, stockholders, and the public generally take a very positive view of the quality circle concept.

The quality circle concept is not without its critics, however. Some critics question the real cost effectiveness of quality circles. They contend that since employees are not performing their normal duties while they meet in circles (most circles meet on company time) and since most circle suggestions generate only minor savings, it is difficult to prove that the savings gained from the groups' suggested improvements justify the time lost from work. Union representatives in particular have had mixed reactions to the quality circle concept. For example, leaders of the United Auto Workers are favorably inclined toward quality circles as long as the programs do not produce layoffs or increase the work pace. They look less favorably on the fact that most circles are not compensated for generating cost-saving solutions.

In addition, the motives of people who volunteer for quality circles are not fully understood. Some people who volunteer for the program may do so in order to get away from the assembly line and gain a sanctioned work break. Others may join merely to voice their frustrations and complain about their jobs rather than to offer constructive suggestions. Only recently has research focused on the attributes of quality circle volunteers. The results suggest that circle participants are likely to be more highly educated, younger, in jobs of greater responsibility, and more satisfied with their jobs than are employees who show no interest in membership.[42] One study of the level of job satisfaction of quality circle members found an increase over several years. However, the level of member job satisfaction returned to the earlier, pre-circle level after three years.[43]

Because they are by definition voluntary, it is not possible to study circles in a rigorous scientific fashion.[†††] Some quality circle improvements may be due to nothing more than a Hawthorne effect (see Chapter 1). An additional concern relates to the longevity of quality circle programs. One review reported that nearly 75 percent of the initially successful circle programs in the United States were no longer operating after only a few years.[44] Continuing

---

[†††]Random assignment of employees to conditions is not possible (se Chapter 2) because it violates the voluntary nature of a quality circle.

interest in and support for circles may be difficult to sustain in many organizations. It is also possible that some of the attractiveness that has surrounded quality circles may be wearing off as firms recognize the limitations of the programs.

Even in Japan (where three times the percentage of manufacturing employees are involved in quality circles as the United States), disenchantment has been reported.[45] For example, roughly one-third of Toyota's employees feel that circle participation is a "burden."[46] At Mitsubishi Chemical Industries, some employees report a sense of obligation to attend quality circles and a concomitant feeling of monotony during meetings.[47] It appears that in order to rekindle enthusiasm and overcome apathy, well-established quality circle programs must find new ways to challenge and reward circle members.

SELF-DIRECTED WORK TEAMS

Perhaps one of the most exciting new developments in the area of employee motivation in recent years has been the emergence of self-directed work teams. In essence, a **self-directed work team (SDWT)** is a highly trained group of 6 to 18 employees that is fully responsible for creating a specified product.[48] Unlike the traditional view of an employee who has a narrowly defined set of responsibilities, each member of a team shares responsibility for performance. Team members are trained to perform a variety of cross-functional tasks in order to be interchangeable within the unit and provide assistance to others. Additionally, team members share information openly and participate in decision making. Team decisions typically cover domains once reserved for supervisors, such as setting priorities, production planning, and assigning work. Even interpersonal problems, such as excessive absenteeism or poor performance by a team member, are fair subjects for discussions at team meetings. It should be emphasized that SDWTs are truly "revolutionary" in their approach and go far beyond conventional work groups in terms of their role within an organization.

The allure of SDWTs stems from success stories that recount improved productivity coupled with reduced costs. One estimate is that a well-functioning system based on SDWT, compared to a traditionally run organization, can produce twice the output in one-quarter of the work space with one-third the work force. Xerox Corporation plants that use SDWTs report 30 percent greater productivity than their conventionally run plants; productivity gains of 20 to 40 percent have been reported at General Motors plants; and Shenandoah Life reports a 50 percent increase in processing customer services with SDWTs while employing 10 percent fewer people.[49]

Although the notion of work groups certainly is not new, the beginnings of SDWTs can be traced to the 1960s when several organizational "experiments" were undertaken. One of the first was at the Gaines Pet Food Facility in Topeka, Kansas. To combat "blue-collar blues" (the notion of worker alienation in manufacturing firms), General Foods established the pet foods facility based on the team concept. At the Topeka facility, employees rotated job assignments and met frequently to make joint, work-related decisions. The facility was highly successful and became a "showcase plant" visited by managers from around the globe.

Also during the 1960s, Procter and Gamble (P&G) began a series of studies on new manufacturing techniques at its plants in Lima, Ohio, and Augusta, Georgia (where diaper and soap products were produced). Although the team-based studies were deliberately surrounded by a great deal of corporate secrecy, word eventually spread that significant, high levels of output were being achieved while production costs were being reduced. Eventually, SDWTs spread to 18 P&G plants. During the 1980s, other large firms adopted the SDWT approach (see Table 7.3). The 1990s has witnessed the spread of the SDWT concept to firms outside the manufacturing sector. Because of the globe-spanning nature of corporate ownership and the sharing of information, SDWTs have become a worldwide phenomenon, with reports of SDWTs being installed in the former Soviet Union, Eastern Europe, and Saudi Arabia.

The essential defining elements of SDWTs consist of team meetings, mandatory job rotation, skill-based pay, and increased training opportunities. At regular team meetings, members make decisions on performance-related issues as well as self-discipline issues (for example, dealing with a poor performer or a member who is frequently late to work). Leadership at these meetings is sometimes shared or rotated.[‡‡‡] In some instances, a team member is elected leader for a fixed period of time. The team leader does not make unilateral decisions, but instead facilitates discussion and consensus.

Mandatory job rotation is a key element of SDWTs. By rotating assignments, members gain knowledge of a broader range of tasks and are able to help out other team members who may need assistance. The team thus gains in versatility and flexibility. Because members become, in a sense, interchangeable as a result of shared knowledge, there is less "downtime" due to a single member lacking the know-how to remedy problems. Mandatory job rotation, which usually occurs at 6- or 12-month intervals, has the added advantage of eliminating "turf wars" that sometimes develop in work units. That is, no one "owns" a particularly enjoyable, or cushy, job, and everyone eventually spends some time doing the least enjoyable job in the unit. Because of rotation, no employee can obtain a permanent position that is removed from the work flow or that would provide a form of "early retirement with pay."

The compensation scheme for SDWTs also differs from traditional forms. Pay is skill-based in such systems. Employees move up the hourly- or salary-rate compensation ladder by demonstrating proficiency in a given task. Employees thus have an incentive to learn a greater variety of tasks or skills in their work units. The employee benefits by gaining more marketable job skills and a sense of competency, while the organization gains by having a more flexible and more talented work force. Because of the skill-based nature of the compensation system, employees welcome the opportunities provided by job rotation. In some SDWT systems, a gain-sharing program also provides bonuses to members of a department or plant for increased productivity.

In order to learn new skills, employees must spend more time in on-the-job training. When a person rotates into a new assignment, he or she must

---

[‡‡‡]Perhaps the most extreme, but reportedly effective, form of rotation is used by Eaton Corporation of South Bend, Indiana, where each team member routinely rotates into the leader position for one day at a time.

TABLE 7.3
MAJOR FIRMS USING SDWTs

Company	Year Started
Boeing	1987
Caterpillar	1986
Champion International	1985
Digital Equipment	1982
General Electric	1985
LTV Steel	1985
A. O. Smith	1987
Tektronix	1983

Source: J. Hoerr, "The Pay-off from Teamwork," *Business Week*, July 1989, 58.

spend some time learning the ropes (often looking over the shoulder of another individual, asking questions, and trying out equipment). This added training requires that some additional slack be built into the unit to accommodate needed learning time. Typically, however, the gains in increased output and reduced costs more than compensate for the time lost by employees in a training phase. In addition, the opportunity to learn new skills tends to have a positive motivational effect, which also helps to make up for time lost due to training.

SDWTs are often introduced as part of a broader shift in organizational philosophy toward enhancing the quality of output or services. Because of global competition and a perception that levels of quality are not sufficient, some organizations have embraced the Total Quality Management perspective. **Total Quality Management (TQM)** is a set of principles that embodies a strong emphasis on establishing and maintaining a high level of quality. The key principles associated with TQM involve (1) getting it right the first time (that is, reducing errors by improved techniques and processes), (2) focusing on the customer or client (that is, being close to and understanding the needs of one's constituencies), (3) emphasizing continuous improvement (that is, making an emphasis on quality part of "the way we do things around here"), and (4) fostering mutual respect among coworkers (that is, eliminating fear based on hierarchical organizational designs and replacing that fear with autonomy and participation based on power-sharing). SDWTs are seen as a vehicle for advancing a TQM philosophy in an organization. As the above points suggest, SDWTs are relevant to TQM as a device for instilling mutual respect through power-sharing.

CONSEQUENCES OF SDWTs Although the potential payoff for successfully implementing SDWTs is highly attractive, there are also some downside features to SDWTs. However, these potential problems can sometimes be ameliorated. Also, it should be understood that for every success story involving SDWTs, there may be a failed attempt at implementation. Sometimes even successful introductions of SDWTs did not occur on the first attempt, and the notion of learning from one's mistakes especially applies to introducing SDWTs.

OB Focus
Teamwork in a Global Marketplace

Today, the word *teamwork* is used to refer to a variety of forms of employee involvement, of which quality circles are the oldest and most widely used format in the United States. Besides quality circles, companies have tried using special-purpose teams, which carry the quality-circle approach a step farther, involving workers in higher-level decisions, such as designing new technology and meeting with suppliers and customers. An even higher level of worker participation comes from self-managing teams that produce an entire product instead of individual components, with workers rotating among many jobs and making managerial decisions, such as scheduling employees and ordering materials.

Quality circles first became popular in the United States in the 1970s, based on the success of this technique in Japanese companies. According to a 1987 survey of 476 large companies by the U.S. General Accounting Office,

70 percent had instituted the use of quality circles for at least some of the work force.

Since the mid-1980s, U.S. companies have begun moving to forms of teamwork that more closely reflect the American rather than the Japanese culture. In American-style teamwork, employees not only have a voice in shop-floor operations, they also take on such traditionally managerial duties as scheduling work and vacations, ordering materials, and hiring new team members. Also, in American companies, union officials often demand a role as consultants or participants in plant-wide decisions such as production scheduling, capital expenditures, and the introduction of new technology. With these shifts, special-purpose teams and self-managing teams became more popular beginning in the 1980s.

In contrast, in Japan, teamwork is not designed to give workers more autonomy. Rather,

quality circles are designed simply to help them identify problems in the production line so that the company does not produce defective goods. The U.S. approach seems to parallel more closely the approach taken in Sweden, where at two Volvo plants teams of workers assemble large units of a car or even an entire car with little supervision.

These changes help American industry meet the need to manufacture more customized products in a global marketplace. When work practices are flexible and workers know how to perform a variety of tasks, they can quickly change over to new models and products. At a General Electric plant in Salisbury, North Carolina, for example, teamwork enables employees to change product models a dozen times a day, which has increased productivity by 250 percent.

Source: John Hoerr, "The Payoff from Teamwork," *Business Week*, July 10, 1989, 56–62.

A necessary consequence of implementing SDWTs is the elimination of the need for a number of supervisory positions. As noted earlier in the discussion on job redesign, fewer supervisors are required as employees take on more responsibility. Supervisors sense this likelihood and often offer resistance to the proposed introduction of SDWTs. Generally, after SDWTs are introduced supervisors are given different responsibilities. For example, they may become more involved in coordinating and integrating communications.[50] Also, former supervisors who are retained as higher-level area managers whose jobs now entail coordinating team efforts need to learn the new skills required for being facilitators and resource personnel, rather than acting as overseers who assign work, monitor production, and administer discipline. For some former supervisors, the transition can be very difficult as it involves abandoning a set of hierarchical values for a set of more egalitarian values.§§§

§§§It must be emphasized that SDWTs are rarely totally autonomous (that is, there is still a need for a level of supervision). However, the manager who oversees a set of teams and interacts with the teams' leaders does have a challenging task of balancing the need to give the team members sufficient autonomy, while being prepared to intervene if a team does not accept its responsibilities or conform to the organization's goals.

Another consequence of SDWTs is that the emerging, transformed organization is likely to be much "flatter," with fewer levels of administration and far fewer job titles. In some plants, the term *technician* is used in place of job titles. This term reflects the technical orientation of many jobs and the continual skill-learning aspect of these positions. Except for hat colors or other minor distinguishing features, differences among employees tend to be minimized (for example, there are often a common entrance and parking lot as well as a common cafeteria, rather than separate facilities for supervisors or managers).

A further necessary consequence of the introduction of SDWTs is the requirement of a sizable investment in training. Additional training staff and facilities are likely to be needed. Also, more attention to individual limitations in learning abilities may be warranted. Skills that are deficient in some individuals (for example, problem-solving techniques and interpersonal skills) may need to be taught by the firm in order to have the teams work efficiently. As a result, human resources development staff take on a more important role in firms that are committed to SDWTs.

POTENTIAL PROBLEMS AND CRITICISMS OF SDWTs   One of the more troubling problems for members of SDWTs occurs when they have learned all the tasks in their work units. An employee who has been in the unit for a relatively long time (more than 6 to 10 years) may have learned, through job rotation, all of the jobs in the unit, and may have reached the maximum level of pay that is possible (sometimes termed *plant rate*). For employees who have "topped-out" by reaching plant rate, there are no new mountains to climb, and the psychological lift that came from relatively frequent pay boosts is no longer visible on the horizon. For such individuals, firms might suggest changing to a significantly different work unit, working on special projects, or pursuing formal education that would lead to a different career path. Often, firms will offer to underwrite part of the educational expenses of employees who wish to seek additional formal education that may lead to another job. However, the preference is to support educational pursuits that may translate into a skill desired by the employer (for example, computer or office-related skills). As noted earlier, the introduction of a gain-sharing program can also help to maintain a sense of financial incentive.[51]

Another potential problem for SDWTs involves the unionized work force. SDWTs have been introduced in unionized settings (with labor's agreement, of course). Although hard evidence is not available, it appears that SDWTs in unionized settings are far less productive than those in nonunionized settings. However, this may not be a fair comparison (SDWTs in unionized settings should probably be compared with those in other unionized settings). Despite the obstacles posed by being unionized, firms continue to **retrofit**—that is, to introduce SDWTs to existing work forces. A more common practice in recent years has been to begin afresh by establishing a new facility in a new location with a new work force. In such a setting, successful introduction of SDWTs has been reported to be far more likely (the Topeka, Kansas, Gaines Pet Food facility provides an example). This technique is termed establishing a **green-**

field site—from, often literally, starting in an open field to build a brand-new facility based on SDWT principles.

It should be mentioned that even organizations that have successfully established SDWTs are not immune from being driven out of business. One firm, although operating quite successfully with SDWTs, went bankrupt because of a change in the price of raw materials and the inability to pay off a bank loan. In another instance, a high-level strategic decision was made to shift to a different market, and one extremely successful "showcase" SDWT was simply closed down. In short, a highly successful SDWT implementation, even when profitable, offers no guarantee of continued employment (although firms using SDWTs do strive to reduce layoffs in order to enhance employee loyalty and commitment).

Organized labor, understandably, has criticized the SDWT concept on the grounds that it eliminates long-established principles of seniority-based job assignments, puts supervisory responsibility on the shoulders of employees without paying supervisory wages, makes employees expendable by making them interchangeable, and reduces the size of needed work forces. Michael Parker and Jane Slaughter have drawn comparisons between SDWTs and traditional industrial supervision.[52] In their assessment, the labels may have changed, but the reality is still hierarchical and exploitive. For example, in traditional industrialist terminology:

> The foreman holds a meeting of his group and announces the week's productivity and scrap figures or discusses the latest safety memo. The foreman's "gofer" takes care of vacation schedules and work gloves,

while in the more modern terminology:

> Hourly workers are organized into teams which meet with their advisor to discuss quality and work procedures. A team leader takes care of vacation scheduling and supplies (page 4).

Critics of the SDWT approach would also question whether it is ethical to try to build employee commitment in a calculated and deliberate manner.

Proponents of SDWTs would counter these arguments by pointing out that a fundamental difference in power-sharing exists in the SDWT-based system. The traditional industrialist view is based on a simple top-down, parent-to-child relationship, while the SDWT view is based on a cooperative, adult-to-adult relationship oriented toward collaborative problem-solving. Moreover, SDWTs combine a pay-for-knowledge compensation scheme with ongoing opportunities for retraining. Additionally, the environment in which organizations must now operate requires that new forms of management–labor relations be devised, as the traditional form of confrontation-based management-labor relations no longer provides a sufficient base for global competition.

The ethical issue surrounding the deliberateness of efforts to build employee commitment is very much open to debate. Organizations that have work forces with high levels of commitment and loyalty have an advantage in competitive settings. Perhaps the key point lies in determining whether a given management is seeking to exploit its employees or to attain a level of organizational effectiveness that is mutually beneficial.

THE FUTURE OF SDWTs   For the future, SDWTs are likely to spread to a greater variety of organizations (for example, not-for-profit and small firms). Many of the principles of SDWTs are easily transferable to nonmanufacturing settings. Also, it is likely that SDWTs will make the jump from rank-and-file operatives to office workers. At the Topeka pet food facility, for example, lower-level office positions have been rotated since the plant's creation. Upper-level positions, which require highly specialized training (for example, accounting and computer programming), are exempted from rotation.

Many observers of the SDWT movement predict that such programs will continue to gain acceptance and that SDWTs will likely replace quality circles at many firms. Viewed from an evolutionary perspective, quality circles may be seen as a transitional form of employee participation that will be supplanted by the stronger form of employee empowerment represented by SDWTs.**** Present estimates from surveys of the largest firms in North America and Europe show that roughly 70 percent are using task forces to tackle specific problems, 50 percent use quality circles, and 25 percent use SDWTs. It is interesting to speculate on what may be the next phase in the evolution of labor-management relations, or the next fad in employee motivation. Certainly, the trend through the 1900s has been toward greater employee empowerment. Whether the future will take us toward a form of still greater organizational democracy (that is, greater power sharing and greater autonomy) or a return to a more hierarchical form is not as yet foreseeable.

SUMMARY

1. Distinguish between extrinsic and intrinsic rewards.

Extrinsic rewards come from sources outside of the individual, while intrinsic rewards are self-administered.

2. Compare various types of rewards on the dimensions of average importance, flexibility, frequency, and visibility.

Table 7.1 summarizes ratings along these dimensions for pay, promotion, fringe benefits, status symbols, and awards and certificates.

3. Evaluate the merits of different pay-for-performance schemes.

Table 7.2 summarizes the merits of salary and bonus rewards when productivity, cost effectiveness, and supervisor rating methods are used to rate employees in relation to the individual, group, or organization.

4. Explain why incentive plans have lost popularity.

Incentive plans have run into problems because they may foster an adversarial attitude in employees; because they can lead to a sense of class distinctions between workers and managers; and because of the impact of societal changes, such as the increasingly interdependent nature of jobs and workers' desires for more challenging and meaningful work.

****Work teams in Western industrialized nations have tended to emphasize power sharing and active participation in decision making, whereas teams in the Orient (for example, Japan) have retained a more deferential, or obedient, posture with respect to management ranks. Some observers have suggested that this difference has the potential to produce greater innovation, more creative solutions, and stronger commitment in Western teams, where the best ideas must stand on their own merits, regardless of their source. As yet, there is little firm evidence that clearly demonstrates the superiority of either approach.

5. Describe three attributes of goals that are important for improving performance.

Three goal attributes that are especially important for improving performance are (1) the specificity of the goal, or the preciseness with which a goal or objective is stated; (2) the difficulty of the goal; and (3) the acceptance of the goal by employees.

6. Describe management-by-objectives and some of its advantages and possible problems.

MBO is a process in which employees participate with management in setting goals for the employee's performance. After an established period of time, employee and supervisor meet again to review the employee's performance based on the goals. Advantages are that goals are specific and measurable and that MBO programs have the potential to improve performance. However, problems can arise from lack of top-level support, management's discomfort with employee participation, personality conflicts between employee and manager, and the potential for neglect of the qualitative aspects of performance.

7. Give some examples of the power of self-fulfilling prophecies.

Children develop in response to the expectations of parents and teachers. In one study, children performed in school according to their teachers' beliefs about their aptitude. Similarly, a group of men in a welding course performed in accordance with their teacher's expectations. Soldiers labeled as having high potential displayed superior performance. In all these studies, the labels were assigned randomly. A bank run is another example of the power of expectations.

8. Describe some ways of constructively managing self-fulfilling prophecies.

People can manage SFPs by being more sensitive to how others perceive their behavior. They can also pay more attention to controlling their behavior and speech so as to communicate positive expectations to everyone. Displaying enthusiasm for the group's goals is another way to manage SFPs constructively, as is attempting to help poorer performers.

9. Describe methods of job redesign used to reduce worker discontent.

Some methods of job redesign are job enlargement, which increases the variety of an employee's activities; job rotation, which rotates personnel in various tasks; and job enrichment, which is an expansion of an employee's autonomy and self-regulation in a job. Other methods include flextime, modified workweeks, and telecommuting.

10. List the job characteristics that enhance a sense of the meaningfulness of one's work, a sense of responsibility, and knowledge of the results of one's work.

The job characteristics that enhance a sense of meaningfulness are skill variety, task identity, and task significance. A sense of responsibility is enhanced by autonomy, while knowledge of results is enhanced by feedback from the job.

11. Discuss some obstacles to job redesign.

Employees often are comfortable with the existing informal power systems. Unions may see job redesign as a way to extract more work from employees with an increase in pay. Supervisors fear that giving employees more self-control or self-monitoring will reduce the need for supervisors. Failure to involve employees in the planning can also lead to problems. Other problems can arise when new employees are hired; they have not experienced the initial impact of the program and take the present conditions for granted.

12. Describe the essential elements of quality circles.
Quality circles are employee committees that meet regularly to discuss production and service-related problems. Members, who volunteer for quality circles, are given training in problem-solving techniques and encouraged to offer solutions and monitor their outcomes. For quality circles to be effective, there must be (1) support from top-level management, (2) group facilitator support, (3) guarantees of job stability, and (4) recognition for quality circle contributions.

13. Explain how self-directed work teams operate, and identify major consequences and problems of such teams.
Self-directed work teams are groups of 6 to 18 employees who have a significant responsibility for delivery of a product or services. In addition to frequent meetings to discuss a range of work-related issues, teams engage in mandatory job rotation and frequent retraining. Compensation in such teams is based on pay-for-knowledge. SDWTs require fewer supervisors and produce flatter organization structures. In order to produce a multiskilled work force, greater investment is required in human resources training. Potential problems include "topping-out" on compensation ladders; and resistance from continuing, especially unionized, employees and first-line supervisors.

KEY TERMS

Extrinsic reward
Intrinsic reward
Gain sharing
Goal specificity
Goal difficulty
Goal acceptance
Management-by-objectives (MBO)
Self-fulfilling prophecy (SFP)
Employee empowerment
Job enlargement
Job rotation
Job enrichment

Job characteristics theory
Job diagnostic survey
Employee growth-need strength
Flextime
Modified workweek
Telecommuting
Quality Circles
Self-directed work team
Total Quality Management
Retrofit
Greenfield site

REVIEW AND DISCUSSION QUESTIONS

1. Give two examples of extrinsic rewards and two examples of intrinsic rewards.

2. What are some advantages of using pay as a reward for employees? Only a small percentage of workers in the United States see a link between how much they are paid and how hard they work. What are some possible reasons for this discrepancy?

3. Based on Table 7.2, what kind of pay schemes are likely to be most successful? What kind of pay schemes are likely to enhance cooperation among group members?

4. Explain the reasons incentive pay schemes have lost their appeal. Do you think incentive pay will become more popular in the future? Why or why not?

5. What are some advantages of compensating employees with profit sharing, gain sharing, and stock ownership?

6. Martha Wilson is the manager of Best Foot Forward, a shoe store in a neighborhood shopping center. She is concerned that all her sales personnel feel motivated to work together and do their best. She meets privately with each of her salespeople and says, "I have set a goal for you that you increase your sales performance each month. I know you can do an excellent job, and if you need any help, please come talk to me." Does Martha's goal have the attributes of a goal that will improve performance? Explain your answer.

7. Acme Ace Company has instituted a new MBO system. Some goals developed by members of the accounting department follow. State whether these are good MBO goals and support your answer.

   • Process accounts receivable records faster.

   • Reduce paperwork costs by June 15.

   • Increase sales by 5 percent by the end of the fiscal year.

   • Institute a training program for bookkeepers by May 1.

8. Bert Burton, marketing vice president for Dynamo Power Tools, likes to give all his personnel helpful guidance. He had been watching Winston Brash, a sales rep who broke all the sales records but also disrupted most meetings by talking constantly. One day Bert called Winston into his office. "Winston," he said, "you're a fine sales rep, but I'm afraid you're just not cut out to be a manager." That afternoon at a sales meeting, Winston was about to make a suggestion, but caught himself as he remembered Bert's words to him. Two weeks later, Winston left Dynamo Power Tools for a sales job at another company. How did Bert's expectations affect Winston? How could Bert have used his influence positively?

9. How does a company benefit from job specialization? What are some limitations of this approach?

10. Explain the differences between job enlargement, job rotation, and job enrichment as job redesign strategies.

11. What characteristics of a job enrich it? Should a company be responsible for enriching jobs and using techniques such as flextime and modified workweeks, even if doing so hurts profitability? Why or why not?

12. What is a quality circle? How do quality circle programs work? What kinds of programs are most likely to succeed?

13. Is it ethical for an organization to deliberately seek to build a high level of employee commitment?

CRITICAL INCIDENT

Is Job Redesign Needed?

Healthcare America, Inc. is a large health insurance company that operates in 46 states. At its corporate headquarters, there is a great deal of reliance on a word processing department. There are 22 people working in this department, with one supervisor and an assistant supervisor. They type a wide variety of documents that are supplied by the various departments. Some of the work involves forms and letters while other work centers around lengthy manuscripts. Most of the work is performed against a deadline.

The work is given to the individual typist by the supervisor. The supervisor attempts to equally distribute the work and monitor progress. The supervisor also checks to make sure everything is in order before giving it to the typist. If it is not, it is sent back to the originator.

Because of the importance surrounding the exactness of the work, completed documents are sent to proofreaders for review. These people then forward the documents or return them for corrections. However, many complaints are still received about an excessive amount of errors and deadlines not being met. In addition, the department has experienced high absenteeism and turnover.

As a consultant, you have been asked to analyze this situation and offer some recommendations.

1. What do you believe is causing the problems in this department? Why?
2. Consider redesigning the job of the word processor/typist according to the principles of job enlargement and job enrichment.
3. What are the advantages and disadvantages of each approach?

Source: Written by Bruce Kemelgor, University of Louisville; used by permission.

EXPERIENTIAL EXERCISE

Goal Setting and Performance

This activity is designed to help you understand and examine the relationship between the process of setting goals and the resulting performance of an individual in an organization. To the extent that the process of goal setting contributes to organizational behavior, this activity seeks to have you analyze the methods used by your manager to use objectives in relation to your job.

1. Think of your present job or a job you held recently. If you have not been employed, use your "job" as a student and consider one of your instructors as the manager. The following statements refer to that job and to the objectives associated with it. Please read each statement carefully and then circle the appropriate number indicating how true or untrue you believe each statement to be.

	Definitely Not True	Generally Not True	Slightly Not True	Uncertain	Slightly True	Generally True	Definitely True
1. Management encourages employees to define job objectives.	−3	−2	−1	0	1	2	3
2. If I achieve my objectives, I receive adequate recognition from my supervisor.	−3	−2	−1	0	1	2	3
3. My objectives are clearly stated with respect to the results expected.	−3	−2	−1	0	1	2	3
4. I have the support I need to accomplish my objectives.	−3	−2	−1	0	1	2	3
5. Achieving my objectives increases my chances for promotion.	−3	−2	−1	0	1	2	3
6. My supervisor dictates my job objectives to me.	−3	−2	−1	0	1	2	3
7. I need more feedback on whether I'm achieving my objectives.	−3	−2	−1	0	1	2	3
8. My supervisor will "get on my back" if I fail to achieve my objectives.	−3	−2	−1	0	1	2	3
9. My job objectives are very challenging.	−3	−2	−1	0	1	2	3
10. Management wants to know whether I set objectives for my job.	−3	−2	−1	0	1	2	3
11. My supervisor will compliment me if I achieve my job objectives.	−3	−2	−1	0	1	2	3
12. My objectives are very ambiguous and unclear.	−3	−2	−1	0	1	2	3
13. I lack the authority to accomplish my objectives.	−3	−2	−1	0	1	2	3
14. Achievement of objectives is rewarded with higher pay.	−3	−2	−1	0	1	2	3
15. My supervisor encourages me to establish my own objectives.	−3	−2	−1	0	1	2	3
16. I always have knowledge of my progress toward my objectives.	−3	−2	−1	0	1	2	3
17. My supervisor will reprimand me if I'm not making progress toward my objectives.	−3	−2	−1	0	1	2	3
18. My objectives seldom require my full interest and effort.	−3	−2	−1	0	1	2	3
19. Management makes it clear that defining job objectives is favorably regarded.	−3	−2	−1	0	1	2	3
20. My supervisor gives me more recognition when I achieve my objectives.	−3	−2	−1	0	1	2	3
21. My objectives are very concrete.	−3	−2	−1	0	1	2	3
22. I have sufficient resources to achieve my objectives.	−3	−2	−1	0	1	2	3
23. My pay is more likely to be increased if I achieve my objectives.	−3	−2	−1	0	1	2	3
24. My supervisor has more influence than I do in setting my objectives.	−3	−2	−1	0	1	2	3
25. I wish I had better knowledge of whether I'm achieving my objectives.	−3	−2	−1	0	1	2	3
26. If I fail to meet my objectives, my supervisor will reprimand me.	−3	−2	−1	0	1	2	3
27. Attaining my objectives requires all my skills and know-how.	−3	−2	−1	0	1	2	3

2. For each of the nine subscales (A through I), compute a total score by summing the answers to the appropriate questions. Be sure to subtract minus scores.

A. Question
  1. + ( )
 10. + ( )
 19. + ( )
Total

B. Question
  3. + ( )
 12. + ( )
 21. + ( )
Total

C. Question
  6. + ( )
 15. + ( )
 24. + ( )
Total

D. Question
  4. + ( )
 13. + ( )
 22. + ( )
Total

E. Question
  7. + ( )
 16. + ( )
 25. + ( )
Total

F. Question
  9. + ( )
 18. + ( )
 27. + ( )
Total

G. Question
  5. + ( )
 14. + ( )
 23. + ( )
Total

H. Question
  2. + ( )
 11. + ( )
 20. + ( )
Total

I. Question
  8. + ( )
 17. + ( )
 26. + ( )
Total

3. Plot the score from each of the subscales on the graph below. Use an X to indicate the appropriate scale value. Next, connect the nine subscale values by drawing a line from value A to value I. This provides you with a profile of your responses.

Subscale

A	−9	−7	−5	−3	−1	+1	+3	+5	+7	+9
B	−9	−7	−5	−3	−1	+1	+3	+5	+7	+9
C	−9	−7	−5	−3	−1	+1	+3	+5	+7	+9
D	−9	−7	−5	−3	−1	+1	+3	+5	+7	+9
E	−9	−7	−5	−3	−1	+1	+3	+5	+7	+9
F	−9	−7	−5	−3	−1	+1	+3	+5	+7	+9
G	−9	−7	−5	−3	−1	+1	+3	+5	+7	+9
H	−9	−7	−5	−3	−1	+1	+3	+5	+7	+9
I	−9	−7	−5	−3	−1	+1	+3	+5	+7	+9

4. Answer the following question: How satisfied are you with this job?
   a. Highly satisfied
   b. Satisfied
   c. It's OK
   d. Somewhat dissatisfied
   e. Very dissatisfied
5. Form small groups based on your (honest) response to this question. As a group, address the following questions:

a. Is there a common pattern in your questionnaire responses?

b. Do certain subscale values (A through I) suggest appropriate managerial use of objectives? Which one(s)?

c. Are certain subscales representative of the characteristics of objectives? Which one(s)?

6. Remain in your small group. Your instructor will ask each group for a representative to describe its predominate profile. Look for similarities among and differences between the group responses.

7. What do you believe accounts for these differences? What characteristics of objectives and the managerial use of objectives contribute to satisfaction within organizations?

Source: Based in part on P. Lorenzi, H.P. Sims, Jr., and E.A. Slusher, "Goal Setting, Performance and Satisfaction: A Behavioral Demonstration," *Exchange: The Organizational Behavior Teaching Journal* 7, no. 1 (1982): 38–42.

Notes

1. E.E. Lawler III, *Pay and Organizational Effectiveness* (New York: McGraw-Hill, 1971); E.E. Lawler III, "New Approaches to Pay: Innovations that Work," *Personnel* 53 (1976): 11–23; E.E. Lawler III, *Pay and Organization Development* (Reading, Mass.: Addison-Wesley, 1981); E.E. Lawler III, "Whatever Happened to Incentive Pay?" *New Management* 1 (1984): 37–41.

2. Lawler, "Whatever Happened to Incentive Pay?"

3. H.C. Handlin, "The Company Built upon the Golden Rule: Lincoln Electric," *Journal of Organizational Behavior Management* 12 (1992): 151–163; "Lincoln Electric's Past Enhances the Future," *Management Review* (1984): 40–41.

4. E.E. Lawler III, "Reward Systems," in *Improving Life at Work*, ed. J.R. Hackman and J.L. Suttle (Glenview, Ill.: Scott, Foresman, 1977).

5. Lawler, "Whatever Happened to Incentive Pay?"

6. Ibid.

7. J. Ramquist, "Labor-Management Cooperation," *Sloan Management Review* 23 (1982): 49–55; E. Leefeldt, "Profit-Sharing Plans Reward Productivity," *The Wall Street Journal,* November 15, 1984, 1.

8. Lawler, "Whatever Happened to Incentive Pay?"

9. T. Curry and K. Jackson-Fallon, "Workers' Risks and Rewards," *Time,* April 15, 1991, 42–43.

10. G.P. Latham and G. Yukl, "A Review of Research on the Application of Goal-Setting in Organizations," *Academy of Management Journal* 18 (1975): 824–845; E.A. Locke, "Job Satisfaction and Job Performance: A Theoretical Analysis," *Organizational Behavior and Human Performance* 5 (1970): 484–500; P.M. Wright, "A Test of the Mediating Role of Goals in the Incentive–Performance Relationship," *Journal of Applied Psychology* 74 (1989): 699–705; J. Hollenbeck, C. Williams, and H. Klein, "An Empirical Examination of the Antecedents of Commitment to Difficult Goals," *Journal of Applied Psychology* 74 (1989): 18–23; P.C. Earley, T. Connolly, and G. Ekegren, "Goals, Strategy Development, and Task Performance," *Journal of Applied Psychology* 74 (1989): 24–33; M. Tubbs, "Goal Setting: A Meta-analytic Examination of the Empirical Evidence," *Journal of Applied Psychology* 71 (1986): 474–483; A.J. Mento, R.P. Steel, and R.J. Karren, "A Meta-analytic Study of the Effects of Goal Setting on Task Performance," *Organizational Behavior and Human Decision Processes* 39 (1987): 52–83; G.P. Latham and E. Locke, "Self-Regulation Through Goal-Setting," *Organizational Behavior and Human Decision Processes* 50 (1991): 212–247.

11. S.E. White, T.R. Mitchell, and C.H. Bell, "Goal Setting, Evaluation Apprehension, and Social Cues as Determinants of Job Performance and Job Satisfaction in a Simulated Organization," *Journal of*

Applied Psychology 62 (1977): 665–673.

12. H. Tosi, J.R. Rizzo, and S. Carroll, "Setting Goals in Management-By-Objectives," *California Management Review* 12 (1970): 70–78.

13. P.F. Drucker, *The Practice of Management* (New York: Harper, 1954); A.P. Raia, *Managing by Objectives* (Glenview, Ill.: Scott, Foresman, 1974); S.J. Carroll and H.L. Tosi, *Management by Objectives: Applications and Research* (New York: Macmillan, 1973); J. Kondrasuk, "Studies in MBO Effectiveness," *Academy of Management Review* 6 (1981): 419–430.

14. R. Rodgers and J.E. Hunter, "Impact of Management by Objectives on Organizational Productivity," *Journal of Applied Psychology* 76 (1991): 322–336; R. Rodgers, J.E. Hunter, and D.L. Rogers, "Influence of Top Management Commitment on Management Program Success," *Journal of Applied Psychology* 78 (1993): 151–155.

15. R.A. Jones, *Self-Fulfilling Prophecies: Social, Psychological, and Physiological Effects of Expectancies* (Hillsdale, N.J.: Erlbaum, 1977); J.S. Livingston, "Pygmalion in Management," *Harvard Business Review* 47 (1969): 81–89.

16. R. Rosenthal and L. Jacobson, *Pygmalion in the Classroom: Teachers' Expectations and Pupil Intellectual Development* (New York: Holt, Rinehart and Winston, 1968).

17. A.S. King, "Managerial Relations with Disadvantaged Work Groups: Supervisory Expectations of the Underprivileged Worker" (Ph.D. diss., Texas Tech University, 1970).

18. D. Eden and A.B. Shani, "Pygmalion Goes to Boot Camp: Expectancy, Leadership, and Trainee Performance," *Journal of Applied Psychology* 67 (1982): 194–199; D. Eden, "Pygmalion Without Interpersonal Contrast Effects: Whole Groups Gain from Raising Manager Expectations," *Journal of Applied Psychology* 75 (1990): 394–400.

19. R. Rosenthal and K. Fode, "The Effect of Experimental Bias on the Performance of the Albino Rat," *Behavioral Science* 8 (1963): 183–189.

20. R.S. Kaufman and F.D. Sheffield, "A Methodological Flow in ESP Experiments" (Paper presented at the Annual Meeting of the Eastern Psychological Association, 1952).

21. A. Smith, *An Inquiry into the Nature and Causes of the Wealth of Nations* (New York: Modern Library, 1937; first published in 1776).

22. A.C. Filley, R.J. House, and S. Kerr, *Managerial Process and Organizational Behavior* (Dallas: Scott, Foresman, 1987).

23. F. Herzberg, B. Mausner, and B. Snyderman, *The Motivation to Work* (New York: Wiley, 1959).

24. L.E. Davis and A.B. Cherns, *The Quality of Working Life. Volume Two: Cases and Commentary* (New York: Free Press, 1975).

25. R.A. Guzzo, R.D. Jette, and R.A. Katzell, "The Effects of Psychologically Based Intervention Programs on Worker Productivity: A Meta-analysis," *Personnel Psychology* 38 (1985): 275–292; R.E. Kopelman, "Job Redesign and Productivity: A Review of the Evidence," *National Productivity Review* 4 (1985): 237–255; R.A. Melcher, "Volvo and Renault: Marriage May Be the Answer," *Business Week*, November 23, 1992, 50–51; S. Prokesch, "Edges Fray on Volvo's Brave New Humanistic World," *New York Times*, July 7, 1991, C5; M. Fein, "Job Enrichment: A Reevaluation," *Sloan Management Review* (Winter 1974): 69–88; S.A. Levitan and W.B. Johnston, "Job Redesign, Enrichment—Exploring the Limitations," *Monthly Labor Review* (July 1973): 35–41; W. Paul, K.B. Robertson, and F. Herzberg, "Job Enrichment Pays Off," *Harvard Business Review* (1969): 83–98.

26. C.L. Hulin and M.R. Blood, "Job Enlargement, Individual Differences, and Worker Responses," *Psychological Bulletin* 69 (1968): 41–55.

27. M.R. Blood and C.L. Hulin, "Alienation, Environmental Characteristics and Worker Responses," *Journal of Applied Psychology* 51 (1967): 284–290.

28. R.P. Vecchio, "Individual Differences as a Moderator of the Job Quality–Job Satisfaction Relationship: Evidence from a National Sample," *Organizational Behavior and Human Performance* 26 (1980): 305–325.

29. J.K. White, "Individual Differences and the Job Quality–Worker Response

Relationship: Review, Integration, and Comments," *Academy of Management Review* 3 (1978): 267–280.

30. J.R. Hackman and G.R. Oldham, "Motivation Through the Design of Work: Test of a Theory," *Organizational Behavior and Human Performance* 16 (1976): 250–279; J.R. Hackman and G.R. Oldham, *Work Redesign* (Reading, Mass.: Addison-Wesley, 1980).

31. J. Kelly, "Does Job Design Theory Explain Job Re-design Outcomes?" *Human Relations* 45 (1992): 753–774; Y. Fried and G.R. Ferris, "The Validity of the Job Characteristics Model: A Review and Meta-analysis," *Personnel Psychology* 40 (1987): 287–322; C.R. Berlinger, W.H. Glick, and R.C. Rodgers, "Job Enrichment and Performance Improvements," in *Productivity in Organizations*, eds. J.P. Campbell and R.J. Campbell (San Francisco: Jossey Bass, 1988); J.B. Miner, *Theories of Organizational Behavior* (Hinsdale, Ill.: The Dryden Press, 1980); T. Taber and E. Taylor, "A Review and Evaluation of the Psychometric Properties of the Job Diagnostic Survey," *Personnel Psychology* 43 (1990): 467–500.

32. A.R. Cohen and H. Gadon, *Alternative Work Schedules: Integrating Individual and Organizational Needs* (Reading, Mass.: Addison-Wesley, 1978).

33. V.E. Schein, E.H. Maurer, and J.F. Novak, "Impact of Flexible Working Hours on Productivity," *Journal of Applied Psychology* 62 (1977): 463–465.

34. R.T. Golembiewski and C.W. Proehl, "A Survey of the Empirical Literature on Flexible Workhours: Character and Consequences of a Major Innovation," *Academy of Management Review* 3 (1978): 837–855; D. Dalton and D. Mesch, "The Impact of Flexible Scheduling on Employee Attendance and Turnover," *Administrative Science Quarterly* 35 (1990): 225–257.

35. P. Dickson, *The Future of the Workplace* (New York: Wybright and Talley, 1975); J. Pierce and R. Dunham, "The 12-Hour Work Day: A 48-Hour, Eight-Day Week," *Academy of Management Journal* 35 (1992): 1086–1098.

36. J.M. Ivancevich and H.C. Lyon, "The Shortened Workweek: A Field Experiment," *Journal of Applied Psychology* 62 (1977): 34–37.

37. Cohen and Gadon, *Alternative Work Schedules*.

38. D. Wallechinsky, A. Wallace, and I. Wallace, *The Book of Predictions* (New York: William-Morrow, 1981).

39. J.N. Goodrich, "Telecommuting in America," *Business Horizons* (1990): 31–37.

40. R. Cole, *Work, Mobility and Participation: A Comparative Study of American and Japanese Industry* (Berkeley: University of California Press, 1980); E. Yeager, "Quality Circles—a Tool for the '80's," *Training and Development Journal* (August 1980): 60–62.

41. J.D. Blair, S.L. Cohen, and J.V. Hurwitz, "Quality Circles: Practical Considerations for Public Managers," *Public Productivity Review* 10 (March 1982): 14.

42. R.P. Vecchio, "Employee Attributes and Interest in Quality Circles," *Proceedings of the Southeast Regional Meeting of the American Institute for Decision Sciences*, 1985, 106–108; S.A. Zahra, W.J. Lundstrom, and D.R. Latham, "An Empirical Investigation into the Dynamics of Volunteerism for Quality Circle Participants" (Paper presented at Southern Management Association, 1983); M. Marks, "The Question of Quality Circles," *Psychology Today* 20 (1986): 36–46; M. Marks, P. Miruis, E. Hackett, and J. Grady, "Employee Participation in a Quality Circle Program: Impact on Quality of Work Life, Productivity, and Absenteeism," *Journal of Applied Psychology* 71 (1986): 61–69; J. Brockner and T. Hess, "Self-Esteem and Task Performance in Quality Circles," *Academy of Management Journal* 29 (1986): 617–622.

43. R.W. Griffin, "Consequences of Quality Circles in an Industrial Setting: A Longitudinal Assessment," *Academy of Management Journal* 31 (1988): 338–358.

44. Blair, Cohen, and Hurwitz, "Quality Circles: Practical Considerations."

45. J. Lincoln, M. Hanada, and K. McBride, "Organizational Structures in Japanese and U.S. Manufacturing," *Administrative Science Quarterly* 31 (1986): 338–364.

46. R. Cole, "Made in Japan—Quality Control Circles," *Across the Board* 16 (1979): 72–78.

47. T. Wada and R.P. Vecchio, "Quality Circles at Mitsubishi," *Quality Circles Journal* 7 (1984): 33–34.

48. J.D. Osburn, L. Moran, E. Musselwhite, J.H. Zenger, and C. Perrin, *Self-directed Work Teams* (Homewood, Ill.: Irwin, 1990).

49. J. Hoerr, M. Pollock, and D. Whiteside, "Management Discovers the Human Side of Automatic," *Business Week*, September 1986, 70–76; A. Bernstein, "GM May Be Off the Hook," *Business Week*, September 1987, 26–27.

50. E.L. Harrison, "The Impact of Employee Involvement on Supervisors," *National Productivity Review* (1992): 447–452.

51. E.E. Lawler, "The New Plant Revolution Revisited," *Organizational Dynamics* (1990): 5–14; E.E. Lawler, *High Involvement Management* (San Francisco: Jossey-Bass, 1986); E.E. Lawler, *Pay and Organizational Development* (Reading, Mass.: Addison-Wesley, 1981); R.W. Griffin, "Effects of Work Redesign on Employee Perceptions, Attitudes, and Behaviors: A Long-term Investigation," *Academy of Management Journal* 34 (1991): 425–435; J. Cordery, W.S. Mueller, and L Smith, "Attitudinal and Behavioral Effects of Autonomous Group Working: A Longitudinal Field Study," *Academy of Management Journal* 34 (1991): 464–476; R.J. Magjuka and T. Baldwin, "Team-based Employee Involvement Programs: Effects of Design and Administration," *Personnel Psychology* 44 (1991): 793–812; K. Thomas and B. Velthouse, "Cognitive Elements of Empowerment: An 'Interpretive' Model of Intrinsic Task Motivation," *Academy of Management Review* 15 (1990): 666–681; C. Leana, R. Ahlbrandt, and A. Murrell, "The Effects of Employee Involvement Programs on Unionized Workers' Attitudes, Perceptions, and Preferences in Decision Making," *Academy of Management Journal* 35 (1992): 861–873.

52. M. Parker and J. Slaughter, *Choosing Sides: Unions and the Team Concept* (New York: A Labor Notes–South End Press, 1988).

CHAPTER

8

It is only when one is
pursued that one becomes
swift.
— Kahlil Gibran

They say what really matters
is not if you win or lose, but
how you played the game.
Trouble is—the best way to
figure how you played the
game is by whether you won
or lost.
— Anonymous

Let us be thankful for the
fools. But for them, the rest
of us could not succeed.
— Mark Twain

Performance Appraisal

LENIENT EVALUATIONS CAN HURT AN ORGANIZATION

It happens every workday at thousands of organizations all across America. In evaluating employee performance, managers shy away from awkward criticism and instead produce dull appraisals that lack specifics, substance, and developmental guidelines. Evaluating employees becomes a perfunctory ritual rather than a substantive review of performance and a detailed plan of action.

One of the most difficult aspects of appraising employee performance is providing objective feedback to the employee. Too often, supervisors are reluctant to provide employees with honest feedback about suboptimal performance. Rather than confront an employee whose performance has been substandard, evaluators avoid presenting honest feedback and rationalize that a lenient evaluation is harmless.

Inflated performance evaluations do hurt. They have detrimental effects on employees, their peers, and the company as a whole.

Because performance evaluations guide many other activities in the organization, such as deciding who to promote and the size of future pay adjustments, the evaluator has a responsibility to identify and communicate the employee's strengths and weaknesses. Without honest feedback, employees are unaware of weaknesses, have little motivation to change their behaviors, and are prevented from realizing their full potential.

If supervisors have not been trained to provide objective appraisals, lenient evaluations of employee performance may become the norm. In this case, organizational performance would ultimately suffer, with a preponderance of people performing at suboptimal levels. Moreover, terminating employees with a history of "satisfactory" performance is difficult. Increasingly, organizations are defending themselves against wrongful discharge lawsuits. To defend these charges, organizations must show documentation that communicates a history of inadequate performance. Employees who receive objective feedback from the start are much easier to weed out than are employees who receive lenient evaluations.

Employees who are meeting and exceeding expectations deserve good evaluations; they are the third victims of lenient appraisal practices. Employees who are truly doing a good job compare their rewards for their performance with those received by other employees in the organization. When outstanding performers compare their rewards with those of under-performers, they often get the message that extraordinary behavior is not valued. As a result, they either contribute less effort to performing the job or retaliate in other ways. Eventually, even good performers reduce their effort.

Inflated performance appraisals can be costly in more ways than one. To prevent lenient appraisals, evaluators must be trained to document performance and deal with negative appraisal situations. Documentation of employee performance must be an ongoing activity for all evaluators. Evaluators must be trained to provide employees with objective feedback; this training will help them feel confident and will remove the confrontational character of the process. Training techniques should consist of modeling or role playing to provide evaluators with opportunities to try out constructive communication techniques. People charged with

(continued on following page)

(continued from previous page)
conducting employee appraisals must be made to realize that lenient evaluations hurt everyone in the organization.

This chapter discusses the purposes of performance appraisal and ways to appraise performance effectively. It includes some suggestions for conducting appraisal interviews and guidelines for developing appraisals that are fair and that help the organization avoid legal action resulting from discriminatory appraisal processes.

Source: Barbara H. Holmes, "The Lenient Evaluator Is Hurting Your Organization," *HR Magazine* (June 1993): 75–78.

Productivity is a function of the ways in which monetary, technical, and human resources are managed. While monetary and technical resources can be managed by specialists in finance, accounting, and engineering, the management of human resources is the responsibility of all those who supervise others, regardless of function specialty. In order to develop human resources with an eye toward maximizing productivity, it is essential that supervisors periodically assess the performance of each subordinate. The results of the performance assessment, or appraisal, should then be shared with the subordinate in a constructive manner that can help the individual to correct any deficiencies or maintain excellence.

The topic of performance appraisal is central to the field of organizational behavior. Because performance appraisal involves aspects of learning, perception, personality, motivation, and incentive systems, it integrates many of the topics that we have considered in previous chapters. In this chapter, we will approach the notion of performance appraisal much as a newspaper reporter would, by asking why, when, what, how, and by whom performance appraisal is, and should be, conducted. Finally, we will conclude by considering some legal issues that currently surround the topic of performance appraisal.

WHY APPRAISE PERFORMANCE?

We have already suggested that performance appraisals are done with the goal of maintaining or improving performance. Beyond this important consideration, there are several additional reasons for conducting formal periodic appraisals. Chief among these is to aid supervisors in making decisions about relative compensation. Any organization that uses a pay-for-performance scheme should deliberately design its compensation plans around its performance appraisal system. The appraisal process should convey a sense of equity to all who are involved.

Periodic appraisals also help managers evaluate subordinates' suitability for training and development, and for job changes, such as promotions, transfers, demotions, or dismissals. Sending a subordinate to a training program can be costly; therefore, supervisors need to be selective. Similarly, supervisors must make wise decisions about whom to promote or transfer. During harsh economic times, performance appraisals can also be used to decide who to demote or temporarily lay off.

A further reason for conducting performance appraisals is to open lines of communication between supervisors and subordinates. Communication about performance-related topics is an essential first step in any program that is designed to enhance productivity. Of course, simply having a superior and a subordinate discuss their perspectives on performance issues is not a guarantee that performance will be enhanced. A subordinate, for example, may not accept the supervisor's views or interpretations of the current state of affairs. Reaching agreement on the need for performance enhancement, as well as the manner in which it can be achieved, is a critical part of a performance appraisal session. Later in this chapter, we will consider how to conduct a performance appraisal session in order to avoid potential communication problems.

Finally, performance appraisals provide subordinates with useful feedback about how they are doing in their jobs. Virtually all employees want to know how their superiors view their performance. Unfortunately, in many organizations there is often little time or inclination for both parties to sit down and discuss personal strengths and weaknesses. Performance appraisal sessions, in a sense, force a superior to meet with each subordinate and provide concrete feedback.

A performance appraisal system serves many important functions within an organization. As we shall see, however, there are many potential obstacles to the conduct of proper appraisals.

WHEN SHOULD PERFORMANCE BE APPRAISED?

In most organizations, formal performance reviews are carried out on an annual basis. To be sure, one can argue that *informal* performance feedback from superiors should be a daily affair. But an important distinction must be made between formal and informal reviews. Informal feedback can, and should, be given with great frequency. Formal feedback, however, involves greater preparation from the evaluator and requires more time.

Annual reviews for all employees are often done on a common review date. This format is widespread because many organizations set their budgets on an annual basis. As a consequence, raises (which are tied to performance reviews) are associated with a particular time of each year. Some organizations, however, conduct annual reviews based on the anniversary date of the subordinate's hiring or entering a particular job. With this system, evaluation can be spread throughout the year so that supervisors are not swamped by the task of conducting numerous appraisals in a short period of time.

In some cases, naturally occurring events mark the need for a formal appraisal. One of these is the completion of an initial probationary period. In entry-level positions, when a person is hired without much relevant work experience, a probationary period of one or more months may be required. At the end of this probationary period, a formal appraisal is conducted and a decision is made about whether to continue the individual's employment. The completion of a major project that has spanned many months or years can also prompt a formal appraisal. Top-level employees are especially likely to be evaluated on such a basis.

WHO SHOULD APPRAISE PERFORMANCE?

Initially, one might think that the only answer to this question is a subordinate's immediate supervisor. However, there are a number of perspectives from which to assess subordinate performance, each of which has certain advantages and disadvantages.

THE IMMEDIATE SUPERVISOR

On logical grounds, one can argue that it is most fitting for an employee's immediate superior to evaluate his or her performance. According to the reasoning, the immediate superior is in the best position to observe each subordinate. Furthermore, it is the immediate supervisor's responsibility to direct the behavior of subordinates. Thus, the immediate supervisor should, by virtue of his or her position, be able to judge the relative contribution of each subordinate to the overall performance of the organizational unit.

Upon careful reflection, however, it becomes clear that supervisors are often *not* in the best position to observe subordinate behavior. In fact, supervisors are frequently too far removed from their subordinates. They may actually spend a great deal of their time on activities such as meeting with other unit leaders, traveling, preparing budgets, and writing reports rather than on the direct monitoring of their subordinates. In addition, subordinates' activities may remove them from their superior's direct supervision, as in the case of traveling sales representatives.

Despite these possible disadvantages, employees are most frequently evaluated by their immediate superiors. As reported by Lazer and Wikstrom, roughly 95 percent of all performance appraisals involve the immediate supervisor as a rater.[1] In addition, some appraisal systems involve evaluations by (1) the individual subordinate (13 percent), (2) groups or committees (6 percent), and (3) personnel department officers (6 percent).* Although they constituted less than 1 percent each, other sources of appraisal include consultants, coworkers (or peers), and subordinates.

SELF-APPRAISAL

Many people are surprised to learn that self-appraisals are sometimes used in organizations. To be sure, such self-ratings are likely to be inflated and show little agreement with supervisor ratings, but in certain situations and with reasonable caution, self-ratings can be helpful.[2] One possibility is to combine self-ratings with supervisor ratings.[3] In such a situation, the subordinate and the superior complete identical appraisal forms. At a subsequent formal interview session, the two then compare their responses. For each question, the supervisor and subordinate discuss why they agree or disagree in their perceptions of the individual's conduct. If such a discussion can be carried out in a nonthreat-

---

*The percentages represent frequency of use and total more than 100 percent because of the occasional use of multiple sources of evaluation.

ening and supportive manner, it can provide a rich opportunity for the subordinate to gain insights and suggestions about his or her workplace behavior. In addition, the supervisor may gain understanding of the subordinate's behavior. In the process, both the supervisor and the subordinate can gain an enhanced sense of working together to improve performance.

A second use of self-rating is in conjunction with participative goal setting. In management-by-objectives (MBO) programs (see Chapter 7), a subordinate will be asked to appraise his or her own performance periodically with respect to attaining specific performance goals. Such required self-appraisals can help subordinates view their own accomplishments more honestly.

Self-ratings are also useful in self-development. In training settings, where self-insight is a primary goal, self-ratings can help a subordinate to gauge the degree of learning that has occurred.

Despite their usefulness in certain settings, self-ratings rarely have much influence on decisions about promotions, raises, transfers, and the like.

PEERS OR COWORKERS

Appraisals by peers are rarely used, but their worth should not be ignored.[4] As you might imagine, peers are frequently able to observe a given subordinate for a longer period of time and in a wider variety of situations than is an immediate supervisor. As one result of this greater contact, peers are likely to generate more accurate assessments and predictions of each other's performance.[5] As an illustration, consider that your classmates probably know you better as a student (in terms of your study habits, interest in coursework, personal mores, and so on) than your instructors know you. Yet your instructors, with whom you usually have only very limited and formal contact (much like an immediate supervisor), will ultimately evaluate your academic performance by assigning a grade to you.

In comparison to self-rating, peer ratings are generally less inflated.[6] Not too surprisingly, peer ratings and ratings by superiors show little agreement.[7] This lack of agreement probably occurs because subordinates tend to change their behavior when in the presence of their superior.

Peer ratings are not used in most organizations because they are susceptible to a number of potential biases. Their vulnerability to friendship effects constitutes one major liablility: People are likely to rate their friends more highly.[8] Also, raters are likely to rate members of their own race more highly.[9] When there is serious competition for promotions and raises, better performers may receive harsher evaluations due to their peers' attempts to improve their own chances of obtaining rewards.

Despite these shortcomings, peer appraisals can be useful in certain situations. Most notable among these is when a group of coworkers is completing a training program (or other period of close contact) and is about to be assigned to geographically dispersed locations or distinct job assignments. If the assignments are predetermined and therefore independent of the appraisal exercise, peer evaluations may yield useful and accurate information for making forecasts of subsequent success or failure.

■ FIGURE 8.1
SOURCES OF PERFORMANCE APPRAISAL INFORMATION

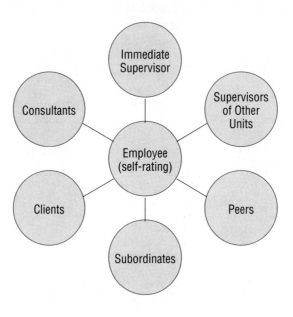

SUBORDINATES

Another intriguing but rarely used approach to appraisal is to request anonymous performance evaluations from an individual's subordinates. Subordinates do, in fact, have a very different perspective on a supervisor's performance, although their impressions may not be uniform.[10] Of course, subordinates are likely to resist being involved in such appraisals out of fear of reprisal; when a work group is small, anonymity may be difficult to safeguard. Most subordinates also feel that it is not their responsibility to evaluate their boss, or that they are not in the best position to observe the boss's performance.

Despite these and other very rational objections, a number of organizations, including Exxon and Weyerhauser, have experimented with subordinate appraisal systems.[11] Generally, the problems inherent in such appraisals outweigh their limited potential value. Nonetheless, they should not be totally dismissed. When used as a source of personal feedback, with the intent of improving performance or self-diagnosis, subordinate appraisals may be of some value. For example, college teachers typically ask their students to complete evaluation forms at the end of a course. The resulting information can help both instructors and college administrators identify areas of deficiency. However, when students' evaluations are used for making major decisions related to promotions and raises, as they are used at some schools, there is a real danger that academic standards may slip as a result of the instructors' attempts to curry favor with their evaluators.

OTHER SOURCES OF APPRAISAL

In addition to superiors, workers themselves, peers, and subordinates, people outside of the immediate work unit may be asked to assist in performance appraisal. These may include customers or clients, who may be surveyed for their impressions, and committees composed of managers who are one level above the individual being appraised. Sometimes an external consultant or group of consultants may be hired to conduct performance appraisals. Because of the inherent cost, this practice is usually limited to the evaluation of higher-level managers. When consultants are brought in, they usually canvass a variety of sources including the employee, peers, subordinates, superiors, and external clients before finalizing their assessment. In essence, all who would have information on the employee in question would be queried. Collecting evaluative information from a full range of sources is termed **360-degree feedback.**

Figure 8.1 summarizes the common sources of information for appraising performance, and Table 8.1 lists the advantages and disadvantages of these sources. As this table suggests, no single rater or group of raters can be endorsed as satisfactory for all settings. Instead, a careful judgment must be made in each work setting.

WHAT SHOULD BE APPRAISED?

Before considering the actual appraisal process, we must examine what an evaluator will be asked to appraise. Since performance is complex and multifaceted, it cannot be assumed to have any simple or general meaning. Rather,

TABLE 8.1
ADVANTAGES AND DISADVANTAGES OF DIFFERENT APPRAISAL SOURCES

Source of Appraisal	Advantages	Disadvantages
Immediate supervisor	Makes decisions on rewards	Personal bias possible
	Has perspectives on all subordinates	Supervisor may be removed from subordinates
Self	Unique perspective	Likely to be too lenient
	A useful basis for comparison	
	Useful for self-insight	
Peers	Greater exposure to appraisee	Competitive atmosphere confounds usage
	More accurate assessment	
Subordinates	Can give diagnostic-type feedback	Can subvert the leader's authority
Superiors of other units	Can be less subjective	Too removed from the individual
Customers or clients	Gives input from immediate client group	Only sees limited facet of appraisee
Consultants	Complete, thorough appraisal	Too expensive for use with all employees

performance must be defined in terms of the actual behaviors that an employee is expected to display in a given job. Only after performance has been defined for a given job can assessment of an employee's performance be attempted in a meaningful way.

Defining the major dimensions of performance requires a job analysis. Although there are a number of different approaches to conducting such an analysis, the common goal of each is a precise statement of the activities that constitute a job.[12] Typically, a job analysis is performed by an observer who carefully examines all available data on a given job. In the course of gathering data, the observer will usually interview the current holders of the job and the immediate supervisor. The outcome is a **job description,** a concise summary of the duties to be performed by someone who occupies the job in question. The job description consists of a series of simple descriptive statements defining the responsibilities of the job holder. For example, the job description of a secretary might include such statements as "Answers the telephone promptly" and "Handles requests for price quotations from outside vendors." A statement from the job description of a sheet-metal worker might be "Sets the cutting blades of the splicer to meet customer's requested specifications" or "Cleans up workstation area at the end of the day." As these examples suggest, the focus in a job description is on actual behaviors that are central to the conduct of the job. Job descriptions play an important role in designing an effective appraisal system because appraisals that are based on job descriptions possess greater relevance.[†]

For many positions, there are additional on-the-job behaviors that are not encapsulated in job descriptions but that reflect discretionary action on the part of the employee. These voluntary actions go beyond formal job descriptions, and are important in promoting the smooth operation of an organization. Dennis Organ, of Indiana University, has developed a five-dimensional model of these "good soldier" behaviors. According to the model, **organizational citizenship behavior (OCB)** includes altruism, courtesy, sportsmanship, conscientiousness, and civic virtue.[13] Table 8.2 provides examples of questions that measure the construct of OCB.

TABLE 8.2

SAMPLE STATEMENTS ILLUSTRATING ORGANIZATIONAL CITIZENSHIP BEHAVIOR

1. Helps others who have been absent.
2. Goes out of the way to help new employees.
3. Gives advance notice when unable to come to work.
4. Conserves and protects organizational property.
5. When not asked, assists supervisor with his/her work.

Source: L. Williams and S. Anderson, "Job Satisfaction and Organizational Commitment as Predictors of Organizational Citizenship and In-Role Behaviors," *Journal of Management* 17 (1991): 601–617.

[†]Also, if challenged in court as being discriminatory, an appraisal system that is not based on a job analysis is more likely to be judged unfair.

OB Focus
To Pay or Not To Pay for Performance?

What role should performance evaluations play in determining an employee's pay? One current trend is to separate pay adjustments form performance reviews, while another trend is to reward employees with one-time or profit-tied bonuses for their performance.

With the first trend, a good performance appraisal no longer implies an immediate raise in pay. Companies such as Harley Davidson, Avon Products, and American Express's IDS Financial Services unit are deliberately separating compensation reviews from evaluations of employee performance. The rationale for separating performance and salary appraisals is that employee evaluations should focus on career development, individual job skills, and employee growth. Salary reviews, on the other hand, consider the value of the worker to the company. Employees at Alumax Mills Products, a Hinsdale, Illinois aluminum company, feel they get more out of their appraisals since evaluations of performance and pay have been split.

Other companies have adopted quite different philosophies. Organizations such as AT&T, General Mills, and PepsiCo give bonuses that are a function of employees' individual contributions and company profits. These pay-for-performance plans are particularly appropriate when employees are evaluated on achieving pre-established, short-term goals, such as cutting inventories or meeting sales targets. A case in point is provided by a team of General Mills managers responsible for Yoplait yogurt. Thanks to General Mills's policy of basing bonuses equally on business unit results and managers' individual performance, the Yoplait management team received bonuses of about 50 percent of their base salaries for doubling the targeted 40 percent increase in operating earnings. According to one General Mills product manager, "Here, if you do a great job, you get a bigger reward."

The jury is still out as to which strategy produces more motivated employees. As long as organizations can adequately harness their employees' energies and creative efforts, the decision of whether to pay for performance may appropriately vary from company to company.

Sources: Julie Amparano Lopez, "Companies Split Reviews on Performance and Pay," *The Wall Street Journal,* May 10, 1993, B1; Shawn Tully, "Your Paycheck Gets Exciting," *Fortune,* November 1, 1993, 83–98.

Research on OCB has found that employees who display more OCBs are more satisfied and more committed, and perceive their work environments as being more fair.[14] These findings suggest that OCBs can be encouraged by creating a work setting that emphasizes fairness, and by seeking to maximize employee satisfaction and commitment. Additionally, employee appraisal systems and, perhaps more important, reward systems should identify and compensate individuals who display OCBs.

HOW SHOULD APPRAISALS BE CONDUCTED?

Intuitively, one might think that the best appraisal system is one that is *totally objective.* In fact, such a system is not obtainable. Consider the study on psychokinesis cited in Chapter 7 that showed that even the perception of simple objective events is influenced by prior expectations. Results of that study suggest that a strong belief in an employee's ability (or lack of ability) can influence the way in which performance is observed, and ultimately interpreted. One might still argue that a "hard" measure of performance, such as annual sales, is beyond question an index of performance. However, as any salesperson will quickly tell you, sales volume is in large part a function of the quality of a territory and the quality of the product line that one is given to sell. The interpretation of sales figures, therefore, requires consideration of the extent to which external factors affect individual performance.

In addition, performance encompasses many aspects and cannot easily be assessed by a single quantifiable measure. For example, bank tellers are typically assessed on a performance measure called "daily over-or-short balancing"—that is, whether their drawer is over or short by any amount of money at the end of the workday. Most bank tellers strongly protest the use of this measure as an index of performance. Nonetheless, the banking industry prefers it because it is relatively "hard" and summarizes a single aspect of performance—accuracy in monetary transactions. Other aspects of teller performance, such as courteousness and the speed or volume of transactions, are ignored. As this example suggests, the "hardness" of a performance measure does not ensure its relevance.

Given the need to rely on a subjective appraisal of a range of job behaviors, which are condensed over time into an overall impression in the mind of an evaluator, let us consider the major methods of performance appraisal. Each of these methods has both strengths and limitations.

GRAPHIC RATING SCALES

The most widely used performance appraisal device is the **graphic rating scale.** Such scales typically consist of a continuum of points that are anchored by mutually exclusive descriptive adjectives. For example:

Cooperative :_____ : _____ : _____ : _____ : _____: Uncooperative
                 1   2   3   4   5

Industrious :_____ : _____ : _____ : _____ : _____: Lazy
                  1   2   3   4   5

The evaluator places a check over the position on each continuum that best reflects his or her appraisal of an employee on that dimension.

Such rating scales are widely used, largely because they are easy to construct and complete. Unfortunately, they are also plagued by a variety of problems. One major shortcoming is the common reliance on anchors that are of little or no relevance to the actual conduct of a given job. As a result, such scales may provide little more than a format for recording a supervisor's general like or dislike of an employee. Furthermore, relying on anchors that are not explicitly tied to job behaviors may result in ratings that largely reflect sexual or racial biases. Although the research results are mixed, bias in rating does, nonetheless, appear to be quite possible.[15] A reliance on ratings that are based on behavior-specific rating formats can, however, reduce bias.[16]

When using graphic rating scales (as well as some other devices that we will consider), raters are also prone to commit a variety of reporting errors. Among the most common are halo, central tendency, leniency, and harshness errors. **Halo errors** occur when an evaluator completes all rating scales in accord with an overall impression based on only one aspect of the employee's performance, instead of judging each scale independently. In a sense, the rater's overall impression of the employee shades the entire evaluation.

Central tendency, leniency, and harshness errors are three examples of a rater's tendency to restrict his or her evaluation to a limited part of the scale. In a **central tendency error,** the rater uses only values that are in the middle range of each scale. In **leniency** and **harshness errors,** the rater generally gives extremely favorable or extremely unfavorable appraisals to the employees being rated.[‡] Despite these potential pitfalls, somewhat more than half of all large organizations use graphic rating scales in their performance-appraisal systems.[17] Training programs designed to help raters reduce the tendency to commit certain types of errors have been found to be effective.[18]

RANKINGS

Although used with less frequency than rating scales, ranking techniques offer a useful format for appraising employee performance. An **alternating ranking technique** requires that an appraiser first write down the name of the best performer in the work unit. Next, she writes down the name of the poorest performer in the unit. Then, she writes the name of the second best performer, followed by the second poorest performer, and so on. A major advantage of this simple exercise is that it forces the appraiser to "sort out" the appraisees, since everyone cannot receive the same evaluation. By spreading out the employees on a performance dimension, it is easier to make decisions about who should receive merit raises or be considered for other rewards or sanctions.

A variation on this ranking technique is the **paired comparison,** which requires the evaluator to think of each employee in conjunction with all other employees before making a judgment. Often, a paired comparison involves the creation of a matrix to aid the evaluator. Figure 8.2 shows such a matrix for a work group of five subordinates. In the cells of the matrix, the evaluator enters the name of the appraisee who is judged superior in a one-on-one comparison

FIGURE 8.2
ILLUSTRATION OF THE PAIRED COMPARISON RANKING TECHNIQUE

	Bill	Pete	Jackie	Julie	Mario
Bill					
Pete	Pete				
Jackie	Jackie	Pete			
Julie	Julie	Julie	Julie		
Mario	Mario	Pete	Mario	Julie	

[‡]Perhaps better than anyone, college students are familiar with all four kinds of rating errors. Halo errors sometimes occur when an instructor's grade for a student's term paper is based more on the student's performance on objective exams and daily attendance in class than on the quality of the paper. Some instructors assign grades according to a normal curve (central tendency error), while others are very generous (leniency error) or very stingy (harshness error) in assigning high grades.

with each of the other subordinates. A simple tally of the number of times a person "wins" a comparison provides a summary of the relative standing of each subordinate. From the results of this tally, it is clear that Bill is the poorest performer (having won no comparisons), while Julie is the best performer (having won all comparisons). A major advantage of a paired comparison approach is its requirement that each subordinate be consciously considered in the ranking process. No individual can be accidentally overlooked by an evaluator who has to consider all subordinates simultaneously. Also, middle-range performers, who may be difficult to distinguish among as a subgroup, must be deliberately considered against one another.

A serious potential shortcoming of the paired comparison technique is that more and more comparisons must be made as a work group increases in size. When there are 5 subordinates, only 10 comparisons need be made. But with 20 subordinates, 190 comparisons become necessary.[§]

Yet another ranking format is the **forced distribution.** Used at Exxon, this technique requires that the evaluator assign specified percentages of employees to each of several classifications.[19] For example, he may be required to assign 10 percent of the employees to each of the categories *excellent* and *unacceptable,* 20 percent to each of the categories *above average* and *poor,* and 40 percent to the category *average.* This approach also forces the evaluator to sort out his subordinates. But while avoiding some errors, such as leniency and harshness, it may introduce another: an imposed distribution that is unjustifiable. For example, a normal performance distribution may be imposed, which would assume that most performance falls in the average range. Such an assumption may be unwarranted because entire units can be expected to differ in terms of performance. Some units may be composed of mostly superior performers, while others may contain many poor performers.

One possible problem with any ranking technique is that the results may be difficult to share with subordinates who receive low rankings. Employees tend to have a difficult time accepting the assessment that they are below average (although, by definition, half of the employees in any group must be considered below average).[**]

BEHAVIORALLY ANCHORED RATING SCALES

In recent years, there have been several attempts to develop performance rating scales that are more closely tied to actual employee behavior. **Behaviorally anchored rating scales (BARS)** use examples of employee behavior as anchors for performance dimensions.[20,††] When carefully constructed, BARS are potentially very accurate devices for appraising employee performance.

The creation of a BARS system involves several steps. First, statements that describe competent, average, and incompetent behavior are gathered

---

[§]A simple equation can be used to determine the number of comparisons to be made: $n(n - 1)/2$, where n is the number of employees. Therefore, with 7 employees, the number of comparisons is $7(6)/2 = 21$.

[**]One can extend this simple relative assessment notion of "average" to generate some surprising statements. For example, consider that one-half of all medical doctors graduated from medical school in the bottom half of their class!

[††]Behaviorally anchored rating scales (BARS) are called behavioral expectation scales (BES) by some authors.[21]

from employees and supervisors. Supervisors then categorize the statements in terms of performance dimensions, such as interpersonal skills, technical know-how, and so on, and discard those statements that are ambiguous or not classifiable. A group of judges (made up of supervisors from other units or specialized job analysts) are then asked to rate each incident on a seven-point scale in terms of whether the incident represents outstanding (7), average (4), or poor (1) performance. Specific incidents are then selected to serve as anchors or benchmarks on the final scale, with the average of the judges' ratings of an incident used as the numerical index for that anchor. Figure 8.3 shows an example of a BARS for the performance dimension of motivation.

BARS have several distinct advantages as tools for appraising performance. Because the scales are phrased in job-relevant terminology, they are more meaningful to raters than scales that attempt to assess traits. Also, the initial involvement of raters (and sometimes ratees) in the creation of the scales helps to persuade the participants of the relevance and importance of the appraisal process. In addition, the behavioral emphasis of BARS can help the rater to identify a worker's specific strengths and weaknesses, which can then be discussed at a performance feedback session.

A practical problem that sometimes arises with BARS is that a rater may have difficulty seeing any similarity between the specific behavioral anchors and a subordinate's performance. In such instances, raters are likely to rely more on their expectations than on their observations. A second problem is that BARS are relatively time consuming and expensive to construct. Because they are tailored for specific jobs and because job requirements tend to change over time, BARS cannot necessarily be used across jobs or over a long period for the same job.

■ FIGURE 8.3
EXAMPLE OF A BEHAVIORALLY ANCHORED RATING SCALE

Motivation—the Desire and Willingness to Work Hard

7	After job responsibilities are met, worker could be expected to help coworkers complete their assignments.
6	
5	Worker could be expected to do the job when the supervisor is not present.
4	
3	Worker could be expected to refuse request to work overtime.
2	
1	Worker could be expected to criticize coworkers who work more rapidly than others.

An Inside Look
Performance Appraisal Goes High Tech

One of the latest innovations to help supervisors rate employee performance more effectively is Employee Appraiser, a $129 software package that provides the evaluator a framework for rating employee performance.

Employee Appraiser presents the evaluator with a menu of more than a dozen evaluation categories, including communication, dependability, initiative, decision making, judgment, leadership, planning, and productivity. Within each evaluation category are numerous performance factors. For example, the factors for communication are verbal communication, writing, listening skills, receptivity to feedback and criticism, keeping others informed, ability to focus on desired results, and openness.

The manager evaluates each factor, presented as a Behaviorally Anchored Rating Scale, by selecting the phrase that best describes the employee's behavior. Employee Appraiser then generates sample

text. To demonstrate how this works, Employee Appraiser provides an illustrative example that uses Elias Whitney, inventor of the cotton gin. If Whitney had been evaluated as "is sometimes unclear" for the factor "verbal communication," Employee Appraiser would produce the following text:

Elias usually presents his ideas clearly and concisely. However, he sometimes uses terminology that is unclear to others. Elias would be more effective in his communications if he used less jargon and fewer technical terms.

As the manager evaluates each performance factor, the program generates a thorough, detailed report. An editing function allows the user to edit and customize the report, and add additional comments and feedback. Employee Appraiser overcomes

the weaknesses of traditional evaluations that lack detail and substance by automating the writing of employee evaluations and drawing on a collection of concepts and behaviors that are important for job performance. The program promotes the use of specific, nondiscriminatory language, and gives evaluators examples of constructive criticism. To make ongoing documentation of an employee's performance easier, the program encourages managers to log events in the program's memory throughout the year for review when the evaluator conducts the formal appraisal.

By providing a template for performance evaluations, Employee Appraiser produces a more thorough, expeditious report. Moreover, by making managers less wary of the evaluation process, the program helps them become more perceptive and articulate in providing objective performance feedback.

Source: Peter H. Lewis, "A Way to Rate Employee Performance More Effectively," *New York Times*, December 19, 1993, F10.

BEHAVIORAL OBSERVATION SCALES

Another behavioral approach to appraising employee performance has been developed by Gary Latham and Kenneth Wexley.[22] Their **behavioral observation scales (BOS)** are developed using a critical incident technique (like that for BARS) in which jobholders and supervisors generate examples of performance behaviors that characterize an entire job. Any behavioral statements judged too rare to be observed ("Has the smell of liquor on his breath" is one example Latham and Wexley cite) are then excluded from the final product.

BOS differ from BARS in that BOS require the evaluator to indicate the *frequency* with which a worker exhibits a specific behavior, whereas BARS ask the evaluator to define superior versus inferior performance. Also, with BOS the focus is on the frequency with which a ratee is observed engaging in the specific behaviors, whereas with BARS the ratee is judged on having displayed a particular behavior during a specific rating period.

Figure 8.4 shows several statements from a BOS that was designed for a department store salesclerk. Note that these items focus on specific performance-related actions. As such, they are very close in content to the kinds of statements that are included in job descriptions based on job analyses. Thus, BOS can greatly enhance performance feedback sessions by helping to focus the discussion on specific behaviors instead of personal feelings and emotions.

In order to help the rater interpret the numerical values of BOS items, Latham and Wexley suggest that the following guidelines be used:

Assign a Numerical Rating of	If the Behavior Is	Observed % of the Time
1	_____	0–64
2	_____	65–74
3	_____	75–84
4	_____	85–94
5	_____	95–100

A rater thus selects a numerical value that corresponds to the percentage of the time that the employee displayed the behavior.

Because BOS are a fairly recent innovation, there is relatively little evidence on their limitations.[23] However, in comparing BOS with BARS in terms of reducing rater bias and errors, Bernardin found that BOS were as good as BARS, and Bernardin, Alvares, and Cranny found that they were better.[24]

MANAGEMENT-BY-OBJECTIVES

In Chapter 7, we considered management-by-objectives (MBO) as a means of *motivating* individual performance. But MBO can also be used in *evaluating* individual performance. Recall from our earlier discussion that the essential elements of an MBO program are (1) the supervisor and each subordinate meet to establish specific goals and the means to attain them, (2) the supervisor aids the subordinates in their efforts to reach the established goals, and (3) the supervisor and each subordinate meet at a later prespecified time to review the extent of goal attainment. The third element in this process, the review and

FIGURE 8.4

EXAMPLE OF A BOS FOR A SALESCLERK

1. **Stops talking to another salesclerk as soon as a customer approaches him/her.**
   Almost Never   1   2   3   4   5   Almost Always

2. **Closes a sale by saying "thank you" to the customer.**
   Almost Never   1   2   3   4   5   Almost Always

3. **Comes to work without wearing company uniform.**
   Almost Never   1   2   3   4   5   Almost Always

appraisal of goal attainment, represents a performance appraisal exercise. The deliberate tying of organizational rewards to goal attainment can also have a powerful impact on enhancing performance.

Despite their virtues, MBO programs are not without potential pitfalls. For example, they generate additional paperwork and time-consuming meetings—two things most workers prefer to avoid. In some instances, when rewards (such as merit pay) are tied to goal attainment, subordinates may try to set easy goals and resist taking responsibility for their failure to attain goals. Also, the focus of MBO on attaining specific goals may lead to greater success in some areas while sacrificing accomplishment in other areas that are not being explicitly measured. For example, a sales manager may actively seek to increase the number of new clients because a goal has been set on this dimension. As a result of focusing so much effort and time on acquiring new clients, however, less attention may be paid to maintaining the satisfaction of former, more established clients—something that was not explicitly included in the MBO goals statement. The net result of some MBO programs may be success on certain emphasized (and usually quantifiable) performance dimensions, at the sacrifice of performance on unemphasized, and often less easily quantifiable, dimensions.

ASSESSMENT CENTERS

Perhaps the most elaborate method of appraising managerial ability is through an assessment center. An **assessment center** is a site where appraisals of individual managerial skills are conducted over a period of several days. The appraisal includes interviews, testing, simulations, peer appraisals, and appraisals by experts who observe candidates during their stay at the center. Strictly speaking, assessment centers are designed to appraise individuals' *current* managerial ability as opposed to their *past performance*. The estimate of present ability is then frequently used in forecasting whether an individual is suitable for promotion to a higher-level management position.

Before their adoption by American industry during the 1950s, live-in centers where candidates were appraised by observing their performance in simulations and games were used by the German, British, and United States military during World War II.[‡‡] As part of their remilitarization during the 1930s, the German High Command devised a live-in situational testing scheme for assessing military officers. Their assessment focused on whether the officers possessed a "practical disposition." To document this disposition, hidden cameras recorded candidates' facial expressions while they engaged in stress-inducing tasks, such as pulling an expanding-spring exerciser that sent out increasing levels of electric current as it was pulled. Although less interested in stress tolerance, the British and Americans created assessment centers in the 1940s to close an emerging "assessment center gap" with the Germans. The American assessment centers were largely used by the Office of Strategic Service (the forerunner of the CIA) for selecting army volunteers to serve as spies. The OSS

---

‡‡The original creation of situational assessment, however, is credited to Imperial China, circa 220 B.C.[25]

model for assessment centers became the foundation for later centers in American organizations, such as AT&T, SOHIO, and IBM.

A typical schedule of events at an assessment center (then and now) might include a lengthy interview covering personal and work history, a battery of mental ability and personality tests, participation in a leaderless group discussion or a formal debate (in which participants are asked to discuss a controversial topic while a group of assessors records each individual's reactions and mannerisms), role playing in front of an audience, and peer appraisals.

In recent years, it has become very common to include an *in-basket exercise*—a simulation in which a participant is asked to go through a stack of papers (consisting of memos, production reports, letters, and the like) that are allegedly taken from a manager's basket of incoming mail. During a one- or two-hour period, the participant must decide how to handle each document contained in the in-basket. For example, in response to a certain memo, a participant may decide to send a letter, schedule a meeting with subordinates, or do nothing at all. The participant's responses are then scored by trained judges in accordance with fairly elaborate grading schemes. In essence, an in-basket exercise simulates the daily activities of most managers. As a simulation, it can help to identify individuals who have the judgment necessary to make high-quality decisions.[26]

One might conjecture that some people could "fake their way" through a three-day assessment. Such an occurrence would be highly unlikely because it would be difficult to maintain a facade for such an extended period. During the course of the experience, observers also keep fairly constant watch on the participants. For example, at athletic events and social functions (such as cocktail parties in the evening), the observers mentally take notes on the conduct of participants. And if a participant clearly displays a tendency to "fake it," this becomes another bit of evidence that will be "grist for the mill" in the final appraisal.

Based on their observations, the assessment center's staff prepares a report on each participant's suitability for promotion. The report is usually fairly detailed and describes the observed strengths and weaknesses of the individual.

A number of studies have been conducted to determine whether the reports generated by assessment center personnel can predict an individual's later success as a manager.[27] By and large, the results suggest that assessment centers can successfully predict later job performance, job progress in terms of pay, and job potential. Several especially well-designed studies, in which the reports from the assessment center were withheld from the candidate's supervisor in order to eliminate the possibility of a self-fulfilling prophecy (see Chapter 7), also concluded that assessment centers can identify individuals who possess key management abilities.

Assessment centers are not without shortcomings, however. The cost of sending a single employee to an assessment center can vary from $600 to as much as $1,000. In addition, the work-group dynamics may change after an individual has been sent to an assessment center. Coworkers may label such a person a "fast-tracker." This can either lead to serious resentment or help guarantee the individual's later success due to a self-fulfilling prophecy.[28]

Another potential drawback is that the center's observers may not be sufficiently familiar with a specific organization or with the positions within an organization to provide useful forecasts of success. Instead, the observers may rely on stereotypes or thumbnail sketches of the jobs for which candidates are being appraised. To avoid such problems, an organization may employ its own managers to serve as observers. These managers, who are usually one or two levels above the candidates, are then trained to administer the exercises and serve as observers. The use of upper-level managers as observers also helps to "sell" the results of the assessment center to the people who will be most interested in the outcome.

THE FEEDBACK INTERVIEW

No matter what instrument or appraisal method is used, the results must be constructively conveyed to the subordinate in order to produce the desired effects on performance.[29] Most researchers agree that knowledge of appraisal results can enhance employee performance and that the best forum for providing such information is the **feedback interview.** Although the goal of such a session is to establish a give-and-take atmosphere that will encourage corrective changes, the more frequent outcome is emotional tension and defensiveness. Managers invariably report that performance feedback interviews make them very uncomfortable.[30] Subordinates likewise find the experience unpleasant because they frequently disagree with their superiors' appraisals.[31] The tendency to reject superiors' suggestions stems from the fact that most employees view their performance as above average. For example, Carrol and Schneier asked 249 managers to rate themselves as below average, average, or above average on a number of performance dimensions.[32] The mean response across all dimensions was that 67 percent viewed themselves as above-average performers! Furthermore, the person giving the feedback may not have sufficient credibility or power to be effective.[33] An evaluator must be viewed as credible before an appraisee will respect and accept feedback. And if the evaluator also has power (that is, the ability to reward and punish), the appraisee is even more likely to accept his or her comments. When the appraiser lacks credibility or power, the employee is likely to look for other sources of feedback about performance, such as coworkers, himself or herself, subordinates, or the job itself. If the other sources disagree with the evaluator, the employee may adopt their views as a way of protecting his or her self-esteem. Because of these obstacles, many organizations, such as GTE, provide training programs for supervisors on how to conduct a feedback interview.[34]

CONDUCTING A FEEDBACK INTERVIEW

When conducting a performance feedback interview, an evaluator can take a number of steps to enhance the process's likelihood of success.[§§]

[§§]Many of the techniques discussed in this section were originally summarized in a reivew of the literature by Burke, Weitzel, and Weir.[35]

PREPARATION   To be effective in conveying his or her point of view, the evaluator must be able to support comments with facts. Thus, it is important for the evaluator to prepare carefully for the interview. This entails gathering and reviewing all available records of the candidate's performance. For example, the evaluator should examine the candidate's record on a variety of dimensions, such as absenteeism, quantity and quality of output, tardiness, and the like, to get a total picture of the individual's performance and to note specific instances that call for comment. Most good evaluators also prepare an outline of the points that they intend to cover, which enables them to stay on track during the interview.

Out of fairness, the employee should be given advance notice of the meeting and information about its primary purpose—that is, whether it will pertain to merit raises, personal development, performance goal setting, or another area. This will give the employee time to prepare his or her thoughts and comments.

As an opening to the interview itself, many appraisers like to ask employees to comment on their own performance. For example, the evaluator may begin by saying, "Tell me how you view your own progress and problems in your job." Such an opening invites the employee's participation, which is a highly desired reaction, since the more subordinates are permitted to express their opinions during a feedback interview, the more satisfied they are likely to be with the appraisal experience.[36]

PHRASING COMMENTS   When providing explicit (and especially critical) appraisal information to a subordinate, an effective evaluator will focus on problems and avoid personalities. For example, the evaluator will not make comments about personal traits, such as, "You don't strike me as a very ambitious person," but rather will keep the feedback fairly specific and behaviorally based. Thus, instead of saying, "You're tardy too often," the evaluator will say: "You've been late for the start of your shift eight times during the past six months. Since we expect an employee to be late no more than once a month, can you suggest some ways that you might be able to achieve this standard in the coming months?" And in place of "You need to improve the quality of your work," an effective evaluator will say: "During the past year, our quality-assurance crew has had to reject 22 percent of the output from your machine. The average reject rate for all other operators is only 2 percent. How can we reduce your reject rate to make it closer to the average?"

Sometimes, an appraiser has strong feelings about a subordinate's personal characteristics and behaviors. For example, he or she may not like the way an employee dresses or talks. If personal characteristics are relevant to the job—as dress and speech are for salesclerks, repairers who visit customers in their homes, and many other workers—they can be legitimately discussed during a feedback interview. But if attire and other personal habits are not job relevant, it is best for the appraiser to try to develop greater tolerance for human diversity.

When it is impossible to avoid criticizing an individual, an effective evaluator will state his or her criticisms without hostility and clearly explain why the action or inaction cannot be continued. For example, the evaluator will point out the consequences of poor performance for people both inside and outside the organization. After voicing criticism, the evaluator should carefully and with an open mind listen to any explanations that the subordinate may offer. Following a complete discussion, the two should work out a series of steps for remedying the problem and set a follow-up date for appraising the progress toward change.

THE SANDWICH APPROACH   In a feedback interview, the identification of good performance is as important as the correction of substandard performance. In light of this, some performance appraisal specialists suggest that the evaluator highlight the positive points of an employee's performance early in the interview. The evaluator can then lead the discussion to the negative aspects of performance and, finally, close the conversation with several additional positive points. This positive-negative-positive sequence is called the **sandwich approach** to providing feedback. Many appraisers find themselves using this technique almost instinctively. Perhaps this is due to a natural tendency to try to minimize defensiveness by starting out with upbeat comments and to maintain good working relations by ending on a positive note. Critics, however, contend that the sandwich technique may actually blunt the intended purpose of a critical evaluation. The use of positive statements at the beginning and end of the session may mask the intended message of the need for improvement. At present, there is no evidence on the sandwich technique's effectiveness in enhancing the communication of feedback or in changing subsequent performance.

LIMITING CRITICISM   If criticism will be a major focus of a feedback session, the evaluator should limit the comments to one or two problem areas to avoid overwhelming the employee and to decrease the potential for defensiveness and conflict. Under even the best circumstances, most people have a very low tolerance for criticism and, when it is given in heavy doses (even if well packaged and presented as a problem-solving exercise), many people find criticism impossible to accept.

CLOSING THE INTERVIEW   As the feedback interview draws to a close, it is useful to rephrase the agreed-upon steps for improving performance. For example, the supervisor might say, "Let's review our agreement. Next Thursday, you'll talk with Bud about getting his department to respond more quickly to our requests for materials. Then I'll speak with Bud's supervisor the following week if there's no change in their response to our needs."

In closing the session, the appraiser should offer his or her assistance to the subordinate. This offer should be explicit and genuine. By offering to help the subordinate (especially by removing obstacles), a supervisor can minimize his or her role as judge and enhance the subordinate's perception of the supervisor as counselor or coach.

Finally, a supervisor should not wait for a company-mandated appraisal session to provide feedback to subordinates. Daily informal feedback about an employee's positive and negative performance will actually aid in making formal appraisals more effective. Informal appraisals let employees know that the supervisor understands and is concerned with their performance. As a comparison, consider that most sports figures work with their coaches daily rather than waiting until contract negotiation time to discuss performance enhancement.

LEGAL ASPECTS OF PERFORMANCE APPRAISAL

Performance appraisal systems form the basis for many important personnel decisions. Promotions, salary raises and cuts, layoffs, and demotions are based on the outcomes of such systems. Given the significant consequences of performance appraisals and the possibility of bias entering into the evaluation process, a number of government regulations have been created to safeguard the groups of employees (especially women and minorities) who are most likely to be victimized by such bias.[37] These government regulations, which include the Equal Pay Act of 1963, the Civil Rights Act of 1964, the Age Discrimination in Employment Act of 1967, the Vocational Rehabilitation Act of 1973, and the Americans with Disabilities Act of 1992 require that performance be documented in accordance with certain standards when making personnel-related decisions. The Civil Rights Act of 1964 even created a separate federal agency (the Equal Employment Opportunity Commission) to oversee employers' compliance with a set of uniform guidelines for protecting employees' rights.[38] (cf Federal Register, 1978).*** When employees have charged their employers with discriminatory practices in appraisal (as well as initial hiring) systems, the courts have frequently ruled in favor of the employees when one or more specific shortcomings have been identified.

ADVERSE IMPACT

A primary issue in discrimination suits is whether the company's actions have an **adverse impact** on a legally protected group. For example, an employer may be accused of having a policy (either formal or informal) that prevents members of a protected group from being promoted. To determine if the allegation is true, the employer's record for promoting individuals from the protected group would be compared with percentages for the same group in the population at large. For example, a construction firm in a large metropolitan area may have only 2 percent of its supervisory positions held by blacks. If data (usually taken from Department of Labor surveys of labor pool availability) suggest that 15 percent is a more reasonable expected proportion, the employer may be liable for discriminatory practices in promoting or hiring or both.

One of the more common checks for adverse impact is to compare a company's rejection rates of protected and nonprotected group members, a process known as applying the **four-fifths rule**. According to this rule, adverse impact

---

***Strictly speaking, the Civil Rights Act prohibits discrimination only on the basis of sex, race, religion, color, or national origin. Discrimination on the basis of age or physical disability is covered by separate legislation, but enforcement is overseen by the Equal Employment Opportunity Commission.

exists if a protected group's selection rate for employment decisions (that is, hiring, promotion, and so on) is less than four-fifths, or 80 percent, of the selection rate of the nonprotected group. For example, a said company's promotion rate is 40 percent for males and 10 percent for females. Given that 10 percent is less than four-fifths of 40 percent ($.8 \times 40 = 32$ percent), adverse impact may exist for female employees. Of course, the four-fifths rule is simply a rule of thumb and, as such, is usually interpreted as merely suggesting discrimination. Other evidence, such as how recently female employees have been hired for certain positions and the company's overall record in providing equal employment opportunities, would have to be considered in determining whether an employer is guilty of discrimination.

Interestingly, an employer can still use appraisal systems that have adverse impact as long as the systems are shown to be valid—that is, as long as they are highly relevant to the job and accurately predict subsequent performance. Also, an appraisal system does not have to be validated if there is no initial evidence of discriminatory impact.[†††] Of course, it requires a serious commitment from an organization to establish that its employment practices are job relevant and predictively useful. In essence, federal (and many state) regulations simply require that employers subscribe to sound principles derived from the behavioral side of management. To ignore these principles leaves an employer vulnerable to charges of discrimination.

PENALTIES

The penalties for being found guilty of discrimination can be substantial (running into the millions of dollars). They may include back pay settlements to all members of a protected group who were excluded from promotion or transfer opportunites, the forced promotion and training of members of the aggrieved group, fines, court costs, the loss of federal contracts, and/or the hiring of a compliance officer to monitor subsequent employment practices to ensure cooperation with the imposed goals for promotions and hiring.

LEGALLY DEFENSIBLE APPRAISAL SYSTEMS

To avoid such problems, an employer should know what attributes make a performance appraisal system legally defensible. In a review of this issue, Klasson, Thompson, and Lubben identified a number of critical features.[39] First, an ideal appraisal system would be formal and standardized. It would, therefore, be done in accordance with a written policy, and all appraisees would be treated alike, regardless of sex, race, and so on. The appraisal system would be based on a thorough job analysis that would lead to clear standards and fixed measures of performance. Subjective evaluations by a single supervisor would be only one component of an appraisal process that included input from the

---

[†††]It can be said that an appraisal system may even be fairly stupid (such as feeling for lumps on a person's head) as long as it is stupid fairly (that is, it does not reject a larger percentage of protected group members as compared with other candidates).

appraisee and performance-based data. In addition, the appraisers would be given training in how to rate employees. In the present litigious atmosphere, it is essential that every decision to promote, transfer, or terminate an employee on any basis other than seniority be documented with substantial evidence.‡‡‡

The court case of *Rowe v. General Motors* helps to identify many of the shortcomings that still exist in today's performance appraisal systems. In this case, the recommendations of supervisors (all of whom were white) were based on vague and subjective standards. These recommendations led to a lack of promotions for black employees and, consequently, discriminatory treatment. The court's ruling that discrimination existed was based on five points:

1. The supervisor's recommendations were the critical factor in the promotion process.
2. Supervisors were not instructed on the qualifications needed for promotion.
3. The standards were subjective and vague.
4. Employees were not given notification of opportunities for promotion.
5. The appraisal system had no safeguards against discriminatory practices.

In light of these potential shortcomings, it is worth considering how some of the performance appraisal techniques discussed in this chapter measure up to regulations against discriminatory treatment.

Latham and Wexley contend that both BARS and BOS satisfy the requirements of federal legislation in two ways: They allow employees to participate in the identification of a job's critical elements and they focus on actual job behaviors rather than on subjective traits.[41]

The possibility that assessment centers may have adverse impact on women and minorities has been closely studied. In a study of nearly 5,000 women, Moses and Boehm found that the same factors that predicted success for male managers (such as leadership, decision-making ability, and organizing skills) also predicted success for female managers.[42] In another study, Huck reported that assessment centers were as valid for females and blacks as they were for males and whites.[43]

Other performance appraisal devices, such as graphic rating scales and rankings, although not inherently biased, are frequently regarded with suspicion by the courts if they are not clearly derived from an analysis of a job's content. Management-by-objectives systems have not been seriously studied from the standpoint of discrimination against protected groups. It is likely that MBO and other goal-setting systems are fairly defensible, however, and that they minimize disparate tretatment if they are properly established and used in accordance with an appropriate and consistent philosophy.

---

‡‡‡For further information on discriminatory issues, the interested reader should consult Arvey.[40] Several important court decisions have served to direct legal thinking in the area of employer appraisal: *Griggs v. Duke Power Co.*, 3 FEP Cases 175 (1972); *Moody v. Albermarle Paper Co.*, 10 FEP Cases 1181 (1975); *Rogers v. International Paper Co.*, 10 FEP Cases 404 (1975); *Rowe v. General Motors Corp.*, 4 FEP Cases 445 (1972); *Brito v. Zia Co.*, 5 FEP Cases 1207 (1973); *Wade v. Mississippi Cooperative Extension Service*, 372 F. Supp. 126, 7 FEP 282 (1974); *James v. Stockham Values and Fittings*, 15 FEP 827 (1977); *Watson v. Fort Worth Bank and Trust*, 108 S. Ct. 2777, 2790-91 (1988); *Wards Cove Packing Company v. Atonio*, 109 S. Ct. 3115 (1989).

MANAGING AND VALUING DIVERSITY

In recent years, there has been a recognition of a changing demographic mix in the U.S. work force. The term *work force diversity* gained popularity following a 1987 study entitled *Work Force 2000: Work and Workers for the 21st Century* (commissioned by the U.S. Department of Labor).[44] One major conclusion of the *Work Force 2000* study was that a large proportion of the new entrants to the labor force for the near future would be from demographic categories other than that of white males. Many leading-edge firms have chosen to respond to the challenge of an increasingly diverse work force by seeking to actively manage diversity for competitive advantage.

To some managers, this recent concern with the management of diversity reflects the newest stage in the evolution of affirmative action and equal employment opportunity issues. Other managers, however, view diversity as an opportunity for increased productivity and competitiveness. The most frequently cited avenues include more effective recruiting of talented women and minorities, entry to new marketing opportunities, and the maximization of each employee's unique ability to contribute. Yet, despite common use of the term *diversity,* there is little agreement within the business community as to its precise meaning or how it should be specifically "managed."

The definition of *diversity* itself also lacks consensus. Some firms emphasize only gender, race, and age, while others include military experience and regional origins. Still other firms emphasize religious beliefs or sexual orientation. In a sense, the definition of diversity is fairly well customized to each firm. Avon Products, considered a pioneer in the area of diversity, includes in its definition: gender, race, disability, job function, lifestyle, age, tenure with the employer, sexual orientation, geographic region, and employment by companies acquired by acquisitions and mergers. IBM, by contrast, holds to the definition of "all the different characteristics that make one individual different from another."

Diversity programs within companies, such as Monsanto and Mobil Oil, typically include several elements, most frequently training in which managers are given opportunities to develop greater sensitivity to and awareness of diversity. For example, participants might be asked to consider how their lives might be different had they been born or were living their lives as one of the following: a divorced, older woman responsible for elderly parents; a gay male in his midthirties living with a partner; a 46-year-old disabled veteran; or a young, black female high school graduate. Participants are also asked to consider their implicit preferences in promoting others (for example, their often unstated preferences for promoting people in a certain age range or of a given ethnic background, race, religion, height, sexual orientation, and so on).

Another common element in diversity programs may be termed communication. Communication includes speeches by senior executives, inclusion of diversity in corporate vision statements, the publication of a diversity brochure, and inclusion of diversity as a topic in new employee orientation. In addition to formal training and communication, diversity programs also often include an element of career development, such as mentoring programs designed to aid women and minorities, and special internship opportunities.

Although many executives view diversity as an important issue, they also recognize many obstacles to implementing diversity initiatives. Chief among these are competition with other issues, belief that forecasted demographic shifts will not impair corporate ability to attract talent, lack of top- and middle-management support, and fear of a backlash from white males. Additionally, it is not clear how one can deliberately use identifiable group or aggregate differences to manage a work force competitively, given that the historical trend in civil rights legislation has been to mandate equal treatment of individuals rather than distinctive treatment based on group membership. Also, many managers (and researchers) report that they have observed far greater differences *within* groups of people than *between* groups of people. Therefore, the case for group differences appears to have been overstated for political reasons. As a consequence of these reservations, the rhetoric that emphasizes the *management* of diversity may be in the process of shifting to that of the *valuing* of diversity. Valuing of diversity implies acceptance of other individuals and tolerance of individual differences, with less of an implied emphasis on making (potentially illegal) human resources decisions based on assumptions of group differences. The valuing of diversity also holds the potential of avoiding the most serious pitfalls of ignoring diversity: diminished individual commitment, tarnished corporate image, and monetary cost resulting from high turnover, lawsuits, and grievance filing.§§§

SUMMARY

1. List reasons for appraising performance.
The basic goal of performance appraisal is to maintain or improve employee effectiveness. Other objectives are to help supervisors decide on relative compensation; to help in evaluating subordinates' suitability for training and development; to help in making appropriate job changes; to open communication between supervisors and subordinates; and to provide subordinates with feedback about their performance.

2. Describe different timetables for performance appraisals.
Annual reviews on a common review date help organizations set budgets that incorporate raises based on the reviews. Annual reviews based on the anniversary of an employee's hiring spread evaluation throughout the year, so that supervisors avoid the burden of appraising everyone at once. Appraisals at naturally occurring events fulfill the need for feedback, as after a probationary period or completion of a major project.

---

§§§The limited evidence available on the impact of increasing diversity in work units suggests that for tasks that require a range of inputs and perspectives, more diverse work units will generate higher-quality solutions. However, the process may take more time relative to more homogeneous work units. Also, increases in unit diversity have been found to precede increases in member turnover.45

3. Discuss the relative merits of performance appraisal by the immediate supervisor, the employee being appraised, peers or coworkers, subordinates, and people outside the work unit.

Table 8.1 shows advantages and disadvantages of appraisal by these different sources.

4. Describe the process of job analysis.

Job analysis states precisely the activities a job comprises. An observer examines all available data on a given job, including information gathered from interviews with those doing the job and with their supervisor. The observer then writes a job description describing the actual behaviors that are central to the conduct of the job.

5. Explain why performance appraisal cannot be totally objective.

Prior expectations influence even the perception of objective events. The supervisor's beliefs about the employee's ability influence his or her observations of the employee's performance. Also, performance includes many behaviors, some of which can be difficult to measure.

6. List methods of performance appraisal.

Performance appraisal methods include graphic rating scales; rankings, including the alternating ranking technique, paired comparison approach, and forced distribution; behaviorally anchored rating scales (BARS); behavioral observation scales (BOS); management-by-objectives; and assessment centers.

7. Describe sources of tension in feedback interviews.

Tension can arise because subordinates frequently disagree with the supervisor's appraisal of their performance. Also, the evaluator may not have enough credibility or power for the feedback to be effective.

8. List the elements of a successful feedback interview.

The elements of a successful feedback interview are preparation; comments that focus on problems, not personalities; a positive-negative-positive sequence of comments (the sandwich approach); placing a limit on the amount of criticism; and closing the interview on a positive note and with an offer of assistance.

9. Describe how courts evaluate whether a company's actions have had an adverse impact on a group.

The courts review the employer's record for promoting individuals from the group and compare this to percentages for the group in the population at large. Another way is to compare a company's rejection rates of protected and nonprotected group members.

10. Describe the characteristics of a legally defensible appraisal system.

A legally defensible appraisal system should be valid; formal and standardized; based on a thorough job analysis leading to clear standards of performance; based on input from the supervisor, employee, and performance-based data; and given by supervisors trained in how to use the system. Promotions, transfers, and terminations should be documented.

11. Discuss the issues surrounding managing and valuing diversity.

Diversity programs, which are generally unique to each firm, typically include training, communication, and career development components. Obstacles to diversity initiatives include competition with other issues, skepticism of the projected impact of demographic trends, lack of management support, concern with a backlash from white males, legal trends that mandate equal treatment, and the beliefs that differences between groups are less substantial than differences within groups. Problems associated with ignoring diversity issues include reduced employee commitment, tarnished corporate image, and monetary costs.

KEY TERMS

360-degree feedback
Job description
Organizational Citizenship
   Behaviors
Graphic rating scale
Halo error
Central tendency error
Leniency error
Harshness error
Alternating ranking technique

Paired comparison
Forced distribution
Behaviorally anchored rating scales
   (BARS)
Behavioral observation scales (BOS)
Assessment center
Feedback interview
Sandwich approach
Adverse impact
Four-fifths rule

REVIEW AND DISCUSSION QUESTIONS

1. How do companies benefit from performance appraisal systems?

2. Should performance appraisals take place every day? Explain your answer.

3. How can self-appraisal be used as part of the process of performance appraisal? Do organizations generally use self-appraisal as the basis for a promotion or a raise?

4. Which of the following are appropriate components of a job description? Explain your answers.

   a. Types reports accurately and neatly.

   b. Is courteous to customers.

   c. Performs accounting tasks.

   d. Maintains weekly production log.

5. Describe the advantages and disadvantages of the following appraisal techniques: graphic rating scales, ranking, behaviorally anchored rating scales, behavioral observation scales, management-by-objectives, and assessment centers.

6. Carol Skinner is about to give a feedback interview for the first time. Remembering that she has often felt tense when being appraised by her own supervisor, Carol wants to understand why feedback interviews can be so uncomfortable. What reasons can you give her? How can she make the meeting go more smoothly?

7. Don Direct, manager of the housewares department of Big Buys department store, is not the most tactful supervisor. Salespeople often storm out of his office following their annual feedback interview. In fact, a few employees have even quit during a feedback interview. Following are comments Don has made to employees; suggest a more appropriate alternative for each:

   a. "You're too sloppy."

   b. "You don't seem very ambitious."

   c. "I don't like your tone of voice."

8. When Beatrice Bean evaluates the lab technicians in the microbiology lab she supervises, she likes to discuss all the negative points first, to get them over with. What do you think of this approach? Can you suggest a better alternative?

9. How can an organization set up a performance appraisal system that will reduce its vulnerability to charges of discrimination?

10. Evaluate the concept of adverse impact. Is it beneficial to companies? To employees?

CRITICAL INCIDENT

Is an Improvement Needed?

Omicron Photo Processing Co. is a fairly large organization that processes film from many different retail outlets, such as drugstores, discount stores, and so on. They have over 60 employees and use a graphic rating scale to assess worker performance.

Last week the personnel director called you with a concern about the performance appraisal system. The staff of the personnel department believe that the present system does not provide the information needed to improve job performance and allows the raters to permit personal bias to enter the picture. There is also concern about the inadequacy of information to develop and/or improve needed training programs.

When representatives of the department met with the various supervisors and managers to voice these concerns, the supervisors claimed that there are no problems with the present system and that they know who the better performers are. They were also concerned that any other system would place more demands on their time.

The staff in personnel would like to adopt a Behaviorally Anchored Rating Scale (BARS) system. They believe such a system would provide more reliable and valid information than the present system.

The personnel director would like to demonstrate the advantages of a BARS system to the supervisors. He would like your advice on the following questions:

1. What are the advantages and disadvantages of a BARS system as compared with the graphic rating scale?

2. Would a BARS system be more reliable and valid than the present system? Why?

3. Briefly, design a demonstration to show that a BARS system would be more effective than the present system.

Source: Written by Bruce Kemelgor, University of Louisville; used by permission.

EXPERIENTIAL EXERCISE

Designing Behaviorally Anchored Rating Scales

The text material emphasizes the many advantages that Behaviorally Anchored Rating Scales (BARS) have over the typical trait-oriented appraisal instrument. First, BARS are job oriented. They focus specifically on what employees do, not on vague personality traits, such as loyalty, initiative, or creativity. Second, BARS enable the employee to understand why a particular rating was given. Feedback to the employee is job related. BARS also make it easy for the supervisor to tell the employee what he or she must do to improve the ratings. Finally, BARS are a quantitative technique that generates a total point rating for each employee. Thus, BARS scores can be easily tied to personnel decisions involving compensation, training, or promotion.

This activity asks you to work with several of your classmates to create a BARS for the position of college instructor.

1. As a member of the entire class, you should participate in generating a list of five to ten job dimensions for the position of college instructor. Such dimensions might include "classroom presentation skills" or "being well prepared for class."

2. Your instructor will divide the class into several groups of five to seven students. Each group will select one of the job dimensions. Using the job dimension (for example, "use of examples in class"), develop a list of 10 to 15 specific incidents that represent both effective and ineffective behavior.

3. Each group member independently should rate each of the behavioral incidents according to the following scale:
   10 = Excellent performance
    8 = Good performance
    6 = Moderately good performance
    4 = Moderately poor performance
    2 = Poor performance
    0 = Very poor performance

4. As a group, examine the incidents for high rater agreement. You should discard those incidents where there is wide variance among the ratings. For those incidents that will be used, compute an average rating.

5. Prepare the BARS for your particular job dimension. A model scale is provided. (This sample scale is one of many job dimensions for the position of salesperson.) Use the average rating given each incident to place them in an appropriate order.

Client Relationship

Works hard to establish client rapport. Respects every client and appreciates opportunities.	**10** This person has the highest regard for all clients. Looks at even the smallest client as V.I.P. Clients are constantly made to feel important and respected. Constant appreciation for client's business.
	–8– This person is appreciative for his/her clients and the client knows it. A good working relationship between this person and his/her clients. Clients show a dependency on this person.
	–6– This person grooms clients and gleans from the top. Desires to work only with the best and only with a number of clients that can be handled properly. Does not object to passing prospect names to other sales personnel.
Clients regarded as sources of money. Does not work to establish relationship.	This person works with any client who can be approached. Looks for the income vs. developing a continuous business relationship. Not necessarily the right person to represent the company's best interests.
	–4– This person is primarily an order taker. Good manners, but may never see the client. The client forms an opinion of the company from communicating with this person.
	–2– This person accepts clients as a means to receiving an income. This person is never close to the client. A company-client relationship does not exist.
Lacks respect for clients and possibly self in this position. Very marginal contribution.	This person gives the employer short days. Fabricates daily reports. Frequently turns clients off. Company growth is marginal.

6. Your instructor may choose to use one of many options to present the results to the entire class. Using the BARS instrument that you have developed, discuss the following questions:

   a. What do you perceive to be the relative advantages of BARS versus the instructor evaluation form that is presently being used at your institution?

   b. How could the *process* of constructing BARS be helpful to both instructors and students?

Source: Written by Bruce Kemelgor, University of Louisville; used by permission.

NOTES

1. R.I. Lazer and W.S. Wikstrom, *Appraising Managerial Performance: Current Practices and Future Direction.* Conference Board Report No. 723 (New York: The Conference Board, Inc., 1977), 26.

2. R.W. Beatty, C.E. Schneier, and J.R. Beatty, "An Empirical Investigation of

Perceptions of Rater Behavior, Frequency, and Rater Behavior Change Using Behavioral Expectation Scales," *Personnel Pscyhology* 33 (1977): 647–658; G.L. Thornton, "Psychometric Properties of Self-Appraisals of Job Performance," *Personnel Psychology* 33 (1980): 236–271.

3. K.S. Teel, "Self-Appraisal Revisited," *Personnel Journal* 57 (1978): 364–367.

4. F.J. Landy and J.L. Farr, "Performance Rating," *Psychological Bulletin* 87 (1980): 72–107.

5. A.K. Korman, "The Prediction of Managerial Performance: A Review," *Personnel Psychology* 21 (1968): 295–322.

6. M.J. Kavanaugh, A.C. MacKinney, and L. Wolins, "Issues in Managerial Performance: Multi-trait, Multi-method Analyses of Ratings," *Psychological Bulletin* 75 (1971): 34–39; E.E. Lawler III, "The Multitrait–Multirater Approach to Measuring Managerial Job Performance," *Journal of Applied Psychology* 51 (1967): 369–381.

7. K.N. Wexley, "Roles of Performance Appraisal in Organizations," in *Organizational Behavior,* ed. S. Kerr (Columbus, Ohio: Grid Publishing Co., 1979).

8. A.S. DeNisi and J.L. Mitchell, "An Analysis of Peer Ratings as Predictors and Criterion Measures and a Proposed New Application," *Academy of Management Review* 3 (1978): 369–374.

9. J.E. DeJung and J. Kaplan, "Some Differential Effects of Race of Rater and Ratee on Early Peer Ratings of Combat Attitude," *Journal of Applied Psychology* 46 (1962): 370–374; N. Schmitt and M. Lappin, "Race and Sex as Determinants of the Mean and Variance of Performance Ratings," *Journal of Applied Psychology* 65 (1980): 428–435.

10. G. Graen, "Role-making Processes Within Complex Organizations," in *Handbook of Industrial and Organizational Psychology,* ed. M.D. Dunnette (Chicago: Rand McNally, 1976), 1201–1245.

11. P.W. Maloney and J.R. Hinrichs, "A New Tool for Supervisory Self-development," *Personnel* 36 (1959): 46–53; G. Latham, C.H. Fay, and L.M. Saari, "The Development of Behavioral Observation Scales for Appraising the Performance of Foremen," *Personnel Pscyhology* 32 (1979): 299–311.

12. E.J. McCormick, *Job Analysis: Methods and Applications* (New York: AMA-COM, 1979); C.O. Longnecker and D.A. Gioia, "The Executive Appraisal Paradox," *Academy of Management Executive* 6 (1992): 18–28.

13. D.W. Organ, *Organizational Citizenship Behavior: The Good Soldier Syndrome* (Lexington, Mass.: Lexington Books, 1988).

14. D.W. Organ and M. Konovsky, "Cognitive versus Affective Determinants of Organizational Citizenship Behavior," *Journal of Applied Psychology* 74 (1989): 157–164; C.O. Reilly and J. Chatman, "Organizational Commitment and Psychological Attachment: The Effects of Compliance, Identification, and Internalization on Prosocial Behavior," *Journal of Applied Psychology* 7 (1986): 492–499; D.W. Organ, "The Motivational Basis of Organizational Citizenship Behavior," in *Research in Organizational Behavior,* eds. B.M. Staw and L.L. Cummings (Greenwich, Conn.: JAI Press, 1990); R.H. Moorman, "Relationship Between Organizational Justice and Organizational Citizenship Behaviors: Do Fairness Perceptions Influence Employee Citizenship?" *Journal of Applied Psychology* 76 (1991): 845–855; B.P. Niehoff and R.H. Moorman, "Justice as a Mediator of the Relationship Between Methods of Monitoring and Organizational Citizenship Behavior," *Academy of Management Journal* 36 (1993): 527–556; L. Williams and S. Anderson, "Job Satisfaction and Organizational Commitment as Predictors of Organizational Citizenship and In-Role Behaviors," *Journal of Management* 17 (1991): 601–618.

15. C.E. Schneier and W.E. Busse, "The Impact of Sex and Time in Grade on Management Ratings in the Public Sector: Prospects for the Civil Service Reform Act," *Proceedings, Academy of Management National Meetings,* Detroit, 1980; Schmitt and Lappin, "Race and Sex as Determinants"; E. Pulakos, L. White, S. Oppler, and W. Borman, "Examination of Race and Sex Effects on Performance Ratings," *Journal of Applied Psychology* 74 (1989): 770–780; D. Waldman and E.J. Avolio, "Race Effects in Performance Evaluations: Controlling for Ability, Education, and Experience," *Journal of Applied Psychology* 77 (1991): 897–901.

16. G.A. Brugholi, J.E. Campion, and J.A. Basen, "Racial Bias in the Use of Work Samples for Personnel Selection," *Journal of Applied Psycholgy* 64 (1979): 119–123.

17. C.W. Downs and P. Moscinski, "A Survey of Appraisal Processes and Training in Large Corporations" (Paper presented at the Annual Meeting of the Academy of Management, 1979).

18. C.H. Fay and G.P. Latham, "Effects of Training and Rating Scales on Rating Errors," *Personnel Psychology* 35 (1982): 105–116.

19. R. Levering, M. Moskowitz, and M. Katz, *The 100 Best Companies to Work for in America* (Reading, Mass.: Addison-Wesley, 1984).

20. P.C. Smith and L.M. Kendall, "Retranslation of Expectations: An Approach to the Construction of Unambiguous Anchors for Ratings Scales," *Journal of Applied Psychology* 48 (1963): 149–155; M. Piotrowski, J. Barnes-Farrell, and F. Esrig, "Behaviorally Anchored Bias," *Journal of Applied Psychology* 74 (1989): 823–826.

21. G.P. Latham and K.N. Wexley, *Increasing Productivity through Performance Appraisal* (Reading, Mass.: Addison-Wesley, 1981).

22. Ibid.

23. R.S. Atkin and E.J. Conlon, "Behaviorally Anchored Rating Scales: Some Theoretical Issues," *Academy of Management Review* 3 (1978): 119–128.

24. H.J. Bernardin, "Behavioral Expectation Scales versus Summated Rating Scales: A Fairer Comparison," *Journal of Applied Psychology* 62 (1977): 422–427; H.J. Bernardin, K.M. Alvares, and C.J. Cranny, "A Recomparison of Behavioral Expectation Scales to Summated Scales," *Journal of Applied Psychology* 61 (1976): 564–570.

25. P.H. Dubois, *A History of Psychological Testing* (Boston: Allyn and Bacon, 1970); M.L. Bowan, "Testing Individual Differences in Ancient China," *American Psychologist* 44 (1989): 576–578.

26. A. Howard, "An Assessment of Assessment Centers," *Academy of Management Journal* 17 (1974): 115–134.

27. J.L. Moses, "Assessment Center Performance and Management Progress," *Studies in Personnel Psychology* 4 (1972): 7–12; B.M. Cohen, J.L. Moses, and W.C. Byham, "The Validity of Assessment Centers," *Journal of Industrial and Organizational Psychology* 10 (1973): 1–43; J.R. Hinrichs, "An Eight-Year Follow-up of a Management Assessment Center," *Journal of Applied Psychology* 63 (1978): 596–601; B. Gaugler and G. Thornton, "Number of Assessment Center Dimensions as a Determinant of Assessed Accuracy," *Journal of Applied Psychology* 74 (1989): 611–618; T.H. Shore, G.C. Thornton, and L. M. Shore, "Construct Validity of Two Categories of Assessment Center Dimension Ratings," *Personnel Psychology* 43 (1990): 101–116.

28. D.E. Lupton, "Assessing the Assessment Center—A Theory Y Approach," *Personnel* 50 (1973): 15–22.

29. M. Erez, "Feedback: A Necessary Condition for the Goal-Setting Performance Relationship," *Journal of Applied Psychology* 62 (1977): 624–627.

30. Thornton, "Psychometric Properties of Self-Appraisals."

31. H.G. Heneman II, "Comparisons of Self and Superior Ratings of Managerial Performance," *Journal of Applied Psychology* 59 (1974): 638–642.

32. S.J. Carrol and C.E. Schneier, *Performance Appraisal and Review Systems* (Glenview, Ill.: Scott, Foresman, 1982), 165.

33. D.R. Ilgen, C.D. Fisher, and M.S. Taylor, "Consequences of Individual Feedback on Behavior in Organizations," *Journal of Applied Psychology* 64 (1979): 349–371.

34. "Training Managers to Rate Their Employees," *Business Week,* March 17, 1980, 178.

35. R.J. Burke, W. Weitzel, and T. Weir, "Characteristics of Effective Employee Performance Review and Development Interviews: Replication and Extension," *Personnel Psychology* 31 (1978): 903–919.

36. M.M. Greller, "Subordinate Participation and Reaction to the Appraisal Interview," *Journal of Applied Psychology* 60 (1975): 544–549; W.F. Nemeroff and K.N. Wexley, "Relationships Between Performance Appraisal Interview Outcomes by Supervisors and Subordinates" (Paper presented at the Annual Meeting of the Academy of Management, Orlando, Florida, 1977); K.N. Wexley, J.P. Singh, and G.A. Yukl, "Subordinate Personality as a Moderator

of the Effects of Participation in Three Types of Appraisal Interviews," *Journal of Applied Psychology* 58 (1973): 54–59; C.M. Giannantonio, "The Effect of Recruiter Friendliness, Verifiable Job Attributes, and Nonverifiable Job Attributes on Reactions to the Employment Interview" (Ph.D. diss., University of Maryland, College Park, 1988).

37. V.E. Schein, "Relationships Between Sex Role Stereotypes and Requisite Management Characteristics among Female Managers," *Journal of Applied Psychology* 60 (1975): 340; K.M. Bartol and D.A. Butterfield, "Sex Effects in Evaluating Leaders," *Journal of Applied Psychology* 61 (1976): 446–454; H.A. Brown and D.L. Ford, "An Exploratory Analysis of Discrimination in the Employment of Black MBA Graduates," *Journal of Applied Psychology* 62 (1977): 50–56; J.R. Terborg, "Women in Management: A Research Review," *Journal of Applied Psychology* 62 (1977): 647–664; B. Rosen and T.H. Jerdee, "Too Old or Not Too Old?" *Harvard Business Review* 55 (1977): 97–106; P.E. Varca and P. Pattison, "Evidentiary Standards in Employment Discrimination: A View Toward the Future," *Personnel Psychology* 46 (1993): 239–258.

38. Federal Register, *Adoption by Four Agencies of Uniform Guidelines on Employee Selection Procedures*, vol. 43, no. 166, Friday, August 25, 1978, 38295–38309; G. Barrett and M. Kernan, "Performance Appraisal and Terminations: A Review of Court Decisions Since *Brito v. Zia* with Implications for Personnel Practices," *Personnel Psychology* 32 (1987): 489–503.

39. C.R. Klasson, D.E. Thompson, and G.L. Lubben, "How Defensible Is Your Performance Appraisal System?" *Personnel Administrator* 25 (1980): 77–83.

40. R.D. Arvey, *Fairness in Selecting Employees* (Reading, Mass.: Addison-Wesley, 1978).

41. Latham and Wexley, *"Increasing Productivity Through Performance Appraisal."*

42. J.L. Moses and V. Boehm, "Relationship of Assessment Center Performance to Management Progress of Women," *Journal of Applied Psychology* 60 (1975): 527–529.

43. J.R. Huck, "Assessment Centers: A Review of the External and Internal Validities," *Personnel Psychology* 26 (1973): 196–212.

44. R.P. Vecchio, "The Impact of Differences in Subordinate and Supervisor Age on Attitudes and Performance," *Psychology and Aging* 8 (1993): 112–119; W.B. Johnston and A.E. Packer, *Work Force 2000: Work and Workers for the 21st Century* (Washington, D.C.: U.S. Department of Labor, 1987); Conference Board, *Work Force Diversity: Corporate Challenges, Corporate Responses* (New York: Conference Board, 1992); T.H. Cox and S. Blake, "Managing Cultural Diversity: Implications for Organizational Competitiveness," *Academy of Management Executive* 5 (1991): 45–56; D. Thomas, "From Affirmative Action to Affirming Diversity," *Harvard Business Review* 68 (1990): 107–117.

45. S. Jackson, J. Brett, V. Sessa, D. Cooper, J. Julin, and K. Peyronnin, "Some Differences Make a Difference: Individual Dissimilarity and Group Heterogeneity as Correlates of Recruitment, Promotions, and Turnover," *Journal of Applied Psychology* 76 (1991): 675–689; A. Tsui and C.A. O'Reilly, "Beyond Simple Demographic Effects: The Importance of Relational Demography in Superior-Subordinate Dyads," *Academy of Management Journal* 32 (1989): 402–423; M.E. Shaw, *Group Dynamics*, 3d ed. (New York: McGraw-Hill, 1981); R. Lattimer, "Managing Diversity for Competitive Advantage," *Textbook Authors Conference of American Association of Retired Persons* (Washington, D.C., 1992): 23–26; W. Watson, K. Kumar, and L. Michaelson, "Cultural Diversity's Impact on Interaction Process and Performance: Comparing Homogeneous and Diverse Task Groups," *Academy of Management Journal* 36 (1993): 590–602; A. Tsui, T. Egan, and C. O'Reilly, "Being Different: Relational Demography and Organizational Attachment," *Administrative Science Quarterly* 37 (1992): 549–579.

VIDEO CASE

ARE YOU READY FOR THE WORKPLACE OF THE 21ST CENTURY?

The 21st century promises to be an exciting and challenging time to be a manager. The global economy, rapid technological change and an increasingly diverse work force will require managers to be flexible, tolerate uncertainty, and inspire leadership in their employees. *The New Workplace* describes many of the changes we can expect to see in organizations over the coming years.

To compete in a rapidly changing economy, the organization must increasingly invest in the education of its work force. As work becomes more knowledge-oriented, employees are required to infuse creativity into their jobs, tolerate ambiguity, and accept responsibility and accountability for their work. In the 21st-century organization, new kinds of relationships will develop, with terminology changing to reflect these relationships. Increasingly, managers will be known as coaches and facilitators, and not as managers or supervisors. Supervisor–subordinate and coworker relationships will change considerably. The relationship between the organization and its employees will be considered a partnership, in which all employees are partners working for the organization's success. Work will become more interdependent as the use of interdisciplinary teams continues to grow. At the same time, organizations will rely more on contract and part-time employment, using fewer traditional workers to perform work. Managing diversity—racial, ethnic, gender, age, lifestyle preference, and ability—will become increasingly important, particularly as more handicapped individuals are assimilated into the work force pursuant to the Americans with Disabilities Act (ADA) of 1992.

Employees will have different expectations of their working environment in the new workplace. Increasingly, employees want to understand the organization's "big picture" and their role in the organization's operations. If employees are expected to be partners in the operation of the business, they must be informed about those operations. Employees are no longer willing to work unquestioningly as cogs in a machine. They want to help set the direction of the organization, and help the organization move forward. At the same time, they expect their employers to acknowledge their multiple roles in life. The importance of balancing work and family is becoming increasingly important to employees, and they expect some degree of flexibility from their employers to accommodate family responsibilities.

Likewise, employers' expectations are changing. Employers want their employees to give all they have in terms of skills, experience, expertise, and intelligence. Employees are expected to think critically and initiate changes that will benefit the company. If employees are empowered and self-directed, there exists in the organization potential for benefit for both the organization and its employees.

Closely linked to employees' and employers' expectations will be performance appraisals, and they will change to accommodate the demands of the new organization. Evaluations will be better known as "feedback," and 360-degree feedback—feedback from coaches, subordinates, team members, peers, and customers—will become more popular. Team feedback will be particularly important in helping the organization develop effective, interdisciplinary teams. Thus, increasingly feedback will be used to guide developmental plans to strengthen the employee's weaknesses. Whereas traditional performance evaluations review past performance, feedback will take a more proactive approach to employee development, both reviewing past performance and establishing plans for developing an employee's weaknesses.

The carrot-and-stick approach to motivating employees will be replaced by participative climates in which employees take ownership and pride. It is these climates that foster intrinsic motivation to work. Moreover, managers will be called upon to foster learning environments. Employees develop an intrinsic motivation to work in a learning environment, and rely less upon extrinsic motivators to get the job done. Celebrations, rituals, rites of passage, and learning systems will reinforce performance and strengthen an employee's passion for the job.

Managers will have to lead the change toward the 21st-century organization, building workers' trust and facilitating a cooperative, harmonious environment. Managers will need to help employees rethink business, become knowledge workers, and channel their knowledge of the workplce into a vision of a 21st-century organization. All human resources in an organization will have to be creative change agents, willing to accept risks and negotiate conflict. Employees who engage in a continual learning process and learn from their mistakes will successfully lead their organizations into the 21st century and beyond.

Are you ready to be a 21st-century facilitator? Complete the following scale to determine your readiness for the challenges that lie ahead.

The following are ten management foundations recommended by the American Assembly of Collegiate Schools of Business (AACSB) as skills and personal characteristics that should be nurtured in college and university students of business for success in the new workplace of the 21st century. Rate yourself by placing the number 1–7 on the line before each of the ten management foundations that best describes your frequency of this behavior. Be honest; you will not be asked to share your score in class.

Usually	Frequently	Often	Sometimes	Infrequently	Seldom	Rarely
7	6	5	4	3	2	1

_____ 1. *Resistance to stress.* I get the job done under stressful conditions.

_____ 2. *Tolerance for uncertainty.* I get the job done under ambiguous and uncertain conditions.

_____ 3. *Social Objectivity.* I act free of racial, ethnic, gender, and other prejudices or biases.

_____ 4. *Inner work standards.* I personally set and work to high performance standards on my own.

_____ 5. *Stamina.* I work long, hard hours.

_____ 6. *Adaptability.* I'm flexible and adaptable to change.

_____ 7. *Self-confidence.* I'm consistently decisive and display my personal presence.

_____ 8. *Self-objectivity.* I evaluate my personal strengths and weaknesses and understand my motives and skills relative to tasks I need to do.

_____ 9. *Introspection.* I learn from experience, awareness, and self-study. (I don't make the same mistake twice.)

_____ 10. *Entrepreneurism.* I address problems and take advantage of opportunities for constructive change.

_____ Total. Add up the ten numbers and place your score on the continuum below.

70- - - - - - - 60- - - - - - - -50- - - - - - 40- - - - - - 30- - - - - - 20- - - - - -10
Strong Management Foundations   Weak Management Foundations

CASE QUESTIONS

1. What aspects of an organization's environment are changing?

2. What effects has work force diversity had on organizations?

3. How will the day-to-day nature of managerial work change in the coming years?

4. Based on the assessment of your managerial foundations, which specific managerial foundations need work? What could you do to develop those foundations?

Source: Adapted from exercise created by Robert N. Lussier, in John Schermerhorn, James G. Hunt and Richard N. Osborn, *Managing Organizational Behavior*, 5th ed. Copyright 1994 by John Wiley & Sons, Inc. Sourced from Robert N. Lussier, 1993, and adapted from the assessment "A 21st Century Manager?"

Case written by Melissa Waite, State University of New York, University at Buffalo, and Susan Stites-Doe, State University of New York College at Brockport.

IV

Group Processes

CHAPTER

9

The secret of success is sincerity. Once you can fake that, you've got it made.
— Jean Giraudoux

To be clever enough to gain real power over others, one must be dumb enough to want it.
— G. K. Chesterton

Nice guys finish last.
— Leo Durocher

Contrary to the cliché, genuinely nice guys most often finish first, or very near it.
— Malcolm Forbes

LEARNING OBJECTIVES

After studying this chapter, you should be able to:

1. *Define and distinguish power, authority, influence, and politics.*
2. *Identify and describe three primary influence processes.*
3. *List and define five bases of power.*
4. *Describe some differences between formal and informal power.*
5. *Distinguish the kinds of power organizations use, name a type of organization corresponding to each type of power, and describe the nature of member involvement in an organization that uses that type of power.*
6. *Describe the cycle of approaches that supervisors use to influence subordinates.*
7. *Identify several political tactics, including devious political tactics and political blunders.*
8. *Explain several techniques for coping with organizational politics.*
9. *Support an argument that pressures to conform are powerful.*
10. *Cite evidence that the predisposition to obey authority is strong.*

Power, Politics, and Influence

WHAT ARE THE LIMITS OF AN EMPLOYER'S POWER?

Directing employee behavior inside the corporation is an appropriate use of authority. But does your company have any right to influence your behavior outside of working hours? It may be very subtle, but companies do intrude into the personal lives of employees.

One of the more common pressures employers exert is in controlling their workers' physical well-being. Many organizations have adopted health and wellness programs for a very straightforward reason: Healthy workers cost less. A study of 46,000 Du Pont employees conducted in the late 1980s confirmed that those with healthier lifestyles cost employers less. For example, companies incur an additional $960 in medical claims and sick days each year for the average smoker; $401 for an overweight person; $369 for an alcoholic abuser; $370 for a worker with high cholesterol; and $343 for a worker with high blood pressure. Since 1986, Turner Broadcasting has refused to hire smokers. The city of North Miami requires applicants to sign an affidavit that they have not used tobacco products in the previous year.

Other companies have introduced additional measures to encourage workers to lead healthier lives. Workers at General Mills may have health insurance premiums reduced by as much as 20 percent if they live healthfully. Healthful behaviors include wearing seat belts, not smoking, avoiding alcoholic beverages, and controlling weight and blood pressure. Starting in 1994, the 5,000 employees of Butterworth Hospital of Grand Rapids, Michigan, will receive financial incentives to live healthfully. Employees who live healthfully will find up to $25 extra in their biweekly paychecks. However, $25 will be withheld from the paychecks of those employees who fail to cooperate or score poorly on tests. The policy is not uniformly accepted by all employees. Some workers consider it overbearing, believing that their employer is trying to control their behavior.

Drug testing is also on the rise. The American Management Association surveyed members and found that 85 percent conducted drug testing on employees, primarily new hires, in 1993, up from 50 percent in 1990. All contractors doing business in excess of $20,000 with the federal government are required to conduct random tests on a cross-section of workers. Many companies subject all new hires to drug testing, and Motorola intends to test all employees every three years, regardless of company tenure. However, one group attempting to lessen drug testing requirements is the airline industry. The federal government requires that all carriers randomly test 50 percent of their pilots, flight attendants, mechanics, and dispatchers every year, at a cost of almost $100 per test. Recognizing this as a significant operating cost, airlines are trying to reduce the coverage rate to 10 percent of affected employees.

Clearly, some employees resent their employer's power to control their behavior off the time clock. As resentment builds, worker motivation may wane and could ultimately compromise organizational performance. Power is wielded in many ways in organizations. This chapter explores what power is and what its sources are. It also considers types of power and methods of influence used in organizations, as well as organizational politics, conformity, and obedience.

Source: Lee Smith, "What the Boss Knows about You," *Fortune,* August 9, 1993, 89–93.

At one time or another, all of us have resisted attempts to be controlled or influenced by others. Likewise, each of us has attempted to control or influence those around us. Control—by others and of others—lies at the very heart of organizational relationships. This give-and-take among people is responsible for much of what is actually accomplished in a work unit, as well as for a fair amount of social friction.

DISTINGUISHING POWER AND INFLUENCE

Power is an essential feature of a manager's role. Without some degree of power, a manager would find it very difficult to direct the efforts of subordinates. Thus, power underlies a manager's effectiveness. Subordinates also possess forms and degrees of power. For example, subordinates can control the work flow or withhold support from their manager. Therefore, to some extent, each member of an organization possesses power.

Because power is intangible, it is very difficult to define clearly and precisely. Also, our language has several similar terms that we tend to confuse with power, such as authority and influence. In the interest of clarity, we shall define **power** as the ability to change the behavior of others. It is the ability to cause others to perform actions that they might not otherwise perform.[1]

Power is not always legitimate. Therefore, we speak of **authority** as the *right* to try to change or direct others. Authority includes the notion of legitimacy. It is the right to influence others in the pursuit of common goals that are agreed upon by various parties. Power, in contrast, does not always pursue common goals and may, at times, be clearly directed to pursuing only a single individual's goals.

Another term, **influence**, is also frequently used when discussing the notion of power. Influence tends to be subtler, broader, and more general than power. Although both influence and power can be defined as the ability to change the behavior of others, power embodies the ability to do so with regularity and ease. Influence is weaker and less reliable than power. Also, power rests on a number of specific sources or foundations, which will be examined in a subsequent section of this chapter. Influence relies on particular tactics and often employs face-to-face interactions. Thus, the exercise of influence tends to be more subtle than the exercise of power.

INTERPERSONAL INFLUENCE PROCESSES

In a classic article, Kelman distinguished among three primary reasons for an individual to yield to another person's attempt to be directive.[2] If an employee accepts a manager's influence attempt because she believes she will be rewarded or avoid being punished, her response is one of **compliance.** For example, an employee may skip lunch in order to finish typing a report for her supervisor. She may actually hope to receive an expression of appreciation from the supervisor or she may merely wish to avoid the hard feelings that will result if the report is not finished on time. The employee's behavior is strictly motivated by concern with rewards and punishments. Supervisors who strive for consistent compliance must (1) be certain that they can in fact deliver rewards or punishments and (2) be in a position to frequently monitor their subordinates' behavior.

A second influence process, **identification,** occurs when one person follows another's direction because of a desire to establish or maintain a personally satisfying relationship. When a subordinate admires his manager, seeks his approval, and perhaps tries to imitate him, we infer that the subordinate has a strong desire to identify with the manager. One example of this process occurs when a junior executive who greatly admires the CEO of his organization espouses the CEO's philosophy and beliefs when addressing the employees in his own work unit.

In both compliance and identification, the performance of an action in itself is not necessarily personally satisfying. Rather, the action may be due to a desire for specific outcomes (compliance) or an attraction to the source of influence (identification).

Sometimes employees' actions stem from a third reason: the belief that the behavior is congruent with their value systems. **Internalization** occurs when an employee accepts an influence attempt because he or she believes that the resulting behavior is correct and appropriate. For instance, assume that a high-level executive announces that the organization is participating in a United Way fund-raising campaign. Some of her managers may actively encourage subordinates to contribute to the fund because they strongly believe in the goals of United Way. These managers are not motivated by threats or rewards or admiration for their superior but rather by a personal commitment to a set of values.

THE FIVE BASES OF POWER

Who gets what, when, and how are important concerns for every member of an organization. People at all levels are interested in and affected by the acquisition and distribution of rewards and resources. Of course, power plays a central role in such allocation processes. To explain how power operates, we will first examine the five distinct sources of power proposed by John French and Bertram Raven: reward power, coercive power, legitimate power, referent power, and expert power.[3]

REWARD POWER   **Reward power** is the ability to determine who will receive particular rewards. As long as the rewards are valued, a person who is able to distribute or withhold them can enjoy strong power over others' behavior. Granting promotions, giving raises, and conferring preferred job assignments are some typical rewards most managers can control. Unfortunately, this is not always the case. For example, when a work force is unionized, salary increases and job assignments are based more on seniority and the specifics of a labor contract than on the judgment of a manager or supervisor. As noted in our discussion of motivation (Chapter 6), the relationship between performance and rewards should always be clear. When a manager lacks the ability to administer both extrinsic and intrinsic rewards, it becomes extremely difficult to direct subordinates' behavior. Reward power gives a manager a distinct advantage in obtaining desired ends from his or her work group.

COERCIVE POWER   If reward power can be termed "the carrot," then coercive power is "the stick." **Coercive power** stems from the capacity to produce fear in others. The threat of punishment can be a strong means of invoking compliance. The most obvious examples of punishments are demotions, salary cuts, suspension, removal of such perquisites as a company car or an expense account, and dismissal. However, coercive power can also be more subtle. For example, criticism and the denial of emotional support and friendship may also be effective forms of coercion.

The application of coercive power requires good social judgment. In some instances, a manager is actually expected to be coercive—as when a subordinate is extremely unproductive or interferes with the productivity of others. In such a situation, other employees and managers will rightly expect the supervisor to take firm action.

On the other hand, a manager must be careful when applying coercive power. If he or she is too heavy-handed and indiscriminately inflicts punishment on all employees, morale and productivity are likely to suffer. Such a manager may find that the unit's turnover rate is very high as people seek employment elsewhere. In addition, injured employees may retaliate by sabotaging the unit's operations or withholding useful suggestions for improving the unit's performance.

Despite its potentially negative effects, coercive power underlies much of the routine compliance that occurs in organizations. Decisions to arrive at work on time, meet deadlines, and so forth are often largely due to fear of being fired, ridiculed, or reprimanded. Rightly or wrongly, coercive power is frequently used in most organizations.

LEGITIMATE POWER   **Legitimate power** stems from the willingness of others to accept an individual's direction. They feel an obligation to follow the individual's lead and submit to his authority. There are two sources of legitimate power. The first is social conditioning: From early childhood, people are conditioned to accept the direction of authority figures. They learn that teachers and crossing guards, as well as foremen and managers, have the right to lead or direct others. The second source of legitimate power is designation: A person can gain power by being designated an authority figure by someone who already possesses legitimate authority. For example, the president of a company may assign a vice president the authority to make important decisions on the company's behalf. The president thus gives the vice president legitimate power to act as his representative and exercise authority accordingly.

Legitimate power can be effective only if it is accepted by the people it is intended to control. If the people withdraw their support from the system that is the basis of power, the power ceases to exist. Such withdrawals of support occur in revolutions, when ruling classes and their social systems are over-thrown, and in riots, when a spontaneous but limited rebellion is made against authority.

REFERENT POWER   People with attractive personalities or other special qual-ities possess a form of power. Their appearance, poise, interpersonal style, or values can inspire admiration and cause others to identify with them. The re-sulting ability to influence behavior is called **referent power.** It is often easy to identify an individual who possesses such power. For example, most people would agree that successful politicians, athletes, and entertainers—such as Bill Clinton, Michael Jordan, and Oprah Winfrey—have this attribute. However, it is extremely difficult to define exactly what gives these people their charisma. Usually, vigor and the appearance of success play important roles. But other characteristics that contribute to referent power can be very difficult to pinpoint (consider, for example, that Adolf Hitler was judged to be charis-matic in the eyes of his countrymen).

Referent power derives from people's desire to identify with the qualities of an attractive individual. Advertising that uses a celebrity to endorse a prod-uct is based on referent power, since the sponsor hopes that the audience will buy the product in an attempt to imitate the celebrity's behavior and attitudes.[*]

EXPERT POWER   Individuals with **expert power** are able to direct others be-cause they are perceived as knowledgeable or talented in a given area. Most of us readily seek and follow the advice of experts, such as our family physician or athletic coach. So too are we likely to follow the directions of a coworker who is seen as having expertise in our field of work. This form of power is usu-ally limited to a fairly narrow and specific realm, however, and does not spread to other areas of social interaction.

Most subordinates presume that their superiors possess expert power in the form of understanding all jobs in the work unit. Generally, greater levels of experience and job-relevant knowledge do give a manager an edge in exper-tise. However, in highly technical job settings, it may happen that some subor-dinates have more expert knowledge about certain aspects of their jobs than do their managers. In fact, some managers may be highly dependent on the technical expertise of their subordinates in order to successfully manage their work units. In such a situation, expert power can lead to an atypical reversal of the usual manager–subordinate relationship.

INTERPLAY AMONG THE POWER BASES

A manager can possess each of the five sources of power to varying degrees, and his or her use of one power base can affect the strength of another. For ex-ample, a person can gain greater legitimacy by being promoted to a higher-level position. Of course, a position of greater legitimate power usually entails

---

[*]This logic parallels the notions of balance theory (see Chapter 4).

more opportunities to use rewards and coercion. The exercise of coercion, however, could reduce the manager's referent power because, as discussed in Chapter 5, coercion tends to produce immediate compliance but may have negative side effects.

Above all, the manager should bear in mind that the tendency to use power can lead to greater effectiveness, while the failure to use power can have the opposite effect. Managers who exercise power with some frequency can be counted on to continue such behavior in future settings and are, therefore, given greater deference by subordinates. More passive managers may have difficulty if they suddenly decide to use their power because their subordinates will have become accustomed to their lack of assertiveness.

Distinctions can be drawn among the five power bases. Expert and referent power bases are more informal in nature, while legitimate, reward, and coercive power bases are more formal. The informal power bases have a greater capacity to affect overall employee satisfaction and performance. The formal power bases, in contrast, have potentially greater impact on immediate behavior. Although formal power can elicit a quick response from an employee, it will not necessarily produce agreement and commitment. For example, a worker may comply with a manager's order but still resent having been coerced.

Many centuries ago, the Italian philosopher Machiavelli contended that people who have formal power tend to remain in their positions of authority longer than people who rely on informal power. This observation makes some sense in that the informal bases of power can be more easily eroded, since they depend on people's perceptions. For example, a manager may lose his expertise due to changes in technology or his appeal may diminish following a series of unpopular actions or personnel changes. While expert power can be regained through technical training, there are no surefire ways of increasing referent power.

In general, informal power resides in the personal characteristics of the manager, whereas formal power resides in the position itself. It can be forcefully argued, however, that all sources of power can really be reduced to a single category: control over reinforcers. As shown in Chapter 5, the most effective way to control others' behavior is to control when and how they receive reinforcement.

AN ORGANIZATIONAL ANALYSIS OF POWER

In his analysis of how complex organizations attempt to direct the behavior of their members, Etzioni identified three kinds of organizational power.[4] One type of organizational power can be characterized as coercive. Such organizations try to extract compliance from members through threats and punishment. Examples of coercive organizations include prisons, some mental institutions, and divisions within the military (such as boot camp).

Most business organizations, of course, do not rely on coercion, but instead offer contingent incentives: If employees follow directives, they can expect to be rewarded. Such organizations are said to use **utilitarian power** because of their emphasis on the utility of conforming to directives.

A third set of organizations relies on **normative power.** In this type of organization, members accept directives because of their sense of affiliation with the organization and its espoused values. Professional associations (such as the American Dental Association) and religious organizations typically use normative power to influence their members.

All three types of power can be useful in obtaining people's cooperation in organizations. However, the relative effectiveness of each approach depends on the organizational members' orientation or involvement. Etzioni contends that members' involvement can be broadly categorized as alienative, calculative, or moral. Members with **alienative involvement** have hostile, rejecting, and extremely negative attitudes. Members with **calculative involvement** are rational and oriented toward maximizing personal gain. And members with **moral involvement** are committed to the socially beneficial features of their organizations.

According to Etzioni, the three types of organizational power can be matched with the three types of involvement. According to this logic, only one type of power is most appropriate for each type of member involvement. Attempts to use types of power that are inappropriate for the type of involvement can reduce effectiveness. Figure 9.1 illustrates Etzioni's model of power and involvement.

TYING IT ALL TOGETHER

Sussmann and Vecchio formally compared the three models of power and influence put forth by French and Raven, Kelman, and Etzioni.[5] A good deal of similarity was identified among all three views. For example, French and Raven's concepts of reward and coercive power have a strong similarity to Kelman's notions of compliance. Referent power, in turn, is allied to Kelman's notion of identification, and legitimate and expert power overlap to a great ex-

FIGURE 9.1
ETZIONI'S MODEL OF POWER AND INVOLVEMENT

Types of Power

	Coercive	Utilitarian	Normative
Alienative	X		
Calculative		X	
Moral			X

Types of Involvement

The cells on the primary diagonal of the matrix (denoted by X) represent match-ups of types of power and involvement.

tent with the process of internalization. Both Etzioni and Kelman identify three forms of power (or influence), but while Etzioni focuses on the organizational level of analysis, Kelman focuses on the interpersonal level. Table 9.1 summarizes the comparison of the three views.

In a sense, the multiple forms of power identified correspond to the need-level views of Maslow and others (Chapter 6). The correspondence lies in the recognition that there are several levels of motivation or forms of influence. One level is fairly rudimentary: reward and punishment. A higher level is more social in nature: referent or identification. And the highest level is fairly psychological in nature: internalization or legitimacy.

A Social Influence View of Supervisor Behavior

Sussmann and Vecchio also proposed that a supervisor's attempts to exert influence follow a cycle in which he or she tries one of three approaches to influence a subordinate in accordance with the three levels of needs and the three forms of power.[6] This view suggests that a supervisor (or evaluator) will attempt to use compliance, identification, or internalization to influence an individual. Respectively, he or she may try threats, appeals to a subordinate's sense of organizational membership or affiliation, or appeals to the subordinate's value system.

Such attempts will succeed or fail to the extent that the individual is disposed to accept incentives or threats, identity-related appeals, or value-related appeals. For certain types of subordinates, a particular type of disposition may be more prevalent, as is suggested by Etzioni's notion of involvement. Acceptance of the supervisor's influence attempt leads to behavioral intentions on the part of the subordinate to act in the desired direction. The actual behavior of the subordinate is then compared to the standards that are held in the mind of the supervisor. If the influence attempt is judged to have failed, the supervisor will likely try another attempt, but perhaps with a different type of influence (for example, appealing on a different level). This model suggests that su-

TABLE 9.1
A Comparison of Three Views of Power and Influence

Interpersonal Influence Process (Kelman)	Power Bases (French and Raven)	Organizational Power (Etzioni)
Internalization	Legitimate Power	Normative
	Expert Power	
Identification	Referent Power	Normative
Compliance (reward-based)	Reward Power	Utilitarian
Compliance (punishment-based)	Coercive Power	Coercive

pervisors need to be sensitive to differences in subordinates' preferences for inducement schemes. It is possible that supervisors who are aware of and make use of subordinate preferences for inducements are relatively more effective than other supervisors.

POLITICS: THE FACTS OF ORGANIZATIONAL LIFE

The terms *politics* and *power* are sometimes used interchangeably. Though they are related, they are nonetheless distinct notions. Pfeffer defines **organizational politics** as "those activities taken within organizations to acquire, develop, and use power and other resources to obtain one's preferred outcomes in a situation in which there is uncertainty or [disagreement] about choices."[7] In a sense, the study of organizational politics constitutes the study of power in action. It may also be said that politics involves the playing out of power and influence.

The word *politics* has a somewhat negative connotation. It suggests that someone is attempting to use means or to gain ends that are not sanctioned by the organization. Actually, political behavior, as we've defined it, is quite neutral. Similarly, power is not inherently negative. Whether a person views power and politics as unsavory topics depends on a number of considerations, most important perhaps being where the individual stands on a specific issue in a given situation. Nonetheless, most managers are reluctant to admit to the political character of their own work settings.

A further point is that all members of an organization may exhibit political behavior. In our previous discussion of power, we took a fairly formal and traditional approach to the topic of influence. Thus, we looked at power from the perspective of a supervisor or manager who directs others. Yet, in the area of politics, everyone is a player. Subordinates, as well as their managers, can engage in the give-and-take of organizational politics.[†]

POLITICAL TACTICS

Several authors have identified a variety of political tactics used by employees at virtually all levels.[8] In this section, we will examine a number of these activities.

INGRATIATION   This tactic involves giving compliments to or doing favors for superiors or coworkers. Most people have a difficult time rejecting the positive advances of others. Ingratiation usually works as a tactic insofar as the target often feels positive toward the source even if the ingratiation attempt is fairly blatant and transparent.

In the behavioral sciences, the notion of "social reciprocity" has been offered to help explain the process of ingratiation. In social reciprocity, there is a feeling of a social obligation to repay the positive actions of others with

---

[†] Nonetheless, it is widely believed that political behavior is far less common and less intense among employees in lower-level positions than among employees in higher-level positions.

similar actions. For example, if someone pays you a compliment, there is a strong expectation that you should respond with a compliment of your own. If you fail to do so, you may be judged as being rude. Similarly, ingratiation involves giving positive strokes to a person with the expectation that he or she will feel obligated to return them in some form.

FORMING COALITIONS AND NETWORKS   Another political tactic consists of befriending important people. These people may not be in positions of any obvious political value. However, their jobs may provide them with information that could be useful to have. Some people find that forming friendships with people in upper-level management can help them gain access to important information. They may also find that by being on good terms with their boss's secretary, they can sometimes gain inside information and easier access to the boss.

IMPRESSION MANAGEMENT   A simple tactic that virtually everyone uses from time to time is the management of their outward appearance and style. Generally, most organizations prefer a particular image that consists of being loyal, attentive, honest, neatly groomed, sociable, and so forth. By deliberately trying to exhibit this preferred image, an individual can make a positive impression on influential members of the organization.

INFORMATION MANAGEMENT   A further tactic consists of managing the information that is shared with others. The nature, as well as the timing, of information given out can have strong effects on others' conduct. Releasing good or bad news when it is likely to have its fullest impact can greatly promote one person's self-interest or defeat the hopes of others. Similarly, an individual can ask for information (such as sales data or a production report) when it is most likely to make things appear particularly good or bad. People who play the information management game are not likely to lie or spread misinformation, however, because their future credibility would be jeopardized. Instead, they rely on the carefully planned release of valid information to obtain their ends.

PROMOTE THE OPPOSITION   It may sound strange, but one way to eliminate opposition is to aid political rivals. For example, it is possible to eliminate a political rival by helping that person become so successful that he or she is transferred to a desirable position someplace else in the organization. Recommending a rival for a new assignment or even a promotion within another division of the organization can make one's own work life easier.

PURSUE LINE RESPONSIBILITY   Within virtually every organization, some positions are more closely tied to the primary mission of the organization; these jobs are called line positions. They are at the very heart of the organization. People who occupy support positions are said to be in staff positions. Examples of line positions include engineering, manufacturing, and sales in a customer-oriented firm. People in departments such as public relations, market research, and personnel are usually in staff positions. While staff people may come to wield great power within their own territories, it is the line people who usually "call the shots" on major issues. Line people not only make the more important decisions within the organization, they are also more likely to be promoted to top-level executive positions. In many organizations, there is a preferred department of origin and career path for top-level managers. These are usually line positions. Therefore, one way to gain influence within an organization is to be assigned initially to, or be transferred to, a line position. It will often provide more visibility, influence, and upward mobility.

DEVIOUS POLITICAL TACTICS

Some political tactics are quite honest in nature. For example, accumulating seniority, providing copies of your accomplishments to your boss, and hitching your wagon to yourself are all respectable means for gaining influence.[‡] Some other tactics, however, are difficult to defend on moral grounds. In the interest of self-defense, it is worth examining several of these devious political tactics.[9]

TAKE NO PRISONERS   Sometimes it is necessary to do something unpopular or distasteful, such as demote or transfer someone or announce pay cuts. During corporate takeovers, many unpopular actions may be necessary. As a result, political enemies are likely to be made. One tactic for dealing with this potential problem is to ruthlessly eliminate *all* individuals who may resent your past actions by having them fired or transferred.

DIVIDE AND CONQUER   This tactic involves creating a feud among two or more people so that they will be continually off balance and thus unable to mount an attack against you. This is a very old idea that is still practiced in some work settings. An unscrupulous individual who employs this tactic usually encourages bickering between possible rivals by spreading rumors or promoting competition between subordinates or factions. This is a risky tactic, however, as the opponents may eventually compare notes and conclude that someone else is really responsible for creating and maintaining their bad feelings.

EXCLUDE THE OPPOSITION   Another devious tactic involves keeping rivals away from important meetings and social occasions. This can be done simply by scheduling important affairs when the opposition is out of town (on vacation or a business trip) or attending another meeting. With the opposition absent, it is possible to influence decision making or to take credit for a rival's efforts.

[‡] Pure and simple performance remains an essential ingredient of a successful career in virtually all fields of endeavor.

POLITICAL BLUNDERS

Although certain tactics can promote desired ends, others can be costly political mistakes. Among the most common are violating the chain of command, losing your cool, saying no to top management, upstaging your supervisor, and challenging cherished beliefs. These activities constitute serious political blunders or mistakes.

VIOLATING CHAIN OF COMMAND   Occasionally, a person will feel that it is his duty to see his boss's boss, either to complain about his treatment at the hands of his own boss or to serve as an informant. A person may even feel that such an "end run" is justified because he is fervently convinced of the rightness of his position. However, going over the boss's head is often a very strong organizational taboo. Generally, it is expected that an employee will ask the boss's permission before seeing his superior on any matter.

LOSING YOUR COOL   Throwing temper tantrums and acting aggressively toward others are often seen as acceptable and sometimes effective tactics in settings such as sports events. But in office settings, these tactics do not work well at all. Fist pounding and snide remarks usually earn a person a reputation for being hard to deal with, a label that can be extremely difficult to overcome. One devious twist on this tactic is to goad a person who tends to be acerbic and aggressive into displaying these tendencies at the wrong times. In this way, such a person's peers help him or her to commit political suicide.

SAYING NO TO TOP MANAGEMENT   One of the surest ways to stop your own career progress is to reject a request from top-level management. Instead of feeling fortunate to be selected for an assignment, some individuals believe that they are overburdened and that they are being "dumped on," or that they can afford to defy top management because they are indispensable. This represents poor judgment on two counts: First, people in the lower ranks of an organization are rarely indispensable. Second, if workers are overburdened, they should explain the situation to the manager and try to arrange for additional help.

UPSTAGING YOUR SUPERVISOR   Generally speaking, one should avoid publicly criticizing others. For example, it is not considered appropriate for a supervisor to criticize a subordinate in public view. However, the reverse is also true. A subordinate should refrain from implicitly criticizing the boss by upstaging him or her. Upstaging often takes the form of bragging about one's own accomplishments or claiming credit for a unit's success.

CHALLENGING CHERISHED BELIEFS   In many firms, there are a number of cherished beliefs about the nature of the organization, and it is generally considered "poor form" to criticize or challenge such folklore within earshot of company loyalists. Examples of such fond beliefs include "This organization is the best in its field," "Our founder was (or is) an outstanding individual," and

An Inside Look
The Influence of Gift Giving

"During the holiday season, a consultant you've been working with during the year gives you a case of expensive wine as a present. What do you do?" This question is posed to Citicorp employees to facilitate discussion and understanding of the company's policy regarding employees accepting gifts. Many companies have adopted gift receiving policies because the gesture of gift giving is inherently ambiguous. Is the gift giver thanking you for previous business, or exerting subtle influence tactics in an effort to drum up more business?

Given the potential conflict of interest, it's not surprising that almost 90 percent of companies surveyed in 1993 by the Bureau of National Affairs had policies restricting an employee's ability to receive gifts from suppliers, clients, and outside business contacts. One difficulty of corporate gift policies, however, is that many policies

leave ample room for interpretation. Some gift receipt examples are clear-cut cases of political underhandedness, like the Aetna Life and Casualty employee who was dismissed upon admitting he had received an undisclosed sum from one of the company's vendors. However, most cases are more difficult to interpret. In general, gift receiving policies do allow inexpensive gifts, such as calendars, ballpoint pens, t-shirts, and coffee mugs. Gifts at Price Waterhouse may not exceed $50 in value, while Citicorp only allows gifts of "very nominal value." The policies at Aetna, 3M, and Motorola, rather than setting predetermined dollar limits, allow the recipient of the gift to judge its appropriateness.

Price Waterhouse, Aetna, and Polaroid remind suppliers and vendors of their gift receiving policy in writing. Other companies, such as Motorola, take gifts donated by

recipients and give them away as door prizes at company picnics and dinners. An Aetna executive, not wanting to offend the giver, accepted an ornate briefcase from an Asian businessman, then turned it in to the company and bought it back for its appraised value upon his retirement.

Gift receiving policies represent a mixed message in many cases. While some companies denounce receiving gifts from suppliers and customers, it is common for a company's sales force to have generous expense accounts to dine and entertain potential clients and customers.

Influence can be exerted in a variety of ways in organizations, and most employees are not immune from it. Gift receiving policies are one way organizations attempt to thwart subtle influence tactics.

Source: Deborah L. Jacobs, "The Rules for Giving, and for Giving Back," *New York Times*, December 5, 1993, F25.

"People who leave our organization are people that we are better off without." To be sure, all people are entitled to their own opinions, but it can be politically foolish to engage in an open debate about the truth of certain widely held beliefs.

COPING WITH ORGANIZATIONAL POLITICS

Political gamesmanship, when carried to the extreme, has many dysfunctional effects: Morale is weakened, victors and victims are created, and energy and time are spent on planning attacks and counterattacks instead of on productivity. Thus, combating politics must be part of a manager's job.

SET AN EXAMPLE   When a manager plays political games, such as distorting the facts or manipulating people, he or she conveys to subordinates a message that such conduct is acceptable. A manager can create a climate either tolerant or intolerant of dirty tricks. Clearly, a department is better served by a manager who provides a positive role model by encouraging truthfulness and the even-handed treatment of others.

GIVE CLEAR JOB ASSIGNMENTS Politics seem to be more prevalent when overall purposes are unclear and it is difficult to assess the performance of individual employees.[§] One way to counter political activities is to give well-defined, discrete work assignments. When expectations are clear and subordinates understand how they will be assessed, game playing becomes less necessary as a device for gaining personal recognition.

ELIMINATE COALITIONS AND CLIQUES Coalitions and cliques that are detrimental to unit performance can often be reduced in influence or eliminated. Although dismissal and transfer are two possible solutions, individuals may also be rotated through different job assignments. Job rotation encourages an employee's perception of the larger enterprise and helps to counter an us–them view of other departments.

CONFRONT GAME PLAYERS Even in a climate of trust and openness, individuals may make suggestive comments or offer information that has an ulterior motive. A good response in such a situation is simply to ask, "Why are you telling me this about Sam?" or "Why don't you and I go see Sam's boss about this right now? I think you should tell her what you've just told me." Another useful response is to offer to discuss questionable information in a public forum. A manager may say, for example, "I think I understand your concerns on this issue. Let's bring it up for discussion at our next department meeting." Using a public forum to discuss and choose a course of action is an excellent defense to most dubious suggestions. As a rule, a manager should not get involved in any scheme that he or she is unwilling to have discussed in public. Knowing that all suggestions are subject to open discussion invariably discourages people who hope to engage a manager in political games.

MACHIAVELLIANISM

Niccolò Machiavelli (Figure 9.2), an Italian philosopher and statesman (1469–1527), was one of the earliest writers on the topic of political behavior. In his works, Machiavelli examined political effectiveness without regard for ethics or morality. Machiavelli simply ignored moral considerations in exploring not how people *should* behave, but how they actually *do* behave. Because of his uncompromising view of political reality, Machiavelli has sometimes been called the ultimate pragmatist. In recent years, his name has come to be synonymous with the use of political treachery and maneuvering. Thus, to say that someone is Machiavellian is a serious insult.[**]

[§] The attributes of an open-ended purpose and difficulty in measuring individual performance are especially relevant to academic departments.

[**] Other world cultures have also had their own version of Niccolò Machiavelli. About 300 B.C., both Lord Shang of China and Koutilya, a prime minister in the south of India, wrote much the same philosophy as Machiavelli. All three writers shared several common themes: Humankind is basically weak, fallible, and gullible; therefore, a rational person takes advantage of situations and protects himself or herself from the implicit untrustworthiness of others.

FIGURE 9.2
NICCOLÒ MACHIAVELLI: THE FATHER OF MODERN POLITICS

Source: Historical Pictures Service, Inc. Reprinted with permission.

Christie and Geis have tried to assess the extent to which an individual's personal style is Machiavellian in nature.[10] To do so, they converted certain basic tenets of Machiavelli's writings into an attitude scale that can be used to measure the extent to which an individual agrees with Machiavelli's views. The statements of the Machiavellian scale (or **Mach Scale** for short) focus on several factors. Chief among them are (1) the use of manipulative interpersonal tactics ("It is wise to flatter important people" and "Never tell anyone the real reason you did something unless it is useful to do so") and (2) an unfavorable view of human nature ("Generally speaking, people won't work hard unless they are forced to do so" and "Anyone who completely trusts anyone else is asking for trouble").

A good deal is known about people who score high in agreement with Machiavelli's views.[11] Generally, they are able to control social interactions and effectively manipulate others. They are also especially effective in using their skills in face-to-face settings. A series of studies among college students found that highly Machiavellian students were more likely to be involved in medicine as a career and were more critical of their fellow students.[12] They also admitted to having strong feelings of hostility. In one contrived study, when students were induced to cheat and then accused of doing so, highly Machiavellian individuals looked their accuser in the eye and denied cheating longer than did less Machiavellian individuals.

Still other research indicates that Machiavellianism is positively correlated with occupational attainment (that is, job prestige and income) for individuals with above-average education, while for individuals with below-average education Machiavellianism is inversely related to occupational attainment. These results make sense in that highly Machiavellian individuals require situations that offer considerable latitude for improvisation and interpersonal manipulation (as is characteristic of white-collar jobs). Individuals in blue-collar jobs, where standards of performance are more objective and disciplinary measures are relatively coercive, may be penalized in proportion to their degree of Machiavellianism.[13]

In general, Machiavellian individuals are thought to be socially domineering and manipulative, and they are assumed to engage in political behavior more often than other organizational participants. They are lacking in (1) emotional display in interpersonal relations (that is, they remain cool and distant, and treat others as objects to be manipulated), (2) concern for traditional morality (that is, they find deceit useful rather than reprehensible), and (3) ideological commitments (that is, they prefer to maintain personal power in situations, rather than adhere to relatively inflexible ideals).

CONSEQUENCES OF USING INFLUENCE TACTICS

Research on attempts to influence others has begun to focus on the specific techniques people use at work. After conversations with employees, David Kipnis and Stuart Schmidt developed a questionnaire for measuring six tactics for influencing others.[14] These tactics include:

1. Reason: relies on using data, logic, and discussion
2. Friendliness: interest, goodwill, and esteem are demonstrated to create a favorable impression.
3. Coalition formation: other people in the organization are mobilized to support requests
4. Bargaining: relies on negotiation and exchanging favors
5. Assertiveness: relies on directness and forcefulness in communication
6. Appeal to higher authority: the influence of those higher in the organization is invoked to back up a request.

From responses to their questionnaire, Kipnis and Schmidt grouped employees into four influence styles:

1. Shotguns: people who refuse to take "no" for an answer and who use all of the preceding tactics to achieve their ends

2. Tacticians: people who try to influence others through reason and logic

3. Ingratiators: people who rely on ingratiation and flattery

4. Bystanders: people who watch the action rather than attempt to influence it.[15]

Comparisons of performance evaluations for the four types of employees revealed that people who assertively attempted to influence their supervisors (Shotguns) were viewed less favorably. Both male and female Shotguns received equally low evaluations from their supervisors. Male supervisors tended to give the highest ratings to male Tacticians, who relied on reason and logic. Women who received the highest ratings were likely to be Ingratiators and Bystanders. In responding to these findings, male supervisors explained that both male Tacticians and female Ingratiators were seen as deferential and thoughtful.

Salary was also found to be associated with influence style. In a comparison of the income of 108 male CEOs, Tacticians earned the most ($73,240), followed by Bystanders (60,270), Shotguns ($56,480), and Ingratiators ($52,700). Based on both evaluations and income, it seems that Tacticians are valued more than their peers who use other styles. Also, Shotgun-style individuals reported more job tension and personal stress than their counterparts.

Kipnis and Schmidt argue, from these and other findings, that books and training programs that are designed to "put people in charge" (in essence, teach a Shotgun style) are questionable. They contend that people should not be taught to be overly assertive as the best tactic for achieving their desires. Instead, training programs should emphasize less vigorous influence styles that rely on reason and logic.[16] Also, it is interesting to contrast managers' preferred styles when trying to influence superiors versus subordinates. Kipnis and Schmidt report that reason is preferred for trying to influence both superiors and subordinates. However, assertiveness is far more likely to be used with subordinates than with superiors, while coalition formation is more likely to be used to influence superiors than to influence subordinates.

OTHER INFLUENCE TECHNIQUES

Beyond the influence tactics discussed thus far are several other, more subtle, mechanisms by which people can be influenced. One effective technique is to create the appearance of higher *status*. Research has shown that people who merely appear to have higher status by virtue of their manner of dress or the use of titles exert greater influence. For example, in one study, a man violated the traffic light when crossing the street. In half the instances, the man was dressed in a well-tailored business suit, while in the remaining instances, he wore a work shirt and trousers. Of interest was the number of pedestrians who would cross the street with the man. As would be predicted from a status influence view, the well-dressed jaywalker influenced $3\frac{1}{2}$ times as many people to cross the street with him.[17]

A second subtle form of influence is to create the appearance that a behavior is *normative*. For example, bartenders often place a few dollars into a tip glass to create the appearance that tipping is a proper action, and that green-backs, not change, are commonly given. Also, "ringers" are sometimes planted in the audiences of preachers, with instructions to come forward on cue with donations or "cures."[††] The apparent popularity of an action generally tends to induce compliance. For example, in one study, several individuals stared upward at the sky over New York City for a prolonged period of time. Within a short while, most passersby were also gazing at the empty sky.[18]

Lastly, people can sometimes be influenced to comply with a request for a sizable favor that they would otherwise not agree to, if they are first asked to do a small favor. This **foot-in-the-door principle** was once demonstrated in a study in which researchers asked people to install a large "Drive Carefully" sign in their front yards. Only 17 percent agreed to post a large sign. However, individuals who were initially asked to display a small 3-inch sign in their windows (which nearly all agreed to do) yielded 76 percent of the time when asked two weeks later to post the large sign.[19]

THE ETHICS OF ORGANIZATIONAL POLITICS

Figure 9.3 presents a model for incorporating ethical considerations into deciding whether to act in a political manner. This model, proposed by Gerald Cavanagh, Dennis Moberg, and Manuel Velasquez, provides guidance on whether a political behavior (PB), or course of action, should be followed in a particular situation.[20] From their perspective, a political behavior is ethical and appropriate only if (1) the behavior respects the rights of all affected parties and (2) the behavior respects the canons of justice—a self-evidently correct judgment of what is equitable and fair. In essence, the model encourages the adoption of nonpolitical behaviors (where such alternatives exist), and the rejection of behaviors that interfere with the canons of justice.

To illustrate their model, Cavanagh and his associates suggest a case in which two research scientists, Sam and Bill, are in competition in a new-product development lab. Each has prepared a proposal to win a significant cash award for the best new-product idea. Blind reviews of the proposals by other scientists indicate that both are equally meritorious. Sam inquires periodically about the outcome of the bidding process, while Bill wages an open campaign in support of his proposal. Specifically, Bill seizes every opportunity to point out the relative advantages of his proposal to individuals who may have some impact on the final decision. He does this after freely admitting his intention to Sam and others. His campaign of informal pressure is effective and his proposal is funded, while Sam's is not.

Using the decision tree, we first ask whether the outcome, in terms of the broad interests of society and the company, will be optimal. Since both proposals were judged to be equivalent in the blind reviews, we must answer yes

---

[††] The use of ringers to induce behavior in others in a calculated fashion dates from Parisian opera houses in the 1820s, where members of the audience were paid to applaud or cheer on cue during the performance. The modern descendent of this practice is the television laugh track.

FIGURE 9.3

A DECISION TREE FOR INCORPORATING ETHICS INTO POLITICAL BEHAVIOR DECISIONS

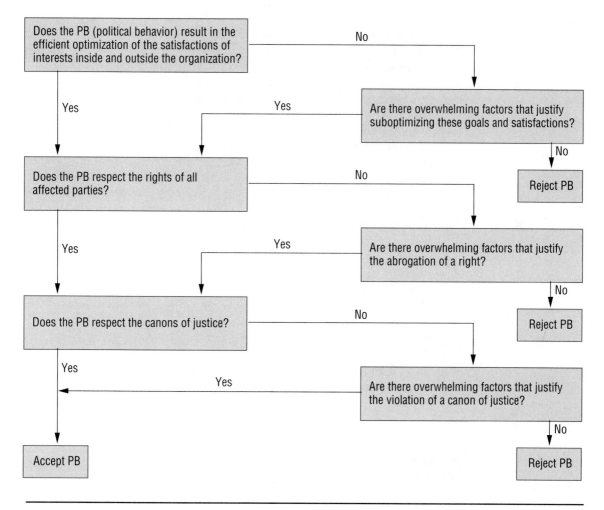

to the first question. The second question focuses on whether Bill's behavior respected the rights of Sam. Because Bill told Sam he intended to campaign actively for his proposal, Bill cannot be accused of deceit. Also, Sam's inaction may be viewed as implied consent. The third question highlights the suspect nature of Bill's actions in pointing out irrelevant differences between the proposals. Given the equivalent merit of the proposals, other considerations (for example, which scientist was most qualified to implement the proposal, or other evidence of past performance) should have been incorporated in the funding decision.

RESPONDING TO SOCIAL INFLUENCE: CONFORMITY

When a person changes behavior or beliefs in response to real or imagined pressure from others, we say that he or she seeks **conformity.** The word *change* is important in this definition because it suggests that the individual deviated from an earlier position or preference.

In organizations, social pressures to conform can be very powerful. An individual who dares to deviate from the preferred line of conduct or belief runs the risk of being ostracized or treated with hostility. "To get along, go along" is an old saying in organizational parlance that summarizes much of what we learn in school and in organizational settings about how to survive.

The power of social pressure to conform was illustrated in a series of now-famous studies by Solomon Asch.[21] In one experiment, college students were asked to indicate which of three lines on Card B was the same size as the line on Card A (Figure 9.4). This task was repeated with the identical-sized line being in the first, second, or third position in various trials. Invariably, the students were able to identify the appropriate line. At a later session, a student who had not taken the test before was placed in a group with seven to nine other subjects and asked to identify the identical line. In this instance, the other subjects were confederates of the experimenter and had been trained to give wrong, but uniform, answers to the task. By contrivance, the new subject was asked to respond after nearly all the other subjects had given the same erroneous answer. The critical question was whether the new subject would answer honestly or be induced by group pressure to deliberately give a wrong answer. In 32 percent of the judgments made on the critical trials, the subjects went along with the unanimous opinion of the group. However, some subjects resisted the group pressure throughout the study.

FIGURE 9.4

A SET OF LINES USED IN THE ASCH EXPERIMENT IN CONFORMITY

In a subsequent study using the same method, it was found that having another subject (also a confederate) present who defied the group and consistently gave the correct response greatly strengthened the new subject's resistance to the group's pressure.

These results illustrate that behavior can be influenced by the pressures of others. People will even reject relatively clear objective data, if others are predisposed to reject it. With more ambiguous and subjective data, such as social information, the power of group pressure is likely to be stronger. When the desire to be liked by others is very strong or when continuing group involvement is likely—as is the case in the workplace—the power of pressure to conform becomes even greater.

RESPONDING TO AUTHORITY: OBEDIENCE

For managers to meet their goals, they must rely on their subordinates to obey their directions. Obedience to authority is a strongly ingrained predisposition for most people. Without this predisposition, society would not be able to function. Usually, the depth of our predisposition to obey orders can only be guessed at. Occasionally, we hear of instances of blind obedience to authority, as in the war-crime trials of Adolf Eichmann and Lieutenant William Calley, but we tend to discount such cases as extreme and unusual.

In the early 1960s, Stanley Milgram of Yale University conducted a series of studies to examine the extent to which people would obey, even if the demands of authority violated their moral responsibilities.[22] As part of this research, 40 adult males from a wide variety of occupations were paid to serve as subjects in a learning experiment. Each subject was told that he was participating in a study of the effects of punishment on learning. The subject was then asked to help another adult (actually the researcher's confederate) learn a lengthy list of word pairs by using electric shock as a penalty for each incorrect answer.

The subject (teacher) met with the alleged learner and then watched as the learner was strapped into an apparatus that looked like an electric chair. The experimenter then took the subject into the next room and showed him how to communicate with the learner through an intercom system (Figure 9.5). The experimenter also explained how to administer the punishment for any errors the learner might make in responding to stimulus words in the list of word pairs. The shock generator contained 30 switches, one for each of 30 different voltage levels ranging from 15 to 450 volts. The switches were also labeled in terms of the increasing strength of the voltage: slight shock, moderate shock, strong shock, very strong shock, intense shock, extreme intensity shock, danger: severe shock, and XXX.

After reading the list of word pairs to the learner, the teacher was to begin quizzing the learner. For each incorrect response, the teacher was to administer an electric shock, and for each additional incorrect response, the teacher was to apply the next higher voltage level on the generator.

The trials passed uneventfully until the learner began to make numerous mistakes. Then, in short order, the teacher found himself administering fairly

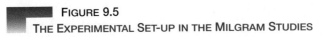

FIGURE 9.5
THE EXPERIMENTAL SET-UP IN THE MILGRAM STUDIES

When the "learner" makes an error, the experimenter prods the "teacher" to deliver a painful electric shock.

Source: Psychology, 3/e by Spencer A. Rathus, p. 657. Copyright ©1987 by Holt, Rinehart and Winston, Inc., reprinted by permission of the publisher.

high levels of voltage to the learner. At that point, the learner would begin to protest, saying that he wanted to drop out of the experiment because his heart was bothering him and the pain of the shocks was too much for him. If the teacher hesitated, the experimenter would encourage him to proceed, saying, for example, "Please go on" or "It is essential that you continue." If the teacher refused to proceed after four verbal encouragements, the experiment was discontinued.

As the voltage levels increased, the confederate (in accord with the experiment's protocol) would voice even stronger objections: He would pound on the wall and, at one point, scream loudly. Beyond a certain voltage level, the learner would no longer answer any of the teacher's questions, giving the impression that he was injured or dead. When this silence occurred, the experimenter would tell the teacher to treat the learner's failure to respond as an incorrect response, to administer the punishment, and to continue on with the next word pair.

Given these conditions, you would probably assume that very few subjects would obey the experimenter. But the actual results revealed that a majority of the subjects administered the maximum voltage on the shock generator and continued their participation in the experiment despite the learner's objections.

Table 9.2 displays the point at which each of the 40 subjects broke off his participation. As the table shows, 26 out of 40, or 65 percent, of the participants administered the maximum level of electric shock. We should note,

TABLE 9.2
VOLTAGE LEVELS WHERE SUBJECTS BREAK OFF THEIR PARTICIPATION

Voltage Level	Number of Subjects Stopping
Slight Shock	
15	0
30	0
45	0
60	0
Moderate Shock	
75	0
90	0
105	0
120	0
Strong Shock	
135	0
150	0
165	0
180	0
Very Strong Shock	
195	0
210	0
225	0
240	0
Intense Shock	
255	0
270	0
285	0
300*	5
Extreme Intensity Shock	
315	4
330	2
345	1
360	1
Danger: Severe Shock	
375	1
390	0
405	0
420	0
XXX	
435	0
450	26

* At 300 volts, the learner no longer responded to the teacher.

however, that although most subjects gave the maximum level of shock to the learner, they did not enjoy doing so. Typically, the subjects displayed strong signs of nervous tension, such as nail biting, trembling, and groaning. Many of them also laughed nervously whenever the learner protested or pleaded. However, the constraints of the situation compelled the subjects to continue their participation.‡‡

The high level of obedience displayed by Milgram's subjects suggests that the predisposition to follow authority is very strong. In this case, the experimenter relied on his expertise and legitimacy to give the subject orders. Despite the fact that all subjects received their pay in advance and participated voluntarily, most felt a strong desire to avoid disobeying authority, even in light of the suffering they inflicted on another person.

These results suggest that society may be too successful at socializing its members to obey authority. When people take on roles that prescribe obedience (such as those of research subject, student, soldier, or employee), the sense of responsibility for the outcomes of their own conduct is likely to be diminished. The evidence from Milgram's work implies that human conscience cannot be relied on to step in and halt activities that are injurious to others. It can be inferred that organizational members generally will carry out orders given by those in authority, regardless of the content or consequences of the actions. This suggests that forms of socialization that emphasize personal responsibility to others may be lacking in our society.

Milgram's findings have raised a number of questions. One of the more intriguing is whether there are cultural differences in the predisposition to obey authority. For example, considering the Holocaust—the persecution and extermination of European Jews by Nazi Germany—one might hypothesize that the level of obedience would be higher in Germany than in other countries. To test this notion, the conditions of Milgram's original study were recreated in several different countries: Canada, England, Jordan, and the former West Germany. The results yielded essentially similar findings, suggesting that the level of obedience to authority in the Milgram condition is fairly constant across different societies.[23] By inference, the atrocities that occurred in Nazi Germany could happen elsewhere in the world.§§

In addition, the level of obedience in the Milgram study may have been near the "baseline" for injurious behavior. The victim (learner) in Milgram's original study was an innocent 47-year-old man. If the victim had been someone whom the subject disliked for any number of possible reasons (race, reli-

---

‡‡When each subject completed the experiment, he met with the learner and discovered that in fact no shocks had been given. The true purpose of the study was then explained to each subject.

§§Such mass atrocities have in fact happened again—witness Cambodia, Uganda, Mao's China, and Stalin's Russia. In an interview with Morley Safer for the news program "Sixty Minutes," Milgram stated that "if a system of death camps were set up in the United States of the sort we had seen in Nazi Germany, one would be able to find sufficient personnel for those camps in any medium-sized American town".[24] However, other evidence from cross-national studies is somewhat suggestive of cultural differences. In a less well publicized self-decision condition (wherein the "teacher" was allowed to choose the shock level in each trial), various studies found extremely low levels of total shock administered by all national samples. However, the levels administered for German and Jordanian samples were somewhat higher than those observed for Australian and U.S. samples.[25]

OB Focus
Obeying Unethical Orders

When an organization's leaders are pursuing legitimate goals, obedience is a necessary ingredient in the organization's smooth functioning. But if a leader's orders are unethical, obedience can do great damage. For Regina Company, an unethical CEO and obedient subordinates brought about the bankruptcy of the organization.

That CEO was Donald D. Sheelen, who launched his business career as a stockbroker with Bache and Co., after he earned his MBA. He joined Regina in 1980, eventually becoming the vacuum cleaner company's marketing chief. Sheelen's colleagues were impressed by his good ideas backed by an intense drive to succeed. He added new products and boosted the company's profits. Four years after he joined the company, Sheelen was named its chief executive officer. In the following years, the company reported tremendous earnings growth.

But the numbers being reported masked some growing problems. To support Sheelen's eagerness to boost sales, the company was skipping testing procedures on new products. By the spring of 1987, Regina was being swamped by returned merchandise. In one quarter alone, customers returned more than 40,000 of the company's Housekeeper vacuum cleaners, 16 percent of sales.

To keep the company's stock price high, Sheelen in December 1987 ordered his chief financial officer, Vincent P. Golden, to not record the returned products. Golden initially protested that this would be unethical accounting, but he gave in and had his staff alter the company's computer systems to make the change. His reason for obeying, he reported later through his lawyer, was to protect his job.

Now that he had Golden's cooperation, Sheelen was able to build on the initial deceit. He told Golden to juggle the books to show $180 million in sales, and earnings per share of $1.20. Golden managed to do this by adjusting the way the company reported sales, by understanding expenses, and by generating about 200 phony invoices.

Sheelen's final deceit again involved the company's products. In a meeting with Wall Street analysts (whom Sheelen hoped would recommend Regina's stock), Sheelen demonstrated the purported superiority of the Housekeeper vacuum cleaner by showing how well it cleaned up the corn flakes he sprinkled on the carpet. Unknown to the analysts, engineers had rigged the demonstration model to have greater suction than the machines actually being sold to customers.

But even with the support of his subordinates, Sheelen could not maintain the deceit indefinitely. In the fall of 1988, he reported the company's troubles and resigned his post. After pleading guilty to mail and securities fraud, he was sentenced to a year in a prison work center and fined $25,000. Golden also pleaded guilty, and received half of the same sentence. The following year, Regina began reorganizing under Chapter 11 of the bankruptcy code.

Source: John A. Byrne, "How Don Sheelen Made a Mess That Regina Couldn't Clean Up," *Business Week*, February 12, 1990, 46–47.

gion, or politics) or had the subject possessed a strong commitment to the purpose of the study in which he was involved, or expected to be continually involved with persons in the study, the level of obedience might well have been much higher.

The study of the personalities of participants in the Milgram experiments has yielded some interesting findings. Subjects who were relatively more obedient were significantly more authoritarian, as measured on the F-scale (see Chapter 3). This result confirms the notion that a major component of the authoritarian personality is one of uncritical submission to an idealized authority.[26] Individuals who defied the experimenter were at a higher stage of moral development than those who were obedient, as measured in Kohlberg's system of moral development (also discussed in Chapter 3). Yet another correlate of defiance of authority was social intelligence. In one study, it was found that subjects who did not comply fully with the experimenter's commands were individuals who scored higher on a measure of social intelligence.[27] People who are more socially intelligent (that is, who are more astute observers of others and who have the ability to effectively influence the outcomes of situations) are probably better able to understand and manage situations using available social cues.

Since the time of Milgram's studies, greater concern has arisen over research ethics and specifically the need to protect subjects from traumatic experiences. Because of these concerns about the rights of subjects, it has become exceedingly difficult to obtain peer approval to conduct and publish similar research. Therefore, something of a moratorium exists on conducting studies such as Milgram's that may involve unpleasant experiences for the subject. As a result, it cannot be determined whether the present level of obedience is lower than in the past. Some national experiences, such as the Watergate scandal and the Vietnam War protests, have certainly made it more socially acceptable to oppose authority. It is probably safe to say that it is now somewhat more difficult to extract conformity in a variety of settings (including work, school, and government) than it has been in the past.

In summary, Milgram's research suggests that people placed in a conflict situation pitting moral values against authority will tend to follow the dictates of authority. Perhaps the most sobering aspect of this discovery lies in how little real power an authority figure needs in order to succeed in directing others. Of course, opportunities for the abuse of authority also occur in business organizations. Because of this reality, it is essential that managers recognize the magnitude of their power over others and act in accordance with the responsibility that such power entails.

SUMMARY

1. Define and distinguish power, authority, influence, and politics.
Power is the ability to change the behavior of others; it may be legitimate or illegitimate, used to attain common goals or personal gain. Authority is the legitimate use of power in the pursuit of common goals. Influence is also defined as the ability to change other people's behavior, but in subtler, more specific, and less reliable ways. Politics constitutes the actions taken to obtain, develop, and use power.

2. Identify and describe three primary influence processes.
Kelman identified three reasons a person yields to another's influence: compliance, identification, and internalization. Compliance entails yielding to influence in the hope of receiving a reward or avoiding a punishment. Identification arises out of the desire to establish or maintain a satisfying relationship with the person exercising the influence. With internalization, the person being influenced believes the behavior is correct and appropriate.

3. List and define five bases of power.
According to French and Raven, five bases of power are reward power, coercive power, legitimate power, referent power, and expert power. Reward power

is the ability to determine who will receive particular rewards. Coercive power is the ability to punish or produce fear in others. Legitimate power arises from willingness to accept an individual's direction because of social conditioning or designation. Referent power is the ability to influence others because of one's attractiveness or ability to inspire. Expert power is the power that arises from being perceived as knowledgeable or talented in some area.

4. Describe some differences between formal and informal power.

Managers with informal power—expert and referent power—have greater capacity to affect the satisfaction and performance of employees, whereas formal power—legitimate, reward, and coercive power—potentially has more impact on immediate behavior. Formal power will not necessarily produce agreement and commitment. Informal power bases are more easily eroded and can be harder to control. In general, informal power resides in the manager's personal characteristics, while formal power resides in the position itself.

5. Distinguish the kinds of power organizations use, name a type of organization corresponding to each type of power, and describe the nature of member involvement in an organization that uses that type of power.

According to Etzioni, organizations attempt to direct the behavior of their members with three kinds of power: coercive, utilitarian, and normative. Coercive power is used by prisons, some mental institutions, and divisions within the military. Members of these organizations are characterized by alienative involvement. Most businesses rely on utilitarian power and characteristically have members with calculative involvement. Organizations that rely on normative power include professional associations and religious organizations. The involvement of their members is moral in nature.

6. Describe the cycle of approaches that supervisors use to influence subordinates.

According to Sussmann and Vecchio, supervisors' attempts to influence a subordinate follow a cycle in which the supervisor tries using compliance (by threatening), identification (by appealing to the subordinate's sense of membership), or internalization (by appealing to the subordinate's values). If one influence attempt fails, the supervisor then tries a different type of influence.

7. Identify several political tactics, including devious political tactics and political blunders.

Political tactics include ingratiation, forming coalitions and networks, impression management, information management, promoting the opposition, and pursuing line responsibility. Political tactics considered devious include eliminating all enemies, creating a feud between potential rivals, and excluding the opposition. Common political blunders are violating the organization's chain of command, losing one's cool, rejecting a request from top management, upstaging one's boss, and challenging cherished beliefs of the organization.

8. Explain several techniques for coping with organizational politics.

A manager can create a positive climate for subordinates by setting an example of truthfulness and even-handed treatment. A manager can make expectations for performance clear by giving well-defined, discrete work assignments.

Coalitions and cliques that interfere with group performance can be eliminated through dismissal, transfer, or job rotation. Managers can bring game playing into the open by confronting the players or offering to discuss the situation in a public forum.

9. Support an argument that pressures to conform are powerful.

In a series of studies by Solomon Asch, many subjects rejected even clear objective data in order to conform to the group's consensus. With more subjective or ambiguous data, the power of group pressure is likely to be even greater. It is also likely to be greater for group members who probably will be involved on a continuing basis and who have a strong desire to be liked by the group.

10. Cite evidence that the predisposition to obey authority is strong.

In a study conducted by Stanley Milgram, subjects obeyed the authority of the researcher, even though the researcher's authority was limited and the subjects were aware that they were severely hurting an innocent person. This research suggests that the predisposition to follow authority is very strong and that when people take on roles that prescribe obedience, their sense of responsibility for the outcome of their conduct is diminished.

KEY TERMS

Power	Expert power
Authority	Utilitarian power
Influence	Normative power
Compliance	Alienative involvement
Identification	Calculative involvement
Internalization	Moral involvement
Reward power	Organizational politics
Coercive power	Mach Scale
Legitimate power	Foot-in-the-door principle
Referent power	Conformity

REVIEW AND DISCUSSION QUESTIONS

1. Dan Williams, vice president of research and development, is so charming that his colleagues invariably take his side in meetings. As a result, the R&D budget has grown 10 percent every year since 1988. Does Dan have power? Authority? Explain your answers.

2. Bernice Wilson supervises production workers in a small widget assembly factory. She believes that the best way to use her influence is to use rewards and punishments to achieve compliance with company rules. Although Bernice prefers to spend hot summer days in her air-conditioned office, she goes out into the plant at the end of each day to ask questions and find out who should be rewarded and who punished. What is Bernice forgetting?

3. According to French and Raven, what are the five bases of power? Give an example of each.

4. Should a manager exercise power frequently, or would the manager's power have more impact if he or she saved it for unusual occasions? Explain your answer.

5. Why might people with formal power tend to remain in their positions of authority longer than those who rely on informal power?

6. Sue Blue, sales manager for Acme Hospital Supply, notices that sales are slipping in New Mexico and flies down to visit the New Mexico sales rep, Jean Green. Sue tells Jean, "The hospitals in this state really need our supplies to save patients' lives. Because the hospitals do such important work, you really should try harder." The next month, Sue is disappointed to find that sales in New Mexico have not improved. Based on Etzioni's model of power, offer Sue a possible explanation for her failure to influence Jean.

7. French and Raven, Kelman, and Etzioni describe three models of power and influence. How can these models be reconciled?

8. When Todd McCrae was a teller, nothing motivated him like the fear of being fired. Now that the bank has put him in charge of the tellers, Todd intends to motivate them all in the way that worked for him. After all, he knows first-hand that it works. Do you agree with Todd? Why or why not?

9. Why might ingratiation be a successful political tactic even when the person is using it blatantly?

10. What is a line position? In what ways might it be advantageous to hold a line position in an organization?

11. Name two characteristics that would lead you to consider a person "Machiavellian." Would you expect such a person to engage in political behavior relatively frequently or relatively infrequently?

12. Stanley Milgram's research suggests that people obey authority figures even when they question whether their own behavior is ethical. Do you think the results of his research apply to the people in your community today? Why or why not? Is this good or bad for your community?

CRITICAL INCIDENT

Warner Memorial Hospital

Warner Memorial Hospital is located in a moderate-sized community, approximately 45 miles from a major metropolitan area. It is a 240-bed facility that employs about 300 people. During the past year, there have been wide fluctuations in the patient census. The chief negotiator for the Allied Health Workers Union, Betty Gordon, was visibly concerned about the new labor contract negotiations that were to begin in two days. She was afraid that the union would be asked to agree to wage and benefit concessions. Remembering the last contract negotiations, which resulted in a 41-day strike, did little to ease her concern. At those negotiations three years ago, few of the more critical issues separating labor and management were really settled.

The head of labor relations for the hospital, Bill Lenox, was also thinking about the upcoming negotiations. He recalled the last contract negotiations and some of the unrealistic demands that were presented by the union. Given that this was a healthcare service and delivery organization, Bill was convinced that the workers, especially the nurses and technicians, would be better off without the union.

The union holds a very strong position at Warner Memorial. Most of the eligible workers belong, which affects all aspects of hospital operations. The hospital could not easily replace these employees during a strike. Betty firmly believes that the union members are seeking improvements in wages and benefits. She is not convinced that management wishes to reach an equitable contract agreement. The union members also believe that if management really wanted to attract more patients, they would be investing in newer equipment and initiating a marketing program.

Bill and his staff have been spending weeks getting ready for the negotiations. They have pages of data in support of the need for concessions or at least a wage freeze. Bill is convinced that the union will adamantly oppose any request for concessions and that volatile, emotional arguments are inevitable. The hospital is not in a position to grant meaningful increases in wages and benefits and can ill afford a strike. Perhaps some patients as well as workers would be lost forever to the hospital's market-intensive competitors in a nearby city, 45 miles north.

QUESTIONS

1. What bases of power are evident in this case for Betty? For Bill?
2. What political tactics or games can be identified in this case?
3. What do you predict is likely to happen? What do you propose as a possible solution?

Source: Written by Bruce Kemelgor, University of Louisville; used by permission.

EXPERIENTIAL EXERCISE
Who Has Power?

In organizational settings, there are usually five types of power: legitimate, reward, coercive, referent, and expert. An individual may have one or more of these kinds of power; also, the person who possesses power is not necessarily considered a manager or leader.

This exercise examines power across several sets of individuals or occupations. For example, set 1 considers the power your professor, as the focal person, has over a student, the significant other. Thus, you should check which kind of power the professor has over students. But also in set 1, you should consider another possibility; that is, in the reverse sense, what power might the student as the focal person possess over the professor as the significant other?

Complete the table for the eight sets, indicating on the first line the power of the focal person over the significant other and on the second line the power of the significant other over the focal person.

QUESTIONS

1. On balance, which person—the focal person or the significant other—has the most power? Make this judgment for each set.
2. Indicate, for each set, which of the five types of power is the most significant.
3. Can you identify instances in which a power base is equally divided between the focal person and the significant other? If so, can you explain why this occurs?

Set	Focal Person	Significant Other	Power				
			Legitimate	Reward	Coercive	Referent	Expert
1	Professor Student	Student Professor					
2	Manager—grocery store Cashier/checker	Cashier/checker Manager—grocery store					
3	President of the U.S. U.S. citizens	U.S. citizens President of the U.S.					
4	Secretary Executive	Executive Secretary					
5	Audit supervisor, IRS Agents for IRS	Agents for IRS Audit supervisor, IRS					
6	Mentor Mentee	Mentee Mentor					
7	University president Deans	Deans University president					
8	Car salesperson Customer	Customer Car salesperson					

Source: Ricky W. Griffin and Thomas C. Head, *Practicing Management*, Second Edition. Copyright © 1987 by Houghton Mifflin Company. Used with permission.

NOTES

1. D.C. McClelland, *Power: The Inner Experience* (New York: Irvington, 1975); D.C. McClelland, "Power Is the Great Motivation," *Harvard Business Review* 54 (1976): 100–110.
2. H.C. Kelman, "Processes of Opinion Change," *Public Opinion Quarterly* 25 (1961): 57–78.
3. J.R.P. French, Jr., and B.H. Raven, "The Bases of Social Power," in *Studies in Social Power*, ed. D. Cartwright (Ann Arbor: University of Michigan, Institute for Social Research, 1959); T. Hinkin and C. Schriesheim, "Development and Application of New Scales to Measure the French and Raven Bases of Social

Power," *Journal of Applied Psychology* 74 (1989): 561–567.

4. A. Etzioni, *A Comparative Analysis of Complex Organizations,* rev. ed. (New York: Free Press, 1975); R. Mayer, "Understanding Employee Motivation through Organizational Commitment" (Ph. D. diss., Purdue University, 1989).

5. M. Sussmann and R.P. Vecchio, "A Social Influence Interpretation of Worker Motivation," *Academy of Management Review* 7 (1982): 177–186; R.P. Vecchio and M. Sussmann, "Preference for Forms of Supervisory Social Influence," *Journal of Organizational Behavior* 10 (1989): 135–143.

6. Ibid.

7. G.R. Ferris and K.M. Kacmar, "Perceptions of Organizational Politics," *Journal of Management* 10 (1992): 93–116; J. Pfeffer, *Power in Organizations* (Boston: Pitman Publishing Co., 1981).

8. R.W. Allen, D.L. Madison, L.W. Porter et al., "Organizational Politics: Tactics and Characteristics of Its Actors," *California Management Review* 12 (Fall 1979): 77–83; A.J. DuBrin, *Winning at Office Politics* (New York: Ballantine, 1978); R.H. Miles, *Macro Organizational Behavior* (Santa Monica, Calif.: Goodyear, 1980), 174–175; Pfeffer, *Power in Organizations.*

9. DuBrin, *Winning at Office Politics.*

10. R. Christie and F.L. Geis, eds., *Studies in Machiavellianism* (New York: Academic Press, 1970).

11. G.R. Gemmil and W.J. Heisler, "Machiavellianism as a Factor in Managerial Job Strain, Job Satisfaction, and Upward Mobility," *Academy of Management Journal* 15 (1972): 53–67.

12. R.V. Exline, J. Thibaut, C.O. Hickey et al., "Visual Interaction in Relation to Machiavellianism and an Unethical Act," in *Studies in Machiavellianism,* eds. R. Christie and F.L. Geis (New York: Academic Press, 1970), 53–75; D. Kipnis and S.M. Schmidt, *Profiles of Organizational Influence Strategies* (San Diego: University Associates, 1982); S.M. Schmidt and D. Kipnis, "The Perils of Persistence," *Psychology Today,* November 1987, 32–34; D. Kipnis, *The Powerholders* (Chicago: University of Chicago Press, 1976); P. Block, *The Empowered Manager* (San Francisco: Jossey-Bass, 1988).

13. C.F. Turner and D.C. Martinez, "Socioeconomic Achievement and the Machiavellian Personality," *Sociometry* 40 (1977): 325–336.

14. Kipnis and Schmidt, *Profiles of Organizational Influence Strategies;* C. Schriescheim and T. Hinkin, "Influence Tactics Used by Subordinates: A Theoretical and Empirical Analysis and Refinement of the Kipnis, Schmidt, and Wilkinson Subscales," *Journal of Applied Psychology* 75 (1990): 246–252; G. Yukl and J.B. Tracey, "Consequences of Influence Tactics Used with Subordinates, Peers, and the Boss," *Journal of Applied Psychology* 76 (1992): 525–535; C. Falbe and G. Yukl, "Consequences for Managers of Using Single Influence Tactics and Combinations of Tactics," *Academy of Management Journal* 35 (1992): 638–652; D. Brass and M. Burkhardt, "Potential Power and Power Use: An Investigation of Structure and Behaviors," *Academy of Management Journal* 36 (1993): 441–470.

15. Schmidt and Kipnis, "The Perils of Persistence."

16. Kipnis, *The Powerholders;* Block, *The Empowered Manager;* D. Kipnis, S.M. Schmidt, C. Swaffin-Smith, and I. Wilkenson, "Patterns of Managerial Influence: Shotgun Managers, Tacticians, and Bystanders," *Organizational Dynamics* (1984): 58–67; S.M. Farmer, D.B. Fedor, J.S. Goodman, and J.M. Maslyn, "Factors Affecting the Use of Upward Influence Strategies," *Proceedings of the Academy of Management* (1993): 64–68.

17. M. Lefkowitz, R.A. Blake, and J.S. Mouton, "Status Factors in Pedestrian Violation of Traffic Signals," *Journal of Abnormal and Social Psychology* 51 (1955): 704–706.

18. S. Milgram, L. Bickman, and L. Berkowitz, "Note on the Drawing Power of Crowds of Different Size," *Journal of Personality and Social Psychology* 13 (1969): 79–82.

19. J.C. Freedman and S.C. Fraser, "Compliance Without Pressure: The Foot-in-the-Door Technique," *Journal of Personality and Social Psychology* 4 (1966): 195–202.

20. G.F. Cavanagh, D.J. Moberg, and M. Velasquez, "The Ethics of Organizational Politics," *Academy of Management Review* 6 (1981): 363–374.

21. S.E. Asch, "Effects of Group Pressure upon the Modification and Distortion of Judgments," in *Groups, Leadership and Men,* ed. H. Guetzkow (Pittsburgh: Carnegie Press, 1951); S.E. Asch, "Studies of Independence and Conformity: A Minority of One against a Unanimous Majority," *Psychological Monographs* 70, whole no. 416 (1956); S.E. Asch, "Effects of Group Pressure upon Modification and Distortion of Judgments," in *Readings in Social Psychology,* 3d ed., eds. E.E. Maccoby, T.M. Newcomb, and E.L. Hartley (New York: Holt, Rinehart, 1958), 174–183.

22. S. Milgram, "Behavioral Study of Obedience," *Journal of Abnormal and Social Psychology* 67 (1963): 371–378.

23. S. Milgram, *Obedience to Authority* (New York: Harper, 1974); M.E. Shanah and K.A. Yahya, "A Behavioral Study of Obedience in Children," *Journal of Personality and Social Psychology* 35 (1977): 530–536.

24. CBS News, Transcript of "Sixty Minutes" segment, "I Was Only Following Orders," (March 31, 1979): 2–8; D.M. Mantell, "The Potential for Violence in Germany," *Journal of Social Issues* 27 (1971): 101–112; M.E. Shanah and K.A. Yahya, "A Cross-Cultural Study of Obedience," *Bulletin of the Psychonomic Society* 11 (1978): 267–269; W. Kilham and L. Mann, "Level of Destructive Obedience as a Function of Transmitter and Executant Roles in the Milgram Obedience Paradigm," *Journal of Personality and Social Psychology* 29 (1974): 696–702; S.R. Shalala, "A Study of Various Communication Settings Which Produce Obedience by Subordinates to Unlawful Superior Orders" (Ph.D. diss, University of Kansas, 1974).

25. T. Blass, "Obedience to Authority: Some Issues and Significance," in *Perspectives on Stanley Milgram's Contributions to Social Psychology* (Symposium conducted at the Annual Meeting of the American Psychological Association, Boston, Mass., August 24, 1990).

26. A.C. Elms and S. Milgram, "Personality Characteristics Associated with Obedience and Defiance toward Authoritative Command," *Journal of Experimental Research in Personality* 1 (1966): 282–289; A.C. Elms, *Social Psychology and Social Relevance* (Boston: Little, Brown, 1972); S. Milgram, *Obedience to Authority: An Experimental View* (New York: Harper and Row, 1974).

27. P.M. Burley and J. McGuiness, "Effects of Social Intelligence on the Milgram Paradigm," *Psychological Reports* 40 (1977): 767–770.

CHAPTER

10

LEARNING OBJECTIVES

*After studying this chapter,
you should be able to:*

1. *Define leadership.*
2. *List some attributes that
   are associated with leadership.*
3. *Describe ways in which
   leader behavior is related to
   employee attitudes and performance.*
4. *Explain the importance of
   leadership.*
5. *Explain why some people
   seek leadership positions.*
6. *Identify three major approaches to studying leadership.*
7. *Compare and contrast the
   major models of leader
   traits and behaviors.*

Leadership
Individual and Behavioral Processes

THE LEADER BEHIND DELL COMPUTER CORP.

An entrepreneur from the start, Michael Dell at age 12 netted $2,000 by selling stamps through the mail. Seven years later, while still in college at the University of Texas at Austin, he started his own business with $1,000 in savings. Dell's business focused on buying surplus IBM computers at cost, upgrading them with graphics cards and hard drives, then reselling them through phone sales. Within a year, the company began assembling its own PC designs. Workers designed and assembled PCs with off-the-shelf components and sold them directly over the phone, eliminating dealers and distributors, and providing excellent customer service. Dell, who had dropped out of college, had 40 employees on the payroll, worked 18-hour days and slept on a cot in his office.

Dell's hard work paid off. In 1987, the company's name was changed from PCs Limited to Dell Computer Corp., in honor of its enterprising founder. Today, Dell has a staff of over 4,600 employees and holds 11 patents. By early 1993, Dell Computer revenues were $2 billion a year, and the business was ranked fourth largest PC maker in America, behind IBM, Apple, and Compaq.

Despite his successes, recent events have tested Michael Dell's leadership abilities. At age 28, Michael Dell is one of the youngest CEOs in America. As the company continues to grow, he faces a difficult rite of passage that will test his ability to transform his company from startup to sustained growth. Some entrepreneurs, such as Bill Gates of Microsoft Corp., have been able to make this transition, while others, such as Steve Jobs of Apple Computer Inc., have not. Although Dell Computer's sales and profits rose during fiscal 1993, net margins were down as a result of increased capital expenditures, PC price wars, and higher taxes. Moreover, within a two-month period in 1992, Dell lost two top executives and received some bad press about currency speculation, resulting in a 10 percent drop in stock price.

In 1993, Dell learned that archrival Compaq Computer would begin marketing PCs through direct sales, threatening to cut into Dell Computer's niche of service and price. However, the PC market is continually changing, and Dell readily admits the company constantly reinvents itself. Dell Computer is trying to retain its niche in customer service by as-

sembling machines on a just-in-time basis. Rather than carrying inventories of finished PCs, machines are assembled after the customer has specified the particular configuration needed. Realizing the direct sales market is being invaded by other direct sales companies, such as Gateway 2000, and low-price electronics superstores, such as BestBuy and CompUSA, Dell Computer has recently started selling in superstores, such as Sam's Club, Price Club, and CompUSA.

Dell Computer's board of directors and executive team have seen a change in Michael Dell's leadership style. International President Andrew R. Harris recalls Dell's intense style during the middle to late 1980s: "He wasn't a very good public speaker. He wasn't good at running meetings. He wasn't laughing a lot." Regarding the Michael Dell of the 1990s, Harris says, "He's a very charismatic leader, a great speaker. He can go into any department and know what hot button to push" to motivate his staff. Many credit Lee Walker, president and COO of Dell Computer from 1986 to 1990, with transforming Dell into a polished executive. Walker has been an important mentor for

Michael Dell, providing him financial and managerial experience, and preparing him to meet the challenging future of the PC world.

By helping managers develop as leaders, companies obtain people who are able not only to manage but also to inspire subordinates. This chapter explores the important role of leadership. It discusses evaluative techniques that may be used to distinguish leaders from managers, and examines characteristics of effective leaders.

Source: Stephanie Anderson Forest, Catherine Arnst, Kathy Rebello, and Peter Burrows, "The Education of Michael Dell," *Business Week*, March 22, 1993, 82–88.

What makes a manager an effective leader? What personal attributes distinguish effective leaders from ineffective leaders? And what situational factors can help a person be more effective as a leader? These are the questions asked by both managers and the people who study organizational behavior. In an effort to answer these questions, managers have at times helped researchers by serving as subjects in studies of leadership. The results of both empirical and conceptual investigations of leadership have produced an enormous body of knowledge.

In the most recent edition of the *Handbook of Leadership,* a fairly complete compendium of research on the topic, Bernard M. Bass identified over 5,000 studies and treatises dealing with the behavioral aspects of leadership.[1] Trying to make sense of such a mass of information is no simple task. Nonetheless, certain themes and consistencies can be identified. In this chapter, we will begin by examining the nature of leadership and its defining characteristics. We will then consider a variety of approaches to understanding the leadership process by examining the roles of individual differences and behavioral issues. In the following chapter, we will explore the role of situational influences in determining leader effectiveness.

THE NATURE OF LEADERSHIP

Although many definitions have been offered for *leadership,* most contain certain common elements. A distillation of these elements suggests that **leadership** can be defined as a process through which a person tries to get organizational members to do something that the person desires. This definition overlaps, to a great extent, with the way in which we defined influence in the previous chapter. Therefore, leadership must be viewed as an influence process.

Typically, we think of leadership as being associated with the role of manager. However, *leader* and *manager* are not equivalent terms. Someone may be an outstanding manager without in fact being a work group's leader. Although the group's manager performs planning, organizing, and controlling activities, the real leader may actually be one of the subordinates. So, too, a work group's nominal head may be a great leader, while requiring that others handle the functional duties of planning, organizing, and controlling for the unit.

Leadership thus implies something more than mere supervisory responsibility or formal authority. It consists of influence that extends beyond the usual influence that accompanies legitimacy as a supervisor. Therefore, it can be said that leadership is the *incremental influence,* or additional influence, that a person has beyond his or her formal authority. Incremental influence can exist to varying degrees in every member of a work group. As a result, it is not uncommon to find situations in which a subordinate who lacks formal authority actually possesses substantial incremental influence. We would call such an individual an **informal leader**. Informal leaders are often invaluable to their groups because they can aid coworkers in a number of different ways. For example, an informal leader may possess technical expertise that even the formal leader lacks. Or an informal leader may have special social skills (such as the ability to make people feel good about themselves or their accomplishments) that can maintain or improve group morale.

The presence of an informal leader (or leaders) may sound like a distinct plus for a manager. However, this is not always the case. Occasionally, an informal leader's values may not coincide with those of the formal leader. Sometimes the informal leader may encourage his or her peers to be less productive or more demanding in order to extract greater rewards from the formal leader. In so doing, an informal leader may become a political opponent. Clearly, the presence of an informal leader is not inherently a good or bad thing. The ultimate value of an informal leader depends on whether he or she supports or opposes the goals of the organization.

Thus, the differences between leadership and headship can be quite distinct, and leadership may exist on both formal and informal levels. While it might not be technically correct to use the terms *leader* and *manager* interchangeably, we will do so throughout the remainder of this chapter, because most views on the topic of leadership refer primarily to formal leaders, or managers, and do not maintain the distinction between leadership and headship.

DOES LEADERSHIP MAKE A DIFFERENCE?

One can make a good argument that leadership should have only a modest impact on group performance as work-unit accomplishments result more from the efforts of the unit's members than of one individual. For example, the players on a sports team would seem to be more important than the head coach in terms of final points on the scoreboard. Also, organizations have rules and policies that govern member behaviors. Yet, one also has a sense that a leader, under the right circumstances, can have a powerful impact on unit performance.

One interesting way to learn whether leaders can have an impact is to study the effects of leader succession. That is, what are the results of changing leaders for units that are performing well or poorly? In most work units, change of leadership is precipitated by poor performance by the group. Occasionally, the group's leadership is truly to blame, but in some instances, the leader is a scapegoat for other problems. By and large, financial problems do predict changes in organizational leadership.[2] Also, rates of executive succession tend to be higher in larger organizations.[3] Research on the consequences of leader succession suggests that group performance can be either enhanced or impaired by succession. For well-performing groups, succession can be disruptive and lead to greater personnel turnover. However, for poorly performing groups, succession offers an opportunity for performance enhancement. In studies that have examined such diverse positions as baseball coaches, mayors, and board chairpersons, evidence suggests that succession (hence leadership) can have strong effects on measurable performance outcomes.[4] A frequent change of leaders (that is, a high rate of succession), however, is associated with declines in performance (although such declines may be a cause of leader turnover rather than an effect).

WHAT DO MANAGERS ACTUALLY DO?

Before examining the major studies of leadership, it is instructive to consider what managers do during a typical day. By considering what managers actually do, we can develop an appreciation of what such jobs are like.

Studies of actual on-the-job behavior reveal that most managers perform a large number of brief, highly varied, and fragmented activities. The results of these studies, which are usually obtained through direct observation or by having a manager maintain a daily log of activities, suggest that the popular notion of the harried executive is fairly accurate. One such study found that on only nine occasions during a 4-week period did a manager remain uninterrupted for 30 minutes or longer.[5] In another study, it was found that CEOs averaged over 50 written and verbal contacts per day, with half of these activities taking less than 9 minutes and only one-tenth taking more than an hour.[6] Other researchers also have argued that most of a manager's time is devoted to face-to-face or telephone communications. The recurring nature of the problems tackled by a manager over a period of time is difficult to describe succinctly. However, one colorful summarization suggested by Marples is that "the manager's job can usefully be pictured as a stranded rope made up of fibers of different lengths—where length represents time—each fiber coming to the surface one or more times in observable 'episodes' and each representing a single issue."[7]

Given the nonroutine nature of managerial work, it is reasonable to ask where managers find time to communicate with their people on a personal level or to attempt to motivate them. Often, there is truly little time for such activities. More typically, managers are involved in "putting out fires" and managing problems than in developing the human resources within their work units.

According to Katz, managers at different levels within organizations are generally assumed to require different mixes of three broad types of skills: technical, human, and conceptual. Technical skills comprise the knowledge and ability that relate to job-specific techniques and operations. An ability to work with others and an aptitude for relating well with people are human skills. Conceptual skills include the abilities to engage in effective planning, to develop models, and, to obtain a deeper understanding of processes. At the lowest levels of management (for example, the supervisory level), conceptual skills are thought to be less important than technical skills. As a person rises through organizational levels, technical know-how becomes less important and conceptual skills become more important. Human skills are assumed to be important at all levels of management. Figure 10.1 displays the shift in emphasis that occurs at different organizational levels.

WHY DO SOME PEOPLE SEEK LEADERSHIP ROLES?

Individuals differ in the extent to which they aspire to managerial positions. John Miner, of the State University of New York at Buffalo, has conducted research on the **motivation to manage.** His research relies on a unique projective test comprising a series of incomplete sentences (for example, "Giving orders . . . ," "Athletic contests . . . ," and "My relationship with my boss . . ."). The responses have been found to predict success as a leader in hierarchical organizations.[8] From his work, Miner concluded that a successful manager must:

1. be able to maintain good working relations with authority figures,

2. desire to compete for recognition and rewards,

FIGURE 10.1
CHANGES IN THE NEED FOR THREE TYPES OF SKILLS ACROSS ORGANIZATIONAL LEVELS

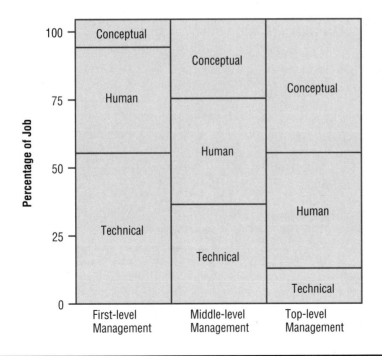

Source: Adapted from R. L. Katz, "Skills of an Effective Administrator," *Harvard Business Review* 33 (1955): 33–42.

3. be assertive,

4. wish to exercise influence over subordinates,

5. desire to be visibly different from subordinates, and

6. be willing to stay on top of routine administrative tasks.

Of course, not all individuals desire to stand apart from others, regulate others, or deal with routine minutiae. Hence, Miner's work identifies preconditions for interest in a managerial career. Success in the context of Miner's model, however, presupposes a hierarchical, competitive environment.[9] For many nonhierarchical or nonbureaucratic settings (such as professional organizations or smaller firms), Miner's formulations for success as a leader may not hold.

OVERVIEW OF APPROACHES TO STUDYING LEADERSHIP

Attempts to study leadership in a systematic manner have produced three major **paradigms** (frameworks that suggest how variables should be arranged in a causal sequence). Most research conforms to one of the following paradigms: the trait approach, the behavioral approach, and the situational approach. Figure 10.2 displays the arrangement of variables in each of the three approaches.

FIGURE 10.2
MAJOR APPROACHES TO STUDYING LEADERSHIP

A.   Trait Approach

Leader Traits and Skills → Effectiveness Measures

B.   Behavioral Approach

Leader Behavior → Intervening Variables → Effectiveness Measures

C.   Situational Approach

Leader Traits, Skills, Behaviors → Effectiveness Measures

Situational Variables →

Source: Adapted from Gary Yukl, *Leadership in Organizations,* 3/e, © 1994, pp. 12–14. Adapted by permission of Prentice Hall, Englewood Cliffs, New Jersey.

In the trait approach, researchers identify and study attributes of leaders in order to determine which traits and skills distinguish superior leaders. The behavioral approach focuses on what leaders actually do in their positions, and how these actions (that is, the intervening variables [see Chapter 2]) relate to effectiveness. The situational approach follows the logic of the contingency approach (see Chapter 1) wherein important contextual factors are identified and studied. For example, research based on the situational approach might examine the influences of subordinate differences in motivation and loyalty, the influence of clients, or the role of reward systems in determining the impact of leader behaviors and traits on unit effectiveness. In the remainder of this chapter, we will examine the results of trait-based research and behavioral research. In the following chapter, we will explore the situational view of leadership, and controversies surrounding the importance of leadership in organizational settings.

THE TRAIT APPROACH

Before the 1950s, researchers sought to understand leadership by comparing leaders with followers and effective leaders with ineffective leaders. This search for features of leaders, or leader traits, was prompted by a belief that leaders somehow possessed distinguishing traits that set them apart from other people. The logic of this approach is simple: To understand what makes some individuals more effective as leaders, merely measure such people on a large number of psychological, social, and physical attributes and note how they differ from most others.

As the research progressed (mostly during the 1930s and 1940s), the number of traits of suspected importance began to grow. Moreover, the results became increasingly mixed and did not follow a clear pattern. Finally, in 1948, Ralph Stogdill published a review of the trait researchers' findings that was so devastating it seriously curtailed the amount of trait research subsequently conducted.[10]

By and large, the trait studies did not show any simple pattern of traits that was both strongly and consistently related to leadership.[11] At first glance, this seems surprising. Based on personal experience and observations, we might expect to find consistent differences between effective and ineffective leaders. However, if we consider a large number of effective leaders, we reach a different conclusion. For example, observations and experience may lead one to believe that effective leaders are likely to be outgoing and socially assertive. Yet, there have been outstanding leaders who were relatively shy and withdrawn, such as Abraham Lincoln and Mahatma Gandhi.

The search for leader traits, however, was not a total failure. Several traits do appear to be very modestly but inconsistently associated with leadership. Chief among these traits is intelligence. It appears that people who hold leadership positions tend to be somewhat more intelligent. On the other hand, there is good reason to believe that highly intelligent people are not likely to attain or maintain leadership in many settings.[12] According to this line of reasoning, individuals who are much brighter than their potential followers may have difficulty in communicating and relating to them.* In essence, there may be an optimal level of intelligence for a leader in a given situation.

Although intelligence has been shown to correlate only modestly with leadership, work by Fred Fiedler and his associates suggests that under special circumstances, leader intelligence and other cognitive attributes can be highly correlated with effectiveness.[13] In particular, Fiedler found that in situations combining a leader's ability to be directive and a stress-free environment, intelligence can be used to predict work-unit performance with a fairly high degree of accuracy. Called **cognitive resource theory,** this view argues that directive leaders who are intelligent and possess relevant job experience will be more effective if they are in stress-free settings with subordinates who are supportive. This fairly straightforward perspective of what makes for effective leadership is, in fact, the logic that underlies much of the hiring of managers. That is to say, when selecting supervisors, it is common to search for experienced managers possessing a fair degree of intelligence plus social skills that can be used to build supportiveness and reduce interpersonal stress. Research on the validity of cognitive resource theory has tended to be conducted primarily by the theory's originator. An independent test of the proposed processes further confirmed the critical hypothesis that leader intelligence is related to group performance as stress in the work setting is diminished.[14] Future research on the theory will likely be directed toward differentiating the impact of various types of stress (interpersonal, time-based, and so on) and the role of unique intellectual abilities in determining group performance.

Recent research by Robert Sternberg of Harvard has suggested that intelligence may be better conceptualized as comprising several major components (rather than being a single, unitary factor). In Sternberg's **triarchic model of intelligence,** intellectual functioning is viewed as consisting of analytical reasoning ability, social intelligence, and creativity.[15] Analytical reasoning refers to the ability to solve problems that have an abstract element. Problem solving that seeks to identify a single, correct answer exemplifies this ability. An individual who easily solves math problems can be said to have a high level of analytical reasoning ability. Analytical reasoning also includes the ability to use deductive thinking. Social intelligence refers to the ability to understand the motives and actions of others and to interact effectively with others. Individuals who possess relatively more social intelligence are expected to be capable of understanding and influencing others. Social intelligence is akin to what most of us refer to as "street smarts." Creativity refers to the ability to identify many possible solutions to a given problem. What is particularly novel about Sternberg's model is its suggestion that individuals who are especially able on any one dimension may not be regarded as effective if the setting in which they operate does not call for a specific cognitive ability. Hence, people who may be especially competent at analytical reasoning may be quite unsuccessful if they lack social intelligence in a setting that requires competency on this dimension.

---

* This argument is sometimes raised in political commentary to explain why the candidates for the presidency of the United States are usually not terribly intellectual (that is, a majority of the voting populace would have a difficult time identifying with an intellectual president).

Sternberg's model further implies that managerial jobs can be analyzed in terms of their requirements on the dimensions of analytical reasoning, social intelligence, and creativity, and that individuals can be assessed on these dimensions and "matched" to job requirements. For example, some jobs could require high levels of creativity and social intelligence and little analytical ability (for example, R&D and marketing research), while others might require high levels of analytical reasoning (for example, financial analysis). Managers could then be selected and developed based on their abilities across the three dimensions. To date, Sternberg has developed some reasonable measures of all three components, and these measures are available to industry. However, research on the optimal matching strategy has not yet been conducted. As suggested by Vecchio and others, Sternberg's work offers a promising new direction for research on managerial intelligence.[16]

Several other traits have also been linked to successful leaders. For example, Stogdill has argued that leaders can be characterized by task persistence, self-confidence, tolerance of interpersonal stress, and the ability to influence others' behavior.[17] One somewhat surprising finding is a low but positive correlation between leadership status and height, which suggests that taller individuals have something of an advantage in gaining leadership positions. This may reflect a desire on the part of many people to "look up" to their leaders.

Table 10.1 lists the traits and skills that have been frequently linked to effective leaders.[18] However, the usefulness of these traits as predictors of effectiveness depends to a large extent on the specific situation. One can conclude from the modest findings of the trait approach that the assumption that "leaders are born, not made" is not at all defensible. It appears that effective leadership

TABLE 10.1
ATTRIBUTES OF SUCCESSFUL LEADERS*

Traits	Physical Factors	Skills
Adaptable to situations	**Activity level**	**Conceptually skilled**
Alert to social environment	Appearance	Creative
Ambitious and achievement oriented	Height	Diplomatic and tactful
Assertive	Weight	Fluent in speaking
Cooperative		**Intelligent**
Decisive		**Knowledgeable about group task**
Dependable		
Dominant (desire to influence others)		Organized (administrative ability)
Persistent		Persuasive
Self-confident		Socially skilled
Tolerant of stress		
Willing to assume responsibility		

*Boldface attributes have the greatest association with leadership.
Source: G. Yukl, *Leadership in Organizations*, 1981, p. 70. Prentice-Hall Publishing Co., Englewood Cliffs, N.J.

depends less on the leader's predispositions than on how well the leader can adapt to the unique needs of different situations.

THEORY X AND THEORY Y   Another line of reasoning about the leadership process that has received significant attention is Douglas McGregor's suggestion that leaders differ in their underlying philosophy of management. These underlying assumptions are presumed to be related to effectiveness. Specifically, McGregor, working from Maslow's notions of a need hierarchy (see Chapter 6), offered a contrast between two distinct views of people, labeled **Theory X** and **Theory Y**.[19] The Theory X view of humankind assumes that employee behavior is directed toward lower-level, basic needs. Therefore, people are presumed to lack ambition, be passive, and prefer to be led. Moreover, people are assumed to dislike responsibility, be self-interested, and seek to avoid work. The Theory X view implies that managers should devote their energies to rewarding, punishing, and overseeing the behavior of employees. In contrast, Theory Y assumes that employee behavior is directed toward satisfying higher-order needs in Maslow's system. Hence, people are assumed to have ambition, seek greater responsibility, and be active. In this view, employees desire self-direction and can be trusted to perform their jobs. Within the Theory Y perspective, managers should involve employees in decision making and establish an atmosphere of trust and supportiveness. Figure 10.3 contrasts the assumptions defined by Theory X and Theory Y.

Little research has been conducted on the relative effectiveness of these two philosophical viewpoints. To be sure, managers do differ in their underlying philosophy of management (some are more trusting and open, while others are less so). However, hard evidence that espousing a particular philosophy is related to effectiveness is not available. Also, an individual's values are not always related to that individual's acts (see Chapter 4), as situational constraints also influence behavior. In recent years, McGregor's writings have come to be seen as outlining stereotypic views of workers. It is hard to make the case that all (or even most) employees are consistently passive or active, irresponsible or responsible, and so on. Instead, it is more widely accepted that employees have

FIGURE 10.3
ASSUMPTIONS OF THEORY X AND THEORY Y

Theory X assumes employees are:	Theory Y assumes employees are:
Passive	Active
Lacking ambition	Ambitious
Averse to responsibility	Desirous of responsibility
Willing to be led	Interested in self-control
Self-interested	Supportive of the organization
Aversive to work	Willing to work

the capacity to be responsible, trustworthy, and so on when treated in a manner that elicits and sustains such behavior (the converse is true as well). McGregor's work can be seen as underscoring certain prejudices that managers may hold (either pessimistic or optimistic) concerning employee values. Today, the assumptions outlined by Theory X seem archaic and very much out-of-step with current thinking. This is not to say that Theory X managers cannot still be found;[†] however, the dominant rhetoric in managerial circles, especially in larger firms, is decidedly more toward the Theory Y end of the continuum. Whether Theory X or Theory Y is in any sense a better viewpoint to adopt seems to depend heavily on the unique circumstances that confront an individual manager.

GENDER ISSUES   Most views of leadership have ignored the possibility that men and women may display different traits, values, or behaviors. As more women enter leadership positions, interest has increased regarding whether female managers are at a disadvantage relative to male managers. A comprehensive review by Eagly and Johnson of the available literature on male-female differences revealed that men and women tend to differ in their leadership styles.[20] Women are somewhat more democratic in their orientation, while men are somewhat more directive in their styles. The overlap between the two groups, however, is substantial, rendering the magnitude of these differences small. Also, comparisons of males and females on other leadership dimensions have not substantiated reliable and meaningful differences. In a review of the evidence, Gary Powell of the University of Connecticut observed that there is little reason to believe that either women or men will be superior in the role of manager, or that either group offers a distinctive type of management.[21] In short, both groups can produce superior, mediocre, and poor managerial performers, and the constructs that determine the success and failure of any manager are the same for both genders.[‡]

It is important to note, however, that because of their relatively recent entry in sizeable numbers to managerial ranks, and because of certain social dynamics, female managers do not often experience the same ease of entry and advancement afforded to males. For example, it has been observed that mentoring (a practice in which a senior manager helps a younger manager by offering advice and other forms of support) can be a significant aid in the advancement of a manager's career. Because many senior managers are male, and female managers tend to be younger, there is little opportunity for young female managers to find same-sex mentors. Crossing the "gender barrier" to find a mentor can be a problem for younger managers as there is a good deal of sensitivity surrounding the situation (both female and male managers fear

---

[†]McGregor believed that Theory X was the prevalent view among managers when he published his ideas in 1960.

[‡]Despite the limited evidence of male-female differences on leadership dimensions, it should not, of course, be inferred that there is no evidence whatsoever of sex differences in behavior. For some time, males have been found to be, in the aggregate, somewhat more aggressive, self-assertive, and rough in their manner and language than females, while females have been found to be more expressive of compassion and emotion than males.[22] However, the relevance of these differences to job behavior is minimal.

OB Focus
A New Approach to Executive Education

Many organizations take deliberate steps to develop top managers into effective leaders. Some large organizations send their top brass to elite business schools, such as Harvard, Stanford, and Columbia, for executive education programs. Many companies, however, are rethinking executive training. Traditional executive education programs are like mini-MBA programs that broaden the intellectual and analytical skills of executives by providing them courses in business basics. These programs have been criticized by some for focusing too much on improving analytical skills and not enough on producing inspiring leaders. In response to this criticism, innovative executive education programs are popping up across the country.

Some elite business schools offer short courses in executive development. Forty companies in Boston recently collaborated to develop executive education programs that were unavailable at local universities, and many business schools now customize courses to teach employees of a particular company.

Today, many companies want managers to focus more on managing and leading skills, and less on analytical skills. According to Frank Morgan, director of executive education at the University of Virginia's Darden School, "Leadership programs are growing fastest. It's a big change from five years ago. Now what's wanted are courses like the global perspective or the enterprise perspective."

As organizations change, leaders need the skills to bring people together to achieve a common purpose. Culture change is facilitated by strong leaders who move the organization and its members to the desired end. To do this, leaders often learn from other organizations. Leaders increasingly are looking to other companies that excel in a particular area for insight on how to achieve success. In

one of Darden's recent courses, "Creating the High-Performance Workplace," a Federal Express courier was brought in to discuss how FedEx managers make work enjoyable.

The Leadership Institute for Managers was the brainchild of Horace Parker, head of executive education at Weyerhauser, and James Bolt, former head of human resources planning at Xerox. The institute was created in response to a felt need for more customer-oriented executive training. Weyerhauser's top brass now spend two to four weeks in executive education, and customer satisfaction levels are beginning to rise as a result.

Organizations are realizing that learning is an ongoing process rather than a one-shot activity. Executive education is an important element in developing leaders who can face the challenges of the future.

Source: Brian O'Reilly, "How Execs Learn Now," *Fortune*, April 5, 1993, 52–58.

appearing to have a sexual relationship, which would compromise their credibility).[23] As an alternative to traditional senior-junior mentoring, it has been suggested that young female managers use peer relationships as the basis for career development.[24]

THE BEHAVIORAL APPROACH

As interest in the early trait approach to leadership began to decline, researchers focused their attention on leaders' actions rather than on their attributes. These studies of leader behavior tried to identify specific styles of leader conduct and attempted to discover whether leader behavior was associated with employee attitudes and performance.

UNIVERSITY OF IOWA LEADERSHIP STUDIES   Some of the earliest studies of leader behavior, conducted at The University of Iowa, addressed the question of whether a democratic style of leadership is more effective than an authoritarian or a laissez-faire style. To compare these styles of leadership in a controlled situation, Lewin, Lippett, and White randomly assigned 10-year-old boys to one of three groups involved in hobby activities after school hours.[25] In these groups, the boys did such things as make toy boats and papier-maché masks. Each group was under the direction of an adult who behaved in either a democratic, an authoritarian, or a laissez-faire style.

In the authoritarian condition, the adult leader assigned specific tasks to each individual, decided what was to be done without consulting the boys, assigned work partners, was subjective in his praise, and remained aloof from the group's activities. In contrast, the democratic leader allowed the group to decide who was to perform which task, permitted the boys to pick their own work partners, gave specific feedback on how to improve craftsmanship, and tried to be an involved member of the group. The laissez-faire leader was very detached from the group's activities. He gave the group members complete freedom to do what they wished and provided information only when he was specifically asked.

The boys' reactions were greatly influenced by the style of leadership to which they were subjected. Boys in the democratically led group were more satisfied and displayed less aggression toward one another than did boys in the autocratically led group. Although there was a slight tendency for the boys in the authoritarian setting to produce more items, judges rated the quality of output to be highest in the democratically led group. Another interesting finding from this study was that boys in the autocratically led group tended to stop working and engage in horseplay whenever the leader left the room.

It is possible to argue, however, that an autocratic style of leadership may not always be inappropriate. Sometimes a situation may call for urgent action, and in these cases an autocratic style of leadership may be best.[26] In addition, most people are familiar with autocratic leadership and, therefore, have less difficulty adopting that style. Furthermore, in some situations, subordinates may actually prefer an autocratic style. For example, a group of truckers may have difficulty respecting a truck dispatcher who tries to be participative rather than authoritarian in decision making.[27]

BALES'S INTERACTION PROCESS ANALYSIS SYSTEM   During the 1950s, researchers turned their attention to the behaviors that members exhibit in groups. R. F. Bales developed a system for coding the social interaction that occurs in groups. His system consists of 12 content categories within which the behaviors of group members are coded[28] (see Table 10.2). In using the system, two or more coders listen to a group discussion and code each individual's remarks into one of the categories. For example, member A might ask a question ("What do you think will happen if we don't complete this task in the time allotted?"), member B might offer an opinion ("It probably doesn't matter"), and member C might crack a joke (which would be coded as "tension release"). Although it may seem remarkable, all group discussion can be broken down into these 12 categories.

The use of Bales's system for groups that lacked a designated leader revealed some interesting findings. For example, some members tended to take on specific, identifiable roles within a group. That is, one member tended to make comments and show behaviors that fit mostly into the first six categories

TABLE 10.2

THE 12 CATEGORIES OF BALES' INTERACTION PROCESS ANALYSIS SYSTEMS

1. Shows solidarity; raises others' status; gives help, rewards
2. Shows tension release; jokes; laughs; shows satisfaction
3. Agrees; shows passive acceptance; understands; is concerned; complies
4. Disagrees; shows passive rejection; shows formality; withholds help
5. Shows tension; asks for help; withdraws out of field
6. Shows antagonism; deflates others' status; defends or asserts self
7. Gives suggestion or direction, implying autonomy for others
8. Gives opinion, evaluation, analysis; expresses feeling, wish
9. Gives orientation, information; repeats; clarifies; confirms
10. Asks for orientation, information, repetition, confirmation
11. Asks for opinions, evaluation, analysis, expression of feeling
12. Asks for suggestion, direction, possible ways of action

listed in Table 10.2, while another member tended to make comments and show behaviors that fit mostly into the last six categories. Still other members might be categorized as relatively unresponsive—they contributed little to the group discussion. The first six categories are concerned with socio-emotional issues, while the second six are largely concerned with accomplishing the group's given task. From these results, Bales concluded that groups have two roles that must be fulfilled for effective functioning: a task-oriented role and a socio-emotional role. In other words, groups need members to attend both to social relations maintenance issues and to task accomplishment issues. Of special interest is the finding that different members tend to emerge as socio-emotional leaders and task leaders. That is, a single individual rarely rises to occupy both roles. Such findings suggest that, for groups to be effective, they must have some attention shown to getting the job accomplished and helping to steer the group to meet its goals, as well as some attention to concerns for the feelings and welfare of members, and the social atmosphere within the group. In work groups, we would expect to find leaders expressing concern for both **task orientation** issues and **employee orientation** issues.[§]

OHIO STATE LEADERSHIP STUDIES   Although many researchers have studied these dimensions of leadership, one group of researchers at Ohio State University came to be noted for its efforts. These researchers proposed that consideration and initiating structure are two primary dimensions of leadership that parallel the styles of employee and task orientations. **Consideration** is defined as the extent to which the leader has job relationships that rely on mutual trust, respect for subordinates, and sensitivity to subordinates' feelings. **Initiat-**

[§]The pervasiveness of this need for groups to attend to the dual function of social issues and task issues has been suggested in cross-cultural research. Also, it has been suggested that one of the most basic social groups, the family, embodies these two functions in the traditional role definitions of mother (that is, the socio-emotional leader) and father (that is, the task leader).

ing structure is the extent to which a leader defines and structures the work that subordinates perform, with an eye toward successful task accomplishment.

These two dimensions of leader behavior are assumed to be independent of each other, so that a leader may possess either a high or a low predisposition toward each dimension. The combination of the two dimensions for an individual suggests that several different types of managers can be identified (Figure 10.4). Manager A in Figure 10.4 would be described as highly considerate of subordinates, while lacking a concern for employee production. Manager B, on the other hand, lacks concern for the feelings of employees but is moderately concerned with unit output. Manager C is apparently devoted to maximizing both production and employee well-being. This third case exemplifies what some see as an ideal style, in that it combines the best of both dimensions.

Research on the Ohio State dimensions of consideration and initiating structure has generated some interesting findings. Questionnaires completed by both subordinates and leaders (Table 10.3 provides a sample of the questions) showed that high consideration was related to lower rates of grievance filings and lower turnover. However, beyond a certain point, increases in supervisory considerateness did not appear to decrease turnover and grievances further. In addition, the study found that highly considerate leaders could structure work more without risking an increase in grievances and that supervisors can, to some extent, compensate for displaying a high degree of structure if they increase their considerateness. In contrast, supervisors who are low on considerateness cannot eliminate their negative impact by being less concerned with the creation of structure. Low considerateness apparently has a strong

FIGURE 10.4
THE OHIO STATE LEADERSHIP DIMENSIONS

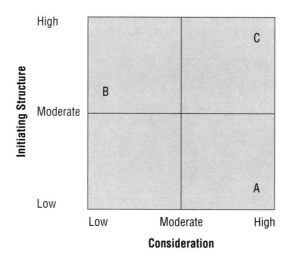

TABLE 10.3

SAMPLE QUESTIONS FROM A QUESTIONNAIRE USED IN OHIO STATE RESEARCH ON LEADER BEHAVIOR

How Frequently Does Your Leader Do Each of the Following?
Never, Seldom, Occasionally, Often, or Always?

Structure	Consideration
Lets work unit members know what is expected of them	Is friendly and approachable
Decides what shall be done and how it should be done	Puts suggestions made by the work unit into operation
Maintains definite standards for performance	Does little things to make it pleasant to be a member of the work unit

Source: R.M. Stogdill, 1963, *Manual for Leader Behavior Description Questionnaire—form XII.* Columbus, Ohio, Ohio State University Bureau of Business Research.

and persistent negative effect on relations with subordinates.[29] In addition, other research has rather consistently found that low considerateness is associated with employee dissatisfaction with supervisors.[30]

Although early results suggested that the combination of high consideration and high initiating structure constitutes the most successful managerial style, other studies have not corroborated this finding.[31]** Some researchers attempted to state the conditions under which consideration and structure are related to employee satisfaction and performance.[32] Their efforts suggest that many variables can affect the relationship between leader style and subordinate reactions. Table 10.4 lists a number of important subordinate, supervisor, and task variables that can have a moderating influence.

TABLE 10.4

VARIABLES FOUND TO MODERATE THE RELATIONSHIP BETWEEN LEADER BEHAVIOR AND OUTCOME

Subordinate Characteristics	Supervisor Characteristics	Task Characteristics
Expertise	Influence with superiors	Time urgency
Experience	Attitude similarity with superior	Physical danger
Competence	Similarity of behavior with higher management	External stress
Knowledge of job		Autonomy
Job level		Job scope
Expectations concerning the leader		Ambiguity
		Importance of task
		Meaningfulness of task
		Tolerable error rate

Source: Adapted from F. Landy and D. Trumbo, *Psychology of Work Behavior,* Homewood, Ill.: Dorsey, 1980.

** In fact, the early assumption that the high-consideration/high-structuring combination was optimal has come to be known as the "hi-hi myth."

THE MANAGERIAL GRID   Practicing managers have found the Ohio State dimensions of leadership to be an appealing concept. In fact, Robert Blake and Jane Mouton have adapted the Ohio State approach to a managerial training program that explains leadership styles in the context of a grid.[33] In their Managerial Grid, the various combinations of a concern for people and a concern for production define five major leadership styles (Figure 10.5) as follows:

1. *Authority/obedience management,* or a 9,1 style, emphasizes efficiency in operations that results from arranging work conditions in such a way that human elements can interfere only to a small degree.

2. *Country-club management,* or a 1,9 style, involves thoughtful attention to the needs of people, because such satisfying relationships are expected to lead to a comfortable, friendly organizational atmosphere.

3. *Laissez-faire or impoverished management,* or a 1,1 style, is characterized by minimal effort to get the required work done and sustain organization membership.

4. *Organization man management,* or a 5,5 style, is concerned with balancing the necessity to get the work out while maintaining morale at a satisfactory level. The goal is adequate performance.

5. *Team management,* or a 9,9 style, relies on interdependence through a common stake in the organization's purpose. This interdependence leads to

FIGURE 10.5
THE MANAGERIAL GRID

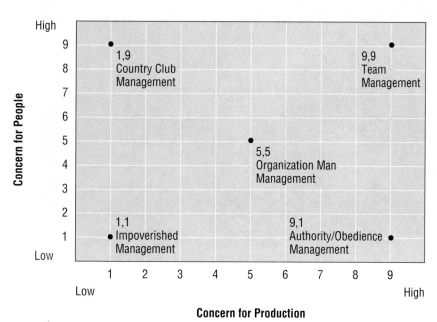

Source: R. Blake and J. Mouton, 1978, *The New Managerial Grid,* Houston: Gulf Publishing Co., p. 11.

relationships based on trust and respect, and work accomplishment from committed employees.

The Managerial Grid model assumes that there is one best or most effective style of management—the team management, or 9,9 style. Managers who emphasize both concern for people and productivity are presumed to be more successful. As mentioned earlier, however, the evidence for a single best style of management is not convincing.[††]

DIRECTIVE VERSUS PARTICIPATIVE LEADERSHIP In addition to socioemotional and task issues, the dimension of participative versus directive leadership has received a great deal of attention from behavioral researchers. Although participative leadership can be defined in many ways, all definitions incorporate the notion of power-sharing. Power-sharing can occur to varying degrees: from genuine control over the final decisions that are made, to providing input to the final decision, to consultation, to mere tokenism and the misuse of the term *participation* to manipulate others. Tannenbaum and Schmidt have suggested that participation and its complement, direction, are based on the amount of authority used by a superior in relation to the amount of freedom permitted to subordinates.[35] Their views can be represented on a continuum ranging from boss-centered leadership to subordinate-centered leadership. Figure 10.6 summarizes Tannenbaum and Schmidt's view of directive versus participative leadership.

FIGURE 10.6
DIRECTIVE VERSUS PARTICIPATIVE LEADERSHIP

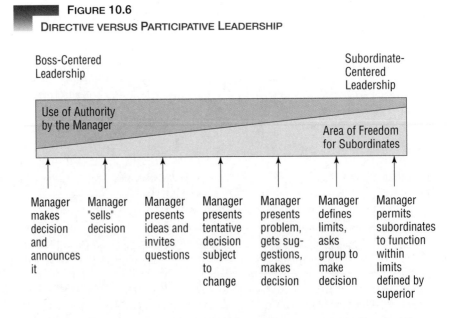

Source: Adapted from R. Tannenbaum and W. Schmidt, "How to Choose a Leadership Pattern," *Harvard Business Review* 36 (March–April, 1958), pp. 95–101. Reprinted by permission.

[††] In response to such evidence, however, Blake and Mouton offer conceptual rather than empirical arguments as to why the 9,9 style *should* work when conditions are favorable.[34]

Studies of the costs and benefits of participative versus directive leadership have not shown convincingly that either style of leadership is commonly superior. In some instances, the costs of employee participation may offset the benefits. In many other instances, however, participation is favored over directive leadership. For example, employee acceptance of decisions is generally greater following participative leadership. Also, employee job satisfaction, loyalty, and commitment tend to be much greater in settings that are more participative. However, a comprehensive review by Locke and Schweiger of the question of whether participation enhances productivity did not find clear support.[36] It seems that participation has the potential to affect performance favorably (see Chapter 7). However, the obstacles to effective implementation of genuine participation are substantial. Therefore, it is unlikely that productivity will be enhanced with a leader who simply engages in relatively participative actions.[‡‡]

CHARISMATIC LEADERSHIP   Some of the most fascinating research in the behavioral vein is being done on the quality of charisma. *Charisma* is a Greek word that refers to a divinely inspired gift (for example, being able to perform miracles or to predict the future). In the area of leadership, it refers to a type of social influence based on follower perceptions of the leader rather than on the leader's formal authority. **Charismatic leadership** is closest in meaning to the notion of referent power (see Chapter 9). Until recently, the topic has been discussed only in sociological and political contexts. In the 1980s, however, organizational researchers began to tackle the topic.

It is generally agreed that charismatic leaders exude self-confidence and a sense of purpose, and have the ability to articulate a view that subordinates are already likely to accept. Studies of identifiable charismatic individuals indicate that charismatic types often are rejecting of formal authority and willing to take personal risks because of their strong convictions.[37] Hence, charismatic leaders in formal organizational settings must be willing to accept the organization's primary norms, or face expulsion.

Although many researchers have assumed that charismatic leadership is exceedingly rare and not amenable to study, recent investigations have revealed that charismatic leadership can be found in all varieties of organizations (not-for-profit, large, small, volunteer, entrepreneurial, and so on) and at all levels within organizations. Also, the phenomenon has proven measurable. Perhaps the most widely used device for measuring charismatic leadership was developed by Bernard Bass and Bruce Avolio.[38] A respondent to their Scale of Charismatic Leadership is asked to indicate the extent to which "I have complete faith in him/her," "This person is a model for me to follow," "This person makes me proud to be associated with him/her," and "This person has a sense of mission that is transmitted to me." Research with the scale has found

---

[‡‡] In the following chapter, we will return to the issue of participative versus directive leadership and consider how situational factors can aid in deciding when to be more participative or directive.

An Inside Look
Tenneco's Determined Leader

CEO Mike Walsh took over Tenneco, a $13 billion faltering conglomerate of farm and construction equipment manufacturers, natural gas pipeline companies, shipbuilders, and other concerns, in September 1991. He immediately put into place plans to turn the conglomerate around, company by company, by streamlining operations, reducing capacity, eliminating thousands of jobs, and cutting 1992 expenses by $250 million. At the core of his fix-it strategy was "no-excuses management," an approach that required company executives to meet targeted goals, regardless of external economic forces.

In the midst of this massive reorganization, Walsh was diagnosed as having an inoperable form of brain cancer. Despite his uncertain prognosis, Walsh has continued at the helm, undergoing extensive radiation and chemotherapy treatments while engineering Tenneco's reorganization. By late 1993, Walsh had gained progress on both fronts. The company's value had nearly doubled since 1991, and Walsh's brain cancer had gone into remission.

Although Tenneco's reorganization is still under way, one of Walsh's goals has been to inspire in his employees the tenacity to confront challenges, as he has done over the years. Leaders, he says, must create an encouraging environment to motivate people. Good leaders can find employees who share their desire for change and capitalize on their shared vision. Just as important, says Walsh, leaders must make themselves visible and accessible. CEOs have to be on the front line, where the real problems occur, so that employees can see the leader's commitment to change. Organizational restructuring requires employees to adopt the organizational vision and take responsibility to help the organization achieve its goals. According to Walsh, all employees must see themselves as mini-CEOs by identifying what needs to be done and then executing a plan to accomplish the change.

Trying to break through the bureaucracy at Tenneco hasn't been easy. But Walsh's swift actions and lofty performance expectations have generated enough momentum to have a major impact on the bottom line. Debt-to-capital ratio has been cut by more than 20 points and operating earnings are up by $1.1 billion. These numbers represent a substantial turnaround over a short period of time. In more ways than one, Mike Walsh is blazing a determined path to recovery.

Sources: "A Master Class in Radical Change," *Fortune,* December 13, 1993, 82–40; Wendy Zellner, "The Fight of His Life," *Business Week,* September 20, 1993, 54–64.

that charismatic leaders are rated more highly on their effectiveness as leaders, and have subordinates who are more highly satisfied with their leadership.

More recently, Bass has introduced the distinction between transactional leadership and transformational leadership.[39] **Transactional leadership** refers to the everyday exchanges that take place between leaders and subordinates as they routinely perform their duties. Such exchanges are based on the offer of contingent rewards for specific performance. **Transformational leadership,** a broader concept than charisma, implies reshaping entire strategies of an organization (although the terms *charisma* and *transformational leadership* overlap to a great extent in highlighting the influence of a leader's personal attributes and the trust of followers). Transformational leadership elevates the goals of subordinates and enhances their self-confidence to strive for higher goals. Bass contends that transformational leadership is potentially strongest at the highest levels of management. Bass's view underscores the importance of vision, intellectual stimulation, and individualized consideration in leadership, and the major role that leadership can have during times of change and crisis. However, the research base in this area is not as well established as in other domains of leadership. Therefore, practical applications of the features of transformational and charismatic leadership cannot as yet be offered.

The phenomenon of charismatic leadership also has its "dark side." Although we can identify instances of positive charismatic leadership (for example, Franklin Roosevelt, John F. Kennedy, Lee Iacocca, and Mahatma Gandhi), we can also identify instances of charismatic leadership that were clearly negative in their consequences (for example, Adolph Hitler, Reverend Jim Jones, and David Koresh). One suggested measure for determining whether charismatic leadership is positive or negative is to examine whether charismatic leaders intentionally try to create devotion to themselves among their followers, rather than commitment to ideological principles.[40] The "dark side" of charisma is typically revealed by efforts that encourage devotion to self. In such cases, ideological principles eventually become vehicles for enhancing personal devotion and power. Positive charismatics focus on enhancing follower commitment to ideological principles, and sometimes actively avoid excessive limelight. Because of the difference in these basic goals, the two types of charismatic leadership have differing consequences for followers (follower enhancement versus follower destruction). Furthermore, it is possible that some negative charismatics begin as positive charismatics (initially placing ideology ahead of personal goals), but eventually are seduced by the experience of self-glorification.

There is reason to believe that early childhood experiences may predispose people to be negative charismatics.[41] Specifically, people whose parents were rejecting and emotionally unresponsive may develop beliefs that others cannot be depended upon for support. As a consequence of such emotional deprivation, these individuals develop narcissistic preoccupations concerning the attainment of prestige and success, along with an exaggerated sense of self-worth. Human relationships are simplified into good/bad or friend/enemy dichotomies, and real or imagined slights are interpreted as evidence of serious disloyalty. The narcissistic personality base serves as the foundation for undertaking self-glorifying projects in which personal credit is accumulated for any positive accomplishments and blame is fixed on others for any shortcomings.

TYING IT ALL TOGETHER: A TAXONOMY OF LEADER TRAIT AND BEHAVIORAL ASPECTS

We have considered a number of perspectives for characterizing leaders in terms of trait and behavioral differences. Although these views of leadership seem disjointed, they have a number of common features. Table 10.5 lists the major elements of the ten models covered in this chapter. A comparison of the terms used in each model reveals a considerable degree of convergence. The models often use different terminology to describe essentially similar features of leadership. For example, the Ohio State University and the University of Iowa studies, plus the work of Bales and Katz, all identify a consideration/socio-emotional dimension to leadership. Similarly, a task/structuring dimension can be deduced across most of the models. In fact, we can develop our own meta-model of leadership by creating an integrative taxonomy that highlights the common features of the various models. Table 10.6 provides this general taxonomy of leadership. Our meta-model identifies six commonly

TABLE 10.5

A COMPARISON OF 10 MAJOR MODELS OF LEADERSHIP

	Trait Theory	Cognitive Resource Theory	Sternberg's Triarchic Model	Katz	University of Iowa	Ohio State University	Bales	Tannenbaum and Schmidt	McGregor	Charismatic
Concern for inter-personal relations	Socially skilled	—	Social intelligence	Human skills	Democratic style	Consideration	Socio-emotional orientation	Participative	Theory Y	Compelling vision
Concern for task accomplishment	Task expertise	Leader experience	Creativity	Technical skills	—	Initiating structure	Task orientation	—	—	—
Conceptual-analytical skills	Intelligent	Leader intelligence	Analytical reasoning	Conceptual skills	—	—	—	—	—	—
Self-confidence	Self-confident	—	—	—	—	—	—	—	—	Self-confident, sense of purpose
Desire to be directive	Socially dominant	—	—	—	Autocratic style	—	—	Directive	Theory X	—
High energy level	High activity level	—	—	—	Laissez-faire	—	—	—	—	Vigor

TABLE 10.6
A TAXONOMY OF EFFECTIVE LEADERSHIP

1. Concern with interpersonal relations
2. Concern for task accomplishment
3. Conceptual-analytical skills
4. Self-confidence and sense of purpose
5. Desire to be directive
6. High energy level

cited aspects of leadership: (1) concern for interpersonal relations, (2) concern for task accomplishment, (3) conceptual-analytical skills, (4) self-confidence and a sense of purpose, (5) a desire to be directive, and (6) a high energy level. Any complete characterization of the leadership process should be mindful of these aspects of leadership. In the following chapter, we will examine additional models that seek to explain leadership by introducing situational variables. These models, however, often will draw from the components of the general taxonomy of leadership that we have just developed, and seek to specify the conditions in which one should be relatively more or less directive, relatively concerned with interpersonal relations, and so on.

SUMMARY

1. Define leadership.

Leadership is a process through which a person tries to get organizational members to do something the person desires. The leader's influence extends beyond supervisory responsibility and formal authority.

2. List some attributes that are associated with leadership.

Table 10.1 shows attributes that have been associated with successful leaders. Those having the strongest association are the desire to influence others, self-confidence, high activity level, intelligence, and knowledge of the group's task.

3. Describe ways in which leader behavior is related to employee attitudes and performance.

A democratic leadership style may lead to greater employee satisfaction and higher-quality output. Autocratic leadership may lead to a greater quantity of output, accompanied by decreased quality and employee satisfaction. Up to a point, high consideration for the employee may be related to employee satisfaction, and low consideration may lead to employee dissatisfaction. Both the Ohio State and the Managerial Grid models presume that the most successful managers emphasize concern for both people and productivity.

4. Explain the importance of leadership.

Leadership has been shown to make a difference in the performance of groups and organizations. Studies of the impact of changing leaders reveal that the performance of poorly performing groups can be enhanced. Excessive turnover of leaders, however, can be detrimental to unit performance.

5. Explain why some people seek leadership positions.

John Miner's research on individual motivation to manage shows that successful managers must (1) be able to maintain good working relations with authority figures, (2) desire to compete for recognition and rewards, (3) be assertive, (4) want to exercise influence over subordinates, and (5) be willing to stay on top of routine administrative tasks. These aspects of the motivation to manage are especially relevant to success in hierarchical-bureaucratic organizations.

6. Identify three major approaches to studying leadership.

Three major approaches to the study of leadership are the trait approach (which seeks to identify traits and skills that distinguish superior leaders), the behavioral approach (which examines what effective leaders actually do in their positions), and the situational approach (which focuses on the role of contextual factors in determining optimal leader style).

7. Compare and contrast the major models of leader traits and behaviors.

The ten major models of leadership (trait theory, cognitive resource theory, the triarchic model, Katz's skill model, University of Iowa view, Ohio State University view, Bales's dual-orientation view, Tannenbaum and Schmidt's directive-participative model, Theory X–Theory Y, and the charismatic leadership view) can be understood to have six common themes. The six themes, which constitute effective leadership are: concern for interpersonal relations, concern for task accomplishment, conceptual-analytical skill, self-confidence and a sense of purpose, desire to be directive, and a high energy level.

KEY TERMS

Leadership
Informal leader
Motivation to manage
Paradigm
Cognitive resource theory
Triarchic model of intelligence
Theory X

Theory Y
Task orientation
Employee orientation
Initiating structure
Consideration
Charismatic leadership

REVIEW AND DISCUSSION QUESTIONS

1. Contrast the roles of leader and manager. Is the manager of a group always its leader?

2. What are some attributes of an effective leader? Are these traits clearly related to successful leadership? Can a person without these attributes be a leader?

3. Explain the terms *consideration* and *initiating structure*. What is typically considered the optimal combination of these characteristics? Is this conclusion well founded?

4. Prepare a debate on the opposing points of view that (a) leadership is of no consequence to group performance versus (b) leadership is of great importance in determining group performance.

5. Research on the advancement of women in managerial ranks suggests that a "glass ceiling" may operate that makes top-level advancement especially difficult. What are the issues surrounding the advancement of women to top-level positions?

6. Why do some people deliberately avoid managerial responsibility? What does research suggest about those who seek to attain leadership positions?

7. What are the major shortcomings of the trait approach and the behavioral approach to the study of leadership?

8. Can an individual deliberately try to be a charismatic leader? What are the preconditions for the existence of charismatic leadership?

CRITICAL INCIDENT

Hal's Halo

Hal Baines has been employed by IFP Financial Services Corporation for more than ten years. Two years ago he was promoted to unit supervisor. Hal has always been a very loyal employee and has worked hard to follow and support the company's policies and procedures. In talking with any of Hal's superiors, one gets the impression that he is well liked and viewed as an asset to the organization.

Because employee dissatisfaction has become more pronounced in Hal's unit, you have been asked to assess the situation. In private talks with his employees, you discover that they think Hal is consumed with the desire to please upper-level management. They don't feel he "goes to bat" for the unit. For example, at each of the past two budget hearings, their department has received little or no increase. Also, whenever new ideas or suggestions from one of the employees are given to Hal to pass on, nothing ever comes of them. This has resulted in frustration and a general feeling of being unappreciated. Finally, whenever a request is made of Hal's department, regardless of whatever else is being done, Hal always promises to get it done immediately. This has meant additional work and long hours without compensation or recognition for many employees.

As the consultant, how would you address the following questions?

1. In terms of the leadership theories discussed in this chapter, how would you portray Hal's leadership style?

2. If you met with Hal right now, what advice or suggestions would you offer to alter his style of leadership?

3. Do you think a leadership skills training program would be helpful to Hal? If so, what should it consist of?

Source: Written by Bruce Kemelgor.

EXPERIENTIAL EXERCISE

Your Leadership Style

Transactional leadership is characterized by low-emotion, uninspirational leader-follower exchanges. Transactional leadership induces followers to achieve routine, agreed-upon performance, but not aspire to higher goals. Transformational leadership, on the other hand, inspires followers to elevate their performance goals. The leader instills confidence in followers through charisma, inspiration, intellectual stimulation, and individualized consideration.

The following leadership questionnaire assesses your personal propensity for transformational or transactional leader style. It will help you develop an understanding of leadership characteristics and aid your understanding of the similarities and differences in leadership styles and types of leaders.

For each of the following ten pairs of statements, divide five points between the two according to your beliefs or your perceptions of yourself, or according to which of the two statements better characterizes you. The five points may be divided between the A and B statements in any way you wish with the constraint that only whole positive integers may be used (that is, you may not split 2.5 points equally between the two).

1.___ A. As a leader, I have a primary mission of maintaining stability.
   ___ B. As a leader, I have a primary mission of change.

2.___ A. As a leader, I must cause events.
   ___ B. As a leader, I must facilitate events.

3.___ A. I am concerned that my followers are rewarded equitably for their work.
   ___ B. I am concerned about what my followers want in life.

4.___ A. My preference is to think long range: What might be.
   ___ B. My preference is to think short range: What is realistic.

5.___ A. As a leader, I spend considerable energy in managing separate but related goals.
   ___ B. As a leader, I spend considerable energy in arousing hopes, expectations, and aspirations among my followers.

6.___ A. While not in a formal classroom sense, I believe that a significant part of my leadership is that of teacher.
   ___ B. I believe that a significant part of my leadership is that of facilitator.

7.___ A. As a leader, I must engage with followers at an equal level of morality.
   ___ B. As a leader, I must represent a higher morality.

8.___ A. I enjoy stimulating followers to want to do more.
   ___ B. I enjoy rewarding followers for a job well done.

9.___ A. Leadership should be practical.
   ___ B. Leadership should be inspirational.

10.___ A. What power I have to influence others comes primarily from my ability to get people to identify with me and my ideas.

___ B. What power I have to influence others comes primarily from my status and position.

SCORING KEY

Transformational Your Point(s):	**Transactional** Your Point(s):
1. B_____	1. A_____
2. A_____	2. B_____
3. B_____	3. A_____
4. A_____	4. B_____
5. B_____	5. A_____
6. A_____	6. B_____
7. B_____	7. A_____
8. A_____	8. B_____
9. B_____	9. A_____
10. A_____	10. B_____

Column Totals: _____   _____

The higher column total indicates that you agree more with, and see yourself more like, either a transformational leader or a transactional leader.

Source: Experiential Exercise created by W. Warner Burke, Ph.D. In John R. Schermerhorn, James G. Hunt, and Richard N. Osborn, *Managing Organizational Behavior*, Fifth Edition. Copyright 1994 by John Wiley and Sons, Inc. Reprinted by permission of John Wiley & Sons, Inc.

NOTES

1. B.M. Bass, *Bass and Stogdill's Handbook of Leadership,* 3rd ed. (New York: Free Press, 1990).

2. W.G. Wagner, J. Pfeffer, and C.A. O'Reilly, "Organizational Demography and Turnover in Top-Management Groups," *Administrative Science Quarterly* 29 (1984): 74–92; K.B. Schwartz and K. Menon, "Executive Succession in Failing Firms," *Academy of Management Journal* 28 (1985): 680–686.

3. G.R. Salancik, B.M. Staw, and L.R. Pondy, "Administrative Turnover as a Response to Unmanaged Organizational Independence," *Academy of Management Journal* 10 (1980): 422–437.

4. S. Lieberson and J.F. O'Connor, "Leadership and Organizational Performance: A Study of Large Corporations," *American Sociological Review* 37 (1972): 117–130; N. Weiner and T.A. Mahoney, "A Model of Corporate Performance as a Function of Environmental, Organizational, and Leadership Influences," *Academy of Management Journal* 24 (1981): 453–470; G.R. Salancik and J. Pfeffer, "Constraints on Administrator Discretion: The Limited Influence of Mayors on City Budgets," *Urban Affairs Quarterly* 12 (1977): 475–498; D. Miller, "Some Organizational Consequences of CEO Succession," *Academy of Management Journal* 36 (1993): 644–659; A. Cannella and M. Lubatkin, "Succession as a Sociopolitical Process: Internal Impediments to Outsider Selection," *Academy of Management Journal* 36 (1993): 763–793; S. Friedman and K. Saul, "A Leader's Wake: Organization Member Reactions to CEO Succession," *Journal of Management* 17 (1991): 619–642; D. Hambrick and G. Fukutomi, "The Seasons of a CEO's Tenure," *Academy of Management Review* 16 (1991): 719–742.

5. R. Stewart, *Managers and Their Jobs: A Study of the Similarities and Differences in the Ways Managers Spend Their Time* (London: Macmillan, 1967).

6. H. Mintzberg, "The Manager's Job: Folklore and Fact," *Harvard Business Review* 53 (July–August 1975): 49–61; H. Mintzberg, *The Nature of Managerial Work* (New York: Harper and Row, 1973).

7. D.L. Marples, "Studies of Managers—A Fresh Start," *Journal of Management Studies* 4 (1967): 282–299.

8. J.B. Miner, "Student Attitudes Toward Bureaucratic Role Prescriptions and the Prospects for Managerial Shortages," *Personnel Psychology* 27 (1974): 605–613; J.B. Miner, "Twenty Years of Research on Role Motivation Theory of Managerial Effectiveness," *Personnel Psychology* 31 (1978): 739–760.

9. Bass, *Handbook of Leadership,* 554.

10. R.M. Stogdill, "Personal Factors Associated with Leadership: A Survey of the Literature," *Journal of Psychology* 25 (1948): 35–71.

11. R.M. Stogdill, *Handbook of Leadership* (Glencoe, Ill.: Free Press, 1975); Bass, *Handbook of Leadership.*

12. E. Ghiselli, *Exploration in Managerial Talent* (Santa Monica, Calif.: Goodyear, 1971).

13. F.E. Fiedler and J.E. Garcia, *New Approaches to Effective Leadership* (New York: John Wiley and Sons, 1987); F.E. Fiedler, "The Contribution of Cognitive Resources and Behavior to Leadership Performance" (Paper presented at the Annual Meeting of the Academy of Management, Boston, Mass., 1984); F.E. Fiedler and A.F. Leister, "Leader Intelligence and Task Performance: A Test of a Multiple Screen Model," *Organizational Behavior and Human Performance* 20 (1977): 1–14; J. Blades, "The Influence of Intelligence, Task Ability, and Motivation on Group Performance" (Ph.D. diss., University of Washington, 1976); R.P. Vecchio, "Cognitive Resource Theory: Successor to the 'Black Box' Model of Leadership," *Contemporary Psychology* 33 (1988): 1030–1032.

14. R.P. Vecchio, "A Theoretical and Empirical Examination of Cognitive Resource Theory," *Journal of Applied Psychology* 75 (1990): 141–147.

15. R.K. Wagner and R.J. Sternberg, "Street Smarts," in *Measures of Leadership,* eds. K.E. Clark and M.B. Clark (West Orange, N.J.: Leadership Library of America, 1990).

16. Vecchio, "A Theoretical and Empirical Examination of Cognitive Resource Theory.

17. Stogdill, *Handbook of Leadership.*

18. G. Yukl, *Leadership in Organizations* (Englewood Cliffs, N.J.: Prentice-Hall, 1981).

19. D. McGregor, *The Human Side of Enterprise* (New York: McGraw-Hill, 1960).

20. A.H. Eagly and B.T. Johnson, "Gender and Leadership Style: A Meta-analysis, " *Psychological Bulletin* 108 (1990): 233–256; A. Eagly, M. Makhijani, and B. Klonsky, "Gender and the Evaluation of Leaders: A Meta-analysis," *Psychological Bulletin* 111 (1992): 3–22.

21. G.N. Powell, "One More Time: Do Female and Male Managers Differ?" *Academy of Management Executive* 4 (1990): 68–75.

22. L.M. Terman and C.C. Miles, *Sex and Personality: Studies on Masculinity and Femininity* (New York: McGraw-Hill, 1936); M.E. Shaw, *Group Dynamics* (New York: McGraw-Hill, 1971).

23. R.A. Noe, "Women and Mentoring: A Review and Research Agenda," *Academy of Management Review* 13 (1988): 65–78.

24. K.E. Kram and L.A. Isabella, "Alternatives to Mentoring: The Role of Peer Relationships in Career Development," *Academy of Management Journal* 28 (1985): 110–132.

25. K. Lewin, R. Lippitt, and R.K. White, "Patterns of Aggressive Behavior in Experimentally Created Social Climates," *Journal of Social Psychology* 10 (1939): 271–301.

26. B. Bass, *Leadership, Psychology, and Organizational Behavior* (New York: Harper and Row, 1960); C. Gibb, "Leadership," in *The Handbook of Social Psychology,* 2d ed., eds. G. Lindzey and E. Aronson, 5 vols. (Reading, Mass.: Addison-Wesley, 1969), 4:205–282.

27. V.H. Vroom and F.C. Mann, "Leader Authoritarianism and Employee Attitudes," *Personnel Psychology* 13 (1960): 125–140.

28. R.F. Bales, "The Equilibrium Problem in Small Groups," in *Working Papers on the Theory in Action,* ed. T. Parson, R.F.

Bales, and E.A. Shills (Glencoe, Ill.: Free Press, 1953).

29. E.A. Fleishman and E.F. Harris, "Patterns of Leadership Behavior Related to Employee Grievance and Turnover," *Personnel Psychology* 15 (1962): 43–56.

30. Stogdill, *Handbook of Leadership;* Yukl, *Leadership in Organizations.*

31. L.L. Larson, J.G. Hunt, and R. Osburn, "The Great Hi-Hi Leader Behavior Myth: A Lesson from Occam's Razor," *Academy of Management Journal* 19 (1976): 628–641.

32. S. Kerr, C.A. Schriesheim, C.J. Murphy et al., "Toward a Contingency Theory of Leadership Based upon the Consideration and Initiating Structure Literature," *Organizational Behavior and Human Performance* 12 (1974): 62–82; Stogdill, *Handbook of Leadership;* Yukl *Leadership in Organizations.*

33. R.R. Blake and J.S. Mouton, *The New Managerial Grid* (Houston: Gulf Publishing Co., 1978).

34. R.R. Blake and J.S. Mouton, "A Comparative Analysis of Situationalism and 9,9 Management by Principle," *Organizational Dynamics* 24 (Spring 1982): 21.

35. R. Tannenbaum and W.H. Schmidt, "How to Choose a Leadership Pattern," *Harvard Business Review* 36 (1958): 95–101.

36. E.A. Locke and D.M. Schweiger, "Participation in Decision Making: One More Look," in *Research in Organizational Behavior,* vol. 1, eds. B. Staw and L.L. Cummings (Greenwich, Conn.: JAI Press, 1979).

37. L.K. Hall, "Charisma: A Study of Personality Characteristics of Charismatic Leaders." (Ph.D. diss., University of Georgia, Athens (1983); J.A. Conger and R.N. Kanungo,

"Behavioral Dimensions of Charismatic Leadership," in *Charismatic Leadership: The Elusive Factor in Organizational Effectiveness,* eds. J.A. Conger and R.N. Kanungo (San Francisco: Jossey-Bass, 1988); J.A. Conger and R.N. Kanungo, "Toward a Behavioral Theory of Charismatic Leadership in Organizational Settings," *Academy of Management Journal* 12 (1987): 637–647; R. House, W.D. Spangler, and J. Woycke, "Personality and Charisma in the U.S. Presidency: A Psychological Theory of Leader Effectiveness," *Administrative Science Quarterly* 36 (1991): 364–396.

38. B.M. Bass, *The Multifactor Leadership Questionnaire—Form 5* (Binghamton: State University of New York, 1985); B.M. Bass and B.J. Avolio, "Phototypicality, Leniency, and Generalized Response Set in Rated and Ranked Transformational and Transactional Leadership Descriptions," Binghamton State University of New York Center for Leadership Studies, Report Series 88-2, (1988).

39. B.M. Bass, "Policy Implications of Transformational Leadership," in *Research in Organizational Change and Development,* eds. R.W. Woodman and W.A. Pasmore (Greenwich, Conn.: JAI Press, 1988); J.M. Burns, *Leadership* (New York: Harper and Row, 1978).

40. S.J. Musser, "The Determination of Positive and Negative Charismatic Leadership" (Unpublished paper, Grantham, Penn.: Messiah College).

41. M.R. Kets de Vries and D. Miller, *The Neurotic Organization: Diagnosing and Changing Counter-productive Styles of Management* (San Francisco: Jossey-Bass, 1984); M.R. Kets de Vries and D. Miller, "Narcissism and Leadership: An Object-relations Perspective," *Human Relations* 38 (1985): 583–601.

The President doesn't want any yes-men and yes-women around him. When he says no, we all say no.
— Elizabeth Dole

Charlatanism is to some degree indispensable to effective leadership.
— Eric Hoffer

We have, I fear, confused power with greatness.
— Stewart Udall

LEARNING OBJECTIVES

After studying this chapter, you should be able to:

1. *Identify the factors underlying situational favorableness and explain how they influence a leader's effectiveness.*

2. *Explain how leaders can clarify paths to goals to motivate employees.*

3. *Describe the components of subordinate maturity and the relevance of subordinate maturity to leadership style.*

4. *Describe the decision-making styles of the Vroom–Yetton model and explain how to use a decision tree to select the appropriate style.*

5. *Describe a way to evaluate leadership style taking into account managers' views of different employees.*

6. *Identify similarities and differences among the major situational leadership models.*

7. *Define leadership substitute and leadership neutralizer and give examples of each.*

8. *Offer some major reasons why managers fail.*

9. *Explain how you would manage the leadership process.*

HOW TO MANAGE A COMPANY'S CREATIVES

One of an organization's most important assets is found in the minds of those who create the company's products and services. All organizations have a nucleus of creative talent whose jobs are to create the product the organization markets. Creatives, as these imaginative powerhouses are called, are self-motivated and thrive on ambiguity and risk. Whether it's software engineers at Microsoft, greeting card designers at Hallmark, or R&D scientists at Du Pont, organizations may need to manage these people in a completely different way, and can help focus their energies by embracing the following rules.

- **Accommodate.** Ideas can pop into the minds of creatives at any hour of any day. The creative may stare out an office window all day, then awake suddenly that night from a deep sleep with a brilliant idea. Managers need to realize that these people have creative surges and droughts, and give them some creative slack. Managers may also need to let them redefine their jobs. A former director of R&D at Du Pont would not write progress reports or speak to his peers. His supervisor tried, without success, to modify his behavior. Because he was

such a valuable resource, Du Pont adjusted to accommodate his style of work. Supervisors must also be supportive of creatives. Even the most invigorating thinkers come up with more bad ideas than good ones. Failure is a necessary side effect of the creative's endeavors, and supervisors must nurture them through good times and bad.

- **Stimulate.** Hallmark's staff of more than 600 artists, writers, and designers are the self-proclaimed largest creative staff in the world. Hallmark management has introduced a variety of novel approaches to enhance creativity. Writers and artists are sent to intriguing destinations to stimulate creative energies and consider how the ambiance of their surroundings can be reproduced in a greeting card. And employees are treated to some 20 speakers a year to stimulate their creative abilities. Creative juices often flow readily during lunch among a group of employees in physical research at Bell Labs, as scientists gather to scribble down ideas on napkins in the company cafeteria.

- **Recognize and reward.** Traditional rewards may be less invigorating to creative employ-

ees than less tangible rewards, such as recognition and autonomy. Creatives are self-starters who thrive on freedom, self-expression, and the ability to see their ideas carried out by the organization. Financial rewards may be secondary to the nontangible rewards creatives value. But increasingly, organizations will need to reward creatives for their innovative developments or risk other organizations luring creatives away with a bigger paycheck and the same opportunities for autonomy and self-expression.

- **Give feedback.** Creatives learn a lot by understanding how their products are used in the marketplace. Software writers at Lotus Development meet with customers to learn more about their preferences and desires. Software architects at Microsoft observe individuals using new software from behind a one-way mirror, so that they can see firsthand what difficulties the user has with the new software.

- **Offer protection.** Some members of the organization may not understand the idiosyncrasies or apparent aloofness of creatives. Managers may need to explain the peculiarities of

(continued on following page)

(continued from previous page)
creatives to prevent antagonism and jealousy from disrupting employee relations.

- **Share creativity.** Many jobs in an organization could use a spark of creativity. Hallmark enrolled 80 of its executives in its creative leadership course, which required them to design and produce a line of greeting cards. Experiencing firsthand the pressures of spontaneous creativity gave executives a better appreciation of the creative's job demands.

Clearly, the creative resources of any company can be its competitive advantage. Poorly managed, creatives can quickly walk out the door and find employment with a competitor. If properly managed, creativity can become contagious throughout the organization, resulting in improved individual and organizational performance.

By its very nature, leadership is not a static activity. Various situations require different leadership responses. This chapter considers situations in which the traits of good leadership may vary or take second place to other considerations.

Source: Alan Farnham, "How to Nurture Creative Sparks," *Fortune*, January 10, 1994, 94–100.

In the previous chapter, we learned that the behavioral approach to leadership was fairly popular into the mid-1960s, at which time there was a growing recognition that leadership could not be explained solely in terms of leader behavior, and that features of the context in which leadership occurred (for example, subordinate and task attributes) also needed to be examined in order to gain a more complete and accurate understanding of leadership. In this chapter, we will examine a number of different leadership models that explicitly consider situational attributes.

SITUATIONAL APPROACHES

FIEDLER'S CONTINGENCY MODEL

Fred Fiedler was one of the earliest proponents of a leadership model that explicitly incorporated situational features. The underlying assumption of his **contingency model of leadership effectiveness** is that group performance is a function of the combination of a leader's style and several relevant features of the situation.[1]

Within the model, leadership style and the situation are defined with a high degree of precision. Leadership style is assessed with a semantic differential attitude scale (see Chapter 4) that measures esteem for the **least preferred coworker**, or **LPC**. The scale asks that a person describe the coworker, past or present, with whom he or she has had the most difficulty working. Sample items from the scale are:

Pleasant :	_ : _ : _ : _ : _ : _ : _ : _	: Unpleasant
	8 7 6 5 4 3 2 1	
Helpful :	_ : _ : _ : _ : _ : _ : _ : _	: Frustrating
	8 7 6 5 4 3 2 1	
Warm :	_ : _ : _ : _ : _ : _ : _ : _	: Cold
	8 7 6 5 4 3 2 1	

An Inside Look
Coaching Leadership Skills

Modern companies expect their employees to work harder, produce more, and work interdependently. To accomplish these goals, managers and their employees need to establish solid working relationships. It is no wonder then that many companies are using the services of executive coaches to improve the communication and managerial skills of promising executives.

Among the major companies contracting the services of an executive coach are American Express, AT&T, Citibank, Colgate, Levi Strauss, Northern Telecom, and Proctor and Gamble. The job of an executive coach, simply enough, is to improve an executive's managerial and communication skills. Many managers have ascended to their current positions because of their technical expertise. Many players, as the managers being coached are known, are dedicated and ambitious, but their difficulties in getting along

with others limit their opportunities for further advancement.

Most players fall into one of two categories. The first is often a white, middle-aged man with outstanding technical skills who has recently been promoted to a position in which he now deals with people of diverse abilities. His management style is characterized by shouting, interrupting others while they speak, and making employees feel uncomfortable in his presence. The second archetype is a woman, about a decade younger then her male counterpart, whose hard work and dedication have allowed her to scale the organizational hierarchy. She's now at a new managerial level, where she perceives male chauvinism to operate, and she lacks the acumen of the old-boy network. She deliberately limits her interaction with others in the company.

Rather than simply firing these interpersonal messes, many organizations have decided to

build on their investments in employees through the intervention of an executive coach. Moreover, the technical expertise of these employees makes them valuable assets to their organizations.

Executive coaches adopt different philosophies and techniques to get their players to overcome their limitations, ranging from drilling communication skills in the same way an athlete learns a game, to pseudo-psychoanalysis in which the coach uncovers deep-rooted problems that fuel the players' dysfunctional behaviors.

Regardless of the methodology chosen, long-lasting behavioral change is less likely to occur if the manager does not receive reinforcements for changed behaviors. Without continual reinforcers, the player will eventually revert to old behaviors, and the organization will continue to suffer the consequences of dysfunctional interpersonal behaviors.

Source: Lee Smith, "The Executive's New Coach," *Fortune*, December 27, 1993, 126–134.

A person who completes the LPC scale by giving relatively lenient responses receives a fairly high total score, while a person who gives harsh marks will obtain a relatively low score. Fiedler infers that people who attain high LPC scores are motivated to achieve positive social relations in their work groups. People with low LPC scores are judged to be less relationship-oriented and more satisfied by task accomplishment. In short, high-LPC individuals are more relationship-motivated, while low-LPC types are more task-motivated. Clearly, Fiedler's LPC notion borrows heavily from the behavioral approach to leadership.

Actual work situations are multifaceted. To describe them, Fiedler proposed a single, broad definition of a critical situational dimension (favorableness) and several specific underlying attributes that define this larger dimension. According to his model, situations differ in terms of how favorable they are for a leader. **Situational favorableness,** therefore, is a broad notion of how easy or difficult a setting might seem to be for a manager.

Three factors are believed to underlie situational favorableness. In order of relative importance, they are (1) leader–member relations, (2) task structure, and (3) position power.

Leader–member relations reflect the extent to which a leader is accepted and generates positive emotional reactions from his or her subordinates. A situation in which leader–member relations are relatively good is potentially much easier to manage than a situation in which such relations are strained.

Task structure is the degree to which the job at hand can be clearly specified. Such structure is evident in rules, job descriptions, and policies. When tasks are relatively structured, there is little ambiguity about how they should be approached. In addition, goals are clear, performance measures are understood, and multiple solutions or approaches to a problem are unlikely to exist. With low task structure, the opposite holds true.

Position power is the extent to which a leader has recourse to formal sanctions. That is, can a leader control the fate of subordinates by offering rewards or threatening punishment? Other things being equal, situations in which a leader has position power are considered easier to manage than situations in which such power is lacking.

If we combine these three situational attributes, we obtain eight possible combinations, or octants, representing a range of situations (Figure 11.1). Situations to the left side of this arrangement are highly favorable (that is, they possess attributes that should make is easy to lead), while situations to the right side are highly unfavorable (possessing attributes that make it difficult to lead).

To illustrate these situations, consider octant 1. This is a situation in which all lights are "green." The subordinates and leader get along, the task is clearly structured so that all know what they should be doing, and the leader can fall back on his or her position power if need be. Such a situation might be enjoyed by a foreman in a nonunionized manufacturing setting who is admired by his subordinates. Octant 8, in contrast, has many obstacles to group

■ FIGURE 11.1
FIEDLER'S CONTINGENCY MODEL

	Most Favorable							**Least Favorable**
Leader–Member Relations	Good	Good	Good	Good	Poor	Poor	Poor	Poor
Task Structure	Strd.	Strd.	Unstrd.	Unstrd.	Strd.	Strd.	Unstrd.	Unstrd.
Position Power	Strong	Weak	Strong	Weak	Strong	Weak	Strong	Weak
Octant	1	2	3	4	5	6	7	8

performance. Here, the leader and the group's members have poor interpersonal relations, the task in which they are engaged is ambiguous, and the leader lacks any real base of power to reward or coerce. Such a situation might arise when an unpopular individual is asked to chair an ad hoc committee to prepare a report on how to ensure the quality of work life in the 21st century. In this situation, all lights are "red."

Fiedler applied his contingency model to a large variety of work groups (service station crews, basketball teams, laboratory groups, bomber crews, and others). The results of this data gathering suggested that high-LPC (interpersonlly oriented) leaders were more effective than low-LPC (task-oriented) leaders only in certain octants. Low-LPC leaders were found to be more effective in the remaining octants. Generally, low-LPC leaders were determined to be more effective than high-LPC leaders in extremely favorable and unfavorable situations, while high-LPC leaders were relatively more effective in octants of moderate favorability. Figure 11.2 summarizes Fiedler's original findings.*

An important question remains: *Why* should high-LPC leaders be more effective in moderately favorable situations, while low-LPC leaders are more effective in the remaining situations? Presently, there is no satisfactory answer to this question. Even Fiedler admits that the model is still largely a "black box" in that no one has a fully satisfying explanation as to why the observed relationships should be as they were reported.[2] Perhaps the most popular

FIGURE 11.2
SUMMARY OF FIEDLER'S ORIGINAL FINDINGS

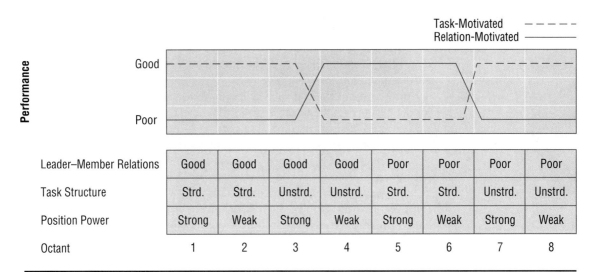

	1	2	3	4	5	6	7	8
Leader–Member Relations	Good	Good	Good	Good	Poor	Poor	Poor	Poor
Task Structure	Strd.	Strd.	Unstrd.	Unstrd.	Strd.	Strd.	Unstrd.	Unstrd.
Position Power	Strong	Weak	Strong	Weak	Strong	Weak	Strong	Weak
Octant	1	2	3	4	5	6	7	8

Source: *Leadership and Effective Management* by F.E. Fiedler and M.M. Chemers, 1974, Scott, Foresman & Company.
*Although Figure 11.2 illustrates the essential points of the contingency model, it is not, strictly speaking, accurate in that average levels of performance are not compared between octants, only within octants.

explanation is still the original one offered by Fiedler when he first proposed the model. At the time, he contended that leaders who are task-oriented will be successful in favorable situations because they will emphasize task accomplishment in a situation that merely requires persistence. So, too, in extremely difficult situations (octants 7 and 8) what is needed is firm, task-oriented leadership. In these unfavorable situations, if anything at all is going to be accomplished, the leader must have a strong desire to see results. Interpersonally oriented leaders, however, may have an advantage in settings that emit "mixed" signals. In these situations, such leaders can apply their social skills to overcoming the more manageable obstacles to performance.

Because the model was induced from empirical findings on group performance, other explanations can be offered for the pretzel-shaped relationship portrayed in Figure 11.2. One currently popular alternative interpretation is that the findings reflect a "matching" of leader complexity with situational complexity. This line of reasoning holds that high-LPC individuals are cognitively complex: They are able to perceive people and events in shades of gray, rather than in simple black-and-white terms. This is reflected by their tendency to give some positive ratings in addition to negative ratings to their least preferred coworker. Low-LPC leaders, on the other hand, may be more cognitively simple in that they judge people and objects in a fairly simplistic fashion (good-bad, black-white) without seeing or accepting complexities and nuances. So, too, we can conceptualize situations as being relatively simple versus complex. Simple situations would be those in which the major attributes are largely congruent—that is, all good or all bad. Examples of such simple situations would be the highly favorable and highly unfavorable octants of the contingency model. Complex situations are those in which the signals are mixed, as in the middle octants.

According to this complexity interpretation, cognitively complex people are better as leaders in relatively complex settings, while cognitively simple people do better as leaders in relatively simple settings. As yet, no one has offered any evidence that clearly refutes a complexity-matching interpretation of Fiedler's original findings.

Critics point out that the lack of a strong explanation for the dynamics of the model means that the model is still little more than a "black box." Because the model relies exclusively on a single method of measuring leadership style (LPC), the model may be viewed as being method-bound (see Chapter 6).

Also, Fiedler's initial results were gathered from a large survey of a variety of work groups. Because of the possibility that these early results may reflect chance, it is necessary that other researchers replicate Fiedler's findings with a different set of work groups. Such efforts have generated very mixed results, so that considerable controversy still surrounds the validity of the contingency model.[3]

IMPLICATIONS OF THE CONTINGENCY MODEL   Perhaps the most basic conclusion to be drawn from Fiedler's model is that a leader who is effective in one situation may be ineffective in another. Managers need to recognize this fact and understand the limitations that a situation may place on them.

Fiedler suggests that leaders should attempt to engineer facets of their work setting in order to enhance their personal effectiveness rather than try to change their leadership style.[4] He contends that personal style is fairly difficult to change, even for an individual who strongly desires to do so. Therefore, it can sometimes be easier to change the situational attributes to fit one's own style. This may mean deliberately trying to change the situational favorableness by enhancing relations with subordinates, changing the amount of structure in a task, or gaining more formal power with the goal of achieving a more conducive work setting based on personal leadership style.

Finally, there is reason to believe from available studies that performance actually declines across octants as we move toward the unfavorable end of situational favorability.[5] Within each octant, we might hope to find the predicted orderings of group performance based on leader LPC. However, groups in octant 1, led by low-LPC leaders, would likely do better than groups under other leaders in all other octants. Figure 11.3 represents the expected performance decrement across the octants. From this reasoning, the notion of engineering situations for optimal performance leads to the unusual prediction that we should try to make all settings into octant 1 (that is, good leader–member relations, structured task, and strong position power) with low-LPC individuals as leaders. Changes in any of the octant parameters or changes in leadership style should produce relatively poorer performance. As yet, this notion has not been formally tested and the model continues to be discussed from a within-octant basis for predicting performance.

FIGURE 11.3
SUGGESTED PERFORMANCE CURVES ACROSS OCTANTS

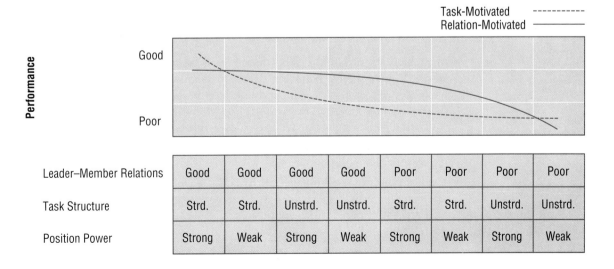

Leader–Member Relations	Good	Good	Good	Good	Poor	Poor	Poor	Poor
Task Structure	Strd.	Strd.	Unstrd.	Unstrd.	Strd.	Strd.	Unstrd.	Unstrd.
Position Power	Strong	Weak	Strong	Weak	Strong	Weak	Strong	Weak

Path–Goal Theory

Martin Evans[6] and Robert House[7] have proposed another perspective on how leaders can be effective. Their **path–goal theory** suggests that leaders can affect the satisfaction, motivation, and performance of group members in several ways. A primary means is by making rewards contingent on the accomplishment of performance *goals*. (This notion is similar to Bass's notion of transactional leadership, discussed in Chapter 10.) In addition, a leader can aid group members in obtaining valued rewards by clarifying the *paths* to these performance goals and by removing obstacles to performance.

In order to accomplish these ends, a leader may be required to adopt different styles of leadership behavior as the situation dictates. House has identified four distinct types of leader behavior:

1. **Directive leadership** involves giving specific guidance to subordinates and asking them to follow standard rules. It is similar to the high-structure/low-consideration style in the Ohio State scheme, which was discussed in the previous chapter.

2. **Supportive leadership** includes being friendly to subordinates and sensitive to their needs. It is similar to the low-structure/high-consideration style.

3. **Participative leadership** involves sharing information with subordinates and consulting with them before making decisions. It is much like the high-structure/high-consideration style.

4. **Achievement-oriented leadership** entails setting challenging goals and emphasizing excellence, while simultaneously showing confidence that subordinates will perform well. It is not really equivalent to any of the Ohio State styles of management.

House contends that all four styles can be, and often are, used by a single leader in varying situations.

A number of propositions have been generated from path–goal theory regarding the impact of certain leader behaviors on subordinate performance and satisfaction. Chief among these are:

- In ambiguous situations, subordinates will be more satisfied with leaders who exhibit directive behavior. This satisfaction results from the subordinates' appreciation of the supervisor's help in increasing the probability of their obtaining a desired reward. In situations with greater task or goal clarity, such directive behavior will be of less value to subordinates.

- In stressful environments, supportive leader behavior will ameliorate subordinate dissatisfaction.

- Leaders who possess influence with their own superiors (upward influence) can enhance unit performance and satisfaction. With upward influence, a leader is better able to help subordinates be successful and receive appropriate rewards.

Thus far, there has been little research on path–goal theory. Available evidence suggests that when subordinates are involved with ambiguous tasks, di-

OB Focus
The New Style of Manager

Call them leaders, sponsors, facilitators, coaches. Just don't call them managers. More and more companies are adopting new philosophies about how to get work done, and are standing old management techniques on their ear. Take the case of Cindy Ransom, a middle manager at Clorox. In 1990, Ransom charged her employees with redesigning the business operations of the 100-person plant in Fairfield, California. The team of hourly employees created training programs, established absenteeism policies, and reorganized the plant into five customer-focused business units. Ransom intervened only occasionally to answer questions, and as workers increasingly accepted managerial responsibilities, Ransom was able to spend more time with customers and suppliers. The following year, Clorox named the Fairfield plant most improved in the company's household products division.

Drypers, an emerging disposable diaper company out of Houston, has another cut on shared leadership. The office of the chief executive actually consists of five managing directors, all sharing equal power. Each of the five has a functional responsibility, such as marketing, finance, or manufacturing. Major decisions are made only after the group of five has shared information, tinkered with ideas, and arrived at consensus. This style of teamwork allows all group members to have a shared vision, and allows products to get to market faster and more efficiently.

The new-style manager helps workers understand the problem at hand, gather information, and make decisions on their own. At a division of R.R. Donnelly & Sons, America's largest printer, the group manager's role is to instruct, enlighten, and reassure members of the work unit until they are able to accept the responsibilities of a manager: hiring, firing, and scheduling vacations.

An important element of group success is for all group members to become teachers and learn from one another. Group members should be given plenty of information and should be self-motivated. The new-style manager encourages others to participate in the decision-making process, share information, and contribute to the organization's success.

Self-managed work teams are believed by many to be critical to the success of American organizations. According to James Champy, CEO of CSC Index, a consulting firm specializing in reengineering organizations, managers with a deep-felt commitment to coaching and empowering their employees will not be seen in great numbers in corporate America until the mid-to-late 1990s. But the line has been drawn in the sand and a new style of management is upon us.

Source: Brian Dumaine, "The New Non-manager Managers," *Fortune*, February 22, 1993, 80–84.

rective leadership can increase satisfaction and motivation. With fairly unambiguous tasks, however, directive leadership can decrease satisfaction and motivation.[8] Also, supportive leader behavior typically is associated with increased subordinate satisfaction. When subordinates are employed on tasks that are inherently distasteful or frustrating, supportive leader behavior can enhance subordinate satisfaction.[9] Although path–goal theory remains as yet largely untested, its greatest theoretical strength seems to lie in its integration of leader behavior such expectancy theory notions (Chapter 6) as providing contingent, valued rewards for performance.

THE HERSEY–BLANCHARD SITUATIONAL THEORY

Of the various situational approaches to leadership, the **Hersey–Blanchard situational theory** has been the least researched.[10] Yet it is widely used in management training programs. The theory is closely based on the leadership styles generated by the Ohio State model. The unique contribution of the model lies in its emphasis on matching a particular leadership style to the "maturity" of the followers.

Subordinate maturity is defined as the capacity to set high but attainable goals, the willingness to take on responsibility, and the possession of relevant education and/or experience. Maturity is judged in relation to a given task. Therefore, a particular subordinate may be quite mature in relation to one task and immature in relation to another. Subordinate maturity contains two components: **job maturity,** or technical knowledge and task-relevant skills, and **psychological maturity,** or feelings of self-confidence and the willingness and ability to accept responsibility. A subordinate who is highly mature possesses both technical competence and self-confidence for a given task. A subordinate who is low on maturity for a task lacks both ability and confidence. Although Hersey and Blanchard acknowledge other variables as potentially important (for example, time pressures), they focus primarily on follower maturity as the critical situational attribute.

The central thesis of their model is that as follower maturity increases, a leader should rely more on relationship-oriented behavior and less on task-oriented behavior. Beyond a certain point on this maturity dimension, however, the leader should rely less on both task-oriented and relationship-oriented behaviors. This pattern is depicted in Figure 11.4. With subordinates who are highly immature (situation M1), the leader should emphasize task-oriented behavior and be very directive and autocratic. In essence, this is a style of leadership that involves *telling* subordinates what to do. For situation M2, subordinates who are still on the somewhat low side of maturity, a leader should focus on being more relationship-oriented. Such a leader works on *selling* his or her ideas to the subordinates. Subordinates who are somewhat high in maturity (M3) will also need a fair degree of support and considerate treatment. The appropriate style in this case is one of *participating* with subordinates. Lastly, subordinates who are highly mature (M4) are self-motivated and can be trusted to rely on their own self-direction. In fact, highly mature employees may actually expect to be given a great deal of autonomy. The preferred style of leadership with such subordinates is one of *delegating.*

Hersey and Blanchard offered their theory with little empirical evidence of its validity. Available research suggests that their model may only be partially correct in that less experienced (that is, less mature) subordinates may be somewhat more responsive to greater direction. Furthermore, the theoretical aspects of the model have recently been criticized for not giving a coherent or precise rationale for the proposed relationships.[11] Nonetheless, this model possesses an intuitive appeal that makes it an attractive instructional device for practicing managers. It also emphasizes the need for flexible, adaptable leader behaviors. But until more evidence is available, it is not possible to claim that the Hersey–Blanchard model is superior to other perspectives.

THE VROOM–YETTON LEADERSHIP MODEL

Victor Vroom and Philip Yetton developed a very promising model that deals with one specific facet of leadership: how to select a leadership style for mak-

FIGURE 11.4

THE HERSEY–BLANCHARD SITUATIONAL MODEL

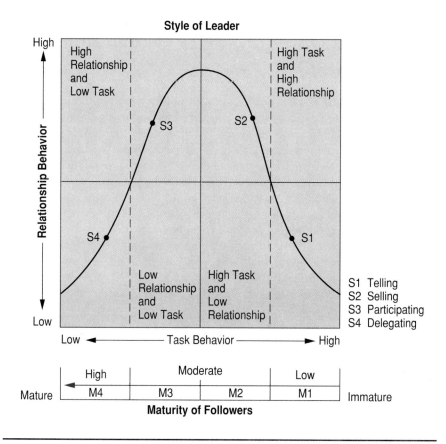

Style of Leader

Source: P. Hersey and K. Blanchard, *Management of Organizational Behavior* (Englewood Cliffs, N.J.: Prentice-Hall, 1982), 152.

ing a decision.[12] Their work is built on Tannenbaum and Schmidt's views of directive versus participative leadership, which were discussed in the previous chapter. The **Vroom–Yetton model** suggests that there are five decision-making styles, ranging from highly autocratic to highly participative. In order of increasing participation, the five styles are:

- *Autocratic I (AI)*—A manager solves a problem using the information that is already available.

- *Autocratic II (AII)*—A manager obtains additional information from subordinates and then solves the problem.

- *Consultative I (CI)*—A manager shares the problem with subordinates on an individual basis and obtains their ideas and suggestions. Again, the manager chooses a solution to the problem at hand.

- *Consultative II (CII)*—A manager shares the problem with subordinates as a group. The final decision may or may not reflect subordinate input.
- *Group (G)*—A manager meets with subordinates as a group. However, the manager acts as a chairperson who focuses and directs discussion, but does not impose his or her will on the group. True subordinate participation, in a democratic sense, is sought.

Which of these five styles is most appropriate for a given situation depends on a number of important considerations. In total, Vroom and Yetton identify seven questions that must be answered to determine the appropriate style. These underlying contingencies (or decision rules) focus on such issues as whether sufficient information is available to make a good decision and whether subordinates can be trusted to approach the problem from a perspective that is congruent with organizational goals. The seven questions can be arranged in a sequential fashion that permits us to follow a logical path in matching a single, preferred leader style to a given situation.

Figure 11.5 shows the decision tree that Vroom and Yetton devised for selecting a best or most appropriate style. The seven decision rules are listed across the top of the model. For each question, a manager is to provide a yes or no repsonse. At the end of each branch in the tree is a designated style, denoted by AI, AII, CI, CII, or G.

To see how a manager would use the decision tree, imagine a case in which a manager must deal with an order typist who is not typing enough purchase orders each day (the answer to question A is yes). If the manager has a clear understanding of why the typist is a poor performer (B = yes), if the subordinate must accept the manager's decision in order for the solution to work (D = yes), and if the manager is also certain that his decision will be accepted by the subordinate (E = yes), then the manager should take a nonparticipative approach to dealing with the problem (AI).

As another example, consider a manager who is contemplating the introduction of flexible work schedules (Chapter 7). For such a decision to be successfully implemented, it is worthwhile to consider what the Vroom–Yetton model suggests. In this situation, one solution is likely to be more rational than another (A = yes), but the manager does not know the extent of individual preferences and job-related obstacles (B = no). The problem is relatively unstructured (C = no), while acceptance by subordinates is critical to implementation (D = yes). As the manager cannot be reasonably certain that an imposed solution will be accepted by subordinates (E = no), the final choice of style depends on whether subordinates are judged to share the organization's goals. If the manager believes that the subordinates share the organization's goals, then a highly participative approach is in order (G). Otherwise, a less participative strategy (CII) is appropriate.

The Vroom–Yetton model provides a useful device for diagnosing a situation. It prescribes a specific type of behavior for a leader who is confronted with a specific problem. As such, it is much more precise and somewhat more practical than the other models we have examined.

FIGURE 11.5
THE VROOM-YETTON MODEL

Decision Quality | Subordinate Acceptance

A
Does the problem possess a quality requirement?

B
Do I have sufficient information to make a high-quality decision?

C
Is the problem structured?

D
Is acceptance of the decision by subordinates important for effective implementation?

E
If I were to make the decision by myself, am I reasonably certain that it would be accepted by my subordinates?

F
Do subordinates share the enterprise goals to be attained in solving this problem?

G
Is conflict among subordinates over preferred solutions likely?

No — 1: AI, AII, CI, CII, G
Yes
Yes — 2: AI, AII, CI, CII, G
No — 3: G

No — 4: AI, AII, CI, CII
Yes
Yes — 5: AI, AII, CI, CII
No
6: G
Yes — 7: CII
Yes
No — 8: CI, CII

Yes
No
Yes — 9: AII, CI, CII
No
10: AII, CI, CII
11: CII
Yes

No
Yes
Yes — 12: G
No
No
14: CII, G — 13: CII

Yes
Yes
No
No
No

Decision-Making Methods
AI = Autocratic decision without subordinates' input
AII = Autocratic decision using information gathered from subordinates
CI = Consultative decision with problem discussed individually with each subordinate
CII = Consultative decision with problem discussed with subordinates as a group
G = Group decision
Note: The numbers 1–14 denote Problem Types.

Source: Reprinted from *Leadership and Decision Making*, by Victor H. Vroom and Philip W. Yetton, pp. 41–42, by permission of the University of Pittsburgh Press. © 1973 by University of Pittsburgh Press.

Further studies have tended to support the validity of the Vroom–Yetton model. Work by the original researchers as well as by independent investigators indicates that the model closely describes the actual decision process of most managers.[13] Also, the model is widely used by organizations that specialize in managerial training (for example, Kepner Tregoe).[14]

Recently, Vroom and Jago have attempted to address several shortcomings of the model.[15] For example, it can be very difficult to always answer the seven decision rules with a simple yes or no response. Often, a manager has only a sense of what is likely to occur. In such cases, the manager may be able to give probability estimates but not simple, firm answers. To address this and other problems, Vroom and Jago have made a number of modifications, such as permitting probabilistic responses. As a result, the model is evolving into a very complex and unwieldy set of mathematical equations. Nonetheless, managers who are not particularly interested in precise mathematical advice, perhaps because they lack the time or a computer program to work out the equations, will probably continue to use the decision tree presented in Figure 11.5 as a quick guide to selecting a leadership style.

GRAEN'S VERTICAL DYAD LINKAGE MODEL

A further perspective on the leadership process is provided by the **vertical dyad linkage model** (sometimes termed the leader–member exchange model[16] of leadership proposed by George Graen and his associates.[17] In some respects, this model is similar to the other approaches we have considered in that it focuses on the influence of subordinates on leader behavior and the topic of subordinate participation in decision making. In all other ways, however, the model is unique.

Graen and his associates contend that much of the past theorizing on the leadership process presumes the existence of an average leadership style that a manager exhibits toward all members of a work group. But careful considerations reveals that leaders do not typically display a uniform style of leadership or set of behaviors toward all group members. Instead, they behave somewhat differently toward each subordinate. The model contends that each *linkage*, or relationship, that exists between the leader and a subordinate is likely to differ in quality. Thus, the same supervisor may have poor interpersonal relations with some subordinates and fairly open and trusting relations with others. In each work unit, these pairs of relations, or *dyads*, can be judged in terms of whether an individual is relatively "in" or "out" with the supervisor. Members of the in-group (or, more correctly, in-subgroup) are invited to share in decision making and are given added responsibility. Members of the out-group, however, are supervised within the narrow terms of their formal employment contract. In essence, an in-group member is elevated to the unofficial role of "trusted assistant," while an out-group member is assigned the role of "hired hand." In-group members, in many respects, enjoy the benefits of enriched jobs with many opportunities to participate in decision making. Out-group members are not given these opportunities. Further, it is hypothesized that in-group members will display greater job satisfaction, superior performance, higher commitment, and lower turnover.

Panel *a* in Figure 11.6 portrays the traditional view of how leaders and subordinates are perceived, in that all subordinates are seen as being treated equally by a supervisor—that is, they have equal access to the leader, equal influence in decision making, equal information exchange, and equal social dis-

FIGURE 11.6
CONTRASTING VIEWS OF LEADER-SUBORDINATE RELATIONS

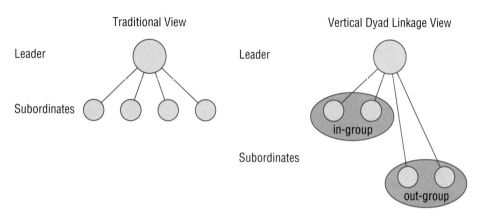

tance from the leader. Panel *b*, however, reflects the vertical dyad linkage perspective, wherein a subset of the subordinates (the in-group) has better working relations with the leader than another subset (the out-group). The differing distances of the individual subordinates from the leader reflect differences in the equality of the working relationships, and, therefore, differences in influence, authority, and information access.

How people come to be members of the in-group or the out-group is not as yet fully understood. Preliminary evidence suggests, however, that the leader's initial impression of an employee's competency plays an important role. Certainly, leaders and in-group members strongly believe that competency is the distinguishing characteristic between in-group members and out-group members. Out-group members, however, are just as firmly convinced that ingratiation, favoritism, and politics are more important than competency in the selection of in-group members. In fact, interpersonal attraction probably does play some role in the selection process. However, it is likely that perceived competence plays a much larger and complementary role in most instances.

The existence of in-groups and out-groups is easy to demonstrate. In the original studies on the vertical dyad linkage (VDL) model, employees and their superiors were asked to identify who in each unit was rela_.vely more or less trusted by the superior. Generally, people had little difficulty identifying such a hierarchy. Overall, the membership status of a particular individual (in versus out) is understood by all group members, especially the individual in question.

The original and validating studies on the VDL model generally have provided support for the model's central hypotheses, which are that in-group members are more satisfied and are judged to be superior performers. That in-group and out-group status may be related to employee turnover, however, has received far less consistent support.[18] An additional finding is that in-group members tend to see job-related problems in much the same way as their superiors. Graen and Schiemann observed that in-group members' reports of job problems correlated more closely with their superior's perceptions than did the reports of out-group members.[19]

As is usually the case, the model and its supporting research can be criticized on several counts.[20] For example, in a review of VDL research, John Miner noted that the research has often relied on ratings of subordinate performance rather than on objective measures of performance, that most tests of the model had been made by its developer, and that the model's principles may be limited to white-collar employees.[21] Yet a subsequent study that addressed many of the shortcomings identified by Miner found good support for the model's major hypotheses.[22]

In summary, it seems that leaders do distinguish among their subordinates by inviting some to join an inner cadre, while excluding others. Initial impressions of the competency of subordinates can lead to categorization as in- or out-group members, which may affect their subsequent performance and promotion or turnover.

A COMPARISON OF THE MAJOR SITUATIONAL LEADERSHIP MODELS

The major situational models of leadership have many similarities and differences, as summarized in Table 11.1. The similarities include a general focus on leader behaviors as being primarily oriented toward either task accomplishment or social supportiveness. Although the models categorize leadership style in somewhat different ways, all models generally recognize that leaders differ in their behavior and that leader behavior can make a difference in unit outcomes. Other similarities among the models include their frequent attempt to predict performance as an index of effectiveness and their expectation that satisfaction will be influenced by various leadership principles. The models differ greatly in terms of the specified situational variables.

One common situational thread in the models, however, is a focus on the importance of followers. Fiedler's model incorporates leader–member relations, path–goal theory acknowledges the role of subordinate characteristics, Hersey–Blanchard makes subordinate maturity a cornerstone principle, Vroom–Yetton focuses on the issue of subordinate acceptance of a decision and subordinate knowledge, and the vertical dyad linkage model emphasizes subordinate competence and loyalty. As yet, there is less understanding of the dimensions of follower behavior than the dimensions of leader behavior. Recent interest in the topic of followership, however, suggests that followers can be thought of as possessing styles as well. Figure 11.7 outlines a two-dimensional model of followership that sorts follower behavior into four quadrants, defined by the dimensions of loyalty–hostility and compliance–defiance.[23] Subordinates who are close to the intersection of the axes may be viewed as "survivors" who display little uniqueness, while members at the ends of the quadrants represent extreme types.

TABLE 11.1
COMPARISON OF MAJOR SITUATIONAL LEADERSHIP MODELS

Model	Leader Behaviors	Situational Variables	Outcomes/Criteria	Level of Empirical Support
Fiedler's Contingency Model	Task–oriented (low LPC) Relationship–oriented (high LPC)	Leader–member relations Task structure Position power	Performance	Mixed
Path–Goal Theory	Directive Supportive Participative Achievement–oriented	Task structure Subordinate characteristics	Satisfaction Motivation Performance	Good
Hersey–Blanchard	Concern for people Concern for task	Subordinate maturity	Effectiveness	Limited
Vroom–Yetton	Autocratic Participative	Decision quality Decision acceptance	Quality of decision Acceptance of decision by subordinates	Good
Vertical Dyad Linkage	Differential treatment of subordinates	Subordinate competence Subordinate loyalty	Satisfaction Performance Turnover	Good

Although the models (with the exception of Fiedler's) possess a fairly strong intuitive appeal, the amount and quality of empirical evidence supporting each model differ considerably. For some models, such as Hersey–Blanchard,

FIGURE 11.7
DIMENSIONS OF FOLLOWERSHIP

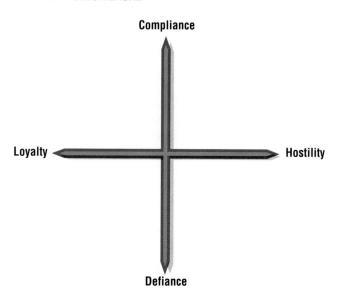

Source: R.P. Vecchio, "Effective Followership: Leadership Turned Upside Down," *Journal of Business Strategies* 4 (1987): 39–47.

very little evidence is available. Other models, such as Fiedler's contingency model, have generated a great deal of research. Nonetheless, the results of such research have also been varied. For Fiedler's contingency model, the results have been mixed, while the vertical dyad linkage model has had good success in predicting subordinate satisfaction and performance, but only mixed success in predicting turnover.

A manager's choice of a particular leadership model as a guide to personal conduct depends on his or her goals and on the specific situation. An initial issue is whether the individual hopes to maximize a given outcome, such as satisfaction or performance. Some models, such as Fiedler's contingency model, are silent on the dimension of satisfaction, and therefore might be eliminated from competition. The next step is to examine the situational variables identified by the models to determine if they are pertinent to the actual work setting. Such an exercise can provide insights into which model is most appropriate to a given manager in a specific situation.

SUBSTITUTES FOR LEADERSHIP

Steven Kerr and John Jermier have suggested, somewhat controversially, that leader behavior may sometimes be unnecessary or superfluous because factors in the situation offer sufficient aid to subordinates.[24] Such factors might include subordinate ability, training, or experience. The notion that leaders may not play a crucial role in all settings can help to explain why some work groups do quite well despite the presence of a poor leader. In other words, there can be situations in which leadership is unimportant or redundant.

Kerr and Jermier have suggested two types of variables to account for cases in which leadership may be redundant or unimportant: leadership substitutes and leadership neutralizers. The presence of a **leadership substitute** will make leadership redundant or unnecessary, while the presence of a **leadership neutralizer** prevents a leader from taking action in some fashion. Table 11.2 lists some possible leadership substitutes and neutralizers for two styles of leader behavior.

The essence of Kerr and Jermier's proposal is that leadership is only one factor in successful work-group performance. The notions of substitutes and neutralizers help us keep a proper perspective on the role of leadership in work groups. Although leadership can be critical to unit performance, certain preconditions are necessary. In addition, the idea of leadership substitutes and neutralizers helps to account for the largely mixed results of research on most leadership theories. Studies of leadership that ignore the effect of neutralizers and substitutes may fail to uncover hypothesized relationships because the particular leadership process is irrelevant, rather than because the theory is invalid.

OBSTACLES TO PERSONAL EFFECTIVENESS IN LEADERSHIP POSITIONS

As noted earlier, leadership can sometimes be irrelevant to a given situation because of subordinate, task, or organizational characteristics. Leaders in such

TABLE 11.2
SUBSTITUTES AND NEUTRALIZERS FOR
SUPPORTIVE AND INSTRUMENTAL LEADERSHIP

Factor	Supportive Leadership	Instrumental Leadership
Subordinate Characteristics		
1. Experience, ability, training		Substitute
2. "Professional" orientation	Substitute	Substitute
3. Indifference toward organizational rewards	Neutralizer	Neutralizer
Task Characteristics		
1. Structured, routine task		Substitute
2. Task feedback		Substitute
3. Intrinsically satisfying task	Substitute	
Organizational Characteristics		
1. Cohesive work group	Substitute	Substitute
2. Leader lacks position power	Neutralizer	Neutralizer
3. Formalization of goals and plans		Substitute
4. Rigid rules and procedures		Neutralizer
5. Physical distance between leader and subordinates	Neutralizer	Neutralizer

Note: Supportive and instrumental leadership are analogous to leader consideration and leader structuring (See Chapter 10).
Source: G. Yukl, *Leadership in Organizations* (Englewood Cliffs, N.J.: Prentice-Hall, 1981).

settings may find their assignments particularly difficult because of such realities. Leaders can also face a rough road for reasons beyond their control or for failing to follow some widely accepted management wisdom. J. K. Van Fleet has compiled a list of the biggest mistakes that managers make.[25] Any one of these mistakes can be fatal to a manager's career, and many of these principles are not readily deducible from existing theory. Following is a selected list of the top ten mistakes:

1. Failing to stay abreast of developments in your field and limiting yourself to your own specialty area
2. Refusing to seek higher responsibility or to take responsibility for your own actions
3. Failing to make sure that assignments are understood, supervised, and accomplished
4. Refusing to assess your own performance and abilities realistically
5. Using your position for personal gain or failing to tell the truth
6. Not setting a positive, personal example for subordinates
7. Trying to be liked rather than respected
8. Emphasizing rules rather than skill

9. Failing to keep criticism in a constructive vein

10. Not attending to employee gripes and complaints

Additional research on why managers fail has been conducted by the Center for Creative Leadership in Greensboro, North Carolina.[26] From detailed interviews with managers who were initially successful in their careers but eventually failed (that is, they plateaued, retired early, or were dismissed), it was learned that failure was sometimes influenced by external factors, such as economic downturns or uncontrollable events. Four sets of individual factors, however, also were associated with failure:

1. Defensiveness: trying to hide mistakes or fix blame on others, rather than taking responsibility and seeking to remedy errors

2. Emotional instability: engaging in emotional outbursts or displaying moodiness, rather than projecting confidence and a calm demeanor

3. Poor interpersonal skills: lacking sensitivity and tact, and being arrogant or abrasive

4. Weak technical and cognitive skills: lacking technical know-how for upper-level jobs, possessing a narrow perspective based on a single specialty, or trying to micro-manage the work of subordinates who possess substantial technical competence.

A PRACTICAL MODEL FOR MANAGING THE LEADERSHIP PROCESS

In both the previous and present chapters, we have reviewed a variety of perspectives on the leadership process. Now we will consider how the various models can be used to actively manage the phenomenon of leadership. Figure 11.8 outlines a practical model for managing the process of leadership. The model relates known aspects of the leadership process in a meaningful sequence. In the model, we begin with a situational needs assessment (step 1) that focuses on critical aspects of the situation. Specifically, we first consider the context in which leadership takes place. This includes such variables as organizational level, group size, focus on quality, and formality of authority and communication. Additionally, a situational needs assessment examines the specific requirements of a given task, detailing the technical expertise required of a leader. Finally, members' needs are reviewed. These needs include expectations for leader behavior, levels of self-efficacy, and openness to inspirational leadership. At this point, it is important to consider how organizational, task, and member characteristics act as substitutes or neutralizers of leadership.

Following a situational needs assessment, we define the individual abilities expected of a leader. These abilities include cognitive-intellectual skills and stylistic dimensions, such as participative orientation, as well as such aptitudes as capacity to develop needed technical know-how and adapt to changes in the situation. A situational needs assessment also allows us to specify outcome criteria against which a leader is evaluated (step 2). These criteria include em-

FIGURE 11.8
A PRACTICAL MODEL FOR MANAGING THE LEADERSHIP PROCESS

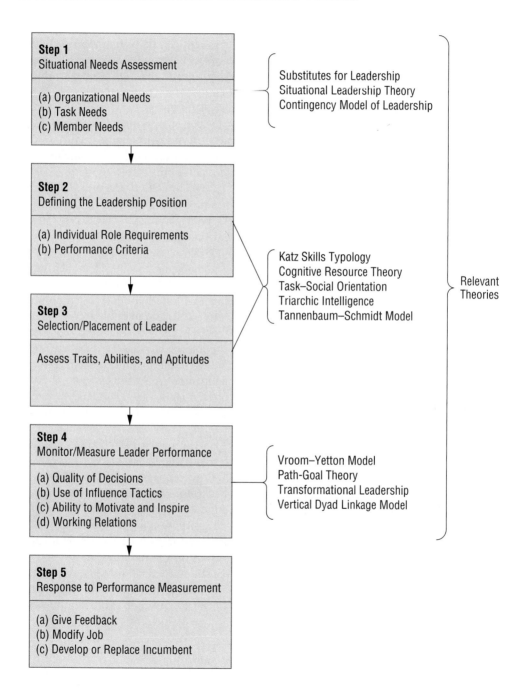

Source: P. Hersey and K. Blanchard, *Management of Organizational Behavior* (Englewood Cliffs, N.J.: Prentice-Hall, 1982) 152.

ployee satisfaction and turnover, along with relatively "hard" performance measures.

After defining the ideal leader for the given situation, step 3 consists of selecting (or placing) a leader from among available candidates, based on matching traits, abilities, and aptitudes. If no single candidate matches on all important dimensions, it will be necessary to consider providing leadership development experiences (for example, training programs or job rotation) that would strengthen an individual's capabilities.

Following the appointment of the preferred candidate, the individual's performance in the role of leader is measured and monitored (step 4). Beyond traditional outcome measures, we are interested in (1) the quality of decisions made by the individual (for example, the optimal level of inclusion of employee participation as articulated in the Vroom–Yetton model), (2) the appropriate use of social influence tactics (cf. Kipnis and Schmidt, Chapter 9), (3) the ability to motivate (through path–goal theory principles) and inspire others (that is, the ability to use referent power in a charismatic fashion), and (4) the quality of working relations that emerges (the vertical dyad linkage perspective).

Ultimately, a formal response is made to this performance assessment (step 5). Ideally, no changes will be required. It might prove necessary, however, to modify the job if the leader is unable to handle certain components of the role (for example, an administrative assistant may be needed to help with accounting issues), or because of changes in the job's demands over time. Also, the assigned leader may need further personal development experiences, which can be gained, for example, by attending seminars on time management or on how to handle difficult clients and subordinates. At the extreme, the appropriate response may be to replace the present leader and search for a replacement, paying special attention to closing the gap between the failed leader's deficiencies and the situation's demands.

The model depicted in Figure 11.8 can be used as a framework for aligning the major theories of leadership. Each theory has greater relevance to specific components of the model. The lower portion of Figure 11.8 aligns the various theories with each step in the figure. In addition to its use for selecting, placing, and replacing leaders, the model in Figure 11.8 can be used by an individual as a framework for analyzing situational demands (for example, before taking a leadership assignment) and for comparing personal capabilities (following self-assessment) to the situation's demands. The outcome of this comparison would indicate whether the individual should take on a specific assignment. It would also indicate the components that the individual might wish to alter (by changing aspects of the situation or personal abilities) before accepting a leadership position.

SUMMARY

1. Identify the factors underlying situational favorableness and explain how they influence a leader's effectiveness.

A favorable situation exists when leader–member relations are good, task structure (the degree to which the job can be clearly specified) is high, and the leader's position power (the extent to which the leader has recourse to formal sanctions) is high. Interpersonally oriented leaders are more effective in moderately favorable situations, whereas task-oriented leaders are more effective in situations that are extremely favorable or unfavorable.

2. Explain how leaders can clarify paths to goals to motivate employees.
Path goal theory suggests that leaders can affect satisfaction, motivation, and performance by basing rewards on the accomplishment of performance goals and by clarifying the paths to these goals and removing obstacles to performance. Depending on the situation, the leader does this by choosing one of four types of leader behavior: directive leadership, supportive leadership, participative leadership, or achievement-oriented leadership.

3. Describe the components of subordinate maturity and the relevance of subordinate maturity to leadership style.
Subordinate maturity consists of job maturity (technical knowledge and task-relevant skills) and psychological maturity (feelings of self-confidence and self-respect). The Hersey–Blanchard theory proposes that the leader should change his of her style to match the employee's level of maturity.

4. Describe the decision-making styles of the Vroom–Yetton model and explain how to use a decision tree to select the appropriate style.
A manager can solve a problem by (1) using already available information; (2) obtaining additional information from subordinates and then making an individual decision; (3) sharing the problem with subordinates individually, obtaining their ideas, and making an individual decision; (4) sharing the problem with subordinates as a group and possibly using subordinates' ideas in reaching a solution; or (5) meeting with subordinates as a group, focusing and directing discussion, but not imposing his or her will. To use a decision tree in a particular situation, the manager answers the questions from left to right, moving along a branch of the tree. At the end of each branch is the style designated appropriate for the particular decision.

5. Describe a way to evaluate leadership style taking into account managers' views of different employees.
In the vertical dyad linkage model, employees are members of an in-group or an out-group in the eyes of the manager. In-group members are invited to share in decision making and are given added responsibility, whereas out-group members are supervised within the narrow terms of their employment contract.

6. Identify similarities and differences among the major situational leadership models.
The leadership models generally focus on leader behaviors as being primarily oriented to either accomplishing tasks or providing social support. They all recognize that leaders behave differently, and that leader behavior can influence unit outcomes. The models frequently see performance as an index of effectiveness and expect that leadership principles will affect employee

satisfaction and turnover. However, the models differ greatly in their consideration of situational variables.

7. Define leadership substitute and leadership neutralizer and give examples of each.
A leadership substitute is a factor that makes leadership redundant or unnecessary; one example would be an extremely cohesive work group. A leadership neutralizer is a factor that prevents a leader from being effective; one such factor would be subordinates who are indifferent to organizational rewards. Other examples of each factor are shown in Table 10.5

8. Offer some major reasons why managers fail.
Managers fail for a variety of reasons. Along with external influences, failure can arise from such personal factors as defensiveness, emotional instability, poor interpersonal skills, and weak technical and cognitive skills.

9. Explain how you would manage the leadership process.
First, conduct a situational needs assessment. Then define the leadership role and select or develop a candidate. Next, measure and monitor the leader's conduct against such criteria as the ability to motivate, the quality of decisions made, the quality of working relations, and the appropriate use of influence tactics. Following this assessment, modify the job, offer developmental opportunities, or change the job incumbent.

KEY TERMS

Contingency model of leadership
   effectiveness
Least preferred coworker (LPC)
Situational favorableness
Leader–member relations
Task structure
Position power
Path–goal theory
Directive leadership
Supportive leadership

Participative leadership
Achievement-oriented leadership
Hersey–Blanchard situational theory
Subordinate maturity
Job maturity
Psychological maturity
Vroom–Yetton model
Vertical dyad linkage model
Leadership substitute
Leadership neutralizer

REVIEW AND DISCUSSION QUESTIONS

1. What is a high-LPC leader? Why might a high-LPC leader be most effective in moderately favorable work situations?

2. Martha Muffin has just been appointed to chair a committee set up to explore future markets for the company's products (special-purpose gaskets). Although the committee will consist of people from several departments, Martha is dismayed to learn that she is unpopular with most committee members because of a record-keeping procedure she instituted recently. Martha has just read about Fiedler's contingency model, from which she learned that a task-motivated leader would be most effective in this unfavorable situation. Martha sees herself as socially motivated, however, and

she wonders how she can change her leadership style. What do you suggest?

3. Describe the types of leader behavior identified in path–goal theory. Which approach works best in ambiguous situations?

4. Hersey and Blanchard suggest that a leader's style should change as subordinates develop job maturity. How should the leader's style change? What are some shortcomings of this approach to leadership?

5. Use the decision tree shown in Figure 11.5 to choose a leadership style appropriate for each of the following situations. Give the name of the decision style and describe how it works.

   a. John Apple notes that Sam Slow, one of the programmers in his group, has not been meeting the deadlines for his portion of the database system John's department is developing. John has also noticed that Sam regularly starts the day late and spends more time on the phone with his girlfriend than on the computer. John wants to inspire Sam to work harder, but he thinks Sam will doubt his assessment that Sam isn't trying hard enough. In the meantime, the other programmers in the office wish Sam would do better, because everyone will get a bonus if the group finishes its project ahead of schedule.

   b. Irma Bloom, production manager at Marvelous Metal Castings, Inc., shares the workers' concern over the recent increase in accidents. No one is quite certain why the accident rate has risen, but the consensus is that some changes should be made. Because Irma has 20 years' experience in the plant, she is confident that workers will respect her ideas for improving safety.

6. According to the vertical dyad linkage model of leadership, leaders do not treat all subordinates in the same way. How does treatment differ? Is this fair? Explain your answer.

7. What does the existence of leadership substitutes and leadership neutralizers tell us about the role of leadership?

8. Choose a leadership theory and analyze it in terms of the model portrayed in Figure 11.8.

CRITICAL INCIDENT

Crisis at Holy Cow Frozen Yogurt

Dave Kimball started out as a management trainee at Holy Cow Frozen Yogurt fifteen years ago and eventually worked his way up to president, a position he has held for the past four years. Holy Cow, located in a small midwestern town, produces an extensive line of frozen yogurt flavors, sold in pints at grocery stores throughout the midwest and central plains states. With demand for low-fat frozen desserts growing in the past five years, the company has recently expanded its work force to 230 employees, and has recently moved operations into a new factory just outside of town. The factory is equipped with new, high-tech machinery, and all employees have recently undergone four days of training in operating the new machinery.

Dave has worked hard to maintain a friendly working atmosphere at Holy Cow. He knows each one of his employees by name and frequently visits the factory floor to chat with them and check on operations. Dave has ardently maintained an open-door policy, always encouraging employees to come to him with concerns and suggestions. Many employees have commented that Holy Cow is like a big family. Managers and employees show sincere concern and appreciation for one another, and Holy Cow regularly holds company-wide picnics, family days, and other social gatherings.

Holy Cow sales have grown steadily in the past few years. Consumers have turned to frozen yogurt products to satisfy their appetites for low-fat frozen desserts. Holy Cow's most successful product to date has been a flavor called Heavenly Holstein—frozen vanilla yogurt with crushed chocolate cookies. Trying to build on Heavenly Holstein's success, the company is about to introduce a new flavor, Chocolate Peanut Udder—frozen chocolate yogurt with crushed peanut butter cups. A product development group headed by Dave took joint responsibility for creating and naming the new flavor, designing the artwork on the pint container, and selecting the advertising campaign.

Dave knows the success of Chocolate Peanut Udder will be critical to meeting the sales projections set for Holy Cow's current fiscal year. Dave projects sales growth of 20 percent this year, up from 15 percent a year ago. Holy Cow made its 15 percent goal last year, and the company shared the success with employees through a generous profit-sharing plan. Dave thinks that the 20 percent goal is challenging, but attainable.

The night before the first shipment of Chocolate Peanut Udder is scheduled to go out, one of the new machines in the factory malfunctions, causing an ammonia leak. Dangerous fumes fill the surrounding town, necessitating the evacuation of several dozen families from their homes. The fire department is brought in to secure the leak and ensure the safety of the plant. Dave is notified of the emergency and goes immediately to the plant. As soon as the fire marshal has declared the plant safe, Dave instructs his plant managers to conduct safety checks and assess losses. The following afternoon, the managers report to Dave that over $1 million in inventory has been lost.

He calls all managers together and asks them to come up with a contingency plan outlining the ways in which current sales goods remain viable. Recognizing that insurance coverage will provide a cushion in that regard, he asks them to consider how seriously the emergency has affected future sales, and to come up with a complete game plan. Arrangements are made to convene in 24 hours to brainstorm and reach some sort of consensus.

QUESTIONS

1. Which theory of leadership best describes the leadership at Holy Cow?
2. Identify the specific leadership styles used by Dave. Give specific examples from the case to support your answer.
3. Is Dave an effective leader? Explain.

Source: "Crisis at Holy Cow Frozen Yogurt," written by Melissa Waite, State University of New York, University at Buffalo, and Susan Stites-Doe, State University of New York, College at Brockport.

EXPERIENTIAL EXERCISE

*Leadership Style Profile**

According to situational leadership theory, there is no one best way to influence people. Most of the research on leadership indicates that leader behavior is a combination of task and relationship orientations. Task behavior is the extent to which a leader provides direction. Telling people what to do and/or setting goals for them and defining their roles is indicative of a task orientation. Providing support, being open, and being a good communicator are some of the behaviors of a relationship-oriented leader.

One's leadership style is, therefore, a combination of task and relationship behaviors. This exercise is designed to provide you with a profile of your leadership style.

Assume you are involved in each of the following 12 situations. Read each item and then circle the letter of the alternative that would most closely describe your behavior in the situations presented.

Situation 1 The employees in your program appear to be having serious problems getting the job done. Their performance has been going downhill rapidly. They have not responded to your efforts to be friendly or to your expressions of concern for their welfare.

a. Reestablish the need for following program procedures and meeting the expectations for task accomplishment.
b. Be sure that staff members know you are available for discussion, but don't pressure them.
c. Talk with your employees and then set performance goals.
d. Wait and see what happens.

Situation 2 During the past few months, the quality of work done by staff members has been increasing. Record keeping is accurate and up-to-date. You have made sure that all staff members are aware of your performance expectations.

a. Stay uninvolved.
b. Continue to emphasize the importance of completing tasks and meeting deadlines.
c. Be supportive and provide clear feedback. Continue to make sure that staff members are aware of performance expectations.
d. Make every effort to let staff members feel important and involved in the decision-making process.

Situation 3 Performance and interpersonal relations among your staff have been good. You have normally left them alone. However, a new situation has developed, and it appears that the staff members are unable to solve the problem themselves.

a. Bring the group together and work as a team to solve the problem.

b. Continue to leave them alone to work it out.

c. Act quickly and firmly to identify the problem and establish procedures to correct it.

d. Encourage the staff to work on the problem, letting them know you are available as a resource and for discussion if they need you.

Situation 4 You are considering a major change in your program. Your staff has a fine record of accomplishment and a strong commitment to excellence. They are supportive of the need for change and have been involved in the planning.

a. Continue to involve the staff in the planning, but you direct the change.

b. Announce the changes and then implement them with close supervision.

c. Allow the group to be involved in developing the change, but don't push the process.

d. Let the staff manage the change process.

Situation 5 You are aware that staff performance has been going down during the past several months. They need continual reminding to get tasks done on time and seem unconcerned about meeting objectives. In the past, redefining procedures and role expectations has helped.

a. Allow your staff to set their own direction.

b. Get suggestions from the staff, but see that the objectives are met.

c. Redefine goals and expectations and supervise carefully.

d. Allow the staff to be involved in setting goals, but don't pressure them.

Situation 6 You have just been appointed director of a program that had been running smoothly under the previous director. She had the reputation of running a tight ship. You want to maintain the quality of the program and the service delivery, but you would like to begin humanizing the environment.

a. Do nothing at the present time.

b. Continue with the administrative pattern set by the previous director, monitoring the staff and emphasizing the importance of task accomplishment.

c. Get the staff involved in decision making and planning, but continue to see that objectives are met and quality is maintained.

d. Reach out to staff members to let them feel important and involved.

Situation 7 You are considering expanding your unit's responsibilities. Your staff members have made suggestions about the proposed change and are enthusiastic. They operate effectively on a day-to-day basis and have shown themselves willing to assume responsibility.

a. Outline the changes and monitor carefully.

b. Reach consensus with the staff on the proposed changes and allow the staff members to organize the implementation.

c. Solicit input from the staff on proposed changes, but maintain control of the implementation.

d. Let the staff handle it.

Situation 8 Staff members have been working well. Interpersonal relations and morale are good. The quality of service delivery is excellent. You are somewhat uncomfortable with your apparent lack of direction of the group.

a. Be careful not to hurt your relationship with the staff by becoming too directive.

b. Take steps to assure that staff members are working in a well-defined manner.

c. Leave the staff alone to work as they have been.

d. Discuss the situation with the staff, and then initiate the necessary changes.

Situation 9 You have been appointed to replace the chairman of a task force that is long overdue in making requested recommendations for certification requirements. The group is not clear on its goal. Attendance at meetings has been poor. Frequently, the meetings are more social than task oriented. Potentially, task force members have the knowledge and experience to complete the task.

a. Let the group members work out their problems.

b. Solicit recommendations from the group, but see that the objectives are met.

c. Redefine and clarify the goals, tasks, and expectations, and carefully supervise progress toward task completion.

d. Allow group involvement in setting goals, but don't push.

Situation 10 Your employees are usually able to take responsibility. However, they are not responding well to your recent redefinition of performance standards.

a. Supervise carefully to ensure that standards are met.

b. Solicit input from the staff on performance standards. Incorporate their suggestions and monitor their progress toward meeting the standards.

c. Allow staff involvement in the redefinition of performance standards, but don't push.

d. Avoid confrontation. Apply no pressure and see what happens.

Situation 11 You have been promoted to the position of manager. The previous manager appeared to be uninvolved in the affairs of the staff. They have adequately handled their tasks and responsibilities. Their morale is high.

a. Become active in directing the staff toward working in a clearly defined manner.

b. Involve your staff in decision making and consistently reinforce good contributions.

c. Discuss past performance with your staff and then examine the need for new procedures.

d. Continue to leave the staff alone.

Situation 12 You have recently become aware of some internal difficulties on your staff. They had been working well together for the past year. The staff has an excellent record of accomplishment and staff members have consistently met their performance goals. All are well qualified for their roles in the program.

a. Allow your staff members to deal with the new problem themselves.

b. Tell the staff how you propose to deal with the situation and discuss the necessity for these procedures.

c. Make yourself available for discussion, but don't jeopardize your relationship with the staff by forcing the issue.

d. Act quickly and firmly to nip the problem in the bud.

SCORING

1. Circle the letter you chose for each situation in both the following charts, labeled Flexibility and Effectiveness. For example, if you answered alternative C for situation 1, circle the C in row 1 of the Flexibility chart and the C in row 1 of the Effectiveness chart.
2. Add the total number of letters you circled in each column of the Flexibility chart on page and enter these totals in the boxes labeled S1, S2, S3, and S4.
3. Still focusing on the Flexibility chart, place the total of each column in the corresponding quadrant of the following style matrix. That is, the S1 score

Flexibility						Effectiveness				
	S1	S2	S3	S4		−2	−1	+1	+2	
1	A	C	B	D		D	B	C	A	1
2	B	C	D	A		A	B	D	C	2
3	C	A	D	B		C	B	A	D	3
4	B	A	C	D		B	A	C	D	4
5	C	B	D	A		A	D	B	C	5
6	B	C	D	A		A	D	B	C	6
7	A	C	B	D		A	C	D	B	7
8	B	D	A	C		B	D	A	C	8
9	C	B	D	A		A	D	B	C	9
10	A	B	C	D		A	D	C	B	10
11	A	C	B	D		A	C	D	B	11
12	D	B	C	A		D	B	C	A	12

Situation Number

Situation Number

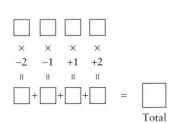

S1   S2   S3   S4

×   ×   ×   ×
−2   −1   +1   +2
‖   ‖   ‖   ‖

☐ + ☐ + ☐ + ☐   =   ☐

Total

Style 3 ☐ High Relationship Low Task	Style 2 ☐ High Task High Relationship
Style 4 ☐ Low Relationship Low Task	Style 1 ☐ High Task Low Relationship

goes in the Style 1 box (high task, low relationship), the S2 score goes in the Style 2 box (High task, high relationship), the S3 score goes in the Style 3 box, and the S4 score goes in the Style 4 box.

4. Add the total number of letters you circled in each column of the Effectiveness chart and enter these totals in the boxes below each column.
5. Multiply each number in the boxes by the number directly under it (be sure to indicate + or − as appropriate). Put the answer in the next box below that.
6. Add the four numbers and enter the total in the box labeled Total. Again, be sure to include the + or − sign.
7. On the following Effectiveness Scale, find the number in the Total box and mark it with an arrow.

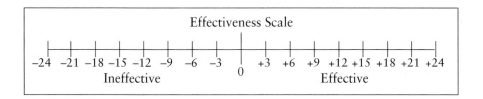

Effectiveness Scale

−24 −21 −18 −15 −12 −9 −6 −3   0   +3 +6 +9 +12 +15 +18 +21 +24

Ineffective   Effective

8. What does your style matrix tell you? How balanced are your scores? Do you have one predominant quadrant (this is not uncommon)? Do you have the potential flexibility to use all four leadership behaviors?
9. In terms of Effectiveness, how well did you do? The most appropriate behavior in each situation is indicated in the +2 column of the Effectiveness chart. You may want to go back to each situation and attempt to discover why that leadership behavior was best.

Your instructor may choose to discuss the results and implications of this exercise for leadership effectiveness.

NOTES

1. F.E. Fiedler, *A Theory of Leadership Effectiveness* (New York: McGraw-Hill, 1967).

2. F.E. Fiedler, "The Contribution of Cognitive Resources and Behavior to Leadership Performance" (Paper presented at Annual Meeting of the Academy of Management, Boston, Mass., 1984).

3. R.P. Vecchio, "Cognitive Resource Theory: Successor to the 'Black Box' Model of Leadership," *Contemporary Psychology* 33 (1988): 1030–1032; R.P. Vecchio, "A Theoretical and Empirical Examination of Cognitive Resource Theory," *Journal of Applied Psychology* 75 (1990): 141–147. R.P. Vecchio, "An Empirical Investigation of the Validity of Fiedler's Model of Leadership Effectiveness," *Organizational Behavior and Human Performance* 19 (1977): 180–206; M.J. Strube and J.E. Garcia, "A Meta-analytic Investigation of Fiedler's Contingency Model of Leadership Effectiveness," *Psychological Bulletin* 90 (1981): 307–321; R.P. Vecchio, "Assessing the Validity of Fiedler's Contingency Model of Leadership Effectiveness: A Closer Look at Strube and Garcia (1981)," *Psychological Bulletin* 93 (1983): 404–408; M.J. Strube and J.E. Garcia, "On the Proper Interpretation of Empirical Findings: Strube and Garcia (1981) Revisited," *Psychological Bulletin* 93 (1983): 600–603.

4. F.E. Fiedler, "The Leadership Game: Matching the Man to the Situation," *Organizational Dynamics* 4 (1976): 6–16.

5. Vecchio, "An Empirical Investigation of the Validity of Fiedler's Model."

6. M.G. Evans, "The Effects of Supervisory Behavior on the Path–Goal Relationship," *Organizational Behavior and Human Performance* 5 (1970): 277–298; M.G. Evans, "Extensions of a Path–Goal Theory of Motivation," *Journal of Applied Psychology* 59 (1974): 172–178.

7. R.J. House, "A Path–Goal Theory of Leader Effectiveness," *Administrative Science Quarterly* 16 (1971): 321–338.

8. A.D. Szilagyi and H.P. Sims, "An Exploration of the Path–Goal Theory of Leadership in a Health-Care Environment," *Academy of Management Journal* 17 (1974): 622–634; C.A. Schriesheim and A.S. DeNisi, "Task Dimensions as Moderators of the Effects of Instrumental Leadership: A Two-Sample Replicated Test of Path–Goal Leadership Theory," *Journal of Applied Psychology* 66 (1981): 589–597.

9. R.J. House and G. Dessler, "The Path–Goal Theory of Leadership: Some Post Hoc and A Priori Tests," in *Contingency Approaches to Leadership,* eds. J.G. Hunt and L.L. Larson (Carbondale, Ill.: Southern Illinois University Press, 1974); H.K. Downey, J.E. Sheridan, and J.W. Slocum, "Analysis of Relationships among Leader Behavior, Subordinate Job Performance, and Satisfaction: A Path–Goal Approach," *Academy of Management Journal* 18 (1975): 253–262.

10. P. Hersey and K.H. Blanchard, *Management of Organizational Behavior,* 3d ed. (Englewood Cliffs, N.J.: Prentice-Hall, 1977).

11. C.L. Graeff, "The Situational Leadership Theory: A Critical Review," *Academy of Management Review* 7 (1983): 285–291; G. Yukl, *Leadership in Organizations* (Englewood Cliffs, N.J.: Prentice-Hall, 1981); R.P. Vecchio, "Situational Leadership Theory: An Examination of a Prescriptive Theory," *Journal of Applied Psychology* 72 (1987): 444–451.

12. V.H. Vroom and P.W. Yetton, *Leadership and Decision Making* (Pittsburgh: University of Pittsburgh Press, 1973).

13. V.H. Vroom, "Leadership Revisited," in *Man and Work in Society,* eds. E.L. Case and F.G. Zimmer (New York: Van Nostrand Reinhold, 1975); V.H. Vroom and A.G. Jago, "On the Validity of the Vroom–Yetton Model," *Journal of Applied Psychology* 63 (1978): 151–162; R.H. Field, "A Test of the Vroom–Yetton Normative Model of Leadership," *Journal of Applied Psychology* 67 (1982): 523–532; W.C. Wedley and R.H. Field, "The Vroom–Yetton Model: Are Feasible Set Choices Due to Chance? *Academy of Management Proceedings* (1982): 146–150; R.H. Field and R.J. House, "A Test of the Vroom–Yetton Model Using Manager and Subordinate Reports," *Journal of Applied Psychology* 75 (1990): 362–370.

14. B. Smith, "The TELOS Program and the Vroom–Yetton Model," in *Crosscurrents*

in Leadership, eds. J.G. Hunt and L. Larson, (Carbondale, Ill: Southern Illinois University Press, 1979): 39–40.

15. V.H. Vroom and A.G. Jago, "Leadership and Decision Making: A Revised Normative Model" (Paper presented at Annual Meeting of the Academy of Management, Boston, Mass., 1984).

16. R.M. Dienesch and R.C. Liden, "Leader–Member Exchange Model of Leadership: A Critique and Further Developments," *Academy of Management Review* 11 (1986): 118–134; D. Duchon, S. Green, and T. Tabor, "Vertical Dyad Linkage," *Journal of Applied Psychology* 71 (1986): 56–60.

17. F. Dansereau, G. Graen, and W.J. Haga, "A Vertical Dyad Linkage Approach to Leadership within Formal Organizations: A Cognitudinal Investigation of the Role-Making Process," *Organizational Behavior and Human Performance* 15 (1975): 46–78; G. Graen and J.F. Cashman, "A Role-Making Model of Leadership in Formal Organizations: A Developmental Approach," in *Leadership Frontiers,* eds. J.G. Hunt and L.L. Larson (Kent, Ohio: Kent State University Press, 1975): 143–165; R.C. Liden and G. Graen, "Generalizability of the Vertical Dyad Linkage Model of Leadership," *Academy of Management Journal* 23 (1980): 451–465; R.P. Vecchio, "Are You IN or OUT with Your Boss?" *Business Horizons* 29 (1987): 76–78; R.P. Vecchio, "A Dyadic Interpretation of the Contingency Model of Leadership Effectiveness," *Academy of Management Journal* 22 (1979): 590–600; K. Dunegan, D. Duchon, and M. Uhl-Bien, "Examining the Link Between Leader–Member Exchange and Subordinate Performance: The Role of Task Analyzability and Variety as Moderators," *Journal of Management* 18 (1992): 59–76.

18. J. Miner, *Theories of Organizational Behavior* (Hinsdale, Ill.: The Dryden Press, 1980); R.P. Vecchio, "Predicting Employee Turnover from Leader–Member Exchange," *Academy of Management Journal* 28 (1985): 478–485; G. Ferris, "Role of Leadership in the Employee Withdrawal Process: A Constructive Replication," *Journal of Applied Psychology* 70 (1985): 777–781.

19. G. Graen and W. Schiemann, "Leader–Member Agreement: A Vertical Dyad Linkage Approach," *Journal of Applied Psychology* 63 (1978): 206–212.

20. R. Katerberg and P.W. Hom, "Effects of Within-Group and Between-Groups Variation in Leadership," *Journal of Applied Psychology* 66 (1981): 218–223; R.P. Vecchio, "A Further Test of Leadership Effects Due to Between-Group Variation and Within-Group Variation," *Journal of Applied Psychology* 67 (1982): 200–208; R.P. Vecchio, R.W. Griffeth, and P.W. Hom, "The Predictive Utility of the Vertical Dyad Linkage Approach," *Journal of Social Psychology* 126 (1987): 617–625.

21. Miner, *Theories of Organizational Behavior.*

22. R.P. Vecchio and B.C. Gobdel, "The Vertical Dyad Linkage Model of Leadership: Problems and Prospects," *Organizational Behavior and Human Performance* 34 (1984): 5–20.

23. R.P. Vecchio, "Effective Followership: Leadership Turned Upside Down," *Journal of Business Strategies* 4 (1987): 39–47.

24. S. Kerr and J.M. Jermier, "Substitutes for Leadership: Their Meaning and Measurement," *Organizational Behavior and Human Performance* 22 (1978): 375–403; S. Kerr, "Substitutes for Leadership: Some Implications for Organization Design," *Organization and Administrative Sciences* 8 (1977): 135; P.M. Podsakoff, B. Niehoff, S. MacKenzie, and M.L. Williams, "Do Substitutes for Leadership Really Substitute for Leadership? An Empirical Examination of Kerr and Jermier's Situational Leadership Model," *Organizational Behavior and Human Decision Processes* 54 (1993): 1–44.

25. J.K. Van Fleet, *The 22 Biggest Mistakes Managers Make* (West Nyack, N.Y.: Parker, 1973).

26. M. McCall and M. Lombardo, *Off the Track: Why and How Successful Executives Get Derailed—Technical Report No. 21* (Greensboro, N.C.: Center for Creative Leadership, 1983).

When it is necessary to make a decision, sometimes it is necessary to not make a decision.

— Lord Falkland

If you come to a fork in the road, take it.

— Yogi Berra

Originality is the art of remembering what you hear but forgetting where you heard it.

— Not sure who said this

LEARNING OBJECTIVES

After studying this chapter, you should be able to:

1. *Describe the types of decisions managers make.*
2. *List the steps of a highly rational decision-making process.*
3. *Describe some constraints on the decision-making process.*
4. *Identify obstacles to effective decision making.*
5. *Define groupthink and list its symptoms.*
6. *Describe techniques to improve decision making.*
7. *Identify characteristics of creative organization members.*
8. *Describe the steps in the creative process.*
9. *Identify ways that groups and individuals can enhance creativity.*
10. *List ways organizations can establish a climate that encourages creativity.*
11. *Explain how ethics training is being used in larger corporations.*

Decision Making

WHO DECIDES?

At Semco, Brazil's largest manufacturer of marine and food-processing machinery, president Ricardo Semler believes in treating his 800 employees "like responsible adults." In his view, this includes letting them make the decisions.

The company's policy of democratic decision making means that employees collectively make decisions that in most companies would be the province of the executives. For example, when the company's marine division needed a larger plant, Semco first hired real estate agents to find a location, but they found nothing. The company then asked the employees for help; over the first weekend they found three nearby factories for sale. The division shut down for a day, and all the workers went out to inspect the three buildings. Then the workers voted on which plant they wanted.

As it turned out, the plant that won the vote was not a plant that management wanted. However, the company went along with the decision on the assumption that letting the workers participate in the decision would enhance motivation and morale. In fact, once the workers were in the new plant, the division's productivity, in dollars per year per employee, shot up from $14,200 in 1984 to $37,500 in 1988.

The logic of letting employees make their own decisions extends to day-to-day concerns, such as what to wear, when to report to work, and whether to fly first-class. The company abolished its dress code and its rules about travel expenses. About the travel policy, Semler says, "If we can't trust people with our money and their judgment, we . . . shouldn't be sending them overseas to do business in our name."

Semco has also eliminated time clocks, relying instead on the employees' maturity and their desire to benefit from the company's policy of paying regular bonuses of 23 percent of profits. The flex-time policy worked out even better than expected, with no abuses or production interruptions. Quite the contrary: In one work area, a man wanted to start at 7:00 A.M., but he couldn't get the parts he needed until 8:00, when the forklift operator showed up. The employees discussed the problem and resolved it by having everyone in that work area learn to operate a forklift. The union didn't object, because the idea came from the workers.

This responsibility for decision making commits the employees to carrying out their decisions. For example, factory workers set their own schedule, so they are committed to fulfilling their plans.

One group decided to make 220 meat slicers during a month. When the end of that month came, the slicers were ready except for the motors; the supplier still hadn't sent them. Two employees drove to the supplier and arranged to have the motors delivered at the end of that day, the 31st. The motors arrived, and the whole work force stayed overnight, finishing the meat slicers at 4:45 the next morning.

Of course, good decision making requires informed decision makers. So that workers understand the impact of their decisions, Semco trains all of them to read financial reports, then provides them with a monthly balance sheet, profit-and-loss statement, and cash-flow statement for their division.

Even with such training, many company executives would be reluctant to delegate so much decision-making authority. However, no matter who makes the decisions in an organization, certain pitfalls can impede the selection of the best option. This chapter discusses how an organization's members make decisions and ways to improve decision making. It also describes obstacles to avoid in the decision-making process. The chapter concludes by considering creativity, which can enhance the quality of decisions.

Source: Ricardo Semler, "Managing without Managers," *Harvard Business Review* (September–October 1989): 76–84.

It can be reasonably argued that decision making is the most central activity of management, that it is the very essence of a manager's job. The nature of a manager's decisions, of course, is quite varied. They can range from such major issues as deciding whether to create a new product line to such seemingly minor issues as deciding where to take a client to lunch. In a given day, a manager will make a great number of decisions. The quality of these decisions can have a powerful impact on unit performance and, perhaps ultimately, on the performance of the entire organization.

TYPES OF ORGANIZATIONAL DECISIONS

Before considering the major models of decision making, let us first examine the variety of decisions a manager may make. Two useful classifications focus on whether decisions are (1) personal versus organizational and (2) programmed versus nonprogrammed.

PERSONAL VERSUS ORGANIZATIONAL DECISIONS

Every day we engage in **personal decision making.** Such decisions directly affect ourselves, rather than others. For example, each of us decides what clothes to wear on a given day and whether to ride our bike, take a bus, or drive a car to work. Although personal decisions are often fairly trivial, they can sometimes be quite important. Selecting a college or a field in which to major, as well as applying for a particular job, are personal decisions that can have profound effects on the course of a person's life.

In contrast, **organizational decision making** involves decisions that pertain to the problems and practices of a given organization. Like personal decisions, some organizational decisions can be fairly trivial, such as deciding which brand of typewriter ribbon to order. But others may have a major impact on the organization, such as choosing an advertising campaign or deciding whether to acquire a competing firm. The essential distinction between personal and organizational decision making lies in the object of the process. Personal decision making focuses on the actions and life of an individual, while organizational decision making focuses on the practices and performance of an organization.

PROGRAMMED VERSUS NONPROGRAMMED DECISIONS

Another useful way to distinguish among decisions has been proposed by Herbert Simon, who contends that decisions can be characterized in terms of whether they are fairly routine and well structured, or novel and poorly structured.[1] Well-structured decisions are termed **programmed decisions,** while poorly structured decisions are termed **nonprogrammed decisions.**

A good example of a programmed decision is when a clerk checks the on-hand inventory against a preestablished minimum standard. If the on-hand inventory falls below that standard, the clerk knows that it is time to order more stock.

With decisions that are unique and nonroutine, taking a preprogrammed approach becomes difficult. For example, the leaders of a nation may have trouble deciding how much to spend on military armaments for national defense, because of the uniqueness of political relations with neighboring countries and the difficulty of predicting the intentions of other world leaders. Not surprisingly, such nonprogrammed decision making may rely more on an individual's intuition and experience in similar situations.

By combining these two types of decisions (personal versus organizational and programmed versus nonprogrammed), we can create four classes or varieties of decisions (Figure 12.1). Personal programmed decisions involve simple, repetitive personal matters. Most people devote very little time to such decisions and tend to rely on established habits or simple decision rules. For example, an employee may usually park her car in the same spot in a parking lot, but on days that it rains, she may park in a different spot.

Personal nonprogrammed decisions arise during rare but significant events in an individual's personal life. For example, choosing which company to work for or whom to marry are personal decisions that people make only rarely. While some personal nonprogrammed decisions can be directly job-related, as when a person decides to quit one firm in hopes of finding a better position with another, others that are not so obviously job-related can also affect workplace behavior. For example, a person's choice of a marriage partner may mean having to relocate to be with him or her.

Organizational programmed decisions are typically handled according to established guidelines, rules, or procedures. Many simple problem situations can be dealt with by merely referring to a manual or rulebook that outlines the appropriate solution. In most organizations, lower-level personnel are responsible for handling organizational preprogrammed decisions. For example, a worker may be responsible for monitoring a control panel that provides information on the temperature and pressure within a vat. If the readings indicate that these values are outside of a predetermined range, the worker is instructed to adjust the necessary mechanisms in order to maintain control of the process.

FIGURE 12.1
TYPES OF DECISIONS

	Personal	Organizational
Programmed	Daily Routines Habits	Standard Operating Procedures Rulebooks and Manuals
Nonprogrammed	Job Choice Career Selection	Strategic Planning Issues Crisis Management

Organizational nonprogrammed decisions pertain to rare and unique situations that have potentially significant impact on the organization. Major planning issues and problems are often the topic of such decision making. How to acquire capital, whether to sell off unprofitable corporate divisions, and whether to launch a new product line are examples of organizational nonprogrammed decision issues. Because of the critical nature of such decisions for the very well-being of the organization, they are more typically handled by high-level personnel. Organizational nonprogrammed decision making affords the greatest opportunities for creativity.

CLASSICAL DECISION THEORY

The traditional approach to understanding decision making, often called **classical decision theory,** assumes that decision making is, and should be, a highly rational process. The classical theory of decision making is often referred to as the **rational-economic model** because of the model's presumption that decision makers are rational and its strong ties to the classical economic view of behavior. The process can be described in terms of a sequence of steps that a decision maker should follow in order to enhance the probability of attaining a desired goal. Figure 12.2 illustrates the proposed steps in classical decision theory.[2]

As the figure shows, a situation must exist that triggers the decision-making process. A set of circumstances leads the decision maker to recognize the existence of the problem or opportunity that demands action. Recognition is an essential early step in decision making because unless a person believes a

FIGURE 12.2
STEPS IN THE DECISION-MAKING PROCESS: THE CLASSICAL VIEW

Opportunity or Problem Situation
↓
Opportunity or Problem Recognition
↓
Opportunity or Problem Definition
↓
Generate Alternatives
↓
Gather Information
↓
Evaluate Alternatives
↓
Select One Alternative
↓
Implement Selected Alternative

Evaluate Effectiveness of Alternative

problem or opportunity exists, the decision-making process will not occur. Following recognition, the decision maker defines the nature of the situation. This definition leads to the generation of alternative approaches to coping with the situation. The manner in which the situation is defined will dictate the nature and variety of alternatives. The next steps in the process entail gathering information about each alternative (such as its relative cost and likelihood of success) and evaluating its desirability by weighting and combining the obtained information. From this evaluation, a single best course of action will emerge. This course of action is the one that will be implemented and subsequently evaluated in terms of its effectiveness in eliminating the problem or taking advantage of the opportunity. By monitoring the effectiveness of the solution, the decision maker can judge the extent to which it was appropriate and determine whether further action can or should be taken. It may be that the problem or opportunity will need to be redefined in light of the results. In essence, this step in the model provides feedback about how well the decision-making process was carried out.

The classical view is in fact popular with many scholars.* It does a fairly good job of describing how a decision *should* be made; in particular, the view points to the features managers should focus on when trying to improve the caliber of the decision-making process. Yet, the classical view is largely inaccurate as a description of *how* managers typically make decisions. Furthermore, its prescriptions for making better decisions are often in error.

One major set of deficiencies in the classical approach lies in its assumptions that all alternatives will be considered, that the consequences of each alternative will be considered, that accurate information is available at no cost, and that decision makers are totally rational beings.

In reality, a manager rarely considers all possible alternatives, since there often are too many to list. Additionally, many alternatives may not even occur to the decision maker. The assumption that the consequences of each alternative are considered is similarly impractical. In many circumstances, it may be impossible to estimate all the consequences. But even when full consideration is possible, examining all alternatives may require too much time and effort.

Rarely, if ever, is a manager's information perfectly accurate. More typically, the available information is often dated (because it takes time to gather, distill, and digest information) and only partially relevant to the question at hand (because information is often gathered for purposes other than a manager's specific needs). Also, information is not a free good. The cost of generating or purchasing needed data adds another constraint to the decision-making process. As a consequence, a manager is often forced to make decisions based on incomplete or insufficient information.

Furthermore, studies show that decision makers do not have the mental ability needed to store and process all of the data required to select the single best alternative. Available evidence suggests that people are simply not capable of performing the cognitive calculus that the classical view requires.[3]

---

*Most economists subscribe to the classical view of decision making.

Finally, there are a number of real-world constraints on a manager's decision making. For example, a manager may not have sufficient time to devote to making a decision. Despite a decision's importance, the need for prompt action may rule out a formal analysis of the situation.

A BEHAVIORAL THEORY OF DECISION MAKING

Given the shortcomings of the rational-economic model, an alternative perspective has emerged that provides a more descriptive view of managerial behavior. This approach is termed a **behavioral theory of decision making,** sometimes called the **administrative model.**[4] Figure 12.3 illustrates the essential steps in the administrative model of decision making.

The administrative model explicitly acknowledges the real-world limitations on managers' decision making. Specifically, it holds that decision makers must work within conditions that provide a **bounded rationality.** Bounded rationality means that managers are restricted in their decision-making processes and must, therefore, settle for something short of an ideal or optimal solution. Bounded rationality recognizes that (1) all possible alternatives and their associated consequences cannot be generated, (2) both the available information and the definition of the situation are likely to be incomplete and inadequate to some degree, and (3) the final decision may be based on criteria other than simple optimization or outcome maximization.[†]

Due to the personal and situational limitations on managerial decision making, managers tend to make decisions that are "good enough" for the situ-

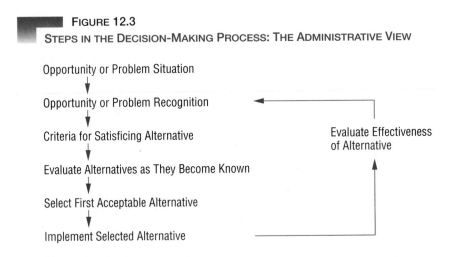

FIGURE 12.3

STEPS IN THE DECISION-MAKING PROCESS: THE ADMINISTRATIVE VIEW

Opportunity or Problem Situation
↓
Opportunity or Problem Recognition ←
↓
Criteria for Satisficing Alternative   Evaluate Effectiveness
↓   of Alternative
Evaluate Alternatives as They Become Known
↓
Select First Acceptable Alternative   ↑
↓
Implement Selected Alternative

[†]It is interesting to consider what an organization would be like if it were staffed with totally rational beings. In point of fact, it is because organizations are not staffed with collections of individuals like Mr. Spock *(Star Trek*'s science officer) that organizations pose many intriguing problems for the field of organizational behavior (in addition to making organizational life much more exciting).

ation at hand. When managers seek solutions that are "good enough" rather than "ideal," they **satisfice** rather than **maximize**. When maximizing, a manager attempts to find the best or optimal solution. In contrast, when satisficing, a decision maker considers each alternative until one arises that is reasonably acceptable. Such an alternative meets all necessary requirements for a solution, but may not be the very best choice. March and Simon have provided a very useful illustration of the essential difference between satisficing and maximizing: Maximizing (or optimizing) is analogous to searching through a haystack for the sharpest needle to be found, whereas satisficing is much like searching through a haystack until a needle can be found that is sharp enough to sew with.[5]

Also included in the administrative model is the notion of **bounded discretion,** which suggests that optimal solutions are sometimes not feasible courses of action because they are ethically improper. In some circumstances, the best or optimal solution may actually involve morally questionable behavior. A retailer, for example, may reason that one way out of a difficult financial situation is to set her store on fire in order to collect the insurance. Or a food processor may have the option of significantly reducing product quality (perhaps by decreasing the amount of meat and increasing the proportion of filler in a hamburger patty) as a means of lowering costs and thereby raising profits. Most managers (but, of course, not all) prefer to avoid such unethical behavior. Therefore, bounded discretion represents a further constraint on the decision-making process.

In addition, Simon and others contend that managers often follow rules of thumb, or **heuristics,** when making decisions.[6] Because of the volume, variety, and complexity of business decisions, managers frequently use simplified decision rules to achieve satisficing solutions. For example, a heuristic for some investors is that if a stock drops 10 percent or more below its purchase price, they will decide to sell. These investors use this heuristic with great consistency and regardless of other circumstances to avoid holding on to a potentially disastrous, but previously attractive, stock.

The administrative model provides an interesting comparison to the rational-economic model. The two differ, most fundamentally, in their approaches to how decisions *should be* and *are* made. Each is successful in its own domain: The rational-economic model provides a useful summary of how decisions *should be made*, while the administrative model gives a good description of how decisions typically *are made*.

THE INFLUENCE OF JUDGMENTAL STRATEGIES

Recently, researchers have come to recognize that decision makers frequently go beyond the information they are given when making inferences. Daniel Kahneman and Amos Tversky have identified two judgmental strategies (sometimes termed judgmental heuristics) on which people frequently rely.[7] The strategies, unfortunately, oftentimes mislead people into making erroneous inferences.

An Inside Look
A Trend Toward Labor–Management Cooperation

Union members are helping managers make important decisions in more and more U.S. companies. This change in decision participation is spurred on partially by empowerment and employee involvement programs that have become popular over the past several years, and partially because unions are struggling to maintain their diminishing power base.

Gone are the days when management told workers to "check your brains at the door." Committees and teams of managers and union employees now engage in joint problem solving, creating new ways to improve quality and boost production.

In return for sharing their operating expertise and creative solutions, unions want companies to share their cost and profit data as well as guarantee union workers job security. These are legiti-mate requests if employees are to earnestly consider more efficient ways of working.

Participative decision making has gained support among steel, rubber, textile, and communications workers, and from such companies as AT&T, Goodyear, Xerox, and Ford Motor. In fact, Xerox was one of the earliest companies to realize the benefits of participative decision making. Upon learning the company would close its wire-harness manufacturing unit outside of Rochester, New York, because the parts could be purchased less expensively from Mexico, the union was given the opportunity to devise a cost-cutting plan that would be competitive with the Mexican bid. The union succeeded, and participative decision making has become widespread throughout Xerox.

At National Steel, cooperative reform with the United Steelworkers, a union that lost 45 percent of its membership in the 1980s, has been widely accepted. Teams of employees are now empowered to shut down the production line and conduct their own safety inspections. Management at National Steel, for its part, is enjoying labor peace and higher productivity.

Some union traditionalists think that unions are moving in the wrong direction and selling out to management. However, with the steady decline in union membership and the trends toward teamwork and participation, union leaders realize that cooperative decision making may help prevent the demise of America's labor unions.

Source: Peter Nulty, "Look What the Unions Want Now," *Fortune*, February 8, 1993, 128–135.

The first judgmental strategy, termed the **availability heuristic**, reflects the influence of the relative availability of objects or events (that is, their accessibility through memory, perception, or imagination). Occasionally, the availability heuristic can be misleading. Consider a pollster who asks adults in the United States to estimate the current level of national unemployment. It is likely that a bias will be reflected in these estimates such that unemployed individuals will tend to overestimate the rate of unemployment, while employed individuals will underestimate it. Many people would not recall newspaper or television accounts of estimates of unemployment or attempt to compensate for their possible bias by deliberately considering the impact of their own experiences on their beliefs.

The second judgmental strategy proposed by Kahneman and Tversky, termed the **representativeness heuristic**, involves the application of one's sense of resemblance between objects or events. In applying this heuristic, a person assesses the extent to which an object or event possesses features that would enable that person to categorize the object or event appropriately. As an illustration of this tendency, consider the following: I have a friend who is a professor. He likes to write poetry, is rather shy, and is small in stature. Which of the following is his field of expertise—Chinese studies or psychology?

If you are inclined to answer "Chinese studies," you have been seduced by the representativeness heuristic. That is to say, you judged the personality profile to be a better fit for the stereotype of a sinologist than a psychologist. However, the odds are that any person is more likely to know psychologists, and psychologists are far more numerous than sinologists. In light of this more critical base-rate information, the better answer (from a statistical standpoint) would be "psychology."

Numerous decision-making tasks, of course, rely on accurate estimation and categorization. Therefore, both the availability heuristic and the representativeness heuristic are important tools in drawing inferences. Although they often may lead us to correct inferences, they have the potential to lead to erroneous judgments as well. It should also be understood that Kahneman and Tversky's notions of availability and representativeness are not, strictly speaking, heuristics, in the sense of being explicit and invariant devices or formulae for making decisions. Rather, they represent automatic and nonconscious processes that are frequently involved in judgment and decision-making processes.

OBSTACLES TO EFFECTIVE DECISION MAKING

A number of potential obstacles to effective decision making have been identified. In this section, we will examine four of the most common: judgmental biases, escalation of commitment, groupthink, and the willingness of groups to take risks.

JUDGMENTAL BIASES

When the availability heuristic and the representativeness heuristic lead us to erroneous conclusions, they may be termed *biases*. Along with the availability bias and the representativeness bias are a number of common biases that have been found to influence decision making. These include:

1. *Implicit favorite bias:* The tendency of a decision maker to have a preferred alternative and, though not fully aware of this preference, to engage in a process of considering alternatives that merely confirms the initial prejudice.[8]

2. *Loss-aversion bias:* The tendency of a decision maker to treat potential losses as more important than potential gains, even though the objective values of both losses and gains are truly equal.[9]

3. *Selective perception bias:* The tendency of a decision maker to be influenced by prior expectations to interpret only certain, selected information (for example, a supervisor who believes strongly in a particular subordinate may interpret information on that worker's performance in only favorable terms).

4. *Personal experience bias:* The tendency of a decision maker to be so influenced by strong, personal experiences that he or she ignores other information

(for example, a manager who has had a bad experience in a unionized setting might believe all employees are hostile to their employers).

ESCALATION OF COMMITMENT

Barry Staw has suggested that people are sometimes unwilling to change a course of action despite unequivocal evidence showing that their decision was incorrect.[10] In essence, a person may decide to "stay the course" because he or she has already invested substantial time, effort, and/or money in the existing situation. All the more remarkable is the tendency of people to invest still more resources in a course of action that appears doomed to failure. As examples of escalating commitment, Staw cites the following:

> *Imagine a person who has purchased a stock at $50 a share. Yet, when the stock drops in price to $20, he buys more shares at the lower price. When the price drops still further, the individual must decide whether to buy more, sell out, or hold on to what he has purchased.*
>
> *Consider a person who spends several years working toward an academic degree in a field which offers minimal job prospects (for example, in the humanities). Yet, the person invests still more time and money in completing the degree (rather than changing fields). Ultimately, the person is faced with the choice of being unemployed, underemployed (that is, working in a job which is below his capabilities), or starting over in another field or career path.*
>
> *During the early phase of U.S. involvement in the Vietnam War, the Undersecretary of State (George Ball) wrote to President Johnson: "The decision you face now is crucial. Once large members of U. S. troops are committed to direct combat, they will begin to take heavy casualties in a war they are ill-equipped to fight in a noncooperative, if not downright hostile, countryside. Once we suffer large casualties, we will have started a well-nigh irreversible process. Our involvement will be so great that we cannot—without national humiliation—stop short of achieving our complete objectives. Of the two possibilities, I think humiliation would be more likely than the achievement of our objectives." (Memo dated July 1, 1965.)[11]*

We have all seen situations in which people stay committed to a specific course of action despite negative feedback. By committing additional resources to a losing strategy, they in essence throw good money after bad. There are several explanations of this phenomenon. One is that people pursue a course of action *in spite of* negative feedback largely *because of* negative feedback. This argument suggests that people value tenacity, or stick-to-it-iveness. They feel that a "damn the torpedoes, full speed ahead" stance has a certain social value. Because people generally admire those who stick to their principles, a decision maker may adopt a persistent approach in response to perceived social pressure. A second explanation suggests that people will forsake a more rational approach to difficult decision situations out of concern for establishing consistency.

To test the notion that social norms explain managerial consistency, Staw and Ross used practicing managers, college business majors, and other undergraduate students as subjects in a study.[12] Each subject was presented with a case study summary of a manager's behavior. The case portrayed the manager as being either consistent or experimenting (less consistent) in following a course of action. In addition, the manager's behavior was described as ultimately leading to either success or failure. In the consistency condition, the manager adhered to a single course of action despite a series of negative results. In the experimenting condition, the manager initially tried one course of action, then shifted to a second and a third course when negative results were obtained.

The subjects responded most favorably to the managers who followed a consistent course of action and were successful in the end. In addition, the hypothetical manager who persisted to an ultimately successful outcome was judged more highly than would be predicted from the separate effects of the variables of consistency and outcome success. In essence, Staw and Ross found a form of "hero effect" in which a manager who remained committed despite two setbacks *and* succeeded in the end was regarded quite positively. Furthermore, the researchers found that the subjects' reactions to consistency varied across groups of raters. Practicing managers showed the strongest appreciation, followed by college business majors and then other undergraduates. This suggests that consistency is viewed as important to effective management and that this perception may be acquired through participation in business roles.[‡]

Escalation of commitment is most likely to occur in certain predictable settings. Among these are situations in which a person feels a strong sense of personal responsibility, as when selecting a career or setting a policy with which the individual will be publicly associated. To counter the escalation tendency, Staw suggests employing outside advisers who do not feel personal responsibility for previous losses or gains.[14] It may also be wise to rotate decision-making responsibility across managers if there is a history of losses due to the tendency to escalate commitment.

GROUPTHINK

Irving Janis has identified a fascinating phenomenon that can lead groups to commit serious errors in decision making. In describing this situation, which he called **groupthink,** Janis proposed that highly cohesive working groups (that is, groups whose members enjoy a high degree of interpersonal attraction) are in danger of taking a distorted view of situations that confront them.[15][§] As a result, the group's decision-making processes may be slanted toward seeking *consensus* rather than exploring alternative courses of action. Because dissent and critical analysis are not encouraged in discussion sessions, the group may select a course of action that ignores potential dangers and pitfalls.

[‡]Research on the escalation of commitment phenomenon has been criticized for not yet employing decision-making situations in which the continued commitment of resources is explicitly inadvisable on economic grounds.[13]

[§]Janis selected the term *groupthink* to label this phenomenon because it had Orwellian overtones (cf. *newspeak* in George Orwell's novel *1984).*

Janis has provided a number of illustrations of groupthink, including the Watergate cover-up by the Nixon administration, the escalation of U.S. military involvement in Vietnam, the failure of the Roosevelt administration to prepare for the Japanese raid on Pearl Harbor, the space shuttle *Challenger* disaster, Nazi Germany's decision to invade the Soviet Union in 1941, Ford Motor Company's decision to market the Edsel, and—perhaps the most clear-cut example—the Bay of Pigs incident during the presidency of John Kennedy (the incident in which President Kennedy and his top advisers unanimously decided to adopt a CIA proposal to invade Cuba and overthrow Fidel Castro).[16] None of Kennedy's advisers voiced opposition to the proposal. The operation was spearheaded by 1,400 Cuban exiles who were given air and naval support by the U.S. military and the CIA. The invasion, which occurred at the Bay of Pigs on the south coast of Cuba, was a total failure within a few days of the invasion, with a majority of the invaders being taken prisoner by the Cuban army.**

In retrospect, Kennedy and his advisers appear to have been victims of groupthink.[17] Their decision to proceed with the invasion was based on a certain amount of wishful thinking in that the plan relied heavily on a popular uprising by the Cuban people in support of the invaders. Kennedy and his advisers assumed that the invasion would be a simple operation that could not fail and would quickly lead to Castro's overthrow. They also gave no advance consideration to the possible adverse consequences of a failed invasion—the most significant of which were the anger of normally friendly Latin American and European countries, and the growth of closer military ties between the Soviet Union and Cuba. Later, Castro's concern for defense led to the installation of Soviet-built nuclear missiles in Cuba, within 90 miles of the United States. This defensive move precipitated a further problem for the Kennedy administration—the Cuban Missile Crisis.

Following the Bay of Pigs invasion, the confidence of Kennedy and his top advisers (such men as Robert McNamara, Robert Kennedy, Dean Rusk, and Arthur Schlesinger, Jr.) was deeply shaken as they came to realize their own tendencies toward self-deception. In writing about the decision process, Schlesinger observed that

> Had one advisor opposed the adventure, I believe Kennedy would have canceled it. No one spoke against it. . . . Our meetings took place in a curious atmosphere of assumed consensus. . . . In the months after the Bay of Pigs, I bitterly reproached myself for having kept so silent . . . though my feelings of guilt were tempered by the knowledge that a course of objection would have accomplished little save to gain me a name as a nuisance. I can only explain . . . that one's impulse to blow the whistle on this nonsense was simply undone by the circumstances of the discussion (Janis, 1972, pp. 39–40).

**To the credit of Kennedy and his policy advisers, they recognized the mistakes they made during the Bay of Pigs invasion and tried to compensate by having open and frank discussions when coping with the Cuban Missile Crisis.

Janis has proposed eight main symptoms or signs of groupthink:

1. *An illusion of invulnerability.* Group members may develop a sense of powerfulness that leads them to ignore obvious danger signals. They may take extreme risks as a result of being overly optimistic.

2. *Rationalization.* The members may discredit or ignore evidence that contradicts the group's consensus. Sources of disagreeable information may be attacked, or elaborate rationalizations may be offered to explain away the information.

3. *An assumption of morality.* Group members may view themselves as highly ethical and above reproach. The views of outsiders are then defined as intrinsically immoral or evil. Adopting a stance of self-righteousness makes it easier for the group to follow a course of action that is morally questionable because the members view themselves as pursuing a higher morality.

4. *Negative stereotyping.* Groups that suffer from groupthink may come to view opponents and people outside the group in simple negative stereotypic terms. By casting outsiders in negative terms, the group makes them easier to ignore because their opposition is to be expected.

5. *Pressure to conform.* The expression of dissent is suppressed by the group's members. Persons who voice objections or express doubts may be ostracized or expelled.

6. *Self-censorship.* Each member of the group may carefully monitor his or her own thoughts and suppress personal objectives, in essence withholding dissent.

7. *An illusion of unanimity.* As a result of self-censorship, no reservations are expressed. The consequence of this lack of dissent is the apparent unanimous endorsement of proposals.

8. *Mindguards.* Certain individuals in the group may take it upon themselves to serve as mindguards, guarding a manager's thoughts in the same way a bodyguard protects a leader's personal safety. These mindguards will act against sources of information or dissenters by deflecting them or their objections.

As this discussion of groupthink suggests, the existence of an apparently admirable condition—group cohesion—can have detrimental effects on the quality of decision making. Janis suggests that several steps be taken if a highly cohesive decision-making body is disposed to groupthink. Specifically, group members should be encouraged to voice criticisms, doubts, and objections. To promote open debate, managers should avoid stating their preferred positions during the early stages of group discussion. It may also be valuable for the group to invite outside experts to sit in on their sessions occasionally and offer suggestions.

Another tactic for countering groupthink is to assign several group members to teams that will investigate the advisability of alternative courses of action. After gathering evidence in support of an assigned position, the teams can present their arguments and participate in a directed debate. Such a confrontation of alternative points of view can lead to new insights on the issues underlying a decision-making situation.

A somewhat related technique is to appoint a group member to serve as a devil's advocate at each group meeting.[††] This person's responsibilities would include actively criticizing the proposals (and the implicit assumptions) raised by all group members.

Another suggested technique is the scheduling of a **last-chance meeting** at which all group members are encouraged to raise any nagging doubts or hesitations they may have.

Last, and perhaps most important, a manager can help to overcome groupthink through a willingness to accept criticism. Setting an example of openness to criticism, as opposed to resentment or fear of subordinates' objections, can help to promote serious discussion of the pros and cons of alternative courses of action.

RISK TAKING WITHIN GROUPS

Imagine that you are a manager who must make a decision that entails a fair amount of risk—for example, deciding whether to expand your production facilities into a politically unstable country in Latin America. The risks are great in that your entire investment could be lost if the country is taken over by extremists who intend to nationalize all industry. However, the potential profits will be substantial if the country does not experience a revolution. Would you make the final decision on such an investment by yourself or would you turn it over to a committee?

Most people would argue that committee decisions tend to be conservative and that individuals, in comparison, are not constrained by the dynamics of debate or the doubts that might be raised within a committee. Boldness and initiative are more typically associated with individuals than with committees.[‡‡]

James Stoner, while a graduate student at MIT, was one of the first people to investigate whether groups are more cautious than individuals in decision making that involves risky propositions.[18] In his research, he devised a series of cases involving the propensity (or willingness) to take risks. The cases dealt with such diverse topics as (1) choosing between a secure though modest-paying job with one employer versus taking a high-paying job with a newly founded but financially less sound firm in a highly competitive field, and (2) choosing between calling a football play that would likely result in a tie versus calling a play that is riskier but could result in a victory.

In his research, Stoner found that individuals tended to take a less risky route, while groups favored riskier actions. When the individuals were placed in a group setting, they shifted their endorsement to a riskier position. This phenomenon, in which a group endorses a riskier position than would its individual members, is called the **risky shift.**

[††]The procedure of appointing a "devil's advocate" originated with a Catholic church practice of assigning someone the role of arguing against the canonization of a candidate for sainthood.

[‡‡]As an illustration of the belief that committees tend to be conservative, consider the old saying, "A camel is a horse that was designed by a committee."

A number of explanations have been offered to account for the risky shift. One of the more popular is the concept of **diffusion of responsibility.** This line of reasoning holds that when individuals are in groups, they may feel less personal responsibility for the consequences of their actions. The diffusion of responsibility concept has also been used to account for the failure of an individual to come to the aid of an injured person if a large number of people are nearby. Thus, a mugging victim who is lying on the floor of a subway station is less likely to receive aid as the size of the crowd increases. Similarly, group decision making may sometimes reflect this sense of personal anonymity in endorsing a course of action. From studies of incidents similar to the subway station mugging, researchers have inferred that risky shifts can even occur in the absence of group discussion.[19]

Although the shift toward endorsing risk within groups has been found in a variety of settings,[20] there have been occasions where groups opted for the more cautious alternative action. For example, in one study, groups of housewives and students were asked whether a married couple should abort a pregnancy when future complications in the pregnancy could endanger the life of the mother. In this decision scenario, groups endorsed a more cautious course (abortion) than did the members acting alone.[21] In another study, groups were again more cautious than individuals in recommending that a couple not go ahead with their plan to be married when the couple expressed disagreement on a number of issues.[22] The tendency of groups to move in a more conservative direction than would individuals is called the **cautious shift.**

Clearly, the risky shift and the cautious shift are contradictory in their predictions of how groups will behave when faced with a decision that involves an element of risk. A close examination of the studies that have identified both risky and cautious shifts suggests that the prior inclination of the group's members (that is, when they make their premeeting judgment of their preferences) is an important factor in determining whether a shift will occur in a cautious or a risky direction. If the premeeting inclination is toward caution, the group's decision tends to go to the extreme of the cautious direction. If the premeeting inclination is toward risk, however, the group's decision is likely to go toward the risky extreme. For example, a group that is meeting to determine the level of punishment a student should receive for cheating is likely to opt for a more severe penalty than the members in isolation would have selected. Yet, a group that is betting on horses will be more conservative than its members acting alone.[23]

The tendency of groups to move toward extremes has been termed **group polarization.**[24] This phenomenon is most probably the result of several factors. First, the premeeting inclinations of the group's members encourage a certain bias during discussions that leads the group to explore and endorse arguments and information that support the members' initial positions. Throughout discussions, the group's members will voice, and thereby encourage, additional rationales for being either conservative or risky, depending on their original bias.

Group polarization can also be explained by the tendency of groups to make decisions that endorse dominant cultural values. The content of the decision then becomes an important issue in predicting whether a cautious or a risky shift will occur. For business- and career-related decisions, the dominant cultural value favors risk taking. Within our culture, taking chances in competitive arenas is greatly admired and seen as an often necessary step in attaining success. Other topics, such as weighing the value of a mother's life versus the life of an unborn child, are traditionally decided more conservatively. Thus, a group would probably favor preserving the mother's life rather than the child's. In general, group members try to endorse the prevalent social view on the appropriateness of risk versus conservatism in a given situation. Nonetheless, the observed instances of groups endorsing risk appear to outnumber the instances of groups endorsing caution.

TECHNIQUES FOR IMPROVING DECISION MAKING

INDIVIDUAL VERSUS GROUP DECISION MAKING

In the previous discussion of individual versus group decision making, it was noted that groups tend to endorse extreme positions when confronted with decisions involving an element of risk. In situations where risk is not great or where achieving a high-quality solution is the primary goal, the question of the relative advantages of group versus individual decision making can be raised. A good deal of research has been devoted to the issue of whether solutions generated by decision-making groups are superior, inferior, or equal to the solutions generated by individuals working alone on the same problem.

Studies of individual versus group decision making have typically relied on one of two approaches: (1) individuals initially work alone on a problem and subsequently work on similar problems in groups (and vice versa), or (2) some individuals work alone on several problems, while other individuals simultaneously work in groups on the same problems. The problems studied ranged from simple puzzles to complex reasoning tasks. Performance has frequently been measured in terms of quality of solution, time required to reach a solution, and sheer number of problems solved.

Despite variations in their designs and samples, these studies overall have yielded quite similar results. By and large, research that has pitted individuals against groups has shown that groups will outperform individuals working in isolation. That is, the group's solutions to problems are typically of higher quality than the average of the individuals' solutions. One interesting additional finding is that the best solitary worker may often outperform the group. But in general, and for a variety of tasks, groups can be expected to outperform the vast majority of individuals who work alone.

Precisely why groups have an advantage over individuals has also been the subject of much research. One self-evident explanation is that groups can pool information and abilities. By pooling these resources, the group gains access to a collection of knowledge that is greater than any single individual's. This knowledge enables the group to reject obviously incorrect approaches and provides a check on the possibility of committing errors.

Being in a group also tends to motivate and inspire group members. The stimulation of being in a social setting can enhance an individual's level of contribution. In addition, there are social rewards for making a significant contribution to a group's efforts. For example, praise, admiration, and feeling valuable to the group can be strong incentives for an individual to exert greater effort.

Finally, depending on the situation, it may be possible to divide a group's general assignment into smaller, more manageable tasks that can then be delegated to individual group members. Thus, groups have the potential for employing division of labor.

Despite these advantages, problems may arise. As we noted earlier, highly cohesive groups sometimes encourage a restricted view of alternatives (groupthink). Groups may also polarize toward extreme points of view if an appreciable element of risk is involved (risky and cautious shifts). Although it has not been formally studied yet, it is possible that groups may be successful in exerting social pressure on a manager to escalate commitment to a losing course of action because of the manager's desire to appear consistent in the eyes of the group's members.

In addition to these potential disadvantages, group decision making has other likely drawbacks. For example, group decision making tends to be much more costly than individual decision making. Given the time and energy that meetings can consume, it is usually best to reserve group decision making for more important decisions that require high-quality solutions. Group discussions can also give rise to hostility and conflict. This is especially likely when group members have divergent and strongly held opinions on alternative courses of action. In addition, decision making in groups tends to be influenced by the relative status of group members. Thus, when a group member who possesses relatively little status offers an objectively good suggestion, it may be rejected. But if the same suggestion is offered by a group member with high status, the likelihood of its being adopted is greatly increased.[25]

As Table 12.1 illustrates, there are many advantages and disadvantages to entrusting decision making to groups rather than to individuals. Before choosing a format for decision making, a manager should examine the points

TABLE 12.1
ADVANTAGES AND DISADVANTAGES OF GROUP DECISION MAKING

Advantages	Disadvantages
Pooling of information	Groupthink
Social arousal of participants	Endorsement of extreme positions
Social rewards for participation	Escalation of commitment
Division of labor	Greater cost in time and energy
Higher-quality solutions	Split positions can generate conflict
Sharing of resources	Status biases in member involvement

OB Focus
Peer Review Can Resolve Disputes

Peer review is a method of handling employee disputes that is gaining popularity in many U.S. organizations. The peer review system uses a team of about five employees and managers to solve employee disputes. The team investigates, hears, and makes a binding decision on each case.

Peer review team members are typically selected from a pool of volunteer employees who have received extensive training in communication and listening skills, corporate policies and procedures, workplace privacy and confidentiality, and fact-based decision making. Peer review teams should reflect employee diversity and represent workers from different levels of the organization.

Parameters should limit the scope of the team's authority in terms of hearing cases and recommending restitution. For example, the peer review system at Merrill Industries of Adrian, Michigan, is restricted to reviewing discharge decisions only. Public Service Company of New Mexico allows performance appraisal ratings to be challenged, but prohibits peer review of terminations. Reinstatement, performance reevaluations, and payment of back wages are some of the remedies peer review teams can recommend.

The benefits of the peer review process are straightforward. Peer review offers a fair, impartial process that builds on participative decision making to ensure employee disputes are resolved quickly and effectively. Because peers are directly involved in the decision making, employees are more likely to have confidence in the system. Disputes can be handled on a timely basis, and peer review often prevents employee disputes from turning into expensive lawsuits.

Placing decision making squarely on the shoulders of fellow employees fosters trust and effective problem solving. Even if a peer review team is never selected, both parties benefit by having a trained group of volunteers who are better informed about company policies. Peer review represents an innovative way companies are putting the decision-making abilities of employees to good use.

Source: Paula Ann Hughes and Richard Charles Grote, "Peer Review Places Trust with Employees," *HRMagazine*, June 1993, 57–62.

outlined in the table to determine if any specific conditions strongly advise for or against the use of groups.

THE NOMINAL GROUP TECHNIQUE

One approach that attempts to capitalize on the positive feature of group decision making, while avoiding many of the potential pitfalls, is the **nominal group technique (NGT)**. In this technique, seven to ten individuals are brought together to participate in a structured exercise that includes the following steps:

1. The members silently and independently record their ideas about how to tackle a problem.

2. In turn, each member presents one of his or her ideas to the group. As each idea is offered, it is summarized and recorded on a chalkboard or wall chart, without discussion of its merits.

3. A discussion is held in which all ideas are clarified and evaluated.

4. Individuals silently and independently vote on each idea. This voting may involve a rating of the proposals or a rank ordering. The group's decision is then derived by pooling the votes or rankings into a single preferred alternative.[26] Table 12.2 shows the results from a typical NGT session.

The nominal group technique is a quite popular means of reaching a group decision because it avoids many of the potential problems of group decision making outlined in Table 12.1. For example, a decision can be reached in a

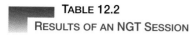

TABLE 12.2

RESULTS OF AN NGT SESSION

Nominal Grouping Technique Form

Group Name: *Industrial Engineering Department*

Date: *January 27, 19—*   Facilitator: *D. Scott Sink*

Number of Group Members: *14*   Number of Objectives to be Ranked: *8*

Problem: Identify specific objectives the Industrial Engineering Department should strive to accomplish during the next year.

Objectives (Ranked in Preference)	Votes Received (Most Important = 8)	Total (Number of Votes/ Total Vote Score)
1. Faculty development	8-8-8-8-8-8-8-7-6-5-4-4-1	13/83
2. Graduate student recruitment	8-7-7-7-5-5-5-4-3	9/51
3. Industry relations	8-8-7-6-6-4-4-3-2-2	10/50
4. Faculty support	7-7-7-6-6-3-3	7/39
5. Intradepartment communication	7-6-5-2-2-2-1	7/25
6. Working paper series	8-6-4-3-1	5/22
7. Ph.D. program development	6-4-4-2-1-1	6/18
8. Course content coordination	4-3-3-3-2-1	6/16
9. National conference attendance	5-5-5-1	4/16
10. Co-op program	8-3-2-2	4/15
11. Interdisciplinary research	7-6-1	3/14
12. Graduate student support	7-4-3	3/14
13. Timely information on funding opportunities	6-5-3	3/14
14. Beginning and ending course evaluations	6-5-3	3/14
15. Manufacturing institute	5-4-2	3/11
16. Faculty performance indices	7-3	2/10
17. Material handling/plant layout course	6-4	2/10

Note: Forty-one objectives were identified; 33 received votes; the top 17 are listed above.

Source: Adapted from D. Scott Sink, "Using the Nominal Group Technique Effectively," *National Productivity Review* 2 (Spring 1983): 181.

reasonable amount of time without being greatly influenced by the leader's preferred position. Also, the technique can be used effectively in a variety of organizations (for example, General Electric, ARA Services, government agencies, and universities have employed the technique). Perhaps the strongest drawback of NGT is its high degree of structure. As a result, the group may tend to limit its discussion to a single and often highly focused issue.

THE DELPHI TECHNIQUE

Another technique for capitalizing on a group's resources while avoiding several possible disadvantages of relying on group decision-making processes was developed by the Rand Corporation.[27] This approach, called the **Delphi technique,** is similar to NGT in several respects, but also differs significantly in that the decision makers never actually meet. The steps in the Delphi technique are:

1. Select a group of individuals who possess expertise in a given problem area, for example, forecasting social trends or technical breakthroughs.

2. Survey the experts for their opinions via a mailed questionnaire.

3. Analyze and distill the experts' responses.

4. Mail the summarized results of the survey to the experts and request that they respond once again to a questionnaire. If one expert's opinion differs sharply from the rest, he or she may be asked to provide a rationale. This rationale could then be forwarded to the other participants.

5. After this process is repeated several times, the experts usually achieve a consensus. If not, the responses can be pooled to determine a most preferred view.

The Delphi technique has a number of advantages and disadvantages. Its greatest advantage is that it avoids many of the biases and obstacles associated with interacting groups (that is, groups where the members meet face-to-face). It has also been shown to generate fairly useful information and high-quality solutions.[28] A strong disadvantage stems from the amount of time it takes to complete the entire Delphi process—rarely less than several weeks, and often as long as five months. Clearly, urgent problems cannot be solved in this manner. Finally, like NGT, the Delphi technique follows a highly structured format. As a result, it does not offer much flexibility if conditions change. And, obviously, since respondents never meet face-to-face, social interaction and free dialogue are lost.

In an interesting comparison of three approaches to group decision making—interacting groups, NGT, and Delphi technique—Van de Ven and Delbecq gave an identical problem to 60 different seven-person groups.[29] Twenty of the groups tackled the problem in an interacting format, while the remaining groups were assigned to either NGT or Delphi approaches. In terms of effectiveness, the NGT groups were somewhat more productive, followed in turn by the Delphi and interacting groups. Members of NGT groups also reported higher satisfaction than did members of the other groups. These results suggest that the presence and increased involvement of others can sometimes diminish the quality of decision making.

SOCIAL LOAFING AND THE STEPLADDER TECHNIQUE

In one well-known set of studies, the performance of individuals working alone was compared with the performance of the same individuals working in a group.[30] It was observed that some of the group members produced at less than their maximum capability when working in the group setting. This phenomenon, whereby a member of a group slacks off because of the experience of being in a group, is termed **social loafing.** There is some evidence that social loafing is greater in larger groups.[31] This is probably because members of larger groups believe that they are less noticeable, have less likelihood of affecting results, and are less likely to share in any rewards.

A problem-solving structure recently proposed as a solution to social loafing is termed the **stepladder technique.** The technique is intended to improve group decision making by structuring the entry of group members into a core group. Initially, a small core group of, for example, two members work together on a problem. Then, a third member joins the core group and presents his or her preliminary suggestions for solving the same problem. Next, the member's presentation is followed by a three-person discussion. Each additional member—fourth, fifth, and so on—joins the expanding core group and presents his or her preliminary solutions. At each step, there is a discussion. The technique has four requirements. First, each member is given sufficient time to think about the task before entering the core group. Second, the new member must make a preliminary solution presentation before hearing the core group's ideas. Third, sufficient time is allocated to discuss the problem as each member is added. Fourth, the final decision occurs only after the entire group has been formed. These steps make it difficult for a member to "loaf," or hide in the group. Research on the effectiveness of the stepladder technique has shown that stepladdered groups produce higher-quality decisions than conventional groups.[32]

EXPERT SYSTEMS

Expert Systems (sometimes called bootstrapping) is a device for improving both individual and group decision making.[§§] It is derived from the efforts of decision scientists to understand how managers and other decision makers actually formulate alternatives and make choices. To an observer, it often seems that decision makers do not follow a clear or consistent set of decision rules when making judgments. However, by recording the actual decision-making process in a group or having a solitary manager "think out loud" as he or she makes a decision, it is possible to uncover the information that was used, the relative weight that was assigned to each piece of information, and the decision rule that was employed. By examining enough decision-making episodes, it is possible to capture the process that is actually being used. Under scrutiny, an apparently haphazard and unpredictable decision-making process often turns out to be quite reasonable and understandable. A flowchart based on the results constitutes a model of the decision-making process that can be used as an aid in making subsequent decisions. Research suggests that such a flowchart can be used to make consistently high-quality decisions. Thus, by explicitly stating a poorly understood set of rules, a decision maker can improve the effectiveness of later decisions. He or she can then consistently follow an established set of principles, whereas previously the decision-making process followed the implicit logic in an inconsistent fashion.[***]

[§§]The term *bootstrapping* is based on the notion that a decision maker begins with nothing more than apparent intuition and "lifts himself by his own bootstraps" to arrive at a formal decision model.[33]

[***]Following a discussion of decision-making techniques, it must be noted that effective decision making is not equivalent to effective decision implementation. Simply being able to decide on the best course of action does not ensure a particular outcome. Decision implementation is actually the concern of much of the field of OB in that effective implementation involves influencing others, managing group meetings, and building consensus.

CREATIVITY AND DECISION MAKING

Many problems, especially nonprogrammed decisions that are broad in scope and consequences, require creative solutions. Given the competitive nature of business, it can be argued that those firms that can generate creative strategies for coping with decisions may enjoy an important competitive edge.

Creativity can enter the decision-making process at any step. The way in which a problem situation is defined, the generation of alternatives, the perception of opportunities, and the actual implementation of a solution can all be enhanced by creative perspectives.

In this section, we will discuss several aspects of creativity. Initially, we will consider the characteristics of creative individuals and how individual creativity can be measured. Then we will examine the steps in the creative process and some methods for enhancing creativity.

CHARACTERISTICS OF CREATIVE INDIVIDUALS

People vary in the extent to which they are creative. Although one widely held belief is that highly creative individuals are the products of peculiar childhoods, the available evidence does not support such a view.

Although the results are not highly consistent, some studies have found that in the United States, creativity is greater in females than males after about age 10.[34] In India, however, boys have been found to be more consistently creative than girls.[35] These results suggest that cultural differences in emphasizing the appropriateness of being creative can be important.

The impact of age on creativity has also been heavily researched, with more conclusive results. A study of professionals in a variety of fields, including both the arts and the sciences, found that most individuals tended to be most creative between the ages of 30 and 40.[36] The peak period of creative productivity, however, seems to vary somewhat by discipline. In the field of music and other arts, creative accomplishment peaks during the period from age 35 to 39, while in the sciences the peak creativity period appears to be from age 30 to 34. It should be pointed out, of course, that people can still make creative contributions later in life (that is, they may continue to take out patents or compose symphonies). However, the frequency of creative productivity tends to decrease for most people as they age.

In terms of personality, creative individuals typically have a wide range of interests, value independence, and enjoy aesthetic impressions.[37] In analyzing creative executives, Raudsepp concluded that some of their more salient characteristics include:

- A willingness to give up immediate gain to reach long-range goals
- A great amount of energy
- An irritation with the status quo
- Perseverance
- A pursuit of hobbies and specialized interests
- A belief that fantasy and daydreaming are not a waste of time[38]

Other studies of creative individuals have offered further insights. One study found that highly creative engineers did not identify as strongly with their employing organization as did their less creative coworkers.[39] In addition, highly creative people are more likely to change jobs frequently, although the precise reasons for this higher turnover are not yet understood.[40]

MEASURING INDIVIDUAL CREATIVITY

Especially in occupations related to research and development, advertising, and mass media, individual creativity is an important resource. To optimize the creative resources of their employees, managers must understand how to measure individual creativity.

One simple device for assessing the creative potential of employees is to observe their actions in situations that call for creative responses. For example, a manager may give an employee a challenging assignment, such as designing the cover of a newsletter, and then carefully monitor both the employee's problem-solving process and the final product. A more direct approach is to administer a paper-and-pencil test of creativity. Organizations that are strongly interested in creativity are more likely to use standardized creativity tests or devise their own. For example, the AC Spark Plug Division of General Motors has developed its own test of creativity for engineers and supervisors.[41]

Numerous tests of creativity are available. Although they appear to identify the general ability to be creative, they may not be particularly relevant to a given occupation. To illustrate this point, consider these sample items from some typical tests of creativity:

- Write a four-word sentence in which each word begins with the following letters: K . . . U . . . Y . . . I . . .
- In the next 30 seconds, name fluids that will burn.
- During the next 60 seconds, write words beginning with the letter J.

Another test asks a person to envision the consequences of various situations. For example:

- In a two-minute period, write down as many answers as you can to the question "What would happen if people no longer needed or wanted to sleep?"

STEPS IN THE CREATIVE PROCESS

Most students of the creative process divide it into five stages.[42]

1. *Opportunity or problem recognition.* In this phase, an individual becomes aware of the existence of a problem or opportunity that needs attention. For example, an employee may remark, "There must be a better way of doing this."
2. *Immersion.* At this stage, the individual collects and recalls information that is relevant to the situation. He or she also generates hypotheses without appraising their value, for example, "I think I recall reading somewhere that some firms use a different set of procedures."

3. *Incubation.* At this point, the information simmers in the person's subconscious. The individual does not appear to be actively focusing on the problem, yet is subconsciously rearranging the available information into new patterns.

4. *Insight.* While a person is engaged in an unrelated activity, an integrative idea will come to mind—for example, "A new reporting system that keeps both departments simultaneously apprised of our needs should do the trick!" Many people report that at this stage it is usually a good idea to jot down the creative insight, as it may quickly be forgotten.

5. *Verification.* Finally, the individual tests out the solution by logic or actual experimentation. At this point, tenacity may be critical, because other people often resist innovative ideas or quickly reject them as impractical.

Although this list of steps suggests that the creative process follows a certain order, creative insight does not happen in such an orderly or neat fashion. For example, incubation may occur during verification. Furthermore, the process is often repetitive because initial ideas may be unsatisfactory and require further revision.

METHODS OF ENHANCING CREATIVITY

Several methods are suggested for enhancing or "freeing up" individual creativity. Studies show that attempts to improve creative ability through training techniques are frequently successful. In fact, one review of 40 studies in the area of increasing creativity found that 90 percent of such efforts succeeded.[43]

We have already considered two of the more popular ways of maximizing group output: the nominal group technique and the Delphi technique. In the area of creativity enhancement, both of these techniques have applicability.

Brainstorming may also be used to train individuals to be more creative and to tackle complex problems. In a brainstorming session, a group of people are encouraged to exchange ideas freely in an atmosphere that is nonjudgmental and noncritical. When presented with a problem, group members try to generate as many ideas or solutions as they can. At this point, the quality of the ideas is not important. Instead, sheer quantity is emphasized. Outlandish ideas are especially encouraged because they may serve as springboards to useful solutions. Later, the recorded proposals are refined and evaluated.

A study of the effectiveness of having individuals brainstorm in isolation versus in groups found that individuals in isolation produce more and better ideas than do an equivalent number of people in groups.[44] These results suggest that the presence of others, despite any possible instructions of group leaders to the contrary, inhibits personal creativity and reduces the range of ideas that are generated.

Another technique in the creativity arsenal is called **grid analysis.** In this technique, ideas or materials of possible relevance to a problem are listed on the sides of a two-dimensional grid. Then each possible combination of ideas is created and examined for its usefulness as a solution. For example, a marketing firm may be interested in promoting alternative uses for its current products. To uncover such novel uses, they may list their products on a horizontal dimension and target audiences or other products that they do not manufacture on the vertical axis. The resulting combinations may suggest new markets for their products, or the possible conversion of their equipment or goods to the manufacture of other products.

Andrew DuBrin has suggested a number of techniques that individuals can use to increase their creativity.[45] Although these techniques do not offer formal guidance for solving specific problems, they can be valuable aids to personal development.

DON'T BE AFRAID TO TRY AND FAIL   Many people find it intimidating that a large proportion of their attempts at creativity are likely to fail. In fact, it is the *absolute number* of successful new ideas that counts and not the *percentage*. Roger Von Oech summarizes this point by saying, "We learn by trial and error, not by trial and rightness."[46]

LET YOUR PLAYFUL SIDE COME OUT   One way to get into a creative state of mind is to think humorously. Approaching a problem with humor can generate novel perspectives and insights.

IDENTIFY YOUR CREATIVE TIME PERIOD   Some people have a specific time of day when they are most likely to be creative. By recognizing this and scheduling work sessions accordingly, they can capitalize on peak periods. Some people find they are most creative while exercising or traveling. Others feel most creative shortly after a rest. Most people, however, report that one of their most creative periods occurs just before falling asleep.

BORROW IDEAS   Studying ideas already in use in related fields can suggest new approaches to one's work problems. Reading books, magazines, and newspapers and contacting people who have related interests may give rise to ideas that, if appropriately modified, can be converted into workable solutions.

MAINTAIN AN IDEA NOTEBOOK   Because many novel ideas are generated and lost in the course of daily activities, a notebook can be a practical means of recording flashes of insight for future reference. Some executives keep a separate "idea file" for storing bits of information that are useful in themselves or that may serve as the basis for other useful ideas.

ESTABLISHING A CLIMATE FOR CREATIVITY

As the previous discussion suggests, creativity must be encouraged if it is to flourish. The proper environment is crucial to fostering creative thought. For example, an organization that shows intolerance of change and a lack of trust in its employees can greatly inhibit creativity. On the other hand, the following factors encourage creativity within an organization:

1. Tolerance of risk taking and failure
2. Open channels of communication within the organization and with the outside environment
3. Tolerance for a variety of personality types
4. Freedom for employees to interact and set goals (that is, individual autonomy)
5. Rewards for being creative
6. Use of creativity-enhancing techniques, such as suggestion boxes and brainstorming

Managers can play a crucial role in the establishment of a climate for creativity by expressing an openness to ideas, encouraging different approaches to problem solving, and allocating rewards for creative efforts.

ETHICS IN DECISION MAKING

In recent years, there has been a growing recognition of the need to explicitly consider ethical issues when engaging in decision making. This interest in being ethical stems partly from a desire to avoid legal action and the resulting adverse public reaction, as well as from a desire to satisfy concerns of personal conscience.[47] Moreover, ethical conduct is believed to offer a strategic advantage over competitors. It has been estimated that over two-thirds of larger firms have a code of ethics and 44 percent of larger firms provide some form of ethics training for their managers.[†††] Ethical training is intended to aid decision making by helping people recognize ethical aspects of decisions, by clarifying rules and norms, by reducing confusion concerning issues of responsibility, and by providing decision-making frameworks for analyzing ethical options.[48]

Most ethics training programs include statements from the top officer emphasizing the importance of ethical decision making, discussion of the corporation's code of ethics, and discussion of specific procedures for reporting unethical conduct. Many programs, such as those in use at Chase Manhattan, General Electric, and Allied, incorporate case discussion, exercises for developing higher levels of ethical maturity, and discussion of ethical frameworks for analyzing decisions. The cases that are discussed are often created from actual corporate-specific instances of difficult decision making. Efforts to raise the ethical maturity level of managers have often relied on Kohlberg's theory of moral development (see Chapter 3). Although evidence is limited, there is some suggestion that individuals exposed to ethical training (especially when couched in Kohlbergian terminology) may show evidence of higher moral reasoning as measured within the context of Kohlberg's theory.[49] Three ethical

---

[†††]Interest in, and support of, ethical training seems to be characteristic of mostly larger firms. Smaller firms, which have fewer surplus resources to devote to managerial training, are far less involved in ethical training. Unfortunately, it is widely believed that smaller organizations are responsible for a sizable proportion of unethical conduct.

frameworks are invariably discussed in training programs: utilitarian, the categorical imperative, and the human nature frameworks. The utilitarian framework focuses on the consequences of actions. It emphasizes the course of action that creates the greatest benefit for the greatest number of people. The categorical imperative framework emphasizes the use of rules and principles (rather than focusing on results) for guiding actions. For example, the Golden Rule (treat others as you wish to be treated) represents such a principle. The human nature framework emphasizes respecting the potentiality of human beings (in terms of their future, as yet undeveloped, abilities), and the goodness of each human being. The basis for selecting a course of action is whether it is compatible with advancing inherent human capacities.[50] What enhances human capacity is "good," while what deters human capacity is "bad."[‡‡‡]

SUMMARY

1. Describe the types of decisions managers make.
Personal programmed decisions involve simple, repetitive personal matters. Personal nonprogrammed decisions arise during rare but significant events in an individual's personal life. Organizational programmed decisions pertain to relatively simple problem situations in an organization and are handled according to established guidelines or procedures. Organizational nonprogrammed decisions pertain to rare or unique situations that have a potentially significant impact on the organization.

2. List the steps of a highly rational decision-making process.
When a situation triggers the decision-making process, recognize the existence of a problem or opportunity that demands action. Define the nature of the situation. Generate alternative ways to cope with the situation. Gather information about each alternative and evaluate its desirability. From this evaluation, arrive at a single best course of action. Implement this alternative. Evaluate the decision's effectiveness.

3. Describe some constraints on the decision-making process.
Constraints on the decision-making process include inability to generate all possible alternatives and their associated consequences, unavailability of accurate information, ethical restrictions on otherwise optimal solutions, and managers' tendency to use heuristics and to satisfice (consider alternative actions only until a reasonably acceptable one is found).

4. Identify obstacles to effective decision making.
Obstacles to effective decision making include judgmental biases, escalation of commitment, groupthink, and the tendency of groups to endorse extreme positions when confronted with decisions involving an element of risk.

[‡‡‡]Some ethical theorists debate the legitimacy of the third, or human nature, framework, arguing that utilitarianism and the categorical imperative views exhaust the realm of ethical theories. Also, the human nature framework is on shaky ground because of its questionable assumptions that all humans have the same inherent capacities and that all people are basically good (rather, they seem to be selfish and aggressive much of the time). Perhaps more important, the human nature view does not provide clear rules to use in ethical decision making.

5. Define groupthink and list its symptoms.

Groupthink is the tendency of highly cohesive groups to take a distorted view of situations. Symptoms of groupthink include an illusion of invulnerability, rationalization, an assumption of morality, negative stereotyping of outsiders, pressure to conform, self-censorship, an illusion of unanimity, and the presence of mindguards (who deflect critics and criticisms).

6. Describe techniques to improve decision making.

Weigh the advantages and disadvantages of group versus individual decision making when choosing a format for making a decision. To take advantage of the positive features of group decision making, use the nominal group technique, the Delphi technique, and the stepladder technique. The expert systems approach—the procedure of analyzing an individual's decision-making process and using the resulting model—is a technique for improving both individual and group decision making.

7. Identify characteristics of creative organization members.

Characteristics of creative people include willingness to forgo immediate gain in favor of long-term goals, high energy, irritation with the status quo, perseverance, pursuit of hobbies and specialized interests, belief that fantasy and daydreaming are not a waste of time, relatively weak identification with their employing organization, and greater likelihood of changing jobs.

8. Describe the steps in the creative process.

The first step is opportunity or problem recognition, during which an individual becomes aware that a problem or opportunity needs attention. Next comes immersion, during which the individual collects and recalls relevant information and generates hypotheses. Next is the incubation stage, when the individual subconsciously rearranges the available information. In the insight stage, while a person is engaged in an unrelated activity, an integrative idea will come into his or her consciousness. Finally, in the verification stage, the individual tests the solution with logic or experimentation.

9. Identify ways that groups and individuals can enhance creativity.

Groups can improve creativity with brainstorming and grid analysis. People can enhance their own creativity by being unafraid of failure, permitting playfulness, identifying creative time periods in each day, borrowing ideas, and maintaining an idea notebook.

10. List ways organizations can establish a climate that encourages creativity.

Organizations can encourage creativity by tolerating risk taking and failure, opening communication channels, tolerating various personality types, giving employees autonomy, rewarding creativity, and using techniques such as brainstorming that enhance creativity.

11. Explain how ethics training is being used in larger corporations.

It is considered "good business practice" to follow ethical guidelines when making decisions. A majority of large firms have codes of ethics, and many require training in ethical decision making. Training programs typically consist of case discussion, exercises designed to enhance ethical awareness, and discussion of ethical frameworks for analyzing decisions.

KEY TERMS

Personal decision making
Organizational decision making
Programmed decision
Nonprogrammed decision
Classical decision theory
Rational-economic model
Behavioral theory of decision
  making
Administrative model
Bounded rationality
Satisfice
Maximize
Bounded discretion
Heuristics
Availability heuristic
Representativeness heuristic
Implicit favorite bias

Loss-aversion bias
Selective perception bias
Personal experience bias
Groupthink
Last-chance meeting
Risky shift
Diffusion of responsibility
Cautious shift
Group polarization
Nominal group technique (NGT)
Delphi technique
Social loafing
Stepladder technique
Expert systems
Brainstorming
Grid analysis

REVIEW AND DISCUSSION QUESTIONS

1. Give an example of each of the following kinds of decisions:
   a. Personal programmed decision
   b. Personal nonprogrammed decision
   c. Organizational programmed decision
   d. Organizational nonprogrammed decision

2. The classical view of decision making describes how a decision *should* be made. In what ways does it fall short in describing how managers actually make decisions? List the steps a typical manager takes in making a decision.

3. In what type of situation is a manager's commitment to a policy likely to intensify, even if the policy is leading to failure? How can an organization counter this tendency?

4. At its staff meeting, the accounting department is discussing the likelihood that the company's recent performance will look bad in a soon-to-be-published financial report. Several members of the department are advocating that numbers in the company's books be changed to look more favorable. These employees argue that they can make the changes in a way that no one will be able to detect and that changing a few numbers is a small matter next to the important goal of keeping the company alive so that hundreds of workers can keep their jobs. It appears that other employees are afraid to argue against this view. Lynette Hayes, manager of the accounting department, is concerned that the department may succumb to groupthink. What are some ways she can prevent this?

5. What causes some groups to adopt a riskier position than individuals would? Why do groups tend to make decisions at the extremes?

6. What are the advantages of making decisions in a group? What are the disadvantages?

7. Daniel Beach is executive vice president of marketing for Trustworthy Savings and Loan Association. He is concerned that consumer interest in individual retirement accounts has been lagging and wants to develop other ways to build interest in saving at Trustworthy. Daniel's plan is to meet with key managers next Thursday to explore possibilities and to begin implementing an idea within the following month. Because he wants to avoid some of the pitfalls of group decision making, Daniel wants to use either the nominal group technique or the Delphi technique. What is involved in each of these approaches to decision making? Which approach do you recommend? Why?

8. Amanda Crisp wants to hire creative people to work in her advertising agency. How can she identify such people?

9. Amanda has hired a staff of people she thinks are creative. How can she help them to work creatively as a group? What advice can she give them as individuals?

10. How does creativity improve the quality of decision making? What would an organization be like if all its employees were highly creative? In some situations, might creativity be seen as an undesirable trait?

The Root of All Evil

The Ajax Toy Corporation is a medium-sized firm located in southern Michigan. The firm designs and manufactures toys and games. The wage and salary program of the company operates on a low-profile basis; that is, no information on salary ranges in regard to grade classification is given to employees and they are not given minimum, medium, or maximum pay ranges attainable in their present job levels. When employees are formally evaluated each year, a merit increase, when given, is usually a small percentage increase, with management retaining any information as to how much money is available for merit increases. When management was asked by employees why merit increases and salaries were handled in this manner, the standard answer was, "It is company policy that this information cannot be given to employees. Only staff personnel have knowledge of this information."

The employees of the Research and Development Department for new products are due for a performance appraisal. Their current minimum and maximum levels of wages are $25,000 and $44,000 per year. These salaries are average for the industry. Last year, the company's conservative wage and salary policies resulted in two of the best people in the department being pirated by Ajax's largest competitor, hurting the performance of the Research and Development Department this year. Pirating of employees in other departments has also been a problem for the past two years.

A new director of Research and Development has recently been hired and management has charged her with proposing recommendations to reduce the pirating of people from her department, while also conducting the department's individual performance appraisals and merit distribution. The manager of Human Resources will later review her ideas against the present system to determine what changes, if any, the department may wish to make.

Additional information about the Research and Development Department and its employees is as follows:

Roger Ballard: 60 years of age; 20 years' experience with Ajax; has not designed any new products during the past year, but works well with others to develop their ideas. Current salary: $44,000 (top of his salary range).

John Connelly: 45 years of age; 10 years with Ajax; is seldom late for work, but doesn't work well with others in the department; was a very good friend of the previous manager; has designed only one new product this year. Current salary: $39,000.

David Browing: 32 years of age; 4 years with Ajax; has designed two new products this year, one of which has been completed; past evaluations have shown him as an average performer, but this year his work has been very good. Current salary: $31,000.

Karen Harding: 24 years of age; was hired 10 months ago to replace one of the pirated employees; has designed two new products that have been completed and are doing very well; has ideas for three more new products; is currently working on these three new ideas with help from Roger; has not received a raise since joining Ajax. Current salary: $25,000.

The director of Research and Development was confidentially informed by the company that she has $12,000 to distribute for use as merit increases. Her recommendation for distribution of the merit dollars requires your approval. As Human Resources manager, you have just received the following merit increase recommendations from the director of Research and Development:

1. Roger Ballard . . . $2,000
2. John Connelly . . . $1,000
3. David Browing . . . $4,750
4. Karen Harding . . . $4,250

QUESTIONS

1. As Human Resources manager, would you agree with the distribution of the merit money among the four employees?
2. Defend and explain your decision.

Source: From Jack L. Simonetti, *Experiential Exercises and Cases for Human Resource Management* (New York: Allyn and Bacon, 1987).

EXPERIENTIAL EXERCISE

How Creative Are You?

In recent years, several tests have been developed to measure creative abilities and behavior. Although certainly useful, they do not adequately tap the complex network of behaviors—the particular personality traits, attitudes, motivations, values, interests, and other variables—that predispose a person to think creatively.

To arrive at assessment measures that would cover a broader range of creative attributes, one organization developed an inventory type of test. Part of this instrument is featured below.

After each statement, indicate with a letter the degree or extent with which you agree or disagree:

A = Strongly agree
B = Agree
C = In between or don't know
D = Disagree
E = Strongly disagree

Mark your answers as accurately and frankly as possible. Try not to "second guess" how a creative person might respond to each statement.

1. I always work with a great deal of certainty that I'm following the correct procedures for solving a particular problem.   _____

2. It would be a waste of time for me to ask questions if I had no hope of obtaining answers.   _____

3. I feel that a logical step-by-step method is best for solving problems.   _____

4. I occasionally voice opinions in groups that seem to turn some people off.   _____

5. I spend a great deal of time thinking about what others think of me.   _____

6. I feel that I may have a special contribution to give to the world.   _____

7. It is more important for me to do what I believe to be right than to try to win the approval of others.   _____

8. People who seem unsure and uncertain about things lose my respect.   _____

9. I am able to stick with difficult problems over extended periods of time.   _____

10. On occasion I get overly enthusiastic about things.   _____

11. I often get my best ideas when doing nothing in particular.   _____

12. I rely on intuitive hunches and the feeling of "rightness" or "wrongness" when moving toward the solution of a problem.   _____

13. When problem solving, I work faster when analyzing the problem and slower when synthesizing the information I've gathered.   _____

14. I like hobbies that involve collecting things.   _____

15. Daydreaming has provided the impetus for many of my more important projects.   _____

16. If I had to choose from two occupations other than the one I now have, I would rather be a physician than an explorer.   _____

17. I can get along more easily with people if they belong to about the same social and business class as myself.   _____

18. I have a high degree of aesthetic sensitivity.   _____

19. Intuitive hunches are unreliable guides in problem solving.   _____

20. I am much more interested in coming up with new ideas than I am in trying to sell them to others.   _____

21. I tend to avoid situations in which I might feel inferior.   _____

22. In evaluating information, the source of it is more important to me than the content.   _____

23. I like people who follow the rule "business before pleasure."   _____

24. One's self-respect is much more important than the respect of others.   _____

25. I feel that people who strive for perfection are unwise.   _____

26. I like work in which I must influence others.   _____

27. It is important for me to have a place for everything and everything in its place.   _____

28. People who are willing to entertain "crackpot" ideas are impractical.   _____

29. I rather enjoy fooling around with new ideas, even if there is no practical payoff.   _____

30. When a certain approach to a problem doesn't work, I can quickly reorient my thinking.   _____

31. I don't like to ask questions that show ignorance.   _____

32. I am able to more easily change my interests to pursue a job or career than I can change a job to pursue my interests.   _____

33. Inability to solve a problem is frequently due to asking the wrong questions.   _____

34. I can frequently anticipate the solution to my problems.   _____

35. It is a waste of time to analyze one's failures.   _____

36. Only fuzzy thinkers resort to metaphors and analogies.   _____

37. At times I have so enjoyed the ingenuity of a crook that I hoped he or she would go scot-free.   _____

38. I frequently begin work on a problem that I can only dimly sense and not yet express. _____

39. I frequently tend to forget things, such as names of people, streets, highways, or small towns. _____

40. I feel that hard work is the basic factor in success. _____

41. To be regarded as a good team member is important to me. _____

42. I know how to keep my inner impulses in check. _____

43. I am a thoroughly dependable and responsible person. _____

44. I resent things being uncertain and unpredictable. _____

45. I prefer to work with others in a team effort rather than solo. _____

46. The trouble with many people is that they take things too seriously. _____

47. I am frequently haunted by my problems and cannot let go of them. _____

48. I can easily give up immediate gain or comfort to reach the goals I have set. _____

49. If I were a college professor, I would rather teach factual courses than those involving theory. _____

50. I'm attracted to the mystery of life. _____

SCORING INSTRUCTIONS

To compute your score, circle the value assigned to your answer for each question, as indicated below, and then add all the values.

	Strongly Agree A	Agree B	In-between or Don't Know C	Disagree D	Strongly Disagree E
1.	−2	−1	0	+1	+2
2.	−2	−1	0	+1	+2
3.	−2	−1	0	+1	+2
4.	+2	+1	0	−1	−2
5.	−2	−1	0	+1	+2
6.	+2	+1	0	−1	−2
7.	+2	+1	0	−1	−2
8.	−2	−1	0	+1	+2
9.	+2	+1	0	−1	−2
10.	+2	+1	0	−1	−2
11.	+2	+1	0	−1	−2
12.	+2	+1	0	−1	−2
13.	−2	−1	0	+1	+2
14.	−2	−1	0	+1	+2
15.	+2	+1	0	−1	−2

	Strongly Agree A	Agree B	In-between or Don't Know C	Disagree D	Strongly Disagree E
16.	−2	−1	0	+1	+2
17.	−2	−1	0	+1	+2
18.	+2	+1	0	−1	−2
19.	−2	−1	0	+1	+2
20.	+2	+1	0	−1	−2
21.	−2	−1	0	+1	+2
22.	−2	−1	0	+1	+2
23.	−2	−1	0	+1	+2
24.	+2	+1	0	−1	−2
25.	−2	−1	0	+1	+2
26.	−2	−1	0	+1	+2
27.	−2	−1	0	+1	+2
28.	−2	−1	0	+1	+2
29.	+2	+1	0	−1	−2
30.	+2	+1	0	−1	−2
31.	−2	−1	0	+1	+2
32.	−2	−1	0	+1	+2
33.	+2	+1	0	−1	−2
34.	+2	+1	0	−1	−2
35.	−2	−1	0	+1	+2
36.	−2	−1	0	+1	+2
37.	+2	+1	0	−1	−2
38.	+2	+1	0	−1	−2
39.	+2	+1	0	−1	−2
40.	+2	+1	0	−1	−2
41.	−2	−1	0	+1	+2
42.	−2	−1	0	+1	+2
43.	−2	−1	0	+1	+2
44.	−2	−1	0	+1	+2
45.	−2	−1	0	+1	+2
46.	+2	+1	0	−1	−2
47.	+2	+1	0	−1	−2
48.	+2	+1	0	−1	−2
49.	−2	−1	0	+1	+2
50.	+2	+1	0	−1	−2

Very creative	80 to 100	Below average	20 to 39
Above average	60 to 79	Noncreative	−100 to 19
Average	40 to 59		

Source: E. Raudsepp, *Personnel Journal*, April 1979. Further information about this test is available from Princeton Creative Research, Inc. P.O. Box 122, Princeton, NJ 08542.

NOTES

1. H.A. Simon, *The New Science of Managerial Decision Making*, 2d ed. (Englewood Cliffs, N.J.: Prentice-Hall, 1977).

2. A. Ebling, *Behavioral Decisions in Organizations*, 2d ed. (Glenview, Ill.: Scott, Foresman, 1978).

3. H.A. Simon, *Administrative Behavior*, 3d ed. (New York: Free Press, 1976); K.R. MacCrimmon and R.N. Taylor, "Decision Making and Problem Solving," in *Handbook of Industrial and Organizational Psychology*, ed. M.D. Dunnette (Chicago: Rand-McNally, 1976).

4. H.A. Simon, *Models of Man* (New York: Wiley, 1957).

5. J.G. March and H.A. Simon, *Organizations* (New York: Wiley, 1958).

6. Simon, *Models of Man*.

7. D. Kahneman and A. Tversky, "Subjective Probability: A Judgment of Representativeness," *Cognitive Psychology* 3 (1972): 430–454; D. Kahneman and A. Tversky, "On the Psychology of Prediction," *Psychological Review* 80 (1973): 237–251; A. Tversky and D. Kahneman "Judgment Under Uncertainty: Heuristics and Biases," *Science* 185 (1974): 1124–1131; A. Tversky, "Features of Similarity," *Psychological Review* 84 (1977): 327–352; D. Kahneman and A. Tversky, "Intuitive Prediction: Biases and Corrective Procedures," *Management Science* 62 (1980): 250–257.

8. P.O. Soelberg, "Unprogrammed Decision Making," *Industrial Management Review* (1987): 19–29; D.J. Power and R.J. Aldag, "Soelberg's Job Search and Choice Model: A Clarification, Review, and Critique," *Academy of Management Review* (1985): 48–58.

9. A. Tversky and D. Kahneman, "The Framing of Decisions and the Psychology of Choice," *Science* 211 (1981): 453–458.

10. B.M. Staw, "The Escalation of Commitment to a Course of Action," *Academy of Management Review* 6 (1981): 577–587.

11. Ibid., 577.

12. B.M. Staw and J. Ross, "Commitment in an Experimenting Society: An Experiment on the Attribution of Leadership from Administrative Scenarios," *Journal of Applied Psychology* 65 (1980): 249–260.

13. C.F. Northcraft and G. Wolf, "Dollars, Sense, and Sunk Costs: A Life Cycle Model of Resource Allocation Decisions," *Academy of Management Review* 9 (1984): 225–234; M. Bowen, S. Goltz, and R. Vecchio, "Learning and Contextual Influences on Escalation in Decision Making" (Paper presented at Midwest Academy of Management Meeting, 1989); E. Conlon and J. Parks, "Information Requests in the Context of Escalation," *Journal of Applied Psychology* 72 (1989): 344–350; H. Garland, "Throwing Good Money After Bad: The Effect of Sunk Costs on the Decision to Escalate Commitment to an Ongoing Project," *Journal of Applied Psychology* 75 (1990): 728–731; J. Ross and B.M. Staw, "Organizational Escalation and Exit: Lessons from the Shoreham Nuclear Power Plant," *Academy of Management Journal* 36 (1993): 701–732; J. Brockner, "The Escalation of Commitment to a Failing Course of Action: Toward Theoretical Progress," *Academy of Management Review* 17 (1992): 39–61.

14. Staw, "The Escalation of Commitment."

15. I.L. Janis, *Victims of Groupthink* (Boston: Houghton-Mifflin, 1972); G. Whyte, "Groupthink Reconsidered," *Academy of Management Review* 14 (1989): 45–56.

16. I.L. Janis, "Sources of Error in Strategic Decision Making," in *Organizational Strategy and Change*, ed. J.M. Pennings (San Francisco: Jossey Bass, 1985).

17. C. McCauley, "The Nature of Social Influence in Groupthink: Compliance and Internalization," *Journal of Personality and Social Psychology* 57 (1989): 250–260; M.E. Turner, A.R. Pratkanis, P. Probasco, and C. Leve, "Threat, Cohesion, and Group Effectiveness: Testing a Social Identity Maintenance Perspective on Groupthink," *Journal of Experimental and Social Psychology* 63 (1992): 781–796; R. Aldag and S. Fuller, "Beyond Fiasco: A Reappraisal of the Groupthink Phenomenon and a New Model of Group Decision Processing," *Psychological Bulletin* 113 (1993): 533–552

18. J.A.F. Stoner, "A Comparison of Individual and Group Decisions

Involving Risk" (Master's thesis, Sloan School of Management, MIT, 1961).

19. A.F. Teger and D.G. Pruitt, "Components of Group Risk Taking," *Journal of Experimental Social Psychology* 3 (1967): 189–205.

20. N. Kogan and M.A. Wallach, "Group Risk Taking as a Function of Members' Anxiety and Defensiveness," *Journal of Personality* 35 (1967): 50–63.

21. J.A.F. Stoner, "Risky and Cautious Shifts in Group Decisions: The Influence of Widely Held Values," *Journal of Experimental Social Psychology* 4 (1968): 442–459.

22. N. Kogan and M.G. Wallach, *Risk Taking: A Study of Cognition and Personality* (New York: Holt, Rinehart and Winston, 1964).

23. R.E. Knox and R.K. Safford, "Group Caution at the Racetrack," *Journal of Experimental Social Psychology* 12 (1976): 317–324.

24. D.G. Myers and H. Lamm, "The Group Polarization Phenomenon," *Psychological Bulletin* 83 (1976): 602–627; M.F. Kaplan, "The Influencing Process in Group Decision Making," in *Group Processes,* ed. C. Hendrick (Newberry Park, Calif.: Sage, 1987).

25. M.E. Shaw, *Group Dynamics,* 3d ed. (New York: McGraw-Hill, 1981).

26. A.H. Van de Ven and A.L. Delbecq, "The Effectiveness of Nominal, Delphi, and Interacting Group Decision-Making Processes," *Academy of Management Journal* 17 (1974): 605–621.

27. N. Dalkey, *The Delphi Method: An Experimental Study of Group Opinions* (Santa Monica, Calif.: The Rand Corporation, 1969).

28. A.L. Delbecq, A.H. Van de Ven, and D.H. Gustafson, *Group Techniques for Program Planning* (Glenview, Ill.: Scott, Foresman, 1975).

29. Van de Ven and Delbecq, "The Effectiveness of Nominal, Delphi, and Interacting Group Processes."

30. S. Harkins, B. Latané, and K. Williams, "Social Loafing: Allocating Effort or 'Taking It Easy,'" *Journal of Experimental Social Psychology* 16 (1980): 457–465.

31. R. Albanese and D. Van Fleet, "Rational Behavior in Groups: The Free Riding Tendency," *Academy of Management Review* 10 (1985): 244–255; J. George,

"Extrinsic and Intrinsic Origins of Perceived Social Loafing in Organizations," *Academy of Management Journal* 35 (1992): 191–202.

32. S.G. Rogelbert, J.L. Barnes-Farrel, and G.A. Lowe, "The Stepladder Technique: An Alternative Group Structure Facilitating Effective Group Decision Making," *Journal of Applied Psychology* 77 (1992): 730–737.

33. R.M. Dawes, "A Case Study of Graduate Admissions: Applications of Three Principles of Human Decision Making," *American Psychologist* 26 (1971): 180–188; J.S. Wiggins, *Personality and Prediction: Principles of Personality Assessment* (Reading, Mass.: Addison-Wesley, 1973).

34. E.P. Torrance and N.C. Aliotti, "Sex Differences in Levels of Performance and Test–-Retest Reliability on the Torrance Tests of Creative Thinking Ability," *Journal of Creative Behavior* 3 (1969): 52–57.

35. Ibid.

36. H.C. Lehman, *Age and Achievement* (Princeton, N.J.: Princeton University Press, 1953).

37. D.W. MacKinnon, "Assessing Creative Persons," *Journal of Creative Behavior* 1 (1967): 303–304.

38. E. Raudsepp, "Are You a Creative Manager?" *Management Review* 58 (1978): 15–16.

39. T. Rotondi, "Organizational Identification: Issues and Implications," *Organizational Behavior and Human Performance* 13 (1975): 95–109.

40. E.P. Torrance, "Is Bias Against Job Changing Bias Against Giftedness?" *Gifted Child Quarterly* 15 (1971): 244–248.

41. R.M. Guion, *Personnel Testing* (New York: McGraw-Hill, 1965).

42. J.F. Mee, "The Creative Thinking Process," *Indiana Business Review* 3 (1956): 4–9; F.D. Randall, "Stimulate Your Executives to Think Creatively," *Harvard Business Review* (July–August 1955): 121–128.

43. S.J. Parnes and E.A. Brunelle, "The Literature of Creativity, Part I," *Journal of Creative Behavior* 1 (1967): 52–109; D.J.Treffinger and J.C. Gowan, "An Updated Representative List of Methods and Educational Programs for

Stimulating Creativity," *Journal of Creative Behavior* 5 (1971): 127–139.

44. D.W. Taylor, R.C. Berry, and C.H. Black, "Does Group Participation When Using Brainstorming Techniques Facilitate or Inhibit Creative Thinking?" *Administrative Science Quarterly* 3 (1958): 23–47.

45. A.J. DuBrin, *Contemporary Applied Management* (Plano, Texas: Business Publications, Inc., 1985).

46. R. Von Oech, *A Whack on the Side of the Head: How to Unlock Your Mind for Innovation* (New York: Warner Books, 1984).

47. S. Harrington, "What Corporate America Is Teaching about Ethics,"

Academy of Management Executive 5 (1991): 21–30.

48. E. Jansen and M.A. Von Glinow, "Ethical Ambivalence and Organizational Reward Systems," *Academy of Management Review* 10 (1985): 814–822.

49. B.D. Penn and B.D. Collier, "Current Research in Moral Development as a Decision Support System," *Journal of Business Ethics* 4 (1985): 131–136.

50. T. Donaldson and P.H. Werhane, "Introduction to Ethical Reasoning," in *Ethical Issues in Business*, eds. T. Donaldson and C.H. Werhane (Englewood Cliffs, N.J.: Prentice-Hall, 1983): 5–17.

A committee is a group that keeps minutes but squanders hours.
— Anonymous

To get along—go along.
— Sam Rayburn

There is no monument dedicated to the memory of a committee.
— Lester J. Pourciau

LEARNING OBJECTIVES

After studying this chapter, you should be able to:

1. *Contrast formal and informal groups, and open and closed groups.*
2. *List some reasons people join groups.*
3. *Describe influences on the degree to which people are attracted to one another.*
4. *Describe stages of group formation and development.*
5. *List some important group properties that affect performance.*
6. *List factors that induce and sustain cohesiveness in a group.*
7. *Describe types of groups commonly used in modern organizations.*
8. *Discuss ways to improve the effectiveness of meetings.*

Group Dynamics

LEADERSHIP ROTATES AT THERMOS

In 1990, Thermos, best known for its Thermos bottles and lunch boxes, embarked on a new product development project and a new style of management, both of which would become major boons to the company. Having previously established itself in the electric and gas grill market, Thermos wanted to reinvigorate the market with a new grill that would be radically different from the current assortment of black, boxy grills.

The first step in creating a bold, new product was to assemble a team of experts that would take complete control of the project from beginning to end. The team planned to identify market needs and consumer preferences, capitalize on Thermos's engineering finesse and manufacturing abilities, and design a new product that would create a niche in the outdoor grill market. The six-person product development team consisted of middle managers from such functions as engineering, marketing, manufacturing, and finance. The group became known as the Lifestyle Team because its assignment was to understand and produce a product that reflected consumers' lifestyles. Thus, from the beginning, the focus was on the customer, not the product. The Lifestyle Team was fortified with experi-

enced external consultants to provide expertise and help the team with market research and design.

One key element of the team's success was that no one individual took sole leadership responsibility for the entire project. Rather, leadership rotated as a function of the task at hand. When the team conducted market and field research, the marketing team member took the lead. Research and Development took the reins when technical issues came to the fore, and manufacturing took over from there. But all members of the Lifestyle Team worked together throughout the project to provide alternative perspectives that kept the project on track.

To identify the target market, the team, led by marketing representatives, traveled to Boston, Los Angeles, and Columbus, Ohio, to learn what consumers were looking for in outdoor grills. The Lifestyle Team held focus groups, talked to consumers, and videotaped people in their backyards barbecuing. They discovered that people found charcoal messy, that backyard decks and patios were increasingly popular, and that rusty, boxy grills were unsightly. Moreover, they learned that potential customers faced grilling constraints: Condominium and apartment dwellers were often forbidden

from using gas grills on their balconies, and charcoal starter fluid was banned entirely in parts of Southern California.

After digesting this information, the Lifestyle Team came up with an idea for an electric grill that would eliminate the need for charcoal and lighter fluid, appeal to condo and apartment dwellers, look like an attractive piece of furniture, and cook food that tasted great. It was a radical new idea, particularly because electric grill sales represented less than 2 percent of the market. Consumers simply didn't like electric grills because the configuration of the heat rod in conventional electric grills baked food rather than grilled it. In response to this, engineering team members explored electric grill technology. The team ultimately built on Thermos's core competency—the vacuum technology that allows Thermos bottles to keep liquids either cold or hot. They came up with a domed grill that would contain the heat. Incorporating the electric heat rod directly into the grill's surface made the grill hot enough to sear meat and give food those characteristic grill lines.

The design team members took over next. Determined to break the black box mold and include value-adding features, they

(continued on following page)

(continued from previous page)
came up with a Mickey Mouse–inspired look—two round side tables protruding from the circular grill. The Lifestyle Team tested the prototype in several retail outlets and incorporated consumer feedback into the design. By the summer of 1992, 100 Thermos employees had taken home grills to test them for themselves. The side tables were found to be too weak; stronger ones were installed on the grills before they ever went to market.

So far, unit sales have been good. Thermos's revenues grew about 13 percent in 1993 primarily because of new products like the electric grill. But the benefits of this project go beyond dollar signs at Thermos. By bringing key people into the process from the start, the team was able to work more effectively and efficiently at producing a new product. Thermos has adopted this new style of management throughout the organization and believes the use of interdisciplinary teams can help revitalize the company.

As this story illustrates, groups, large or small, are an important part of organizations. Groups can alter work processes and affect organizational performance. This chapter explores the dynamics of groups and their role in organizations.

Source: Brian Dumaine, "Payoff from the New Management," *Fortune,* December 13, 1993, 103–110.

Managers spend a sizable proportion of their day working in groups and dealing with groups. As a member of a work group and as a representative of a firm who interacts with various groups both inside and outside the organization, a manager must understand the dynamics of groups.

Groups constitute an essential part of organizations and can strongly influence the total level of accomplishment. They can also satisfy the social needs of their members. Thus, it is fair to say that groups have the potential to satisfy the needs of both individuals and organizations. The extent to which these needs are met, and the processes by which they can be met, are the concerns of this chapter. We will examine the nature of groups, the reasons for joining groups, group formation and development, the major variables that affect group performance, and the various kinds of groups that are typically found in modern organizations. Managers who understand the basic principles of group dynamics often find it easier to direct the efforts of a group in a desired direction.

THE NATURE OF GROUPS

People are social animals—they seek the company of others both to satisfy social needs and to pool resources for improved effectiveness. The presence of others can satisfy a great variety of needs. Hence, people participate in groups. For our purposes, we can define a **group** as two or more people who interact with each other, share certain common beliefs, and view themselves as being members of a group. At a minimum, to be considered a group, at least two people must deal with one another on a continuing basis. Before they interact with each other, they are likely to share common beliefs that impel them to band together. Over time, other shared values may emerge and be solidified. As a consequence of continuing interaction and awareness of shared beliefs, the individuals will come to see themselves as belonging to a distinct entity—the group.

FORMAL VERSUS INFORMAL GROUPS

In organizations, people are frequently assigned to work groups. These teams, which are essentially task oriented, are classified as **formal groups.** For example, employees are typically assigned to departments or work crews. A committee is another example of a formal group. It can be said that every organizational member must belong to at least one formal organizational group—that is, every employee must have at least one formal role. Some organizational members may hold two or more formal group memberships (for example, by being on several different committees). Such multiple members can serve as "linking pins" within the organization who can enhance integration by sharing information across groups and passing on directives to lower levels.[1] Figure 13.1 shows how managers who belong to several groups may serve as linking pins.

Informal groups arise from social interaction among organizational members. Membership in such groups is voluntary and more heavily based on interpersonal attraction. Sometimes the activities or goals of an informal group are attractive to prospective members. For example, department softball and bowling teams are informal groups whose activities attract interested individuals. Not all informal groups, however, have a specific set of activities. Often, they are simply composed of coworkers who share common concerns. For example, a department head may informally meet with other managers to share information (or rumors) about an impending merger.

Informal groups are not inherently good or bad for an organization. When the informal group's goals are congruent with the organization's—such as when both seek to maximize customer satisfaction and produce a high-quality product—then all is well and good. In other instances, however, an informal group may oppose the organization's goals, as when employees decide to restrict daily output. In fact, informal groups are often sources of resistance to organizational change. They sometimes oppose approaches to job redesign

FIGURE 13.1
A LINKING PIN VIEW OF GROUP MEMBERSHIP

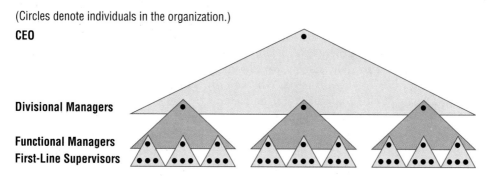

(Circles denote individuals in the organization.)
CEO

Divisional Managers

Functional Managers
First-Line Supervisors

and organizational restructuring. Because of the status and personal satisfaction they derive from their affiliation, members of informal groups can be counted on to resist attempts to disrupt or disband their social arrangement.

OPEN VERSUS CLOSED GROUPS

Groups in organizational settings can also be classified in terms of whether they are open or closed.[2] An **open group** frequently changes its membership, with people constantly moving in and out of the group. In contrast, a **closed group** has a relatively stable membership. In addition, most closed groups have well-established status relationships among their members, whereas open groups tend to fluctuate on dimensions of individual power and status. Open groups are also more subject to disruption because of their changing membership and are less able to focus on long-term issues because of their relative instability. Nonetheless, open groups have certain advantages. For example, their high rate of turnover permits the infusion of "new blood," and therefore new ideas and talents. They are also more adaptable to changes in their surrounding circumstances.

Certain types of activities are better performed by each type of group. For example, for long-range planning, a closed group is likely to be more effective because it has a stronger commitment to dealing with the future. For developing new ideas or new products, an open group is likely to be more effective because of its more fluid and change-oriented atmosphere. Closed groups possess a stronger historical perspective, while open groups are more tolerant of developing and implementing new perspectives.

REASONS FOR JOINING GROUPS

By and large, people join groups for two reasons: to accomplish a task or goal and to satisfy their social needs. These two reasons are not perfectly distinct, however, because many group activities satisfy both task and social needs. In fact, a review of the various needs that were considered in Chapter 6—such as those in Maslow's hierarchy—would reveal that to some extent, nearly all needs can be satisfied by joining a group.

SECURITY AND PROTECTION   Group membership can give an individual a sense of security and a real degree of protection. Being one member of a large organization can generate feelings of insecurity and anxiety, but belonging to a small group can reduce such fears by providing a sense of unity with others. During times of stress, such as when an organization is changing direction or leadership, belonging to a stable and supportive work unit can reduce individual anxieties.

By virtue of sheer numbers, groups afford a degree of protection that an individual might not otherwise enjoy. This principle is embodied in the union movement, which attempts to give members a sense of protection through highly organized collective strength.

AFFILIATION An individual's need for affiliation and emotional support can be directly satisfied by membership in a group. Acceptance by others is an important social need. Feeling accepted by others at work can help to enhance one's feeling of self-worth.

ESTEEM AND IDENTITY Groups also provide opportunities for an individual to feel important. They can give a person status and provide opportunities for praise and recognition. Many work-related achievements may not be appreciated or understood by people unfamiliar with the nature of the job. But in joining a group that does understand the job (either within organizations or through professional associations), people gain opportunities to receive recognition and esteem for their accomplishments.

Membership in a group also helps people to define who they are in the social scheme of things. Seeing oneself as a salesperson, an economist, or a teamster helps foster a feeling of identification with a larger purpose. Through membership in a work group, a person gains a formal title and a sense of purpose.

TASK ACCOMPLISHMENT A primary reason that groups are created is to facilitate task accomplishment. A group can often accomplish more through joint effort than can an equal number of individuals working separately. In fact, many goals are attainable only through cooperative group effort. By sharing ideas, pooling resources, and providing feedback to members, a group can be an effective mechanism for attaining otherwise difficult goals.*

INTERPERSONAL ATTRACTION

People sometimes join and remain in groups because of interpersonal attraction. Three key determinants of interpersonal attraction are physical distance, psychological distance, and similarity.

PHYSICAL AND PSYCHOLOGICAL DISTANCE

Having an opportunity to interact is an important determinant of attraction to others, especially for informal groups. Generally, people who are physically closer to one another develop closer relationships than those who are farther apart. This principle of proximity has been found to hold not only in work settings but also in relationships among neighbors.[3]

In addition to actual physical distance, psychological distance is important. Figure 13.2 shows how two sets of offices can be arranged either to facilitate social interaction or to discourage it. The top office arrangement (A) encourages social interaction by providing a common access to elevators and a shared secretarial-reception area. The lower office layout (B) discourages

---

*It has been suggested that early in the history of humankind, it was recognized that members benefited from cooperative effort. For example, members of a primitive tribe would work together in relays to wear out a game animal that the tribe would then share as a meal. No individual alone could defeat the animal, but together it was easy (and even something of a sport).

FIGURE 13.2

TWO OFFICE LAYOUTS

A is designed to encourage social interaction, while B is arranged to discourage it.

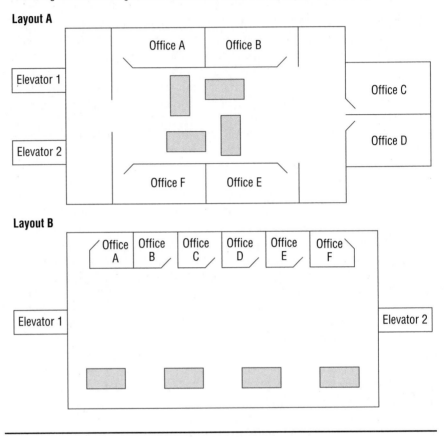

Layout A

Office A | Office B

Elevator 1

Office C

Office D

Elevator 2

Office F | Office E

Layout B

Office A | Office B | Office C | Office D | Office E | Office F

Elevator 1   Elevator 2

Source: H.J. Reitz, *Behavior in Organizations* (New York: Irwin, 1981).

interaction by offering two avenues of entry and exit that reduce overlapping traffic patterns. People on each side of the layout would tend to use only the nearer elevator. In addition, the placement of the office doors does not encourage eye contact as people enter and leave their work spaces. Although the physical distance separating the office workers in both layouts is not great, the psychological distance is greatly augmented in layout B because of the impact that the physical arrangements will have on social relations. As a result, the office workers in layout B would *feel* farther apart than those in layout A. Therefore, managers can consciously structure work settings, depending on whether the goal is to create camaraderie and group spirit, or to reduce informal contacts.

SIMILARITY

There has been a fair amount of debate on the issue of whether "opposites at-tract" or "birds of a feather flock together." That is, do people who are dis-similar in terms of sex, race, income, age, religion, and the like find each oth-er's company more satisfying than people who are highly similar on these dimensions? Although much of the research on this topic points to the poten-tial for both processes, attraction among similar people appears to be some-what more common and more easily produced in formal studies.[4]

One particularly powerful and reliable finding in this area deals with simi-larity of attitudes. The proportion of similar attitudes that two people have in common (that is, whether they share a small, moderate, or high percentage of similar attitudes) appears to be a very strong determinant of interpersonal at-traction. The greater the proportion, the greater the degree of attraction.[5] In fact, this finding has been found with such a high degree of reliability that it is sometimes termed the **law of attraction.**[†]

Although the notions of "opposites attract" and "birds of a feather flock together" may seem contradictory, one does not necessarily exclude the other. Most social scientists agree that individuals who possess similar *attitudes* and complementary *needs* and *abilities* will be highly attracted to one another. Peo-ple often find each other's needs and abilities highly attractive because, by joining forces, they can achieve a form of need-completion or personal fulfill-ment. For example, in a successful business partnership, two partners may share common goals and values, yet one of them will be skilled at managing the financial aspects of their enterprise, while the other excels at marketing, public relations, and innovation.

In their **social exchange theory,** Thibaut and Kelley define *reward* as any satisfaction that is derived from a relationship.[6] Investments (such as time and energy) as well as social problems (such as embarrassment and conflict) that are associated with a relationship are considered *costs*. According to this the-ory, a person is continuously monitoring rewards, costs, and the difference be-tween rewards and costs—or *outcomes*. If rewards exceed costs, so that a per-son greatly benefits from a relationship, we would expect the relationship to continue. But if costs greatly exceed rewards, we would perhaps intuitively ex-pect the relationship to cease.

Actually, the theory suggests much more than the notion of "rewards minus costs." Thibaut and Kelley propose that a person will judge the out-comes of a relationship against two standards: a comparison level (CL) and a comparison level of alternatives (CL_{alt}). The **comparison level** is the magni-tude of outcomes that the individual expects as a result of past experiences and knowledge of similar relationships. Knowing that others in similar jobs are treated in much the same way (for example, given the same title or equivalent

---

[†]Most social scientists believe that these and other findings in the area of social attraction can be explained in terms of reinforcement or reward principles—that is, we like those who reaffirm our beliefs and are likely to re-ward us for holding a particular point of view.

respect) will be an important determinant of a worker's satisfaction with how he or she is treated. Therefore, whether an employee's outcomes (rewards minus costs) exceed, equal, or fall short of the CL will determine the degree of satisfaction with a relationship.

Although the comparison of outcomes to CL determines satisfaction, it does not solely or directly determine the length of the relationship. According to this theory, an individual's desire to remain in or leave a relationship will depend largely on what alternative relationships are available. The highest level of outcomes that an individual could hope to attain from another relationship is termed the **comparison level of alternatives** (CL_{alt}). If a person is in a dissatisfying relationship but it is the best available relationship at that time, he or she is likely to remain in that relationship until a better opportunity arises.

Table 13.1 summarizes the predictions of social exchange theory for the various combinations of outcomes in relation to CL and CL_{alt}. These predictions are for the issues of employee satisfaction and employee propensity to remain in or leave a relationship.

STAGES IN GROUP DEVELOPMENT

Groups are not static, but change and develop over time. Tuckman has offered a popular view of the four stages through which groups pass as they develop.[7]

In the earliest stage of a group's development, members are concerned with testing each other's reaction to determine which actions are acceptable and unacceptable. In addition, the members depend on each other for cues about what is expected in the way of contribution and personal conduct. Problems associated with starting a group (for example, scheduling, finding a location, and obtaining resources) are also a significant part of this stage. Tuckman calls this initial stage **forming.**

The second stage, **storming,** involves intragroup conflict. Hostility and disagreement arise as the group's members wrestle with how power and status

TABLE 13.1

PREDICTIONS FOR SATISFACTION AND LONGEVITY OF RELATIONSHIPS

	Outcomes exceed CL_{alt}	Outcomes below CL_{alt}
Outcomes exceed CL	Satisfied and stable relationship	Satisfied but uncommitted to the relationship
Outcomes below CL	Dissatisfied but continuing relationship	Dissatisfied and uncommitted to the relationship

will be divided. Members may resist the formation of a group structure and ignore the desires of the group's leader.

During the third stage, **norming,** feelings of cohesiveness develop. New standards and roles are adopted, and opinions about task accomplishment are freely voiced. The members' attraction to the group is strengthened, and job satisfaction grows as the level of cohesiveness increases. Cooperation and a sense of shared responsibility are primary themes of this stage.

In the final stage, **performing,** the group has established a flexible network of relationships that aids task accomplishment. Internal hostility is at a low point as the group directs its energies toward the successful performance of valued tasks.

Of course, not every group goes through these four stages in a fixed sequence. For more formal groups, for example, in which the division of power may be less subject to debate, storming may be virtually eliminated. Also, as a group experiences change, it may return to an earlier stage. For example, if an established group receives a new leader, it may temporarily give up performing and return to storming or norming. Figure 13.3 outlines Tuckman's sequence of group development.

IMPACT OF GROUP PROPERTIES ON PERFORMANCE

THE MERE PRESENCE OF OTHERS

Perhaps the most fundamental feature of groups is the presence of other people. Some interesting research has focused on the effects of the mere presence of others on an individual's task performance. In these studies, an individual is asked to perform a task without interacting with others who are present. Results of such studies indicate that having others nearby tends to facilitate performance on relatively simple and well-rehearsed tasks.[8] However, for fairly

■ **FIGURE 13.3**
STAGES OF GROUP FORMATION AND DEVELOPMENT

Stages	Concerns
Forming	Testing and Dependency
Storming	Division of Power
Norming	Rule Making
Performing	Accomplishing Goals

complex tasks, the presence of others can have a detrimental effect. The positive effect of others being present is called the **social facilitation effect,** while the detrimental effect is termed the **social inhibition effect.**

You may have noticed such effects greatly magnified if you have ever been asked to perform in front of an audience. If your assigned task was relatively simple, such as giving your name or reciting other well-rehearsed information, you probably had little difficulty. But if you were asked to solve a problem that you had never encountered before, you probably did poorly.‡ The reasons for these effects are twofold. First, when we expect others to evaluate us, we feel apprehensive (regardless of whether we are actually being judged). Second, the presence of others can increase arousal because of greater self-evaluation of performance. Such self-evaluation can aid performance of a simple task, but impair performance of a difficult task.[9] The implications of this line of research are fairly direct: For tasks that are simple and repetitive, the presence of coworkers can have positive effects, while for complex and novel tasks, working in isolation is preferable.

SIZE

Group size has detectable effects on group performance. In larger groups, the potential impact and contribution of each individual are somewhat diminished, but the total resources of the group are increased. Administering a larger group also creates unique problems for managers.

Although most organizations settle on groups of five to seven persons to handle most problem-solving tasks, some organizations use much larger "spans of control" for simple tasks. Hard evidence about an ideal size for groups is sparse, yet several conclusions seem possible.

First, members appear to become more tolerant of authoritarian and directive leadership as group size increases. Apparently, group members recognize and concede the administrative difficulties that can arise in a larger work unit. In addition, as unit size increases, it becomes more difficult for a handful of subordinates to be influential, and members may feel inhibited about participating in group activities.

Second, larger groups are more likely to have formalized rules and set procedures for dealing with problems. Despite this greater formality, larger groups require more time to reach decisions than smaller groups. Additionally, subgroups are not committed to the full group's formal goals and prefer instead to pursue the more selfish interests of a few members.

Third, in a review of research on group size, Steers suggests that job satisfaction is lower in larger groups.[10] This probably occurs because people receive less personal attention and fewer opportunities to participate. It is also likely that employees in smaller work units feel that their presence is more cru-

---

‡An illustration of the facilitation effect is reported by people who jog. Most joggers report feeling energized when running with another person, even though they are not truly competing with one another. Perhaps one of the more intriguing aspects of the social facilitation effect has been the pervasiveness of the phenomenon across species. It appears that even ants, cockroaches, and chickens demonstrate a social facilitation effect with well-rehearsed behaviors when in the presence of other members of their species!

cial to the group and therefore are inclined to be more involved. For blue-collar workers, absenteeism and turnover also increase in larger work units. Cohesion and communication diminish with increased group size, making a job inherently less attractive and lessening the worker's desire to attend. In white-collar jobs, on the other hand, employees may have other sources of satisfaction to draw on.

Fourth, as group size increases, productivity reaches a point of diminishing returns because of the rising difficulties of coordination and member involvement. This may be a primary reason that five-member groups are so popular. Groups of five have several advantages. The group size is not intimidating, so that a member who disagrees with the majority is less inclined to remain silent. Having an odd number of members means that a tie or split decision can be avoided when voting. Members of such a group also have less difficulty in shifting roles within the group.[11]

As noted in the previous chapter, an interesting problem that tends to arise in larger groups is *social loafing*. In an early study of this phenomenon, Ringelmann, a German psychologist, had workers pull as hard as they could on a rope. Each subject performed this task first alone and then with others in groups of varying sizes while a meter measured the strength of each pull. Although the total amount of force tended to increase as the size of the work group increased, the amount of effort exerted by each person actually decreased. In other words, the average productivity per group member decreased as the size of the work group increased. Latane, Williams, and Harkins, who later replicated Ringlemann's finding, have argued that such social loafing occurs because each individual feels that the needed effort will be shared by the group's members and that he or she can count on others to take up any necessary slack.[12] The social loafing phenomenon suggests that under some circumstances, a group's effort may actually be less than the expected sum of individual contributions.[§]

COMPOSITION

How well a group performs a task depends in large part on the task-relevant resources of its members. The diversity versus redundancy of members' traits and abilities, then, is an important factor in explaining group performance. Groups composed of highly similar individuals who hold common beliefs and have much the same abilities are likely to view a task from a single perspective. Such solidarity can be productive, but it may also mean that members will lack a critical ingredient for unraveling certain kinds of problems. As we saw in our discussion of individual versus group problem solving (Chapter 12), one of a group's greatest assets in comparison to individuals acting alone is the likelihood of achieving higher-quality solutions. Carrying this logic a step farther, we can reasonably expect that diversified groups tend to do better on many problem-solving tasks than do homogeneous groups of highly similar individuals.[13]

[§]This line of reasoning is very similar to the concept of *diffusion of responsibility* considered in Chapter 12.

OB Focus
A Firsthand Perspective of Teamwork

To get a personal perspective on the teamwork revolution sweeping through American manufacturers, a *Business Week* reporter spent a week at Freudenberg-NOK, a Ligonier, Indiana auto parts manufacturer. Rather than observing the dynamics of employee teams from afar, he actually joined a team to learn firsthand the efficiencies of teamwork.

The 12 members of his team had been given a short deadline and specific goals for their section of the plant: boost capacity by 20 percent, raise productivity by 15 percent, and reduce work-in-process by 50 percent. They were given four days to scrutinize work processes, and suggest and test alternatives. If successful, their recommendations would spread throughout the plant. Additional teams brainstormed other work processes. Some 40 G.R.O.W.T.H. teams—Get Rid Of Waste

through Team Harmony—are planned for 1994.

Following a brief training session, the team, led by a plant quality manager and equipped with stopwatches and white lab coats, headed for the factory floor. They timed the operations of every work process and then discussed inefficiencies. Before long, they identified a major bottleneck and outlined a plan to cut two minutes off the operation without affecting quality.

The following morning two team members conferred with the third shift to learn about the workers' perspectives of the work processes. At breakfast, team members formed subteams and were given new problems to tackle. The next two days were spent testing and retesting ideas.

On the final day, the team reconvened and shared their results with the senior vice president in

charge of the division. Two of the three goals had been met—work-in-process inventory was down 50 percent and productivity gains exceeded the 15 percent goal. The team fell short of upping capacity by 20 percent, but they had identified the problem: Unplanned downtime was running far higher than plant managers realized.

The benefits of teamwork were indisputable at Freudenberg-NOK. The team of 12 employees spent four days identifying inefficiencies and suggesting improvements. Within a month of their work, all but one of their recommendations had been implemented. CEO Joseph Day expects to invest $2 million in teamwork and in implementing teams' suggestions by the end of 1995, and anticipates a payback between $12 million and $20 million. He readily admits that would be a nice return on his investment.

Source: James B. Treece, "Improving the Soul of an Old Machine," *Business Week*, October 25, 1993, 134–136.

The diverse abilities and experiences of the members of a heterogeneous group offer an advantage for generating innovative solutions, provided the skills and experiences are *relevant* to the task. Thus, merely adding more people to a problem-solving group to broaden the pool of skills and experience will not guarantee a better job. Attention must be paid to the relevance of the members' attributes and the mix of these attributes within the group. Additionally, the more *competent* members of a work group must also be the most *influential* members. As noted by Maier, if the people who are the least informed are the most influential group members, the quality of the decision will be diminished.[14]

One interesting finding about group composition is that members are more socially conforming in mixed-sex groups than in same-sex groups.[15] This suggests that members of mixed-sex groups focus more on interpersonal relations and therefore conform more than members of same-sex groups. Members of same-sex groups tend to be more concerned with accomplishing the task at hand.**

** Although this finding suggests that managers should segregate the sexes or mix them depending on whether task accomplishment or social conformity is a major goal, it is difficult to defend any contention that espouses segregating the sexes within work settings.

ROLES

Every member of a group has a differentiated set of activities to perform. The set of expected behaviors relating to an individual's position within a group is called a **role**. Although the term *role* seems familiar enough (we can each easily define the roles of schoolteachers, managers, students, and others), it can be viewed in several different ways.

A person's **expected role** is the formal role that is defined in a job description or manual. This role may be conveyed through both a written job description and the signals that other members of a work unit send as they teach newcomers how to perform their jobs. An individual's expected role, however, may differ from his or her perceived role. A **perceived role** is the set of activities that an individual believes he or she is expected to perform. The perceived role may or may not greatly overlap with the expected role that originates with other members of the organization. Finally, an **enacted role** is a person's actual conduct in his or her position. It is more likely to reflect the individual's perceived role than the expected role.

Figure 13.4 illustrates how individuals receive information about their role and adjust their behavior accordingly. As this figure suggests, the process generally begins with the standards that are held by evaluators, such as managers, supervisors, peers, and subordinates. These standards or expectations are then communicated to the individual. Because communication is often imprecise, the expected (or sent) role may not be identical to the perceived (or received) role. Furthermore, due to constraints on actual behavior, the enacted role is observed by the evaluators, who then compare it to the standards they have set. This feedback then completes a single **role episode.** If the individual's behavior does not come sufficiently close to the standards, another role episode may be initiated.

It should be noted that steps 1 and 2 of a role episode involve the group members who surround the individual, while steps 3 and 4 involve the thoughts and actions of the individual alone. Also, steps 1 and 3 are mental and perceptual in nature, while steps 2 and 4 involve actions and the transmittal of information.

As the figure suggests, many things can go wrong in a role episode. Sometimes the evaluators do not send consistent signals. For example, your superior

FIGURE 13.4
A REPRESENTATION OF A ROLE EPISODE

Step 1	Step 2	Step 3	Step 4
Evaluators' Standards	Expected Role	Perceived Role	Enacted Role

Step 5   Feedback

Source: Adapted from D. Katz and R. Kahn, *The Social Psychology of Organizations,* 2d ed. (Newy York: Wiley, 1978).

may assign you a task, while his or her superior, in turn, may later tell you that you should not perform that duty, perhaps because it is not your responsibility or not included in your job description. Different groups sometimes send different signals, as when a supervisor's subordinates indicate that they would like less pressure for production, while his or her superiors simultaneously insist on higher levels of output. Differing signals from evaluating groups and individuals result in **role conflict.** On occasion, the messages that evaluators send are not clear, or they give incomplete information, which leads to **role ambiguity.** At each step in the role episode depicted in Figure 13.4, poor communication and other obstacles may interfere with the process.

Although role conflict and role ambiguity seem to be undesirable, there are some indications that in modest amounts and under the right conditions, they may actually have positive effects.[16] In fact, a work setting that is totally devoid of conflict and ambiguity can be dull and uninspiring. Thus, in order to avoid stagnation and encourage innovation, managers should perhaps seek to create a productive level of conflict and ambiguity. This novel proposal will be considered in greater detail in Chapter 14.

Gross has compiled a list of the roles that employees most commonly assume in a work group.[17] Although Gross's categories do not fit into a workable model of role episodes, they do provide an insightful view of the dominant ways in which individual group members tend to behave:

- *Task-oriented employees:* Those who can be counted on to "get the job done" and "deliver the goods."
- *People-oriented employees:* Those who are the Good Samaritans and social leaders.
- *Nay-sayers:* Those who oppose most proposals, have thick skins, and find fault with nearly everything.
- *Yea-sayers:* Those who counter the nay-sayers and help to circumvent the opposition.
- *Regulars:* Those who are "in," accept the group's values, and are accepted by the group.
- *Deviants:* Those who depart from the group's values—the mavericks.
- *Isolates:* The "lone wolves" who depart farther from the group than the deviants.
- *Newcomers:* Those who know little and need to be taken care of by others; people who are expected to be "seen but not heard."
- *Old-timers:* Those who have been around a long time and "know the ropes."
- *Climbers:* Those who are expected to get ahead, often on the basis of potential rather than ability.
- *Cosmopolitans:* Those who view themselves as members of a larger professional or cultural community.
- *Locals:* Those who are firmly rooted in the organization and the local community.

STATUS

Status is the social ranking or social worth accorded an individual because of the position he or she occupies in a group. Although we typically speak of status as a single notion, it is in fact made up of numerous factors, such as salary, title, seniority, and power. However, a difference on only one of these dimensions is often sufficient to confer status. For example, a group of tool-and-die makers may all have equivalent job titles, but the oldest member of the department, due to seniority, may enjoy higher status and, as a result, greater deference. Of course, status must exist in the eyes of those who confer it. If the other tool-and-die makers in the work unit do not respect seniority, then the oldest individual will not in fact enjoy high status (although he may still feel that he deserves it).

Although status is often conferred on the basis of achievement, personal characteristics, and the ability to administer rewards, it is perhaps most frequently associated with formal authority. Symbols of status, such as titles and perquisites, are designed to communicate difference and distinction, and serve several purposes.[18] Status symbols *provide stability* to the social order, which helps to reduce uncertainty about the appropriateness of conduct and role expectations. In addition, they can *provide incentives* for people to strive for superior performance. Finally, status symbols *provide a sense of identification* by giving individuals information about group membership and reminding them of the group's values.

If all attributes of a high-status individual are greater than those of low-status individuals, the high-status individual is said to be congruent on all dimensions of status. For example, if the highest-level executive is also the oldest, most expert, most experienced, best educated, and best paid member of that organization, then he is similar, or congruent, on all aspects of status. If, however, that executive holds the highest level on all attributes except pay (that is, if another member of the organization were highest paid but lacked equal standing on the other dimensions), the executive would experience **status incongruence.**

Status incongruence can have an unsettling effect on group relations. In progressive organizations, people are more likely to be promoted for personal achievement than for length of service. In such organizations, status incongruence can be prevalent as younger, talented managers are promoted over their more senior colleagues. A situation in which a subordinate is substantially older than his or her superiors can be uncomfortable for both an older person and a fast-track manager. As a consequence, some amount of jealousy and hostility can be expected in group situations involving status incongruence.[††]

Status differences may also have undue influence on group decision making. In a well-know study by Torrance, bomber crews were assigned a task that could not be easily completed.[19] After struggling with the task for some time, the men took a break during which one member of each crew (either the pilot or the tail gunner) was given a clue to the problem's solution. In crews

---

[††]In order to appreciate how uncomfortable a person can be in situations involving status incongruence, imagine taking a high-level math course that is taught by a professor who is 17 years old.

where the clue was planted with the pilot, the suggestion was frequently adopted. But in crews where the tail gunner offered the new approach, the suggestion was adopted much more rarely. Pilots and tail gunners differ sharply on a number of status-related dimensions: pilots are older, more highly educated, hold higher military rank, have greater responsibility, and have more flying time than tail gunners. Thus, it is safe to conclude that the crews showed a bias toward favoring high-status individuals, rather than objectively assessing the quality of the proposal.

NORMS

Norms are rules of conduct that are established to maintain the behavioral consistency of group members. They may be written (as in a code of professional ethics) or unwritten. Deviation from norms is frequently punished by ostracism and verbal attacks. Other more formal sanctions may also be used, as when an unethical lawyer is disbarred. As we saw in the Bank Wiring Room Study in Chapter 1, work-group norms can be a powerful determinant of output.[20]

Norms have two primary purposes: (1) they give members a useful frame of reference for explaining and comprehending their group, and (2) they identify appropriate and inappropriate conduct. In addition, norms ensure that group members will focus their efforts in a common direction. This uniformity of purpose improves the group's chances of attaining its goals. J. R. Hackman has identified five major characteristics of norms:[21]

1. *They represent the structural characteristics of the group.* Group norms are analogous to individual personalities in that they reveal the underlying processes that regulate behavior.
2. *They apply strictly to behavior and not to private thoughts and feelings.* Private acceptance of group norms is not necessary. What really matters is public compliance.
3. *They are developed only for behaviors that are judged to be important by the majority of group members.*
4. *Although they usually develop slowly, norms can be developed rapidly if the need arises.*
5. *Not all norms apply to all members.* High-status individuals may be exempted from certain norms, but new group members may be expected to comply closely with all norms. Often it is expected that distasteful tasks will be handled by initiates.

As is true of many social phenomena in isolation, group norms are neither good nor bad. Their value to an organization depends on whether they are directed to enhancing, rather than restricting, productivity. If norms lead a work group to produce a high-quality product or to be the best in its industry, they are highly desirable. But norms that encourage workers to reduce productivity are clearly undesirable because they undercut management's goals.

As a manager, you may find yourself enforcing group norms when they are congruent with your own goals or opposing them when they are incongruent. Alvin Zander has developed a set of guidelines for achieving both ends.[22] If you wish to enforce group norms, these guidelines should be followed:

1. Show a group member that the difference between the group's wishes and his or her wishes is not great, and that there is little need to resist group pressures.

2. Develop methods for rewarding employees who conform to group standards, such as bonuses, honor rolls, public recognition, and trophies.

3. Help members to understand how their contributions help the group accomplish its purposes.

4. Give participants a say in establishing standards, since standards are more closely followed by those who set them.

5. Make it known that members who do not conform to the group's standards will be removed from the team (while also helping anyone who is removed to overcome the resulting guilt and loss of self-esteem).

If the work group's standards are in opposition to your own, the following guidelines should be employed:

1. Recognize like-minded members and ally yourself with them.

2. Try to establish joint opposition with like-minded members by discussing your views and plans with them.

3. Do not give up legitimate professional preferences in order to prevent disharmony.

4. Hold out against social pressures by concealing from others what you do or think.

5. Attempt to publicize the value of cooperation and resultant rewards.

COHESIVENESS

Cohesiveness is the extent to which members are attracted to a group and desire to remain in it.[23] Cohesiveness is sometimes described as the sum of all forces acting on individuals to remain in the group. As the term implies, cohesiveness pertains to how group members "stick together." Listed below are the factors that induce and sustain cohesiveness in groups, and the effects of cohesiveness on group members and the organization.

FACTORS THAT INDUCE AND SUSTAIN GROUP COHESIVENESS

1. *Similarity of attitudes and goals.* As mentioned in the discussion of interpersonal attraction, when group members have similar attitudes, they find each other's company pleasurable. So, too, individual members will be attracted to a group whose goals and ambitions are similar to their own.

2. *Threats.* The presence of external threats can help to increase group cohesion in that sharing a mutual fate can lead to greater awareness of interdependence. Competition from sources outside the group can also enhance cohesiveness, whereas competition among group members will tend to decrease cohesion.

3. *Unit size.* Smaller groups tend to be more cohesive than larger groups because smaller groups offer greater opportunities to interact with all members. Since diversity (and therefore dissimilarity of attitudes and values) tends to increase with group size, larger groups are likely to be less cohesive. In addition, in large units, the need for more rigid work rules and procedures reduces the informal nature of relations and communication among group members.

4. *Reward systems.* Cohesiveness can also be enhanced by offering rewards on a group, rather than an individual, basis. Group incentives, such as bonuses based on team performance, encourage a perception of a common fate and enhance cooperation. In contrast, reward schemes that encourage competition among group members—such as a winner-take-all bonus system for the single best performer in a unit—tend to diminish group cohesiveness.

5. *Work unit assignments.* The deliberate composition of work units based on interpersonal attraction, similarity of values, and common goals can facilitate cohesion. In a classic study, Van Zelst assigned carpenters and bricklayers to teams based on a prior secret balloting of preferred workmates.[24] The work teams that were formed on the basis of personal preferences had higher levels of job satisfaction than did the randomly assigned work units that served as a control group.

6. *Isolation.* Generally, groups that are isolated from others are more likely to be cohesive. Groups in isolation come to view themselves as unique and different. Isolation also helps to foster group members' sense of a common fate and need for defense against outside threats.

THE EFFECTS OF COHESIVENESS

1. *Satisfaction.* Members of highly cohesive groups are generally much more satisfied than members of less cohesive groups. This is, of course, to be expected, since the very definition of group cohesion implies a strong attraction among group members.

2. *Communication.* Communication among group members is significantly greater in highly cohesive groups than in less cohesive groups. Because members of cohesive groups are likely to share common values and goals and to find their own company satisfying, they are inclined to greater communicativeness. This communication in turn tends to foster greater personal revelation and depth of understanding, which cements positive social relations.

3. *Hostility.* Hostile and aggressive acts are more frequent in highly cohesive groups, but such hostility is usually directed toward people who are not members of the group.[25] Cohesion apparently creates a sense of superiority

among group members, which can result in hostility toward, and rejection of, outsiders.

4. *Productivity.* Some researchers have found cohesive groups to be very productive, while others have found that highly cohesive groups are not as productive as less cohesive groups. Still other researchers have reported no relationship between productivity and group cohesion.[26] It appears that a primary determinant of the effect of cohesion on productivity is whether the group's goals are congruent with those of the organization. If the goals of a cohesive group include high performance, then high performance can be reasonably expected. Conversely, if a highly cohesive group values reduced productivity, then a relatively low level of productivity can be expected. In short, cohesive groups are more likely to attain their goals than are less cohesive groups. In a study of 228 small work groups in a manufacturing setting, Seashore found that cohesive groups also tended to be less variable in their performance regardless of their absolute level of output.[27] This occurred because cohesive groups tend to emphasize compliance with work norms. Whether its norms endorse high or low productivity, a group will probably produce within its own relatively narrow but prescribed range of output. Despite evidence of less variance for highly cohesive groups, one recent review of 27 studies of the relationship between cohesiveness and performance did find that, on average, highly cohesive groups outperformed less cohesive groups.[28] Unfortunately, many of the groups examined in the review (sports teams, military units) were not typical of groups found in organizations, where antagonism to performance measurement may be greater.

5. *Resistance to change.* Although it is less well documented, social scientists generally believe that highly cohesive groups are more resistant to change than are less cohesive groups. Changes that disrupt the status quo threaten a group's networks and social supports and are, therefore, likely to be resisted. Attempts at job redesign that ignore the existing social relations among employees run a greater risk of failing.[29]

USE OF GROUPS IN ORGANIZATIONS

Modern organizations rely on groups to perform many activities. In this section, we will examine several of the more frequently used kinds of groups: task forces and committees, and boards and commissions. In addition, we will examine several techniques for enhancing the usefulness of meetings.

TASK FORCES AND COMMITTEES

As we have suggested before (Chapter 12), under the proper circumstances, groups can outperform individuals.[‡‡] Two formal embodiments of an organization's desire to have a task handled by a group are the task force and the

---

[‡‡]Of course, it can be argued that a committee will never be able to create the equivalent of a Rembrandt painting.

An Inside Look
Saturn's Growing Pains

The cooperative working relationship between management and workers at Saturn Corp. represents unprecedented group harmony for an American auto manufacturer. Saturn workers have a major stake in running the company. Factory-floor teams of 15 employees are responsible for everything from hiring to budgeting. Union officials have a voice at every level, including choosing suppliers, developing products, and creating advertising campaigns. This spirit of cooperation between Saturn management and the original group of 3,200 United Auto Workers has been crucial to Saturn's market success.

The collaborative atmosphere, however, may be in jeopardy. Employees have been working overtime to meet the high demand for Saturn cars, and the strain of overwork is beginning to take its toll. Moreover, 1,800 UAW members have been added to the payroll since late 1990 and many of them are lukewarm about Saturn's emphasis on cooperative management techniques. The cause of new-worker apathy may be management's decision to cut new-worker training by more than 50 percent. Training has been credited with helping the original work force learn crucial participa-tive skills. In January 1993, most of the 5,000 UAW Saturn employees voted to maintain the current partnership with management, yet 29 percent voted for a more traditional, adversarial relationship with management.

Part of the problem may be a side effect of the 1990 General Motors–UAW agreement that Saturn hire only workers laid off from other GM plants, rather than any UAW member. The result is a smaller pool of applicants, many of whom are disinterested in a participative work environment. Moreover, having been laid off from another GM plant, many don't trust management and are coming to Saturn merely to pick up a paycheck, not create labor–management history.

New hires receive truncated training so that they can more quickly get out on the shop floor to relieve veteran workers. Training programs have dropped from 700 to 175 hours, with team-skills training the largest casualty. New employees now focus more on job-skills training, such as power-tool operation, and far less on the conflict management and team-skills training that fostered the efficiencies of Saturn's original teams.

Union and management are at a crossroads that may ultimately cause the demise of the collaborative spirit at Saturn. Saturn's union leader insists new workers need more up-front training to enlighten them about the work climate at Saturn and to teach them the value of self-managed work teams. Although demand for Saturn cars is high, the company has suffered losses and must cut costs and boost productivity to break even. Managers see extensive training of new hires as a luxury they simply can't afford. Moreover, they're experimenting with the Saturn system. Management suggested reducing team size and offered $3,000 bonuses to workers if Saturn turned a profit by mid-1993.

Although Saturn management isn't worried that growing employee discontent will damage Saturn quality or productivity, some experts believe Saturn cars have become a top seller because the cooperative environment at Saturn fosters quality work at all stages of the production process. If management and labor cannot work out their differences, it may be difficult to maintain the same level of quality in Saturn cars.

Source: David Woodruff, "Saturn: Labor's Lost Love?" *Business Week*, February 8, 1993, 122–124.

committee. Task forces are usually formed to handle a fairly specific problem. They exist as long as necessary to deal with the problem, and then they are dissolved. Problems that span several organizational units or departments usually require the creation of special task forces. Representatives from each unit are assigned to the task force based on the relevance of their expertise and training.

Committees, or standing committees, are typically designed to operate over a long period in order to handle a continuing need or problem. Examples of standing committees include ethics committees, college curriculum review committees, and executive decision-making committees.

BOARDS AND COMMISSIONS

Boards typically comprise individuals who are elected or appointed to manage an institution. For example, the stockholders of a corporation will select a board of directors to manage company operations. Communities elect school board members to select principals and determine educational policies. Board members are usually more concerned with the desires of constituencies outside of an organization than are members of task forces and standing committees.

Commissions resemble boards in that members of commissions also possess decision-making authority for larger organizational issues. However, they are usually appointed by government officials rather than elected. Examples of commissions include the Federal Trade Commission and the Securities and Exchange Commission.

These various forms of groups have several common advantages and disadvantages. Dale suggests that the advantages of such groups include:

1. Better quality decisions
2. Enhanced likelihood of implementation
3. Improved coordination
4. Controlled training for managers
5. Dispersion of power to reduce the potential for abuse.

The disadvantages of relying on groups include:

1. Premature agreements and mediocre compromises (for example, the group-think phenomenon)
2. Domination by the group leader
3. Diffusion of responsibility
4. Wasting of time and money.[30]

INCREASING THE EFFECTIVENESS OF MEETINGS

Managers devote a substantial proportion of their day to meetings. By one estimate, meetings can consume as much as two-thirds of a typical workday.[31] It has also been estimated that up to one-half of the time spent in meetings is actually wasted. Because of these considerations, techniques for enhancing the effectiveness of meetings need to be considered. Peter Turla and Kathleen Hawkins suggest that:

1. The group's goals should be defined in advance to reduce discussion of that topic.
2. The group's authority should be specified in advance so that members know whether they are to investigate, advise, or recommend.
3. The size and composition of the group should be based on the feasibility of a given number of members and the need for various kinds of expertise.
4. An agenda and supporting material should be distributed to the members in advance of each meeting.

5. Meetings should start and stop on time. When an ending time is announced at the outset, members can better budget the time allotted to presentations and discussions.[32]

Group leaders also need to understand how to manage a meeting. Anthony Jay has offered the following seven rules for leading a meeting:

1. Control the garrulous.
2. Draw out the silent.
3. Protect the weak.
4. Encourage the clash of ideas.
5. Watch out for the suggestion-squashing reflex.
6. Come to the most senior people last.
7. Close on a note of achievement.[33]

SUMMARY

1. Contrast formal and informal groups and open and closed groups.
Formal groups are task-oriented groups to which people are assigned; informal groups arise from voluntary social interaction among members of the organization. Open groups frequently change their membership; closed groups have a relatively stable membership.

2. List some reasons people join groups.
People join groups for security and protection, for affiliation and emotional support, for esteem and a sense of identity, and to accomplish tasks.

3. Describe influences on the degree to which people are attracted to one another.
The less the distance between people, the greater their interpersonal attraction. Distance can be either physical or psychological. People with similar attitudes or complementary needs and abilities feel greater attraction.

4. Describe stages of group formation and development.
A popular view is that groups pass through four stages as they develop: (1) forming, during which group members look to each other for clues about what actions are acceptable and expected; (2) storming, a stage of intragroup conflict during which power and status are allocated; (3) norming, the development of feelings of cohesiveness; and (4) performing, the accomplishment of valued tasks.

5. List some important group properties that affect performance.
Performance is affected by the mere presence of others, the size and composition of the group, the roles and status of group members, the norms of the group, and the degree of cohesiveness of the group.

6. List factors that induce and sustain cohesiveness in a group.
These factors include similarity of attitudes and goals, the presence of external threats, small group size, reward systems based on group performance, work

unit assignments based on personal preferences, and isolation from other groups.

7. Describe types of groups commonly used in modern organizations.

Typically occurring groups are task forces, usually formed to handle a fairly specific problem; committees, typically designed to operate over a long period; boards, which comprise individuals elected or appointed to manage an institution; and commissions, which comprise individuals who have decision-making authority and were appointed by government officials.

8. Discuss ways to improve the effectiveness of meetings.

Some specific procedures are defining goals and specifying authority in advance; selecting the size and composition of the group based on feasibility and needs; distributing the agenda in advance; starting and stopping the meeting on time; controlling talkative participants and drawing out quiet ones; protecting weak participants; encouraging conflicting ideas; avoiding dismissing suggestions prematurely; coming to the most senior person last; and closing on a note of achievement.

KEY TERMS

Group	Social facilitation effect
Formal group	Social inhibition effect
Informal group	Role
Open group	Expected role
Closed group	Perceived role
Law of attraction	Enacted role
Social exchange theory	Role episode
Comparison level	Role conflict
Comparison level of alternatives	Role ambiguity
Forming	Status
Storming	Status incongruence
Norming	Norms
Performing	Cohesiveness

REVIEW AND DISCUSSION QUESTIONS

1. Give an example of a formal and an informal group. What characteristics of open and closed groups can help a manager choose between them for a given task?

2. When Betty Lee started her new job with Acme Auto Insurance, one of the other claims adjusters invited her to join a group of people who always eat together in the cafeteria. Within weeks, Betty found she prefers to have lunch with these people every day. What are some possible explanations for Betty's desire to be part of a group?

3. In terms of forming groups, do opposites attract?

4. Sam Samson is in charge of the new committee to recommend activities for next year's orientation program for first-year students. It seems to him that

most of the first meeting was spent in bickering and game playing, and the second meeting is going even worse. Sometimes when Sam tries to call the meeting back to order, everyone ignores him. Sam wonders whether he should quit or ask for a new group of committee members. What information about group development might encourage Sam?

5. Would a bagger in a grocery store likely perform the job better working alone or in the presence of others? What about the executive who is planning marketing strategy for the grocery store chain?

6. Marlene Megabyte wants all the systems analysts in her division to be top performers, so she goes to great lengths to be sure that they experience no conflict or ambiguity about what they are supposed to be doing. In general, what causes of role conflict and role ambiguity should Marlene be aware of? Is she correct about the benefits of eliminating conflict and ambiguity?

7. What are some sources of status? What benefits do status symbols provide? How does status influence groups?

8. Generally, a manager is expected to enforce the organization's norms. However, managers sometimes find themselves in situations where the group makes a decision that does not mesh with the manager's personal norms. For example, imagine that you are the sales manager in a company that has decided to continue manufacturing a product when tests do not clearly indicate it is safe. What might you do? Assume that you can't leave the organization immediately.

9. Over lunch, the six researchers at A-1 Pharmaceuticals usually discuss the latest research and the likelihood that A-1 will make further cut backs in the research department. The researchers doubt that any other employees really appreciate the importance of their work; at company functions, talk seems to focus only on sales and production. Probably no one else understands enough about microbiology to follow a conversation about research anyway. Would you say this group of researchers is cohesive? What are some advantages and disadvantages of this degree of cohesiveness (or lack of it)?

10. What are some advantages of using groups rather than individuals to make decisions? What are some disadvantages?

11. Marv Marvelous assembled a group of people to review the company's sales goals and evaluate whether they should be revised. To make sure that all ideas would be considered, he invited two people from every department, for a total of 16 people. The meeting was scheduled for 2:00 P.M. At 2:15, Marv said, "Well, everyone is here except one, so we might as well get started. Please pass around these copies of the agenda I prepared for you." Then Marv turned to the most senior vice president in attendance, Sid Senior, and asked him, "Perhaps you would start us off by suggesting some guidelines for evaluating the sales figures." Suggest some ways in which Marv could have made his meeting more effective.

The Bread II Team

By early 1995, the five-member team at Wilson Appliance, a small appliance manufacturer in Youngstown, Ohio, had been working for more than twelve months on "Bread II," a new electric breadmaker. The self-managed interdisciplinary work team was a first for the company. If it operated successfully, the teamwork concept would spread throughout the company. Julia Kendall, leader of the Bread II team, knew a lot was riding on the team's success.

Electric breadmakers had become a hot consumer item the past few years, and Wilson's Bread I machine, introduced in 1990, had been a popular model, but sales had recently leveled off. Wilson executives decided to adopt a team approach to developing a new breadmaker. The team, representing employees from marketing, engineering, manufacturing, and finance, was given a blank slate and a mission to create a new breadmaker that would be different from those already on the market.

Although Julia was the team's leader, as manager of the household appliance division, she had extensive responsibilities beyond the Bread II project. Her role with regard to Bread II was to keep the team on track and intervene when there were problems.

The team members worked interdependently, making important marketing, design, and product decisions by consensus. In addition to Julia, the team consisted of Linda Killington, and Michael Delcamp from marketing; Henry Kichner, Wilson's engineering genius; Maggie Dresser from finance; and Jim Summers from manufacturing.

Focus groups with current owners of breadmakers and potential customers had revealed customers were universally dissatisfied with one aspect of currently available breadmakers. The process of electronic breadmaking, although it merely required the user to accurately measure ingredients and turn the appliance on, took nearly three hours from start to finish for each loaf. Families with children found one loaf of bread was consumed within two days. To produce enough bread for a family of four, the breadmaker would have to be in use two or three times per week. With this information, the team decided to introduce a breadmaker that would simultaneously bake two loaves of bread (hence the name Bread II) without compromising taste or quality.

Over the past year, the group had worked very well together. Despite some initial difficulties with the team format, the Bread II team had made substantial progress toward their September 1995 goal to introduce the Bread II to the market in time for holiday sales.

Following a meeting last week, Henry and Jim began a spirited discussion of the political changes that had occurred in recent years. Henry was very outspoken about his disapproval of women holding important political positions. Linda, Michael, and Maggie joined the discussion, intrigued by Henry's perspective. Before long the conversation got out of hand, and Henry and Linda became embroiled in a heated confrontation. Four days later the two were still not speaking to one another. With Bread II on a tight deadline, Julia knew she would have to intervene to return cohesion to the group. She was not sure how to handle the situation, particularly because she, too, felt Henry's comments were out of line. Realizing the conflict would grow deeper with each passing day, she headed for the conference room in which the Bread II team was about to meet.

QUESTIONS

1. What stage was the group in before the conflict erupted? After?
2. What factors have sustained the group's cohesiveness? What factors have fractured the group's cohesiveness?
3. What should Julia do?

Source: "The Bread II Team," written by Melissa Waite, State University of New York, University at Buffalo; and Susan Stites-Doe, State University of New York, College at Brockport.

EXPERIENTIAL EXERCISE

Group Effectiveness Checklist

The ability to work in groups is a skill increasingly called upon in today's businesses. Working effectively in groups will be an important skill to develop in both your personal and professional lives. The following 20 items provide a checklist for you to use in describing the effectiveness of a group or groups to which you belong. If you have been using groups to do role plays, cases, or other exercises in your Organizational Behavior class, use one of these groups as your point of reference.

	Mostly Yes	Mostly No
1. The atmosphere is relaxed and comfortable.	_____	_____
2. Group discussion is frequent and usually pertinent to the task at hand.	_____	_____
3. Group members understand what they are trying to accomplish.	_____	_____
4. People listen to each other's suggestions and ideas.	_____	_____
5. Disagreements are tolerated and an attempt is made to resolve them.	_____	_____
6. There is general agreement on most courses of action taken.	_____	_____
7. The group welcomes frank criticism from inside and outside sources.	_____	_____
8. When the group takes action, clear assignments are made and accepted.	_____	_____
9. There is a well-established, relaxed working relationship among the members.	_____	_____
10. There is a high degree of trust and confidence among the leader and subordinates.	_____	_____
11. The group members strive to help the group achieve its goal.	_____	_____
12. Suggestions and criticisms are offered and received with a helpful spirit.	_____	_____
13. There is a cooperative rather than a competitive relationship among group members.	_____	_____
14. The group's goals are set high, but not so high as to create anxieties or fear of failure.	_____	_____
15. The leaders and members hold a high opinion of the group's capabilities.	_____	_____
16. Creativity is stimulated within the group.	_____	_____

17. There is ample communication within the group of topics relevant to getting the work accomplished.   _____   _____

18. Group members feel confident in making decisions.   _____   _____

19. People are kept busy, but not overloaded.   _____   _____

20. The leader of the group is well suited for the job.   _____   _____

Scoring Guidelines: This checklist is designed to help you assess a group's effectiveness. The greater the number of statements to which you answered "Mostly Yes," the more likely the group is productive and its members are satisfied. You can also use this checklist as a development tool. If you want to improve a group's effectiveness, emphasize achieving the 20 qualities described in the checklist.

Source: "Group Effectiveness Checklist," A. J. DuBrin, *Contemporary Applied Management* (Plano, Texas: Business Publications, Inc., 1985), *169–170.* Used by permission of the publisher.

Notes

1. R. Likert, *New Patterns in Management* (New York: McGraw-Hill, 1961).

2. R.C. Ziller, "Toward a Theory of Open and Closed Groups," *Psychological Bulletin* 64 (1965): 164–182.

3. W.H. Whyte, Jr., *The Organization Man* (New York: Simon and Schuster, 1956).

4. H.J. Lott and B.E. Lott, "Group Cohesiveness as Interpersonal Attraction: A Review of Relationships with Antecedent and Consequent Variables," *Psychological Bulletin* 64 (1965): 259–302.

5. D. Bryne and G.L. Clore, "A Reinforcement Model of Evaluative Responses," *Personality: An International Journal* 1 (1970): 103–128; D. Bryne, *The Attraction Paradigm* (New York: Academic Press, 1971).

6. J.W. Thibaut and H.H. Kelley, *The Social Psychology of Groups* (New York: Wiley, 1959).

7. B.W. Tuckman, "Developmental Sequence in Small Groups," *Psychological Bulletin* 63 (1965): 384–399.

8. R.B. Zajonc, "Social Facilitation," *Science* 149 (1965): 269–274.

9. B. Guerin, "Mere Presence Effects in Humans: A Review," *Journal of Experimental Social Psychology* 22 (1986): 38–77; R.G. Green, "Alternative Conceptions of Social Facilitation," in *Psychology of Group Influences*, ed. P.B. Pavles (Hillsdale, N.J.: Erlbaum, 1989); J.M. Jackson, S. Buglione, and D.S. Glenwick, "Major League Baseball Performance as a Function of Being Traded: A Drive Theory Analysis," *Personality and Social Psychology Bulletin* 14 (1988): 46–56; K. Bettenhausen, "Five Years of Group Research: What We've Learned and What Needs to Be Addressed," *Journal of Management* 17 (1991): 345–382.

10. R.M. Steers, *An Introduction to Organizational Behavior* (Glenview, Ill.: Scott, Foresman, 1984).

11. P.A. Hare, *Handbook of Small Group Research* (New York: Free Press, 1962).

12. B. Latane, K. Williams, and S. Harkins, "Many Hands Make Light the Work: The Causes and Consequences of Social Loafing," *Journal of Personality and Social Psychology* 37 (1979): 822–832.

13. M.E. Shaw, *Group Dynamics*, 3d ed. (New York: McGraw-Hill, 1981).

14. N.R.F. Maier, *Problem Solving and Creativity in Individuals and Groups* (Belmont, Calif.: Brooks-Cole, 1970).

15. H.T. Reitan and M.E. Shaw, "Group Membership, Sex-Composition of the Group, and Conformity Behavior," *Journal of Social Psychology* 64 (1964): 45–51.

16. S.P. Robbins, *Managing Organizational Conflict* (Englewood Cliffs, N.J.: Prentice-Hall, 1974).

17. B.M. Gross, *Organizations and Their Managing* (New York: Free Press, 1968), 242–248.

18. W.G. Scott, *Organization Theory* (Homewood, Ill.: Irwin, 1967).

19. E.P. Torrance, "Some Consequences of Power Differences on Decision Making in Permanent and Temporary Three-Man Groups," *Research Studies, Washington State College* 22 (1954): 130–140.

20. F. Roethlisberger and W.J. Dickson, *Management and the Worker* (Cambridge, Mass.: Harvard University Press, 1939); K. Bettenhausen and J.K. Murnighan, "The Emergence of Norms in Competitive Decision-Making Groups," *Administrative Science Quarterly* 10 (1985): 350–372.

21. J.R. Hackman, "Group Influences on Individuals," in *Handbook of Industrial and Organizational Psychology*, ed. M.D. Dunnette (Chicago: Rand McNally, 1976), 1455–1525.

22. A. Zander, *Making Groups Effective* (San Francisco: Jossey-Bass, 1983), 55–56.

23. Shaw, *Group Dynamics*.

24. R.H. Van Zelst, "Validation of a Sociometric Regrouping Procedure," *Journal of Abnormal and Social Psychology* 47 (1952): 299–301.

25. L. Berkowitz and J.A. Green, "The Stimulus Qualities of the Scapegoat," *Journal of Abnormal and Social Psychology* 64 (1962): 293–301; K.L. Dion, "Cohesiveness as a Determinant of Ingroup–Outgroup Bias," *Journal of Personality and Social Psychology* 28 (1973): 163–171.

26. R.M. Stogdill, "Group Productivity, Drive, and Cohesiveness," *Organizational Behavior and Human Performance* 8 (1972): 26–43.

27. S.E. Seashore, *Group Cohesiveness in the Industrial Work Group* (Ann Arbor: University of Michigan Press, 1954).

28. C. Evans and K. Dion, "Group Cohesion and Performance: A Meta-analysis," *Small Group Research* 22 (1991): 175–186.

29. E. Trist and K. Bamforth, "Some Social and Psychological Consequences of the Long-Wall Method of Goal-Setting," *Human Relations* 4 (1951): 1–38.

30. E. Dale, *Organizations* (New York: American Management Association, 1967).

31. P.A. Turla and K.L. Hawkins, "Meaningful Meetings," *Success*, June 1983, 40.

32. Ibid.

33. A. Jay, "How to Run a Meeting," *Harvard Business Review* 54 (1976): 43–57.

CHAPTER

14

Let us never negotiate out
of fear; but let us never fear
to negotiate.
— John F. Kennedy

If compromise continues,
the revolution will disappear.
— Lenin

The secret of managing a
club is to keep the five guys
who hate you away from the
five who are undecided.
— Casey Stengel

LEARNING OBJECTIVES

*After studying this chapter,
you should be able to:*

1. *Define conflict.*
2. *Contrast competition and
conflict.*
3. *Explain how the understanding of conflict has
changed.*
4. *List some sources of conflict.*
5. *Describe strategies for
managing conflict in an organization.*
6. *List ways a manager can
induce desirable conflict.*

Conflict Management

CONFLICT CAN FRACTURE A COMPANY

Herbert Haft is no stranger to confrontation. When he and his wife, Gloria, opened their first discount drugstore in downtown Washington, D.C., in 1954, they quickly ran up against powerful pharmaceutical companies that objected to their selling at below suggested prices. The case went all the way to the Supreme Court, and its landmark decision against price-fixing gave impetus to the growth of the discount industry.

Over the past 40 years, Herbert Haft has built a $1.2 billion discounting empire. He is CEO of the Dart Group, a holding company that includes Crown Books, Trak Auto, and Shoppers Food Warehouse. Holding 57 percent of the stock, he has a controlling interest in these companies. Herbert, Gloria, and their three children helped the businesses grow. Robert, their oldest son, was groomed for business from the start, earning degrees from top-tier business schools and holding positions as president of Dart Group and chief executive of Crown Books. Gloria was corporate secretary at Dart Group, and their two other children, Linda and Ronald, had important but lesser roles in the family empire.

In an emotional toast to Robert on his fortieth birthday, with 80 close friends and family

members watching, Herbert proclaimed Robert to be his proudest achievement. Robert had been a key partner with Herbert in amassing the Haft family retail and real estate empire, and it was widely assumed that Robert would one day succeed his father as Dart Group's CEO.

Although both men were accomplished businessmen who worked well together, they had distinctly different leadership styles. Herbert was aggressive and covert, constantly butting heads with business rivals and divulging as little financial information as possible in annual reports. Robert adopted a more open style with Wall Street, and took a more analytical approach to strategic planning.

Eventually, their different approaches sparked a power struggle that turned Dart Group upside down. In March 1993, the two discussed Herbert's succession. Robert, without Herbert's full consent, began to take control of Dart Group. At a Dart board meeting on April 19, Robert and Herbert publicly disputed the expansion of Total Beverage, a wine, beer, and beverage chain, with Herbert claiming Robert was "trying to destroy the company." Four days later a *Wall Street Journal* article designated Robert the

"de facto chief executive [of Dart] for the last two years" and contained quotes from Robert only. Herbert perceived this as a public grab for power and a humiliating blow to the empire they had built. The fighting continued, and Gloria made an emotional plea for the two to reconcile at the May 24 Crown Books board meeting, to which Herbert and three nonfamily board directors had brought lawyers to represent them. Within two weeks Herbert ousted all family members from the Dart Group board, including Gloria and Robert. By the end of June, new board members, hand-selected by Herbert, fired Robert from his executive positions at Dart and Crown Books, and, despite his million-dollar employment contracts, suspended his pay.

The once close-knit family was now deeply divided. Gloria and Linda initially sided with Robert, while Ronald supported his father. Although Herbert dominated the Dart Group, he did not have a controlling share of the family's extensive privately held real estate holdings of Washington, D.C., shopping centers. Concerned that Gloria, Robert, and Linda would control the real estate holdings, Herbert convinced Ronald to side with him. Together, they pressured Linda to

(continued on following page)

(continued from previous page)
sign a power of attorney granting Herbert and Ronald broad powers to conduct business affairs on her behalf. Linda later demanded they return the paper to her, but they refused.

Since then, Ronald has been named president of Dart Group and has been chosen to succeed Herbert upon this retirement. He is also the largest shareholder of both Dart Group and the family's real estate holdings. Gloria, after 46 years of marriage, has filed for divorce. The terms of Robert's dismissal, as well as covert stock transactions and money transfers conducted by Ronald and Herbert to make Ronald the largest shareholder and protect Herbert's stake in the empire, are being contested in various state courts and may be invalidated in the divorce proceedings.

As this story illustrates, conflict can severely disrupt an organization. Conflict management skills are critical to effective management. This chapter explores elements of conflict and strategies for managing it.

Sources: Kara Swisher, "Father-Son Struggle Splinters Dynasty," *Washington Post,* July 25, 1993, Al, A18–A19; Kara Swisher, "Rift in the Boardroom Leads to Family Purge," *Washington Post,* July 26, 1993, A1, A8; Mark Lewyn, "Behind the Bloody Battle in Dart's Boardroom," *Business Week,* June 28, 1993, 96–98; Mark Lewyn, "This Week on *The Hafts . . .,*" *Business Week,* November 22, 1993, 96–97.

Conflict may well be an inevitable product of organizational life. Although most of us think of conflict as a negative experience to be avoided, it actually has the potential to produce positive organizational outcomes if properly managed. To increase understanding of how conflict can affect performance, we will examine the nature and origins of this phenomenon and some techniques for managing it.

CONFLICT

Conflict is the process that results when one person (or a group of people) perceives that another person or group is frustrating, or about to frustrate, an important concern.[1] Conflict involves incompatible differences between parties that result in interference or opposition.

It is important to distinguish between conflict and competition. Conflict is directed against another party, whereas competition is directed toward obtaining a desired goal without interference from another party. For example, competition may exist between two salespeople who vie for an annual performance award, but conflict (that is, incompatible differences) may not exist so long as the two do not interfere with or oppose each other. Students also compete for grades, yet they are not usually placed in a competitive system that induces conflict. To be sure, *intense competition* can sometimes lead to conflict. But conflict can result without the existence of competition.

If two parties can both gain from their competitive efforts, then competition is less likely to lead to conflict. For example, if two faculty members are trying to obtain a promotion, the efforts of one person need not block the other's success. In such a case, the promotion of both individuals is possible and, therefore, direct conflict is not likely to arise. In essence, the difference between competition and conflict lies in whether actions are taken to interfere with another's goal attainment. This difference suggests that eliminating opportunities for interference is a useful management tactic for preventing the escalation of competition into conflict.

CHANGING VIEWS OF CONFLICT

How social scientists and managers view the topic of conflict has changed over the years.[2] Until the mid-1940s, it was popular to consider conflict as harmful and unnecessary. The existence of conflict was regarded as a sign that something was wrong and required correction. According to this *traditional view,* conflict serves no useful purpose because it distracts managers' attention and saps energy and resources. Thus, conflict should be avoided. In addition, conflict was seen as the result of poor management and the efforts of troublemakers. Through proper management techniques and the removal of troublemakers, conflict could be eliminated and optimal performance could be achieved.

In recent years, management scholars have shifted their view of conflict. Today, conflict is seen as inevitable in every organization and oftentimes necessary to ensure high performance. That conflict can be harmful in some instances is not denied, but emphasis is placed on recognizing that some forms of conflict can be useful in achieving desired goals. According to this perspective, conflict can encourage a search for new tactics and strategies, and help overcome stagnation and complacency. Conflict as a device for directing effort is, therefore, sometimes a desirable state. The focus of this *contemporary view* is on the successful management of conflict rather than its total elimination.

The successful management of conflict involves both sustaining a target level of conflict and selecting a conflict-reduction strategy. In addition, managers may purposely create conflict. In situations that call for creativity and when frank discussions of alternatives are needed (as when resisting a tendency toward groupthink), the stimulation of conflict is advisable.

In itself, conflict is neither desirable nor undesirable. It is only in terms of its effects on performance that the value of conflict can be judged. Figure 14.1 illustrates this notion, which suggests that an optimal level of conflict exists for any given situation. Carried to a high extreme, conflict can lead to chaos and disorder. In contrast, an extremely low level of conflict can result in complacency and poor performance due to lack of innovation.

Identifying the optimal level of conflict for a specific situation is not a simple matter. It requires a good understanding of the individuals involved and the nature of their assignments. Also, a manager needs a degree of creativity to determine strategies and tactics for reducing or, if necessary, increasing the level of conflict. Furthermore, simply increasing conflict when it appears necessary is not in itself sufficient: For conflict to foster creativity, it must be channeled and directed. Maintaining conflict at an optimal, or "Goldilocks," point is also a difficult managerial challenge.[*] In the succeeding sections of this chapter, we will consider techniques for reducing as well as for intentionally stimulating conflict.

---

[*]The Goldilocks point is the point on a curve where the conditions are "just right."

FIGURE 14.1

CONTEMPORARY VIEW OF THE RELATIONSHIP BETWEEN CONFLICT AND PERFORMANCE

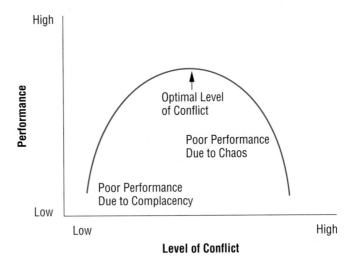

SOURCES OF CONFLICT

Conflict can spring from a variety of sources. These sources can be grouped into three general categories: communication, structural, and personal behavior factors.[3]

COMMUNICATION FACTORS

Managers typically attribute a sizable proportion of the conflicts that arise in organizations to poor communication. If we define true communication as creating a mental picture in the mind of a receiver in exactly the same detail as intended by the sender, then true or perfect communication is certainly rare. Given this inherent imperfection, there are many opportunities for misunderstanding to develop in the communication process. To be sure, conflict stemming from such unsuccessful communication is not the same as conflict based on substantive differences, yet it can still have powerful effects.

Incorrect, distorted, or ambiguous information can create hostility. For example, a manager may fail to communicate clearly to subordinates regarding who will be responsible for performing a distasteful task while she is away on vacation. Upon her return, she may find that the subordinates are "at each other's throats" and that the task remains to be done.

STRUCTURAL FACTORS

SIZE   In a review of studies examining the relationship of conflict to organizational size, Robbins found fairly consistent evidence suggesting that conflict is greater in larger organizations. It is likely that increases in size are associated with less goal clarity, greater formality, increased specialization, more supervisory levels, and increased opportunities for information to become distorted as it passes through more levels.

STAFF HETEROGENEITY   It appears that differences among staff members in terms of authority, longevity, and values may also be sources of conflict. Differences among staff members, however, can also have beneficial effects on performance. As we discussed in Chapter 12, problem-solving groups comprised of relatively diverse individuals have an advantage over homogeneously composed groups. The diversity that exists in heterogeneous groups can serve to bring in different ideas and perhaps create challenges among members that foster superior achievement.

PARTICIPATION   One might expect that greater subordinate participation (for example, in decision making) would reduce conflict. From a human relations perspective, one might even argue that inviting subordinates to participate can satisfy a possible drive to be fully involved. Research on this topic, however, has shown that just the opposite is true: When subordinate participation is greater, levels of conflict tend to be higher. This somewhat unexpected result may occur because increased participation leads to greater awareness of individual differences. Also, simply participating in decision making does not ensure that an individual's point of view will prevail, since a subordinate can be involved in decision making but lack the authority to have his or her preferences put into action. However, as mentioned earlier, the increased conflict associated with greater participation is not necessarily undesirable. If the results of subordinate participation, and the subsequent conflict, enhance the overall performance of a work unit, then the existence of conflict can be productive.

LINE–STAFF DISTINCTIONS   In surveys of managers, one of the most frequently mentioned sources of conflict is the distinction between line and staff units within organizations. Line units perform jobs that are directly related to core activities of the organization. In a manufacturing setting, the production department would be a line unit, while in a customer-oriented setting, the marketing or sales department might be considered line. Staff units perform jobs that support the line function. Examples of staff departments include research and development, public relations, personnel, and marketing research.

Conflict occurs between many line and staff divisions because of the functions they perform, their differing goals, and the values and backgrounds of their members. Line divisions are generally more operations oriented, while staff divisions are more removed from central operating activities. Line personnel are often very loyal to their firm, while staff personnel tend to be (and feel that it is their duty to be) critical of company practices. In fact, staff people frequently identify more strongly with a professional group or discipline than with the organization in which they are employed. For example, personnel officers and marketing researchers may belong to national associations that give them a sense of professional identification. Thus, a staff person may see herself primarily as a public relations specialist who happens to be working at Inland Steel, while a line person's strongest identification is likely to be with his employer. Lastly, the two groups' time horizons often differ—staff people more typically think in terms of long-range issues, while line people are more involved with short-term or day-to-day concerns. Given these differences in orientation, it is not too surprising that line and staff personnel experience a fair degree of conflict.

REWARD SYSTEMS   If one party obtains rewards at the expense of another party, conflict can be easily generated. This form of conflict can arise among individuals and groups as well as among entire organizations. How mutually exclusive reward systems operate is not always obvious. For example, staff people are generally rewarded for being innovative and identifying the need for change. By suggesting and attempting to induce change, they are able to demonstrate their usefulness to the larger organization. On the other hand, most line people strongly prefer to avoid change because for them, it is both disruptive and inconvenient. In fact, line people are generally rewarded for productivity that results from uninterrupted activity.

RESOURCE INTERDEPENDENCE   Typically, groups must compete for the resources of their organization. With a growing supply of money and other resources, such as space, equipment, and materials, conflicts may not arise. However, such bountifulness is not the norm for organizations. As a result, conflict and the resulting lack of coordination and cooperation between divisions exist.

POWER   The distribution of power within an organization can also be a source of conflict. If a group feels that it possesses far less power than it should, or if it believes that an excessive amount of power is held by another group, it is likely to challenge the existing order. If departments are ostensibly equal when in fact they hold differing amounts of power, serious discontent can arise. For example, in many companies, staff people must continually justify their need to exist, be understanding of problems in line departments, and make constant efforts to get along with the line personnel. Similar expectations do not exist for line personnel, however, because the line usually wields greater authority than the staff.[4] Such asymmetry of power distribution can add further tension to an already difficult situation.

PERSONAL BEHAVIOR FACTORS

Another source of conflict lies in differences among individuals. Some people's values or perceptions of situations are particularly likely to generate conflict with others. For example, a manager may highly value the idea that all employees must "pay their dues." His argument might be that he spent much of his early career in an unglamorous lower-level position and that others would benefit from a similar experience. Of course, the imposition of this value on ambitious young subordinates could create serious conflict. Similarly, if a manager tends to perceive people in a certain way (for example, if she is quick to infer laziness or incompetence from only limited evidence), her responses to certain situations can be a source for conflict. In addition, some people simply enjoy being argumentative and combative. For such individuals, whose personal style is especially conflict-prone, life is a continuing series of escalating hostilities and battles.

Studies show that conflict-prone individuals are likely to possess certain traits. For example, highly authoritarian individuals are prone to antagonize their coworkers by escalating otherwise trivial differences. Also, individuals with low self-esteem may more readily feel threatened by others and therefore overreact. Both authoritarianism and low self-esteem can predispose people to feel the need to "defend their turf" against (objectively) trivial threats.[5]

LEVELS OF CONFLICT

Conflict can be examined at several different levels. Conflict that exists within an individual is termed **intrapersonal,** while conflict between two people is termed **interpersonal.**[†] Conflict between groups is labeled **intergroup.** In this section, we will examine specific aspects of intrapersonal and interpersonal conflict.

INTRAPERSONAL CONFLICT

A common form of intrapersonal conflict in everyday life involves choices between mutually exclusive goals. Selecting one option in many instances eliminates any other alternative. Several other types of intrapersonal goal conflict can be identified, depending on the nature of the choices.

APPROACH–APPROACH CONFLICT   **Approach–approach conflict** arises when an individual must choose between two attractive alternatives. For example, an employer faces an approach–approach conflict when she must choose between two highly qualified applicants for a single position. Similarly, a job seeker must cope with an approach–approach conflict when deciding which of two outstanding but equally appealing job offers to accept. Approach–approach conflicts pose a problem for only a brief period of time—that is, of course, if they are not immobilizing. If we model such a situation in terms of the strength of each motive to approach a desired goal, as in panel A of Figure 14.2, we can see that a person should initially be caught between the two alternatives (position X in the graph). However, even slight movement in the direction of one of the choices is enough to break the deadlock and lead to the selection of that particular option.

One interesting aspect of approach–approach conflicts is the change that occurs in the individual's attitude toward the rejected option. Often, he or she

---

[†]Similarly, conflict within an organization can be labeled *intraorganizational*, while conflict between organizations can be labeled *interorganizational*.

An Inside Look
An Ethical Dilemma

Intrapersonal conflict often arises in ethical decisions. In many cases, an ethical choice clashes with some sort of immediate gain to the decision maker, such as money or a boss's approval.

Such was the ethical dilemma faced by Mark Morze in his experience with ZZZZ Best Company, a business with a notorious history. Barry Minkow, a Californian in his late teens, started the carpet-cleaning company in the garage of his parents' home and, over the next several years, through a series of scams and ever-growing loans, built it into a company valued at $200 million. Along the way, Minkow recruited a variety of people to work with him. One of them was Mark Morze.

When he met Minkow, Morze was operating a small bookkeeping business, preparing tax returns for about 100 clients. Initially, Morze was amazed by the lack of paperwork documenting ZZZZ Best's business, but he pieced together what he could, establishing a semblance of financial record keeping.

His first major ethical conflict arose when Minkow was scrambling to get a $400,000 loan from a California company called California Factors and Finance to repay a previous lender. Minkow told Cal Factor the loan was to cover a big restoration job in Arroyo Grande, California. Unfortunately for Minkow, Cal Factor would not lend the money without seeing the job site—which didn't actually exist.

Minkow solicited Morze's help. "So what's the problem?" Morze replied, suggesting that Minkow let Cal Factor see the job site. When Minkow explained that there was no job site, that he had made it up, Morze was in a bind. He knew that the company needed another loan to survive. On a more personal level, ZZZZ Best owed him at least $50,000.

Deciding that a little deception wouldn't do too much damage, Morze rented a car and drove to Arroyo Grande. What he saw was discouraging. He was supposed to document the restoration of an eight-story building, but nothing in the sleepy little town stood over three stories tall. Undeterred, Morze bought a Polaroid camera, selected a two-story building, then lay on his back, seeking an angle that would disguise the true size of the building.

This deception was only the beginning of Morze's involvement in the ZZZZ Best scams. In planning to raise money by taking his company public, Minkow learned that the company would need three years' worth of audited statements. However, such documentation did not exist, and what did often painted an unflattering picture. Again, he turned to Morze, who developed an intricate system of photocopying checks, invoices, bank statements, and tax returns, then cutting and pasting the numbers on them to show ZZZZ Best's status in a more favorable light. Morze knew that he was taking a risk, but he liked to gamble, and he was tantalized by the big money that could result from a public stock offering.

Of course, a business cannot prosper on borrowing alone, and the ZZZZ Best scam eventually began to unravel. Ultimately, Morze was sentenced to eight years in prison and five years' probation, and he was ordered to make restitution in an unspecified amount.

Source: Joe Domanick, *Faking It in America: Barry Minkow and the Great ZZZZ Best Scam* (Chicago: Contemporary Books, 1989).

regrets not having selected that alternative, as when a person buys one of two different cars and afterwards feels the decision was poor. Frequently, a person will then try to reduce this sense of regret by rationalizing that the chosen option is inherently better or by actively trying to avoid information that would suggest that the choice was not superior.[‡]

AVOIDANCE–AVOIDANCE CONFLICT Avoidance–avoidance conflict involves a choice between two equally unattractive options. For example, a person may have a physical disorder that is very uncomfortable, such as ulcers. Yet the

---

[‡]This postdecision regret can be understood in terms of the theory of cognitive dissonance (see Chapter 4).[6]

person may have a strong fear of going to the hospital for surgery. The net result is that the person is caught between the two options. Faced with an avoidance–avoidance conflict, most people will vacillate between the two operations, without resolution of the conflict (point X in panel B of Figure 14.2).

FIGURE 14.2

MODELS OF MOTIVE STRENGTH IN THREE TYPES OF INTRAPERSONAL CONFLICT

A. Approach–Approach Conflict

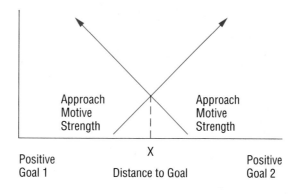

Approach Motive Strength   Approach Motive Strength

X

Positive Goal 1   Distance to Goal   Positive Goal 2

B. Avoidance–Avoidance Conflict

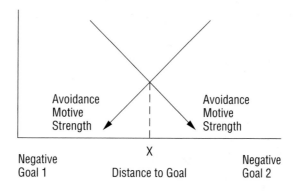

Avoidance Motive Strength   Avoidance Motive Strength

X

Negative Goal 1   Distance to Goal   Negative Goal 2

C. Approach–Avoidance Conflict

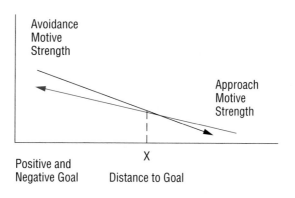

Avoidance Motive Strength

Approach Motive Strength

X

Positive and Negative Goal   Distance to Goal

However, if one of the two motives becomes stronger, the conflict can be resolved. Thus, if the ulcer sufferer's discomfort becomes unbearable, the motive to avoid pain may override the motive to avoid surgery and the conflict will be resolved.

People who are trapped in avoidance–avoidance situations sometimes have another option for dealing with their conflict—leaving the situation. In some settings, it may not be possible, however, to quit one's job or leave one's family. As this discussion suggests, avoidance–avoidance conflict is difficult to resolve as the conflict places the person in a situation of trying to maintain distance between opposing outcomes.

APPROACH–AVOIDANCE CONFLICT   In an **approach–avoidance conflict,** the individual must decide whether to approach or avoid a single goal that has both positive (attractive) and negative (unattractive) qualities. This is not an uncommon circumstance in organizational settings, where many goals have mixed outcomes for an individual. For example, such a conflict could arise when a student considers choosing a college major that offers a greater guarantee of employment on graduation but involves uninteresting course work, or when an employee is offered a promotion to an otherwise attractive position that involves reporting to a person who is difficult to work for. If the motive to avoid the goal is stronger than the motive to approach it, the person will be caught where the strengths of the motives are roughly equal (point X in panel C of Figure 14.2). As the person moves toward or away from the goal, the relatively stronger motive takes over and brings the person back to a point where she vacillates.

The resolution of an approach–avoidance conflict requires the strengthening of one motive over the other. Then it is possible for the person to reach the goal. This can be accomplished if the goal is made more attractive or if the individual does more rationalizing to overcome the conflict. Although the person might thereby reach the goal, the strength of the avoidance motive would still be high and the person would remain highly anxious. Lowering the strength of the motive to avoid the goal is, therefore, also important in finding a tolerable resolution to the conflict.

INTERPERSONAL CONFLICT

Researchers have used a number of contrived situations in laboratory settings to determine which factors influence the tendencies to compete or cooperate when conflict exists. One such contrived conflict scenario is called the Prisoners' Dilemma:

> *Two suspected criminals are taken into custody and separated. The district attorney is certain that they are guilty of a specific crime, but he does not have adequate evidence to convict them at a trial. He points out to each prisoner that each has two alternatives: to confess to the crime the police are sure they have done or not to confess. If they both do not confess, then the district attorney will book them on some very minor, trumped-up charge. . . ; if they both confess, they will be prosecuted, [and] he will recommend [a rather se-*

vere] sentence; but if one confesses and the other does not, then the confessor will receive rather lenient treatment for turning state's evidence whereas the latter will get the "book" slapped at him.[7]

This situation is designed to create mixed motives for the prisoners. If each chooses what is best for him personally and ignores the other's circumstances, he will decide not to confess. However, if one prisoner does not confess and the other does, the holdout will suffer severely (by receiving a longer sentence). The best option for both prisoners, therefore, is to resist the divide-and-conquer strategy of the attorney and stick to their pleas of innocence. Of course, the question is whether they can really trust their partner in crime not to confess. Figure 14.3 shows the outcomes of the various choices for each prisoner. The outcome for each individual depends on the actions of the other participant.[§]

In role-playing studies using college students as subjects and substituting monetary rewards and penalties for threatened jail sentences, it has been found that the tendency of the participants to compete versus cooperate with each other can be influenced by a variety of forces. Chief among these is the penalty–reward structure for cooperating and competing. By altering the rewards and penalties for various actions, it is possible to induce more or fewer choices of competition or cooperation.

As a real-world illustration of how the size of penalties and rewards can influence the choice of a competitive strategy, consider the payoff matrix for the United States and the former Soviet Union with respect to the use of

FIGURE 14.3
OUTCOMES OF CHOICES AVAILABLE IN A PRISONERS' DILEMMA SCENARIO

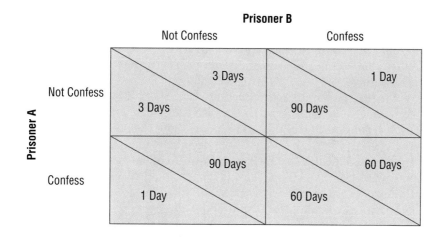

[§]In actuality, the practice of separating suspected criminals and offering these alternatives is effective in extracting confessions.

nuclear weapons during the Cold War. If both countries had attacked each other, the magnitude of total annihilation would have been enormous (this is analogous to the values in the lower right-hand cell of Figure 14.3 being the electric chair). If one country had tried to preemptively (or sneak) attack the other with confidence that the other would strive to be cooperative, the attacker would have gained a clear advantage. However, the retaliatory capability of the attacked country could not be ruled out. Therefore, each found it to its advantage to avoid taking the competitive option of "pushing the button" because the costs were too high. In short, excessive penalties can force a form of cooperativeness (or at least reduced aggression) between otherwise contentious parties.

Other research on situations like the Prisoners' Dilemma also points to the importance of communication between parties as a means of inducing cooperation. This evidence suggests that the availability of "hot lines" between potentially antagonistic parties can help to reduce tension and conflict.

STRATEGIES FOR REDUCING CONFLICT

SUPERORDINATE GOALS

Providing higher-level, or superordinate, goals to antagonistic parties can help to avert or reduce the level of conflict. When people share a common superordinate goal, they must cooperate to achieve a degree of success or avoid disaster.

In a demonstration of the conflict-reducing power of superordinate goals, Sherif conducted a field experiment with groups of 12-year-old boys attending neighboring summer camps.[8] Initially, he established two independent groups of boys who were unaware of the other group's existence. These boys engaged in the usual summer fun and developed norms of behavior within their groups. Sherif then created a degree of conflict by informing both groups that the other camp would be using certain equipment, such as canoes, and that, as a result, they would be unable to engage in that activity. (In essence, he created win-lose situations for the groups.) As a result, the two groups came to resent each other strongly.

As the situation approached open warfare. Sherif experimented with several techniques to induce harmony between the camps. Initially Sherif tried to give each group some favorable information about the other. This effort failed because the boys' negative impressions led them to reject the information. Next, Sherif had the boys eat their meals and attend movies together. This also failed to work, since hostility (such as name calling) erupted when the camp members were near each other. Then Sherif asked the group leaders to negotiate and share favorable information about their groups that could later be conveyed to their respective camps. Once again, the strategy failed because the leaders feared being "dethroned" by their constituents if they were seen to be too friendly to the out-group.

Finally, Sherif attempted to create superordinate goals for the camps by staging situations in which both groups needed to participate in order to benefit their members. These planned situations involved a breakdown of the

OB Focus
Smaller Organizations Need Diversity Training, Too

Although diversity training workshops have become common at large organizations, many smaller companies often lack the resources to educate employees about work force diversity. Yet, smaller organizations are just as prone to ethnic, gender, and religious tensions, and are finding it cost-effective to preempt potential confrontations with diversity workshops.

Take the case of Cardiac Concepts Inc., a Texas outpatient facility that specializes in cardiovascular laboratory tests. After an ongoing year-long argument about religion between two employees, a Roman Catholic and a Jehovah's Witness, president and co-founder Emma Colquitt decided to hire a consultant to conduct a workshop in how to work productively in a diverse work force. Although Cardiac Concepts employs only 11 people, Colquitt felt the $3,000 fee was well spent. Had she done nothing, tensions among workers might ultimately

have affected production or damaged the company's reputation with its patients and the local medical community.

Diversity training workshops can also help employees understand and work more effectively with a company's diverse customer base. Mental Health Systems, of San Diego, Calif., a nonprofit organization that provides mental health treatment, drug and alcohol rehabilitation services, and vocational training, uses diversity training to facilitate better understanding among staff and clients. Nearly a quarter of its employees are ethnic minorities and almost half are disabled. Says Bill Eastwood, executive director of Mental Health Systems, "Understanding breeds better working relationships."

In diversity training workshops, managers and employees generally participate in role-playing exercises and share their backgrounds and beliefs to un-

cover prejudices. In one exercise, staff pair off and list stereotypes of the ethnic groups represented at the workshop. By considering the values and lifestyles of their peers, employees can better understand their own biases.

By the year 2000, the U.S. Department of Labor forecasts that African Americans will constitute 16.5 percent of the U.S. labor force, Hispanics, 14.3 percent, and Asians and others, 5.6 percent. As ethnic multiplicity in the workplace grows, diversity training is an important precaution in heading off workplace tensions. Although diversity training workshops can go a long way in helping employees better understand one another, managerial follow-up is essential for long-lasting results. A partner in the consulting firm International Productivity Institute contends, "If the boss uses diversity training as a Band-Aid, the problems often recur."

Source: Melissa Lee, "Diversity Training Brings Unity to Small Companies," *The Wall Street Journal*, September 3, 1993, B2.

---

camps' food truck (boys from *both* camps were needed to push the truck in order to get it started), a disruption of the camps' water supply, and a cooperative effort to obtain funds to rent a desired film.

Because of the need to meet a common threat, the boys of the two camps eventually adopted friendly and cooperative behaviors. For example, near the end of their stays, when one group had excess funds, it used them to purchase refreshments for both camps, rather than solely for its own members.

The implementation of this strategy in organizational settings has not proved to be easy. In the early 1970s, General Motors attempted to use superordinate goals to unite management and labor in a battle against the threat of foreign competition.[9] The Chevrolet Vega, GM's intended answer to imported subcompacts, was to be manufactured in new production facilities in Lordstown, Ohio. Despite management's efforts to unite workers with managers through an attitude-change campaign focusing on the need to counter the foreign threat, a strike and open violence occurred not long after the plant opened. This experience suggests that a superordinate approach may need to be highly credible if it is to be effective.[10]

STRUCTURAL APPROACHES

A number of options exist for managers who wish to reduce conflict via structural change. One technique is to transfer conflict-prone individuals to other units. Of course, this apparently simple approach cannot always be used, since some employees are nearly indispensable to their unit's performance. In some instances, it is the recognition of their value to the unit that gives such individuals the confidence to engage in battles over what they see as important issues.

One way to overcome line–staff conflict is to appoint one person to serve as moderator (and mediator) at line–staff meetings. This person tries to manage the interaction between the two factions to ensure that relations between the two groups remain constructive. For example, before a meeting takes place, an effective moderator may try to help both groups better understand the nature of their counterparts so that they will be more tolerant of each other. To ensure that the meeting goes smoothly, the moderator may also encourage both sides to "do their homework" and prepare for questions that may arise and encourage staff people to consult with line people as they develop their proposals.

The moderator is expected to serve as a buffer between the units and encourage understanding by both sides. However, because higher management often selects a moderator from among the line people, staff people may question that person's real loyalty and biases. Being the moderator of such conflict, therefore, can pose a serious challenge for anyone asked to serve in such a role. Furthermore, what little evidence is available on the effectiveness of moderators suggests that many organizational members perceive them as having only limited positive impact on line–staff relations.[11]

Conflict management methods can be customized to match specific situations. A common technique is to create an appeals procedure (for example, a grievance system or arbitration) that provides a higher authority for resolving conflicts and a set of specific steps to follow when filing an appeal. One major shortcoming of an appeals procedure, however, is that the losing party often has difficulty in accepting the verdict. Although obliged to go along with the decision in theory, the person may feel compelled to "even the score" at a later time by a subtle, but vengeful, action or inaction. Thus, for an appeals process to succeed, the losing party must be made to bring the two parties closer together.

STYLES OF CONFLICT MANAGEMENT

Managers differ in their ways of dealing with conflict. Ken Thomas has suggested five major styles of conflict management that managers can adopt: forcing, collaborating, compromising, avoiding, and accommodating.[12] Table 14.1 summarizes the characteristics of these styles.

FORCING   In addition to defining the five basic styles of conflict management, Thomas has suggested a two-dimensional framework for comparing them

TABLE 14.1
FIVE CONFLICT-HANDLING STYLES

Conflict-handling Style	Related Term	Proverb
Forcing	Competing Conflictful Moving against the other	Put your foot down where you mean to stand.
Collaborating	Problem solving Integrating Confronting	Come let us reason together.
Compromising	Splitting the difference Sharing Horse-trading	You have to give some to get some.
Avoiding	Moving away from the other Withdrawing Losing–leaving	Let sleeping dogs lie.
Accommodating	Yielding–losing Friendly–helping Moving toward the other	It is better to give than to receive.

Source: K. W. Thomas, "Organizational Conflict," in *Organizational Behavior,* ed. S. Kerr (Columbus, Ohio: Grid, 1979).

(Figure 14.4). According to this framework, the **forcing** style attempts to overwhelm an opponent with formal authority, threats, or the use of power. Its underlying features are assertiveness and uncooperativeness.

COLLABORATING   The **collaborating** style represents a combination of assertiveness and cooperativeness. Collaborating involves an attempt to satisfy the concerns of both sides through honest discussion. Creative approaches to conflict reduction—for example, the sharing of resources—may actually lead to both parties' being materially better off. For this style to be successful, trust and openness are required of all participants.

ACCOMMODATING   An **accommodating** style combines unassertiveness and cooperativeness. At its simplest level, this style may merely involve giving in to another's wishes. Accommodating behavior may be motivated by a desire to be altruistic or prosocial, but sometimes no other approach is feasible for someone in a truly weak position.

AVOIDING   The combination of unassertiveness and uncooperativeness leads to an **avoiding** style, in which a person implies that he or she will either improve a difficult situation or attempt to appear neutral. In some cases, it may not be possible to adopt a truly neutral position, but a manager may nonetheless prefer to avoid the situation. Although a manager who avoids difficult

FIGURE 14.4
A TWO-DIMENSIONAL MODEL OF CONFLICT BEHAVIOR

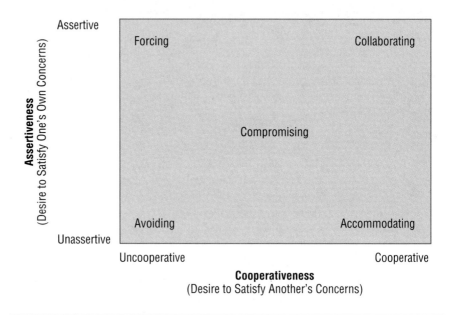

Source: K. W. Thomas, "Organizational Conflict," in *Organizational Behavior*, ed. S. Kerr (Columbus, Ohio: Grid, 1979), 156.

issues is likely to be resented by subordinates, this strategy may be effective under certain circumstances. For example, a manager may initially stay out of a disagreement to avoid escalating the conflict during a particular phase of its development. Later, when she judges the time is right, she may take a more active role in finding a productive solution.

Experienced managers also recognize that action is not always necessary because some problems dissipate over time or are resolved by other organizational processes. For example, an intense conflict between two subordinates may seem to require intervention by their manager. But if the manager knows that one of the individuals will soon be transferred to another department or promoted to another position, it may be advisable to ignore the situation and let the impending changes resolve the difficulty.

COMPROMISING   The fifth style, **compromising,** involves intermediate amounts of assertiveness and cooperativeness and strives for partial satisfaction of both parties' desire by seeking a middle ground. To succeed at compromising, both parties must be willing to give up something.

Although people may be tempted to consider some styles of conflict management more effective than others (for example, collaborating versus avoiding), there is good reason to believe that each style works best in certain situations. Through a survey of chief executives, Thomas has attempted to identify the most effective match-ups of style and situation (Table 14.2).

TABLE 14.2
USES OF FIVE STYLES OF CONFLICT HANDLING

Conflict-handling Styles	Appropriate Situations
Competing	1. When quick, decisive action is vital, e.g., emergencies.
	2. On important issues where unpopular actions need implementing, e.g., cost-cutting, enforcing unpopular rules, discipline.
	3. On issues vital to company welfare when you know you're right.
	4. Against people who take advantage of noncompetitive behavior.
Collaborating	1. To find an integrative solution when both sets of concerns are too important to be compromised.
	2. When your objective is to learn.
	3. To merge insights from people with different perspectives.
	4. To gain commitment by incorporating concerns into a consensus.
	5. To work through feelings that have interfered with a relationship.
Compromising	1. When goals are important but not worth the effort of potential disruption of more assertive modes.
	2. When opponents with equal power are committed to mutually exclusive goals.
	3. To achieve temporary settlements to complex issues.
	4. To arrive at expedient solutions under time pressure.
	5. As a backup when collaboration or competition is unsuccessful.
Avoiding	1. When an issue is trivial, or more important issues are pressing.
	2. When you perceive no chance of satisfying your concerns.
	3. When potential disruption outweighs the benefits of resolution.
	4. To let people cool down and regain perspective.
	5. When gathering information supersedes immediate decision.
	6. When others can resolve the conflict more effectively.
	7. When issues seem tangential or symptomatic of other issues.
Accommodating	1. When you find you are wrong—to allow a better position to be heard, to learn, and to show your reasonableness.
	2. When issues are more important to others than to you—to satisfy others and maintain cooperation.
	3. To build social credits for later issues.
	4. To minimize loss when you are outmatched and losing.
	5. When harmony and stability are especially important.
	6. To allow subordinates to develop by learning from mistakes.

Source: K. W. Thomas, "Toward Multi-Dimensional Values in Teaching: The Example of Conflict Behaviors," *Academy of Management Review* 2 (1977): 484–490.

INTERGROUP CONFLICT

Conflict between groups can result from a variety of causes. Competition for resources, differences in goals, and interpersonal conflict can serve as the basis for conflict among groups or departments. Line and staff conflict, discussed earlier in this chapter, is a prime example of intergroup conflict. The management of conflict between groups or departments can be achieved through a variety of strategies.[13] Table 14.3 lists specific techniques for managing intergroup conflict.

RULES AND PROCEDURES   A fairly direct approach to managing intergroup conflict is the establishment of rules and procedures. This approach is likely to work best if the rules and procedures are set up before conflict arises. However, as a way of sorting out and managing differences even after conflict has emerged, it is still a potentially useful technique. As an example, consider two departments that need to use a specific piece of equipment that can only accommodate one user at a time. To manage the potential conflict in this situation, certain times of day or certain days of the week can be reserved for each department to have exclusive use of the equipment. Rules and procedures often help to avert conflict or defuse tense situations by reducing the amount of contact between groups.

APPEAL TO HIGHER AUTHORITY   In circumstances where rules and procedures are not easily established, a higher authority may be relied on to decide how to best manage the needs of groups. For example, a supervisor may be assigned to make decisions about how each group will have its desires satisfied, with an eye toward satisfying the larger needs of the organization rather than just those of the immediate groups. This technique can also have drawbacks. For instance, group members may try to befriend the supervisor in an attempt to receive unwarranted, additional consideration in scheduling decisions. Also, the supervisor may find that continually trying to manage the interests of these groups is very time-consuming and detracts from time needed to perform other supervisory duties.

BOUNDARY-SPANNING POSITIONS   When the coordination of the efforts and interests of departments becomes increasingly continuous and complex, it is sometimes desirable to assign a person on a full-time basis to manage relations between departments. Such a person's job entails spanning the boundaries, or crossing the divisional lines, between groups. In essence, a **boundary-spanning position** is one that requires a person to serve as a liaison, or communications

■ TABLE 14.3
TECHNIQUES FOR MANAGING INTERGROUP CONFLICT

Rules and Procedures
Higher Authority
Boundary-spanning Positions
Negotiation
Teams
Integrating Departments

link, between groups. Liaison, or boundary-spanning, positions can increase the frequency of contact between groups (through meetings and communiqués). Increased contact between groups can facilitate coordination and, ideally, foster cooperation. On the downside, employees who serve as go-betweens within organizations experience a good deal of job-related conflict and ambiguity concerning their actual role in the organization. This may, in part, account for the finding that boundary-spanners report somewhat lower job satisfaction.[14]

NEGOTIATION   **Negotiation** is an interactive process wherein two or more groups discuss the allocation of resources. It is a commonly used technique for managing conflict. Negotiation typically follows one of two models: distributive bargaining or integrative bargaining. *Distributive bargaining* is an adversarial, win-lose approach to negotiation that focuses on the pool of resources as fixed. *Integrative bargaining* is a collaborative, problem-solving approach that seeks to create win-win outcomes for the parties. Although the integrative bargaining approach has a more attractive appeal, it is difficult to achieve. This difficulty stems partly from the unwillingness of parties to trust each other. For an integrative problem-solving approach to be effective, each party must also have a high degree of concern for the outcomes attained by the other party (see Figure 14.5). In order to move groups from a distributive bargaining approach to an integrative bargaining approach, one should strive to create options that offer mutual gain. In addition, it helps to depersonalize the nature of the conflict and to focus on key interests of the parties.

TEAMS   Teams are collections of employees who are assigned to manage intergroup relations. Teams may be created to manage long-term, continuous intergroup relations, or they may be established to examine a specific problem on a short-term basis. The primary purpose of teams is to tackle recurring

FIGURE 14.5
INFLUENCES ON ATTAINING A PROBLEM-SOLVING APPROACH IN NEGOTIATION

		Low	High
Concern for Others' Outcomes	High	Yield to other party	Problem-solving approach possible
	Low	No action is likely	Fight for own preferences

Source: D. G. Pruitt, "Strategic Choice in Negotiation," *American Behavioral Scientist* 27 (1983): 167–194.

problems resulting from intergroup conflict and to develop remedies for managing the conflict. Typically, such teams comprise employees who hold membership in the competing groups. However, the team members usually have a functional specialty that justifies their membership on the team. Such teams work best, of course, when the members take a problem-solving approach to the task and set aside competitive or antagonistic feelings toward members of the opposing group.

INTEGRATING DEPARTMENTS   At the extreme, groups may require extensive coordination of efforts. Simultaneously, conflict may exist. As an ultimate form of response to such a situation, an organization can create an integrating department. An integrating department actually has few members. It might consist of a head and a few staff members who possess expertise in the specialties associated with the other departments. The **integrating department** is a formal and permanent mechanism with a goal of integrating the efforts of the departments of interest. Initially, an integrating department may not be taken seriously by contesting departments. However, it can be given greater formal authority by providing the head with influence in decision making that affects the affairs, and especially the budgets, of the other departments.

STIMULATING CONFLICT

At the outset of this chapter, we suggested that there is an optimal level of conflict for any situation. Although the optimal level may sometimes be zero, in most cases a modest level of conflict actually encourages involvement and innovation. This indicates that some situations may in fact benefit from the creation of conflict. According to Robbins, some signs that a manager needs to stimulate conflict include an unusually low rate of employee turnover, a shortage of new ideas, strong resistance to change, and the belief that cooperativeness (the principle trait of a "yes-man") is more important than personal competence.[15]

Among the specific techniques that Robbins offers for inducing conflict are:

1. *Appointing managers who are open to change.* In some units, a highly authoritarian manager will tend to suppress opposing viewpoints. The resulting lethargy can be overcome to some extent by the appropriate selection and placement of change-oriented managers.

2. *Encouraging competition.* The use of individual and group incentives to performance, such as pay increases, bonuses, and recognition, tends to enhance competition. And competition, if managed properly, can result in creative conflict.

3. **Restructuring the work unit.** Changing members of work teams, rotating personnel, and altering lines of communication can do much to shake up an organization. Restructuring can also create new jobs to be filled by outsiders whose values and styles will contrast with the prevailing but lethargic set of norms.

An Inside Look
Stirring Up Good Decisions

Some antagonism can be good for an organization's decision makers. Professor Charles R. Schwenk recommends that businesses use devil's advocates to help managers make the right decisions. A devil's advocate can be used in a basic approach or in techniques called *multiple advocacy* and *dialectical inquiry.*

In the basic approach, one person or a group of people takes the role of devil's advocate and criticizes a proposal. The devil's advocate researches the proposal beforehand. Then he or she points out weaknesses, inconsistencies, and problems that may cause the proposed plan or project to fail. Managers can then make their decision with confidence that they have heard all sides of the argument.

Multiple advocacy involves using several devil's advocates from every dissenting faction. Dozens of different opinions may come to the surface with multiple advocacy. Therefore, it is important one person have the role of "custodian of unpopular views." That person makes sure sufficient time is devoted to discussing each issue.

With dialectical inquiry, decision makers are divided into subgroups on the basis of their personalities and problem-solving orientations. The subgroups develop alternatives to the recommended strategy, focusing on the assumptions used to arrive at the recommendation. It is important to question assumptions, because top executives view the company differently than lower-level managers. Because subgroup members have different backgrounds and come from different departments, management gets a variety of opinions on proposals and their underlying assumptions. This technique has been used with success at Eastman Kodak as part of its strategic marketing decision making.

Devil's advocacy works best with unique problems that are difficult to solve. For devil's advocacy to work in an organization, the person making the decision must be willing to listen to other points of view. Also, the devil's advocate should be an objective observer, not a person who is already committed to a proposal.

Source: Walecia Konrad, "Want Better Decisions? Stir Up a Little Conflict," *Working Woman* (November 1985): 28–31; R. Kilmann, K. Thomas, D. Slevin, R. Nath, and S. Jerrell, eds., *Producing Useful Knowledge for Organizations* (New York: Praeger, 1983), 147–166.

SUMMARY

1. Define conflict.
Conflict is the process that results when a person or group perceives that another person or group is frustrating, or about to frustrate, an important concern.

2. Contrast competition and conflict.
Conflict is directed against another party, whereas competition is directed toward obtaining a desired goal without interference from another party. The difference lies in whether one party takes actions to interfere with another's efforts to attain a goal.

3. Explain how the understanding of conflict has changed.
Until the mid-1940s, the popular view was that conflict is harmful and unnecessary. Today, conflict is considered to be inevitable in every organization and often necessary to ensure high performance, although conflict can sometimes be harmful. The value of conflict depends on how the conflict affects performance.

4. List some sources of conflict.
Conflict can arise from poor communication, increased size of the organization, staff heterogeneity, greater subordinate participation, differences

between line and staff personnel, mutually exclusive reward systems, competition for limited resources, unequal distribution of power, and differences among individuals.

5. Describe strategies for managing conflict in an organization.
The manager can provide superordinate goals to antagonistic parties, so that they will cooperate to achieve the common goal. The manager can transfer conflict-prone individuals to other units, or institute an appeals procedure.

6. List ways a manager can induce desirable conflict.
The manager can appoint managers who are open to change, encourage competition, and restructure the work unit to change lines of communication or to create new positions.

KEY TERMS

Conflict	Collaborating
Intrapersonal conflict	Accommodating
Interpersonal conflict	Avoiding
Intergroup conflict	Compromising
Approach–approach conflict	Boundary-spanning position
Avoidance–avoidance conflict	Negotiation
Approach–avoidance conflict	Integrating department
Forcing	

REVIEW AND DISCUSSION QUESTIONS

1. What is the difference between conflict and competition? What insights does this difference give you into how a manager can prevent competition from escalating into conflict?

2. What are some advantages of conflict? What consequences can result from extremely high or low levels of conflict? How can managers maintain an optimal level of conflict?

3. Orville Snorr has found that his subordinates frequently misinterpret his policy memos, surprising him with their dissatisfaction. Furthermore, his procedural memos often confuse his subordinates. When Orville is out of town—and hence unable to explain what he has written—arguments erupt and little work gets accomplished. Orville realizes he has a communication problem and decides that everyone will be happier if they develop policies and procedures jointly in staff meetings. To Orville's surprise, however, he finds that much of the arguing has moved into the meetings. Inviting subordinates to participate in decision making doesn't seem to have helped the conflict at all. Suggest a reason why conflict still exists. Should Orville try to reduce or eliminate the conflict? Why or why not?

4. What are some sources of conflict between line and staff employees? What can be done to manage this conflict?

5. What traits typically characterize a person who is prone to conflicts?

6. An intrapersonal conflict can be an approach–approach conflict, an approach–avoidance conflict, or an avoidance–avoidance conflict. Describe these three kinds of conflicts and give an example of each.

7. The text describes the balance of power between the United States and the former Soviet Union as an example of the "prisoners' dilemma." What is your opinion of this arrangement as a way to control conflict between the two nations? Would some of the other strategies for managing conflict discussed in this chapter be more suitable, or do those strategies apply only to business organizations? Explain.

8. Alice Chalmers is considering whether to redecorate the restaurant in her hotel. Ted Quince argues vehemently for redecoration, saying it would boost business dramatically. He came to the meeting armed with sketches of how the refurbished restaurant would look. Rosalie Bean brought graphs and statistics. She begins earnestly explaining the costs of renovation, making clear her view that spending money on the restaurant will soon drive the hotel into bankruptcy. Ted looks wounded and exclaims that he wouldn't support an idea that would lead to bankruptcy and that clearly Rosalie is exaggerating. Soon the two are trading barbed remarks. Alice breaks in and says, "Leave your information with me. I'll consider what you've said, and we'll talk more later." Is Alice justified in avoiding the conflict between Ted and Rosalie? Why or why not?

CRITICAL INCIDENT

A Manager's Nightmare

Wearever Tire has operated in Happyville, New York, for 45 years. Well known for its superior human relations policies and competitive benefits, Wearever has enjoyed good labor–management relations and has offered what is virtually lifetime employment to several generations of local families. The company has a reputation for being environmentally concerned, and for providing strong community support.

Today, Wearever faces a serious threat. It has just learned that a "bread and butter" account will cut its orders this year due to foreign competition. Bob Stone, Industrial Division manager, has been advised that he must reduce his staff by 20 percent. A thorough plan drafted by the human resources department details his options. Some of the necessary labor cost reduction will come from attrition—that is, from normal levels of turnover and forecasted retirements. The bulk, however, will have to come from "forced" reductions—either early retirements or layoffs.

For those who will be laid off and are too young to retire, Wearever will offer a lump-sum service bonus intended to offset the emotional and financial costs of the layoff, and will offer each laid-off employee the opportunity to utilize outplacement services. The range of outplacement services provided will include career counseling, interviewing skills and job search training techniques, and clerical support for transmission of telephone messages, résumé preparation, cover letter generation, and so on. The placement firm also makes physical facilities available to clients, including desks, telephones, and conference areas.

To encourage early retirement among those close to retirement age, Wearever will offer a "5-5-4" package. Under this arrangement, employees will be given the opportunity to retire five years before normal retirement age; they may add five years to their length of service with the firm (thus increasing their retirement pay); and they get four weeks of pay for every year that they have been employed with the firm as a one-time, lump-sum bonus.

Bob dreads informing the staff at large of the cuts. A companywide assembly will be held at 2:00 to announce the details of the plans, but he wants to forewarn them, so he will call everyone into his office after lunch. He has already drafted a sketch in his mind of who will likely consider the 5-5-4 option. He knows that their decisions will not be easy ones to make. They will be enticed by the offer, yet he would like to make sure that they are acting out of prudent self-interest, and not because the offer is too good to pass up. He also has an idea whom he will target to be laid off. Some of the unfortunate few are his best employees, yet their positions can no longer be protected, and there's no place left in the organization for them to move to.

QUESTIONS

1. Why might employees in their late fifties face approach–avoidance conflict in their decision regarding early retirement?

2. Corporate downsizing causes considerable conflict among both workers who are laid off, and among remaining employees not laid off.

   a. What has Wearever done to mitigate the conflicts for employees targeted for layoff?

   b. List three possible forms of conflict that a remaining Wearever employee might perceive.

   c. What can Wearever do for the remaining employees at Wearever to reduce the conflicts that they might perceive?

Source: Susan Stites-Doe, State University of New York, College at Brockport.

EXPERIENTIAL EXERCISE

How Well Do You Manage Conflict?

Step 1   Listed below are 15 pairs of statements people use to describe why they behave the way they do in conflict situations. Allocate 3 points between the two alternative statements in each pair. Base your point allocation on your assessment of each alternative's relative importance to you as a means of handling conflict.

Allocate the points between the first and second statement as follows:

(a) <u>3</u>   or   (a) <u>2</u>   or   (a) <u>1</u>   or   (a) <u>0</u>
(b) <u>0</u>   (b) <u>1</u>   (b) <u>2</u>   (b) <u>3</u>

There can be no tied allocations and each pair's numbers must add up to 3.

1. I am apt to give up something in order to get something.   (a) _____
   I am usually quite firm in pursuing my goals.   (b) _____

2. I usually work to soothe the other person's feelings to preserve our relationship.   (c) _____
   I try to get all of our concerns immediately out into the open.   (d) _____

3. I usually try to get the other person's help in working out a solution.   (e) _____
   I try to avoid taking a position that is likely to create a controversy.   (f) _____

4. I try to do what is necessary to avoid tensions.   (g) _____
   I sometimes give up my own wishes for the desires of the other person.   (h) _____

5. I usually press to get my points across.   (i) _____
   I usually let the other person have some of his or her wishes if he or she allows me to have some of mine.   (j) _____

6. I am usually quite firm in pursuing my goals.   (k) _____
   I usually try to get the other person's help in working out a solution.   (l) _____

7. I am apt to give up something in order to get something.   (m) _____
   I try to avoid taking a position that would create a controversy.   (n) _____

8. I usually work to soothe the other person's feelings to preserve our relationship.   (o) _____
   I usually let the other person have some of his or her wishes if he or she lets me have some of mine.   (p) _____

9. I usually press to get my points across.   (q) _____
   I sometimes give up my own wishes for the desires of the other person.   (r) _____

10. I am apt to give up something in order to get something.   (s) _____
    I try to get all of our concerns immediately out in the open.   (t) _____

11. I try to do what is necessary to avoid tensions.   (u) _____
    I usually let the other person have some of his or her wishes if he or she lets me have some of mine.   (v) _____

12. I usually work to soothe the other person's feelings to preserve our relationship.   (w) _____
    I am usually quite firm in pursuing my goals.   (x) _____

13. I try to avoid taking positions that would create a controversy.   (y) _____

I usually press to get my points across.   (z) _____

14. I usually try to get the other person's help in working out a solution.   (aa) _____

I sometimes give up my own wishes for the desires of the other person.   (bb) _____

15. I try to get all of our concerns immediately out in the open.   (cc) _____

I try to do what is necessary to avoid tensions.   (dd) _____

Step 2   Score the survey by entering the score you have given to each of the statements and then total the scores for each column.

I	II	III	IV	V
(a) _____	(b) _____	(c) _____	(d) _____	(f) _____
(j) _____	(i) _____	(h) _____	(e) _____	(g) _____
(m) _____	(k) _____	(o) _____	(l) _____	(n) _____
(p) _____	(q) _____	(r) _____	(t) _____	(u) _____
(s) _____	(x) _____	(w) _____	(aa) _____	(y) _____
(v) _____	(z) _____	(bb) _____	(cc) _____	(dd) _____
══	══	══	══	══

These scores reflect your perception of your use of various conflict-handling styles. Your highest total suggests a preferred style; however, we all have the potential to apply various conflict-management approaches depending on the situation. The various styles are labeled: I, compromising; II, forcing; III, accommodating; IV, collaborating; and V, avoiding.

The following steps are optional and may be used at the discretion of your instructor.

Step 3   Read the following brief incident, then join others in your class to discuss this situation and propose a plan of action to resolve it.

Seville Electronics manufactures computer components to be used in industrial and military applications. All parts must be produced according to exacting standards.

Stuart Van Ault was hired recently as vice president of production. Last week he toured the plant and was stopped by one of the production supervisors. This supervisor was visibly upset and shouted, "I'm glad you're here. We can't get anything done with the quality of materials we have to work with and the people personnel sends us!" Stuart was taken aback by this outburst. He asked the supervisor to visit him after work to discuss these problems.

When they met, the supervisor explained that they were having to send more and more materials back to their suppliers because they didn't meet Seville's exacting quality standards. He felt that these standards were unrealistic and that quality control was messing up. The supervisor also complained about the lack of skilled, reliable help. Both absenteeism and turnover were running above industry norms. Finally, he pointed out that various production runs were halted in favor of some other components that, according to the sales department, had to be run immediately.

Step 4   Each group will be asked to report its plan of action. Select one member of your group to act as spokesperson. Be as specific as possible in describing what you would do and why. Look for the implications of these plans for conflict management.

Source: Written by Bruce Kemelgor, University of Louisville.

NOTES

1. K.W. Thomas, "Organizational Conflict," in *Organizational Behavior,* ed. S. Kerr (Columbus, Ohio: Grid, 1979).

2. S.P. Robbins, *Managing Organizational Conflict* (Englewood Cliffs, N.J.: Prentice-Hall, 1974).

3. Ibid.

4. M. Dalton, *Men Who Manage* (New York: John Wiley and Sons, 1959).

5. J.M. Rabbie and F. Bekkers, "Threatened Leadership and Intergroup Competition," *European Journal of Social Psychology* 8 (1978): 19–20.

6. L. Festinger, *Theory of Cognitive Dissonance* (Evanston, Ill.: Free Press, 1957).

7. R.D. Luce and H. Raiffa, *Games and Decisions* (New York: Wiley, 1957), 95.

8. M. Sherif, *In Common Predicament: Social Psychology of Intragroup Conflict and Cooperation* (Boston: Houghton Mifflin, 1966).

9. Robbins, *Managing Organizational Conflict.*

10. J. Lowell, "GMAD: Lowdown at Lordstown," *Ward's Auto World,* April 1972, 29.

11. L.A. Allen, "The Line–Staff Relationship," *Management Record* 17 (1955): 346–349; E.C. Schleh, "Using Central Staff to Boost Line Initiative," *Management Review* 65 (1976): 17–23.

12. Thomas, "Organizational Conflict."

13. J.W. Galbraith, *Designing Complex Organizations* (Reading, Mass.: Addison-Wesley, 1973); J.A. Wall and M.W. Blum, "Negotiations," *Journal of Management* 17 (1991): 273–304.

14. R.T. Keller and W.E. Holland, "Boundary-spanning Activity and Research and Development Management: A Comparative Study," *IEEE Transactions and Engineering Management* (1975): 130–133.

15. Robbins, *Managing Organizational Conflict.*

CHAPTER

15

The fast track in business: B.B.A., M.B.A., C.E.O., . . . D.O.A.

— Jim Fisk and Robert Barron

If my doctor told me I had only 6 months to live, I wouldn't brood, I'd type a little faster.

— Isaac Asimov

It isn't what you know that counts, it's what you think of in time.

— Anonymous

LEARNING OBJECTIVES

After studying this chapter, you should be able to:

1. *Define stress.*
2. *Explain various views of job-related stress.*
3. *Identify personal causes of stress.*
4. *Explain interpersonal causes of stress.*
5. *List organizational causes of stress.*
6. *Describe typical reactions to stress.*
7. *List ways of managing stress.*
8. *Explain the concept of a wellness program.*

Stress

SEVEN HABITS CAN REDUCE STRESS

Why should organizations be concerned about stress? For one reason—it's expensive. It is estimated that businesses spend $150 billion annually on stress-related problems and mental illness by bearing such costs as lost productivity, health insurance, and disability claims. Since 1990, the New York University Medical Center has seen a 70 percent jump in the number of managers and professionals suffering from job-related stress. The strain of corporate mergers, restructuring, and cutbacks can seriously compromise employees' well-being.

To preempt the negative consequences of stress, many companies have embraced the philosophy of Stephen Covey, author of *Seven Habits of Highly Effective People*. The program is reported to result in better working relationships, improved productivity, and lowered stress levels in employees' personal and professional lives. Federal Express, Hewlett-Packard, Milliken, Conoco, and Saturn Corp. have all adopted Covey's program.

Every month, Covey's Leadership Center in Sundance, Utah, hosts 150 CEOs and executives at a cost of $3,500 each for a week of training and inspiration. Even President Clinton has hailed *Seven*

Habits as a book every American should read to "dramatically" boost the nation's productivity. The Seven Habits are surprisingly simple:

1. *Be pro-active.* Take responsibility for your life. Decide what you want to do and do it.

2. *Begin with the end in mind.* In your mind, prepare your own eulogy. How would you like others to remember you when you're gone? Pattern your everyday behavior around this vision.

3. *Put first things first.* Prioritize the important things in your life and find the time to devote to those things that give your life the greatest meaning.

4. *Think win-win.* Don't give up until you find solutions that benefit all parties.

5. *Seek first to understand, then to be understood.* Listen first, speak second. Speak only after you fully understand the other person.

6. *Synergize.* Solicit participation of others and appreciate the differences between people.

7. *Sharpen the saw.* Continually appreciate and renew four elements of your self: physical, mental, emotional-social, and spiritual.

At a time when organizations are undergoing radical surgery to keep up with global business pressures, many companies find the Seven Habits give employees direction in charting the course of their organizations. Adoption of the Seven Habits facilitates changes in corporate culture and total quality programs by encouraging employees and supervisors to accept change and to work on personal and professional self-improvement.

Half of Conoco's 19,000 employees have been trained in the Seven Habits, resulting in better interpersonal relations and improved decision making. Mike Bennett, a top union leader at Saturn Corp., agrees the Seven Habits have resulted in more efficient meetings, reduced waste, and better quality: "It's made the difference between high performance and mediocrity." At Blue Cross and Blue Shield of Michigan, negotiations between the union and management have become less adversarial as both parties, embracing Habits 4 and 5, seek to find win-win situations and listen carefully before speaking.

By attempting to work more effectively using the Seven Habits, employees are better able to deal with stressful situations. Completely

(continued on following page)

(continued from previous page)
eliminating stress from one's life may be an impossible goal, but organizations are learning that employees who manage stress can significantly enhance their personal and professional lives. This chapter explores the causes and effects of stress, the role that stress plays in organizations, and a range of organizational responses to stressful work situations.

Sources: Sana Siwolop, "The Crippling Ills That Stress Can Trigger," *Business Week,* April 18, 1988, 77–78; Emily T. Smith, "Stress: The Test Americans Are Failing," *Business Week,* April 18, 1988, 74–76; John Hillkirk, "Golden Rules Promoted for Work Success," *USA Today,* August 20, 1993, B1–B2; and Joseph Spiers, "Upper Middle-Class Woes," *Fortune,* December 27, 1993, 80–86.

From our daily experiences, we all know that conflict-filled situations produce feelings of physical and psychological discomfort. When a person is confronted with a situation that poses a threat (as when extreme conflict arises), the form of physiological and emotional arousal he or she experiences is termed **stress.** Prolonged exposure to stressful situations is believed to produce serious dysfunctional influences that can affect job performance. In this chapter, we will examine the principal causes of stress, reactions to stress, and techniques for coping with stress.

VIEWS OF JOB-RELATED STRESS

As early as 1700, Bernardino Rammizini (the father of occupational medicine) described in detail how certain diseases were associated with different types of work.[1] Presaging current ecological views, he advocated prevention rather than simple treatment of occupational illness. In the early 1900s, psychologist Hugo Munsterberg studied the effects of fatigue in various occupations.[2] Based on his findings, he recommended the institution of rest periods to improve morale, reduce fatigue, and thereby raise productivity. More recently, Dr. Hans Selye identified three distinct stages of a person's response to stress: alarm, resistance, and exhaustion.[3] These three stages define a **General Adaptation Syndrome** associated with stress.

In the alarm stage of the stress response, muscles tense, respiration rate increases, and blood pressure and heart rate increase. Following this stage, a person experiences anxiety, anger, and fatigue. These responses indicate that the person is resisting stress. During this resistance stage, the person may make poor decisions or experience illnesses. Because a person cannot sustain this resistance indefinitely, exhaustion occurs (see Figure 15.1). During this exhaustion stage, the individual develops such stress-induced illnesses as headaches and ulcers. Also, the capacity to respond to other work-related demands is greatly reduced. Although a person may be able to respond effectively to a threat during one of the earlier stages in this reaction, being unable to cope with a threat in the later stages can have serious detrimental effects for the individual. Selye's view suggests that all people go through the same pattern of response and that all people can tolerate only so much stress before a serious, debilitating condition of exhaustion occurs.

The preceding three-stage response to stress is sometimes termed the "fight or flight" response. It is an automatic form of response to threat that once served our species well when our primary concerns were finding food and

FIGURE 15.1

THE GENERAL ADAPTATION SYNDROME

protecting ourselves from wild animals. In ancient times, the powerful stress reaction was an aid in quickly responding by either fighting or swiftly fleeing from a predator. In the modern world, however, persistent forms of stress (for example, unresolved social problems) have a powerful effect on the nervous system of an individual. Consider the lingering discomfort that results when an employee is harshly reprimanded by his or her supervisor. In such a situation, neither fighting with one's boss nor fleeing from the situation is an appropriate response. Nonetheless, the employee's physiological response prepares him or her to take some form of action when none may be possible. In essence, our physiological response to stress is no longer correct for many situations we currently face.

Despite the drawbacks of stress, its complete or near absence may be less than ideal for performance.[4] In situations where stress is low or absent, employees may not be sufficiently aroused or involved in their tasks. Instead, to maximize performance, low levels of stress are preferable because, in moderate amounts, stress can stimulate individuals to work harder and accomplish more. A certain amount of stress may thus be beneficial. Stress that has positive effects should be termed *eustress* (the prefix *eu-* is Greek for "good"). Eustress occurs when pressure for performance helps a person to achieve. When stress levels rise too high, however, employee performance is impaired. Extreme stress can leave workers feeling emotionally incapacitated, at least in the short run, and sap their energies and drive. The relationship between stress and employee performance follows the curve previously depicted in Figure 14.1.

Two experts in the area of job stress, John Ivancevich and Michael Matteson of the University of Houston, have outlined the major causes of stress as well as reactions to it.[5] In the two sections that follow, we will consider their summary of the major causes and consequences of stress. Following these sections, we will consider techniques for coping with stress.

CAUSES OF STRESS

PERSONAL FACTORS

TYPE A PERSONALITY   Some people are more stress-prone than others. Especially susceptible are individuals who display a cluster of traits known as **type A personality.** Type As tend to be impatient, competitive individuals who feel that they are constantly under time pressure. They also tend to be aggressive, try to accomplish several things at the same time, and have difficulty relaxing. In contrast, individuals with the **type B personality** are relatively more mild-mannered, in less of a hurry, and far less competitive.[6]

In recent years, researchers have used personality tests to assess whether managers are type A or type B personalities. A simple example of one such test is presented in Table 15.1. When type A and type B managers were studied in terms of certain physical disorders, some interesting results appeared. For example, Rosenman and Friedman found that type A men were twice as prone to heart disease and fatal heart attacks as type B individuals.[7] Of 133 heart disease patients, Jenkins found that 94 were classifiable as type A personalities.[8]

The same traits that predispose type A individuals to certain physical disorders also appear to predispose them to certain types of work. For example,

TABLE 15.1

SELF-TEST FOR TYPE A OR TYPE B PERSONALITY

To determine your personality type, circle the number that best represents your own behavior.

Am casual about appointments	1	2	3	4	5	6	7	8	Am never late
Am not competitive	1	2	3	4	5	6	7	8	Am very competitive
Never feel rushed, even under pressure	1	2	3	4	5	6	7	8	Always feel rushed
Take things one at a time	1	2	3	4	5	6	7	8	Try to do many things at once, think about what I am going to do next
Do things slowly	1	2	3	4	5	6	7	8	Do things fast (eating, walking, etc.)
Express feelings	1	2	3	4	5	6	7	8	"Sit" on feelings
Have many interests	1	2	3	4	5	6	7	8	Have few interests outside work

Total points _____ multiplied by 3 = _____ Final Score

Final Score	Personality Type
120 or more	A+
106 to 119	A
100 to 105	A−
90 to 99	B+
Below 90	B

Source: Adapted from R. W. Bortner, "A Short Rating Scale as a Potential Measure of Patterns of Behavior," *Journal of Chronic Diseases* 22 (1966): 87–91.

60 percent of a sample of managers could be clearly identified as type A while only 12 percent were clearly classifiable as type B.[9] Surprisingly, the characteristics that seem most helpful to type A individuals in their rise through managerial ranks (such as persistence, fanatic observance of deadlines, and the like) do not aid them in their performance as top-level managers. Rather, it appears that type B individuals have better performance records in top management positions. The relaxed and patient attitude of type B individuals appears to give them a better perspective on running large organizations. This evidence may seem to suggest that once people reach the top of their professions they should abandon type A behaviors and switch to type B. However, the tendency to display type A traits is fairly well engrained in such individuals, and they find it very hard to adopt the type B behavior style.

CHANGES IN ONE'S LIFE   Another personal factor that can produce stress is both the magnitude and the frequency of changes in an individual's life. For example, a major change such as being fired or the death of a spouse can have a strong impact on a person's health. The frequent occurrence of many less dramatic changes over a short period of time can also have a negative effect. In studying this phenomenon, Holmes and Rahe compiled a list of life changes that are especially stressful and devised a weighting system that reflects the relative severity of each event (Table 15.2).[10] If a person experiences the equivalent of more than 150 points of stressfulness in one year, there appears to be a better than 50 percent chance that he or she will suffer a serious physical disorder during the following year. The chance of illness increases to 80 percent for scores that exceed 300.

DeLongis, Folkman, and Lazarus have studied how immediate, daily events, called "hassles" and "uplifts," can create stress. Research measuring daily hassles and uplifts suggests that predictions about the severity of stress-related disorders can be improved when information on daily hassles is added to information on major stressful events (see Table 15.3). Uplifts, however, do not appear to have a comparable impact.

DEMOGRAPHIC ATTRIBUTES   As level of income increases, stress levels tend to decrease. Americans with income levels above $50,000 report less stress than those with lower earnings. Whites report less stress than minorities, and men have lower stress levels than women. However, minorities and women, in the aggregate, are in lower-quality positions that pay less and have greater demands. Hence, evidence of simple demographic differences in stress level is probably a reflection of differences in job attributes.

INTERPERSONAL FACTORS

JEALOUSY AND ENVY   In recent years, there has been increasing recognition of the role of negative emotion at work. Two powerful, commonplace, and dysfunctional negative emotions are employee jealousy and employee envy. Vecchio has defined **employee jealousy** as a pattern of thoughts, emotions, and behaviors that result from a loss of self-esteem and the loss of outcomes

TABLE 15.2
RELATIVE WEIGHTS OF LIFE CHANGES

Life Event	Scale Value
Death of spouse	100
Divorce	73
Marital separation	65
Jail term	63
Death of a close family member	63
Major personal injury or illness	53
Marriage	50
Fired from work	47
Marital reconciliation	45
Retirement	45
Major change in health of family member	44
Pregnancy	40
Sex difficulties	39
Gain of a new family member	39
Business readjustment	39
Change in financial state	38
Death of a close friend	37
Change to a different line of work	36
Change in number of arguments with spouse	35
Mortgage or loan for major purchase (home, etc.)	31
Foreclosure of mortgage or loan	30
Change in responsibilities at work	29
Son or daughter leaving home	29
Trouble with in-laws	29
Outstanding personal achievement	28
Spouse begins or stops work	26
Begin or end school	26
Change in living conditions	25
Revision of personal habits	24
Trouble with boss	23
Change in work hours or conditions	20
Change in residence	20
Change in schools	20
Change in recreation	19
Change in church activities	19
Change in social activities	18
Mortgage or loan for lesser purchase (car, etc.)	17
Change in sleeping habits	16
Change in number of family get-togethers	15
Change in eating habits	15
Vacation	13
Christmas	12
Minor violations of the law	11

Source: T.H. Holmes and L.O. Rahe, "Scaling of Life Change: Composition of Direct and Indirect Methods," *Journal of Psychosomatic Research* 15 (1971).

TABLE 15.3
A MEASURE OF DAILY HASSLES

How much of a hassle was this item for you today?	Item	How much of an uplift was this item for you today?
0 1 2 3 4	Your child(ren)	0 1 2 3 4
0 1 2 3 4	Time with family	0 1 2 3 4
0 1 2 3 4	Sex	0 1 2 3 4
0 1 2 3 4	Coworkers	0 1 2 3 4
0 1 2 3 4	Your workload	0 1 2 3 4
0 1 2 3 4	Meeting deadlines	0 1 2 3 4
0 1 2 3 4	Having enough money	0 1 2 3 4
0 1 2 3 4	Your physical appearance	0 1 2 3 4
0 1 2 3 4	The weather	0 1 2 3 4
0 1 2 3 4	Your neighborhood	0 1 2 3 4
0 1 2 3 4	Cooking	0 1 2 3 4
0 1 2 3 4	Home entertainment	0 1 2 3 4
0 1 2 3 4	Amount of free time	0 1 2 3 4

Source: Adapted from A. DeLongis, S. Folkman, and R. Lazarus, "The Impact of Daily Stress on Health and Mood: Psychological and Social Resources as Mediators," *Journal of Personality and Social Psychology* 54 (1988): 486–495.

associated with a working relationship.[11] **Employee envy,** often confused with employee jealousy, can be defined as a pattern of thoughts, emotions, and behaviors that result from the loss of self-esteem in response to another individual obtaining outcomes that one personally desires.[*] Feelings of envy at work (that is, resenting the success of another) are generally regarded as petty and reflective of immaturity, while feelings of jealousy (that is, a protective reaction to a threat to a valued relationship) are widely sympathized with by others and more socially accepted. Also, it is not rare (and has probably become more common in recent years) for strong feelings of workplace jealousy and envy to result in extreme violence. Because loss of self-esteem plays a part in both jealousy and envy, it has been suggested that employees with low self-esteem may be more susceptible to these feelings.[12] Supervisors who wish to actively manage potential jealousy and envy should consider how decisions will affect the self-esteem of employees and should institute techniques that promote both cooperation and sharing of resources (for example, the introduction of self-directed work teams, discussed in Chapter 7).[13] Preliminary research on employee jealousy and envy suggests that men express more workplace envy than women (perhaps because men are more attuned to competition), while women express more workplace jealousy than men (perhaps

---

[*]A simple way to distinguish jealousy from envy is to recall that jealousy involves three people, while envy only requires two.

because women are more concerned with maintaining social relations). Additionally, employees who express greater jealousy and envy also express greater intent to quit and lower job satisfaction.[14]

Although we typically think of envy and jealousy as emotions rather than stressors, they are in fact stress inducers in that they arise from the perception of threats in the work environment. These threats imply a loss of self-esteem or social standing. As with other threats that we experience, we are aroused to remedy (that is, eliminate) the threat if possible. Figure 15.2 presents a model proposed by Vecchio to explain employee jealousy and envy. As this model suggests, jealousy and envy arise from certain precipitating events, such as the recognition of a rival or the recognition that desired rewards are being allocated to another. The assessment of this loss is influenced by individual attributes (such as level of self-esteem and gender), as well as work-unit attributes (such as the existence of job rotation and resource sharing) and

FIGURE 15.2

VECCHIO'S MODEL OF EMPLOYEE JEALOUSY AND ENVY

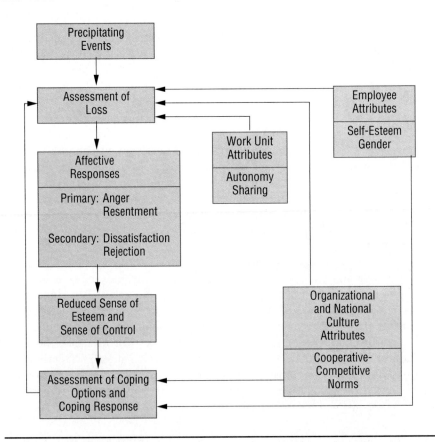

Source: R. P. Vecchio, "It's Not Easy Being Green: Jealousy and Envy in the Workplace," in *Research in Personnel and Human Resources Management,* ed. G. R. Ferris (Greenwich, Conn.: JAI Press, 1995).

cultural attributes (such as norms for cooperation versus competition). The assessment of loss triggers the initial affective responses of anger and resentment followed by job dissatisfaction and a sense of rejection. These affective responses result in a lessened sense of esteem or worth, and a lessening of control or personal efficacy. In response to these reactions, an individual will evaluate, select, and enact one or more coping responses. The ultimate response to the experience of jealousy and envy will be influenced by both individual attributes and cultural attributes.

ORGANIZATIONAL FACTORS

RESPONSIBILITY FOR OTHERS   Alan McLean, a medical researcher, has reviewed a variety of studies suggesting that having responsibility, in general, can lead to greater stress.[15] Beyond that, having responsibility for *other people*, rather than responsibility for the other features of an enterprise, can be highly stressful.[†] For managers who deal with people, the stress associated with recognizing the impact of their actions on others' lives is more immediate and real than it is for managers who deal with things and ideas.

WORKING CONDITIONS   The work environment also plays a role in determining the amount of stress an employee experiences. Certain occupations are noted for the high levels of stress they entail. As you might imagine, it is truly difficult to prove conclusively that one occupation is more stressful than another. Nonetheless, in one fairly direct attempt to study the possible link of occupation to illness, the health records of over 22,000 employees in the state of Tennessee were examined for stress-related disorders. The results of comparisons for over 100 occupations revealed the existence of significant differences (see Table 15.4).[16] Stress was found to be generally greater in such jobs as

TABLE 15.4
HIGH-STRESS VERSUS LOW-STRESS JOBS

High-Stress Jobs	Low-Stress Jobs
Construction laborer	Craft workers
Secretary	Stock handlers
Inspector	College professors
Office manager	Heavy equipment operators
Foreman	
Waitress/Waiter	

---

† In an experiment sometimes called the "executive monkey" study, two rhesus monkeys were strapped into electrified chairs. Five seconds after the illumination of a red warning light, both monkeys received mild electric shocks. After learning that the light served as a warning of the impending shock, an arm of one of the monkeys was released so that he could reach a lever, which would prevent both monkeys from being shocked. After a time, the monkey that had the opportunity to reach the lever came to control the occurrence of the shock reliably. The monkey with the responsibility (the "executive monkey") had to remain constantly vigilant. When the experiment was over, researchers examined the intestinal tracts of both monkeys. The "executive monkey" had begun to develop ulcers, while the companion monkey had not experienced intestinal distress.

construction laborer, secretary, inspector, office manager, foreman, waitress/ waiter, mine operative, air traffic controller, and clinical lab technician. In contrast, stress was relatively low for craft workers, stock handlers, college professors, and heavy equipment operators. In addition, the researchers found that occupational status level was not significantly related to stress-related disorders; that is, both white-collar *and* blue-collar employees, and skilled *and* unskilled workers showed high and low incidences of disorders.

Other research has linked the repetitive and "dehumanizing" work environment created by assembly lines to health-related disorders. One study of 4,000 industrial workers reported that employees in companies using assembly-line technology were more likely to show evidence of early coronary artery disease than were employees involved in other work technologies. Piecework systems have similarly been implicated. Such systems generally lead to higher productivity than do other pay systems, but the toll on the employee can be questioned. For example, the number of accidents is also higher under piece-rate systems than under salaried systems.[17]

The absence of intrinsically enjoyable and rewarding work is associated with feelings of stress, as is being overloaded. For example, a correlation has been found between tax deadlines and illness for accountants.[18]

EMOTIONAL LABOR   An especially stressful aspect of some jobs involves the obligation to project specific emotions. For example, employees at vacation resorts, flight attendants, and salespeople are obliged to display an extremely positive demeanor when dealing with customers and clients, even when their true feelings are far from positive. The additional effort required to maintain these false feelings, or "face work," is termed **emotional labor**.[19] Learning to do one's job well when it requires emotional labor means learning proper affective tone, gestures, appearance, and language. To some extent, every job requires an occupational mask. Examples include supervisors who must enforce disciplinary rules that they don't genuinely believe in, and nurses who must display calm in the face of human suffering.

To cope with the stress caused by this high degree of self-control, employees in such jobs often find outlets for their true feelings. John Van Maanen, a researcher at the Massachusetts Institute of Technology, has provided some interesting behind-the-scenes insights on how employees cope with such stress.[20] Working as an amusement-ride operator at Disneyland, Maanen observed that the ride operators exercised norms for regulating their true feelings. Because ride operators are obliged to project a positive, upbeat, clean-cut image, they are not permitted to display animosity toward "guests," even if a guest is quite rude. Operators cope with such "ducks" (a derisive term used by operators to label unruly customers) by slapping seatbelts harshly across riders, squeezing seatbelts tightly, or arranging "near miss" collisions of ride vehicles that are designed to startle and intimidate guests.‡ Ride operators also cope with the

---

‡J. Marnocha has coined the term *Pagliacci effect* to refer to the emotional breakdown that results from having to maintain a jovial and ingratiating demeanor while simultaneously feeling extreme anger and hurt.

requirement of continuous emotion management by "going robot" or "checking out"—that is, willing emotional numbness while maintaining a smiling exterior.[§] At Disneyland, as well as in other public positions, employees cope with emotional labor by drawing together as cohesive, self-protecting units. Such cohesion helps employees work cooperatively in handling "ducks" and dealing with supervisors.

ROLE CONFLICT   **Role conflict** occurs when two or more sets of demands are made on an employee so that compliance with one set of demands makes it more difficult to comply with another.[21] In essence, an employee is expected to perform contradictory, or conflicting, activities. For example, a supervisor may find that his superior expects increased productivity from his department, while his subordinates expect his support in finding ways to reduce their daily quota. Likewise, a college faculty member may find that she is expected to devote significant amounts of time to preparing and delivering lectures, while at the same time she is expected to publish in highly competitive scholarly journals. If possible, one may resolve the conflict by devoting more time and energy to the most pressing demand in a given situation (for instance, by preparing a lecture as the time for a class approaches). It is well established that employee job satisfaction decreases as role conflict increases.[22] In addition, role conflict has been found to be connected with heart disease, high blood pressure, elevated cholesterol, and obesity.[23] Furthermore, abilities to make high-quality decisions and to be creative are likely to be impaired in situations containing a high degree of role conflict.

ROLE AMBIGUITY   **Role ambiguity** refers to the absence of clarity regarding how to perform one's job. Ambiguity or uncertainty may surround knowing what goals to set and how to best achieve them, and determining one's level of accomplishment. Initially, all newly hired employees experience some degree of role ambiguity when they are assigned to their tasks. However, some jobs are consistently more lacking in clarity concerning how to perform them. For example, managerial jobs generally lack a specific, well-defined set of activities that are to be routinely carried out. Project team managers are also likely to experience greater degrees of uncertainty, especially in the early stages of work.

Role ambiguity is closely associated with a variety of negative consequences. As with role conflict, decreased job satisfaction is thought to be a result of increased role ambiguity. In addition, lower levels of self-confidence, decreased satisfaction with life in general, and increased expression of intentions to quit have been found to be correlated with role ambiguity.[24]

ROLE OVERLOAD   In addition to conflict and ambiguity, role processes can play a part as a source of stress in yet a third fashion: role overload. **Role overload** occurs when too many activities are expected of an employee, given the

[§]Disneyland supervisors try to identify "malcontent" ride operators (the supervisors' term for undesirable operators) by posing as tourists and "ghostriding" various attractions to see if everything is up to snuff.

An Inside Look
Entrepreneurial Couples: Double the Stress

Starting a business is a stress-provoking way to make a living. The hours are long, the responsibility tremendous, the future uncertain. But some couples are willing to risk the even greater stress of starting a business together.

Although mom-and-pop stores have been around for years, the pattern is extending to more complex enterprises as women increasingly move into management and professional careers. These couples risk bringing the tension of the workplace home *and* bringing the tensions of home to the workplace. They must sort out their roles as the way responsibility is shared in a marriage may not work out as well in a business that requires more of a hierarchy of responsibility. As a result of such stresses, working together can destroy both the marriage and the business.

Still, some entrepreneurial couples are finding success and happiness. One strategy is to make sure the roles at work are clearly defined and based on talents rather than gender stereotypes. Susan and Michael Morgan, for example, founded Softview Inc., a computer software concern. Susan served as chief executive while her husband focused on software design. "I was the one better suited to running the company," she explains. "Mike's the shy type. He's more comfortable designing the product and explaining it to me." When Susan wanted to focus on developing and marketing a new product, the Morgans hired an outsider to serve as chief executive.

Similarly, when William Carrico and Judith Estrin started Network Computing Devices, they agreed, in Carrico's words, that "there had to be a CEO and that was me." Estrin agrees that the arrangement is optimal because her husband has more experience. Besides, she adds, "If a couple's ever going to work together, they have to decide who's boss early."

Couples may also look for other ways to minimize stress. For example, they may choose not to emphasize rapid growth, thereby avoiding the intense commitment to work that such a strategy requires. John McClelland and Linda Seaverson decided to develop MTEC Photoacoustics, their high-tech instrument company, gradually. That strategy allows them to balance research with growth, to manage the company themselves, and to spend time with their two young children. As the children get older, McClelland and Seaverson intend to plan for more ambitious expansion.

Source: Udayan Gupta, "And Business Makes Three: Couples Working Together," *The Wall Street Journal,* February 26, 1990, B2.

---

time available and the ability level of the employee. Indications of role overload include working in excess of sixty hours a week, holding down two jobs, and foregoing vacations. Being in a situation where one lacks the necessary time to perform required tasks has been found to be a possible cause of increased blood cholesterol levels.[25] Furthermore, overload has been found to be related to job dissatisfaction, lower self-esteem, increased heart rate, and increased cigarette consumption.[26]

SHIFT WORK   Approximately 20 percent of the U.S. work force (roughly 20 million people) is involved in rotating (afternoon and evening) work schedules as opposed to fixed daytime work schedules.[27] Shift work is unavoidable in a modern, technological society. Certain services must be available twenty-four hours a day, and hence require shifts. Firefighters, police officers, medical and military personnel, and utility operators, for example, must work in shifts around the clock. Because of the unpopularity of afternoon and evening shifts, many employers find it necessary to rotate staff through shifts.

Shift rotation, understandably, has an adverse influence on sleeping patterns and on opportunities for normal social activities. However, the range of

TABLE 15.5

STRESS SYMPTOMS ASSOCIATED WITH SHIFT WORK

Fatigue

Difficulty obtaining sleep

Disturbances in appetite, digestion, and elimination

Increased divorce rate

Increased incidence of sexual problems

Reduced involvement in social and religious organizations

Reduced contact with friends

Lowered productivity

Increased accidents

Reduced commitment to the organization

---

adverse consequences of shift work is substantial. Table 15.5 lists a number of these problems.[28] Although the past ten years have witnessed significant advances in the understanding of biological rhythms (that is, the physiological and behavioral functions that recur at regular intervals), there have not been equivalent advances in the application of this knowledge to the workplace in the form of interventions designed to ameliorate problems caused by shift work.

REACTIONS TO STRESS

PHYSICAL PROBLEMS

As suggested above, a high level of stress has been associated with a host of physical disorders, including heart disease, arthritis, ulcers, high blood pressure, and high levels of cholesterol.[29] There is also some suspicion that stress may be linked to cancer.[30]

Although it is impossible to quantify the personal cost of serious physical ailments for an individual, it is possible to estimate the cost of such problems for an organization. For example, Ivancevich and Matteson have created a worksheet for estimating the yearly costs associated with replacing employees lost to heart disease.[31] For a company that employs 4,000 people, the estimates would be:

1. Number of employees   4,000

2. Men in age range 45 to 65 ($0.25 \times$ line 1)   1,000

3. Estimated deaths due to heart disease per year ($0.006 \times$ line 2)   6

4. Estimated premature retirement due to heart problems per year ($0.003 \times$ line 2)   3

5. Company's annual personnel losses due to heart disorders (sum of lines 3 and 4)   9

6. Annual replacement cost: the average cost of hiring and training replacements for experienced employees (line 5 × $4,300) $38,700

As these figures suggest, heart disease can be a significant cost to an organization, and the absolute number of employees who are likely to die eventually of heart disease is not trivial. Furthermore, the additional costs of hospitalization coverage, lost wages, and lost performance are not included in the above estimate.

To be sure, a single organization cannot assume full responsibility for all employee deaths due to heart disease. In addition to work-related stress, many other factors play a role in the development of heart disease, including heredity, diet, and general state of well-being.

ALCOHOLISM AND DRUG ABUSE

The National Institute on Alcohol Abuse and Alcoholism estimates that between 6 and 10 percent of all employees are alcoholics. Although drug usage is not as widespread as alcohol abuse, it is nonetheless a serious problem. Both alcohol and drug abuse are linked to higher levels of stress among employees. In addition to threatening their own well-being, employees who attend work while under the influence of alcohol or drugs pose a serious threat to the well-being of their coworkers because they are more prone to on-the-job accidents.

ABSENTEEISM, TURNOVER, AND DISSATISFACTION

Research reviews by Porter and Steers, Steers and Rhodes, and Mobley and colleagues have generally pointed to a relationship between stress and increases in such withdrawal behaviors as absenteeism and turnover.[32] A correlation has also been found between dissatisfaction and work-related stress.[33] Because these studies of stress as a predictor of turnover, absenteeism, and dissatisfaction have all been correlational in nature, it is difficult to state conclusively what factors are responsible for the relationship (see Chapter 2). Although little evidence is available, it is also widely believed that hostile actions in the workplace, such as sabotage and violence directed against supervisors and coworkers, may result, at least indirectly, from stress (see Chapter 4). For example, stress associated with feelings of job insecurity (that is, plans to eliminate 130,000 jobs) have been cited as a contributing cause for a wave of shootings by U.S. Postal Service employees.[34]

MASS PSYCHOGENIC ILLNESS

Perhaps one of the strangest suspected responses to the experience of stress is the occurrence of **mass psychogenic illness.** One report of such an instance stated that 30 workers in an electronics assembly facility complained for two weeks of headaches, sleepiness, nausea, and dizziness. Another report involved

27 women in an aluminum furniture assembly plant. Although no chemicals were used in the assembly process, these women reported symptoms of dizziness, lightheadedness, dry mouth, and a bad taste in the mouth after smelling a strange odor. Other employees stated that they had seen a "blue mist" in one section of the plant. As word spread, a near panic among the 300-plus employees resulted in a temporary shutdown of the plant. Despite these problems, an analysis of air samples yielded no evidence of toxic chemicals or other agents. When the plant reopened a few days later, 27 employees (19 of whom were not involved in the initial hysteria) reported similar symptoms.

In a third reported incident, 35 employees in a frozen-fish packing plant complained of headaches, dizziness, and difficulty in breathing shortly after their shift began. A few years earlier, a carbon monoxide leak in the plant had affected several employees, yet the recent symptoms were not those of carbon monoxide exposure. Furthermore, a detecting–recording device showed that the level of carbon monoxide in the air where the employees complained was well below the level necessary to create ill effects.[35]

In the Middle Ages, such outbreaks might have been labeled "demon possessions."** Much later they were termed "assembly-line hysteria" or "epidemic hysteria," and today, such events are called "mass psychogenic reactions." Occupational health professionals are beginning to examine possible causes, and chief among the suspects is work-related stress. Further investigations have suggested that the actual incidence of mass psychogenic illness may be much greater than reported in the medical literature.[36] The number of such outbreaks may be expected to increase as work-related stress combines with greater employee awareness of and sensitivity to issues of toxic chemical exposure and environmental protection.

In recent years, there has been a growing acceptance (for example, by the World Health Organization) of a related phenomenon: sick building syndrome. In one British instance, 94 percent of the office workers in a new building complained of headaches, lethargy, rashes, and nausea. Ironically, 60 employees in the Environmental Protection Agency building in Washington, D.C., reported fatigue and loss of voice. In some cases, the illnesses can be traced to chemicals in carpeting adhesives, pulsating fluorescent lighting, and computer screen glare. However, there are instances where simple explanations are elusive and only speculation remains (typically targeting poor ventilation that recirculates fungi, microbes, and dust mites).[37]

BURNOUT—A COMPANION PROBLEM

Like stress, **burnout** is a reaction to prolonged and energy-depleting difficulties. Its primary symptoms include feeling drained or used up. It typically affects people who are highly conscientious and work in the helping professions, such as police officers, schoolteachers, social workers, and nurses. At some point, such employees may come to feel that they are not receiving the rewards

---

** And a few people would probably have been burned at the stake in order to remove the demons and get on with the business at hand.

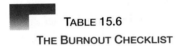

TABLE 15.6

THE BURNOUT CHECKLIST

	Mostly True	Mostly False
1. I feel tired more frequently than I used to.	———	———
2. I snap at people too often.	———	———
3. Trying to help other people often seems hopeless.	———	———
4. I seem to be working harder but accomplishing less.	———	———
5. I get down on myself too often.	———	———
6. My job is beginning to depress me.	———	———
7. I often feel I'm headed nowhere.	———	———
8. I've reached (or am fast reaching) a dead end in my job.	———	———
9. I've lost a lot of my zip lately.	———	———
10. It's hard for me to laugh at a joke about myself.	———	———
11. I'm not really physically ill, but I have a lot of aches and pains.	———	———
12. Lately I've kind of withdrawn from friends and family.	———	———
13. My enthusiasm for life is on the wane.	———	———
14. I'm running out of things to say to people.	———	———
15. My temper is much shorter than it used to be.	———	———
16. My job makes me feel sad.	———	———

Interpretation: The more of these questions you can honestly answer mostly true, the more likely it is that you are experiencing burnout. If you answered twelve or more of these statements mostly true, it is likely you are experiencing burnout or another form of mental depression. If so, discuss these feelings with a physical or mental health professional.

Source: "The Burnout Checklist," A. J. DuBrin, *Contemporary Applied Management*, Plano, Texas; Business Publications, 1982; p. 243. Reprinted with permission. The checklist is based in part on the questionnaire printed on the dust jacket of *Burn Out* by Freudenberger.

that they expected for their efforts to help others. Their frustration leads to feelings of apathy and failure, which may result in physical symptoms such as high blood pressure and ulcers, and mental symptoms such as depression and irritability.[38] In many respects, burnout and stress are highly similar reactions. A checklist for assessing burnout is presented in Table 15.6.

COPING WITH STRESS

Helping a person maintain the level of stress that is best for him or her is the goal of various stress management techniques. By and large, the techniques we will consider focus primarily on the reduction rather than the increase of stress.

FLIGHT OR FIGHT

Flight and fight are two reactions that can serve as a primary means of successful coping. *Flight*, or leaving a distressing situation, is a perfectly reasonable response to stress if an avenue of flight is available. For example, some individuals try their hand at supervising others and find that they simply do not like it. This is not to say that they cannot handle the job, but rather that they prefer other types of assignments or activities. For such individuals, the recognition of this personal preference is an important and useful insight that can help them cope with the stress that may accompany supervisory responsibilities.

Fight, or confronting a threat or stressor, can also be an effective response. The desire to confront a threat may actually be the best way to bring about a change that will reduce the level of stress. For example, the urge to fight may lead an employee to confront her superior on an issue that has been bothering her for some time. The confrontation may then lead to a workable resolution.[††]

EXERCISE

Physical exercise, including participation in sports, enables a person to develop resistance to the detrimental effects of stress. Exercise can both improve health and reduce fatigue. Fatigue plays a key role in stress-producing situations because people who are feeling fatigued are more apt to overreact to frustration. Therefore, tolerance for frustration can be increased by being in better physical health. Regular exercise is also thought to be of value in reducing the likelihood of coronary diseases. Some large organizations, such as Tenneco, Weyerhauser, Johns-Manville, and Exxon, provide a gymnasium at company headquarters to promote employee fitness.

SOCIAL SUPPORT

One means of resisting stress is to have a strong network of social supports. Studies indicate that the availability of sympathetic others (especially coworkers) can help a person deal with job-related stress.[39] The reassurance derived from knowing that others can be called on to help when needed can be invaluable.

JOB REDESIGN

Jobs can be redesigned to minimize the creation of stress. One approach to job redesign that seeks to reduce assembly-line pressures and the dull, repetitive aspects of such work is job enrichment. As discussed in Chapter 7, one way in which job enrichment makes a task more attractive is by giving greater autonomy (usually self-pacing) to the individual worker. Such autonomy is critical to alleviating feelings of pressure and the resultant stress. Two other common ways of reducing stress are to provide employees with opportunities to participate in decision making and to improve communication, both of which can reduce workers' feelings of helplessness and dependence.

RELAXATION TECHNIQUES

Relaxation techniques such as progressive relaxation, yoga, and Transcendental Meditation rely on the idea that relaxation of the major voluntary muscles reduces anxiety levels. The goal of these techniques is to achieve a state of

---

[††]Of course, it might also lead to her dismissal.

physiological and psychological rest, and evidence suggests that such improve-ments can in fact result.[40] Although some corporations (such as New York Telephone Company and Metropolitan Life Insurance) are beginning to ex-plore the sponsored use of relaxation techniques for their managers,[41] evi-dence of the effectiveness of these techniques within organizational settings is not yet available. Also, some large organizations, such as Apple Computer and Intel, allow managers to take sabbaticals (paid time off) to encourage "mental rejuvenation." Universities, for example, have a long tradition of permitting faculty time off to pursue alternative research interests.

DEVELOPING A NEW PHILOSOPHY OF LIFE

One technique for coping with stress is to develop a philosophy of life that in-corporates a more tolerant and broader view of life (versus the "looking out for number one" perspective). In order to achieve a new perspective, some in-dividuals turn to philosophical exercises for enlightenment and understanding. Some approaches to achieving a greater acceptance of oneself and others rely on Eastern thought (such as Taoist or Buddhist philosophy) for insights not found in Western thought.[42]

Siu, a consultant in the field of strategy and decision critique, has offered a set of guidelines that exemplify this approach to seeking contemplative in-sights. He has designed the following list of proverbs to guide the "journey-man-executive" who wishes to become a "philosopher-executive."[43] Five proverbs for planning are

1. The bird hunting the locust is unaware of the hawk hunting him.
2. The mouse with but one hole is easily taken.
3. In shallow waters, shrimps make fools of dragons.
4. Do not try to catch two frogs with one hand.
5. Give the bird room to fly.

Four proverbs for operations are

1. Do not insult the crocodile until you have crossed the river.
2. It is better to struggle with a sick jackass than carry the wood yourself.
3. Do not throw stone at mouse and break precious vase.
4. It is not the last blow of the ax that fells the tree.

Such thought-stimulating proverbs are intended to provide a challenging and provocative stimulus to rethinking one's view of stressful situations. As sug-gested by McLean, a consideration of one's job circumstances from a slightly altered perspective can help to restore a sense of balance.[44]

TIME MANAGEMENT: A PRACTICAL APPROACH TO REDUCING STRESS

One especially useful strategy for coping with job-related stress is effective **time management**. An inability to manage time can result in overcommitment, a lack of planning, and missed deadlines. Strictly speaking, one does not manage time as such, in that time moves at its own rate and is not subject to any effort to manipulate it. In truth, effective time management is really effective self-management. Time-management specialists have developed a number of useful techniques for gaining control over one's work life and, thereby, one's sanity.[45]

TIME LOG   The first step in trying to manage one's time is to develop a time log, or inventory. By jotting down the events that occur in a typical day with the time required for each activity, it is possible to learn where one's time is being spent. The results of a time log (which might be reviewed at the end of a week) can offer surprising insights. For example, some executives are amazed to find that a large percentage of each day is devoted to dealing with interruptions and pointless socializing. The results of such an inventory can help pinpoint sources of time wastage and thus help focus attention on using time more effectively.

STRUCTURING TIME   One can gain greater control over one's life by structuring the day so that time wasters are blocked or eliminated. For example, not being accessible by phone or to visitors for an hour or two in the morning provides a block of uninterrupted time during which mail can be read or writing can be done. Similarly, all visits can be arranged between 2:00 and 4:00 in the afternoon. Meetings can be strategically set one-half hour or an hour before lunch or quitting time to ensure that the participants will help complete the meeting on time.

JUST SAY NO   Sometimes an employee is victimized by a desire to be accommodating to everyone. In such instances, others learn that their requests are seldom refused by such an employee and may take advantage of his or her good nature. For such individuals, an important step in gaining control of their lives is to learn how to say no to requests for their time and energy. Refusing the requests of others requires some delicacy, and should be done politely, but firmly. For people who are already heavily committed to their primary job duties, taking on the added responsibility of managing the office baseball team and the fund-raising drive will likely provide needless stress.

MAKE A LIST   One of the most useful techniques for managing time is to prepare a list of "things to do." Interviews with highly effective managers reveal that they invariably maintain a planning list of activities that aids their memories and focuses their attention and energy. A planning list contains such items as phone calls that must be returned, correspondence that must be prepared, meetings that need to be scheduled, and projects that must be monitored. In addition, the items on the list should be prioritized. The most critical items are labeled "category A," while the next most critical items are labeled "category B," and so on. Then, category A items are handled first, category B items are tackled if time permits, and lower-category items are put off until even later. In maintaining a "to-do" list, it is important to keep the list current, to never give in to the temptation to clean up the "small" or "easy" items first, and to scrutinize the list for items that can be reasonably delegated to subordinates.

OB Focus
Rubbing Stress Away

SNI Companies of Flourtown, Pennsylvania, which provides nurses and consultants to the health care industry, can't afford to build a gym for an employee wellness program. Instead, the company has Harris Fishkin.

Fishkin has the unusual role of full-time corporate masseur at SNI. Every week or every other week, each of SNI's 60 Flourtown employees receives Fishkin's standard 15-minute massage of the back, head, and neck. Employees sit in a small, darkened room, leaning forward on a specially designed chair and listening to New Age music. Fishkin also travels to the Albert Einstein Medical Center in Philadelphia once a week to give massages to SNI's eight critical-care nurses there.

This stress-reduction benefit, known as on-site massage (OSM), became known to the corporate world when David Palmer, who devised OSM, introduced it to Apple Computer in the early 1980s. Now OSM is available to at least some workers at over 30 companies, including American Airlines, AT&T, H.J. Heinz Company, and Pillsbury. The number of OSM practitioners has grown from about 100 since the technique's introduction to over 3,000.

The practice might catch on even faster, except that some managers view massage as having a dubious connotation associated with X-rated massage parlors. In fact, OSM is intended to be strictly therapeutic and involves no undressing or oils. Advocates of the technique claim that it increases blood circulation, stimulates the lymphatic system, calms the autonomic nervous system, reduces lactic acid in the muscles (allowing them to stay relaxed), and boosts productivity and morale. Lynn Fauerbach, an employee of SNI, credits her weekly massages with putting an end to severe headaches.

Some preliminary data, while only suggestive, support the idea that massage is an effective stress-reduction technique. A dozen nurses at two Philadelphia-area hospitals took a standardized stress test and then received a series of six massages. When they retook the stress test, ten of the nurses (83 percent) scored lower on stress. Eleven of the nurses received another six massages; afterward, ten of them (90 percent) showed even less stress as measured by the test.

If further evidence supports the benefits of OSM, perhaps regular back rubs will eventually become part of the daily work routine.

Source: Sandy Bauers, "There's the Rub: Masseurs Tackle Stress on Job," *Chicago Tribune*, February 19, 1990, sec. 4, p. 3.

WELLNESS PROGRAMS

Following a discussion of work-related stress, it is fitting to recognize the growth of the "wellness" movement in the United States and Canada. The movement represents a proactive rather than reactive approach to the issue of health management. Prevention, the core notion of the wellness movement, has gained recognition as a wise investment, as employers are faced with the burden of the rising cost of health care. In essence, it is more prudent to promote employee health, or wellness, than to cope with illness. **Wellness programs** involve educating employees on health-risk factors (for example, smoking, obesity, poor nutrition), providing physical exams (for example, blood pressure checks), and offering plans for assisting employees in reducing health risks. The variety of existing wellness programs is quite broad. Some organizations simply distribute literature to employees regarding health-related topics, while others provide on-site exercise equipment and uniforms. American Telephone and Telegraph Co., along with other firms, has adopted "stress-down days" when employees come to work wearing casual attire, including jeans and sweatshirts.

Control Data Corporation's "Staywell Program" provides an outstanding example of a wellness program. The program, which is available to employees and their spouses at many company locations throughout the United States, includes medical screening, health education, and activities designed to change life-styles. The medical screening includes a physical exam, blood sampling, a blood pressure check, and a "computerized health-risk profile." Participants may also attend one-hour health-awareness courses that cover such topics as drug abuse and cancer detection. Programs designed to change life-styles focus on such issues as nutrition, obesity, hypertension, and smoking. In these programs, ongoing employee support groups are formed.

The Control Data wellness program has been credited for significant reductions in health-care costs due to decreased smoking and hypertension, and increased exercise. Absenteeism and time lost due to illness have also been reduced. Other corporations that have introduced wellness programs (such as Prudential Insurance, Johnson and Johnson, Campbell Soup, Champion International, Travelers Corp., Tenneco, and Blue Cross and Blue Shield) have reported significant reductions in sickness rates and absenteeism, and improved job performance and work-related attitudes.[46] As a result of these success stories, there are no reports of organizations dismantling wellness programs after they have been installed. Even during times of cutbacks, corporations have maintained in-house fitness centers, partly because they have been shown to pay for themselves and partly because such an action would have a negative effect on morale.

SUMMARY

1. Define stress.

Stress is the extreme physiological and emotional arousal a person experiences when confronted with a threatening situation.

2. Explain various views of job-related stress.

Hans Selye has proposed three stages that characterize a person's response to stress: alarm, resistance, and exhaustion. These stages constitute the General Adaptation Syndrome. Another view holds that a certain degree of stress may be beneficial in that it may increase achievement.

3. Identify personal causes of stress.

A major personal cause of stress is the possession of a type A personality. People with such a personality tend to be impatient and competitive. Another major personal cause of stress is change in one's life (for example, death of a spouse or loss of a job).

4. Explain interpersonal causes of stress.

The negative emotions of jealousy (threats to self-esteem due to loss of a relationship) and envy (threats to self-esteem due to desired outcomes being allocated to another) can induce feelings of stress. Individual attributes, work-unit attributes, and cultural attributes all play a role in perceiving and responding to such social threats.

5. List organizational causes of stress.

Organizational influences include having responsibility for others, being involved in shift work, and working in a stress-inducing occupation or one that requires emotional labor. Role conflict, role ambiguity, and role overload also contribute to the experience of stress.

6. Describe typical reactions to stress.

High levels of stress are associated with physical disorders, including heart disease, arthritis, ulcers, high blood pressure, high levels of cholesterol, and, possibly, cancer. Stress is linked to poor job performance, abuse of alcohol and other drugs, absenteeism, job turnover, worker dissatisfaction, mass psychogenic illness, and burnout.

7. List ways of managing stress.

People can manage stress by weighing the merits of fighting or fleeing a particular situation. Physical exercise and a strong network of social supports help people resist stress. Managers can redesign jobs to minimize the creation of stress. People can reduce stress by using time-management and relaxation techniques, and by developing a more tolerant and broader philosophy of life.

8. Explain the concept of a wellness program.

A wellness program focuses on the prevention of illness. Such programs educate employees about health-related issues, provide physical exams, and assist employees in reducing health risks.

KEY TERMS

Stress	Role conflict
General Adaptation Syndrome	Role ambiguity
Type A personality	Role overload
Type B personality	Mass psychogenic illness
Employee jealousy	Burnout
Employee envy	Time management
Emotional labor	Wellness program

REVIEW AND DISCUSSION QUESTIONS

1. What are type A personality characteristics? Do people with such personality types usually perform best as top-level managers?

2. What are some working conditions that are associated with stress among employees?

3. Lance Lucky marries the woman of his dreams. She is not only beautiful, but also a successful cardiologist. With her income, they will easily be able to travel and live more comfortably than Lance ever imagined he would. They buy a comfortable house, taking out a $195,000 mortgage. Shortly after they move in, Lance receives a phone call; he has just been named "Realtor of the Year" in his community. He is ecstatic; it seems as though everything is going right. But when he goes to his doctor for a checkup, he learns that his blood pressure and cholesterol levels are both high. "I think it's stress," the doctor tells him. Lance is shocked at the diagnosis. How

can Lance be suffering from stress when his life is going so well? Suggest ways he can cope with the stress.

4. What are the major techniques associated with time management? How do they help to reduce job-related stress?

5. Distinguish among role conflict, role ambiguity, and role overload.

6. Bill says that he gets nervous every time he has to make a presentation, and that he experiences "butterflies in the stomach" from the stress. Clayton tells Bill not to worry, that a certain amount of stress is actually good for him. "The trick," he says, "is to get your butterflies to fly in formation." Can Clayton be correct in stating that stress can be beneficial?

7. Len is impatient and highly competitive, while Mel is very relaxed and easygoing. Assuming that Len and Mel typify the type A and type B personalities, what might they be like to work with as coworkers? As bosses?

8. Jobs can be characterized in terms of how stressful they are. Compare the high-stress jobs of office manager, waitress/waiter, and secretary with the low-stress jobs of stock handlers and college professors. What specific aspects of these jobs are responsible for creating differing degrees of stress?

9. What stress symptoms are associated with shift work? How might some of these symptoms be ameliorated?

CRITICAL INCIDENT

No Response from Monitor 23

Loudspeaker: IGNITION MINUS 45 MINUTES.

Paul Keller tripped the sequence switches at control monitor 23 in accordance with the countdown instruction book just to his left. All hydraulic systems were functioning normally in the second stage of the spacecraft booster at checkpoint I minus 45. Keller automatically snapped his master control switch to GREEN and knew that his electronic impulse along with hundreds of others from similar consoles within the Cape Kennedy complex signaled continuation of the countdown.

It used to be an incredible challenge, fantastically interesting work at the very fringe of knowledge about the universe. Keller recalled his first day in Brevard County, Florida, with his wife and young daughter. How happy they were that day. Here was the future, the good life . . . forever. And Keller was going to be part of that fantastic, utopian future.

Loudspeaker: IGNITION MINUS 35 MINUTES.

Keller panicked! His mind had wandered momentarily, and he lost his place in the countdown instructions. Seconds later, he found the correct place and tripped the proper sequence of switches for checkpoint I minus 35. No problem. Keller snapped the master control to GREEN and wiped his brow. He knew he was late reporting and would hear about it later.

Loudspeaker: IGNITION MINUS 30 MINUTES.

Keller completed the reporting sequence for checkpoint I minus 30 and took one long last drag on his cigarette. Utopia? Hell! It was one big rat race and getting bigger all the time. Keller recalled how he once naively felt that his problems with Naomi would disappear after they left Minneapolis and came to the Cape with the space program. Now, 10,000 arguments later, Keller knew there was no escape.

> *Only one can of beer left, Naomi? One stinking lousy can of beer, cold lunch-meat, and potato salad? Leftovers after 12 hours of mental exhaustion?*
>
> *Oh, shut up, Paul! I'm so sick of you playing Mr. Important. You get left-overs because I never know when you're coming home . . . your daughter hardly knows you . . . and you treat us like nobodies . . . incidental to your great Space Program.*
>
> *Don't knock it, Naomi. That job is plenty important to me, to the Team, and it gets you everything you've ever wanted . . . more! Between this house and the boat, we're up to our ears in debt.*
>
> *Now don't try to pin our money problems on me. You're the one who has to have all the same goodies as the scientists earning twice your salary. Face it, Paul. You're just a button-pushing technician regardless of how fancy a title they give you.*

Loudspeaker: IGNITION MINUS 25 MINUTES.

A red light blinked ominously indicating a potential hydraulic fluid leak in subsystem seven of stage two. Keller felt his heartbeat and pulse rate increase. Rule 1 . . . report malfunction immediately and stop the count. Keller punched POTENTIAL ABORT on the master control.

Loudspeaker: THE COUNT IS STOPPED AT IGNITION MINUS 24 MINUTES 17 SECONDS.

Keller fumbled with the countdown instructions. Any POTENTIAL ABORT required a cross-check to separate an actual malfunction from sporadic signal error. Keller began to perspire nervously as he initiated standard cross-check procedures.

"Monitor 23, this is Control. Have you got an actual abort, Paul?" The voice in the headset was cool, but impatient. "Decision required in 30 seconds."

"I know, I know," Keller mumbled, "I'm cross-checking right now."

Cross-check one proved inconclusive. Keller automatically followed detailed instructions for cross-check two.

"Do you need help, Keller?" asked the voice in the headset.

"No, I'm O.K."

"Decision required," demanded the voice in the headset. "Dependent systems must be deactivated in 15 seconds."

Keller read and reread the console data. It looked like a sporadic error signal.

"Decision required," demanded the voice in the headset.

"Continue count," blurted Keller at last. "Subsystem seven fully operational." Keller slumped back in his chair.

Loudspeaker: THE COUNT IS RESUMED AT IGNITION MINUS 24 MINUTES 17 SECONDS.

Keller knew that within an hour after lift-off, Barksdale would call him in for a personal conference. "What's wrong lately, Paul?" he would say. "Is there anything I can help with? You seem so tense lately." But he wouldn't really want to listen. Barksdale was the kind of person who read weakness into any personal problems and demanded that they be purged from one's mind.

More likely Barksdale would demand that Keller make endless practice runs on cross-check procedures while he stood nearby . . . watching and noting any errors . . . while the pressure grew and grew.

Loudspeaker: IGNITION MINUS 20 MINUTES.

The monitor lights at console 23 blinked routinely.

"Keller," said the voice in the earphone. "Report, please."

"Control, this is Wallace at monitor 24. I don't believe Keller is feeling well. Better send someone to cover fast!"

Loudspeaker: THE COUNT IS STOPPED AT 19 MINUTES 33 SECONDS.

"This is Control, Wallace. Assistance has been dispatched and the count is on temporary hold. What seems to be wrong with Keller?"

"Control, this is Wallace, I don't know. His eyes are open and fixed on the monitor, but he won't respond to my questions. It could be a seizure or . . . a stroke."

QUESTIONS

1. Is there any way of avoiding the more serious manifestations (as with Paul Keller) of pressure on the job? Explain.

2. Are there any early warning signs given by employees under stress? If so, what are they?

3. What is the proper role of the supervisor here? Should he attempt counseling?

Source: Adapted with permission from Robert D. Joyce, *Encounters in Organizational Behavior,* pp. 168–172. Copyright 1972, Pergamon Press PLC.

EXPERIENTIAL EXERCISE

Health Risk Appraisal

The Health Risk Appraisal form was developed by the Department of Health and Welfare of the Canadian government. Their initial testing program indicated that approximately one person out of every three who completed the form would modify some unhealthy aspects of his or her life-style for at least a while. Figuring the potential payoff was worth it, the government mailed out over 3 million copies of the questionnaire to Canadians who were on social security. Subsequent checking indicated that initial projections of the number of recipients altering their behavior was correct. Perhaps you will be among the one-third.

Choose from the three answers for each question the one answer that most nearly applies to you. Note that a few items may have only two alternatives.

Exercise

_____ 1. Physical effort expended during the workday: mostly?
  (a) heavy labor, walking, or housework
  (b) —
  (c) deskwork

_____ 2. Participation in physical activities—skiing, golf, swimming, etc., or lawn mowing, gardening, etc.?
  (a) daily
  (b) weekly
  (c) seldom

_____ 3. Participation in vigorous exercise program?
  (a) three times weekly
  (b) weekly
  (c) seldom

_____ 4. Average miles walked or jogged per day?
  (a) one or more
  (b) less than one
  (c) none

_____ 5. Flights of stairs climbed per day?
  (a) more than 10
  (b) 10 or fewer
  (c) —

Nutrition

_____ 6. Are you overweight?
  (a) no
  (b) 5 to 19 lbs.
  (c) 20 or more lbs.

_____ 7. Do you eat a wide variety of foods, something from each of the following five food groups: (1) meat, fish, poultry, dried legumes, eggs, or nuts; (2) milk or milk products; (3) bread or cereals; (4) fruits; (5) vegetables?
  (a) each day
  (b) three times weekly
  (c) —

Alcohol

_____ 8. Average number of bottles (12 oz.) of beer per week?
  (a) 0 to 7

      (b) 8 to 15

      (c) 16 or more

_____ 9. Average number of hard liquor ($1\frac{1}{2}$ oz.) drinks per week?

      (a) 0 to 7

      (b) 8 to 15

      (c) 16 or more

_____ 10. Average number of glasses (5 oz.) of wine or cider per week?

      (a) 0 to 7

      (b) 8 to 15

      (c) 16 or more

_____ 11. Total number of drinks per week including beer, liquor, or wine?

      (a) 0 to 7

      (b) 8 to 15

      (c) 16 or more

Drugs

_____ 12. Do you take drugs illegally?

      (a) no

      (b) —

      (c) yes

_____ 13. Do you consume alcoholic beverages together with certain drugs (tranquilizers, barbiturates, illegal drugs)?

      (a) no

      (b) —

      (c) yes

_____ 14. Do you use painkillers improperly or excessively?

      (a) no

      (b) —

      (c) yes

Tobacco

_____ 15. Cigarettes smoked per day?

      (a) none

      (b) less than 10

      (c) 10 or more

_____ 16. Cigars smoked per day?

      (a) none

      (b) less than 5

      (c) 5 or more

_____ 17. Pipe tobacco pouches per week?

      (a) none

      (b) 1

      (c) 2 or more

Personal Health

_____ 18. Do you experience periods of depression?

(a) seldom
(b) occasionally
(c) frequently
_____ 19. Does anxiety interfere with your daily activities?
(a) seldom
(b) occasionally
(c) frequently
_____ 20. Do you get enough satisfying sleep?
(a) yes
(b) no
(c) —
_____ 21. Are you aware of the causes and dangers of VD?
(a) yes
(b) no
(c) —
_____ 22. Breast self-examination? (if not applicable, do not score)
(a) monthly
(b) occasionally
(c) —

Road and Water Safety
_____ 23. Mileage per year as a driver or passenger?
(a) less than 10,000
(b) 10,000 or more
(c) —
_____ 24. Do you often exceed the speed limit?
(a) no
(b) by 10 mph
(c) by 20 mph or more
_____ 25. Do you wear a seat belt?
(a) always
(b) occasionally
(c) never
_____ 26. Do you drive a motorcycle, moped, or snowmobile?
(a) no
(b) yes
(c) —
_____ 27. If yes to the above, do you always wear a regulation helmet?
(a) yes
(b) —
(c) no
_____ 28. Do you ever drive under the influence of alcohol?
(a) never
(b) —
(c) occasionally
_____ 29. Do you ever drive when your ability may be affected by drugs?
(a) never

(b) —
(c) occasionally
_____ 30. Are you aware of water safety rules?
     (a) yes
     (b) no
     (c) —
_____ 31. If you participate in water sports or boating, do you wear a life jacket?
     (a) yes
     (b) no
     (c) —

General
_____ 32. Average time watching TV per day (in hours)?
     (a) 0 to 1
     (b) 1 to 4
     (c) 4 or more
_____ 33. Are you familiar with first-aid procedures?
     (a) yes
     (b) no
     (c) —
_____ 34. Do you ever smoke in bed?
     (a) no
     (b) occasionally
     (c) regularly
_____ 35. Do you always make use of equipment provided for your safety at work?
     (a) yes
     (b) occasionally
     (c) no

To Score: Give yourself 1 point for each *a* answer; 3 points for each *b* answer; 5 points for each *c* answer. *Total Score:* _____

- A total score of 35–45 is *excellent.* You have a commendable life-style based on sensible habits and a lively awareness of personal health.
- A total score of 45–55 is *good.* With some minor change, you can develop an excellent life-style.
- A total score of 56–65 is *risky.* You are taking unnecessary risks with your health. Several of your habits should be changed if potential health problems are to be avoided.
- A total score of 66 and over is *hazardous.* Either you have little personal awareness of good health habits or you are choosing to ignore them. This is a danger zone.

Source: Dept. of Health and Welfare of Canada as found in J.M. Ivancevich and M.T. Matteson, *Organizational Behavior and Management,* 2d ed. (Homewood, Ill.: BPI/Irwin, 1990), 250. Used with permission of the publisher.

Notes

1. B. Rammizini, *De Morbis Artificum Diatriba* (1713), trans. under the auspices of the New York Academy of Medicine (New York: Hafnor Press, 1964).

2. H. Munsterberg, *Psychology and Industrial Efficiency* (New York: Houghton Mifflin, 1913).

3. H. Selye, *The Stress of Life* (New York: McGraw-Hill, 1976).

4. W.E. Scott, "Activation Theory and Task Design," *Organizational Behavior and Human Performance* (1966): 13–30.

5. M.T. Matteson and J.M. Ivancevich, *Controlling Work Stress* (San Francisco: Jossey-Bass, 1987).

6. M. Friedman and R. Rosenman, *Type A Behavior and Your Heart* (New York: Knopf, 1974); D. Ganster, J. Schaubroeck, W. Sime, and B.T. Mayes, "The Nomological Validity of the Type A Personality among Employed Adults," *Journal of Applied Psychology* 76 (1991): 143–168.

7. R. Rosenman and M. Friedman, "The Central Nervous System and Coronary Heart Disease," *Hospital Practice* 6 (1971): 87–97.

8. C.D. Jenkins, "Psychologic and Social Precursors of Coronary Disease," *New England Journal of Medicine* 284 (1971): 244–255.

9. J.H. Howard, D.A. Cunningham, and P.A. Rechnitzer, "Health Patterns Associated with Type A Behavior: A Managerial Population," *Journal of Human Stress* 2 (1976): 24–31.

10. T.H. Holmes and R.H. Rahe, "Social Readjustment Rating Scale," *Journal of Psychosomatic Research* 11 (1967): 213–218; A. DeLongis, S. Folkman, and R. Lazarus, "The Impact of Daily Stress on Health and Mood: Psychological and Social Resources as Mediators," *Journal of Personality and Social Psychology* 54 (1988): 486–495.

11. R.P. Vecchio, "It's Not Easy Being Green: Jealousy and Envy in the Workplace," in *Research in Personnel and Human Resources Management*, ed. G.R. Ferris (Greenwich, Conn.: JAI Press, 1995).

12. Ibid.

13. Ibid.

14. R.P. Vecchio, "Employee Jealousy: Antecedents, Consequences, and Testable Hypotheses" (Paper presented at the 1993 Meeting of the Western Division of the Academy of Management, San José).

15. A.A. McLean, *Work Stress* (Reading, Mass.: Addison-Wesley, 1979); J.V. Brady, "Ulcers in Executive Monkeys," *Scientific American* 199 (1958): 89–95.

16. M.M. Smith, M. Colligan, R.W. Horning et al., *Occupational Comparison of Stress-related Disease Incidence* (Cincinnati: National Institute for Occupational Safety and Health. 1978).

17. McLean, *Work Stress*, 80.

18. Ibid., 82.

19. E. Goffman, "On Face Work," *Psychiatry* 18 (1955): 215–236; A.R. Hochschild, "Emotion Work: Feeling Rules and Social Structure," *American Journal of Sociology* 85 (1979): 551–575; D.E. Gibson, "Constructing Emotional Maps: Structures in Organizations and Emotions" (Paper presented at the 1993 Meeting of the Western Division of the Academy of Management, San José).

20. J. Van Maanen and G. Kunda, "Real Feelings: Emotional Expression and Organizational Culture," in *Research in Organizational Behavior* 11, eds. B. Staw and L. Cummings (Greenwich, Conn.: JAI Press, 1989), 43–103.

21. R.L. Kahn et al., *Organizational Stress* (New York: Wiley, 1964).

22. Ibid.

23. J. Cassel, "Psychosocial Processes and Stress: Theoretical Formulation," *International Journal of Health Services* 4 (1974): 471–482; W.H. Hendrix, N.K. Ovalle, and R.G. Troxler, "Behavioral and Physiological Consequences of Stress and Its Antecedent Factors," *Journal of Applied Psychology* 70 (1985): 188–201; W.H. Hendrix, "Factors Predictive of Stress, Organizational Effectiveness and Coronary Heart Disease Potential," *Aviation, Space, and Environmental Medicine* (July 1985): 654–659; J. Martocchio and A. O'Leary, "Sex Differences in Occupational Stress," *Journal of Applied Psychology* 74 (1989): 495–501.

24. B.L. Margolis, W.M. Kroes, and R.P. Quinn, "Job Stress: An Unlisted Occupational Hazard," *Journal of Occupational Medicine* 16 (1974): 659–661.

25. Friedman and Rosenman, *Type A Behavior and Your Heart*.

26. J.R.P. French and R.D. Caplan,"Organizational Stress and Individual Stress," in *Failure of Success* ed., A.J. Marrow (New York: AMACOM, 1972).

27. C.M. Winget, L. Hughes, and J. La Don, "Physiological Effects of Rotational Work Shifting: A Review," *Journal of Occupational Medicine* 20 (1978): 204–210.

28. A. Brief, R.S. Schuler, and M. Van Sell, *Managing Job Stress* (Boston: LIttle, Brown & Co., 1981).

29. T.G. Cummings and C.L. Cooper, "A Cybernetic Framework for Studying Occupational Stress," *Human Relations* (1979): 395–418.

30. K. Bammer and B.H. Newberry, eds., *Stress and Cancer* (Toronto: Hogrefe, 1982); D. Ganster and J. Schaubroeck, "Work Stress and Employee Health," *Journal of Management* 17 (1991): 235–271; D. Nelson and C. Sutton, "Chronic Work Stress and Coping: A Longitudinal Study and Suggested New Directions," *Journal of Applied Psychology* 33 (1990): 859–869.

31. J.M. Ivancevich and M.T. Matteson, *Stress and Work* (Glenview, Ill.: Scott, Foresman, 1980).

32. L.W. Porter and R.M. Steers, "Organizational, Work, and Personal Factors in Employee Turnover and Absenteeism," *Psychological Bulletin* 80 (1973): 151–176; R.M. Steers and S.R. Rhodes, "Major Influences on Employee Attendance: A Process Model," *Journal of Applied Psychology* 63 (1978): 391–407; W.H. Mobley, R.W. Griffeth, H.H. Hand, et al., "Review and Conceptual Analysis of the Employee Turnover Process," *Psychological Bulletin* 86 (1979): 493–522.

33. A. Kornhauser, *Mental Health of the Industrial Worker* (New York: Wiley, 1965); J. Schaubroeck, D.C. Ganster, and M.L. Fox, "Dispositional Affect and Work-related Stress," *Journal of Applied Psychology* 77 (1992): 322–335; S. Sullivan and R.S. Bhagat, "Organizational Stress, Job Satisfaction, and Job Performance: Where Do We Go from Here?" *Journal of Management* 18 (1992): 353–374.

34. R. Davis, "Tragic Trend Played Out at Two Sites," *USA Today*, May 7, 1993, 1–2.

35. Smith et al., *Occupational Comparison of Stress-related Disease Incidence*.

36. B. Cohen, M. Colligan, W. Wester, et al., "An Investigation of Job Satisfaction Factors in an Incident of Mass Psychogenic Illness at the Workplace," *Organizational Health Nursing* 26 (1978): 10–16.

37. D. Amrine, *Did You Know?* (New York: Reader's Digest Limited, 1990).

38. A. Shirom, "Burnout in Work Organizations," in *International Review of Industrial and Organizational Psychology*, eds. C.L. Cooper and I. Robertson (Chichester, England: Wiley, 1989), 25–48.

39. McLean, *Work Stress*.

40. R.K. Wallace and H. Benson, "The Physiology of Meditation," *Scientific American* (1972): 84–90; T. Schultz, "What Science Is Discovering about the Potential Benefits of Meditation," *Today's Health*, April 1972, 34–37.

41. A.J. DuBrin, *Fundamentals of Organizational Behavior* (New York: Pergamon Press, 1978), 142.

42. R.G. Siu, "Work and Serenity," *Occupational Mental Health* 1 (1971): 5–6; R.G. Siu, "The Tao of Organization Management," in *Reducing Occupational Stress*, ed. A. McLean, DHEW-NIOSH Publication no. 78–140 (National Institute for Occupational Safety and Health).

43. Siu, "The Tao of Organization Management," 143–144.

44. McLean, *Work Stress*, 108.

45. A. Lakien, *How to Gain Control of Your Time and Your Life* (New York: Peter Wyden, 1973); R.A. MacKenzie, *The Time Trap* (New York: McGraw-Hill, 1972).

46. R. Kreitner, "Personal Wellness: It's Just Good Business," *Business Horizons* (1982): 28; D. Gebhardt and C. Crump, "Employee Fitness and Wellness Programs in the Workplace," *American Psychologist* 45 (1990): 262–272; J. Erfurt, A. Foote, and M. Heirich, "The Cost-Effectiveness of Worksite Wellness Programs for Hypertension Control, Weight Loss, Smoking Cessation, and Exercise," *Personnel Psychology* 45 (1992): 5–28.

VIDEO CASE   MANAGING CONFLICT

Conflict is inevitable in all organizations, and managing conflict is a time-consuming activity. It is estimated that managers spend 20 percent of their time resolving conflicts. Conflict can erupt from interpersonal friction that is either emotional or work-related in nature. *Emotionally charged* conflict entails interpersonal antagonisms arising from employees' competing values, mistrust, and resentment. This type of conflict can occur between a supervisor and staff members, within work groups, and among coworkers. *Work-related conflict* involves disagreement over substantive workplace issues, such as division goals, organizational policies and procedures, and allocation of resources. Both types of conflict can inhibit an organization from operating effectively. With the current trends toward increased participative decision making, downsizing, and restructuring, managing both emotionally charged and work-related conflict has become increasingly important.

Conflict can arise from communication breakdown, tensions due to workplace diversity, changes in organizational size, competition for scarce resources, and unequal bases of power. A number of approaches are available to manage conflict. Among them are providing superordinate goals to antagonistic parties, redesigning the relationship between the conflicting groups, or relegating the resolution of the conflict to a higher level in the organizational hierarchy. A more direct method of managing conflict is provided by the conflict management model.

The conflict management model presented in *Managing Conflict* proposes the use of five conflict management styles that differ along two dimensions: cooperativeness and assertiveness. Cooperativeness refers to the degree to which one person attempts to satisfy the other person's concerns, and assertiveness refers to the degree to which one person attempts to satisfy his or her own concerns.

• *Avoidance,* characterized by uncooperativeness and unassertiveness, falls in the lower left quadrant of the conflict management grid. In Avoidance, the disagreement is downplayed, and one or both parties fail to participate in the situation. When one party engages in Avoidance, little or no attempt is made to satisfy the party's own needs. When both parties avoid, a stalemate occurs as neither party's concerns are satisfied. Both parties feel anger and frustration. An example of Avoidance in *Managing Conflict* is the condominium residents who were disturbed by one another's music. Rather than discussing the situation with each other, one tenant called the condo association president. But instead of leaving a message on the president's answering machine, the tenant who initiated the call chose to do nothing, thereby avoiding the conflict.

• *Accommodation* occurs when one party is unassertive about its own concerns and is highly cooperative with the other party. While attempting to satisfy the other party's concerns, little or no attempt is made to satisfy one's own concerns. In *Managing Conflict*, the sales representative felt pressured by his boss to get new clients. Rather than initiate a hostile confrontation, his boss took over a key new account. Giving in to the other party's wishes and foregoing one's own desires is an example of Accommodation.

• *Competing* represents an uncooperative, highly assertive style. In Competing, the conflict is framed solely in terms of one's own concerns with little concern for the other party. Because one party is determined to work against the wishes of the other party, Competing is the classic type of conflict. In *Managing Conflict*, an inventory accountant and production supervisor, both of whom were members of a work team, were embroiled in a dispute regarding held purchase requisitions and an inventory shortage. The accountant accused the production supervisor of failing to stick to control thresholds, and he derided her for holding his order. If both parties are interested only in protecting their own positions, it may be difficult for either of them, or a neutral third party, to devise a mutually acceptable solution. Conflicts that originate as other styles may eventually degenerate into Competing as both parties become frustrated with the process.

- *Compromising,* a position of moderate assertiveness and moderate cooperation, occurs when both parties seek acceptable solutions rather than optimal solutions. In *Managing Conflict,* the condominium neighbors came to a mutually acceptable agreement in which each would modify the behavior that was causing the conflict. By splitting the difference, both parties try to achieve partial satisfaction.

- *Collaboration* occurs when one party is highly assertive about its own positions and highly cooperative with regard to the concerns of the other party. Collaboration involves finding solutions that benefit both parties. Collaboration requires looking past one's own position to uncover the concerns that underlie that position. Active listening and open, honest communication are required for Collaboration to work. Collaboration succeeds because it defines conflict as a mutual problem and allows both parties to work toward an integrative outcome. Examples of Collaboration in *Managing Conflict* include the sales manager who learns that her sales rep prefers to work autonomously, and the accountant who learns that expanded production has increased inventory requirements, thereby preventing the production supervisor from complying with control thresholds. In Collaboration, each party remains highly assertive about its own concerns, and overcomes the friction to find out what the other party wants. Once a resolution has been determined, Collaboration requires both parties to commit to the ongoing problem-solving and collaborative process.

While true conflict resolution requires problem-solving and a Collaborative style, the other four styles of conflict management can be ap-

propriate under certain circumstances. Avoidance may be appropriate for trivial issues, or if one person needs to relax and regain his or her composure. Accommodation may be used when one party perceives the conflict issue as being more important than does the cooperating party. When quick, decisive action is needed, or if an unpopular decision must be made, Competition may be the appropriate style. When time is scarce, Compromising may help expedite a solution that may be temporary or permanent.

By finding a balance between cooperativeness and assertiveness, it is possible for both parties to identify areas of negotiation and achieve a positive outcome.

QUESTIONS

1. Which of the conflict management styles represent lose-lose situations for both parties? Win-lose situations? Win-win situations?

2. Describe some of the sources of conflict in the scenarios presented in *Managing Conflict.*

3. Think of instances in your own life when you used each of the five conflict management styles. Was it the appropriate style for the situation at hand, or would an alternative style have produced a better outcome?

STYLES OF CONFLICT MANAGEMENT EXERCISE

To attain a better understanding of each of the five styles of conflict management, think about which style would predominate in each of the following hypothetical situations.

1. Angie disagrees with the rest of the team, but does not communicate this to other members in order to keep the peace.

2. Chris goes along with the recommendations of the team.

3. To break an impasse, Amanda suggests a middle-ground alternative.

4. Evan tries to present everyone's concerns so that problems can be resolved in the best possible way.

5. Joel refrains from discussing disagreements with team members.

6. Karen stands firm in her solution to a problem.

7. Jennifer examines problems with fellow team members to find a mutually acceptable solution.

8. Dave steadfastly pursues his own concerns.

9. Jeremy negotiates with coworkers to find an acceptable solution.

10. Meg tries to meet her coworkers' expectations.

QUESTION

How accurate were you at matching the five conflict management styles to the ten situations given? Give a few hypothetical scenarios in which each individual used the appropriate conflict management technique.

Source: Exercise adapted in part from M. Afzalur Rahim, "A Measure of Styles of Handling Interpersonal Conflict," *Academy of Management Journal* (June 1983): 368–376. "Video Case: Managing Conflict," written by Melissa Waite, State University of New York, University at Buffalo; and Susan Stites-Doe, State University of New York, College at Brockport.

VIDEO CASE

ETHICAL DECISION MAKING: MORTON THIOKOL AND THE SPACE SHUTTLE *CHALLENGER* DISASTER

On January 28, 1986, the space shuttle *Challenger* lifted off on the 25th mission of NASA's shuttle program. Its voyage ended tragically with an explosion just 73 seconds into flight. All seven crew members perished. The shock of the tragedy humbled a once-proud agency. It brought months of investigations as a presidential commission searched for the cause.

In its final report, issued June 10, 1986, the commission identified the immediate, technical reason for the disaster as a failed seal of O-rings in the right Solid Rocket Booster field joint due to the freezing temperatures preceding lift-off. The commission singled out the "flawed decision-making process" that led to the launch as a "contributing cause of the accident."

Multiple warnings, some dating back years and others voiced just hours before the fateful launch, were communicated all the way up to the highest levels of NASA. Morton Thiokol Inc. (MTI), the makers of the booster, had initially recommended against the launch during a telephone conference call between MTI and NASA officials the evening before the launch. The MTI engineers and managers were stunned when their unanimous recommendation was challenged by NASA middle-level managers Larry Mulloy and George Hardy. After a half-hour break in the teleconference, the MTI people returned to announce that they had reconsidered their position and had concluded that it was safe to fly.

How could this have happened? As former Morton Thiokol engineer and seal expert Roger Boisjoly pointed out, "We could have stopped it. We had initially stopped it. And then the decision was made to go forward anyways."

DISASTER BY DESIGN

The origins of the *Challenger* disaster may ultimately be traced back to the day NASA selected Morton Thiokol to build the Solid Rocket Boosters, which would propel the shuttle into space. On November 29, 1973, Thiokol won the contract over three competitors, despite earning the lowest rank in engineering design. The main reason: NASA was then drastically cutting costs to live within its shrinking post-Apollo budget. Thiokol's bid represented a sizable cost advantage.

During seven years of development and testing, NASA engineers at Marshall Space Center found the design of the O-ring joints to be "completely unacceptable." In spite of these objections, the joints were certified for flight, and the space shuttle *Columbia* lifted off for the first time on April 12, 1981. By mid-1985, after 19 missions, NASA headquarters acknowledged the increasing erosion problems in the O-ring joints, yet continued to fly, referring to the erosion as "an allowable risk."

NASA had become a victim of its own gung-ho, can-do philosophy. The agency had promoted the still-experimental Space Transport System as an operational space truck, and was pushing for 15 launches in 1986 and 24 a year by 1990. Such a goal was ambitious when contrasted with the 1985 high of 9 missions, but far short of the 60 missions a year originally envisioned by NASA.

Headquarters had underestimated the fragility of the complex system and overestimated its own capability for resolving problems without disrupting its flight schedule. During the summer and fall of 1985, concern over the dangers posed by the faulty boosters was escalating both within NASA and at Morton Thiokol.

On July 31, 1985, Roger Boisjoly, a rocket engineer at MTI and its top expert on the Solid Rocket Booster seals, wrote a memo to his vice president of engineering, Bob Lund, cautioning that "the mistakenly accepted position on the joint problem was to fly without fear of failure" and modify the joint within the limits of the flight schedule. He warned that failure to address the problem would result in "a catastrophe of the highest order—loss of human life." He concluded, "It is my honest and very real fear that if we do not take immediate action to dedicate a team to solve the problem, with the field joint having the number one priority, then we stand in jeopardy of losing a flight along with all the launch pad facilities."

On August 19, 1985, Al McDonald of Morton Thiokol briefed NASA headquarters on the O-ring joint erosion problem. The presidential commission concluded that the briefing was "sufficiently detailed to require corrective action prior to the next flight," and that no correction was made because "meeting flight schedules and cutting cost were given a higher priority than flight safety."

On January 21, 1986, one week before the launch of the *Challenger*, NASA announced it would seek bids for a "second source" to supply shuttle boosters. The contract was worth over $1 billion to Morton Thiokol.

THE TELECONFERENCE

On Monday, January 27, 1986, the lift-off of *Challenger* Flight 51-L was scrubbed for a fourth time. Following right on the heels of the most delayed flight in shuttle history, it was a disappointing setback for NASA. Perhaps even more significantly, that mission was to showcase President Reagan's "Teacher-in-Space" program by carrying the spritely, effervescent Christa McAuliffe as a crew member. Further, the president was scheduled to deliver his annual State of the Union Address the following evening.

The temperature for launch time the next morning was projected to be 23 degrees, with overnight lows forecast in the teens. Marshall Space Flight Center's Stan Reinartz and Larry Mulloy, the Level III third and fourth ranking shuttle launch officials (see Figure 1), were at Cape Kennedy for the launch along with Thiokol's Al McDonald. They asked MTI to assess the effects of the cold snap. In the afternoon, Thiokol's Bob Lund, recalling that the seals nearly burned through at 53 degrees on the January 1985 flight of the *Discovery*, echoed the recommendations of Boisjoly and the rest of his engineering team, informing Reinartz and Mulloy, "It looks to me like 53 degrees is about it. I don't want to fly outside of our experience base." Thiokol was asked to fax its data to the Marshall Space Flight Center in Huntsville, Alabama, and the Kennedy Space Center in

FINAL TELECONFERENCE BETWEEN THIOKOL–MARSHALL–KENNEDY KEY PARTICIPANTS (JANUARY 27, 1986)

	Marshall Space Flight Center (NASA)	Morton Thiokol, Inc.
	George Hardy, Deputy Dir., Science and Engineering John Miller, SRM Technical Asst. Ben Powers, Propulsion Engineer (And 11 others)	**Management** Jerry Mason, Senior VP Joe Kilminster, VP, Space Boosters Bob Lund, VP, Engineering **Engineers** Roger Boisjoly, SRM Seal Expert Arnie Thompson, SRM Cases Expert Brian Russell, SRM Ignition Expert (And 8 others)
Kennedy Space Center	Stanley Reinartz, Manager, Shuttle Project Larry Mulloy, Manager, SRM Project	Allan McDonald, Dir., SRM Project, MTI

Telecon, 8:45 to 11:00 P.M. Includes Thiokol off-link caucus (10:30 to 11:00 P.M.).

FIGURE 1
THE NASA LAUNCH CHAIN OF COMMAND

Level I
NASA Headquarters,
Washington, D.C.

Associate Administrator
for Space Flight
Jesse W. Moore †

Level II
Johnson Space Center (JSC),
Houston, Tex.
(STS Integration)

Manager, National Space
Transportation System
Program Office
Arnold D. Aldrich

Level III
Marshall Space Flight Center
(MSFC), Huntsville, Ala.
(STS Components)

Manager, Shuttle
Projects Office
Stanley R. Reinartz †

Manager, Solid Rocket
Booster Project (SRB)
Lawrence B. Mulloy †

Level IV
Morton-Thiokol, Inc. (MTI)
Wasatch, Utah
(Contractor Solid
Rocket Boosters)

Senior Vice President,
Wasatch Operations
Jerald E. Mason †

Vice President, Space
Boosters Program
Joe C. Kilminster †

Vice President,
Engineering
Robert K. Lund

Vice President &
General Manager,
Space Division
Calvin G. Wiggins

Director, Solid Rocket
Motor (SRM) Project
Allan J. McDonald

Engineer
Robert Ebeling †

Engineer
Brian Russell

Engineer
Roger Boisjoly †

Engineer
Arnie Thompson

†No longer with the organization.

Florida for a full teleconference review to begin at 8:45 P.M.

During the teleconference, Boisjoly and his colleagues presented data suggesting, though not conclusively proving, that the joints would fail at such a cold temperature. Specifically, the data indicated that

1. The temperature would be about 25 degrees colder than any previous shuttle launch.

2. Colder temperatures would make the rubber O-rings harder and less resilient.

3. Harder O-rings would take longer to seal.

4. If the primary O-ring did not seat, the secondary seal might not be able to pressurize in time, although the effect was impossible to precisely quantify.

5. Therefore, the prudent choice was to stay within the experience base and simply wait until the temperature reached at least 53 degrees.

The unanimous recommendation of the Thiokol engineers and management, including Senior Vice President Jerry Mason and Vice Presidents Joe Kilminster, Calvin Wiggins, and Bob Lund, was not to launch. Accustomed to NASA's safety-first philosophy, the MTI participants were caught completely off-guard when Larry Mulloy sharply challenged their recommendations, telling them their data were "inconclusive" and didn't "hang together." "My God, Thiokol," he said, "When do you expect us to launch? Next April? The eve of a launch is a hell of a time to be generating new Launch Commit Criteria!" George Hardy at Marshall added that he was "appalled" at Thiokol's recommendation, but said he would not launch over a contractor's objection.

It was the first time in the history of space flight that a contractor's no-launch recommendation had been challenged. Thiokol was placed in the position of proving that a launch would be unsafe (that is, that the joint would fail), when their entire history with NASA had been to establish why a launch was safe. Nearly to a

man, the Thiokol participants would later testify to the significance of this reversal of philosophy.

The managers at MTI temporarily left the conference to discuss the NASA challenge. When asked by Stan Reinartz to respond to Mulloy's comments, Joe Kilminster instead requested, and was granted, a five-minute break in the telecon so that Thiokol could caucus and reassess its data. As the caucus began, Jerry Mason turned to his three vice presidents and softly announced, "We have to make a management decision." Engineers Arnie Thompson and Roger Boisjoly, fearful of an impending reversal, argued with the managers and urged them to stand by their original decision. Although they knew the launch would be unsafe, they were unable to prove absolutely that the joint would not work. They backed away when it was clear that the managers had no intention of listening to them. Thompson testified that he could not understand "why we just couldn't wait another day."

Bob Lund was the sole holdout among the four senior managers, but after 25 minutes he capitulated when Mason asked him to "take off your engineering hat and put on your management hat." A vote was taken of the four senior managers, who then agreed unanimously to launch.

At 11:00 P.M. Thiokol went back to the teleconference and Kilminster announced their reversal to Stan Reinartz, who promptly accepted the new recommendation. When questioned by the commission about his willingness to accept the decision so hastily, Reinartz testified, "Mr. Chairman, when I asked very clearly and very deliberately on the telecon, while all parties were involved, I asked if there were any disagreements . . . and there was no comment, no objection or anything raised at that time.

Larry Mulloy testified, "I did not discuss with Mr. Aldrich the conversations that we had just completed with Morton Thiokol [because] at that time, and I still consider today, that was a Level III [Marshall] issue. . . . There was no violation of Launch Commit Criteria. There was no waiver required, in my judgment, at that time and still today. . . . It was clearly a Level III issue that had been resolved." Stan Reinartz, who was in the reporting channel to Aldrich and Moore, claims he said nothing of the initial recommendation because he concluded: (1) there was no Launch Commit Criteria violation, (2) there was no Level II requirement violation that required that the information be passed upward, (3) there was, in the end, no disagreement concerning the Thiokol launch recommendation from anyone at Level III, and (4) Thiokol and Marshall had "fully and openly examined the concern and satisfactorily dispositioned that concern."

On January 28, 1986, at 11:38 A.M., *Challenger* lifted off on its final voyage from launch pad 39-B. The overnight lows of 8 degrees at the O-ring joint hopelessly compromised the effectiveness of the seals, as predicted by the Thiokol engineers. The seals were vaporized at ignition and only a fragile seal, formed by the products of combustion, kept *Challenger* from blowing up on the pad. Roger Boisjoly and the other engineers who participated in the teleconference at Thiokol breathed a collective sigh of relief, believing they were home free. Sixty seconds later, the fragile seal shattered and hot gases roared through the joint like a giant blow torch directed against the external fuel tank. At T + 73 seconds, the orbiter broke up. Pilot Michael Smith's last recorded words are, "Uh-Oh." The astronauts survived the breakup, but perished when their flight deck slammed into the Atlantic Ocean at a speed of over 200 m.p.h.

It could—and should—have been prevented.

Questions

1. The presidential commission concluded that the *Challenger* decision-making process was "seriously flawed." If that is the case, who is responsible for the "flaw"? From what you have read and seen, who among the following is *most* to blame for the *Challenger* disaster?

   a. NASA senior management (Levels I and II: e.g., Moore, Aldrich)?

   b. NASA middle-level management (e.g., Level III personnel at Marshall Space Flight Center: Reinartz, Mulloy)?

   c. Morton Thiokol senior management (e.g., Mason, Lund, Kilminster, Wiggins)?

2. Was the decision-making process an example of groupthink? Explain.

3. a. Assume that Thiokol had held firm and recommended against the launch. From what you can infer from the case, what do you think would have been the result? Explore all facets and ramifications (for NASA, Thiokol, particular individuals, and so on).

   b. Assuming the decision had been to delay the launch, how could you prove that delaying it was the right thing to do? How would you be able to know you did the right thing?

4. "To the extent that the Presidential Commission faulted the decision-making process that led up to the launch of the *Challenger* and the death of its seven crew members, it was essentially handing down an indictment of the standard operating procedure which characterizes most of our large-scale organizations." Do you agree or disagree? Explain.

5. Was the decision-making process more reflective of the classical or administrative model of decision making?

Source: "Ethical Decision Making: Morton Thiokol and the Space Shuttle Challenger Disaster," © 1990, Mark Maier, State University of New York at Binghamton. Used by permission.

V

Organizational Structure and Processes

If you don't agree with me, it means you haven't been listening.

— Sam Markerich

If you don't say anything, you won't be called upon to repeat it.

— Calvin "Silent Cal" Coolidge

Fama malum quo non aliud velocius ullum (Nothing travels faster than rumor).

— Virgil

LEARNING OBJECTIVES

After studying this chapter, you should be able to:

1. *List the steps in the communication process and name some obstacles to communication.*

2. *Identify common forms of communication in organizations.*

3. *Explain how a group's pattern of communication affects its performance.*

4. *Describe the nature of downward, upward, and horizontal communication.*

5. *Identify roles a person fills in an organization's communication network.*

6. *Describe how the concepts of transactional analysis aid in understanding the messages an organization's members send.*

7. *Identify basic dimensions of nonverbal communication.*

8. *Describe individual barriers to communication.*

9. *Describe organizational barriers to communication.*

10. *List techniques for improving organizational communication.*

Communication

LISTEN TO ME!

After years of working for big restaurant chains, Keith Dunn and two partners formed their own restaurant, which they named McGuffey's. The three men were determined to avoid mistreating their employees, as Dunn felt he had been when he worked for the chains. In contrast, they were determined to make workers feel appreciated.

To do this, they instituted a two-week training program for new employees, gave them a meal after every shift, allowed them the freedom to give away appetizers and desserts, and provided a week's paid vacation each year. The employees responded by working hard and developing a sense of camaraderie. Sales at the first McGuffey's boomed, so the partners opened a second restaurant, then a third.

As the business grew, Dunn and his partners became overloaded with responsibility. They no longer had time for greeting, talking to, or orienting their workers. Said one partner, "You get pulled in so many directions that you just lose touch." Instead, as sales lagged, the partners responded by adding fringe benefits and trying out a variety of incentive programs.

Employees grew resentful as they found it increasingly difficult to communicate with the top. The service they provided often reflected their attitude. Concerned about the restaurants' suffering performance, Dunn sent employees a questionnaire asking them to rate the owners' performance on a scale of one to ten. Dunn had hoped for reassurance, but he was to be disappointed. One questionnaire, then another, rated him a zero. Other employees gave him a one or a two.

At first Dunn was furious: Weren't the employees grateful about all the benefits they were receiving? Eventually, however, he conceded that the evidence of dissatisfaction was overwhelming. He began to make more efforts to listen to his workers.

Dunn created an associate board, a group consisting of two cooks, two servers, and a bartender from each restaurant. This group met with the owners once a month to serve as a sounding board. Initially Dunn made the mistake of also inviting the restaurant managers, who at times retaliated when their staff members complained at meetings of the associate board. Dunn uninvited the managers.

He also instituted employee focus groups, at which employees would meet with an owner. Each employee was to participate in such a focus group at least once every six months.

As Dunn began listening, employee morale picked up. Turnover fell from an embarrassing 220 percent to only 60 percent—about one-fourth the average for the restaurant industry. "You feel like you're a person here," explains Geri O'Brien, a hostess at the Charlotte, North Carolina, McGuffey's.

Listening is an essential part of the process of communicating. This chapter discusses the way communication works and some of the forces that can interfere with effective communication. The chapter concludes with ideas for improving communication in organizations.

Source: Joshua Hyatt, "The Odyssey of an 'Excellent' Man," *Inc.*, February 1989, 63–69.

A MODEL OF THE COMMUNICATION PROCESS

In Chapter 14, we defined true **communication** as the creation of a mental image in the mind of a receiver in exactly the same detail as intended by the sender. There are also many other definitions of communication. For example, Baskin and Aronoff define communication as the "exchange of messages between persons for the purpose of constructing common meanings."[1] Both of these definitions suggest a view of communication that is interpersonal, involving the use of verbal and nonverbal signs and symbols to create understanding.

True, or accurate, communication is often difficult to achieve because it requires a complex sequence of steps: idea generation, encoding, transmitting via various channels, receiving, decoding, understanding, and responding. As the diagram in Figure 16.1 suggests, potential obstacles to successful communication exist at every step. These obstacles, which can be described as noise, barriers, and filters, have the potential to disrupt or alter the communication process.

To illustrate the communication process, consider the example of an inventory control clerk who determines that the supply of labels needed for packaging a product is running low. The *generation of the idea* that labels must be ordered results in the clerk's *encoding* a message consisting of symbols that will convey the desired information. In this case, the clerk's encoded mes-

FIGURE 16.1
THE COMMUNICATION CYCLE

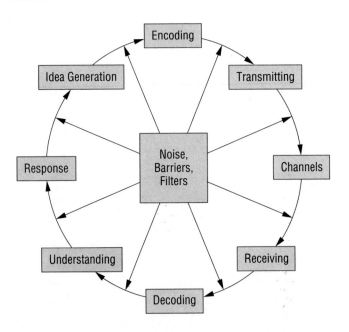

sage is a typewritten form that is sent to the purchasing agent. Encoded messages may also be simple verbal instructions. The encoded message is then *transmitted* via one or more channels. For example, a memo might be transmitted by interoffice mail and a verbal instruction could be delivered personally or over the phone. In addition, several channels may be used simultaneously, as when a person verbally makes a statement and uses appropriate gestures and facial expressions to emphasize its meaning.

Receiving the message involves attending to and actually perceiving a written, spoken, or otherwise transmitted message. Reception is then followed by *decoding,* which involves deciphering the message. The receiver's personality, prior experience, and intellect may intervene at this stage. *Understanding* results from the decoding process. However, understanding is often imperfect. To the extent that the decoded message matches the encoded message, we can say that understanding has been achieved.

The final step in this cyclical process is the receiver's *response* to the communicative effort. This response may take the form of action or inaction. In our example, the purchasing agent may act by ordering more labels, or telling the clerk that labels will no longer be needed because of a change in the packaging process. This response, or action, serves as a form of feedback to the initiator of the process and determines the nature of any subsequent efforts at communication.

Because communication involves so many steps, numerous factors can intervene to confound the process. For example, the encoded message may not accurately correspond to the intended message because of the sender's poor choice of words, or the response may not accurately reflect the intent of the receiver as a result of forces outside of the receiver's control.

As this discussion implies, continually successful communication can be difficult to achieve. This fact contributes to the widespread belief that poor communication is responsible for many problems within organizations and that many larger problems would be resolved if only people tried to improve their communication skills. However, Gary Johns has pointed out that although communication may be at the root of many problems, it is possible to overestimate its role.[2] He contends, for example, that *more* communication is not necessarily *better* communication. Furthermore, difficulties in communication may really be the symptom or outcome of another problem, rather than the cause of the target problem.

To keep the proper perspective, it is crucial to recognize that communication is a social process that includes both perception and influence. The accurate conveyance and reception of a message, plus the impact that the message has on the receiver, are equally important in explaining the phenomenon of communication.

TYPES OF COMMUNICATION

In organizations, there are several common forms of interpersonal communication. By far, the most frequently used form is the spoken word, since it is usually the quickest. In addition, oral communication is likely to be quite accurate because messages can be clarified through ongoing dialogue. Written communication is also important within organizations. Employees devote large portions of their workdays to expressing ideas in written form.[*] Memos, letters, reports, order forms, electronic mail, and the like can serve as permanent records, which enhance their precision and clarity in comparison to oral communication.

A third form of interpersonal communication, **nonverbal communication,** consists of unspoken cues that a communicator sends in conjunction with a spoken or written message. For example, through hand gestures, nodding, and posture, a speaker can underscore his or her spoken words. Sometimes, however, nonverbal cues may seem to contradict the content of the spoken word, as when a speaker smiles while announcing bad news. In such instances, sorting out the intended content can be a challenge for the receiver.

Nonverbal communication may also take the form of symbols. For example, the uniform a person wears or the specific form on which a message is written can convey additional information to the receiver. The topic of nonverbal communication will be examined more closely later in this chapter.

COMMUNICATION NETWORKS

The formal structure of relationships in an organization can affect various aspects of the communication process. Research on the impact of structure on communication has focused on how different kinds of **networks,** or patterns of relationships, influence communication. Of special interest has been the effect of a network's degree of centralization on the communication process. Figure 16.2 illustrates the amount of centralization in five different types of five-person communication networks that have been closely studied. The **centralized networks** are characterized by their members' differing abilities to obtain and pass on information. Note that in each centralized network, information must flow through a pivotal or *central* person (indicated by an X in Figure 16.2). In contrast, in a **decentralized network,** each member has an equal opportunity to participate in the communication process.

The formal study of networks has relied on the creation of experimental conditions in which subjects are placed in cubicles and permitted to communicate only with prespecified members of their group. From such studies, several sets of fairly reliable results have emerged.[4]

Generally, members of decentralized networks report greater satisfaction, while the more centralized a structure is, the lower the satisfaction of its members. Wheel networks generate the lowest satisfaction ratings, while completely connected networks produce the highest ratings. Apparently, the more group members must depend on others for information and decision making, the less they enjoy their participation.

---

[*]In a review of the literature on managerial communication, O'Reilly and Pondy concluded that managers generally overestimate the amount of time they spend reading and writing, and tend to underestimate the amount of time they spend talking.[3]

FIGURE 16.2
FIVE TYPES OF GROUP COMMUNICATION NETWORKS

Centralized

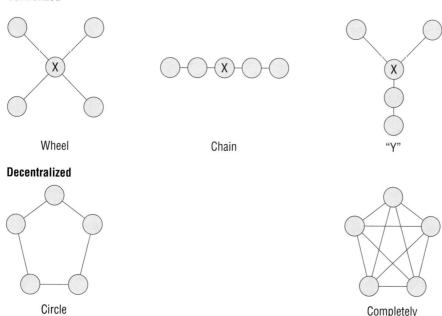

Decentralized

Each circle represents a person and an X indicates the most central position.

The networks also differ in their effectiveness in handling various kinds of problems. For relatively simple and routine tasks, when the goal is to finish a task quickly and make few mistakes, centralized networks are more efficient. But for complex tasks that require the sharing of information, decentralized networks have a relative advantage.

The nature of the task has also been found to influence the formation of a communication pattern. In one study, Faucheux and MacKenzie initially placed subjects in completely connected networks and assigned them several simple problems to solve.[5] Next, they asked the subjects to tackle a set of relatively complex tasks. When the groups worked on the simple tasks, they tended to adopt a centralized structure, converting into a wheel. However, as the tasks became more complex, the persons occupying the more central role felt that the demands on them were too great, and the groups reverted to their original, more decentralized structure.

The appearance of a single leader tends to occur more frequently in centralized networks due to the existence of a hub, or pivotal position. The greater availability of information to the hub occupant, plus the relative dependency of others on him or her for information and decision making, leads to the emergence of the hub occupant as a leader. By being such a critical link in the network, the person in the hub position comes to dominate group accomplishment. Furthermore, this person is typically the most satisfied of the group's members.

Centralized networks are also more prone to information overload. Members who occupy the more central positions experience greater requirements being placed on them to be effective. In a decentralized network, information and, ultimately, decision making are shared. As a result, no single position is easily overloaded.

The implications of the results of communication network research are fairly direct. Communication patterns should be established to best serve the dual purposes of enhancing task accomplishment and group satisfaction. The nature of the task to be performed, to a large extent, dictates the appropriate network, but attention must also be paid to the social consequences of an assigned network or pattern of relationships. Below a certain level, group dissatisfaction can have serious negative effects, including lack of commitment to decisions and increased turnover. Therefore, when selecting a communication structure for a work group, a manager should consider both member morale and the goals of the task.

THE DIRECTION OF COMMUNICATION

In an organization, messages may travel in several directions: downward, upward, and laterally (horizontally).

DOWNWARD COMMUNICATION

Downward communication travels from the upper levels of an organization to the lower levels. Traditionally, such downward flows of communication occur one step at a time, with no intermediate levels excluded. The primary kinds of messages that travel downward in organizations include the job instructions and directives, explanations of tasks and their relationship to other tasks, feedback on individual performance, statements of organizational policies and practices, and statements of mission designed to indoctrinate the members with established goals.[6] Information sent downward often becomes condensed or distorted as it passes through various levels. Therefore, the originator of a downward message should check whether it was accurately received at its intended destination.

Another problem with downward communication is that its recipients tend to interpret it as a sign of dissatisfaction in the upper levels of the organization. This common perception reflects the belief that if upper management takes the time to send a memo, they must have detected an exception to the norm that needs correction.

An Inside Look
Westinghouse's High-Tech Network

At Westinghouse, an advanced computer system enables employees at all levels to communicate through what amounts to decentralized networks. Members of various departments and diverse operations can link into the network to send and receive information throughout the world.

For example, on a Saturday morning, the company's president, Paul Lego, can turn on his home computer and find out how the company is doing in Taiwan, where it is still nighttime. After evaluating the data, he can send it to marketing managers in, say, Texas. Such electronic message sending gives the company a competitive edge in the global marketplace by speeding communications without regard to time zone or distance.

Altogether, the Westinghouse Information Network, as it is called, links more than 600 locations in Europe, Asia, and the Americas. Every day it is used by more than 90,000 people. The

system is an integrated network, which means that it carries voice as well as data transmissions. It provides information for making decisions, selling products, and satisfying customers.

A basic feature of the information network is an electronic mail system, which almost any Westinghouse employee can use to send a message to or receive a message from another employee. The transmitting employee merely enters the message into the computer; the receiving employee can view it on his or her own computer screen when convenient. What is more unusual, employees can tie their home phones into this network, and traveling managers can connect into it with laptop computers or check their messages through voice mail. Not only can the system carry voice messages, it can transmit technical drawings.

Executives also benefit from using the system's video-conferencing technology to hold meet-

ings at which each participant can remain in his or her own office. Higher-quality images and easier-to-use equipment make this technology more desirable than it once was. Besides making life easier for executives, it saves the company money on travel expenses.

Another aspect of the system that is important for internal communications is its EDGE advanced negotiations system. As salespeople carry out complex negotiations, they may need to draw on the knowledge of those responsible for pricing, manufacturing, and delivering the product. The EDGE system includes a database that contains information about each product. Any of the responsible employees can tap into the database, so information can move swiftly among the people who need it. According to Jack Froggatt, manager of information systems for Westinghouse Distribution and Control, this system has "cut the salesperson's negotiation time by 80 percent."

Source: William R. Ruffin, "Wired for Speed," *Business Month,* January 1990, 56–58.

UPWARD COMMUNICATION

Upward communication travels from the lower levels of an organization to the upper levels. The most common kinds of information that flow upward in an organization include suggestions for improving work procedures, information on progress and goal attainment, requests for assistance, and individual reactions to work and nonwork issues.[7]

A number of obstacles may deter upward communication. For example, many employees feel that they will be rebuked if they speak up to their supervisors, and employees who hope to obtain promotions and other rewards are less likely to be outspoken.[8] In addition, like downward communication, upward communication is subject to condensation and distortion.

Upward and downward communication are not simply reverse processes, however. Differences in authority between levels can alter the accuracy, frequency, and effect of these two forms of communication. For instance, lower-level employees are expected to react quickly to communications from above, and high-level employees have the authority to monitor their reactions and issue follow-up orders. On the other hand, higher-level employees are not formally obligated to respond quickly, if at all, to communications from subordinates. In fact, an upper-level employee who is highly responsive to communications from below risks giving the appearance of "letting the tail wag the dog." Furthermore, a lower-level employee is not normally expected to remind superiors of previous messages or to monitor their final reaction to a message. Thus, employees who occupy lower-level positions receive less feedback about the impact of their upward communications than do higher-level employees about their downward communications.

HORIZONTAL COMMUNICATION

Horizontal communication consists of messages sent between employees who occupy the same level within an organization. Examples include communication between members of different departments or between coworkers in a single department. Because employees are grouped into departments, or sometimes work in relative isolation from others who occupy parallel positions, there is typically little opportunity for horizontal communication. Yet, coordination of actions sometimes necessitates that employees communicate quickly without going through the process of sending messages up the organizational hierarchy and then down the appropriate branch.

Some years ago, Henri Fayol suggested that a formal communication channel, or gangplank, should sometimes be laid between units to facilitate cooperation.[9] Figure 16.3 provides an example of how Fayol's gangplank would work. In this situation, units may communicate directly only if they share a linkage, as indicated by the solid lines. If unlinked units wish to communicate, they must send their messages through higher levels of the organization until a shared link is reached. For example, if unit 3 wanted to communicate with unit 11, it would have to route its message up to unit 6, which would then pass the message back down again. To increase speed and accuracy, Fayol would advocate opening a new channel of communication directly between units 3 and 11, as shown by the dotted line.

COMMUNICATION ROLES

The specific functions a person serves in an organization's communication network may constitute his or her **communication role.** Rogers and Rogers have identified four roles that organizational members may play: gatekeeper, liaison, isolate, and cosmopolite.[10]

GATEKEEPERS

A **gatekeeper** is an individual who passes information to others or controls messages. Common examples of gatekeepers are secretaries and assistants to upper-level managers. A gatekeeper who has the ability to control the sub-

FIGURE 16.3
AN ILLUSTRATION OF FAYOL'S GANGPLANK

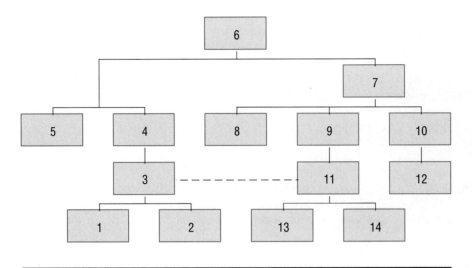

stance and/or the timing of the information that is given to a decision maker can actually influence the final decision.[11] Because the risk of information overload is greater at higher organizational levels, top-level managers come to rely heavily on gatekeepers to condense and edit incoming messages. As a result of this greater trust, gatekeepers tend to have increasing influence at higher levels in an organization.

LIAISONS

An individual who serves as a communication link between groups, but is not a member of either group, is a **liaison.** This person serves as a bridge between groups that need to exchange messages. The gatekeeping function is implicit, to a degree, in the liaison role. Firms that use liaisons to link departments are relatively more effective than firms that do not.[12]

ISOLATES

An **isolate** is someone who has very little or no contact with other members of the organization. Certain jobs, such as night guard and messenger, are characterized by a lack of sustained contact with others in an organization. Yet some people whose jobs offer more opportunities for contact may still remain uninformed. They may consciously choose not to socialize with coworkers or participate in grapevines. Feelings of alienation tend to be associated with such social isolation. Evidence suggests that isolates are somewhat younger, less educated, less satisfied, and poorer performers.[13]

COSMOPOLITES

A **cosmopolite** is a person whose communication network frequently extends into the organization's external environment. By definition, cosmopolites have a greater interest in national, rather than local, affairs and tend to have stronger professional affiliations. They are also more likely to change jobs than are other employees. Like liaisons, cosmopolites can serve a gatekeeping function in that the organization's contact with and information from the outside world must be passed through them.

TRANSACTIONAL ANALYSIS

Eric Berne[14] and Thomas Harris[15] have popularized a simple and useful approach to analyzing interpersonal communication. Although the concepts were used initially in psychotherapy, they have been adopted by organizations to teach employees how to overcome obstacles to effective communication. By relying on terms and concepts that are relatively jargon-free, **transactional analysis (TA)** constitutes a system for understanding the intended and implied messages that people send to each other.

According to TA, each person's personality has three aspects, or ego states: Parent, Adult, and Child. At any given moment, a person acts out of one of these states more than the others.

THE CHILD

The *child ego state* is characterized by immaturity, dependency, and impulsiveness—traits that derive from childhood experiences. Thus, an employee who has an emotional outburst or behaves in a similarly immature manner would be acting out of the child ego state.

THE ADULT

The *adult ego state* is characterized by rational thinking and mature behavior. The experiences of adolescence and adulthood serve as the basis for learning how to behave in a goal-oriented and logical style. This ego state focuses largely on logic and information. In an organizational setting, an employee operates in the adult ego state when he or she gathers facts, generates alternatives, and weighs choices when making logically defensible decisions.

THE PARENT

The *parent ego state* is characterized by authoritarianism and self-righteousness. Sometimes this state may be nurturing, while at other times it may be domineering and controlling. In essence, this state is based on opinions rather than emotions or logic. Supervisors and others act out of a parent ego state when they talk down to employees or adopt a superior, but nurturing, stance.

These three ego states closely mirror the ego states of id, ego, and superego proposed by Sigmund Freud. However, one major difference between the TA ego states and Freud's is that the TA system examines the social interplay between the changing ego states of different people.

When the communication between two people is predictable (for example, if a person acting out of a child ego state is dealing with a person acting out of a parent ego state, the relationship is predictable), it is considered a **complementary transaction.** A supervisor/parent may demand, "Why haven't you turned in your monthly report to me? Can't you handle even the simplest assignments?" To this, the employee/child may respond, "Get off my back. Do you think all I have to do is work on your dumb report?" Other complementary transactions can include child–child, parent–parent, and adult–adult.

Parent–child interactions, although unhealthy for most situations, are believed to be fairly common in organizations because of the formal authority differences that exist between members. Often, the interactions between parent and child ego states appear to be positive. For example, a subordinate may request help on a project in a very submissive and dependent manner, and the superior will agree to help, but will do so in a very superior and paternal fashion. Interactions between two people acting out of their adult ego states are the ideal for organizational settings because, in most business contexts, the logical, problem-solving approach is generally most appropriate. For instance, a superior may ask a subordinate, "Do you have the most recent sales figures?" This adult question would be best answered with an adult answer, such as, "They're not quite ready yet. But as soon as I have them compiled, I will prepare a copy for you."

Noncomplementary transactions occur when an unexpected ego state appears in response to a sender's attempted communication. For example, a manager/adult may say, "Do you have the most recent sales figures?" If, in place of a complementary adult ego state response, this question is met with a child ego state response, such as, "You're not my department head. I'll get a copy of the figures to you when I get around to it," then the transaction is not likely to continue. Noncomplementary transactions cause much of the interpersonal hostility and conflict that occur among organizational members.

Two additional concepts are important to the TA framework: strokes and games. **Strokes** are positive reactions from others, including praise, recognition, and signs of affection. Everyone needs to be stroked. In early childhood, this need demands actual physical contact and stroking from others, but as we grow, the stroking we need becomes more psychological.[†]

Strokes form the basis of social **game playing.** The giving and getting of strokes motivates much of the social interplay of people in organizations. Most of these games are designed to have winners and losers, with the net outcome for the organization being negative because so much time and emotional energy are taken up by such activities.

Based on TA concepts, Fred Luthans and Mark Martinko have identified several common organizational games:

- *Poor Me.* The employee portrays himself or herself to the boss as being helpless, thereby avoiding criticism for poor performance and gaining sympathy.

[†]The notion of strokes can be understood as a simple way of describing the concept of reinforcement (see Chapter 5).

- *Yes, But.* A boss invites participation from subordinates but shoots down each new idea or suggestion by saying "Yes, but . . ." and states reasons why the idea will not work.

- *Hero.* A boss creates situations that employees cannot handle without coming to him or her for help, thereby demonstrating the supervisor's superiority and maintaining the subordinates' dependency.

- *Prosecutor.* Based on details in company regulations or a union contract, an employee creates situations that will force the boss to act in a seemingly arbitrary manner. Then the employee files a grievance or otherwise tries to embarrass the boss.[16]

Transactional analysis is not without its critics, especially since there is not much empirical evidence of TA's validity.[17] Yet the appeal of the approach is very strong, primarily because we know from self-observation that our own thought processes do seem to change from parent to child to adult states across situations and that game playing in organizations unquestionably exists.

NONVERBAL COMMUNICATION

As mentioned at the outset of this chapter, two people can exchange information without the use of words. Through nonverbal communication, people use facial expressions, gestures, manner of dress, and the larger social context to convey silent messages. In popular terms, this type of communication is sometimes referred to as "body language." However, despite the suggestion of several best-selling books on this topic, there is not yet—nor is there likely to be—a "magical way to know employees' or customers' thoughts without having to ask them."[18] There is no precise key for translating nonverbal signals into consistently reliable messages. For example, while a clenched fist may indicate anger, many individuals also clench their fists when they are nervous.

DIMENSIONS OF NONVERBAL COMMUNICATION

Despite these limitations, it is possible to attribute limited meaning to certain general patterns of behavior in many situations. According to Albert Mehrabian, nonverbal communication can be understood in terms of several fairly basic dimensions.[19]

IMMEDIACY   Nonverbal signs may be interpreted in terms of their **immediacy**. Generally, people approach other people and objects that they like and desire, and withdraw from those that they evaluate negatively. This simple concept explains much of the hidden meaning in nonverbal messages. For example, we lean toward someone or ask more questions if we find them interesting or attractive, and we pull away or lean back (or even push our chair back) if we prefer to avoid involvement. When we wish to end a conversation, we often make abbreviated walking-away motions, for example, making little circles as we gradually walk farther away. Such motions are intended to convey the message that we are getting ready to leave (a message that may not be accepted, although it is usually understood, by the other person). Similarly, giving a very firm and long handshake to a person conveys a message of desired immediacy. Too prolonged a handshake, however, can make another person extremely nervous and uncomfortable, especially at a first meeting.

Total attraction toward another person can be understood in terms of the combined effects of the actual spoken words, the vocal expression of the message, and the facial expressions accompanying the message. Spoken words are the actual words in the message and their meaning is self-evident. Vocal expression involves the intonation and inflection in a spoken message.‡ Facial expressions refer to the clearly nonverbal aspects of the message. Mehrabian and Wiener have provided evidence suggesting that the total feeling or reaction one has to another's communication can be understood in accordance with the following approximate equation:[20]

Total feeling = 7% verbal feeling + 38% vocal feeling + 55% facial feeling.

Notice that facial expressions are far more important than verbal content in explaining how people react to a message. Therefore, it is not *what* is said but *how* it is said (that is, facial feeling plus vocal expression) that largely determines meaning. In short, whether the boss is smiling or grimacing while saying you're one of the most unusual employees he or she has ever known makes all the difference!

POWER   A second dimension that enters into the interpretation of nonverbal communication is **power**.[21] Generally, the relative status of individuals can be inferred from how they relate to each other nonverbally. A person of higher status can assume a relaxed posture in the presence of others, but a person of lower status is expected to display a more tense body posture when superiors are present. Asymmetric postures, such as putting your feet on your desk or leaning your head on your arm, are considered acceptable for people of high status but are unacceptable when in the presence of people of higher status. The posture of people of lower status is expected to resemble the military posture of "attention." It has been suggested that the relatively more symmetric body postures of women reflect a lower-status position in society.[22]

Many of the preceding points can be used to explain why people dislike dealing with strangers. The uneasiness that commonly arises from dealing with strangers grows partly out of concern over how the other person will react to us. One study suggests that if a person wants to be liked by others, including strangers, it helps simply to smile more and be more positive in new situations.[23] People differ greatly in their predisposition to be positive or negative when meeting others. Such differences are significant because this predisposition tends to shade the quality of the relationships that later develop.

---

‡Consider how changing the accent in the following sentence can dramatically alter the meaning:
The auditor will be HERE Tuesday.
The AUDITOR will be here Tuesday.
The auditor will be here TUESDAY.

Young people first entering the job market often fail to take advantage of non-verbal ways of conveying interest and positive emotion during job interviews. Many people who might otherwise by very good employees are not hired because they unwittingly convey negativism and dislike to an interviewer by avoiding eye contact and displaying "withdrawing" gestures (as a result of nervousness and self-consciousness). In essence, the greatest need of the "non-verbally handicapped" is an awareness of their own style and the impact that it has on those around them.

PROXEMICS

In his notion of **proxemics,** Edward Hall, an anthropologist, contends that physical space serves an important purpose in communication.[24] People tend to stand at a predictable distance from each other in accordance with the specific roles they occupy. For example, we tend to stand farther away from strangers than from people with whom we are intimate. When we find ourselves thrust together with strangers, as in elevators or on subway trains, we try very hard to avoid giving nonverbal signals that could be interpreted as inappropriate. For example, we do not smile or gaze for very long at a stranger when riding an elevator. If caught staring at someone, we are expected to smile (to show no mean intent) and then to avert our gaze (preferably to watching the elevator's floor indicator or our shoes).

Hall suggests that in the United States there are definable **personal space zones:**

1. *Intimate zone (0 to 2 feet).* To be this close, we must have an intimate association with the other person or be socially domineering.

2. *Personal zone (2 to 4 feet).* Within this zone, we should be fairly well acquainted with the other individual.

3. *Social zone (4 to 12 feet).* In this zone, we are at least minimally acquainted with the other person and have a definite purpose for seeking to communicate. Most behavior in the business world occurs in this zone.

4. *Public zone (beyond 12 feet).* When people are more than 12 feet away, we treat them as if they did not exist. We may look at others from this distance, provided our gaze does not develop into a stare.[25]

Related to the notion of personal space is the concept of **territory.** Unlike personal space, which each of us carries with us, territory is assigned to a specific physical location. In terms of territory, there are many interesting analogies between human behavior in organizational settings and animal behavior. For example, more dominant animals have larger territories than less dominant animals.[26] Dominant animals visit the turf of lesser animals, but lesser animals do not visit the territories of their superiors. If a lesser animal does approach the territory of a dominant animal or the animal itself, it shows signs of nervousness and submission. Similarly, in organizational settings, employees of higher status have larger offices than employees of lower status; supervisors intrude on the work space of employees, but employees do not intrude on the work space of supervisors; and if an employee wants to enter a superior's office, he or she will usually stand at the doorway and ask, "Are you busy?"

In one of his classic works on behavior in work settings, William F. Whyte studied the relations of kitchen workers and other restaurant employees.[27] In the process, he noted that the kitchen workers had a proprietary attitude (akin to a sense of territory) toward the kitchen area itself. If other employees entered the kitchen area, the routine pattern of social interaction was disrupted. Lower-status "invaders" were often openly blocked from entering, while higher-status invaders (who could not be blocked) were tolerated until their departure.

SPATIAL ARRANGEMENTS

The arrangement of furniture, such as desks and chairs, affects the frequency and nature of interpersonal communication. Osmond has suggested that the areas that drive people away from each other should be termed **sociofugal**, while those that bring people together should be termed **sociopetal**. [28] In his studies of hospital waiting areas, he found that arranging furniture around the perimeter of a room was one of the surest ways to decrease social interaction.[§]

Baskin and Aronoff, however, report that simply restructuring the workplace to minimize social communication may not necessarily increase productivity.[30] As an example, they cite the case of a young manager who attempted to increase worker productivity by decreasing the amount of time workers devoted to social interaction. To accomplish this, he rearranged the workers' equipment to make it difficult for them to speak to each other while they were at their posts. Although the amount of social communication on the job did decrease, so did the level of output.

TIME

Although this form of nonverbal communication is more subtle in nature, status can be conveyed by the use of time. The way in which a request is phrased ("As soon as possible . . ." or "At your convenience . . .") implies how urgent the request is and how it should be approached. Arriving late for a social occasion, such as a business meeting or a dinner, may convey any number of different messages, including carelessness, lack of interest, and lack of ambition. Yet, the late arrival of a person of high status invariably reaffirms their relative social superiority. Their tardiness implies that they have a very busy schedule and that others will understand and forgive them. The same generosity does not extend to individuals of low status who are late. People who arrive 15 or so minutes *early* for an event are typically regarded as low in status and also as relatively lacking in sociability.[31]

[§]Intriguingly, the arrangement of furniture in college dormitory lounges tends to be similar to that of dayrooms in mental hospitals.[29]

INDIVIDUAL BARRIERS TO COMMUNICATION

DIFFERENCES IN STATUS

As we have seen throughout this text, status strongly influences people's behavior in organizations. Their willingness to listen to and react to an attempt at communication differs in response to the status of the communicator. Generally, employees are more responsive to, and even solicitous of, communication from people of equal or higher status. Moreover, managers report that they tend to find it more valuable and personally satisfying to communicate with superiors than with subordinates.[32] Given this bias, upward communication is often understandably less effective and less likely to elicit change.

Another barrier related to status is the attempt to convey superiority by using jargon to exclude the uninitiated rather than to clarify a point. Individuals in academia or the professions sometimes use complex phrases to achieve this purpose. To illustrate the silliness of this tendency, Haney has created a "Buzz Phrase Generator" for producing verbose and impressive-sounding but nonsensical phrases.[33] To use the Generator, simply pick any three-digit number from the columns below. For example, the number 262 produces the impressive-sounding but ridiculous phrase "systematized transitional capability."

A	B	C
0. integrated	0. management	0. options
1. total	1. organizational	1. flexibility
2. systematized	2. monitored	2. capability
3. parallel	3. reciprocal	3. mobility
4. functional	4. digital	4. programming
5. responsive	5. logic	5. concept
6. optical	6. transitional	6. time-phase
7. synchronized	7. incremental	7. projection
8. compatible	8. third-generation	8. hardware
9. balanced	9. policy	9. contingency

THE CREDIBILITY OF THE SOURCE

As noted in the discussion of attitude change (Chapter 4), the source of a communication can greatly influence whether the receiver accepts or rejects the message. For communication to be effective, its source should be credible. And a source who combines power and attractiveness with credibility is likely to be an especially effective communicator.

PERCEPTUAL BIASES

According to an old saying, people tend to hear what they want to hear. To be sure, this phenomenon is as common in organizations as it is in society in general. Employees may "tune out" what they do not wish to recognize, which is a form of selective perception keyed to their dominant needs and interests.

When people are confronted with information that they find unsettling or distasteful, they are also likely to ignore it. This process is partly responsible for the failure of employees to accept critical comments during performance appraisal interviews (see Chapter 8).

ORGANIZATIONAL BARRIERS TO COMMUNICATION

INFORMATION OVERLOAD

When an abundance of information is directed to a single position within an organization, decoding and interpreting the messages can become overwhelming. The primary result of such **information overload** is diminished effectiveness. In designing information channels, it is important to consider the amount and complexity of information that can be reasonably handled by one person. In addition, the amount of time it takes to examine and reach an understanding of messages must be taken into account. Two effective ways of eliminating information overload are to encourage employees to screen their messages and to encourage senders to condense their messages and send only essential information.

TIME PRESSURES

The need to take quick action in response to a problem may require that information be sent out or requested on short notice. Such urgency can lead to superficiality and poor timing of communication. For example, data may not be detailed enough or they may arrive too late for employees to act on them. For communication to be effective, it must arrive at an appropriate time, as well as be accurate and complete.

ORGANIZATIONAL CLIMATE

The larger social system within an organization can be a barrier to effective communication. If the climate is one of openness and trust, then incomplete or controversial communications are more likely to be interpreted favorably. But when distrust is the norm, messages may be harshly scrutinized for "hidden meanings," and even good news may be greeted with suspicion and ridicule.

INFORMAL COMMUNICATION

Up to this point, we have focused on formal communication in organizational settings, but most organizations also have numerous pathways of informal communication. Because employees are generally free to exchange information with one another as part of their jobs, little can or should be done to directly control or eliminate such informal communication. Although informal networks may serve useful functions by cutting red tape and leading to greater loyalty through positive social relations, they may also give birth to pathways called **grapevines.**** Although organizational theorists generally regard grape-vines as inevitable outgrowths of organizational structure,[35] most managers believe they have a negative impact on organizational functioning.

Because they are flexible and personal, grapevines may be one of the most rapid communication systems that exist in most organizations. In one out-standing example of the speed of grapevines, Davis found that nearly half the managers in an organization knew within only 13 hours that another man-ager's wife had given birth to a baby (the birth had occurred at 11:00 P.M.).[36] The remarkable speed of grapevines can be attributed to the fact that their messages are oral rather than written. Moreover, people enjoy passing on timely information because it makes them appear in touch and well informed, and there is social value attached to bringing surprising news to others.

Figure 16.4 summarizes three types of grapevines that have been identified by Davis.[37] Some grapevines operate as a single-strand, chain system in which one member tells another, who in turn tells another, and so on. However, such grapevines are actually fairly uncommon. Most organizational grapevines op-erate as a cluster system in which a few individuals inform a cluster, or set, of other people. In one example, over three-quarters of the managers of a firm knew of an executive's plan to resign, but only 11 percent of those managers conveyed the rumor to another person. A third type of grapevine, the gossip

FIGURE 16.4
THREE TYPES OF GRAPEVINE SYSTEMS

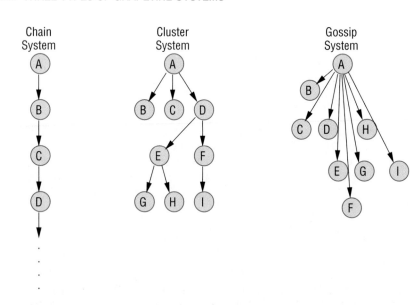

Chain System   Cluster System   Gossip System

****The term *grapevine* is believed to have originated during the Civil War, when telegraph lines were sometimes strung from tree to tree, resembling grapevines. Because of their jerry-rigged nature, these telegraph systems often generated ambiguous and garbled messages. Hence, distorted messages were said to "come from the grapevine."[34]

system, occurs when a single member nonselectively communicates with everyone he or she meets. Most organizational grapevines are cluster systems, with occasional "gossips" rapidly accelerating the rate of spread.

Studies of grapevine behavior have yielded interesting results. One study of the accuracy of 30 rumors dealing with such topics as pay raises, profit sharing, promotions, and transfers found that 16 of the rumors were untrue, 9 were accurate, and 5 were only partly correct.[38] Other studies, however, have indicated that the accuracy of grapevines is usually quite high, especially when the information in noncontroversial.[39] With controversial information, the grapevine can be greatly in error. In light of these findings, it is perhaps not too surprising that a large proportion of employees view grapevines as their central source of information about events within their organizations.[40]

Of the varieties of information that are passed through grapevines, rumors are of special interest. **Rumors** are unverified beliefs that are transmitted from one person to another. Because rumors can harm both individuals and the organization itself, managers must consider how to control and eliminate rumor mills. For example, in one widespread rumor based on a misinterpretation of its corporate logo, which showed a moon and stars, Procter and Gamble was accused of promoting satanism. The company was finally forced to discontinue its use of the emblem. In another case, McDonald's was rumored to be selling hamburgers that contained worms, which forced the company to mount an advertising campaign emphasizing the purity and nutritiousness of its product. These rumors involve customer (rather than employee) perceptions, and show the potential harm that rumors can do to customer relations and possibly sales.

To cope with rumors, DuBrin suggests the following techniques:

1. Try to wait them out. Some rumors dissipate over time and do little actual harm.

2. If waiting does not work, publicly refute the rumor. Refuting and even ridiculing a rumor in public negates its "news value." This approach may also lead people to distrust those who later attempt to pass the rumor along.

3. Feed valid information into the grapevine to counteract the undesired message.[41]

This last point suggests a possible positive feature of grapevines. Managers can use grapevines to serve organizational purposes by "leaking" positive information to grapevine members. For example, through the grapevine, a manager may be able to influence employees' reactions to proposed changes in work procedures.

IMPROVING ORGANIZATIONAL COMMUNICATION

Effective communication of all kinds is crucial to the success of every organization. Chung and Megginson have outlined a number of suggestions for improving the effectiveness of organizational communication.[42]

OB Focus
Contemporary Communication Practice

Organizational communication is heavily influenced by a core group of employees who articulate the sentiments of the larger work force. These individuals are known as peer-opinion leaders, who are adept at persuading fellow workers to share their views. Many organizations are now harnessing the influential power of peer-opinion leaders to create broad support for organizational programs.

Contemporary Communication Practice (CCP), the theory behind peer-opinion leadership, seeks not to exploit workers but to capitalize on the influence of peer-opinion leaders in sending and selling critical messages. Because communication breaks down so easily and is critical to the success of most work projects, the influence of peer-opinion leaders is particularly appropriate for introducing new benefit plans, quality and

productivity programs, customer satisfaction and cost reduction goals, and teamwork initiatives.

To use the efficiencies provided by CCP theory, managers must first identify peer-opinion leaders. It can be difficult to identify individuals who influence the acceptance of communication. Opinion leaders will not necessarily be those individuals who talk the most. Managers must outline strategies for using opinion leaders effectively in order to build a constituency of support among employees. Large organizations should have many peer-opinion leaders to represent the various constituents of the work force.

Peer-opinion leaders have become common because communication easily breaks down in organizations. Widespread organizational restructuring has made employees skeptical of management and cyni-

cal about communications from them. Peers often wield stronger influence than managers. Many employees are flooded with print communication and simply don't have the time to read lengthy memos or letters.

CCP works best when top-down communication is augmented by that from peer-opinion leaders. Peer-opinion leaders are a supplement to, not a substitute for, top-down communication. CCP theory is based on the premise that organizations should rely less on print communication and more on face-to-face communication. Employees should share in the communication process to facilitate acceptance of the communicated message. When employees are involved in the planning and implementation of communication tools, they are more likely to endorse the program being communicated.

Source: David B. Freeland, "Turning Communication Into Influence," *HRMagazine,* September 1993, 93–96.

1. *Use appropriate language.* Words, gestures, and symbols should be appropriate to the receiver's level of understanding.

2. *Practice empathic communication.* The receiver's frame of reference (that is, assumptions and attitudes) should be understood by the communicator.

3. *Encourage feedback.* Two-way communications can improve the communication process. Through feedback, a communicator can check whether a message has been accurately received.

4. *Develop a climate of trust.* Communication is enhanced if the participants have a trusting relationship. Gaining and maintaining the trust of others requires continual effort and the willingness to engage in honest and frank dialogue. At Tandem Computers headquarters, management and employees have regular Friday beer parties to exchange information and ensure that everyone is abreast of what is happening in the company.

5. *Use appropriate media.* Not all forms of organizational communication are equally appropriate for all purposes. Rather, the form of communication should match the situation. Oral communication is best for discussing em-

ployee problems, such as tardiness and poor performance. Written communication is best in matters that require future action, but it is too slow for issues that call for quick action, and too impersonal for discussing employee problems. A combination of oral communication followed by written communication is best for conveying information that requires quick action, job-specific directions, and procedural changes.

6. *Encourage effective listening.* Listening habits can also be improved. Among the techniques that encourage more effective listening are avoiding evaluative judgments, listening to the total meaning of the sender's message, and offering responsive feedback (sometimes called *active listening*) about the listener's degree of understanding. Active listening, which involves restating the speaker's remarks and reflecting on them, conveys the message that the listener is interested in the speaker as a person, and feels that what is being said is important.

7. *Ensure that formal communication efforts are in unison with overall corporate strategy.* At Allstate Insurance Company, a Communication Board (consisting of top management and communication professionals) meets regularly to review public relations efforts as well as internal communication programs involving employees to ensure that the messages being sent are "in synch" with the corporation's overall strategy.[43]

SUMMARY

1. List the steps in the communication process and name some obstacles to communication.
The steps in the communication process are generation of an idea, encoding, transmitting, receiving, decoding, understanding, and responding. Obstacles to communication are noise, barriers, and filters.

2. Identify common forms of communication in organizations.
Common forms of communication in organizations are oral communication, written communication, and nonverbal communication.

3. Explain how a group's pattern of communication affects its performance.
The more group members must depend on others for information and decision making, the less satisfied they are. Centralized communication networks are most effective for quickly and accurately accomplishing simple and routine tasks. Decentralized networks are preferable for complex tasks that require the sharing of information. Centralized networks more often have a single leader. Members of centralized networks are more prone to information overload.

4. Describe the nature of downward, upward, and horizontal communication.
Downward communication travels from the upper to the lower levels of an organization, ideally one step at a time. Upward communication travels from a lower level to upper levels of an organization. Horizontal communication travels between employees who occupy the same level of an organization. Often such communication is informal.

5. Identify roles a person fills in an organization's communication network.

Communication roles consist of gatekeepers, liaisons, isolates, and cosmopolites. Gatekeepers pass information to others or control messages. Liaisons serve as communication links between groups but are not members of those groups. Isolates have little or no contact with other members of the organization. Cosmopolites have communication networks that extend into the organization's external environment.

6. Describe how the concepts of transactional analysis aid in understanding the messages an organization's members send.

In each personality, there are three ego states: (1) parent (authoritarian and self-righteous); (2) adult (rational and mature); and (3) child (immature, dependent, and impulsive). One of these states dominates a person's behavior in any given situation. Complementary transactions (communication that is predictable) can involve parent and child, child and child, parent and parent, or adult and adult. Noncomplementary transactions occur when the receiver of a message reacts with an unexpected ego state. In organizations, adult–adult transactions are generally the most appropriate.

7. Identify basic dimensions of nonverbal communication.

Nonverbal signals may be interpreted in terms of their immediacy (the degree to which people approach or withdraw from others) and the relative status or power of the people in the transaction.

8. Describe individual barriers to communication.

Differences in status inhibit the effectiveness of upward communication. A source that lacks credibility communicates less effectively. Perceptual biases also interfere with communication; specifically, people may tune out messages that are unsettling or distasteful.

9. Describe organizational barriers to communication.

Organizational barriers include information overload (too much information directed to a single position), time pressures, and an organizational climate of distrust.

10. List techniques for improving organizational communication.

Techniques for improving communication in organizations are: using appropriate language; practicing empathic communication; encouraging feedback; developing a climate of trust; using appropriate media; encouraging effective listening; and ensuring that efforts are in unison with overall corporate strategy.

KEY TERMS

Communication	Communication role
Nonverbal communication	Gatekeeper
Networks	Liaison
Centralized networks	Isolate
Decentralized networks	Cosmopolite
Downward communication	Transactional analysis (TA)
Upward communication	Complementary transaction
Horizontal communication	Noncomplementary transaction

Strokes   Territory
Game playing   Sociofugal areas
Immediacy   Sociopetal areas
Power   Information overload
Proxemics   Grapevine
Personal space zones   Rumors

REVIEW AND DISCUSSION QUESTIONS

1. What are the steps in the communication process? Identify those steps in the following example: Bob observes on his computer screen that Ace Carpentry has ordered 200 8-foot two-by-fours from the lumberyard where he works. He prepares an invoice and mails it to Ace Carpentry. At Ace, Judy opens the invoice and writes a check to the lumberyard.

2. What are the characteristics of a centralized communication network? In what situations would a manager want communication to be centralized?

3. What are some potential problems with upward and downward communication? How can managers alleviate these problems?

4. Art director Natasha Blue stopped by the drafting tables to see how work was progressing. "Is that sketch ready for the Morrison Trucking account?" she asked Dennis Green.

   "No, it's not," cried Dennis, "but it's not my fault! People keep coming in here and interrupting me. I can't help it if people keep bothering me."

   "Well, tell them to leave," replied Natasha briskly. "I want that sketch on my desk before you leave here tonight."

   When Natasha had left, Dennis turned to Emily White. "Did you hear that?" he asked. "She's always on my case about something. She just doesn't like me."

   How can Emily explain this transaction to Dennis? What can Dennis do to improve his relationship with his supervisor?

5. How do people interpret the nonverbal messages of immediacy and power?

6. The recipient of a spoken message bases his or her total reaction on the actual words, the speaker's vocal expression, and the speaker's facial expression. Which has the most influence on the recipient's reaction? Which has the least influence? What implications does this have for writing a business letter?

7. Identify the barriers to communication in each of the following situations.

   a. The sales manager sends the vice-president, to whom he reports, a memo describing ways to increase sales. A month later, he still hasn't heard anything.

   b. The new programmer in the company—a recent college graduate—unsuccessfully tries to explain to her colleagues why the system they are developing won't work as effectively as her idea. The department has been developing the system for two years.

8. What are some organizational barriers to communication? How can managers eliminate or reduce these problems?

9. What are some advantages and disadvantages of communications through the grapevine? How can managers cope with rumors?

10. Review the suggestions for improving organizational communication listed at the end of this chapter. Which of these suggestions has your instructor adopted in teaching this course? Which of these suggestions would make the information in this course easier to understand? Which suggestions can you put into practice in your everyday communications?

CRITICAL INCIDENT

A Failure to Communicate

Jeff Williams, M.D., is head of surgery at a major urban hospital. Most of his time is spent in administrative duties such as handling budgets, coordinating facility use, working with staff and resident surgeons, meeting with hospital administrators, serving on hospital committees, and handling complaints.

Dr. Williams relies a great deal on his administrative assistant, Jackie Jones, to handle many of the day-to-day matters. Jackie has worked at the hospital for 12 years, the last 3 in surgery. Dr. Williams has been head of surgery for six months. Because of his position and the nature of surgery, Dr. Williams often works nontraditional hours. He therefore leaves work for Jackie on her desk with brief instructions.

Jackie arrived at work Thursday morning to find a small stack of papers with an accompanying note that read, "Please complete these as soon as possible." Among the papers were a request for transfer and some items concerning the budget. Jackie felt that these were the most important items so she addressed them first. After carefully checking them, she passed them on to a secretary for typing.

It was almost 4:00 and Jackie was preparing to leave. Dr. Williams hurried into her work area and asked for the budget information. Jackie explained that it was being typed and that they would have it sometime the next morning. Dr. Williams became rather agitated because he had a 7:00 A.M. breakfast meeting and needed that information immediately.

Jackie rushed over to the secretary, only to discover that she had not even started typing the budget proposal. Jackie felt there was no other recourse but to type it herself. She returned to her work area to find Dr. Williams waiting. "The budget isn't ready," she explained, "so I'm going to stay and prepare it myself." Dr. Williams was glad to hear that Jackie would have it ready, but he also was concerned that she did not have it available already.

Jackie became rather assertive and said, "Ready now? Nothing in your note said you needed it by this afternoon." Dr. Williams picked up his instruction sheet and said, "It reads, right here, that they should be done as soon as possible."

QUESTIONS

1. What went wrong in the communication process?
2. Which person was in error in terms of failing to communicate?
3. How could this situation have been prevented?

Source: Written by Bruce Kemelgor, University of Louisville.

EXPERIENTIAL EXERCISE

Are You Really Listening?

Listening is probably one of the most important skills anyone can develop. It is used in all interpersonal verbal transactions and is essential for understanding to occur between sender and receiver. Effective listening is more than simply receiving a message, however. Effective listening involves active participation in helping a speaker be understood. Thus, someone who has actively listened has an understanding of both what was said and what was meant.

The skill of active listening involves using responses that do not offer advice or opinion. The response simply captures the listener's understanding of what the speaker is saying and why. This opens up the communication process so that the speaker knows that the listener actually *heard* what was said. A more meaningful conversation, free of initial judgmental roadblocks, can then ensue.

Step 1   Below are some statements that were made by employees to their manager. Read each statement and select the response that best represents active listening by placing an X next to it.

1. Each day brings new problems. You solve one and here comes another. . . . What's the use?
    _____ a. I'm surprised to hear you say that.
    _____ b. That's the way it is. There's no use getting upset over it.
    _____ c. I know it's frustrating and sometimes discouraging to run into problem after problem.
    _____ d. Give me an example so I know what you're referring to.

2. At our meeting yesterday, I was counting on you for some support. All you did was sit there and you never said anything!
    _____ a. I was expecting you to ask for my opinion.
    _____ b. You're evidently upset with the way I handled things at the meeting.
    _____ c. Hey, I said some things on your behalf. You must not have heard me.
    _____ d. I had my reasons for being quiet.

3. I don't know when I'm going to get that report done. I'm already swamped with work.
    _____ a. See if you can get someone to help you.
    _____ b. All of us have been in that situation, believe me.
    _____ c. What do you mean swamped?
    _____ d. You sound concerned about your workload.

4. I've been scheduled to be out of town again on Friday. This is the third weekend in a row that's been messed up!
    _____ a. Why don't you talk with someone higher up and get it changed?
    _____ b. Going on the road must be a burden to you.

_____ c. Everyone has to be on the road—it's part of the job.

_____ d. I'm sure this is the last trip you'll have to make for a while.

5. It seems like other people are always getting the easy jobs. How come I always get the hard ones?

_____ a. You feel I'm picking on you and that I'm being unfair in assigning work.

_____ b. What evidence do you have for saying that?

_____ c. If you'd look at the work schedule, you'd see that everyone has hard and easy jobs.

_____ d. What about that job I gave you yesterday?

6. When I first joined this company, I thought there would be plenty of chances to move up. Here I am, four years later, still doing the same thing.

_____ a. Let's talk about some of the things you could do to be promoted.

_____ b. Maybe you just haven't worked hard enough.

_____ c. Don't worry, I'm sure your chance will come soon.

_____ d. Getting ahead must be important to you. You sound disappointed.

7. Performance evaluations are here again. I wish I could just give all my people good ratings—it sure would be easier.

_____ a. I know, but that's not possible.

_____ b. We all feel that way. Don't get upset over it.

_____ c. Performance evaluations seem to bother you.

_____ d. Just do the best you can.

8. It's the same old thing day in and day out. Any child could do this job!

_____ a. Your work is evidently getting you down and making you feel useless.

_____ b. I always thought you liked your job.

_____ c. What good is complaining going to do?

_____ d. If you've got some ideas on improving your job, I'll be happy to listen.

9. I really appreciate getting the promotion. I just hope I can do the job.

_____ a. Don't worry. I'm sure you'll get better as you get more experience.

_____ b. What makes you think you can't do the job?

_____ c. Don't worry. Most people have those same feelings.

_____ d. I'm sure you can do it, or you wouldn't have been promoted.

10. I'm tired. That last sale really wore me out. I don't think I can handle another customer.

_____ a. Sure you can. Just rest a few minutes and you'll be fine.

_____ b. What have you been doing that's gotten you so tired?

_____ c. You sound like you're exhausted.

_____ d. We all get to feeling that way; don't worry about it.

Step 2   Your instructor has information about the appropriate responses. You can verify your answers with this data.

Notes

1. O.W. Baskin and C.E. Aronoff, *Interpersonal Communication in Organizations* (Glenview, Ill.: Scott, Foresman, 1980), 4.

2. G. Johns, *Organizational Behavior: Understanding Life at Work* (Glenview, Ill.: Scott, Foresman, 1983).

3. C.A. O'Reilly and L.R. Pondy, "Organizational Communication," in *Organizational Behavior,* ed. S. Kerr (Columbus, Ohio: Grid, 1979), 119–150.

4. A. Bavelas and D. Barrett, "An Experimental Approach to Organizational Communication," *Personnel* 27 (1951): 366–371; H.J. Leavitt, "Some Effects of Certain Communication Patterns on Group Performance," *Journal of Abnormal and Social Psychology* 46 (1951): 38–52; M.E. Shaw, *Group Dynamics: The Psychology of Small Group Behavior* (New York: McGraw-Hill, 1976).

5. C. Faucheux and K. MacKenzie, "Task Dependency and Organizational Centrality: Its Behavioral Consequences," *Journal of Experimental Sociology and Psychology* 2 (1966): 361–375.

6. B.L. Hawkins and P. Preston, *Managerial Communication* (Santa Monica, Calif.: Goodyear, 1981).

7. L.W. Rue and L. Byars, *Communication in Organizations* (Homewood, Ill.: Irwin, 1980).

8. A. Vogel, "Why Don't Employees Speak Up?" *Personnel Administration* 12 (1967): 19–23.

9. H. Fayol, *General and Industrial Management,* trans. Constance Storrs (London: Pitman, 1949).

10. E.M. Rogers and R.A. Rogers, *Communication in Organizations* (New York: Free Press, 1976).

11. A. Pettigrew, "Information Control as a Power Resource," *Sociology* 6 (1972): 187–204.

12. P.H. Lawrence and J.W. Lorsch, *Organization and Environment: Managing Differences and Integration* (Homewood, Ill.: Irwin, 1969).

13. K.H. Roberts and C.A. O'Reilly, "Some Correlates of Communication Roles in Organizations," *Academy of Management Journal* 22 (1979): 42–57.

14. E. Berne, *Games People Play* (New York: Grove Press, 1964).

15. T.A. Harris, *I'm OK—You're OK* (New York: Harper and Row, 1969).

16. F. Luthans and M.J. Martinko, *The Practice of Supervision and Management* (New York: McGraw-Hill, 1979), 386–387.

17. D.D. Bowen and R. Rath, "Transactional Analysis in OD: Applications within the NTL Model," *Academy of Management Review* 3 (1978): 79–89.

18. Baskin and Aronoff, *Interpersonal Communication in Organizations,* 102.

19. A. Mehrabian, "Verbal and Nonverbal Interaction of Strangers in a Waiting Situation," *Journal of Experimental Research in Personality* 5 (1971): 127–138; A. Mehrabian, *Silent Messages* (Belmont, Calif.: Wadsworth, 1971).

20. A. Mehrabian and M. Wiener, "Decoding of Inconsistent Communications," *Journal of Personality and Social Psychology* 6 (1967): 109–114.

21. Ibid.

22. A. Mehrabian, "Significance of Posture and Position in the Communication of Attitude and Status Relationships," *Psychological Bulletin* 71 (1971): 359–372; Mehrabian, "Decoding of Inconsistent Communications."

23. Ibid.

24. E.T. Hall, "A System for the Notation of Proxemic Behavior," *American Anthropologist* 5 (1963): 1003–1026.

25. E.T. Hall, *The Hidden Dimension* (Garden City, N.Y.: Doubleday, 1966).

26. R. Ardrey, *The Territorial Imperative* (New York: Atheneum, 1966).

27. W.F. Whyte, "The Social Structure of the Restaurant," *American Journal of Sociology* 54 (1949): 302–308.

28. H. Osmond, "Function as the Basis of Psychiatric Ward Design," *Mental Hospitals* 8 (1957): 23–32; H. Osmond, "The Relationship Between Architect and Psychiatrist," in *Psychiatric Architecture,* ed. C. Goshen (Washington, D.C.: American Psychiatric Association, 1959).

29. S. Van der Ryn and M. Silverstein, *Dorms at Berkeley: An Environmental Analysis* (Berkeley: Center for Planning and Development Research, 1967).

30. Baskin and Aronoff, *Interpersonal Communication in Organizations.*

31. E.H. Marcus, "Neurolinguistic Programming." *Personnel Journal* 27 (1983): 972.

32. E.E. Lawler, L.W. Porter, and A. Tannenbaum, "Managerial Attitudes Toward Interaction Episodes," *Journal of Applied Psychology* 52 (1968): 432–439.

33. W.V. Haney, *Communication and Interpersonal Relations* (Homewood, Ill.: Irwin, 1979).

34. K.E. Davis, *Human Behavior at Work* (New York: McGraw-Hill, 1977).

35. Ibid.

36. K.E. Davis, "Management Communication and the Grapevine," *Harvard Business Review* 31 (1953): 43–49.

37. Ibid.

38. R. Hershey, "The Grapevine—Here to Stay but not Beyond Control," *Personnel* 20 (1966): 64.

39. E. Walton, "How Efficient Is the Grapevine?" *Personnel* 15 (1961): 45–49; Davis, *Human Behavior at Work;* B. Marting, "A Study of Grapevine Communication Patterns in a Manufacturing Organization" (Ph.D. diss., Arizona State University, 1969); E. Rudolph, "A Study of Informal Communication Patterns Within a Multi-Shift Public Utility Organization Unit" (Ph.D. diss., University of Denver, 1971).

40. W. St. John, "In-House Communication Guidelines," *Personnel Journal* (1981): 877.

41. A.J. DuBrin, *Foundations of Organizational Behavior* (Englewood Cliffs, N.J.: Prentice-Hall, 1984).

42. K.H. Chung and L.C. Megginson, *Organizational Behavior: Developing Managerial Skills* (New York: Harper and Row, 1981), 203–204.

43. D. Craib, "Allstate's Communication Strategy: It's a Tool for Growth," *Communication World,* May 1986, 24–26.

17

Properly organized, even crime pays.
— Jim Fisk and
Robert Barron

Corporation: an ingenious device for obtaining individual profit without individual responsibility.
— Ambrose Bierce

No man can serve two masters.
— Matt. 6:24

LEARNING OBJECTIVES

After studying this chapter, you should be able to:

1. *Define decentralization and identify strengths and weaknesses of a decentralized organization.*
2. *Contrast tall and flat organizations.*
3. *Describe unity of command and chain of command.*
4. *Describe the six systems in the behavioral approach to organizational design.*
5. *Describe the relationship between technological and social systems in an organization.*
6. *Describe modern organizational designs.*
7. *Discuss advantages and disadvantages of different organizational designs.*

Organizational Design

P&G's REDESIGN

Procter & Gamble, the corporation known for virtually creating consumer marketing, found that its success required the company to re-create itself. During the mid-1980s, the once phenomenally successful company's profits were beginning to suffer, and leading products such as Crest and Pampers were losing market share. Observers blamed the company's massive size and cumbersome bureaucracy.

Under the leadership of then-CEO John Smale, P&G began to reorganize so that it could respond more quickly to changes in the marketplace. The company started with its sales force. The original system used 11 national sales forces, each selling a single product line such as foods or detergents. This meant that P&G's customers—retail stores—had to meet with different salespeople, all from the same company, but each selling different product lines and using different promotions. The system was awkward for retailers, but P&G was such an important supplier that they put up with the arrangement.

The restructured sales force is based on servicing customers, rather than on pushing products. Under the reorganized system, teams of representatives from finance, distribution, manufacturing, and other functions are assigned to cover the large retailers. The teams move beyond writing up sales to helping these customers improve inventory, distribution, and sales promotion. For example, a team working with Wal-Mart helped that retailer set up a just-in-time inventory system for Pampers and Luvs diapers. When a store's stock of diapers runs low, it transmits an order to a P&G factory via computer; the factory responds by automatically shipping more diapers to the store.

Having reorganized P&G's sales force, Smale turned to the company's celebrated brand management system. At the heart of this system are brand managers, coveted positions responsible for every aspect of a brand, including marketing, advertising, sales, and product development. In the old structure, each brand manager reported to a division head, which meant that each division head had to keep track of the activities of as many as 14 brand managers.

To have a major decision made, a brand manager might have to go through three or four layers of management. One manager reports that he had to wait a year just for approval of a simple change in package design. Furthermore, the brand managers were so focused on a single product that they might use tactics that hurt another P&G product, and no one was able to referee the harmful competition. Says a former employee, "There was a lot of cannibalization. You'd issue coupons at the same time for P&G's liquid and powdered detergents."

Therefore, Smale developed an organizational structure called category management. He divided the company into 39 product categories and assigned them to 26 category managers (some have more than one category). Brand managers report to a category manager, who is responsible for the profitability of the entire product line—for example, all laundry detergents, including Tide, Cheer, and Ivory Flakes. This category manager must ensure that decisions are for the benefit of the entire product line. The category management system also speeds up decision making by authorizing the category managers to make decisions involving expenditures of up to $1 million per project.

These changes are designed to reduce the number of layers of management required for decision making. Says Smale, "The creation of these category profit centers was really a continuation of the basic philosophy that small is good, that you bring focus to a

(continued on following page)

(continued from previous page)
specific business when you create a stand-alone operation."

As Procter & Gamble's executives have found, the way an organization is structured is an ongoing concern. Sometimes a structure appropriate for the company's early years must be changed. This chapter describes some characteristics of the designs that organizations adopt. It also discusses advantages and disadvantages of different organizational designs.

Source: Brian Dumaine, "Marketing Rules," *Fortune,* November 6, 1989, 34–36+.

In the previous chapters of this text, we examined concepts that apply to either individuals or small groups of individuals in organizational settings. In this chapter, we will turn our focus to the impact that the organization has on behavior. Thus, while the previous chapters emphasized the micro aspects of organizational behavior, this chapter will look at some macro influences. In this context, the terms *micro* and *macro* refer to different levels of analysis or conceptualization. The *micro level* examines conditions and processes from a more individually oriented perspective, while the *macro level* deals with conditions and processes involving organizations and the external environment.[*]

In this chapter, we will consider initially the major principles of organizing. Next, we will examine the classical, behavioral, and sociotechnical views of organizational design. Then, we will examine some contemporary notions of organizational design.

PRINCIPLES OF ORGANIZING

Organizations can be described in terms of how their component parts are put together and operate. Researchers who study the concepts of organizational structure and function frequently describe organizations in terms of several important dimensions: decentralization versus centralization, tall versus flat structure, unity of command, and chain of command.

DECENTRALIZATION VERSUS CENTRALIZATION

Decentralization is the degree to which decision making occurs lower down in an institution. In a more centralized institution, there is relatively less participation by employees in a variety of decisions. Decentralized organizations are characterized by less monitoring or checking on decisions made by employees.

It is especially difficult to measure the extent of decentralization that exists in an organization. To be sure, we cannot rely on the statements of top management regarding the extent of decentralization present in their own corporation, since executives tend to endorse the value of decentralization and to perceive its existence. One particularly useful means of assessing the degree of decentralization is to examine the dollar amount of expenses employees are permitted to incur without prior approval by a superior. Generally, the larger the amount of latitude allowed employees on expenditures, the greater the ex-

---

[*] It has been humorously suggested that the micro approach to OB examines employees as if the organization did not matter, while the macro approach to OB examines organizations as if the employees did not matter.

tent of decentralization that may be inferred. In addition, the variety and magnitude of decisions made outside of the top or central office can provide an index of the degree of decentralization.

Although the concept of decentralization has acquired a positive halo,[†] it is not reasonable to endorse the notion of decentralization for all organizations and all situations. Most organizational researchers believe that it is best to think in terms of an optimal level of decentralization for any given organization or its divisions. The identification of the specific forces that dictate the optimal level of decentralization has been a focus of much macro-level research.

Robert Duncan has offered a number of possible weaknesses associated with decentralized organizational structures:

1. Because of a lack of integrative and coordinated direction, there is a tendency to focus on current problems and functions, and to ignore opportunities for growth and innovation.

2. Shared resources (such as computer equipment, staff, and lab facilities) may pose problems because of the need to allocate their usage. Similarly, shared functions (such as research and development and purchasing departments) may create coordinating difficulties.

3. Internal disputes and conflicts may arise. These conflicts may not be easily resolved because each department or division operates with relative independence. Also, potential disputes between units are not as likely to be detected, averted, or well managed if the actions of units are not coordinated.[1]

As these points imply, extreme decentralization can lead to a lack of needed integration and coordination. Nonetheless, decentralization is often touted as a beneficial organizational attribute because of its anticipated enhancement of employee motivation, performance, satisfaction, and creativity. According to this popular line of reasoning, the greater level of autonomy that decentralization affords to employees leads to greater employee involvement and commitment. As a consequence, employees' attitudes and performance are enhanced. Many successful organizations have relied heavily on being decentralized. For example, Digital Equipment Corporation, following the philosophy of its founder, Kenneth H. Olsen, achieved significant growth in large part because of a decentralized organization structure that gave each senior manager substantial responsibility for an individual product line.[2] Evidence in the areas of job enrichment and self-directed work teams (see Chapter 7) generally confirms the positive impact of increasing employees' self-direction and sense of responsibility. Of course, studies in these areas have not typically attempted the sweeping changes that a radical decentralization of an entire organization implies. Hence, the limits of decentralization (that is, the

---

[†] One of the earliest "success stories" of the use of decentralization is reported in the Old Testament. In Exodus 18, Moses is reported to have been overburdened by judicial decision making. On the advice of his father-in-law, Jethro, Moses restructured the process so that a system of judges took responsibility for making many minor decisions.

dysfunctional effects due to the lack of integration and coordination of efforts) have not been carefully studied.

TALL VERSUS FLAT STRUCTURES

Tall structure versus **flat structure** refers to the number of levels of authority and the width (or size) of each level. Tall organizations have more levels, while flat organizations have fewer levels. Figure 17.1 provides examples of both types of organization. Note that the tall organization has five levels of management, while the flat organization has three. Also, both organization structures used in the figure happen to involve the same number of units, 31. Thus, configuration rather than size determines the tallness of flatness or a structure.[‡]

Tall and flat structures also differ in terms of the span of control they employ. **Span of control** refers to the number of employees who report to a single supervisor and thus partially dictates the height of an organization. In the tall organization depicted in Figure 17.1, the span of control is two; in the flat organization, it is five. It can be said that the span of control partially dictates the tallness of the organization. Therefore, the question can be raised, "What

FIGURE 17.1
EXAMPLES OF TALL AND FLAT STRUCTURES

Flat Organization

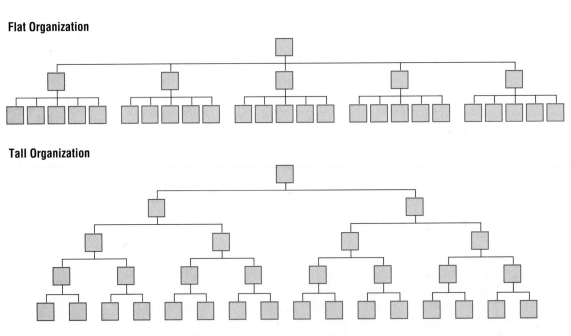

Tall Organization

[‡] Noted management consultant Peter Drucker recommended (in 1954) that seven layers of administration is the maximum necessary for any organization. Thomas Peters, another widely read consultant, insisted that five layers is the maximum for a large organization (based partly on the reasoning that five administrative layers are employed by the Catholic church to oversee 900 million members). For less sizable organizations, Peters recommends three administrative layers as the maximum.[3]

OB Focus
Centralized Structure Positions Ford for Changes in Europe

Trade barriers are coming down in Western Europe. This economic restructuring should bring about a new generation of winners and losers among the companies who do business there. In the auto industry, the changes are expected to bring in more outside manufacturers, especially from Japan. Many companies are likely to establish European subsidiaries, in case the European countries band together to limit imports from outside the European Union.

One company that is expected to be a winner is Ford Motor Company. Ford has production facilities in six European nations, including Spain and Portugal, where labor costs are low. Each of these plants is large enough to serve all of Europe. For example, Ford's trans-

mission plant in the Bordeaux region of France is the region's largest exporter, surpassing even the wine for which Bordeaux is famous.

What is especially important for Ford's competitive edge is the centralized structure of these operations. Under the coordination of Ford of Europe headquarters, the company routinely ships components and assembled vehicles from one nation to another. This setup parallels Ford's North American operations.

This arrangement is no accident. Back in 1967, when it first appeared that the West European nations were headed toward economic unity, Henry Ford II concluded that the company should function as if there were one European market. In response, the

company consolidated its assembly operations and built giant plants to replace older, smaller facilities. Ford continued to use national sales forces, but placed them under the authority of Ford of Europe.

This arrangement made Ford's European operations profitable when performance in the United States was suffering. But most important for the future, the company has already had practice in manufacturing and distributing its cars on a continental scale. Michael Coleman, an attorney with Baker and McKenzie, a law firm specializing in European trade issues, calls Ford "the archetype of the true European firm."

Source: Michael Arndt, "Ford Is Providing a Model for Conquering New Europe," *Chicago Tribune*, December 11, 1989, sec. 4, pp. 1, 4.

is the ideal span of control?" The most widely used logic on this point argues that spans can be larger at lower levels in an organization than at higher levels. Because subordinates in lower-level positions are typically doing much more routine and uniform activities, more subordinates can be effectively supervised at lower levels. In fact, larger spans are often found at lower levels in organizations. However, there is a tendency in many organizations characterized by very large spans (for example, 20 or more subordinates) to employ informal team leaders within a unit. These informal team leaders report to the unit's supervisor. Yet, they may not be officially recognized as a layer of management within the organization. The informal team leader approach allows a supervisor to expand the number of subordinates he or she can effectively supervise and at the same time not create a cumbersome layer of management.

Generally, a taller organization, with its narrower spans of control, allows for closer control of subordinates in that supervisors have more time to devote to monitoring fewer individuals. Therefore, tall organizations tend to discourage decentralization, while flat organizations are more predisposed to use decentralized decision making.

In terms of overall performance, it has traditionally been assumed that tall organizations are superior to flat organizations. However, research conducted by James Worthy on Sears, Roebuck and Company has challenged this assumption.[4] He observed that those Sears stores utilizing flat structures had relatively better sales, profitability, and employee job satisfaction than stores with taller structures. These results suggest that larger spans of control may produce positive advantages. The precise mechanism by which such gains can be achieved is not clearly understood as yet. However, it is likely that flatter structures possess greater decentralization, and decentralization serves as the driving force for improving employee performance and attitudes.

While flatter structures may have some unanticipated advantages, they also can be the source of disadvantages. When carried to an extreme, "flatness" can be dysfunctional. As an illustration, consider the following case of a small, family-owned construction company. The firm initially did relatively simple repair jobs and modest home improvement projects. Soon business improved, and the founder needed to hire additional workers. These workers had to be supervised in teams, since the several groups were geographically dispersed when working on various projects. Eventually, a full-time accountant was needed to handle the financial side of the enterprise. Then, a sales manager was hired to prepare newspaper and radio ads, to meet with clients, and to close deals. Next, a full-time engineer was employed by the firm to draw up and modify construction plans. As business continued to improve, the owner discovered that it would be better to stock and maintain an inventory of needed materials rather than depend on other sources for supplies. The creation of the resulting warehouse operation afforded a new opportunity for revenues: People in the area came to the warehouse to purchase home repair and improvement materials (such as nails, siding, and lumber). As a result, the owner set up a successful outlet store as part of the warehouse operation.

At about this time, he came to recognize that running the firm was simply too burdensome for one individual. The structure of the organization was totally flat. All divisions of the enterprise reported to one person, the company's founder. Whenever a decision had to be made (regarding, for example, how much lumber to stock, whether to start a large project, or the hiring of construction workers), the owner felt obliged to make the decision. As a result, employees were continually approaching him with major, and many minor, issues. As his workweeks came to exceed 80 and 90 hours, the company's founder called in a consultant to recommend ways of improving efficiency and helping him to cope with the demands of the job.

The consultant's recommendation was to redesign the organization so that it would be taller. Specifically, he recommended that two managers be appointed, one to oversee warehouse/office operations and the other to oversee the construction/sales side of the firm. Figure 17.2 illustrates the original and the redesigned organization structures for the firm. As the figure shows, the newer, taller structure affords greater control of each unit because of reduced spans of control. In addition, the founder no longer must coordinate the efforts of a large number of diverse units.

Alternatively, the founder could have tried delegating decision-making authority to the various units (that is, decentralizing the operations of the firm). Instead, he opted for the taller structure, which helped to increase rather than decrease his control of the firm. Given the high personal financial stakes involved in running a firm, it is not uncommon to find that founders are predisposed to seek greater personal control.

FIGURE 17.2
ORGANIZATIONAL STRUCTURES FOR A CONSTRUCTION FIRM

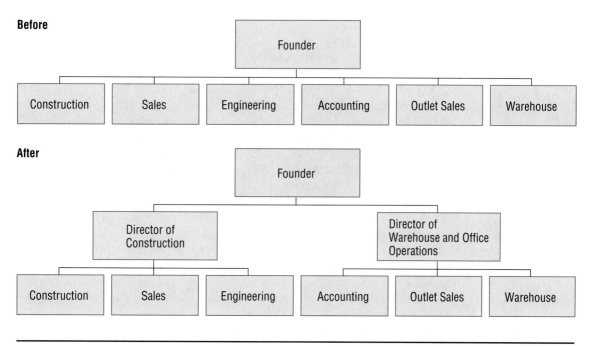

UNITY AND CHAIN OF COMMAND

Unity of command and chain of command are two further principles of organizing. **Unity of command** means that every subordinate should have one and only one supervisor—that is, each subordinate is accountable to and takes orders from a single supervisor. As you might imagine, this notion is intended to improve performance by reducing potential conflicts and ambiguities that might arise if a subordinate dealt with several superiors. By clearly assigning each subordinate to a specific superior, speed of response to problems and information flow should be optimum.

It has long been assumed that unity of command is a cornerstone of organizational efficiency. However, the notion that unity of command must not be violated has recently been challenged by the matrix system, a modern and innovative organizational structure that we will examine more closely later in this chapter.

Chain of command is concerned with the flow of information and authority within an organization. As a principle, chain of command means that information and authority should proceed from level to level in a strict hierarchical fashion without omitting an intermediate level. The need for downward flow of authority is, of course, easy to understand. The converse process, a bottom-up flow of authority, while still within the logic of chain of command, is generally not implied when the term *chain of command* is invoked. Flow of information, however, can be upward or downward within the chain of command. What is critical to the concept in terms of information flow is that each succeeding level of management be completely informed.

The suspected advantages of strict adherence to the chain of command principle are that no higher level of management will be uninformed and that appropriate levels are involved in seeking common goals. By following a chain of command approach, coordination of effort and integration of activities should be more easily achieved. Although it is not widely invoked, a further reason for following chain of command involves simple courtesy to superiors and subordinates. Generally, it is best not to omit or "end-run" individuals within the chain of command, since they are likely to learn about it informally and be resentful of not having been informed or involved in the process.

Organizations differ in the extent to which chain of command is strictly followed. In organizations where uniformity of mission and purpose are important (such as in maintaining orthodoxy in a religious organization), chain of command is likely to be more firmly engrained as a practice. Similarly, in organizations where coordination of effort is highly valued, such as the military, chain of command is also closely followed. Less formally structured organizations (such as voluntary associations or social clubs) may have less serious need to follow the chain of command principle strictly.

THE CLASSICAL APPROACH TO ORGANIZATIONAL DESIGN

In the early part of this century, Max Weber, a German sociologist, outlined a systematic view of organizations based on the notion of bureaucracy. Weber suggested that **bureaucracy** was the best administrative form for the rational and efficient pursuit of organizational goals.[5]

According to Weber, a perfect bureaucracy possesses:

1. *Rules and procedures.* Weber believed that a rational approach to managing tasks should be the dominant principle in organizations. In a bureaucracy, standard operating procedures provide greater certainty and aid in coordinating efforts.

2. *The principle of hierarchy.* In Weber's model, positions are arranged hierarchically, with the lower positions controlled and supervised by the higher ones. Such an arrangement helps to maintain control over the members of the organization and ensures order. In essence, Weber advocated a clear chain of command or hierarchy of authority.

3. *Division of labor and specialization.* Tasks should be broken down and assigned to employees. Each employee should have the expertise needed to master his or her work assignment. The obtainment of such expertise would be aided by making certain that each work assignment is highly specialized. In addition, each employee should be given the authority and resources to perform his or her duties.

4. *Impersonality.* In the idealized bureaucratic system, managers would maintain an air of impersonality toward employees, especially subordinates. This impersonal attitude would help to ensure that rational considerations were the basis for decision making, rather than favoritism or personal prejudice. Maintaining such a formal atmosphere would also make it easier to evaluate employees solely on the basis of actual performance.

5. *Competence.* Technical ability and expertise should be the basis for hiring, job assignments, and promotions. Possession of relevant qualifications and evidence of merit rather than family ties or friendship would determine the receipt of rewards.

6. *Record keeping.* People's memories enable them to recall the outcomes of past dealings with their surroundings and thereby adjust their future conduct in order to obtain advantages. Organizations can, in a sense, possess memories through the maintenance of written records. Such documents enable the organization's members to check on past performance and to record decisions and rules. Written records also aid in the creation of a base of information for training employees to perform specific tasks.

AN ASSESSMENT OF WEBER'S VIEW

Weber advocated the bureaucratic form as an ideal approach to structuring organizations. Clearly, the widespread presence of bureaucracies throughout our nation and the world attests to the appeal of his principles. Yet the many positive aspects of the bureaucratic form are offset in practice by some negative features, as summarized in Table 17.1.[6]

One major drawback of bureaucracy stems from its *emphasis on authority.* Managers in bureaucratic organizations are often unwilling to surrender their authority and are typically interested in acquiring more power. They may also use their authority to preserve their own territory and eliminate challenges. For example, managers in a bureaucracy frequently resist proposed changes in rules and procedures. As a result, bureaucracies can be characterized as *conservative and inflexible,* characteristics that discourage innovation.

Reliance on rules and the maintenance of an impersonal attitude can lead to other dysfunctions, including the inability to cope with unique cases that do

TABLE 17.1

POTENTIAL PLUSES AND MINUSES OF BUREAUCRACY

Pluses	Minuses
Control	Barriers to change
Order	Reduced employee satisfaction
Efficiency	Reduced discretion
Stability	Red tape
Memory	Power seeking
Rule by reason	

not "fit the mold" and for which the rule book does not dictate a solution. Impersonality can also lead to feelings of *frustration* for people who must work in or with a bureaucracy due to the system's lack of a "soft side" or "human face." In addition, the emphasis on rules and procedures can produce *excessive red tape*. The creation of new rules to cover emerging situations and new contingencies can make the official procedures, delays, and inaction of such systems virtually unbearable.

Highly specialized task assignments can lead to feelings of *alienation* or *estrangement* among employees, and the related lack of challenge and novelty can lead to dissatisfaction and turnover. As discussed in Chapter 7, people generally prefer jobs that are not highly fragmented or specialized. Because competence can be difficult to measure in bureaucratic jobs and because a high degree of specialization enables most workers to master their required tasks in little time, there is also a tendency to *base promotions more on seniority and loyalty* than on competence and merit.

For many of us, the term *bureaucracy* has a negative connotation. It conjures up a vision of a large unfeeling institution that is frustrating to deal with. Among the organizations that fit this negative stereotype are agencies of the federal government, such as the Internal Revenue Service and the Defense Department, and state and local government agencies, such as boards of education.

But despite the problems they may create, bureaucratic characteristics have also been associated with positive measures of organizational performance. Specifically, it has been found that greater degrees of bureaucracy (when controlling for differences in the size of various organizations) are associated with higher levels of performance. Organizations that try to maintain a more informal structure do less well if they are relatively large. Smaller organizations of less than roughly 2,000 members tend to have better performance records when they are less bureaucratic.[7] Figure 17.3 portrays this relationship.

Richard Daft suggests that certain organizational attributes dictate that bureaucratic characteristics be avoided.[8] For example, smaller organizations should try to maintain informality by reducing rules and red tape, and they should use face-to-face interactions as the basis of supervision.[9] Professionals do not respond well to bureaucracies either. As a result of their training and the prevailing norms in their fields, researchers, technical specialists, consultants, and the like prefer freedom from rules and procedures. Finally, organizations that are experiencing a high rate of environmental change need to be more free flowing and flexible. A bureaucracy would be too slow moving for organizations that need to adapt frequently or quickly to meet constant changes in customer needs or innovations in technology.

In summary, bureaucracy offers many advantages for improving organizational performance. These benefits can be best realized in larger organizations that function in relatively stable environments and employ workers who are tolerant of the limitations of bureaucracy.[§]

[§] Resistance to bureaucracy may also stem from individual differences in the ability to adjust to the characteristics of bureaucracy. People who react to bureaucracy with strong suspicion due to their own immaturity may be termed *bureauotics;* those who suffer from "bureausis" rarely rise very far in an organization's hierarchy.[10]

FIGURE 17.3
RELATIONSHIP BETWEEN SIZE OF ORGANIZATION, BUREAUCRACY, AND
PERFORMANCE

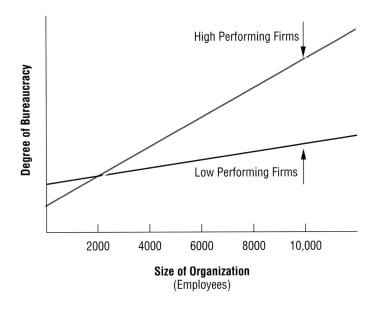

Source: Adapted from John Child, "Managerial and Organizational Factors Associated with Company Performance, Part II. A Contingency Analysis," *Journal of Management Studies* 12 (1975): 12–27.

THE BEHAVIORAL APPROACH
TO ORGANIZATIONAL DESIGN

Given the speed of technological change, an increasing rate of innovation, and growing demands by a more highly educated work force, many scholars suggest that the classical view of organizations will become outdated. In response to the resulting frustration, bureaucracies will begin to fade away and will be replaced by more creative forms of organization. Rensis Likert, a proponent of a behavioral alternative to the bureaucratic approach, has proposed a multi-level classification of organizations (Figure 17.4).[11]

Each of the systems can be characterized in terms of a number of attributes. A System 0 organization is a permissive type of organization characterized by large spans of control and substantial confusion. It might best be characterized as an organization that is in an early, formative stage.

A System 1 organization relies mostly on fear and punishment to motivate employees. Distrust is likely to be high in such organizations, and employee satisfaction low. Because authoritarianism prevails, employees are not consulted before decisions are made.

In a System 2 organization, rewards are used to motivate employees and employees are permitted to comment on directives, but managers still control

FIGURE 17.4
LIKERT'S SIX SYSTEMS OF ORGANIZATION

System 0 Permissive	**System 1** Exploitive Authoritative	**System 2** Benevolent Authoritative	**System 3** Consultative	**System 4** Participative	**System 4T** Total Participation

the decision-making process. Employees may have some freedom in how they conduct their jobs, yet their relations with superiors are guarded and cautious.

In a System 3 organization, subordinates are more readily consulted; however, major decisions are still made by upper management. Threats are avoided as a means of motivating employees, and there is a degree of trust between managers and subordinates. Employee performance and satisfaction are expected to be higher in this system than in Systems 1 and 2.

System 4 is viewed by Likert as an ideal state toward which managers should try to move their organizations. Trust is extremely high among System 4 members, and a variety of economic, ego, and social factors are used as incentives. Communication moves not only downward but also upward and horizontally. Most critically, decision making occurs at all levels and involves all members equally. In a sense, System 4 approaches a democratic, or highly participative, form in that the input of employees is fully incorporated in the decision-making process. As a consequence of these positive attributes, Likert predicted that both employee performance and satisfaction would be greatest in a System 4 organization.

System 4T is a somewhat idealized type of organization in which authority is based on intragroup relationships and overlapping group memberships instead of on a hierarchy. The *T* stands for *total* participation, and implies stable and strong working relationships among members.[12] Performance and employee satisfaction should be maximal in this type of organization.

Research on the accuracy of Likert's model is sparse. In a review of the available evidence, Miner suggests that the model may work best at the level of the work group, since it is largely stated in terms of work group processes.[13] Furthermore, the accuracy of the model probably depends on particular circumstances.[14] However, the model is not sufficiently specific to help a manager identify the appropriate circumstances in advance.

Although Likert's view has value as a guide to consultants who wish to bring about organizational change, one of its underlying premises is difficult to accept. Likert assumed that a single, best solution exists for all settings, an assumption that also underlies Weber's advocacy of the bureaucratic form. As a result, both Weber's and Likert's approaches can be viewed as being somewhat simplistic.

An Inside Look
Restructuring for Customer Service

Likert probably would have approved of the changes instituted in the organizational structure of United Technologies Corporation by Robert F. Daniell, the company's chief executive. In an effort to get managers and workers to assume greater responsibility for satisfying customers, Daniell has been transforming the company from what was in effect a System 1 (exploitative-authoritative) organization to more of a System 4 (participative) organization.

The changes are especially apparent at UTC's subsidiary, Pratt & Whitney Company, which makes jet engines. There, in the two years since the restructuring began, orders have ballooned eightfold.

In the past, autocratic management and an overly intricate bureaucracy left employees with little power to get things done. For example, if the Pratt & Whitney workers making an airplane want to mount an engine a fraction of a millimeter closer to the wing than the blueprint specifies, a good engineer could normally look at the blueprint and decide whether the change would work. But under the old company structure, such a change would have to be approved by nine departments as well as a committee that met only once a week.

Under Daniell's leadership, the company whittled away much of this paperwork. Now a design engineer can make such a decision after obtaining three signatures. Consequently, average response time for approving changes has plummeted from 82 days to 10, and the backlog of requests has shrunk from 1,900 to less than 100.

Employee participation in decision making extends to the company's service representatives in the field. In the past, approval for warranty replacements costing millions of dollars had to come from company headquarters, which could take weeks. Airframe makers that used parts from Pratt & Whitney had to shut down their assembly lines as often as 40 times a month waiting for parts from the company. Under the restructuring, field reps were given authority to authorize replacements on the spot. Now the company causes only an average of two work stoppages a month.

Source: Todd Vogel, "Where 1990s-style Management Is Already Hard at Work," *Business Week,* October 23, 1989, 92–94+.

THE SOCIOTECHNICAL SYSTEMS APPROACH

Eric Trist and his associates at the Tavistock Institute in Great Britain are well known for conducting a series of studies that led to a new, insightful approach to understanding organizational functioning.[15] These studies, which focused on the coal-mining industry in Great Britain, examined the interaction of technological systems and social systems. At the beginning of the studies, coal was mined by a time-honored method known as shortwall mining. This method involved groups of two to eight miners working as teams to extract coal. In addition to being paid as teams for their output, the groups selected their own members and rotated the numerous tasks associated with mining a small section (or seam) of coal. Because of the dangers of working with explosives in dark, confined areas seldom more than three feet high, the men came to develop strong emotional ties with group members. These social relations below ground were closely mirrored in social relations above ground.

As technology advanced, newly developed mining equipment dictated a radically different approach to coal mining. In this new longwall method, the miners were reorganized into large shifts of specialized workers. During the first shift of the day, all of the miners performed the same operation: cutting into the coal wall. The second shift was responsible for shoveling coal into a new type of conveyor. The miners on the third shift worked exclusively at advancing the face of the wall, enlarging gateways, and building roof supports (relatively low-prestige tasks).

In addition, the miners on each shift were spread out along the face of the coal wall at such distances that they could not easily communicate with one another. Similarly, the single supervisor of an entire shift group, consisting of 40 to 50 miners, was not able to monitor the activities of each miner because of the manner in which the men were dispersed.

Although the longwall method had promised to raise productivity, a norm of low productivity emerged. With reduced variety and challenge, the miners found the redesigned work to be unpleasant. They preferred to operate autonomously and to perform *all* the tasks rather than to be solely performing the tasks of cutting, shoveling, or filling.

Although the Tavistock researchers eventually helped to ameliorate the negative consequences of the longwall method, the message was clear: A technological change that appears quite rational from an engineering perspective can disrupt the existing social system so as to reduce greatly the anticipated benefits of the new technology. Of more fundamental importance is the insight gained by the Tavistock researchers on the interplay of technical and social systems. This notion of a **sociotechnical system** arose, therefore, from a consideration that any production-oriented organization involves both a technological system (equipment, task, and process design) and a social system (working relations). While the technological system places demands on the social organization, the social organization has properties of its own, quite independent of the technology, that have an impact on the technological system. Attempts to change the technological and/or social system must be mindful of the relationship between the two systems.

The sociotechnical approach has much to suggest to job redesign (see Chapter 7). In fact, the approach has been used in numerous job redesign efforts. Some of the better publicized redesign efforts have been attempted at General Foods, Rushton Mining, and General Motors. At the Kalmar plant of Volvo, automobile assembly procedures were radically altered from traditional methods in light of an approach that was sensitive to the interface of social and technological systems. By and large, the results of these efforts have netted reduced turnover and accident rates, and superior product quality.[16]

In contrast to the behavioral and classical approaches, the sociotechnical approach does not espouse a simplistic view of organizational processes. However, despite its relative sophistication, the sociotechnical perspective is currently overshadowed by a more recently developed approach, the contingency view of organizational design.

A LOOK AT SOME MODERN ORGANIZATION DESIGNS

Far and away, the most prevalent organization designs in use today are of three varieties: functional, product, and a hybrid of functional and product. Each of the three varieties offers advantages for coping with various contingencies. However, each form also has potential weaknesses.

FUNCTIONAL FORM

Organizations designed along functional lines group personnel and activities according to the resources that are essential to the production process. The contributions of the resulting functional departments aid in the total organizational mission. Figure 17.5 provides an organization chart for a hypothetical firm with a functional design.

A **functional form** is especially appropriate when the most important needs of an organization are collaboration and expertise within a defined set of operations, when the environment is stable, and when only one or a few products are produced. However, the functional form suffers from several weaknesses. It tends to be slow to respond to changes in the organization's environment. It may also result in less innovation and a restricted view of and allegiance to the organization's broader goals. The functional form may also have difficulty in coordinating activities among departments. The measurement of the contribution of each department is also problematic as the end product is a composite result of production, personnel, engineering, design, and marketing efforts. Last, the distinct advantage of the functional form (that is, greater coordination) may become a disadvantage as the organization becomes larger and more complex.

PRODUCT FORM

An organization that selects a **product form** groups personnel and activities according to organizational output. Each product line is provided with its own production, marketing, and development resources as part of the structuring. The primary goals of a product structure are coordination within product

FIGURE 17.5
EXAMPLE OF THE FUNCTIONAL FORM OF ORGANIZATION

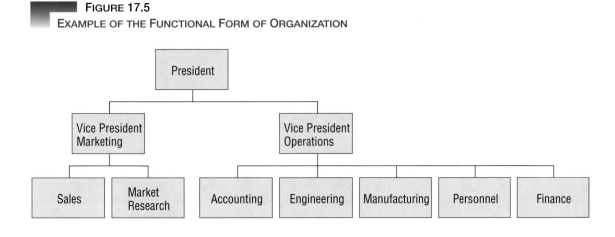

FIGURE 17.6
EXAMPLE OF A PRODUCT FORM OF ORGANIZATION

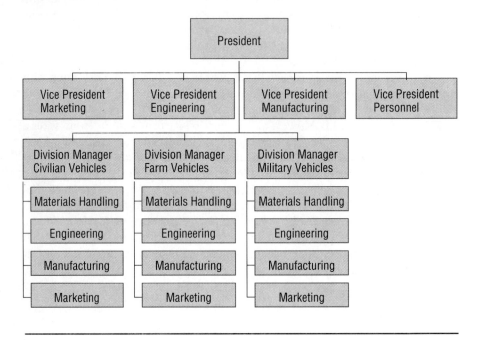

lines and attention to customer desires. Figure 17.6 provides an organizational chart for a hypothetical firm with a product design.

A product form of organization is better suited to adapt to changes in the organization's environment and is especially appropriate for organizations that produce many diverse products or are highly consumer oriented. At the same time, a product form of organization may lead to tremendous losses in economies of scale, redundancy of effort, and little cooperation across product lines. Sharing of competencies and technical advantages is also limited. Internal competition may arise as well. Although competition can be healthy up to a point, the structure of the organization may propel the initial competition into a full-blown power struggle.

HYBRID FORM

As a consequence of either form's limitations, few firms use a pure functional or product structure. More typically, large modern organizations combine the advantages of both functional and product forms into a **hybrid form.** Some functions may be highly specialized and located at corporate headquarters, while other product or market units may be self-contained and located elsewhere. By striving for a balance between functional and product forms, an organization can have the best of both worlds. Hybrids typically provide prod-

FIGURE 17.7
EXAMPLE OF A HYBRID ORGANIZATION STRUCTURE

uct groups with the functional support they need within a product line, while also trying to maintain functional departments for activities that are required by all divisions of the organization. Figure 17.7 presents a sample organization chart of a hybrid organization involved in three distinct product areas.

Of course, an organization's structure is rarely static. More commonly, structure evolves over time as top-level managers attempt to better adapt their firm to the changing features of its surroundings.

MATRIX DESIGN   In some unique situations, a refined balance between functional and product structures is required to give recognition to both functional and product-related issues. When continuous interchange between product and function is necessary, a matrix organizational design may be warranted. In a **matrix design,** the functional and product managers enjoy equal authority. Personnel are required to report to managers from both the functional and product divisions. In essence, a matrix design involves a dual hierarchy.

To illustrate more precisely what is meant by a matrix system, consider Figure 17.8. In this organization, a top-level manager oversees one manager whose responsibilities are functional and one manager whose responsibilities are product related. These two managers, in turn, oversee the single employee whose work relates to both their areas. Thus, in violation of the principle of unity of command, the employee is involved in a two-boss system.**

** Although the concept of a two-boss system may seem very strange, remember that people typically have had a good deal of experience being in a two-boss system: as a child dealing with a mother and a father.

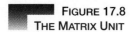

FIGURE 17.8
THE MATRIX UNIT

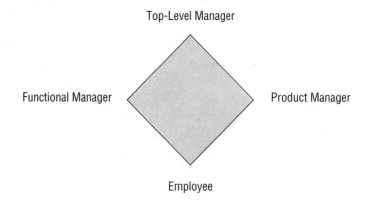

Carrying this illustration a step farther to include an entire management group, we could create the matrix design shown in Figure 17.9. At each intersection of the lines of authority and responsibility for the product and functional divisions, project groups would exist. As this figure suggests, personnel and resources would be grouped together to tackle product-specific problems.

In theory, everyone in an organization could be in the web of a matrix. However, most organizations that employ a matrix design limit its use to management-level personnel and maintain a traditional pyramid-shaped structure for the remainder of the firm.[17] Figure 17.10 illustrates such a configuration.

On the negative side, matrix systems can create significant frustration and confusion, especially for the employee who reports to two superiors. In addition, employees who are not adequately trained in how to adapt to a matrix system may persist in behaving as if they were in a more traditional top-down, one-boss situation. Finally, the use of a matrix design is very time-consuming. Frequent meetings and conflict-resolution sessions are likely to be necessary, and communications must often be duplicated for the benefit of both superiors. Performance evaluation may also become complicated because in appraising a single subordinate, the potentially conflicting views of two superiors must be resolved. In short, many of the problems that one would expect from violating the principle of unity of command will occur in a matrix system if people do not cooperate in resolving conflicts over the sharing of power and resources. A collaborative and collegial spirit is, therefore, necessary if a matrix form of organization is to succeed.

Matrix designs are used in manufacturing, service, professional, and nonprofit organizations. Although matrix systems were first used in the 1960s,[18] their use did not spread until the 1980s. Davis and Lawrence characterize this phenomenon as something of a "quiet revolution" that began largely in the aerospace industry and whose end is not yet in sight.[19]

FIGURE 17.9

EXAMPLE OF A MATRIX ORGANIZATION

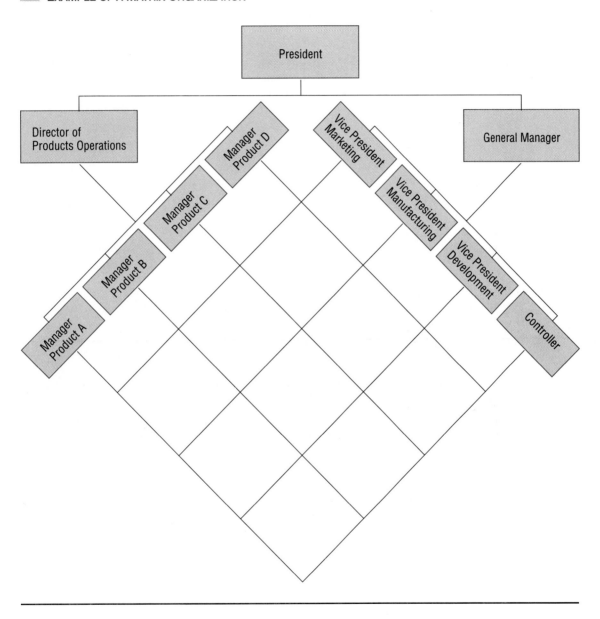

Matrix systems are extremely flexible in their use of both human and material resources, and they can aid in coordinating responses to the dual difficulties created by customer- and production-related pressures.[‡‡] Given their flexibility,

---

[‡‡] Given the continual reshuffling of human and material resources, a good way of describing the dynamics of matrix design is with the three-dimensional analogy of a Rubik's cube.

FIGURE 17.10
A COMBINATION MATRIX AND PYRAMID STRUCTURE

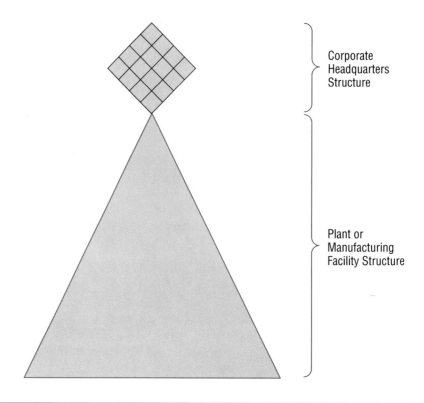

Corporate
Headquarters
Structure

Plant or
Manufacturing
Facility Structure

matrix designs are especially appropriate for organizations that exist in unstable environments, for example, groups that are growing rapidly due to increasing rates of change in technology and consumer preferences.

SUMMARY

1. Define decentralization and identify strengths and weaknesses of a decentralized organization.

Decentralization is the degree to which decision making occurs lower down in an organization. A strength of decentralization is that it can enhance employee motivation, performance, satisfaction, creativity, involvement, and commitment. Weaknesses include a tendency to focus on immediate problems and ignore opportunities for future growth, difficulties in allocating shared resources and coordinating shared functions, and internal conflicts that are difficult to detect and resolve.

2. Contrast tall and flat organizations.

Tall organizations have more levels and narrower spans of control than flat organizations. Generally, tall organizations allow for closer control of subordinates. Tall organizations tend to discourage decentralization, while flat organizations are more likely to be decentralized.

3. Describe unity of command and chain of command.

Unity of command is the idea that every subordinate should have only one supervisor. Chain of command maintains that information and authority proceed from level to level in a hierarchical fashion without omitting any level.

4. Describe the six systems in the behavioral approach to organizational design.

An organization in an early, formative stage may be characterized as permissive, with large spans of control and much confusion (System 0). An exploitative-authoritative organization (System 1) relies on fear and punishment to motivate employees. Decision makers do not consult employees. A benevolent-authoritative organization (System 2) uses rewards to motivate employees. Employees may comment on directives, but managers still make the decisions. In a consultative organization (System 3), managers consult subordinates more readily and avoid using threats, but upper management still makes the major decisions. In a participative organization (System 4), decision making occurs at all levels and involves all members equally. Trust is extremely high, and incentives include economic, ego, and social rewards. An idealized form of organization (System 4T) is based on intragroup relationships and overlapping group memberships.

5. Describe the relationship between technological and social systems in an organization.

Every organization has both a technological system and a social system. The technological system (equipment, task, and process design) interacts with the social system (working relations), each influencing the nature of the other.

6. Describe modern organizational designs.

The functional form of organization groups personnel and activities according to the resources that are essential to the production process. The product form groups personnel and activities according to organizational outputs. The hybrid form often combines functional and product forms. A matrix system is a hybrid design involving a dual hierarchy.

7. Discuss advantages and disadvantages of different organizational designs.

A functional design is useful when collaboration and expertise are needed and the environment is stable. However, a functional design is slow to respond to environmental changes and is less likely to foster innovation. A product design offers greater attention to customer needs and is better suited to respond to environmental changes. A product design, however, incorporates redundancy of effort. A hybrid design strives to balance the functional and product designs. A hybrid design can be highly flexible and can coordinate responses to customer- and production-related pressures, plus offer a greater degree of responsiveness to environmental change. A hybrid design may create problems for evaluating employee performance, as well as generate confusion.

KEY TERMS

Decentralization	Bureaucracy
Tall structure	Sociotechnical system
Flat structure	Functional form
Span of control	Product form
Unity of command	Hybrid form
Chain of command	Matrix design

REVIEW AND DISCUSSION QUESTIONS

1. What is decentralization? What are some benefits and drawbacks of decentralization in an organization?

2. What is a tall organization? Do tall organizations have more units than flat organizations? Does a manager have closer control in a tall organization or a flat one?

3. Susan Floyd reports to two supervisors, each of whom wants his assignments done first. Susan finds that when she tries to please both of them, she winds up satisfying neither. She decides to take matters into her own hands and sends a memo to the person her two supervisors report to, asking this manager to resolve the conflict. In this situation, which two principles of organizing are violated? Explain these principles.

4. Max Weber described a bureaucracy as an ideal form of organization. What are the characteristics of such an organization? Do most organizations actually match this description? What kinds of organizations benefit most from a bureaucratic structure?

5. Phil McGreevy is in charge of planning operations for the refrigerator assembly plant his company is redesigning. Phil and his team have planned for the necessary equipment, and they have studied the assembly process and divided it into the tasks to be done. In planning the refrigerator assembly system, what else should Phil consider? Why?

6. CJS Financial Accountants emphasizes rules and procedures, and respects hierarchy. The company is seeking to hire someone to do routine bookkeeping tasks. One candidate, Linda Burns, has indicated that she is looking for a job that involves challenge, responsibility, and opportunity for growth. Another candidate, George Ronstadt, seemed mainly interested in the salary. Both candidates are qualified; which is most likely to be satisfied? Explain your choice.

7. At General Products, Inc., one vice president is responsible for all aspects of producing and selling breakfast cereal, another has responsibility for frozen pizzas, and a third has responsibility for hosiery. What form of organization does General Products have? What are some advantages and disadvantages of this kind of organization?

8. What is a matrix design? What are some advantages and disadvantages of this type of organizational design?

9. The 2K Company manufactures and distributes floppy disks and cassette tapes. Because of changes in technology and the marketplace, the company frequently encounters customer- and production-related pressures. The management at 2K has decided that reorganizing the company into a matrix system will help it remain competitive. For employees to adapt to the matrix system, what kinds of skills will they need to learn? Do you think employees could learn these skills well enough for a matrix system to work? How practical is a matrix system?

CRITICAL INCIDENT

The Horizontal Corporation

It was clear to Mike O'Reilly, president and CEO of Cambridge Lighting, that the organizational structure of Cambridge was no longer serving the needs of the company. Cambridge, a manufacturer of lamps and lighting fixtures, had developed a hierarchical structure over the years as sales grew and the work force expanded. The organization had been structured according to specialized functions, creating "silos of excellence." Cambridge had multiple layers of management and a formal chain of command. The organization's ability to adapt quickly to change was severely constrained because most key decisions required managerial approval. The hierarchy had become deeply entrenched.

Mike was concerned that the structure was no longer appropriate in the increasingly competitive lighting market. The past few years had seen major changes in the lighting industry. Inexpensive lamps and lighting fixtures were being imported from Pacific Rim countries, and energy-efficient halogen lighting was becoming an increasingly popular alternative. Mike knew that Cambridge would have to respond to these pressures if it wanted to remain a viable competitor in the lighting industry.

After studying the organization for several months, Mike realized that several functional departments had limited interactions. Friction between departments (for example, between marketing and sales and between engineering and manufacturing) had occasionally been intense and had kept the organization from operating smoothly. Mike wondered if a new organizational structure might be in order.

After reading several articles on horizontal corporations, a recent trend in organizational redesign, Mike and his executive team developed a plan to restructure the organization around key processes. In horizontal organizations, leaders identify the core competencies or key processes and design the organization around those. Key processes, such as new product development, sales, and customer support, were identified and specific performance goals defined for each. Because the lighting market had become very competitive, Mike and his team decided that Cambridge should adopt a customer orientation. Therefore, performance goals were defined in terms of customer satisfaction. According to the plan, teams of functional specialists would work on a given key process toward established performance goals.

Following the redesign, teams of employees from different functions would be responsible for every stage of their key process. The multidisciplinary teams would be empowered to make decisions without supervisor input, thereby reducing the chain of command and flattening the organization's hierarchy. To provide better service, teams would meet regularly with suppliers and customers to learn more about their needs and constraints.

The plan looked good on paper, but Mike was concerned about its implementation. On his desk was the 150-page plan book he and his executive team had prepared. They had nicknamed it the "roadmap" because it outlined how Cambridge would proceed from its present vertical structure to its desired horizontal structure. The restructuring process was to begin in about six weeks. But first, Mike and his executive team had to share the entire plan with everyone in the organization. The first meeting to unveil the new organizational structure to upper and middle management was about to begin. With a sigh of both excitement and hesitation, Mike grabbed his roadmap and headed for the conference room.

QUESTIONS

1. How are the managers at this meeting likely to respond?

2. How should Mike respond to managers' and employees' concerns?

3. What role should the human resources management department play in this reorganization?

4. What types of personnel policies should change to reflect the new organizational structure?

5. How does the horizontal structure implemented at Cambridge differ from a matrix organization?

Source: "The Horizontal Corporation," written by Melissa Waite, State University of New York, University at Buffalo; and Susan Stites-Doe, State University of New York, College at Brockport.

EXPERIENTIAL EXERCISE

Bureaucratic Orientation Test

Have you thought about what kind of organization you would like to work for when you finish your studies? The following checklist may help you define what type of organizational structure would be best for you.

Step 1 For each statement, check the response (either Mostly Agree or Mostly Disagree) that best represents your feelings.

	Mostly Agree	Mostly Disagree
1. I value stability in my job.	_____	_____
2. I like a predictable organization.	_____	_____
3. The best job for me would be one in which the future is uncertain.	_____	_____
4. The U.S. Army would be a nice place to work.	_____	_____
5. Rules, policies, and procedures tend to frustrate me.	_____	_____
6. I would enjoy working for a company that employed 85,000 people worldwide.	_____	_____
7. Being self-employed would involve more risk than I'm willing to take.	_____	_____
8. Before accepting a job, I would like to see an exact job description.	_____	_____
9. I would prefer a job as a free-lance house painter to one as a clerk for the Department of Motor Vehicles.	_____	_____
10. Seniority should be as important as performance in determining pay increases and promotion.	_____	_____
11. It would give me a feeling of pride to work for the largest and most successful company in its field.	_____	_____
12. Given a choice, I would prefer to make $30,000 per year as a vice president in a small company to $35,000 as a staff specialist in a large company.	_____	_____
13. I would regard wearing an employee badge with a number on it as a degrading experience.	_____	_____
14. Parking spaces in a company lot should be assigned on the basis of job level.	_____	_____
15. If an accountant works for a large organization, he or she cannot be a true professional.	_____	_____
16. Before accepting a job (given a choice), I would want to make sure that the company had a very fine program of employee benefits.	_____	_____

	Mostly Agree	Mostly Disagree
17. A company will probably not be successful unless it establishes a clear set of rules and procedures.	_____	_____
18. Regular working hours and vacations are more important to me than finding thrills on the job.	_____	_____
19. You should respect people according to their rank.	_____	_____
20. Rules are meant to be broken.	_____	_____

Step 2   Give yourself one point for each statement for which you responded in the bureaucratic direction:

1. Mostly agree	11. Mostly agree
2. Mostly agree	12. Mostly disagree
3. Mostly disagree	13. Mostly disagree
4. Mostly agree	14. Mostly agree
5. Mostly disagree	15. Mostly disagree
6. Mostly disagree	16. Mostly agree
7. Mostly agree	17. Mostly disagree
8. Mostly agree	18. Mostly agree
9. Mostly disagree	19. Mostly agree
10. Mostly agree	20. Mostly disagree

Step 3   Interpret your scores. A very high score (15 or over) would suggest that you would enjoy working in a bureaucracy. A very low score (5 or lower) would suggest that you would be frustrated working in a bureaucracy, especially a large one.

Step 4   Do you think your score is representative of most college students in your major? Discuss with students in your class.

Source: Andrew J. DuBrin, *Human Relations: A Job Oriented Approach,* 5/e, © 1992, pp. 434–435. Reprinted by permission of Prentice Hall, Englewood Cliffs, New Jersey.

NOTES

1. R. Duncan, "What Is the Right Organization Structure?" *Organizational Dynamics* 33 (1979): 66.

2. P. Petre, "America's Most Successful Entrepreneur," *Fortune,* October 27, 1986, 24–32.

3. T. Peters, *Thriving on Chaos* (New York: Harper and Row, 1987), 430.

4. J.C. Worthy, "Organizational Structure and Employee Morale," *American Sociological Review* 15 (1950): 169–179; R.P. Vecchio, "A Cross-National Comparison of Span of Control," *International Journal of Management,* 1995 (in press).

5. M.Weber, *The Theory of Social and Economic Organizations,* trans. A. Henderson and T. Parsons (New York: Free Press, 1947).

6. P.M. Blau, *On the Nature of Organizations* (New York: Wiley, 1974); V.A. Thompson, *Modern Organization* (New York: Knopf, 1961).

7. J. Child, "Managerial and Organizational Factors Associated with Company Performance, Part II. A Contingency Analysis," *Journal of Management Studies* 12 (1975): 12–27.

8. R.L. Daft, *Organizational Theory and Design* (New York: West, 1983).

9. Child, "Managerial and Organizational Factors Associated with Company Performance."

10. Thompson, *Modern Organization.*

11. R. Likert, *The Human Organization: Its Management and Value* (New York: McGraw-Hill, 1967).

12. R. Likert and J.G. Likert, *New Ways of Managing Conflict* (New York: McGraw-Hill, 1976).

13. J.B. Miner, *Theories of Organizational Structure and Process* (Hinsdale, Ill.: The Dryden Press, 1982), 52.

14. J.B. Miner, "Limited Domain Theories of Organizational Energy," in *Middle Range Theory and the Study of Organizations,*

eds. C.C. Pinder and L.F. Moore (Boston: Maritimes Nijhoff, 1980), 273–286.

15. E.L. Trist and K.W. Bamforth, "Some Social and Psychological Consequences of the Longwall Method of Goal Setting," *Human Relations* 4 (1951): 1–38.

16. D.S. Cohen, "The Quality-of-Worklife Movement," *Training HRD* 30 (January 1979): 24.

17. S.M. Davis and P.R. Lawrence, *Matrix* (Reading, Mass.: Addison-Wesley, 1977); W.F. Joyce, "Matrix Organization: A Social Experiment," *Academy of Management Journal* 29 (1986): 536–561.

18. C. Argyris, "Today's Problems with Tomorrow's Organizations," *Journal of Management Studies* 32 (1967): 31–55; J.F. Mee, "Ideational Items: Matrix Organization," *Business Horizons* 7 (1964): 70–72.

19. Davis and Lawrence, *Matrix,* 9.

CHAPTER

18

Going to work for a large company is like getting on a train. Are you going 60 miles an hour or is the train going 60 miles an hour and you're sitting still?
— John Paul Getty

The growth of a large business is merely a survival of the fittest.
— John D. Rockefeller, Sr.

We are very different from the rest of the world. Our only natural resource is the hard work of our people.
— Japanese executive

LEARNING OBJECTIVES

After studying this chapter, you should be able to:

1. *Identify three dimensions that describe an organization's external environment.*

2. *Explain how the environment influences which organizations will succeed and which will fail.*

3. *Explain how organizations handle their dependency on their environment.*

4. *Describe two strategies organizations can use for managing the environment.*

5. *Identify an organization's structural dimensions and contextual dimensions.*

6. *Explain when differentiation is likely to characterize an organization.*

7. *Describe how an organization's structure complements its technology.*

8. *Explain how strategy and structure may be related.*

Environmental Forces

THE VIRTUAL CORPORATION IS COMING

Fascinated by the prospect of a hand-held, pen-based computer, entrepreneur Ron Oklewicz, a veteran of Apple Computer and Xerox Corp., started his own company, TelePad Corp. of Reston, Va. Unlike the organizations from which Oklewicz came, TelePad has only 14 employees on the payroll, including a handful of engineers. With limited in-house talent, the computer was designed and co-developed with GVO Inc., a Palo Alto, Calif., industrial-design company. A crew from Intel Corp. was hired to solve some engineering problems, various companies developed software for the computer, and TelePad is partnering with a battery maker to develop a portable power supply. Rather than incur the considerable start-up costs of a manufacturing site, the computer is assembled in Charlotte, N.C., at an IBM plant with excess capacity. Even the paychecks that TelePad employees receive are issued by an outside vendor, Automatic Data Processing Inc.

Welcome to the virtual corporation. Many experts predict that this will be the dominant organizational form in America's future. The key aspect of the virtual organization is *partnering*, the term used to describe companies that contribute their "core com-petencies"—what they do best—to the organization. Thus, the virtual corporation is merely a temporary network of companies that band together to exploit a specific opportunity, then disband once the opportunity is met. The virtual corporation has no headquarters, no organization chart, no hierarchy, no vertical integration. Organizational borders are blurred; the corporation is fluid and flexible.

This model of organization has actually been around for some time. In both the construction and movie-making industries, companies contribute their own unique talents to the project, then disband once the task is done. As advancements in technology outpace an organization's abilities to keep up, organizations are increasingly relying on partnerships and alliances to remain competitive. James R. Houghton, chairman of Corning Inc., credits its 19 partnerships with allowing the company to develop and sell new products faster.

The information superhighway, endorsed by Vice President Al Gore, will facilitate the growth of virtual corporations. A nationwide information infrastructure would link computers and machinery, allowing companies with divergent missions to locate suppliers, designers, and manufacturers through an information clearinghouse. Computer networks would allow several companies to work on a product simultaneously. Computer technology and sensing devices would allow engineers in Atlanta and designers in Boston to make production changes on a factory floor in Los Angeles.

Perhaps the biggest drawback of the virtual corporation is that it requires surrendering control of business operations to outsiders. Assembling just-in-time talent requires building relationships and forging trust between two business partners. Partnerships must be win-win opportunities for all parties, with each participating company understanding the parameters of its contribution to the project.

For some organizations, the virtual corporation will seem a natural extension of collaborative efforts already underway through strategic alliances and joint ventures. However, the need for adaptability in virtual corporations has broad implications for how organizations operate. Some experts predict the virtual organization will soon have a "vice president for external interactions," an individual responsible for overseeing the numerous collaborations with partners. Organizations

(continued on next page)

(continued from previous page)
that are entering the realm of virtuality should prepare for the changes. The ultimate adaptable company will achieve world-class everything, a feat no single company could accomplish alone.

Many external environmental factors affect an organization's functioning. This chapter explores the environment in which organizations operate and the effect of that environment on organizational performance.

Source: John A. Byrne, Richard Brandt, and Otis Port, "The Virtual Corporation," *Business Week,* February 8, 1993, 98–102.

As we have seen throughout this text, employees' attitudes and behaviors are influenced by the immediate circumstances in their work units, such as their tasks, intragroup relations, and rules and policies. The circumstances that define these subenvironments within the work unit are, in turn, determined by diverse facets of the larger organizational structure.

In Chapter 17, we focused on the influence of the organization's structure, and we emphasized that effective management requires an understanding of how larger structural issues affect individuals. In this chapter, we will examine dimensions of external environments and strategies for actually managing the external environment, with the ultimate goal of controlling the resulting structures and the subenvironments within these structures. Then we will examine the relationship of organizational structure to environment and strategy.

DIMENSIONS OF EXTERNAL ENVIRONMENTS

An organization exists within a particular external environment that is composed of all the various factors (such as the government, legal system, labor pool, suppliers, customers, and state of existing technology) that can affect the organization's functioning. In analogous fashion to a living organism, an organization is influenced by and influences its surroundings. Similarly, the organization is highly dependent on environmental features and must quickly adapt to changes in the environment if it is to survive.

The number of features that constitute an organization's external environment is considerable. However, organizational researchers have attempted to reduce these features to a few critical dimensions. Chief among these schemes for analyzing external environments are those developed by James D. Thompson[1] and Robert Duncan.[2] These theorists have suggested three important dimensions for understanding environments: simplicity–complexity, static–dynamic, and environmental uncertainty.

SIMPLICITY–COMPLEXITY

Environments can be characterized in terms of their intricacy and relative diversity. A simple environment contains few factors that affect the organization and tends to be relatively unvaried. In contrast, a complex environment contains many more elements of importance and is more diverse. As an illustration of a simple environment, consider the environment faced by a manufacturer of washboards at the turn of the century. In such a setting, the technology was relatively simple, and the market was unchanging. In comparison, consider a present-day drug manufacturer. The number of products produced is highly varied, and the customers are quite different (for example, hospitals, doctors, and over-the-counter drugstores). The manufacture, marketing, and distribution of drugs is also highly complex. In addition, there are government regulations covering the preparation and distribution of drugs.

STATIC–DYNAMIC

A second important dimension of environments is the degree of stability or dynamism that characterizes the organization's surroundings. Environments can be said to differ in terms of the rate at which change is occurring; hence, they can be said to differ in terms of predictability. In our example of the washboard manufacturer, we can say that the surrounding environment was relatively static during the beginning of this century. (Washboards were widely used until washing machines became available and affordable later in the century.) Today's drug manufacturer functions in a highly dynamic and changing environment. New drugs are continually being developed and tested. There are continuing changes in the packaging of drugs in response to customer concerns over possible product tampering. In addition, the drug industry is responsive (quickly adapts) to innovations in the drug-manufacturing process.

ENVIRONMENTAL UNCERTAINTY

The degree of uncertainty that characterizes the environment is intricately related to the descriptive dimensions of simplicy–complexity and static–dynamic. According to Duncan, environmental uncertainty is a consequence of the inability to assign probabilities to environmental factors with a high degree of confidence, and a lack of information concerning both the factors that are important to decision making and the costs associated with poor decision making.[3] Duncan has proposed a model to help explain the relationship of uncertainty to the dimensions of simplicity–complexity and static–dynamic (see Figure 18.1). In his model, high degrees of uncertainty are associated with complex–dynamic environments, while low degrees of uncertainty are associated with simple–static environments. Moderate degrees of uncertainty are associated with the combinations of complex–static and simple–dynamic.

Studies of Duncan's model have yielded results that are generally supportive.[4] In addition, results suggest that the static–dynamic dimension may be of greater importance in determining the level of perceived environmental uncertainty.

THE POPULATION ECOLOGY PERSPECTIVE

In recent years, organizational theorists have proposed a new view of how organizations relate to their environments.[5] According to the **population ecology perspective,** organizations seek to find a niche in a highly competitive surrounding so that they will be able to survive. In this view, a niche is defined as a combination of environmental resources and needs that are capable of

FIGURE 18.1

DUNCAN'S MODEL OF ENVIRONMENTAL UNCERTAINTY

Environments With

	Low Perceived Uncertainty	Moderately Low Perceived Uncertainty
Static	1. A small number of similar factors in the environment 2. Factors are unchanging	1. A large number of dissimilar factors in the environment 2. Factors are unchanging
Dynamic	Moderately High Perceived Uncertainty 1. A small number of similar factors in the environment 2. Factors are constantly changing	High Perceived Uncertainty 1. A large number of dissimilar factors in the environment 2. Factors are constantly changing

Environments That Are — Static versus Dynamic

Source: R. Duncan, "The Characteristics of Organizational Environments and Perceived Environmental Uncertainty," *Administrative Science Quarterly* 17 (1972): 320.

sustaining the organization. Initially, a niche may be fairly small. But as the organization grows, it may expand the size of its niche. The population ecology perspective borrows heavily from the notions of natural selection in biology. In both views, entities are seen as competing for survival in a difficult, sometimes predatory, and crowded environment.[*]

In order to maintain its existence, an entity must possess an appropriate **organizational form.** The appropriate organizational form represents a configuration of goals, human resources, products, and technology that will be acceptable to the environment. If an element of the form is inappropriate (for example, the technology is out of date, or the products are not in demand), then the organization risks being rejected by the environment. As is also true of life in the jungle, the population ecology perspective holds that chance, random forces, and continual change are important elements in determining survival and demise.

The population ecology view suggests that there are three stages in the change process: variation, selection, and retention. **Variation** is analogous to the concept of genetic mutation in the theory of evolution. Organizations with unique attributes are continually being born. Often, these new organizations

---

[*] Interestingly, the mortality rates of the young of many species and of young organizations are very high.

are deliberately designed to cope with a particular set of environmental constraints. If the new organization possesses adaptive variations, it will likely be successful. Those organizations that do not possess the needed organizational form will fail. Failure may be due to the organization's lack of skilled personnel, lack of sufficient capital, or chance factors (such as a takeover by another company). Consequently, a process of **selection** occurs. Over a long period, only a few organizations (out of the large number founded every year) can be expected to survive and be reasonably prosperous. **Retention** refers to the institutionalization of certain adaptive organizational forms. As long as the organization's outputs are sought or endorsed by the larger society, the organization will be a critical component of the society. Examples of institutionalized organizational forms include state governments, educational institutions, and automobile manufacturers. In the long term, even these established institutionalized forms may disappear. The key determinants of the longevity of institutionalized organizational forms are the extent of change in the environment and the organization's ability to adapt to such change. Figure 18.2 illustrates the process of change as proposed by the population ecology perspective.

As an example, consider the process of change related to the roadside hamburger stand. In the past, independently owned and operated hamburger stands served an important societal need. As the public became more mobile, roadside dining became a more frequent activity for the average citizen. Over time, chains of franchised hamburger stands (McDonald's, Burger King, Wendy's) came to dominate the roadways by offering the customer a standardized product along with the convenience of fast service and drive-through windows.

At present, the original, independently owned hamburger stands must hold second place (in terms of appeal and sales) to the large institutionalized forms of fast-food restaurants. The clientele of the nonfranchised restaurants are now more likely to be repeat customers who live in the surrounding neighborhood than the traveling public. In this example, we see how the small, independent organizations are gradually being selected out of the environment. With time, it is, of course, possible that the current domination of fast-food restaurants will end. For this to occur: (a) the chains must be supplanted by a new (as yet unforeseen) organizational form that is superior in some fashion,

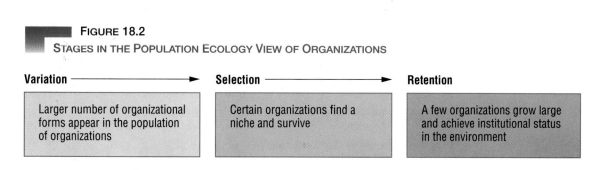

FIGURE 18.2

STAGES IN THE POPULATION ECOLOGY VIEW OF ORGANIZATIONS

Variation ⟶	Selection ⟶	Retention
Larger number of organizational forms appear in the population of organizations	Certain organizations find a niche and survive	A few organizations grow large and achieve institutional status in the environment

Source: R. L. Daft, *Organization Theory and Design* (St. Paul, Minn.: West Publishing, 1983), 521.

(b) the desires of the public will have to change (for example, the public must lose its desire to eat beef, or its desire to eat out must be greatly diminished), and (c) the fast-food chains must fail to respond (or be incapable of responding) to the challenge.

Large retail stores, such as Sears, Roebuck, Montgomery Ward, and J.C. Penney, have long held a leadership role. However, industry experts are forecasting that the long-term prospects of these giants are poor because of the high cost of their operations, shifting demographics that are fragmenting the customer base (traditionally the middle-class homeowner), and the growing competition of discount and specialty chain stores. If they are to survive these challenges, the retail leaders will have to make changes in order to adapt to a new environment.

The population ecology view is particularly useful as a device for explaining organizational change, especially in terms of innovations in organizational design. The evolutionary perspective offered by the notions of variation, selection, and retention help to account for the emergence of new organizational structures, new products, and organizational failures.

THE RESOURCE DEPENDENCE MODEL

Jeffrey Pfeffer and Gerald Salancik have proposed yet another view of how organizations relate to their environments.[6] In their **resource dependence model**, they contend that organizations are highly dependent on their external environments for raw resources and markets. The success of any organization is, therefore, a function of the extent to which the organization can manage its environment. Because organizations are vulnerable to their environments, they must take action to reduce or eliminate their dependency. One approach to this dependency is to purchase or control those forces that can exert influence. For example, a manufacturer who relies heavily on certain raw materials may try to purchase the operations of various suppliers. This represents an attempt to reach out and change the environment (see the next section of this chapter). Also, an organization may attempt an internal change in order to deal with its vulnerability. These internal changes include increases in structural complexity and the creation of boundary-spanning roles.

Increases in organizational complexity reflect the complexity of the external environment. For example, marketing departments are created and specialized in order to identify new markets and understand customer desires and needs. Legal departments interface with federal and state agencies in order to protect the firm from legal constraints. Purchasing agents focus on identifying suppliers and new sources of raw materials. As the complexity of the external environment increases, the complexity of the organization's structure will likely increase in order for the organization to more effectively cope with its surroundings.

An organization needs to have effective relationships with the major elements of its environment. To achieve this end, **boundary-spanning positions** are often created. Boundary spanners seek to understand the external environment and to represent the organization to various constituencies. Examples of boundary-spanning roles include positions in public relations, marketing research, college recruiting, and purchasing. However, the boundary-spanning function is not solely the province of specialized positions. Many employees whose jobs are primarily directed toward performing duties within the organization may occasionally engage in boundary-spanning activities. For example, someone in the finance department may call a friend who works for a supplier in order to learn more about the operations of the supplier, or someone in accounting may meet with a job candidate for a position in another department in order to persuade the candidate to join the organization.

MANAGING THE EXTERNAL ENVIRONMENT

Daft has suggested that it is possible to change the external environment through two major strategies.[7] The first consists of establishing favorable linkages with critical elements in the external environment. The second involves controlling the environmental domain. Each of these strategies can be accomplished through several different methods.

ESTABLISHING FAVORABLE LINKAGES

To improve relations, linkages (or associations) can be set up with elements of the external environment. One useful way of establishing a linkage is to acquire another organization through a merger. Mergers can eliminate dependence on an external factor by gaining control over it. For example, uncertainty about a supplier's ability to deliver sufficient quantities of materials on time can be reduced by acquiring the supplier and thereby guaranteeing preferential treatment. Acquisition of one firm by another with the goal of controlling forces that affect the production process is termed **vertical integration.** Examples of vertical integration include an automobile manufacturer that acquires an auto radio and battery producer, and a food processor that purchases a poultry farm.

Hiring practices can also help to establish favorable linkages. In one approach, a firm may decide to recruit executives from other firms with which it wishes to have good relations. Thus, a defense contractor may hire retired military officers from the Department of Defense to join its contract-negotiating division. Another approach is to select board members who represent various constituencies, such as customers, suppliers, or community interest groups. Membership on a board of directors provides these individuals with an appreciation of, and a continuing interest in, the performance of the firm. A similar tactic involves placing board members of another corporation on your own board. This tactic creates **interlocking directorates.** As a result of sharing board memberships, the individuals experience a sense of common interests.

Last, a firm can attempt to establish favorable linkages by investing in advertising and public relations. Such efforts attempt to enhance the firm's image in the eyes of customers and the public and, as a result, influence the way in which these groups relate to the firm.

OB Focus
Family-Friendly Policies Make Good Business Sense

As the work force becomes more diverse, with more women, single parents, dual-career couples, and an aging population, the boundaries between work and family are becoming increasingly fuzzy. Organizations must not only recognize but also accommodate the personal needs of employees. A case in point is the federal Family and Medical Leave Act that took effect in August 1993. The act guarantees employees as much as 12 weeks per year of unpaid, job-protected leave with medical benefits for childbirth, adoption, or illness of the employee or a family member.

Organizations like AT&T are finding that morale and productivity increase when companies help employees resolve work–family conflicts. Such accommodations also make smart business sense. At AT&T, the average cost of giving up to one year unpaid leave was 32 percent of an employee's annual salary, compared with the 150 percent it would take to replace the employee.

Such innovative arrangements as job sharing, compressed workweeks, and telecommuting are also increasing productivity, and reducing turnover and absenteeism. Programs like these help Aetna Life and Casualty save $1 million per year in costs associated with training new employees.

Technology has been critical to making these innovative programs work. At Aetna, two legal assistants work part-time, but share one job: One works Monday through Wednesday lunch, and the other works Wednesday through Friday. Telephones and electronic mail keep them in touch with what's going on at the office: When one receives a message, it is automatically sent to the other. So far, the job share is successful. Their manager likes the fact that they can work on separate projects and bounce ideas off each other.

American Express Travel Services pondered the idea of allowing employees to work from home, and eventually agreed to try tele-commuting on a trial basis. The program has been so successful that the company plans to expand it. The company installs the hardware, phones, and data lines at a cost of $1,300 in the home of each telecommuting employee. Calls are automatically redirected from office to home, where agents look up fares and book reservations on PCs. One of the unforeseen advantages of telecommuting was lower overhead costs. In New York City, American Express leases office space for about $35 per square foot, equivalent to about $4,400 per year per travel counselor. Productivity is also up considerably. By having fewer distractions at home, the typical agent handles 26 percent more calls, resulting in a 46 percent average revenue increase, or roughly $30,000 more revenue per agent.

As social and technological environments change, some companies are finding that embracing family-friendly environment makes for good employee relations and for good business.

Sources: Sue Shellenbarger, "Whether Firms Are Ready or Not, Leave Law Is Here," *The Wall Street Journal,* August 2, 1993; Michele Galen, Ann Therese Palmer, Alice Cuneo, and Mark Maremont, "Work and Family," *Business Week,* June 28, 1993, 80–88; and Stratford Sherman, "How to Bolster the Bottom Line," *Fortune,* Autumn 1993, 15–28.

CONTROLLING ENVIRONMENTAL DOMAINS

Daft also suggests various means by which an organization can attempt to control the domains in which it operates. One direct approach is simply to buy or sell a product line. This involves seeking or avoiding different suppliers, competitors, government regulations, customer groups, and so on. Additionally, an organization may aggressively diversify into different business arenas, forming **conglomerates**. Conglomerates can sometimes provide built-in markets for products and easier access to supplies. In the Orient, conglomerates have grown to be comparatively large. In Japan, such an enormous corporation is called a *keiretsu*. One of the largest examples of a keiretsu is the Mitsubishi group, which includes such diverse industries as glass, banking, mining, electronics, automotive products, and cement.

A second device consists of joining with other similar organizations that have common goals and interests. For example, coal mine operators may join forces to form a trade association, with the aim of lobbying for their interests. The goals of such associations include encouraging regulators to pass or rescind laws that promote or restrict an industry's well-being. In some technologically advanced industries (for example, robotics and computers), an individual firm may lack the ability to single-handedly develop and market a new product. In such instances, firms may operate cooperatively, sometimes across national boundaries, to form **strategic alliances.**

THE CONTINGENCY VIEW OF ORGANIZATIONAL DESIGN

Today, scholars of organizational design generally subscribe to a view that organizations are **open systems.** As an open system, an organization must deal with its environment by obtaining and consuming resources, and exporting finished goods or services. Organizations do not exist in a vacuum nor can they operate independently from their environment; that is, they cannot function as **closed systems.**

Given this view of organizations as open systems, it is useful to consider how an organization's internal characteristics are influenced by the larger features of the environment and the entire organization itself. These internal characteristics, called **structural dimensions,** include such features as specialization, hierarchy of authority, decentralization, and complexity. Characteristics of the entire organization and its environment, called **contextual dimensions,** include size, technology, and such external constituents as customers, suppliers, competitors, and the government. The goal of the contingency view is to explain how differences in the contextual and structural dimensions are related. As the term *contingency* implies, this approach does not seek simple universal principles that can be used for every situation, but instead seeks to explain how one attribute or characteristic depends upon another. In the search for contingencies, several landmark studies have been conducted.

BURNS AND STALKER'S MECHANISTIC AND ORGANIC SYSTEMS

In a study of 20 firms in England, Burns and Stalker examined the relationships between external environments and the nature of internal organizational structure.[8] Relying on unstructured observations and interviews (a relatively anthropological research approach), they attempted to characterize the manner in which internal management operations were structured and the rate of change in the external environment. Their results indicated that firms in relatively stable or unchanging environments tend to have more highly structured and formal management operations. They termed such organizations **mechanistic** because of their emphasis on rules, procedures, and dominance by a hierarchy of authority. In contrast, firms in more unstable environments tend to have a free-flowing, decentralized, and more adaptive internal organization

TABLE 18.1

FEATURES OF MECHANISTIC AND ORGANIC ORGANIZATIONAL FORMS

Mechanistic	Organic
Specialized tasks	Employee contributions to a common task
Hierarchy of authority	Less adherence to formal authority and control
Hierarchical communication	Network communication
Centralized knowledge and control	Decentralized knowledge and control
Insistence on loyalty and obedience to the organization	Loyalty and commitment given to the project or group
High degree of formality	High degree of flexibility and discretion

that they called **organic.** Table 18.1 summarizes the major differences between mechanistic and organic organizations.

Central to Burns and Stalker's contribution to the area of organizational design is the notion that these two extreme forms of organizational system are most appropriate for different environments: Organic systems are more capable of adapting to change, while mechanistic systems are appropriate to relatively static settings.[†] For example, a computer software company must survive in a dynamic, rapidly changing environment characterized by constant technical innovations, so it needs a more organic form of organization. At the other extreme, a synthetic fabric firm operates in a relatively predictable and stable environment, so it would probably have a more mechanistic form of organization.

EXTENDING BURNS AND STALKER'S MODEL   More recently, Porter, Lawler, and Hackman proposed a model that attempts to relate the mechanistic–organic dimension of organizations to the added dimensions of job type and individual preference.[9] Their model proposes that *congruency*—that is, an appropriate matching of these three dimensions—should result in improved employee attitudes. Individuals who seek challenge and responsibility in their jobs should prefer relatively complex or enriched jobs, and a complex job is more congruent with an organic, rather than a mechanistic, organization. Therefore, the combination of employee higher-order growth need strength with a complex or enriched job in an organic setting should produce greater employee satisfaction because all three factors are congruent.[‡] When any or all of the three factors (individual needs, job type, and system structure) are incongruent, employee attitudes will be less positive.

[†] It should be noted that Burns and Stalker's research did not actually prove that effectiveness is greater when organic systems exist within unstable environments, and so on, but merely that an organic system was associated with environmental change. Nonetheless, the implication is straightforward: Mechanistic organizations are presumed to be limited in their adaptability as a result of their rigidity.

[‡] For explanations of higher-order growth need strength and job enrichment, see Chapter 7.

Vecchio and Keon further refined the model based on the frequent finding that employees typically find complex jobs more satisfying than fairly simple jobs.[10] Using this finding and a set of rules for weighting congruence/incongruence, they proposed the following rank ordering of employee satisfaction in conjunction with congruence among individual needs, job design, and system structure.

Most Congruent	System Structure	Job Design	Growth Need Strength
1	Organic	Complex	High
2	Mechanistic	Complex	High
3	Organic	Complex	Low
4	Mechanistic	Complex	Low
5	Mechanistic	Simple	Low
6	Organic	Simple	Low
7	Mechanistic	Simple	High
8	Organic	Simple	High

Least Congruent

Tests of the predicted rank orderings with satisfaction data obtained in a variety of organizations largely confirmed the accuracy of these predictions: Employees in relatively congruent combinations tend to be more satisfied than employees in less congruent combinations.

LAWRENCE AND LORSCH'S CONTINGENCY RESEARCH

The importance of environmental attributes in determining the effectiveness of organizational systems is also underscored by studies conducted by Lawrence and Lorsch.[11] In their research, they examined the environments of firms in three diverse industries: plastics, food, and containers. Based on interviews with managers in these firms, they found it useful to describe environments in terms of turbulence (or change) and uncertainty, versus stability and certainty. Next, they examined the subenvironments faced by three divisions within each of the firms: production, marketing, and research and development. Environmental uncertainty was found to vary for each division, with uncertainty being greatest in R&D departments, followed in order by marketing and production. The key finding of Lawrence and Lorsch's research was that the nature of structuring within these divisions varied in accordance with environmental uncertainty. Production departments tended to have the highest degree of structure, followed by marketing and, last, R&D. Each department could also be characterized in terms of primary goals and orientations. Table 18.2 summarizes these differences.

Lawrence and Lorsch also examined how units within organizations are related. In the process, they found that organizations differ in terms of integration and differentiation. **Integration** refers to a state of collaboration among departments that seek to achieve unity of effort.[12] It concerns the quality of

TABLE 18.2
DIFFERENCES IN GOALS AND ORIENTATIONS AMONG DEPARTMENTS

	Departments		
Characteristic	Production	Marketing	R&D
Time horizon	Short	Short	Long
Goals	Efficient production	Customer satisfaction	New developments
Formality	High	High	Low

interdepartmental relations. **Differentiation** is reflected in the degree of specialization of labor and the psychological orientation of managers within departments. When department managers feel psychologically distant from managers in other departments, differentiation is greater.

Lawrence and Lorsch observed that differentiation among departments tended to be greater in organizations that operated in more complex and changing environments. Furthermore, these firms also needed more mechanisms designed to achieve integration among units. The plastics firms, for example, were most differentiated and thus needed to establish more mechanisms for coordinating efforts, such as liaison officers who facilitate communication among departments. In the least turbulent environment, that of the container firms, differentiation among departments was low, as was the number of mechanisms needed to integrate the departments.

WOODWARD'S STUDIES OF TECHNOLOGY

Another contextual variable of suspected importance in the structure of organizations is **technology**, the tools, techniques, and knowledge used to transform raw resources into finished goods. Some of the most important studies of the impact of technology were conducted by Joan Woodward, a British industrial sociologist.[13]

In her studies, which focused on 100 firms in England, Woodward initially set out to determine what structural factors were associated with commercial success. The results, however, did not identify characteristics that were more strongly associated with effectiveness (for example, more bureaucratic organizations were not necessarily more or less successful than less bureaucratic organizations). In further analyses on these data, Woodward sought to uncover underlying factors that might help to explain the otherwise meaningless patterns in the data. By reclassifying organizations in terms of type of technology, a set of meaningful results began to emerge suggesting that organizational structure should complement technology. Specifically, Woodward classified the firms into one of three categories: unit (or small-batch) production, mass (or large-batch) production, and long-run process production.

Unit production firms manufacture small orders that are custom-made for the purchaser. Made-to-order products such as furniture, electronics, and specialized construction equipment characterize this type of enterprise. **Mass production** firms manufacture standardized articles that do not require much specialized or varied attention. For example, automobile and mobile home manufacturers employ mass production technology. **Long-run process production** requires mechanization of the entire manufacturing operation. From beginning to end, the process is highly controlled, so the quality of the final product can be very easily predicted. Among the users of long-run process production technology are oil refineries, chemical plants, and distilleries.

Based on this classification system, certain patterns of results suggested that structuring within the sampled firms was indeed related to type of technology. For example, the number of management levels increased from unit to long-run process production—that is, as technological complexity increased.

Woodward also observed several complex patterns in her results. For example, the amount of verbal communication tended to be lowest in mass production organizations, whereas the amount of written communication was greatest. In addition, mass production firms tended to be more highly centralized and to employ more formalized procedures than did the other types of firms. Overall, the unit and long-run process production firms were relatively more organic, while the mass production firms were relatively more mechanistic. Table 18.3 summarizes these findings.

Further analyses by Woodward on the financial success of the same firms, as measured by market share, reputation, and the like, showed that successful firms tended to fit the pattern of structural attributes that was most typical for their technology grouping, as outlined in Table 18.3. For example, successful mass production firms tended to have mechanistic structures, while successful unit or long-run process production firms tended to have organic structures. Other studies in the United States[14] and Japan[15] have corroborated Woodward's findings that technology is related to structure and that appropriateness of structure is related to organizational performance.

TABLE 18.3

MAJOR FINDINGS OF WOODWARD'S STUDIES ON TECHNOLOGY AND STRUCTURE

Structural Attribute	Unit Production	Mass Production	Long-run Process Production
Number of management levels	Low	Moderate	High
Formalization	Low	High	Low
Centralization	Low	High	Low
Verbal communication	High	Low	High
Written communication	Low	High	Low
Overall structure	Organic	Mechanistic	Organic

An Inside Look
Investments in Information Technology

The unveiling of the 1994 Ford Mustang represented a hallmark in auto design for Ford. Today, integrated computer tools, similar to those that created *Jurassic Park*'s dinosaurs, transform a designer's sketches into lifelike images on a computer screen that can be viewed simultaneously at numerous global Ford facilities. Ford designers, engineers, and marketers around the world work interactively at computer workstations to modify model cars. The computers, which read and exchange digital data, are hooked up to design tools at various Ford locations.

Milling machines that create full-sized styrofoam mock-ups of model cars receive their milling instructions directly from the computers. Ford designers use fewer styrofoam models, at a cost of $100,000 each, to examine car designs through computer interaction. Designers literally carve changes into the styrofoam model and a laser scanner, similar to the kind at supermarket checkouts, translates the new shape back into digital data read by the computer. These investments in information technology result in substantial cost savings for Ford and better allocation of scarce human and technical resources.

Similarly, Chris-Craft, a boat manufacturer, installed a $300,000 computer-aided design (CAD) system that has substantially reduced product-development cycles and lowered manufacturing costs. The annual output of new designs has tripled, while development costs have been cut in half since Chris-Craft installed the system four years ago. According to Robert MacNeill, vice president for product development and engineering, CAD is particularly relevant for boatbuilding, where "everything's curved, nothing's level, nothing's plumb, nothing's straight, nothing's square."

Chris-Craft spent nine months designing and building the 268, a 26-foot sport boat that sleeps two. The model immediately filled a market niche and became the company's best seller. Before long, dealers were asking for a smaller version that would sell for $5,000 less than the 268's $35,000 price tag. Realizing it had only a few months before the fall boat-show season, the time when dealers shop for next season's products, the design team was able to turn an idea into a product in just three months, thanks to their CAD system. The smaller boat, a 24-foot version of the 268, is already outselling the 268, contributing to a 34 percent increase in revenues.

In just over a decade, capital outlays in information technology have grown from an average 8 percent of capital investments in 1980 to over 14 percent in 1992. Investments in telecommunications, computer hardware, software, and related high-tech gadgetry will continue to increase as companies try to keep pace with competitors.

Source: Stratford Sherman, "How to Bolster the Bottom Line," *Fortune*, Autumn 1993, 15–28.

THOMPSON'S TYPOLOGY OF TECHNOLOGY

One of the most widely cited approaches to classifying technology is that of James D. Thompson.[16] This typology specifies three varieties of technology: long-linked, mediating, and intensive. According to Thompson, all organizations can be classified with this typology.

A **long-linked technology** involves sequential, or serially linked, operations. A clear illustration of this type of technology is provided by an auto assembly plant. Because of the interdependence that results from the sequential nature of the tasks, this variety of technology is not very adaptable to environmental demands for change.

A **mediating technology** joins otherwise effective independent units of an organization or different types of customers. The "joining" is achieved by the use of standard operating procedures. For example, a commercial bank conducts relatively independent transactions (such as lending funds and receiving deposits). By using standard procedures, the bank serves the diverse needs of its clients. The rigidity of a mediating technology, which results from an adherence to procedures, can interfere with attempts to respond to changing demands.

Last, an **intensive technology** uses skills or services to transform an object. The decision about which skill or service to apply is determined by the results of previous efforts to transform the object. An outstanding example of an intensive technology is a hospital. Here, the object of interest is the patient and the skills and services are the staff and the various techniques embodied in specialties. Depending on how a patient responds to a given treatment, he or she will receive another possible form of therapy. This type of organization requires a high degree of coordination and communication, and is generally more responsive to change than other types of technology.

STRUCTURE AND STRATEGY

An issue of continuing interest to organizational theorists is the relationship between organizational structure and strategy. Specifically, does one influence the other? Does **strategy** (which we will define as a plan of action formulated by top-level management to better prepare the organization to deal with the future) grow out of an organization's structure? Or does structure largely determine an organization's apparent strategy for dealing with the external environment? Further, is it not possible that both structure and strategy influence each other?

In a widely cited study, Alfred Chandler, Jr., a historian, tackled this issue by conducting an in-depth analysis of several large corporations.[17] Using data gathered from company records and interviews with managers, he concluded that structure, especially decentralization, followed from strategy. However, the chief reasons for this tendency to modify organizational structure differed in each corporation. In the case of Du Pont, a more decentralized structure was created in response to a business strategy of product diversification. Standard Oil of New Jersey came to be more decentralized over time, but in an uncoordinated and gradual fashion. Yet, the trend toward decentralization occurred in response to a deliberate business strategy. Sears, Roebuck and Company likewise went through a process of decentralization in response to a specific strategy. Chandler's research further suggested that restructuring was generally in response to a desire to deal with growth. Although it is intuitively appealing to view strategy and structure as being able to influence each other (such that structure has implications for strategy formulation, and strategy has implications for organizational design), available evidence seems to suggest that the mutual influence may not be correct.[18]

SUMMARY

1. Identify three dimensions that describe an organization's external environment.

Environments can be relatively simple or complex; they can be static or dynamic; and they possess varying degrees of environmental uncertainty.

2. Explain how the environment influences which organizations will succeed and which will fail.

To maintain its existence, the organization must have an appropriate form, including goals, human resources, products, and technology. Chance, random forces, and continual change are also important elements in determining which organizations survive. Organizations with varying attributes are continually formed, and those that lack the needed organizational form will fail. A few adaptive forms will survive.

3. Explain how organizations handle their dependency on their environment.

Organizations try to manage their environment. They might try to purchase or control influential forces. They might try to make internal changes that will make them less vulnerable. Such changes include increasing structural complexity and creating boundary-spanning roles.

4. Describe two strategies organizations can use for managing the environment.

Organizations can change the external environment by establishing favorable linkages with critical elements in the environment and by controlling the environmental domain. Establishing favorable linkages includes vertical integration, hiring executives from companies the organization wants to link with, recruiting directors from targeted constituencies, creating interlocking directorates, and investing in advertising and public relations. Controlling environmental domains includes buying or selling a product line and joining with similar organizations having common goals or interests.

5. Identify an organization's structural dimensions and contextual dimensions.

Structural dimensions are internal characteristics of the organization, such as specialization, hierarchy of authority, decentralization, and complexity. Contextual dimensions are characteristics of the organization and its surroundings, and include size of the organization, technology, and external constituents (for example, customers, suppliers, competitors, and the government).

6. Explain when differentiation is likely to characterize an organization.

Differentiation among departments tends to be greatest in organizations that operate in complex and changing environments. These organizations need more mechanisms to achieve cooperation among departments.

7. Describe how an organization's structure complements its technology.

In ascending order of technological complexity, manufacturers can be classified as unit production firms, mass production firms, or long-run process production firms. The number of management levels increases as technological complexity increases. Mass production firms tend to be more mechanistic in structure, while unit and long-run process production firms are relatively organic.

8. Explain how strategy and structure may be related.

Strategy and structure are popularly believed to influence one another. Strategy is believed to have implications for the design of an organization. The design of an organization, in turn, is believed to have implications for how strategy may be formulated. Empirical evidence suggests, however, that structure may be largely influenced by strategy, rather than vice versa.

KEY TERMS

Population ecology perspective	Contextual dimensions
Organizational form	Mechanistic organization
Variation	Organic organization
Selection	Integration
Retention	Differentiation
Resource dependence model	Technology
Boundary-spanning positions	Unit production
Vertical integration	Mass production
Interlocking directorates	Long-run process production
Conglomerate	Long-linked technology
Strategic alliance	Mediating technology
Open system	Intensive technology
Closed system	Strategy
Structural dimensions	

REVIEW AND DISCUSSION QUESTIONS

1. How are an organization's efforts to grow and thrive like those of a living organism?

2. Given that an organization can be reasonably understood as a living entity, answer the following question: Where does the organization go at 5:00 P.M.?

3. For each of the following organizations, indicate whether the environment is simple or complex, static or dynamic. Which of these environments would have the most uncertainty?

   a. A manufacturer of paper clips

   b. A pharmaceutical company

   c. A university

4. Fertile Earth Enterprises sells seeds and garden tools through catalogs mailed to customers nationwide. What are some ways this company is

dependent on its environment? What are some ways in which the company can reduce or eliminate this dependency?

5. In what ways does technology influence organizational design?

6. What is an organization's strategy? Does its strategy grow out of its structure or its structure grow out of strategy, or do they influence each other?

7. The strategic planning committee presents its report to the board of directors of United Board Games. The committee concludes that the environment is changing, but only moderately. Assuming that the directors accept the committee's conclusions, what standards should they set for innovation, control, and development of new ideas?

CRITICAL INCIDENT

Environmental Pressures Intensify at Health-Rite

Robert Gore is president and owner of Health-Rite Equipment Co., Inc., a manufacturer of fitness equipment. The company employs 95 people at its facility in Portland, Oregon. Its physical fitness equipment has been selling well, which has resulted in rapid growth in the number of employees as well as revenue.

The rapid growth has been both a blessing and a curse for Mr. Gore in that he had always managed the firm much like a family business. Now, however, he has had to create an authority structure, employing six supervisors, or managers. The supervisors in charge of the manufacture and assembly of the various lines of equipment handle production scheduling, inventory control, materials procurement, and quality control. Mr. Gore handles all the financial management and personnel matters. He also keeps track of governmental reports and regulations. One manager is in charge of sales, and another, of new product development.

A recent complaint of discrimination was filed with the EEOC (Equal Employment Opportunity Commission), leading to an official inquiry. The matter is under review. In addition, OSHA (Occupational Safety and Health Administration) representatives made a surprise visit a few weeks ago and found several deficiencies. Health-Rite has ten more days to be in full compliance.

Because of the growing interest in personal health and fitness, several competitors have emerged in the past year. And although business has continued to be good, the competitive environment has become much more turbulent.

Finally, Mr. Gore has noticed increasing trouble in filling some orders. Some of the problems stem from suppliers either not shipping enough material or delaying shipments entirely. Other problems have been internal—production delays due to scheduling, quality control, and so forth. This has placed tremendous pressure on Mr. Gore, and he has not had time to address all these problems as he should. Recently, he also has had to deal with above-average turnover. Mr. Gore realizes that some changes need to be made, but he is not sure what to do.

QUESTIONS

1. What types of environmental forces are pressuring Health-Rite now? What forces could enter the picture in the future?
2. What types of changes would you recommend in terms of Health-Rite's organizational design to address these pressures?
3. Would you recommend any other changes? If so, explain.

Source: Written by Bruce Kemelgor, University of Louisville.

EXPERIENTIAL EXERCISE

Assessing Some Dimensions of an External Environment

Many factors influence the external environment of an organization. Complex organizations may find that their various divisions or departments are being influenced by so many different forces that the external environmental domain is heterogeneous (complex) rather than homogeneous (simple).

Using the following table and working either alone or as a member of a small group, describe the various factors that can affect the critical dimensions of an external environment.

Step 1   Your instructor may ask you to form groups of four to six people to complete this exercise, or you may be asked to work independently and discuss your results with the entire class.

Step 2   Using your school's basketball or football team, fill in the following boxes to complete an analysis of the key dimensions of the team's external environment. For example, in the recruitment of student athletes, how diverse is the environment that the recruiter and school must deal with? Using some specific examples, fill in the box under Simplicity–Complexity.

Do the same for each of the remaining boxes. Space has been provided if members of the class can identify another significant element.

Elements of the External Environment	Dimensions of the External Environment		
	Simplicity–Complexity	Static–Dynamic	Uncertainty
Recruiting of student athletes			
Season and single-event ticket sales			
Marketing and promotion			
Media and public relations (sports information)			
Additional element*			

* Must be agreed upon by the entire class

Step 3   Once the table is complete, answer the following questions:

1. Were any of the boxes more difficult than others to complete? Why?

2. Using the information from the chart, what types of strategies might be developed for dealing with these elements?

3. Is this a helpful way to diagnose the external environment and then plan for ways to deal with it? Why or why not?

Source: Written by Bruce Kemelgor, University of Louisville.

NOTES

1. J.D. Thompson, *Organizations in Action* (New York: McGraw-Hill, 1967).

2. R.B. Duncan, "The Characteristics of Organizational Environments and Perceived Environmental Uncertainty," *Administrative Science Quarterly* 17 (1972): 313–327.

3. Ibid.

4. J.B. Miner, *Theories of Organizational Structure and Process* (Hinsdale, Ill.: The Dryden Press, 1982); E. Gerloff, N. Kanoff-Muir, and W.D. Bodensteiner, "Three Components of Perceived Environmental Uncertainty: An Exploratory Analysis of the Effects of Aggregation," *Journal of Management* 17 (1991): 749–768.

5. H.E. Aldrich, *Organizations and Environments* (Englewood Cliffs, N.J.: Prentice-Hall, 1979); M. Sharfman and J. Dean, "Conceptualizing and Measuring the Organizational Environment: A Multidimensional Approach," *Journal of Management* 17 (1991): 681–700.

6. J. Pfeffer and G. Salancik, *The External Control of Organizations* (New York: Harper and Row, 1978); D. Wholey and J. Brittain, "Organizational Ecology: Findings and Implications," *Academy of Management Review* 11 (1986): 513–533.

7. R.L. Daft, *Organization Theory and Design* (St. Paul, Minn.: West, 1983).

8. T. Burns and G.M. Stalker, *The Management of Innovation* (London: Tavistock, 1961); T. Burns, "Industry in a New Age," *New Society* 31 (1963): 17–20.

9. L.W. Porter, E.E. Lawler, and J.R. Hackman, *Behavior in Organizations* (New York: McGraw-Hill, 1975).

10. R.P. Vecchio and T.L. Keon, "Predicting Employee Satisfaction from Congruency among Individual Need, Job Design, and System Structure," *Journal of Occupational Behavior* 2 (1981): 283–292.

11. P.R. Lawrence and J.W. Lorsch, *Organization and Environment: Managing Differentiation and Integration* (Homewood, Ill.: Irwin, 1969).

12. Ibid., 11.

13. J. Woodward, *Industrial Organization* (London: Oxford University Press, 1965).

14. W.L. Zwerman, *New Perspectives on Organizational Theory* (Westport, Conn.: Greenwood, 1970).

15. R.M. Marsh and H. Mannari, "Technology and Size as Determinants of the Organizational Structure of Japanese Factories," *Administrative Science Quarterly* 26 (1981): 33–56.

16. Thompson, *Organizations in Action.*

17. A.D. Chandler, Jr., *Strategy and Structure* (Garden City, N.J.: Anchor Books, 1966).

18. Miner, *Theories of Organizational Structure and Process.*

19

When I hear the word
culture, I reach for my
revolver.
— Hanns Johst

America is the land of
opportunity if you're a
businessman in Japan.
— Lawrence J. Peters

Every nation ridicules other
nations, and all are right.
— Arthur Schopenhauer

LEARNING OBJECTIVES

*After studying this chapter,
you should be able to:*

1. *Define organizational culture and describe influences on its creation and maintenance.*

2. *Explain how organizational culture may influence strategy.*

3. *Explain the importance of research comparing employees across nations.*

4. *Describe characteristics of typical managers in the United States.*

5. *Contrast Japanese and American management styles.*

6. *Give some examples of the differences in social customs and business practices in other cultures.*

7. *Identify two methods of cross-cultural training.*

Cultural Influences

MISTAKES WELCOME

From the beginning, Minnesota Mining & Manufacturing Company was a place where mistakes happened. The company was founded by five Minnesotans—a doctor, a lawyer, two railroad executives, and a meat-market manager—who bought a parcel of land where they planned to mine corundum, an abrasive used in sandpaper. Only after the company bought machinery, hired workers, and started mining did the five entrepreneurs discover that what they thought was corundum was in fact a worthless mineral.

This big mistake forced 3M Company to innovate its way to survival. First, the company introduced an abrasive cloth used for metal finishing. Then, inventor Francis G. Okie came up with 3M's first big hit: a waterproof sandpaper, which the company dubbed Wetordry. The sandpaper produced a better finish on automobiles and created less dust than conventional sandpapers, so it became the standard product used by the auto industry.

Since then, 3M Company has built on its past to develop an atmosphere that encourages experimentation and innovation throughout the company. This means that, among the employees, stories about massive failure are as legendary as tales of spectacular success. Thus, Okie is as well known for his ef- forts to promote rubbing one's cheeks with sandpaper as an alternative to shaving as he is for his invention of Wetordry sandpaper.

Fortunately for 3M, many of its innovations met a need. For example, Scotch tape was invented in 1929 to seal insulation in airtight shipping packages, and eventually grew into a product bringing in three-quarters of a billion dollars annually. Also in the 1920s, 3M inventor Richard G. Drew noticed that painters on automobile assembly lines had difficulty keeping the borders straight on two-tone cars. In response, Drew invented masking tape.

Company policies support the atmosphere of innovation. Divisions are expected to derive 25 percent of sales from products introduced in the preceding five years. Researchers, marketers, and managers visit customers to look for new product ideas. Technological advances made in one division are expected to be shared throughout the company.

The company even provides for workers who have an idea that doesn't seem to fall within the scope of one of the company's divisions. If someone has a product-related idea, that person is allowed to devote 15 percent of his or her time to prove that the idea is workable. The most famous success arising from this policy is Arthur L. Fry's invention of Post-it notes. Fry was looking for a way to keep the bookmark from falling out of his hymnbook. As a result, he developed the light adhesive now applied to the little notes stuck on business reports and refrigerators around the country.

The policies that foster such innovations are deeply ingrained in 3M's history. William L. Mc-Knight, one of the company's early chief executives, who started as an assistant bookkeeper and worked his way up as a salesperson, is viewed by employees as the spiritual founder of the company. After he became chief executive, McKnight wrote, "If management is intolerant and destructively critical when mistakes are made, I think it kills initiative." Tolerance for mistakes and encouragement of innovation are widely credited for the success of a company whose base products are as mundane as sandpaper and tape.

The strong emphasis on risk-taking and innovation at 3M Company is the basis of a distinctive culture. This chapter discusses in greater detail what constitutes an organization's culture, as well as some ways cultures are created and maintained. The chapter also compares Western culture with the cultures of other parts of the world.

Source: Russell Mitchell, "Masters of Innovation," *Business Week*, April 10, 1989, 58–63.

Every organization exists in an external culture and perpetuates its own internal culture. The study of cultural influences, a topic that is central to the field of anthropology, has existed for some time, but its application to business organizations is a recent phenomenon. In this chapter, we will initially examine cultures within organizations. Then, we will turn our attention to the topic of cultural, or national, differences in employee attitudes and behaviors.

ORGANIZATIONAL CULTURE

Although the notion of organizational culture is currently enjoying much popularity, a precise definition of it is difficult to offer. Edgar Schein suggests that organizational culture has been variously defined as a philosophy that underlies an organization's policy, the rules of the game for getting along, and the feeling or climate conveyed by the physical layout of the organization.[1] Ralph Kilmann proposes that organizational culture is largely a matter of norms.[2] Examples of some organizational norms include: Don't say what the boss doesn't want to hear; Don't be associated with an ugly event; Do cheat on your expense account; Don't criticize the company to outsiders; Don't be a bearer of bad news; and (perhaps the most ironic norm) Don't make norms explicit to anyone who inquires about them.[*]

Although there is considerable variation in the suggested definitions of organizational culture, it appears that most contain several common elements. Based on these, we can define **organizational culture** as the shared values and norms that exist in an organization and that are taught to incoming employees.[†] This definition suggests that organizational culture involves common beliefs and feelings, regularities in behavior, and a historical process for transmitting values and norms. Despite its lack of precision, the concept of organizational culture is widely used in management circles, sometimes as a convenient catch-all explanation for why things happen or do not happen in a particular way in a firm, as in, "It's the way we do things here—it's part of our culture."

RITUALS AND STORIES

Organizational rituals and stories (notions borrowed from cultural anthropology) play key roles in maintaining and building organizational cultures. For example, a number of ceremonial rituals may accompany the appointment of a new chief executive officer, including introductory announcements, banquets, meetings, and speeches. Similarly, the public awarding of a lapel pin can take on powerful meaning if employees believe that such an award symbolizes a significant achievement.

---

[*] Intriguingly, Kilmann reported that more than 90 percent of the norms cited by organizational members are negative in tone and connotation.

[†] Strictly speaking, the notions of values and norms already exist in the field of organizational behavior. Also, socialization of new members is a topic in itself. Therefore, the concept of organizational culture continues to be a rather fuzzy notion. In addition, organizations are themselves products of a culture, so it is confusing to speak of cultures existing within a cultural artifact. For many scholars, the debate on the usefulness and meaningfulness of the concept of organizational culture is unresolved.

The function and origin of organizational stories or myths are often un-clear.[3] Occasionally, a story will convey a theme that embodies the values of the corporation's founder or other major figures. Depending on its goal, its tone may be either positive or negative. For example, a positive story may re-count how the president attended a company picnic and displayed great per-sonal warmth toward the spouses and children of the firm's employees. Such a story is meant to convey the underlying concern that the president has for the corporate family. Or a story may retell how all employees in the firm (from the CEO on down) agreed to a 10 percent wage cut during an economically diffi-cult period in order to avoid any layoffs. On a more negative note, a story may be spread of how a former employee was ruthlessly dismissed and his career ruined by being blacklisted for the "crime" of disloyalty. The intent of such a story is, of course, to induce fear and control employees' behavior through in-timidation.

THE MEASUREMENT AND CHANGE OF ORGANIZATIONAL CULTURE

Before the study of organizational culture can make a substantial contribution to the field of organizational behavior in a scientific sense, it is necessary to have a set of methods for studying organizational culture. Unfortunately, the study of organizational culture presents unique challenges. Schein has ob-served that achieving an understanding of an organization's culture can be aided by locating a motivated insider within the organization, someone who is capable of deciphering the organization's culture and is motivated to discuss it.[4] Of course, a researcher is highly dependent on an insider's ability to pro-vide reconstructions of events and the beliefs of others. Therefore, the direct observation of important facets of an organizational culture may not be possi-ble (short of personal membership in an organization).

In addition to interviewing organizational members and joining the orga-nization, surveys can be used to obtain data on insiders' perceptions of the or-ganization's culture. However, the quality of the responses is likely to be lim-ited because the investigator cannot interact with the respondent to probe issues. Furthermore, the use of the survey method presupposes that the investi-gator is already familiar enough with the culture to know what questions and issues need to be investigated.

Although surveys, interviews, and partial membership in an organization are all potentially useful for studying organizational culture, Schein and Kil-mann advocate the use of group sessions by an investigator in order to check his or her emerging perceptions against actual members' views.[5] Kilmann also proposes that group members be asked to list a set of new norms that would facilitate organizational performance. With such lists, one can begin to discuss the changing of norms and, thereby, the changing of a major element of the organization's culture. Kilmann reports that the proposed norms that employ-ees most frequently list include: Treat everyone with respect; Listen to other members' views even if you don't agree with them; Provide recognition to those who suggest new ideas and ways of doing things; and Speak with pride about your organization and department. Such lists of desired norms can serve as a useful starting point for altering an organization's culture. However, the commitment to changing cultural features must of necessity be obtained from top-level administrators if the desired change is to occur and be maintained.

Increasing the potential to change organizational cultures in desired directions may be the greatest benefit of studying corporate cultures. By creating means for developing desired cultural features, the study of organizational culture can make a significant contribution to the field of organizational behavior.

THE CREATION AND MAINTENANCE OF ORGANIZATIONAL CULTURE

Since our research-based knowledge of organizational culture is presently very limited, it is difficult to state, with firm confidence, detailed prescriptions for creating and maintaining organizational cultures. Nonetheless, several observations and cautious suggestions can be made, based on the available understanding of organizational culture. It appears that there are at least four major influences on the origins of organizational culture.[6]

1. The *beliefs and values of the organization's founder* can be strong influences in the creation of organizational culture. During his or her tenure, these beliefs and values can become embedded in the organization's policies, programs, and informal statements perpetuated by continuing members of the organization (akin to the oral tradition of storytelling). For example, James Cash Penney infused his organization with "the Penney idea," consisting of such guiding principles as "Treat everyone as an individual" and "Value loyalty."

2. The *societal norms* of the firm's native or host country can also play a role in determining an organization's culture. That is, the culture of the surrounding society influences the culture of firms existing within it.

3. *Problems of external adaptation and survival* pose challenges for organizations that its members must meet via the creation of organizational culture (that is, norms). For example, the development of strategies and goals and the selection of methods to achieve goals require the creation of norms. At PepsiCo, competition with Coca-Cola has produced an internal atmosphere of extreme competition where careers are made or destroyed by slight fluctuations in market share.

4. *Problems of internal integration* can lead to the formation of organizational culture. For example, setting rules for social relations and the distribution of status, and establishing criteria for group and organizational membership require the development of norms and the acceptance of a set of beliefs.

The maintenance or reinforcement of an organization's culture can be best understood by knowing (1) what managers consider important (what they measure and control); (2) the manner in which top management reacts to crises and critical events; (3) what types of deliberate role modeling are provided by managers; (4) criteria for distributing rewards and status; and (5) criteria for hiring, firing, and promotion.[7] These five elements for understanding the maintenance of organizational culture also provide insights as to how to change an organization's culture. That is, culture may be best changed by altering what managers measure and control, changing the manner in which crises are handled, using different role models for new recruits and altering the socialization/orientation process, establishing different criteria for allocating rewards, and changing the criteria for promotion, hiring, and dismissal.

A FRAMEWORK FOR UNDERSTANDING ORGANIZATIONAL CULTURE

Recently, Smith and Vecchio proposed that the origin, maintenance, and modification of an organization's culture can be understood in terms of the following six central concepts[8] (see Figure 19.1).

CRITICAL DECISIONS OF THE ENTREPRENEUR OR FOUNDING MEMBERS

The founders of an organization, in essence, lay the foundation for the creation of the organization's culture. The vision and aspiration of the founders as well as their values and sense of mission play a critical role in forming norms and values within the organization. Moreover, the founders influence the formation of the organization's culture through such means as key recruiting decisions and critical decisions regarding the firm's market, and through the selection of their successors.

GUIDING IDEAS AND MISSION

The organization's leaders articulate a small set of guiding ideas. These guiding ideas, or superordinate goals, constitute a statement of purpose, or mission. Typically, they embody a belief in a core idea. Examples of guiding ideas

FIGURE 19.1
A FRAMEWORK FOR ANALYZING ORGANIZATIONAL CULTURE

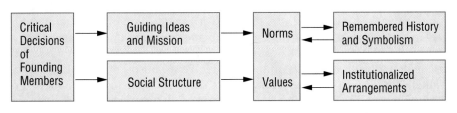

include "IBM Means Service" and, at 3M, "The 11th Commandment is never kill a new product idea." Actions that fulfill this commitment come to define the organization's distinctive identity.

SOCIAL STRUCTURE

The leaders also play a role in creating the organization's social structure. The structure consists of the patterns of interaction among people and groups within the organization. The social structure is a consequence of the leaders' decision on how best to design the organization's structure in light of technical considerations. These task-based issues, in turn, affect the pattern of formal and informal relations that emerges.

NORMS AND VALUES

Norms and values are the heart of what is meant by organizational culture. As the framework suggests, norms and values are influenced by the mission and the social structure. **Norms** are expectations for the behavior of the organization's members, while **values** are preferences among activities and outcomes. By participating in common organizational experiences, members develop greater degrees of shared values and norms, which then serve as aids to further communication and decision making. These norms and values also influence remembered history and institutionalized arrangements.

REMEMBERED HISTORY AND SYMBOLISM

Norms and values can influence the process whereby organizational history is selectively remembered and interpreted. Some events may be exaggerated or distorted, while others may be forgotten. **Symbolism** includes rituals and ceremonies. Symbols communicate values, legitimize practices, and help to socialize members and build loyalty. Remembered history and symbolism thus can influence existing norms and values.

INSTITUTIONALIZED ARRANGEMENTS

Formal policies, reward systems, and lines of authority and communication exemplify **institutionalized arrangements.** These arrangements constitute an organization's "way of doing business" and can have a powerful influence on the attitudes and behaviors of the organization's members. Institutionalized arrangements (for example, the forms people must complete, the training the organization provides, and the promotion and compensation systems) exert a subtle yet powerful form of control over employee actions. These arrangements are a result of norms and values. However, norms and values are continually influenced by the arrangements as well. Both institutionalized arrangements and the remembered history and symbolism help to perpetuate the organization's culture over time.

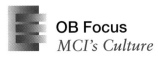

OB Focus
MCI's Culture

According to MCI Communications Corp. Chairman Bert C. Roberts, Jr., the key competitive difference between MCI and its rivals is MCI's strategy, values, and corporate culture. Since the company's beginning, it has used its underdog status against AT&T to inspire and invigorate its work force. Now a $10.6 billion corporation complete with four corporate jets, MCI is a major player in the long-distance communications sector, but its early days of struggle remain a large part of the cultural fabric of the company. MCI leaders take deliberate steps to maintain the spry, entrepreneurial culture as the company continues to grow older and larger.

To "keep the spirit of MCI kindled," Roberts actively uses cultural symbols. He's a regular on MCI's closed-circuit TV network, fervently promoting entrepreneurism. Management meetings are occasionally peppered with his magic tricks, and at a staff caucus he good-naturedly took a pie in the face from a fellow executive. A 1993 Dallas sales meeting, looking more like a political convention, featured a quirky mix of humor and patriotism, complete with red, white, and blue balloons. With patriotic background music, sales teams, dressed as their favorite *Saturday Night Live* characters, gave their revenue projections for the coming year. To the chant of "Bert . . . Bert . . . Bert," Roberts walked onstage to accept his "nomination."

The company's deliberate efforts to prevent the formation of a bureaucratic, hierarchical culture are obvious in the office, too. Most offices at the company's plush new headquarters in Washington, D.C., were deliberately built without doors to encourage unimpeded flow of communication and information. And despite a work force of 31,000, management structure has remained flat, with only two levels between Chairman Roberts and the branches.

Like many organizations, MCI uses symbols and imagery to sustain its culture. The spirit that made the company successful is perpetuated through symbols that reinforce key values to all members of the organization.

Source: Mark Lewyn, "Fun: It's Fundamental," *Business Week*, Enterprise, 1993, 197.

STUDIES OF ORGANIZATIONAL CULTURE

Research on organizational culture has moved beyond a purely descriptive stage and begun to develop and test predictions. One study developed a questionnaire for assessing long-time employees' perception of organizational values, and compared these organizational values with the value preferences of organizational newcomers.[9] Results showed that new employees whose values matched the organizational values on such dimensions as respect for people, team orientation, innovation, and so on had greater commitment and job satisfaction, and less turnover. This suggests that it may be possible to seek a match between an organization's values and new employees' values by screening job applicants for values–culture "fit" along with skill proficiency.

Organizations are now viewed as having a **dominant culture** that espouses the critical, core values shared by most employees. Also, organizations are acknowledged to have many **subcultures,** or sets of values and norms that are unique to a particular unit of the organization. These values and norms may or may not conform to the dominant culture of the organization. Another term often used in the area of corporate culture is **strong culture.** A strong (versus weak) culture is distinguished by whether the organization's values and norms are intensely held and widely endorsed. It is generally believed that a strong culture will provide advantages to an organization in terms of employee commitment and satisfaction. In a series of studies that examined the importance of congruence of values between employees and supervisors, researchers at the University of South Carolina found that employees are both more committed and more satisfied when their values are congruent with those of their supervisor.[10]

Organizations that seek to create strong cultures emphasize employee **socialization,** often investing considerable resources in new employee orientation programs and continuing education. One conspicuous aspect of socialization designed to foster company identification is attention to dress codes. As reported by Rafaeli and Pratt, employee attire influences both employee self-perception and the perception of employees by outsiders.[11]

CULTURE AND STRATEGY

Organizational researchers recognize the importance of an organization's culture in shaping the organization's strategy. The manner in which culture and strategy influence each other is thought to be quite complex. Figure 19.2 presents a simplified view of a mutual influence explanation of the relationships among environment, culture, and strategy. In this view, the perception of the organization's environment by the top management (strategy formulating) team is necessarily influenced by initial values and practices of members (that is, the organization's culture). Culture, therefore, plays a filtering role in terms of which facets of the environment are deemed important and deserving of attention. The top management team's strategic response (that is, its effort to respond to the environment or to manage a portion of the environment) will necessarily be influenced by the existing culture. That is to say, the ability of the top management team to respond quickly to a perceived threat will be affected by existing cultural characteristics of the organization. This suggests that a corporation's culture can sometimes be a liability in that it can impair the corporation's ability to perceive and respond to changes in the environment.‡

The model portrayed in Figure 19.2 argues that organizational culture operates as an intervening variable (see Chapter 2) in that it is a useful construct that cannot be perfectly and directly measured. This model also implies that a key element in judging the usefulness of an organizational culture is whether that culture is in proper "alignment" with the requirements of the organization's strategy. For example, if an organization is in a highly dynamic environment and requires rapid response to new forms of competition, the culture needed is one that endorses flexibility and coordination of efforts. To the degree that the existing culture approximates this ideal state, one can say that the organization's culture is in alignment with its strategy. In essence, cultural alignment is potentially an important determinant of an organization's longevity.

---

‡ Two clear illustrations of "culture as liability" include IBM and General Motors. These firms possess relatively strong cultures that impede their ability to perceive and respond to changes in their environment.

FIGURE 19.2

THE RECIPROCAL INFLUENCE VIEW OF STRATEGY AND ENVIRONMENT AS MODERATED BY ORGANIZATIONAL CULTURE

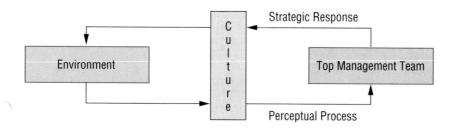

Source: C. G. Smith and R. P. Vecchio, "Organizational Culture and Strategic Management: Issues in the Management of Strategic Change," *Journal of Managerial Issues* 5 (1993): 53–70.

CROSS-CULTURAL RESEARCH

While the study of organizational culture focuses on the conduct of individuals within organizations, cross-cultural research explores the differences and similarities among members of different cultures. Defining what is meant by the term *culture* at this level of analysis is no less problematic. Most often, national boundaries are used as the basis for defining culture, but this is largely a convention of convenience, since the important dimensions of culture are sometimes difficult to specify.[§] In the realm of organizational behavior, it may be more accurate to say that the concern is with cross-national studies or comparative organizational behavior rather than with cross-cultural issues.

Even if we accept a label devoid of the term *culture,* the results of research comparing employees across different countries are still difficult to interpret. This difficulty stems from a lack of theoretical notions for explaining what culture or nationality is, and an inability to predict the effects of culture or nationality on other variables.[13] In short, it is difficult to make sense out of the results of cross-national studies without a theoretical scheme. We are often left simply with results stating that a group of employees in Country A did or did not differ from a group of employees in Country B. Why these results occurred and how any differences were brought about are often unexplained. Additionally, much cross-cultural research may be limited by the use of "made in America" theories. That is, cross-cultural researchers often use theories and derived measures of constructs that were originally designed in the West for studying Westerners. Although much theorizing on organizational behavior issues does originate in the United States, it is probably incorrect to assume that the ideas and constructs relevant to explaining the behavior of North American workers are equally appropriate for explaining the behavior of workers in all other countries.

[§] A good case can even be made that the term *culture* could be dropped or avoided in discussing behavior processes.[12]

TABLE 19.1

THE PACE OF LIFE IN SIX COUNTRIES

	Accuracy of Bank Clocks	Walking Speed	Post Office Speed
Japan	1	1	1
United States	2	3	2
England	4	2	3
Italy	5	4	6
Taiwan	3	5	4
Indonesia	6	6	5

Source: R. Levine and E. Wolff, "Social Time: The Heartbeat of Culture," *Psychology Today,* March 1985, 28–35.

Despite the difficulties of drawing inferences from the results of cross-national research, investigators have continued to make comparisons across nations. Continuing interest is spurred by the belief that cultural processes possess regularity and meaning that will ultimately become better understood, perhaps after more results are gathered and the patterns are examined to identify underlying principles. Further driving forces in cross-national research are the proliferation of multinational corporations (firms that are based in several different countries) and the growth of international trade. Increased contact between employees from different countries has led to a growing awareness of the need to better understand members of other cultures.

CULTURAL DIFFERENCES

Studies of the differences between national groups have uncovered some interesting results. For example, research on the pace of life in various countries suggests that Westerners tend to have fairly precise measures of time and a stronger concern for punctuality than have most other people. Levine and Wolff checked clock accuracy, walking speed, and the average time it took postal clerks to sell stamps in six countries.[14] A rank ordering of their results in terms of fastest to slowest (1 to 6) corroborates anecdotal suggestions that the pace of life differs across countries (Table 19.1). Anthropologist Edward Hall has distinguished two temporal styles: monochronic and polychronic.[15] People who display a monochronic style focus on one thing at a time, separating activities in time and space. People who display a polychronic style focus on several things at once (dovetailing or interspersing other activities). Northern European-derived nations (for example, the United States) tend to be monochronic, while Latin American nations tend to be polychronic. These different styles may underlie some misunderstandings and conflicts that arise when members of different nations interact. Table 19.2 displays a questionnaire developed by Allen Bluedorn, Carol Felker-Kaufman, and Paul Lane for assessing one's temporal style.

TABLE 19.2
A MEASURE OF POLYCHRONICITY

Please consider how you feel about the following statements. Circle your choice on the scale provided.

	Strongly disagree	Disagree	Neutral	Agree	Strongly agree
1. I do not like to juggle several activities at the same time.	5 pts	4 pts	3 pts	2 pts	1 pt
2. People should not try to do many things at once.	5 pts	4 pts	3 pts	2 pts	1 pt
3. When I sit down at my desk, I work on one project at a time.	5 pts	4 pts	3 pts	2 pts	1 pt
4. I am comfortable doing several things at the same time.	5 pts	4 pts	3 pts	2 pts	1 pt

Add up your points, and divide the total by 4. Then plot your score on the scale below.

```
  |        |        |        |        |        |        |        |        |
 1.0      1.5      2.0      2.5      3.0      3.5      4.0      4.5      5.0
monochronic                                                      polychronic
```

The lower your score (below 3), the more monochronic your orientation; the higher your score, the more polychronic.

Source: A. Bluedorn, C. Felker-Kaufman, and P. M. Lane, "How Many Things Do You Like to Do at Once: An Introduction to Monochronic and Polychronic Time," *Academy of Management Executive* 6 (1992): 17–26.

Other research, based on interviews with roughly 1,000 people in each of five countries, identified strong differences in levels of interpersonal trust. Specifically, it was found that the percentage of respondents who agreed that "most people can be trusted" varied as follows:

United States	55%
England	49%
Mexico	30%
Germany	19%
Italy	7%

Further research on cultural/national differences has focused on the need for achievement (see Chapter 6). In an examination of the themes in the literature of different countries, David McClelland noted strong differences.[16] Table 19.3 presents a sampling of his results.

In a comparison of the values of 3,600 managers representing 14 countries, Haire, Ghiselli, and Porter observed a number of similarities in dimensions of leadership and attitudes.[17] Other research by George England on the value systems of 2,600 managers in five countries also found many similarities, suggesting that managers often have common views on business-related activities regardless of national affiliation.[18]

TABLE 19.3

NATIONAL NEED FOR ACHIEVEMENT LEVELS

Country	National Score
Turkey	3.62
India	2.71
France	2.38
Australia	2.38
Israel	2.33
Canada	2.29
U.S.A.	2.24
West Germany	2.14
U.S.S.R.	2.10
Iraq	1.95
U.K.	1.67
Mexico	1.57
Sweden	1.52
Italy	1.33
Japan	1.29
Switzerland	1.20
Chile	1.19
Poland	.86
Belgium	.43

Source: D. C. McClelland, *The Achieving Society* (Princeton: Van Nostrand, 1961).

Certain patterns and clusters of results have also been observed in these and similar cross-national studies. Specifically, it has been found that managers from the United States, Canada, Australia, and Britain tend to hold fairly similar attitudes; Japanese and Korean managers tend to have greater agreement on value issues; Central and South Americans tend to agree; and so on. These clusters of responses suggest that although many similarities may exist among managers worldwide, they can also be sorted into clusters based on historical, religious, linguistic, and racial similarities.

Reliable differences between clusters of countries are frequently reported. In the Haire, Ghiselli, and Porter study and other follow-up studies, it has been found that various clusters of countries often differ on attitudes toward sharing information and the belief that individuals have the capacity for leadership and initiative (Table 19.4).[19] By and large, these results suggest that Anglo-American managers are much more democratic in their orientation, while managers from other countries tend to be more autocratic.

Another attitudinal difference between the United States and other countries can be seen in the extent of gender bias. A failure to appreciate this continuing bias in attitudes toward women in other countries can lead to difficul-

■ TABLE 19.4
ATTITUDES OF 3,600 MANAGERS IN 14 COUNTRIES*

Countries	Individual's Capacity for Leadership and Initiative	Advisability of Sharing Information and Objectives
Nordic-European countries (Denmark, Germany, Norway, Sweden)	−.24	.04
Developing countries (Argentina, Chile, India)	.21	−.59
Latin-European countries (Belgium, France, Italy, Spain)	−.25	.22
Japan	.39	.04
Anglo-American countries (England, United States)	.45	.36

Source: Adapted from M. Haire, E. E. Ghiselli, and L. W. Porter, *Managerial Thinking* (New York: Wiley, 1965).

* Positive average numbers denote democratic values, while negative average numbers denote values that are more autocratic.

ties for those who hope to conduct business in the international arena.** In addition, class consciousness and de facto caste systems are prevalent outside the United States. Even in some European countries, hirings and promotions are still based on social and academic origins rather than on objective merit. Fraternization across management levels and between managers and workers is frowned upon in many countries in the world. However, a limited degree of informal socializing of upper management with the "troops" is regarded quite favorably by most Americans. By and large, Americans object to elitist conduct and class distinctions, while the peoples of many other countries do not hesitate to invoke social rank.[20]

DIMENSIONS OF CULTURAL DIFFERENCES

One of the most ambitious studies of cultural differences as they relate to organizational issues was undertaken by Geert Hofstede, a Dutch scholar.[21] This research involved data on over 116,000 employees of IBM representing 40 countries. Based on his empirical results and a review of evidence in the field of cultural differences, Hofstede deduced four useful criteria for comparing cultures: power-distance, the avoidance of uncertainty, individualism versus collectivism, and masculinity versus femininity.

Power-distance refers to the degree that the members of a culture accept the unequal distribution of power, and the appropriateness of maintaining distance between people. *Avoidance of uncertainty* is the degree to which members of a culture are able to cope with ambiguous or anxiety-provoking situations.

** The United States was the first nation to legally recognize sex discrimination and sexual harassment. Only Australia, Canada, France, New Zealand, Spain, and Sweden also have specific statutes on harassment. In most countries, harassment is handled indirectly (if at all) as a by-product of other laws, such as those dealing with unfair dismissal.

Individualism versus collectivism refers to whether the members of a culture endorse a view that people are expected to take care of only their immediate families (individualism) versus a view that people are expected to care for members of an extended family and offer loyalty to groups (collectivism).

Masculinity versus femininity is concerned with whether members of a culture value traits and attributes that are traditionally defined as masculine versus traits and attributes that are more characteristically feminine in nature. Table 19.5 summarizes the defining endpoints of these four dimensions.

In a comparison of managers from the United States to managers from 39 countries on these four dimensions, Hofstede found that the United States

TABLE 19.5

DIMENSIONS OF CULTURAL DIFFERENCES

Power-Distance

Small Power-Distance	Large Power-Distance
Inequality among people should be reduced	There should be a degree of inequality, where everyone has a rightful place
Leaders and followers consider each other to be just like themselves	Leaders and followers view one another as being different
Those in power should try to appear less powerful	Those in power should try to appear powerful

Avoidance of Uncertainty

Weak Avoidance	Strong Avoidance
There should be few rules	There is a need for written rules
Competition can be used constructively	Competition can unleash aggression and should, therefore, be avoided
Authorities should serve citizens	Citizens lack competence compared to authorities

Individualism versus Collectivism

Individualist	Collectivist
"I" consciousness is dominant	"We" consciousness is dominant
People should strive for themselves and only immediate family	People belong to extended families or clans
Emphasis on initiative and leading	Emphasis on belonging and following

Masculinity versus Femininity

Feminine	Masculine
Men need not be assertive, but can be nurturing	Men should be assertive and women should be nurturing
Equality of sexes is ideal	Men should dominate in society
People and environment are valued	Wealth and goods are valued

Source: G. Hofstede, *Culture's Consequences* (New York: Sage Publications, 1980), 122, 184, 235, 295.

ranked 26th (below average) on power-distance, 32nd on avoidance of uncertainty (again, below average), 1st on individualism (that is, highly individualistic), and 13th on masculinity (above average). In their totality, these results suggest that U.S. managers (in the aggregate and relative to managers in other countries) prefer a small power-distance, feel capable of coping with ambiguity, are highly individualistic, and endorse traditionally masculine values.

JAPANESE MANAGEMENT

Much has been written in recent years about the alleged superiority of **Japanese management** techniques in comparison to the American style of management. The major characteristics of the Japanese approach to management (assuming that it is fair to speak in very general terms of a nation's system of management) have been identified by such writers as Ouchi and Price,[22] Chung and Gray,[23] and Rehder.[24] Contrasting their descriptions with how American firms are structured or tackle similar problems produces some interesting differences.

A major stylistic difference between the two approaches lies in the extent to which consensus is sought when making decisions. Japanese firms involve many more workers in the decision-making process and try to work on a solution until all of those involved are reasonably satisfied. In the United States, decision making is more often an individual manager's prerogative.

A second major difference between the two styles of management lies in their amount of commitment to the worker. Some Japanese firms offer the equivalent of lifetime employment to their employees, thereby creating feelings of security and family membership. U.S. firms, in contrast, tend toward a short-term view of employment, releasing employees when the company finds it necessary.

Third, Japanese evaluation and promotion systems are designed to reward seniority more than merit. A consequence of this feature, coupled with a commitment to employment security, is that individuals must wait a long time to rise through management ranks. In the United States, young managers expect that they will rise rapidly within a firm, or, if they do not, they will seek employment elsewhere.

Other less frequently cited features of Japanese management include intensive socialization of employees to create greater group cohesiveness, emphasis on quality and productivity, and reliance on an informal approach to controlling the behavior of employees. Figure 19.3 summarizes the six major components most frequently identified with Japanese management. William Ouchi, a professor at UCLA, argues that highly successful U.S. firms may be benefiting from the adoption of these six features, which he views as characterizing a unique form of management called **Theory Z.**[25] According to this view, an organization is more likely to be successful to the extent it incorporates the principles of Theory Z.

It is commonly suggested that the features of Theory Z management are responsible for the Japanese economic miracle. Although it is true that Japan's *rate* of productivity growth has been greater than that of the United States in

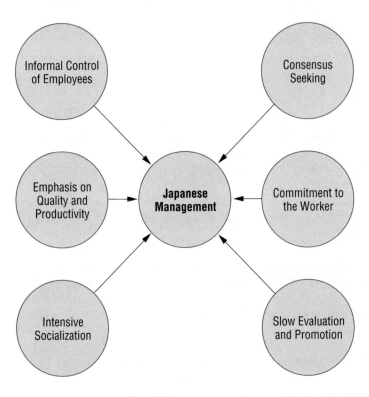

FIGURE 19.3

MAJOR COMPONENTS OF JAPANESE MANAGEMENT

past years, it does not follow that Japanese industry is stronger or that the Japanese approach to management is better in any meaningful sense. The fact that differences exist is not in itself sufficient to explain Japan's productivity gains. Furthermore, Japan's relative economic advantage is only seen in certain areas, such as steel and iron production. The United States leads Japan in terms of quality and technology in aircraft, computers and software, pharmaceuticals, medical equipment, telecommunications equipment and networking, farm equipment, pulp and paper, and printing. In machine tools, steel, and automobiles, the United States is not a leader; but quality and efficiency are improving, and export gains are expected.

If for the sake of argument we assume that Japanese management practices are superior to American practices, we must then consider whether it is feasible to adopt the Japanese approach in the United States. Many students of Japanese management feel that it is not reasonable to think in terms of transplanting many features of Japanese management.[26] For example, the notions of promoting slowly and rewarding heavily for seniority rather than merit would find little acceptance among U.S. employees. Other features, such as seeking consensus in decision making, may be more workable but may also be unnecessary. That is to say, frequent group meetings to achieve consensus may have evolved in Japan because of the difficulty of relying on written communication in the Japanese language. As a result, oral communication may have come to be preferred for business purposes.[27] ††

Finally, many of the vaunted positive features of Japanese management are not common in the country's larger companies. For example, it is estimated that only 30 percent of Japanese workers enjoy the security of a lifetime job guarantee.[28] Also, lifetime employment practices (left over from feudal times) appear to be eroding in recent years due to the difficulty of retaining a large work force during an economic downturn.[29] Some Japanese firms, as a result, are turning to increased subcontracting, temporary help, and women (who can be fired more easily).‡‡ In addition, there are few opportunities for women to enter management ranks. By and large, these and other shortcomings of Japanese business practices argue against a simple transplanting of Japanese management practices to the United States.[31] In addition, it has been suggested that young Japanese employees are less committed to their work than were their predecessors. One comparison found that only 14 percent of young Japanese were satisfied with the workplace versus 70 percent of their U.S. counterparts.§§ A major source of dissatisfaction seems to be the Japanese practice of assigning employees to jobs without regard for their preferences. A cross-cultural comparison by the Aspen Institute for Humanistic Studies found that Japanese (and British) workers reported the greatest disparity between what they desired in a job and what they actually experienced. Although the touted Japanese commitment to work is not in danger of collapse, these and related findings suggest a growing sense of alienation among Japanese workers.[33]

In closing this discussion of differences among managers in various countries, it should be stated that many students of comparative management believe there is a general set of management practices that can be applied across all cultures. Thus, they contend that management can be practiced in a generic sense. One typically finds the major organizational functions (that is, marketing, production, and finance) existing in firms around the world. In short, the principles of effective management may be said to be fairly universal, or lacking a high degree of uniqueness, for various cultures.[34]

DOING BUSINESS OVERSEAS

The increasing globalization of the world economy has produced a growing demand for managers skilled in international business practices. The sophistication required to work effectively with people from other countries takes

†† Gutenberg's invention of printing from movable type—a technique not readily adaptable to the enormous number of Japanese written characters—may, therefore, be responsible for the Western emphasis on written business communications.

‡‡ Although the lifetime employment system in Japan is often cited by foreign observers as a positive attribute, critics point out that the system actually increases management's control of employees by creating a greater employee dependency upon managers.[30]

§§ A survey of Japanese workers found that 40 percent fear they may work themselves into an early grave. In fact, the Japanese have a term for death from overwork—*karoshi*.[32]

considerable time to develop. As a first step in learning to relate with people from other cultures, it is useful to consider how we are seen by others. Following are some observations made by visitors to the United States.[35]

- "Americans seem to be in a perpetual hurry. Just watch the way they walk down the street. They never allow themselves the leisure to enjoy life." (India)

- "Americans appear to us rather distant. They are not really as close to other people—even fellow Americans—as Americans overseas tend to portray. It's almost as if an American says, 'I won't let you get too close to me.' It's like building a wall." (Kenya)

- "Once we were out in a rural area in the middle of nowhere and saw an American come to a stop sign. Though he could see in both directions for miles and no traffic was coming, he still stopped!" (Turkey)

- "The tendency in the United States to think that life is only work hits you in the face. Work seems to be the one type of motivation." (Colombia)

- "In the United States, everything has to be talked about and analyzed. Even the littlest thing has to be, 'Why, Why, Why?' I get a headache from such persistent questions." (Indonesia)

- "The American is very explicit; he wants a 'yes' or 'no.' If someone tries to speak figuratively, the American is confused." (Ethiopia)

- "The first time . . . my (American) professor told me, 'I don't know the answer, I will have to look it up,' I was shocked. I asked myself, 'Why is he teaching me?' In my country, a professor would give the wrong answer rather than admit ignorance." (Iran)

Functioning as a manager in another country requires an understanding of the traditions, customs, and business practices of the host country. Although there is little empirical evidence of the precise requirements to be effective in doing business overseas, the collected wisdom of experienced overseas managers does give some insight on what works (and what doesn't) in specific countries.[36]

LATIN AMERICA   Conducting business in Latin America takes time. Few people rush into business. Although some customs are changing, men and women still congregate into separate groups at social functions (until recently, having a chaperone was still an accepted practice). Latins also stand more closely together than do North Americans when in conversation. Instead of shaking hands, men may embrace. Guests invariably arrive late for functions (although North Americans are expected to be punctual). Several unique traits are the *mañana* concept (meaning a belief in an indefinite future and, therefore, little need to worry about deadlines), *machismo* (an expectation that in business a man will display forcefulness, self-confidence, and leadership with a flourish), and *fatalism* (a resignation to the inevitable, or taking whatever comes, sometimes seen as a heroic posture). As a rule for non-Latins, when in doubt, be formal.

EAST ASIA (JAPAN, THE CHINAS, KOREA)   Initially, business meetings are devoted to pleasantries—serving tea, engaging in inconsequential chitchat, and developing a relationship. Indirect and vague communication is considered acceptable. Sometimes statements are left unfinished so that the listener can reach the conclusion in his or her own mind. Forcing another to admit failure or impotency is to be avoided. Seniority and elderliness command respect. When confronted with a strange, unexpected, or emotionally powerful situation, East Asians may laugh or smile in a seemingly inappropriate manner (as a function of releasing tension rather than finding the circumstance humorous). In addition, many are convinced that East Asians consciously use slowdown techniques as bargaining ploys in the belief that they can exploit a natural inclination of Westerners to be impatient. Finally, it is very much expected that business cards will have one side printed in English and the other in oriental characters (although the presentation of your business card may not always result in your being offered a business card by the other party).

RUSSIA   Notorious for being protocol conscious, Russians expect to do business with only the highest-ranking executives. To Westerners, they appear stiff and dull. When greeting foreigners for the first time, Russians sometimes use the stilted term *gospodin* (citizen). In private, however, Russians are far more expressive and sociable. Written agreements are essential as informal, quid pro quo understandings may not be honored. Unfortunately, writing a contract can be difficult as there are no Russian equivalents for many Western business terms. Contracts, therefore, must be back-translated (that is, translated from English into Russian and then translated from Russian back into English to determine if the exact meaning is retained). In a land of chronic shortages and few choices, the Russians have virtually no advertising experience. The basic sales philosophy can be summarized in the words of a Russian citizen who was asked how he might go about attracting more customers to stay at his hotel. "Well," he responded, "I would hope that all the other hotels were full."

MIDDLE EAST   Middle Easterners are known to occasionally prefer to act through trusted third parties rather than deal directly. Personal honor is given a high premium, and the avoidance of shame is very important. Fatalism influences the view of time. A favorite expression is "Burka insha Allah"—"Tomorrow if God wills." Compared with people of other societies (especially East Asians), Middle Easterners are far more emotionally expressive. They stand closer together, and eye contact is more intense. Also, occasional bodily contact during conversations (for example, gently tapping another's arm or knee) is not unusual. Guests should avoid discussing politics, religion, and the host's family and personal possessions (commenting on the host's female family members is a taboo, and praising a possession implies the host should offer the item as a gift). A signal that a meeting is concluded is given by the offer of coffee or tea.

An Inside Look
The Perils of Uninformed Travel

Why should a manager from the United States be worried about fitting in with the business practices and customs of other cultures? Perhaps the following blunders speak for themselves.

On a trip to Malaysia, a businessman was introduced ceremoniously to someone he thought was named Roger. Throughout the important contract negotiations that followed, he referred to this person as "Rog." Only later did he learn that his potential client was a rajah (a title of nobility), not someone named Roger. He might have avoided tremendous embarrassment by learning ahead of time that one of the states in Malaysia is headed by rajahs (the others are controlled by sultans).

Learning about another country's culture ahead of time can prevent inadvertent insults as well as embarrassment. An American executive with an oil company traveled to a Middle Eastern nation to sign a contract. An hour before the signing ceremony, the executive met for tea with the government official responsible for the contract. The American relaxed by propping his feet on the table, with his soles facing the Arab host. Furious, the official left the room, and the company spent another year in negotiations before the contract was signed. The American executive had not realized that exposing the sole of one's shoe to an Arab is a serious insult.

Some thorough homework might also have prevented the embarrassment experienced by an executive who went to a small Caribbean country to close a sale. He entered the prime minister's conference room and opened his presentation by saying, "Honorable Mr. Tollis and esteemed members of the cabinet." The prime minister suggested that the executive start over. The businessman repeated his opening phrase, to the apparent annoyance of the prime minister, who suggested that he again start over. A sympathetic cabinet minister took the American aside and whispered, "Mr. Tollis was deposed six months ago. You are now addressing the Honorable Mr. Herbert."

Fortunately for their companies, American managers have begun to realize that successful negotiations depend on knowing their customers as well as their products. American businesspeople in Japan, for example, have learned to navigate that country's practices with regard to patents and distribution. But, notes an official of a major Tokyo trading company, some visitors still refuse the customary cup of green tea offered during a company visit. "Why don't they just take it?" wonders the official. "It's so simple, but refusing can throw off the whole pace of a meeting."

The lesson in this complaint is that seemingly minor details can make or break an important contract or business relationship.

Sources: Ted Holden, "The Delicate Art of Doing Business in Japan," *Business Week*, October 2, 1989, 120; and Charles F. Valentine, "Blunders Abroad," *National Business*, March 1989, 54, 56.

METHODS OF CROSS-CULTURAL TRAINING

Cross-cultural training programs have been created to teach members of one culture ways of interacting effectively in another. Programs vary, with the simplest consisting merely of lectures and readings concerning the host culture. More extensive programs may involve role-playing exercises, simulations, and practice in functioning within the host country itself. In this section, we will examine two techniques used in orientation programs: the Culture Assimilator and simulation.

THE CULTURE ASSIMILATOR   The **Culture Assimilator** is a programmed learning exercise designed by social scientists at the University of Illinois under the direction of Harry Triandis.[37] The assimilator is culture-specific—there is a programmed learning exercise for each of a number of countries. The assimilator provides the learner with immediate feedback on his or her response to a hypothetical situation. In addition to simply finding out whether the chosen response is correct, the learner is given an explanation regarding why the response is or is not correct. The following is an example from the Thailand assimilator. The example was developed after a U.S. student reported being bothered by Thai teachers' lack of punctuality. Although Thai students were similarly disturbed, they reported that they would never show these feelings to their professors.

> *One day a Thai administrator of middle academic rank kept two of his assistants waiting about an hour for an appointment. The assistants, although very angry, did not show it while they waited. When the administrator walked in, he acted as if he were not late. He offered no apology or explanation. After he was settled in his office, he called his assistants in; they all began working on the business for which the administrator had set the meeting.*
>
> *If the incident is observed exactly as it is reported in this passage, which of the following best describes the chief significance of the behavior of the people involved?*
>
> 1. *The Thai assistants were extremely skillful at concealing their true feelings.*
>
> 2. *In Thailand, subordinates are required to be polite to their superiors, no matter what happens or what their rank may be.*
>
> 3. *Since no one commented on it, the behavior indicated nothing of unusual significance to the Thais.*

The feedback for each choice is as follows:

1. This is not entirely correct, although it is characteristic of Thais to try to appear reserved under any circumstances. If the assistants were skillful at concealing their true feelings, there would be no doubt about their feelings. Also, the reference to the chief significance of the behavior of the people involved may limit the inference to the assistants.

2. This choice is correct. The information in the episode is fully used. This "deference to the boss" may be observed anywhere in the world, but it is likely to be carried to a higher degree in Thailand than in the United States. Certain clues indicate this choice—the assistants concealed their feelings, the administrator failed to apologize, the tardiness was not mentioned, and the appointment was kept.

3. This answer is completely wrong. Although the behavior in the passage does not seem as significant to the Thais as it might to Americans, why was nothing said about the tardiness? And why were the assistants "very angry" although they "did not show it"?

The Culture Assimilator has been studied extensively, perhaps more than any other cross-cultural training method. In general, the data suggest that assimilator training reduces interpersonal and adjustment problems between the trainees and members of the host country.[38]

SIMULATION   In simulation training, a situation is created through which individuals experience certain elements of behavior they may encounter in another country. Learning is primarily inductive in that participants are expected to draw insight and deeper understanding from the experience. One example is the game "Bafa, Bafa." Bafa, Bafa is a simulation in which participants are assigned membership in one of two artificial cultures, Alpha and Beta. Each group first learns certain customs that characterize its culture (for example, the Alpha culture is warm, friendly, patriarchal, and English-speaking; the Beta do not speak English but are hard workers who seek to maximize points in any game). The two groups are then brought together to play a card game for points, and inevitably experience frustration and hostility in dealing with each other. A post–role-playing debriefing helps participants understand their own and others' negative behavior. Participants are led to realize that fully understanding the subtleties of another culture requires experience. They learn that what is accepted as sensible and reasonable in one culture may seem irrational or unimportant to an outsider, that differences among people are often seen as potentially threatening, and that stereotyping is a fairly natural process.

SUMMARY

1. Define organizational culture and describe influences on its creation and maintenance.
Organizational culture comprises the shared values and norms in an organization that are taught to incoming employees. Influences on the creation of cultures are: the beliefs and values of the organization's founder; societal norms; problems of external adaptation and survival; and problems of internal integration. Maintaining an organizational culture depends on managers' priorities; top management's reactions to critical events; role modeling by managers; criteria for distributing rewards and status; and criteria for hiring, firing, and promotion.

2. Explain how organizational culture may influence strategy.
The perception of an organization's environment by its top management team is affected by, or filtered through, elements of the organization's culture (that is, the initial values and practices of the founding members). This perception affects the team's strategic response to the environment, and that response, in turn, influences the culture. In essence, culture serves as an intervening variable.

3. Explain the importance of research comparing employees across nations.
The research may reveal patterns that will identify underlying principles about cultural processes. Multinational corporations are proliferating, and international trade is growing. As a result, increased contact among nations has heightened the need for better understanding by members of different cultures.

4. Describe characteristics of typical managers in the United States.
In the aggregate, U.S. managers prefer a small power-distance, feel capable of coping with ambiguity, are highly individualistic, and endorse values traditionally considered masculine.

5. Contrast Japanese and American management styles.

Japanese firms involve many more workers in the decision-making process and try to achieve consensus, while in the United States managers more often make decisions individually. Japanese management places more emphasis on job security, whereas U.S. companies tend to take a more short-term view. Japanese systems tend to reward seniority more than merit; in the United States, young managers expect to rise rapidly within a company or they will leave it.

6. Give some examples of the differences in social customs and business practices in other cultures.

In Latin America, there is less attention to punctuality but more physical contact. In East Asia, seniority is given great respect. Russians tend to be formal in public settings, but expressive and sociable in private. Middle Easterners value honor and tend to be emotionally more expressive.

7. Identify two methods of cross-cultural training.

The Culture Assimilator uses a culture-specific programmed learning exercise to explain why people behave differently in different cultures. Simulation training involves role-playing exercises that provide participants with an opportunity to learn more about the values, feelings, and behaviors of members of different cultures.

KEY TERMS

Organizational culture	Subculture
Norms	Strong culture
Values	Socialization
Symbolism	Japanese management
Institutionalized arrangements	Theory Z
Dominant culture	Culture Assimilator

REVIEW AND DISCUSSION QUESTIONS

1. When Don left XYZ Galvanizing, the following story circulated through the grapevine: Don's boss, June, had overheard Don discussing XYZ on the telephone. Don was telling the other party that XYZ was having problems because it was selling products that had been improperly galvanized, and customers were beginning to complain and threaten lawsuits. After June overheard Don, she started reviewing all his outgoing mail and frequently passed by his office in order to keep track of his phone conversations. When the time came for Don's salary review, June told him that he would not be getting a raise. At that time, Don realized that his career at XYZ was over, and he resigned. What norm does this rumor illustrate? How might such a norm have developed?

2. Is research into cross-cultural differences in organizations valid? Consider whether a culture is a meaningful unit for comparison, the benefits of cross-cultural research, and your own opinion of the merits of the findings so far.

For example, does the available research supply information that aids our understanding of other people, or does it merely reinforce baseless stereotypes?

3. People discussing management styles often suggest that a Japanese style of management would greatly improve the performance of U.S. companies. What factors characterize a Japanese management style? Should U.S. companies adopt this style?

4. How might one measure the elements of an organization's culture?

5. Describe the major influences on the origins of organizational culture. How might these influences be used deliberately to change an organization's culture?

6. Do academic institutions have different organizational cultures? In what ways might these cultures be said to differ?

7. Maryann is considering applying for an overseas assignment that would take her to a country that values masculinity over femininity. What are some issues she should be prepared to deal with?

8. You are given an opportunity to work overseas in one of several countries—Mexico, Korea, Russia, or Egypt. Assuming the assignments are equivalent in all major respects, in which country would you prefer to work? Why?

9. Several young managers in your unit are about to be assigned overseas. What steps might you take to help them prepare for their new assignments?

CRITICAL INCIDENT

The Culture at Continental Communications

Six years ago, Continental Communications was founded by two former telephone executives, Bill Schuman and Mark Willis. Their goal was to create a new long-distance telephone company that would compete with the larger long-distance carriers without imposing the bureaucratic culture associated with the larger phone companies. The company, with 400 employees, now provides long-distance service to the entire New England area, and is still owned and headed by its enterprising founders.

Both owners bring a lot of energy and spirit to the company and seek employees with similar levels of drive and determination. Continental recruits at several top business schools, and hires many entry-level managers right out of school. "Newly minted graduates have no preestablished ideas about how communications companies should operate," says Bill. "They are like a blank slate onto which we transfer our company's values." Employees at Continental are youthful and energetic; the median age of the work force is 34.

In an effort to turn Continental into a viable, nationwide long-distance carrier, employees are encouraged to seek innovative solutions, try risky alternatives, and work long hours. Most salaried employees work between 50 and 60 hours a week. From the start, Bill and Mark have maintained open lines of communication with all employees. The official policy states that any employee can discuss problems, issues, or ideas with any other employee at any time. According to Mark, "We're in the business to foster communications. We have an obligation to our customers to facilitate open communication both within and outside our corporate boundaries." Many inside Continental credit the open communications policy for allowing innovative ideas to circulate throughout the company. Employees bounce ideas off one another and proposals often develop into tangible services offered to customers. To maintain an invigorating climate, employees are eligible for a generous annual bonus based on individual and team performance, and company profit measures.

Both Bill and Mark are avid bicyclists, and the company biking team frequently competes in local races. Employees who share the owners' love of biking receive a 12-speed racing bike valued at $1,200 upon completing a continuous 100-mile ride on one of the biking team's regular outings. Many employees remember the time Mark and Bill unknowingly mismarked the route, and employees riding for the complimentary racing bike actually rode closer to 120 miles. Mark and Bill are reminded of the incident whenever their sales or revenue projections seem a little off the mark. To date, over 70 racing bikes have been awarded. Employees also receive a personalized decorative wall plaque denoting entrance into the "100 Mile Club." Similar plaques are awarded to employees who have ridden 50- and 75-mile distances. Through these and other acts, all employees at Continental are made aware of the importance of achieving difficult goals.

QUESTIONS

1. Describe the organizational culture at Continental Communications. What are its main features?

2. List examples of Continental's observable culture, shared values, and common assumptions.

3. Given what you know about its corporate culture, is Continental Communications the type of organization you would like to work for? Why or why not?

Source: "The Culture at Continental Communications," written by Melissa Waite, State University of New York, University at Buffalo; and Susan Stites-Doe, State University of New York, College at Brockport.

EXPERIENTIAL EXERCISE

Is Your Culture Gap Showing?

This activity is designed to help you better understand the culture at your college or university. There are no good or bad cultures per se. The cultural norms either help or hinder the organization in realizing its goals, mission, and purposes.

Following are several sets of paired statements concerning elements that constitute the college culture. Please work quickly and do not read too much into each statement.

Step 1   Complete the following cultural assessment instrument. Respond to each pair of statements in the following manner:

a. Choose the (A) or (B) item in each pair that is the *actual* norm right now. Mark that norm with an A.

b. Label the (A) or (B) norm that is the *desired* condition with a D. This may be the same or the opposite statement you labeled in part a. Thus, you could have one of the following configurations:

(A)   A   (A)   D   (A)   AD   (A)
(B)   D   (B)   A   (B)   (B)   AD

c. Using the following 7-point scale, indicate the importance of the choice (or issue) to you.

7: This is a critical issue.
6: This is very important.
5: This is moderately important.
4: This is a neutral issue.
3: This is moderately unimportant.
2: This is very unimportant.
1: This is an extremely unimportant issue.

	Actual/Desired	Importance
1. (A) The professors go out of their way to help students.	_____	_____
(B) The professors just teach their classes.	_____	_____
2. (A) Channels for expressing student complaints are readily accessible.	_____	_____
(B) Few people pay serious attention to student complaints.	_____	_____
3. (A) Many students here develop a strong sense of responsibility about their roles in contemporary social and political life.	_____	_____
(B) The expression of strong personal belief or conviction is pretty rare around here.	_____	_____
4. (A) Students respect the rules.	_____	_____
(B) Students pay little attention to rules.	_____	_____
5. (A) Most of the professors are very thorough teachers and really probe into the fundamentals of their subjects.	_____	_____
(B) Most of the professors just cover the bare facts.	_____	_____

6. (A) Students are conscientious about taking good care of school property.   _____   _____
   (B) Students are indifferent to or abuse school property.   _____   _____

7. (A) Students set high standards of achievement for themselves.   _____   _____
   (B) Students do just enough to get by.   _____   _____

8. (A) Many students play an active role in helping new students adjust to campus life.   _____   _____
   (B) Most students pay little attention to new students.   _____   _____

9. (A) The administration and faculty make every effort to treat everyone equally.   _____   _____
   (B) Anyone who knows the right people among the faculty or administration can get a better break here.   _____   _____

10. (A) The big college events draw a lot of student enthusiasm and support.   _____   _____
    (B) Major college events are usually greeted with indifference.   _____   _____

11. (A) Academic advisors are knowledgeable and provide quality advice.   _____   _____
    (B) The academic advisors provide little useful information.   _____   _____

12. (A) Information of concern to students, such as the last date to drop a course, is readily available.   _____   _____
    (B) Information of concern to students is not well publicized.   _____   _____

13. (A) The talk among people on campus is warm and friendly.   _____   _____
    (B) People are polite but reserved.   _____   _____

14. (A) Many students get involved in clubs and organizations.   _____   _____
    (B) Only a small number of students seem to be involved in organizations.   _____   _____

15. (A) Faculty members are available for conferences and meetings.   _____   _____
    (B) Faculty members are rarely available for meetings.   _____   _____

16. (A) Students have a high regard for ethics and values.   _____   _____

    (B) Students do not seem interested in
        what's ethical.   _____   _____

17. (A) Most faculty show warmth, interest,
      and helpfulness toward students.   _____   _____
    (B) Most faculty do not seem to care about
        the students as people.   _____   _____

18. (A) Students have a great deal of freedom
      and latitude concerning such things as
      class attendance.   _____   _____
    (B) Students have very few opportunities to
        express freedom of choice.   _____   _____

19. (A) Students respect the value of learning
      and do their own work.   _____   _____
    (B) Students resort to various forms of
        cheating to get by.   _____   _____

20. (A) Residence halls seem to be congenial,
      fun places to live.   _____   _____
    (B) Residence hall life is dull and sterile. _____   _____

21. (A) The administration seems to really care
      about student welfare.   _____   _____
    (B) The administration seems to be indiffer-
        ent toward students.   _____   _____

22. (A) Students help each other with course
      assignments and projects.   _____   _____
    (B) Students regard classwork as "everyone
        for himself or herself."   _____   _____

23. (A) Innovative courses or programs of study
      are introduced and tried.   _____   _____
    (B) The courses and programs seem to be
        always the same.   _____   _____

24. (A) Fraternities and sororities seem to have
      a major impact on the social atmosphere. _____   _____
    (B) Fraternities and sororities exist but seem
        to have little impact on campus. _____   _____

25. (A) Students seem to make extensive use of
      the library as a source of information. _____   _____
    (B) Students do not seem to make use of
        the library resources.   _____   _____

26. (A) It is quite common to find students
      browsing through the bookstore. _____   _____
    (B) The bookstore is only a place to buy
        your texts.   _____   _____

27. (A) Intramural athletic activities and other
      forms of recreation (bowling, ping pong)

seem to be a significant part of student life.   _____   _____

(B) Intramurals and other recreational pursuits are not part of the campus scene.   _____   _____

28. (A) The courses provide students with a basis for improving their social and economic status in life.   _____   _____

(B) The courses provide students with skills and techniques applicable to a job.   _____   _____

Step 2   To score your answers, look for paired statements in which the A and D labels are associated with different norms. Examples: (A) A, (B) D; or (A) D, (B) A.

Using the table below, record the importance score for *only* those items in which a difference exists between Actual and Desired.

Task	Social		Task	Social
1. _____	3. _____		17. _____	14. _____
2. _____	4. _____		18. _____	16. _____
5. _____	6. _____		21. _____	19. _____
9. _____	7. _____		23. _____	20. _____
11. _____	8. _____		25. _____	22. _____
12. _____	10. _____		26. _____	24. _____
15. _____	13. _____		28. _____	27. _____

Step 3   Either as a class or in small groups, examine the results and look for one or two norms where a major difference exists. If the entire class is involved, try to reach a consensus on the predominant area(s) of concern. If small groups are used, each group should focus on a particular area of concern. In either case, develop a brief action plan to address what should be done to reduce the culture gaps. Consider the following when developing your plan:
a. What are the current norms?
b. What would be some ideal norms?
c. Establish some new norms.
d. How can each individual contribute to altering the culture toward the new norms?

Step 4   (For small group situations only) Each small group should be prepared to present its action plan. Comments and discussion are encouraged.

Source: Written by Bruce Kemelgor, University of Louisville.

NOTES

1. E.H. Schein, *Organizational Culture and Leadership* (San Francisco: Jossey-Bass, 1985).
2. R.H. Kilmann, "Corporate Culture," *Psychology Today*, April 1985, 62–68.
3. Schein, *Organizational Culture and Leadership*; H.M. Trice and J.M. Beyer, *The Cultures of Work Organization* (Englewood Cliffs, N.J.: Prentice-Hall, 1993).

4. Ibid.

5. Ibid.; Kilmann, "Corporate Culture."

6. Schein, *Organizational Culture and Leadership.*

7. Ibid.

8. C.G. Smith and R.P. Vecchio, "Organizational Culture and Strategic Management: Issues in the Management of Strategic Change," *Journal of Managerial Issues* 5 (1993): 53–70.

9. C.A. O'Reilly, J. Chatman, and D.F. Caldwell, "People and Organizational Culture: A Profile Comparison Approach to Assessing Person-Organization Fit," *Academy of Management Journal* 34 (1991): 487–516.

10. B.M. Meglino, E.C. Ravlin, and C.L. Adkins, "Value Congruence and Satisfaction with a Leader: An Examination of the Role of Interaction," *Human Relations* 44 (1991): 481–495; E.C. Ravlin and B.M. Meglino, "Effect of Values on Perception and Decision Making: A Study of Alternative Work Values Measures," *Journal of Applied Psychology* 72 (1987): 666–673; B.M. Meglino, E.C. Ravlin, and C.L. Adkins, "A Work Values Approach to Corporate Culture: A Field Test of the Value Congruence Process and Its Relationship to Individual Outcomes," *Journal of Applied Psychology* 74 (1989): 424–432; E.C. Ravlin and B.M. Meglino, "The Transitivity of Work Values: Hierarchical Preference Ordering of Socially Desirable Stimuli," *Organizational Behavior and Human Decision Processes* 44 (1989): 494–508.

11. A. Rafaeli and M.G. Pratt, "Tailored Meanings: On the Meaning and Impact of Organizational Dress," *Academy of Management Review* 18 (1993): 32–55.

12. J. Child, "Culture, Contingency and Capitalism in the Cross-National Study of Organizations," *Research in Organizational Behavior* 3 (1981): 303–356.

13. K.H. Roberts, "On Looking at an Elephant: An Evaluation of Cross-Cultural Research Related to Organizations," *Psychological Bulletin* 74 (1970): 327–350; Meglino, Ravlin, and Adkins, "A Work Values Approach to Corporate Culture"; P.C. Earley, "East Meets West Meets Mideast: Further Explorations of Collectivistic and Individualistic Work Groups," *Academy of Management Journal* 36 (1993): 319–348; C.M. Fiol, "Managing Culture as a Competitive Resource: An Identity-based View of Sustainable Competitive Advantage," *Journal of Management* 17 (1991): 196–211; G. Hofstede, B. Neuijen, D. Ohayv, and G. Sanders, "Measuring Organizational Cultures: A Qualitative and Quantitative Study across Twenty Cases," *Administrative Science Quarterly* 35 (1990): x286–316; N. Boyacigiller and N. Adler, "The Parochial Dinosaur: Organizational Science in a Global Context," *Academy of Management Review* 16 (1991): 262–290.

14. R. Levine and E. Wolff, "Social Time: The Heartbeat of Culture," *Psychology Today,* March 1985, 28–35.

15. E.T. Hall, *The Dance of Life* (Garden City, N.Y.: Anchor-Doubleday, 1969).

16. D.C. McClelland, *The Achieving Society* (Princeton: Van Nostrand, 1961).

17. M. Haire, E.E. Ghiselli, and L.W. Proter, *Managerial Thinking* (New York: Wiley, 1965).

18. G.W. England, *The Manager and His Values* (Cambridge, Mass.: Ballinger, 1975).

19. Haire, Ghiselli, and Porter, *Managerial Thinking;* R. Griffeth, P. Hom, A. DeNisi, et al., "A Multivariate Multinational Comparison of Managerial Attitudes," in *Proceedings of the 40th Annual Meeting of the Academy of Management* (1980): 63–67.

20. R. Vernon and L.T. Wells, *Manager in the International Economy* (Englewood Cliffs, N.J.: Prentice-Hall, 1981).

21. G. Hofstede, *Culture's Consequences* (New York: Sage Publications, 1980).

22. W.G. Ouchi and M. Price, "Hierarchies, Clans and Theory Z: A New Perspective on Organization Development," *Organizational Dynamics* 32 (Autumn 1978): 24–44.

23. K.H. Chung and M.A. Gray, "Can We Adopt the Japanese Methods of Human Resources Management?" *Personnel Administrator* 64 (May 1982): 43–47.

24. R.R. Rehder, "Education and Training: Have the Japanese Beaten Us Again?" *Personnel Journal* 64 (January 1983): 42–47.

25. W.G. Ouchi, *Theory Z: How American Business Can Meet the Japanese Challenge* (Reading, Mass.: Addison-Wesley, 1981).

26. L.S. Dillon, "Adopting Japanese Management: Some Cultural Stumbling

Blocks," *Personnel* 32 (July 1983): 77–81.

27. Ibid.

28. Ibid.

29. H. Befu and C. Cernosia, "Demise of 'Permanent Employment' in Japan," *Human Resource Management* 29 (1990): 231–250.

30. J.J. Sullivan and R.B. Peterson, "A Test of Theories Underlying the Japanese Lifetime Employment System," *Journal of International Business Studies* (1991): 79–97.

31. S. Kamata, *Japan in the Passing Lane* (New York: Pantheon, 1983).

32. "Dying for a Living," *Time*, May 3, 1993, 19.

33. L. Smith, "Cracks in the Japanese Work Ethic," *Fortune*, May 14, 1984, 162–168.

34. R.N. Farmer, "International Management," in *Contemporary Management: Issues and Viewpoints*, ed. J.W. McGuire (Englewood Cliffs, N.J.: Prentice-Hall, 1974).

35. N.J. Adler, *International Dimensions of Organizational Behavior* (Boston: Kent, 1985).

36. P.R. Harris and R.T. Moran, *Managing Cultural Differences* (Houston: Gulf, 1987).

37. F. Fiedler, T. Mitchell, and H.C. Triandis, "The Culture Assimilator: An Approach to Cross-Cultural Training," *Journal of Applied Psychology* 55 (1971): 95–102; H.C. Triandis and W.W. Lambert, eds., *Handbook of Cross-Cultural Psychology: Perspectives* (Boston: Allyn and Bacon, 1980).

38. J. Kline-Harrison, "Individual and Combined Effects of Behavior Modeling and the Cultural Assimilator in Cross-Cultural Management Training," *Journal of Applied Psychology* 77 (1992): 952–962.

How many OD specialists does it take to change a light bulb? Ten: one to change the bulb and nine to relate to the experience.

— Anonymous

A consultant is someone who will take your watch off your wrist and tell you what time it is.

— David Owen

If it ain't broke, don't fix it—unless you are a consultant.

— Winston G. Rossiter

LEARNING OBJECTIVES

After studying this chapter, you should be able to:

1. *Identify external and internal sources of change in an organization.*

2. *Describe the stages of organizational growth.*

3. *List causes of organizational decline.*

4. *Identify factors that lead to an organization's success or failure.*

5. *Describe the phases in the process of change in an organization.*

6. *Identify the components of an organization's readiness for change.*

7. *Describe techniques that organizational design specialists use to help bring about change in organizations.*

8. *Identify the conditions that enhance the likelihood an OD effort will succeed.*

9. *Explain how evaluation researchers evaluate OD programs.*

10. *Evaluate the track record of OD programs.*

Managing Organizational Change and Development

WANT A CHANGE? CREATE A CRISIS

Craig Weatherup, president of a PepsiCo division with sales in excess of $7 billion, privately feared increased competitive pressures, even though earnings were up 10 percent and company profits exceeded those of arch rival Coca-Cola. He realized that he needed to convince the 30,000 people under his charge that a crisis was imminent. At a meeting with his top 11 managers, he candidly stated that 10 percent annual growth in earnings was unacceptable. He said that the company would get run over by the competition if it didn't achieve 15 percent growth. His team caught on. Over the next two years, the organization was restructured, resulting in redesigned work processes and redefined job descriptions. The division was separated into 107 customer-focused units, and three years after Weatherup declared "the crisis," the company is expected to meet its 15 percent earnings growth target.

Doomsday Management is a new technique to inspire radical organizational change. Leaders who use this style envision a crisis, imminent or far-off, and communicate it down the ranks to rile the troops into action. At its foundation is the notion of creating a crisis to upset the established way of doing things. Profitable organi-zations often rest on their laurels, but an impending crisis makes people nervous and readies them for action. To practice Doomsday Management the right way, the leader must share several visions with employees: what will happen if the company does nothing, what the desired end state should be, and what the transition state of getting from here to there will be like. Employees must understand the master plan and be given the resources, time, and trust to acknowledge the crisis and create solutions. A core of steadfast employees will resist the changes, but with appropriate coaching, even the most reticent can be persuaded that a crisis is threatening.

Most crises come in three garden varieties: financial, customer-related, and industrial. Weather-up's crisis was financial. To instill a sense of urgency, three-day meetings involving all 30,000 employees were held over the course of two years to reinforce the imminence of the crisis and to share with employees the vision of a new, customer-focused organization. In training its huge work force, PepsiCo used a "cascade of learning" technique, whereby successive layers of the organization are taught by the layer above them. Weatherup's top 11 man-agers had three months to learn about reengineering work processes, continuous improvement, and work flows, and to apply their newfound knowledge to a company process. They then used their experiences to train the next layer of managers, who went through the same 90-day process and trained the next layer, and so on.

Peter Lewis, CEO of Progressive, a Cleveland insurer of mostly high-risk drivers, discovered that drivers were generally displeased with inflated insurance premiums. Even though customer relations was considered one of the company's strengths, Lewis was able to convince his work force that "our customers actually hate us." Claims processing was ultimately revamped, with claims being settled in 11 days on average (compared to 18 before) with more efficient utilization of claims examiners, and fewer lawyers necessary for processing claims. Profit-sharing was launched in 1992, and the company's stock has appreciated 70 percent over a 12-month period.

Ameritech, a Baby Bell tele-communications giant, had a virtual monopoly in the Midwest, consistently earning a 15 percent annual return on shareholder's equity. Envisioning the evolving,

(continued on following page)

(continued from previous page)
competitive information super-highway, CEO William Weiss embarked on a mission to keep Ameritech competitive and on the cutting edge. The company has become more customer-focused and work processes have been analyzed to cut out waste. For example, a new financial reporting team discovered employees were

preparing financial reports that no one ever read. As a result, the team eliminated six million pages of reports, the equivalent of a stack four times taller than Ameritech's 41-story Chicago headquarters.

Creating a crisis may seem drastic, but many companies lose the ability to adapt after years of profitable, successful operations. With global pressures increasing,

even the most successful companies must keep an eye to the future.

This chapter examines how organizations change and grow, and why some change efforts are successful and others fail. Organizational development is discussed as it relates to the study and implementation of organizational change.

Source: Brian Dumaine, "Times Are Good? Create a Crisis," *Fortune*, June 28, 1993, 123–130.

Organizations are not static, but continuously change in response to a variety of influences coming from both inside and outside. For administrators, the challenge is to anticipate and direct change processes so that organizational performance is enhanced. In this chapter, we will examine what is meant by organizational change and how it occurs. Then, we will consider techniques for managing and evaluating organizational change.

SOURCES OF CHANGE

"The one unchanging principle of life is the principle of change." This old saying contains an important element of truth: Change is an inevitable feature in both the lives of individuals and the lives of organizations. For both people and organizations, some facets of change are slow and nearly imperceptible, while others occur quite rapidly. In addition, the impact of change processes can vary from quite minor to truly substantial. Among the most common and influential forces of organizational change are the emergence of new competitors, innovations in technology, new company leadership, and evolving attitudes toward work.

It is useful to classify the sources of change as either external or internal. *External sources of change* originate in the organization's environment. In addition to competitors and suppliers, the external environment includes customers, the prevailing economic climate, the labor force, and the legal environment. Changes in any of these features of the external environment can have profound positive or negative effects on an organization. The rise and fall of competitors has clear implications for organizational performance, as does the cooperativeness and competencies of suppliers. If the preferences of customers change as a result of changes in taste, the well-being of a product line can be affected. Recessions, periods of inflation, and upturns or downturns in the local or national economy can have both direct and indirect influences on organizations. The education, talents, and attitudes of potential employees also play an important role in an organization's well-being. Changes in these facets of the labor force can lead to a shortage or a surplus of qualified employees. Last, legislation can produce change. Federal legislation, such as the enforcement of the policies of the Equal Employment Opportunity Commission and the Federal Trade Commission, can alter the procedures an organization traditionally uses in its recruiting and marketing functions.

Internal sources of change exist within the organization itself. Examples of internal pressures for change include shifts in workers' attitudes toward their supervisor or their benefits package, declining productivity, and changes in key personnel, whose goals and values influence large populations of the organization. Changes in attitudes among employees (due to increased age or changes in job responsibility) can result in changes in job satisfaction, attendance behavior, and commitment. Changes in top-level and other key individuals in an organization can alter the internal character of the organization. For example, if an incoming president emphasizes corporate ethics and customer service to his or her staff, those concerns will come to be reflected in the creation of new programs, the restructuring of the organization, and the evolution of a different organizational culture.

ORGANIZATIONAL GROWTH AND DECLINE

Organizational change often follows an evolutionary pattern of gradual growth and decline. The study of organizational change at the marco level of analysis reveals that forms of evolution and revolution occur as organizations grow.

In a popular model of organizational growth, Larry Greiner contends that every organization has an ideal structure that corresponds to its stage in the growth process.[1] For example, large organizations need more formalization of procedures and operations than do small, newly created organizations.

Greiner suggests that a series of stages characterize organizational growth. Each stage has a dominant theme or set of issues, and each new stage is preceded by a period of transition, which may be termed a *growth crisis*. Figure 20.1 depicts Greiner's model of organizational growth.

GROWTH THROUGH CREATIVITY

At its birth, an organization is usually fairly informal and loose in structure. The control and moment-to-moment involvement of the organization's founders are likely to be strong. The creative energies of this founding group will help to carry the organization through its birth process. With the growth of the fledgling organization, the nature and variety of problems change. Personnel problems arise as the size of the work force increases. Also, the organization's founders (whose first love may be closer to innovating and marketing than to management, operations, and personnel) may find themselves ill-equipped to lead their growing firm. This represents a *crisis of leadership*. This crisis can be overcome, most often, by acquiring professional managers to direct the organization.

FIGURE 20.1
GREINER'S MODEL OF ORGANIZATIONAL GROWTH

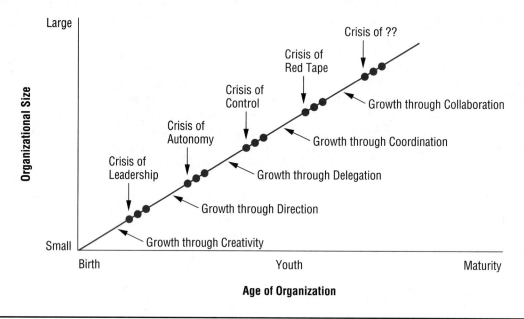

Source: L. E. Greiner, "Evolution and Revolution as Organizations Grow," *Harvard Business Review* 50 (1972): 37–46.

GROWTH THROUGH DIRECTION

Following resolution of the crisis of leadership, the organization enters a stage of growth through direction. Formalization is introduced by the professional managers. Greater bureaucratization takes place as departments and programs are established to help manage the organization. One result of this growth of bureaucracy is the creation of specialized divisions. Such specialization can lead to problems because as individuals within each division become increasingly skilled, they may seek greater control of their operations. These efforts at greater self-direction may be resisted by the same upper-level managers who originally introduced the specialization. The resulting tension can produce a *crisis of autonomy*.

GROWTH THROUGH DELEGATION

The next stage, delegation, follows the successful resolution of the crisis of autonomy. The crisis of autonomy is overcome by delegating greater decision-making power to middle- and lower-level managers, and top management begins to focus on long-range, strategic planning. However, middle- and lower-level managers eventually come to realize that the autonomous divisions sometimes pull in different directions and that performance may suffer due to a lack of control. Thus, the organization faces a *crisis of control*.

GROWTH THROUGH COORDINATION

The crisis of control can be resolved through increased coordination. For example, linkages may be created between members of different departments to enhance communication. Consultants may be hired to assess the extent of coordination needed and to suggest ways of improving efficiency and reducing redundancy. Project groups and task forces may be created to improve coordination, and matrix design concepts may be introduced. However, one consequence of creating these coordinating mechanisms is a profusion of managerial programs, and the resulting complexity may mean that more time and effort are spent on coordinating systems than on increasing actual productivity. The strangulation caused by such a proliferation of programs creates a *crisis of red tape*.

CONTINUED GROWTH THROUGH COLLABORATION

Simplification of programs and systems and reliance on self-control and social norms may eventually replace more formal structures as an organization works its way through the red-tape crisis. Larger organizations often will bring in outside consultants to help them in their continued quest for collaboration. The goal of this stage is to teach managers how to cope with the organization's structure without giving in to the impulse to create additional structure.

MANAGING ORGANIZATIONAL DECLINE

Just as organizations can be said to go through phases of birth, youth, and maturity, they also go through periods of decline.[*] David Whetten defines **organizational decline** as a "cutback in the size of an organization's work force, profits, budget, or clients."[2] This degeneration can occur in any industry and in any size organization. Among the organizations that are currently experiencing decline are the United States steel industry, religious orders, and small liberal arts colleges.

Whetten suggests a number of specific factors that can lead to organizational decline. For example, within the organization itself, atrophy may occur. That is to say, the organization may simply become less efficient over time and lose its will to compete. Further problems may be created by self-complacency, loss of competitive drive, and a recalcitrant work force.

An organization may also be in danger of declining if it is in a vulnerable state. Newly created organizations that are not yet fully established are especially vulnerable because they often lack cash reserves and managers who are experienced in handling crises. Economic downturns and vigorous competitors can also undo vulnerable organizations.

---

[*]Organizations also experience death, although this topic has not received much serious study. Actually, approximately 90 percent of U.S. corporations do not survive more than 25 years. In taking a long-term perspective, it is interesting to note that very few formal organizations have survived since 1500. Among the survivors are the Catholic church, some European guilds, and some universities. Therefore, organizational death is not a rare phenomenon. Somewhat surprisingly, organizations that are dying (that is, being shut down) actually experience an increase in employee productivity, possibly a peculiar form of employee pride.

An Inside Look
Reengineering: The Latest Tool

Reengineering is the latest management tool to catch the attention of corporate America. Unlike some management techniques that have come before it, however, reengineering is a powerful tool recommended only for those companies that need a real shake-up. It differs from other change efforts in that traditional organizational changes merely modify current structures and relationships. The essence of reengineering is to begin with a blank slate and devise new structures and processes to get products out the door.

Reengineering a company requires a hefty investment of time and resources. Over a two-year period, the reengineering prescription for AT&T Global Business Communications Systems called for the following: job descriptions rewritten for hundreds of people, new recognition and reward systems created, computer systems revamped, widespread

training instituted, and considerable changes in financial reporting, manufacturing, shipping, installation, billing, and supplier relations.

Companies experiencing increased competition are often the best candidates for reengineering. Many financial services institutions and telecommunications companies have embraced reengineering in response to increased competition brought on by deregulation. The payoff from reengineering comes in the form of efficiencies, productivity, and profitability. A team of operating and maintenance workers at Union Carbide redesigned their daily processes and generated savings of more than $20 million. All told, Union Carbide has saved $400 million in fixed costs over three years because of reengineering.

To succeed, reengineering has to be driven by a strategic plan. It is a lethal tool that, if applied in-

discriminately, could paralyze a company. Like any change effort, it must have support from top company leaders who can keep the change moving forward. Leaders must induce a sense of urgency to reengineer a company or risk failure as the change effort loses momentum. Processes should be designed around customers. Because customers keep the company in business, all processes should focus on satisfying customers. Employees should help redesign the business processes, and human resource systems, such as recognition and reward systems, staffing, and training, need to reinforce the changes taking place.

Reengineering is certainly not the panacea for all companies, but some organizations are realizing significant gains by redesigning core business processes.

Source: Thomas A. Stewart, "Reengineering: The Hot New Managing Tool," *Fortune*, August 23, 1993, 41–48.

Changes in societal values and consumer tastes can lead to a loss of legitimacy and subsequent decline. For example, an organization that manufactures a product that the buying public no longer desires may well decline. An instance of these processes can be found in the reduced purchase of toy guns by parents during a time of war.

Last, organizations may decline because of insufficient external resources. Needed resources may become scarce, or uncertainty about a reliable supply may make it difficult to produce and deliver a finished good. Dependency on a supplier's ability to obtain and deliver resources can threaten the survival of many organizations.

Managing decline requires many of the same administrative skills as managing growth. The ability to seek creative solutions, the willingness to innovate, and the tactful management of conflict are necessary skills for managers of all organizations, declining or growing. "Toughing it out," minimizing losses, and making it to the next upswing, however, become management's top priorities during periods of decline.

CRITICAL DETERMINANTS OF ORGANIZATIONAL SUCCESS AND FAILURE

The features of organizations that make for success are not always the same ones that lead to failure.[3] Based on reports generated by professional consultants, it is possible to identify the specific factors that contribute most to success and failure. It is also possible to classify these factors as primarily environmental, structural, or management-oriented. Figure 20.2 summarizes this classification system.

FACTORS THAT LEAD TO SUCCESS

Although a successful organization need not possess all the positive attributes shown in Figure 20.2, most successful organizations show more positive than negative attributes. Successful organizations tend to focus on customers and their needs. They invest in ways to improve sales and provide superior service

FIGURE 20.2
FACTORS THAT LEAD TO ORGANIZATIONAL SUCCESS AND FAILURE

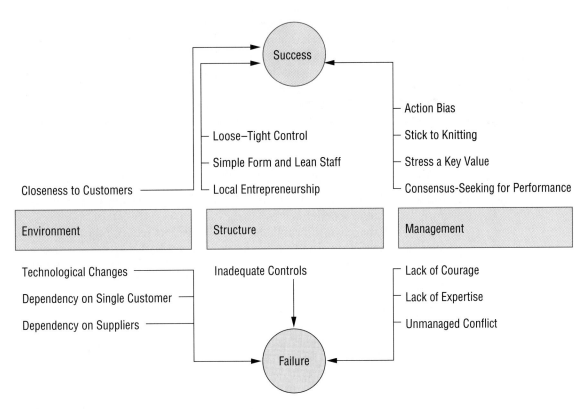

Source: Adapted from R. L. Daft, *Organization Theory and Design* (St. Paul, Minn.: West, 1983).

to clients, and they do not forget that their customers and their customers' needs underlie their organization's existence.

Successful organizations also adapt their structures to the needs of their missions. At the department level, controls may be simultaneously loose, in that managers have autonomy, and tight, insofar as specific performance goals may be set. Highly successful organizations often maintain a simple but appropriate structure that employs an adequate number of staff; they avoid empire building and padding with surplus staff. Also, entrepreneurship is encouraged within the divisions of the organization by rewarding successful innovation and encouraging risk taking.

A major management feature that can lead to success is a deliberate bias toward implementing solutions to problems. Management discourages "paralysis through analysis" of alternatives, and, instead, emphasizes satisficing action (see Chapter 12) that ensures goal attainment. Another management feature in successful firms is a commitment to the organization's original arena of expertise. This is called "sticking to one's knitting." It involves staying close to what the organization knows how to do best and not being led down different paths in pursuit of attractive, but uncertain, alternative product lines.

Successful organizations also tend to stress a single value, such as delivering a quality product, reducing the cost of services to customers, or concern for each customer's unique needs. By emphasizing a single dominant value in their promotional materials and in their training of employees, the organization establishes a useful, distinct reputation for excellence in a specific area.

Finally, managers in successful companies often try to improve performance by achieving the agreement or consensus of employees. Thus, managers and workers may work together to set mutually agreeable performance goals. Employee suggestions are actively sought and a positive work group spirit, which will serve as a basis for enhanced motivation, is encouraged.

FACTORS THAT LEAD TO FAILURE

Different factors in an organization's environment, structure, and management may lead to its failure.

Among the environmental factors, changes in technology are a major cause of organizational failure. Technological innovations by competitors, as well as innovations that cannot be implemented within the organization itself, can lead to lost business.

Two forms of dependency—dependency on suppliers and dependency on a single customer— can also create problems. Difficulties in obtaining raw materials and financing from other institutions can prove fatal for an organization in a competitive environment. In addition, a customer that realizes that another organization is highly dependent on its business may use its resulting power to drive down prices or extract greater concessions by threatening to take its business elsewhere.

In terms of structure, inadequate control mechanisms may contribute to failure. For example, an organization may lack devices for sensing when

OB Focus
Training Pays Off

Training can be essential to organizational change. An organization's ability to realize and sustain its desired vision depends on the training its employees receive. In the process of initiating change, basic skills training often precedes more dramatic change efforts. At Wm. Dudek Manufacturing Co., a small family-owned producer of metal hooks, clips, and clasps, managers tried to teach Total Quality Management principles and methods to its 30 shop-floor employees. It quickly became evident that the employees were not applying the TQM techniques. Although workers were highly knowledgeable about their machines, many could barely read, and most could not interpret a ratio or understand a simple graph.

Nearly 40 percent of the members of the National Association of Manufacturers agree that inadequate math, reading, and technical skills are creating "serious problems" in upgrading factories and enhancing productivity. Fortunately, many companies are realizing the value of education and the payoff it ultimately generates. Solectron Chairman Winston Chen credits training for helping the company win the 1991 Malcolm Baldrige National Quality Award. The company, located in Milpitas, Calif., assembles printed circuitboards and other high-tech components, and has enjoyed an average 59 percent growth in revenues since it began in 1977.

At Solectron, revenue growth and quality go hand-in-hand with education. In 1993, all employees, including Chen, spent about 110 hours—nearly three 40-hour weeks—in training. That's up from an average of 95 hours in 1992. Says Chen: "Technology changes so fast that we estimate 20 percent of an engineer's knowledge becomes obsolete every year. Training is an obligation we owe to our employees."

Motorola is considered by many experts to be the corporate yardstick in worker training. Motorola University, located at corporate headquarters in Schaumburg, Ill., with ten additional education centers around the world, delivered the equivalent of 102,000 days of training to employees, suppliers, and customers in its state-of-the-art facilities in 1992. Computer-equipped classrooms and laboratories teach employees the basics of computer-aided design, robotics, and specialized manufacturing techniques. Other courses focus on corporate quality programs, team management skills, empowerment, and shortening product development cycles.

The 300 faculty members, most of whom are Motorola retirees, have taught outside groups, such as U.S. government agencies, IBM, Digital Equipment, Fiat, and British Telecom, in addition to Motorola's own 107,000 employees. For each $1 spent on training, Motorola estimates a payback of $30 in productivity gains within three years. The company has cut costs by $3.3 billion since 1987 by training workers to simplify work processes and reduce waste. Motorola has a clear commitment to worker training and enjoys a generous payoff from its investment in employees.

Sources: Ronald Henkoff, "Companies That Train Best," *Fortune,* March 22, 1993, 62–75; Barnaby J. Feder, "What's Up at Motorola U.," *New York Times,* October 31, 1993, sec. F, 6.

changes occur that need to be corrected. As a result, product quality may suffer or changes in employee or customer satisfaction levels may be ignored.

Management factors may also contribute to failure. Courageous and decisive leadership can inspire an organization to overcome difficult situations or take quick action. In contrast, a tendency to overanalyze data or to take a "wait-and-see" attitude may cause a firm to lose ground to competitors and may exacerbate internal problems. The kinds of expertise that enable a young organization to thrive may become outdated as an organization matures. The need for professional managers to aid, or replace, the founding group may go unrecognized, and the importance of hiring new talent to revitalize the innovative process may be ignored.

As we saw in Chapters 9 and 14, conflict can lead to serious dysfunction if it is not well managed. Conflicting groups often set their own goals for political and personal gain ahead of organizational goals. For this reason, conflict should be managed to ensure that it remains in desired forms and at desired levels. (Recall that a certain level of internal conflict is probably inevitable and even desirable.)

As Figure 20.2 suggests, success and failure factors are not evenly distributed across the three major sources. For example, more environmental factors may contribute to failure than to success. Conversely, more structural factors are potential sources of success than of failure. And an almost equal number of management factors seem to lead to both success and failure. This analysis, albeit simplistic, suggests a useful insight: Environmental factors are more likely to pose potential threats to an organization's well-being, while structural factors are an organization's major means of achieving success or, at least, coping with threats. It almost goes without saying that management-related factors are potential sources of both organizational success and organizational failure.

ORGANIZATIONAL DEVELOPMENT

Organizational development (OD) is a distinct area within the field of organizational science that focuses on the planned and controlled change of organizations in desired directions. In general, outside consultants rather than organizational members are usually responsible for managing the development process. In essence, OD attempts to change an organization as a totality by changing the organization's structure, technology, people, and/or tasks. Figure 20.3 presents a popular view of OD that emphasizes these four facets of an or-

FIGURE 20.3

INTERDEPENDENT ORGANIZATIONAL ELEMENTS THAT MAY BE THE FOCUS OF CHANGE IN OD

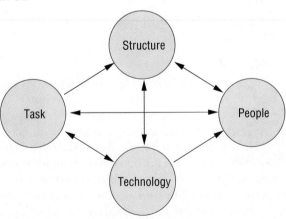

Source: Adapted from H. J. Leavitt and H. Bahrami, *Managerial Psychology-Managing Behavior in Organizations* (Chicago, Ill.: Univ. of Chicago Press, 1988).

ganization. In reality, any facet of an organization is a legitimate target of OD. In our discussion we will focus primarily on change efforts that are directed at people rather than at tasks, structure, or technology. A popular definition of OD, which we can use for discussing the people side of planned change, has been offered by French and Bell. For these authors, OD is a "long-range effort to improve an organization's problem-solving and renewal process . . . through a more effective . . . management of organization culture . . . with the assistance of a change agent . . . and the use of the theory and technology of applied behavioral science."[4]

PHASES IN THE OD PROCESS

All OD specialists recognize the difficulties inherent in bringing about successful, positive changes. Some years ago, Kurt Lewin, a famous behavioral scientist, argued that the process of change involves three basic phases (see Figure 20.4): unfreezing, changing, refreezing.[5] **Unfreezing** begins to occur when a situation is recognized as being deficient or inadequate in some way. The recognition that employees' attitudes or skills are insufficient, or that rules and procedures generate problems that hinder task completion, may trigger the unfreezing process. Sometimes a crisis must occur before a problem is given the attention it deserves. For example, unsafe working conditions may be allowed to continue until a wildcat strike or a life-threatening accident forces management to acknowledge the problem and take action. Unfreezing must occur before OD can succeed because an individual's failure to recognize or accept the existence of a problem can block any desire to change.

The second phase in the process, **changing,** occurs when a new plan or system is implemented in the organization. Such a plan may call for a new recruiting or orientation program, or the introduction of a new accounting system. It may affect the entire organization, as would a total restructuring, or it may focus on only a few key individuals, as would a values-clarification exercise involving the top-level management team.

Refreezing, the third phase in the change process, occurs as the newly created patterns of behavior and techniques become part of ongoing organizational

FIGURE 20.4
LEWIN'S VIEW OF THE CHANGE PROCESS

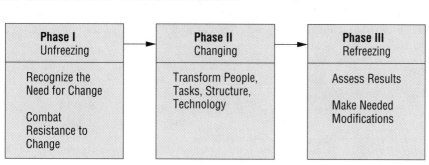

Phase I Unfreezing	**Phase II** Changing	**Phase III** Refreezing
Recognize the Need for Change Combat Resistance to Change	Transform People, Tasks, Structure, Technology	Assess Results Make Needed Modifications

processes. During the refreezing phase, OD specialists usually attempt to appraise the effectiveness of their intervention. If they believe that intervention has failed, they may redirect their efforts to compensate for their program's shortcomings.

RESISTANCE TO CHANGE

Attempts at organizational development are often met with resistance.[†] Employees tend to fear change, partly from a desire for security and contentment with the status quo. Consequently, they may be quick to identify shortcomings in a proposed plan for change and use them to their advantage. If their objections are registered but not redressed, they may act to ensure that the identified problems actually do undercut the program for change.

Resistance to change, one of the most serious challenges for an OD specialist, may be overcome in a number of ways. One of the most common techniques is *education,* not in the formal sense but in terms of meeting with groups of employees to address their concerns and explain the planned changes. *Participation* in the development of plans for change is also an effective way of overcoming resistance. In one well-known study, Coch and French observed that resistance to change can be significantly reduced by having the affected employees actually participate in the design of the change effort.[6] Programs for change that are, in a sense, "owned" by the people who are most affected are often more likely to succeed.[7] Another means of overcoming resistance is *negotiation.* When dealing with employees who have taken a stand against change, this means obtaining statements in writing about trade-offs and concessions that both management and employees will make in order to accommodate change.

In practice, strong-arm tactics, despite their questionable ethical merit, are sometimes used. Chief among these methods are outright *coercion,* such as threatening people with dismissal if they resist the planned change, and *manipulation of opinion* through the careful selection and timing of the information released so as to ensure a favorable impact.

DETERMINING WHETHER AN ORGANIZATION IS READY FOR CHANGE

For change efforts to be effective, they must be supported by favorable conditions. Michael Beer has identified the most important factors and expressed them in a rough formula for predicting change:[8]

$$C = (D \times S \times P) > X$$

where

    C = change
    D = dissatisfaction with the current state of affairs

[†]As noted long ago by Machiavelli, "There is no more delicate matter than to introduce changes. For he who innovates will have for his enemies all those who are well off under the existing order of things, and only lukewarm supporters in those who might be better off under the new."

S = an identifiable and desired end state
P = a practical plan for achieving the desired end state
X = cost of change to the organization

As this formula suggests, change is a function of dissatisfaction, a desired goal, a means to obtain the goal, and a reasonable cost. If dissatisfaction with the status quo is very low (or near zero), then the expression in parentheses in the formula will result in a near zero value. As a consequence, these values will be near or less than the cost of implementing the change. If the various pressures for change are greater than the anticipated costs of the change to key individuals and groups, then change should occur.

As this formula suggests, dissatisfaction, the desired end state, plans for change, and cost must be addressed if change is to occur. For OD specialists, these critical elements must be assessed when determining whether an organization is ready for change.

OD TECHNIQUES

SURVEY FEEDBACK   One of the most widely used sources of information for OD specialists is **survey feedback.** To obtain the information they need, they administer written questionnaires or interview employees. The questions in these surveys typically touch on such topics as satisfaction, leadership, and decision making. The results are summarized and statistically analyzed before they are given back to top-level administrators. Once senior management has examined the results and considered their meaning, the data are fed back to the participants for their consideration and interpretation. In practice, such feedback is often intended to arouse awareness of the need for change. For example, through survey feedback, top management may discover that morale is especially low among members of a particular department, or a group of employees may begin to recognize that they all share a common view of a problem. Following recognition of the need for change, employees' suggestions for designing and implementing change programs are solicited.

Although the OD survey feedback technique may sound similar to the traditional notion of conducting a survey of employees, there are important distinctions between the two approaches.[9] In the traditional approach, data are usually collected only from lower-level employees, but in survey feedback, everyone in the organization is likely to be surveyed. Similarly, in the traditional approach, only top management is likely to see the results, but in the OD variation, everyone in the organization receives feedback at some point. Furthermore, the development of plans to deal with survey results is the prerogative of top management in the traditional approach, but everyone can have input in the survey feedback approach. Because of these essential differences, the survey feedback approach is more likely to achieve productive change.

TEAM BUILDING   Another OD technique, **team building,** has been widely used by specialists in recent years at such diverse organizations as Trans Australia Airlines, Mead Corporation, and Tandem Computers. The hub of team building is existing work groups, called *family groups,* or newly formed groups of employees brought together for a particular purpose, called *special groups.* The goal in both existing work groups and special groups is to improve performance by tackling problems and obstacles.

In a typical team-building effort, a small group of people is brought together at a retreat-like location removed from their place of employment. By getting away from the workplace, they can avoid interruptions and fully concentrate on problem solving.

At their initial meeting, the work group might examine both "hard" and "soft" data that pertain to productivity problems, such as monthly sales figures and customer satisfaction reports. The purpose of examining these data is to encourage the group to enter the unfreezing phase of the OD process and get them to recognize the need for change. During subsequent meetings, the OD specialist attempts to facilitate the process by encouraging frank and open discussions of various aspects of the problem facing the group. Ultimately, the group will be encouraged to develop a specific plan for attaining a desired end state. At later meetings, the group will review the success of the plan and develop and implement refinements of its content.

SENSITIVITY TRAINING   A third technique that has been widely used by OD specialists is **sensitivity training.** Sometimes called T-groups (for training groups), this approach originated in the 1940s at the National Training Laboratory in Bethel, Maine. Over the years, despite some changes in name to *encounter groups* and *laboratory training,* the technique has remained much the same. In a T-group, 8 to 12 individuals are brought together for a series of 2- to 3-hour sessions. The group's trainer does not take an active role in the group's discussions, but instead serves more as a guide or facilitator. The ostensible goal of the sessions is to increase self-awareness and sensitivity to others. To achieve this goal, members are expected to focus on behavior and on giving feedback about their perceptions of one another. Getting to the point at which personal and social learning occurs is sometimes difficult, and, in some cases, group members' reactions may get out of hand. For example, the group may turn on one particular member and severely criticize him or her without reaching a positive reconciliation by the end of the session. Because the group does not have an agenda, some members who are used to working in an ordered and goal-directed social system may become uncomfortable. Often, one member will strive to become group leader to fill the leadership vacuum created by the trainer's refusal to control discussions and behavior. Later, other group members may criticize and resent the individual who attempted to take the leadership role.

For some groups, a state of open and frank discussion is difficult to achieve. This is especially true for groups composed of people who work together in a naturally occurring work unit. To encourage freer discussions, some trainers prefer to work with stranger groups—groups whose members do not know one another—and cousin groups—groups whose members work within the same organization but do not report to one another.

In recent years, T-groups have been declining in popularity due to a variety of factors. One of the chief forces lies in a fear that people "may be taken apart like a clock and not put back together." Team building, with its focus on the enhancement of productivity instead of social skills, has been more widely adopted.

CONFRONTATION MEETINGS   A further technique for bringing about desired change attempts to manage dysfunctional conflict (see Chapter 14) through **confrontation meetings.** In this approach, conflicting groups are brought together in a structured situation that is designed to enhance cooperation.[10]

Most confrontation meetings follow a predictable sequence. First, the conflicting groups' leaders discuss the need for change with the OD specialist. At this session, the leaders and the consultant draw up a specific plan for meetings between the two groups. Next, each group meets separately to create a list that summarizes their views of the other group's attitudes and behaviors. In addition, they attempt to develop a list of impressions that they believe the other group would devise in describing themselves. Next, at a formal joint meeting, a spokesperson for each group reads aloud his or her group's lists. No discussion or reaction is allowed. The groups then meet again in separate rooms to discuss what they have learned about themselves and the other group. Each also draws up a list of issues that need to be resolved.

At the second joint meeting, all members openly discuss the lists of issues that need resolution and develop a plan of action for reducing conflict and achieving cooperation. At subsequent meetings, groups discuss their progress toward implementing their plans and the removal of further obstacles to improved collaboration.

QUALITY OF WORK LIFE   In many Western industrialized countries, there has been a growing recognition of the importance of simultaneously enhancing both the value of employees' psychological experiences at work and employees' productivity. This philosophy is embodied in the **quality of work life (QWL)** approach to OD.‡ QWL is not a set of specific techniques, but rather an approach that seeks to enhance the total work climate in an organization or its subsystems. QWL programs focus on such issues as conflict reduction, employee satisfaction, and worker participation. In terms of actual techniques, QWL programs often encompass job redesign (Chapter 7), employee involvement in decision making (Chapter 12), redesign of pay systems (Chapter 7), and/or the creation of quality circles (Chapter 7). In essence, QWL represents a desired end state that emphasizes the importance of providing opportunities for employees to contribute to their jobs as well as to receive more from their jobs.[11] Successful QWL programs have been used in such firms as AT&T, IBM, Texas Instruments, Xerox, and Procter & Gamble. At present, it appears that QWL programs will continue to enjoy popularity and slow expansion.[12]

---

‡QWL is often pronounced "quill" by OD specialists.

CONDITIONS FOR THE SUCCESSFUL ADOPTION OF OD

From numerous successes and failures in implementing OD programs, practitioners have been able to generate a specific list of conditions that help to ensure that an OD effort will succeed. According to French and Bell, among the most important are:

1. Use of an outsider who is trained in the behavioral sciences as a change agent
2. Recognition by top-level management that problems exist
3. Support and involvement in the program by top-level management, work group supervisors, and opinion leaders
4. Early successes in the OD program that suggest that the program is working and thereby encourage further cooperation
5. Respect for the managerial talents of those whose domain of responsibility is being improved
6. Cooperation and involvement on the part of human resource managers
7. Effective coordination and control of the OD program
8. Measurement of outcomes.[13]

EVALUATING OD INTERVENTIONS

The evaluation of OD programs poses many problems. If we rely on the opinions of those who have a stake in the program's success, such as the OD consultant and the manager who hired the change agent, some bias can be expected. Because of this and other considerations, people who are knowledgeable in the techniques of **evaluation research** may be called in to provide a more objective assessment of the true merits and impact of an OD intervention.

Evaluation researchers rely on the logic of research design when trying to evaluate a program.[14] In the vernacular of research design, there are three major designs: pre-experimental, experimental, and quasi-experimental.

In a **pre-experimental design,** no control is made of the event or program of interest. One simply takes readings or measures following an OD program. For example, an evaluation researcher may conduct interviews with employees on their impressions of the value of a training program after the employees have completed it. If we diagram this example with the simple notation that O represents the taking of observations and X represents the occurrence of the training program, then we have

This diagram is, in essence, an example of a case study. As you may recall (see Chapter 2), a case study merely involves the collection of information and an

attempt to relate the information to some prior event(s). Because the researcher exercises no formal control over the event, it is not possible to say whether X had any effect. Many alternative explanations (that is, events other than X) can be offered to account for whatever values are observed.

A somewhat better pre-experimental evaluation design is the **one-group pretest—post-test design.** In this design, observations are collected both before and after the program is introduced. In our example of studying the effects of a training program, we might survey the program's participants both before and after the introduction of the program.

As a diagram, we would portray this design as

$$O_1 \quad X \quad O_2$$
$$\xrightarrow{\hspace{3cm}}$$
$$\text{Time}$$

Although we might be tempted to draw conclusions about the effects of the program (X) from differences observed at time 1 and 2, we really cannot draw any firm conclusions because several loose ends exist in this design. One problem lies in the fact that other changes in the participants or their jobs may have been occurring at the same time as the training program (for example, the employees may have received salary increments). These simultaneous changes may be partially or largely responsible for changes observed in the measures of employee attitudes or performance. Also, during pre-testing, the employees may have been sensitized to the fact that they are involved in a study. Almost certainly, when employees are questioned a second time on their impressions, they will likely conclude that they are being studied. Their responses at the second time may, therefore, reflect a willingness to show cooperativeness with the apparent purpose of the surveys or a desire to appear consistent by trying to recall their previous answers. Finally, employees in a given department or work unit may be relatively atypical in terms of abilities and attitudes. In order to counter the problem of uniquely group-related differences, employees should be randomly assigned to one of two work groups where a training program is introduced in one group, and not immediately introduced in the other.

A design that is truly *experimental* and that overcomes many of the above problems is:

Random	O_1	X	O_2
Assignment			
Random	O_1		O_2
Assignment			

$$\xrightarrow{\hspace{3cm}}$$
$$\text{Time}$$

The above **pretest—post-test control group design** is a true experiment in that at least one formal comparison is being conducted. Because employees are randomly assigned to treatments and a comparable (control) condition is created that does not experience the training program, it is possible to draw cautious conclusions about the effect of X. One remaining potential problem is respondent **reactivity** to being pretested—that is, the problem of an employee responding in a particular fashion simply because he or she is aware of being involved in a study.

A superior experimental research design examines the question of whether pretesting has sensitized the respondents. It can be diagrammed as:

Random **Assignment**	O_1	X	O_2
Random **Assignment**	O_1		O_2
Random **Assignment**		X	O_2
Random **Assignment**		$\longrightarrow$	O_2

Time

The above design is termed a **Solomon four-group design.**[15] In this design, employees are randomly assigned to one of four conditions that are identical except for the introduction of the training program. Because employees are randomly assigned to groups, we can assume that the four groups are roughly identical at the start of the study. By comparing results obtained for the four groups at time 2 (as well as comparisons between time 1 and time 2 where possible), we can draw conclusions about the causal effect of the training program as well as the influence of pretesting on our results.

Although the Solomon four-group design represents perhaps the highest degree of control, it is very costly. In many organizations, it is very difficult or impossible to introduce such controls as the creation of a comparison group or random assignment of employees to conditions. In the absence of such controls, a variety of **quasi-experimental designs** is available for studying the effects of OD interventions. These designs have the dual strengths of selecting who is measured and when. To illustrate one example of a quasi-experimental design, consider the following:

$$O_1 \qquad O_2 \qquad O_3 \qquad O_4 \qquad X \qquad O_5 \qquad O_6 \qquad O_7 \qquad O_8$$

Time

This **time-series design** greatly extends the frequency of the pretest and post-test observations around our hypothetical training program. Because no formal comparison group exists, we are attempting to use a single group as its own control. As an illustration, consider a series of monthly performance reports taken before and after the introduction of a training program. In this example, it would be possible to draw a cautious inference concerning the impact of the training program (if we are willing to assume that other processes were not operating at the same time, and so on).

Figure 20.5 shows several sets of results we may expect to obtain from a time-series design. Outcome A suggests that the training program had an influ-

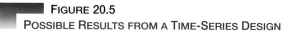

FIGURE 20.5
POSSIBLE RESULTS FROM A TIME-SERIES DESIGN

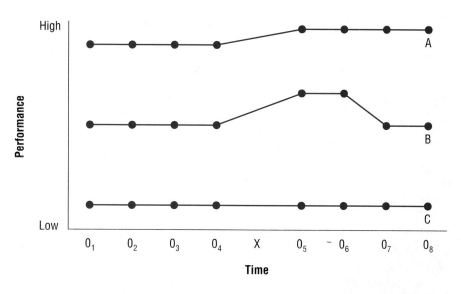

ence on performance that was of considerable duration. Outcome B also suggests that the program had an influence on performance, but this influence was fairly transitory and faded away over time. In Outcome C, the training program had no discernible impact on performance. Although the results of a time-series design cannot tell us conclusively that the training program had a particular effect on an outcome measure of interest, they can provide some insights that may be useful in deciding whether to continue, expand, or curtail a training program.

In practice, however, much of the evaluation of OD programs is fairly simple and unsophisticated. If key personnel are reasonably satisfied that the OD effort has been positive, based on their personal and subjective impressions, then the effort is labeled a success. Sometimes, simple measures of participants' attitudes are taken before and after the OD effort. If the results show "improvement" over time, then a "success" is declared. Unfortunately, improvement or change on an attitude scale can be due to a variety of factors (in addition to real change).

Terborg, Howard, and Maxwell[16] and Golembiewski and Billingsley[17] have suggested that additional complexities need to be considered. These authors suggest that any of three types of change may underlie differences in perceptual report data gathered before and after an OD effort. If an OD program does in fact produce the observed change, we refer to this type of difference as **alpha change**. However, the change may be due to other processes. In **beta**

change, employees change in the way in which they respond to the survey. This occurs when the respondents change their perceptions of the endpoints or ranges of the scales. For example, employees may initially rate their jobs very harshly. After a lecture on job enrichment (as part of a job redesign program) and related topics, they may become more realistic about the possible range of jobs for which they qualify and the constraints on their own job mobility. As a result of this shift in how they view their job (that it's not too bad, all things considered), they may assign a more favorable rating to their redesigned job. This higher rating is not the result of the job being more meaningfully changed, but rather of a shift in how the employee interprets the scale. A third type of shift in response can result when an employee shifts his or her idea or conceptualization of the construct. This is termed **gamma change.** In our example, this could occur if the employees initially viewed their jobs as merely a means to make a living. Following the OD effort, they may come to see their jobs as having some social value. As a consequence of this shift in perception, they may rate their redesigned job more favorably. Of course, no real change in the way in which the job is performed may have occurred. Also, productivity may not increase because work methods have not improved. Yet, the survey results would give the appearance that meaningful change has occurred. Determining whether alpha, beta, or gamma change processes are at work in a set of results requires substantial effort on the part of an evaluator. Fortunately, sophisticated techniques for uncovering these three sources of change are available.[18]

Finally, it should be mentioned that some OD practitioners believe that the effectiveness of OD efforts should be evaluated only at the level of individual personal satisfaction with the experience. This point of view, although not widely prevalent in the field of OD, views the attempt to measure human attributes as a fundamentally impersonal and mechanistic technique that is counter to OD's mission of helping people to achieve personal fulfillment through their work. To suggest measurement and evaluation of OD efforts reveals (to humanistic proponents) that the advocate of such a proposal does not completely understand the concept of what OD strives for in the area of human development. An OD specialist of the humanistic bent would likely suggest that someone who is a proponent of measuring and evaluating OD efforts is a prime candidate for participating in a humanistically oriented OD program![19]

Although the technical knowledge of evaluation research is available, many OD practitioners opt for a simplified approach to evaluating the results of their efforts. This usually consists of a combination of "soft," impressionistic data collected from key individuals and pretest and post-test data on attitudes and performance. A third approach to the evaluation of OD efforts, based on philosophical grounds, is that formal evaluation is impossible and should not even be attempted. This third view, from a humanistic perspective, holds that it is dehumanizing to attach numbers or measures to individuals. Therefore, in respect for human dignity, feelings (for example) should not be formally quantified.

DOES OD WORK?

Despite the difficulty of measuring the effects of OD efforts, it is possible to draw some tentative conclusions about the general value of OD in enhancing organizational effectiveness.

In their examination of 35 studies, Porras and Berg sorted the obtained results into outcome variables and process variables.[20] Outcome variables refer to measures of productivity, efficiency, absenteeism, profits, and so on (relatively "hard" measures), while process variables refer to measures of trust, perceptions of leadership, motivation, and decision making (relatively "soft" measures). In addition, they further divided their sample of studies into categories based on whether the OD efforts were directed at groups, organizations, individuals, or leaders. Their analyses of these studies suggested that group outcome variables (for example, group productivity) were most likely to be enhanced following OD interventions. Individual process variables also showed relatively positive improvement (for example, individual job satisfaction increased in roughly 40 percent of the OD studies in which it was measured). Table 20.1 summarizes these results in order of positive impact.

A further analysis was made of these studies in terms of the impact of various OD procedures. By and large, Porras and Berg observed that the most common OD techniques, such as team building and survey feedback, were reported to have positive effects, while T-groups were somewhat less effective (Table 20.2).

TABLE 20.1

EFFECTS OF OD EFFORTS ON OUTCOME AND PROCESS VARIABLES

Outcome Variables	Examples	Number of Studies	Average Positive Change
Group	Performance, length of meetings	8	63%
Organization	Profit, return on investment	12	47%
Individual	Performance, satisfaction	14	42%
Leader	Performance	3	—
Total		22	51%

Process Variables	Examples	Number of Studies	Average Positive Change
Individual	Self-awareness, self-actualization	10	62%
Group	Trust, involvement	20	49%
Leader	Openness to influence, interaction facilitation	20	45%
Organization	Leadership, decision making	27	36%
Total		35	46%

Source: Adapted from J. I. Porras and P. O. Berg, "The Impact of Organization Development," *Academy of Management Review* 3 (1978): 249–266.

TABLE 20.2
POSITIVE CHANGES IN ASSOCIATION WITH OD TECHNIQUE

Dominant Technique	Percentage Change*	
	Process Variables	Outcome Variables
Eclectic approach	52% (5)	52% (5)
Team building	45% (14)	53% (3)
Survey feedback	48% (4)	53% (3)
T-groups	44% (8)	44% (8)

* Values in parentheses are the number of studies in each classification.
Source: Adapted from J. I. Porras and P. O. Berg, "The Impact of Organization Development," *Academy of Management Review* 3 (1978): 249–266.

Porras and Berg also observed that OD efforts that used four or more techniques (the eclectic approach) were likely to produce more meaningful change. This suggests that a multifaceted approach to achieving organizational change is most appropriate. In addition, they noted that interventions lasting at least six days had superior results, with maximum benefits being reported when the duration was between 10 and 20 days. This suggests that OD efforts should be neither too brief nor too extended.

Despite the methodological shortcomings of many of the studies that Porras and Berg examined and the tendency of OD specialists to report their results in the most positive light (OD failures are less frequently written up), these results suggest that the efforts are usually effective.[§] As Porras and Berg's analysis suggests, the precise nature of OD's impact will depend on the type of technique, its duration, and the measures chosen to evaluate the intervention.

OD IN PERSPECTIVE

Although Porras and Berg's review points to many positive conclusions, the value of OD as commonly conducted is often questioned by both managers and behavioral scientists. Some of this criticism derives from a healthy skepticism on the part of managers and behavioral scientists. However, other factors can partially account for this criticism.[22]

First of all, OD is not a cure-all for every difficulty an organization may face. Its successful use requires skill and expertise, and it is most applicable to interpersonal problems. When used by nonexperts and applied to inappropriate situations, OD cannot be expected to succeed.

Users may also be disappointed to find that OD often does not live up to its stated ideal as described in articles and texts, but the flaw may be traceable to the users' approach. For example, OD is often performed at the lower levels of an organization, following top management's endorsement. The attitude

[§]A specific finding that should increase our caution in drawing inferences about the merits of OD is that the more methodologically rigorous a study is, the less likely it is to report that an OD effort has been successful.[21]

that OD is a task to be delegated to lower-level managers is likely to minimize the impact of most such programs. Yet high levels of participation, support, and concern for OD efforts from top-level management are fairly rare.

As discussed earlier, resistance to change is a significant obstacle to OD efforts. Although resistance on the individual level may be manageable, more difficult challenges arise when resistance stems from the total organizational system and its need to cope with its external environment. The external environment, of course, cannot be meaningfully changed by most OD efforts—and OD efforts are rarely intended to make such changes. Therefore, this larger constraint limits the progress that is possible within the organization.

In addition, organizations may be based on values that can significantly curtail certain forms of change. For example, religiously affiliated organizations typically adhere to specific sets of values, mission statements, and codes of conduct that set limits on what is feasible in the way of change. Thus, the perceived nature of an organization and what it stands for will dictate what changes are deemed permissible by both its members and its constituent groups in the larger society.

It has also been suggested that the chief values espoused by OD specialists—trust, openness, and power sharing—are not appropriate for some organizations. As part of their work, OD practitioners attempt to convert employees to their value system. Then, when the specific OD effort is completed, the employees must function within the larger, as yet unchanged, system of their organization. At this point, OD training may backfire because an employee who attempts to implement a philosophy of openness in a hostile environment may experience frustration and punishment rather than acceptance. In fact, as observed by DuBrin, people who adopt an open style of conduct may have problems competing with the more political and devious members of their organization.[23] In some instances, highly valued, competent, and successful employees may come to so fully embrace the values of openness and honesty that they reject their employment setting because it does not support their new-found values. As a result, the organization may actually lose valuable employees due to a shift in personal values induced by an OD effort. The irony, of course, is that the OD effort was intended to help such individuals perform better rather than encourage them to leave. In such cases, critics may contend that OD has made the employees less able to cope with the real world.

Bennis has suggested that OD practitioners rely largely on "truth and love" as sources of influence.[24] OD is, of course, more appropriate under conditions of openness and collaboration. But, in practice, OD specialists may sometimes rely on the truth–love model when it is inappropriate—that is, in situations characterized by distrust and conflict. This, then, is the basic dilemma for OD specialists: How can they help people in situations of conflict to realize and affirm the values of trust and collaboration? As further noted by Bennis, the truth–love model is more typically endorsed by wealthy and powerful organizations, such as IBM, AT&T, and Union Carbide. But many "disadvantaged organizations" most in need of OD, such as local governments, smaller firms, and social action groups, are less likely to be involved in OD efforts.

In the future, organizations may need to rely more heavily on the services of OD specialists as they are forced to undergo planned change. This need for managed change will result from a variety of emerging forces. Rapid changes in technology, for example, will require organizations to adjust their structure and processes. Also, the environment for many organizations will become more turbulent and uncertain. Contributing to this pressure will be an increasingly global business environment and a shrinking qualified labor pool (caused by both a "baby bust" and an inability of the American educational system to produce even minimally competent individuals). All these forces will require organizations to be more flexible and responsive. The ability to effectively implement planned change will be of great importance in the years to come.

SUMMARY

1. Identify external and internal sources of change in an organization.
External sources of change include competitors, suppliers, customers, the prevailing economic climate, the labor force, and the legal environment. Internal sources of change include shifts in workers' attitudes, declining productivity, and changes in key personnel.

2. Describe the stages of organizational growth.
An organization begins with a loose structure and grows through creativity until a crisis of leadership develops. The organization hires professional managers and enters a phase of growth through direction. A more formal structure leads to tension among specialized divisions and a crisis of autonomy. During the next stage, growth through delegation, middle- and lower-level managers receive greater power to make decisions, and a crisis of control arises. In the next stage, growth through collaboration, programs to increase coordination resolve the crisis of control but create a crisis of red tape. To continue growth through collaboration, the organization simplifies programs and systems.

3. List causes of organizational decline.
Organizations decline as a result of atrophy within the organization, self-complacency, loss of competitive drive, a recalcitrant work force, vulnerability because of low resources or inexperienced management, economic downturns, vigorous competition, changes in societal values, and lack of external resources.

4. Identify factors that lead to an organization's success or failure.
Organizations that succeed emphasize customers and their needs, exercise loose control at the departmental level but tight control over specific goals, have a simple structure, encourage entrepreneurship within the organization, emphasize action, maintain a commitment to original areas of expertise, stress a key value, and seek consensus among employees. Factors leading to failure include technological changes, dependency on suppliers or a single customer, inadequate control mechanisms, hesitancy to make change, lack of expertise, and unmanaged conflict.

5. Describe the phases in the process of change in an organization.
The first phase, unfreezing, begins with recognition that a situation is deficient.

The second phase, changing, occurs with implementation of a new plan or system. The third phase, refreezing, occurs as the newly created patterns of behavior and techniques become part of ongoing organizational processes.

6. Identify the components of an organization's readiness for change.

An organization is relatively ready for change if dissatisfaction with the status quo is high, an identifiable and desired solution exists, a practical plan for change exists, and the cost of change is low.

7. Describe techniques that organizational design specialists use to help bring about change in organizations.

OD specialists use feedback from surveys to obtain information and arouse awareness of the need for change. Another technique, team building, uses discussion of problems as a way to improve performance. Sensitivity training attempts to increase self-awareness and sensitivity to others. The goal of confrontation meetings is to manage dysfunctional intergroup conflict. Quality of work life programs use such techniques as job redesign, employee involvement in decision making, redesign of pay systems, and quality circles to enhance the total work climate.

8. Identify the conditions that enhance the likelihood an OD effort will succeed.

Conditions favorable to success include the use of a trained outsider, top-level management recognition that problems exist, leader support of and involvement in the program, early successes in the OD program, respect for the talents of the affected managers, cooperation and involvement from human resources managers, effective coordination and control of the OD program, and measurement of outcomes.

9. Explain how evaluation researchers evaluate OD programs.

Evaluation researchers sometimes use one of three major designs to evaluate a program. In a pre-experimental design, observations are taken either after or before and after implementing an OD program. An experimental design overcomes many of the problems of a pre-experimental design by including a control group that does not experience the OD program. When the controls necessary for experimental research are unavailable, a quasi-experimental design may be desirable.

10. Evaluate the track record of OD programs.

The success of an OD program depends on the type of technique, its duration, and the way the results are measured. Overall, research suggests that OD programs are usually effective. Efforts using four or more techniques and lasting 10 to 20 days are likely to produce more meaningful change.

KEY TERMS

Organizational decline	Survey feedback
Organizational development (OD)	Team building
Unfreezing	Sensitivity training
Changing	Confrontation meetings
Refreezing	Quality of work life (QWL)

Evaluation research

Pre-experimental design

One-group pretest–post-test design

Pretest–post-test control group
  design

Reactivity

Solomon four-group design

Quasi-experimental design

Time-series design

Alpha change

Beta change

Gamma change

REVIEW AND DISCUSSION QUESTIONS

1. What are some external sources of change in organizations? What are some internal sources?

2. What crises can arise at each stage of an organization's growth? How can the organization overcome each crisis?

3. Are large organizations immune to organizational decline? Why are new organizations particularly vulnerable to decline?

4. Danielle Irons learns that the restaurant next door to her bookstore is for sale. Danielle's bookstore has been very profitable this year, so she thinks it would be a good time to expand, and a restaurant sounds like a fun business to expand into. Danielle goes to see her banker about getting a loan to buy the restaurant. "Ms. Irons," says her banker, "before we discuss your application, I have a word of advice: Stick to your knitting." What does the banker mean? How is this advice relevant to Danielle's business?

5. Futuristic Computing is a new company set up to make special high-speed computers for the U.S. Defense Department. The company had a relatively easy time getting the government contract because their product is at the cutting edge of computing technology. Futuristic Computing is ready to start production; all key positions have been filled except for the Quality Control Manager. Company executives have been considering applications for this position for the past five months; they hope to be able to select a candidate in a few weeks but don't want to be hasty. Futuristic Computing is vulnerable to some of the factors that can lead to organization failure. Which of these factors should the company's executives be concerned about?

6. What is organizational development (OD)? What are the phases of the OD process?

7. Burt Stilgoe, chief executive officer of Quick & True Appraisal Company, wants to give individual appraisers more autonomy. As soon as Burt announces his plan, some employees at Quick & True begin raising objections to this change. How can Burt overcome this resistance? Which techniques do you recommend and why?

8. Robin Finch is an OD specialist who has contracted with Clean Sweep Incorporated, a janitorial services company that provides cleaning services in most of the city's largest office buildings. Clean Sweep has asked Robin to help the company improve its productivity. Describe some techniques Robin might use. Should she select a single technique, or more than one?

9. What are some advantages and drawbacks of the pre-experimental, experimental, and quasi-experimental research designs?

10. Should the effectiveness of an OD program be measured in terms of changes in employee performance, or in terms of individual personal satisfaction? If the goal of OD is personal fulfillment, who should be responsible for this? Are the values of OD appropriate for all organizations? Explain.

CRITICAL INCIDENT

Staunch Resistance at Metropolitan Police Department

Jerry Spore was disgusted. As commander of the 10th Division of the Metropolitan Police Department (MPD), he had just issued an ultimatum to Deputy Chief Robert Powell. All officers not in compliance with the new uniform standards within two weeks' time would be issued official reprimands that carry time-off-without-pay sanctions. He just couldn't understand what the problem was.

It all began two years ago, when a group of city officials responded to complaints from citizens about the Gestapo-like design of MPD officers' uniforms. Until that time, officers still donned the 1940s-style eight-pointed hat. Their other accessories were also traditional in style. Leather Sam Browne belts were worn over leather pants belts. Gun holsters, cuffs, and other equipment pertinent to the job were attached to the Sam Browne belts. City officials perceived citizens' comments to be reflective of the total MPD image, and they prompted Spore to work on improving that image by modifying the uniforms.

Spore took the task seriously. He formed a committee of local citizens and businesspeople to research and evaluate possible uniform modifications. Uniform suppliers called on the committee and encouraged them to adopt coordinated uniforms and accessories designed to maximize utility. The committee's conclusions were that they could get a lot of "bang for their buck" by simply changing key accessories in the uniform. They recommended that the city purchase new Sam Browne belts, new pants belts, and new rounded-top hats for the officers. The committee recommended that the uniforms be introduced in the police academy, and then adopted by the entire force over a period of six months, allowing for ample acquisition and distribution time.

All new recruits, therefore, were issued new belts and hats, as were all experienced officers. The hats were accepted almost without comment, but the belts met with resistance. The outside of the pants belt was Velcro as was the inside of the Sam Browne belt, thus allowing them to be conveniently attached. Belt closures were also Velcro. The belts required less maintenance and were slightly less expensive than the former standard belts.

Officers claimed that the rigid Velcro backing cut the pants loops. They also said that the belts were uncomfortable to wear. Spore observed that the problem probably related more to obesity than to the belt design. The more portly officers were accustomed to wearing their belts low, under their abdomens, and the backing material on the new belts did not cooperate. A few of the older officers also complained that the new belts were dangerous. They argued that each officer placed tools necessary for protection in a slightly different spot on the belts, and that this change could actually cost an officer's life in an emergency situation.

Most officers fresh out of the academy had replaced the issued Velcro-style belts, which they had discarded, with leather versions. Anyone seen with a Velcro belt was labeled as "green," or "nerdy." The change had been completely ignored by the other officers, and apparently Powell had been reprimanded by the now-disbanded committee about the waste of its time and money.

Meanwhile, Powell had been given the task to shape up these guys. Powell sensed that there was a lot more than logic behind the officers' resistance. Powell judged that Spore had made one key mistake in handling this whole uniform business, and that was affecting the entire change process. He didn't blame the officers for their gripes, but he also knew that his own neck was on the line. Powell was only one year from retirement, and didn't want to blow things now.

QUESTIONS

1. What do you think Spore's key mistake was?

2. What were the forces for change behind the uniform issue?

3. Use Kurt Lewin's model of change to recommend an ideal plan for making the change to the new uniform.

Source: Adapted by Susan Stites-Doe, State University of New York, College at Brockport. Used with permission from pages 444–446 of ORGANIZATION AND PEOPLE, Fourth Edition by J. B. Ritchie and Paul R. Thompson; Copyright © 1988 by West Publishing Company. All rights reserved.

EXPERIENTIAL EXERCISE

Introducing a Change—A Role Play

Most changes in organizations go far beyond the technical aspects of doing work; they usually involve alterations that influence the work satisfaction of the employees. In fact, change is often encountered on a personal level by most people. And frequently their reaction to change is one of resistance—not necessarily to the change itself but to what the change represents: the loss of known satisfaction.

As a manager, one might think of a continuum of approaches to introducing change, not unlike a leadership continuum (Chapter 11). At one end is telling/selling, where facts and arguments are presented showing the advantages of the change. In the middle is consultation, where the manager discusses the need for change with subordinates, solicits their ideas, and makes the decision. At the other end is collaboration, where the manager and the subordinates discuss the need for change and reach a consensus on a plan for implementing the change. The nature of the discussion that the manager initiates, plus the valence or attractiveness of what's at stake, will go a long way toward affecting the forces for and against change.

Step 1   This activity is a role play that concerns a change that must be introduced. The change affects everyone personally. Four volunteers will be selected for the roles. The remaining class members will serve as observers. Your instructor will provide each role player with a description of his or her role (the role descriptions are provided in the *Instructor's Manual*). If you are a role player, you should *not* let anyone else know the role situation you are in.

Step 2   The remaining class members will receive an observer's form from the instructor. It is very important for this activity that you fulfill your responsibilities as an observer. Having read and interpreted the roles, each role player should move to the front of the classroom. Four chairs arranged in a semicircle will represent the supervisor's office. On the instructor's signal, the group supervisor should begin the meeting.

Step 3   Once the role play has resulted in an acceptable outcome, the entire class can reconvene to discuss the observer's responses. The questions posed to the observers explore the dynamics of change in a manner that seeks recognition of the importance of power, influence, communication, motivation, and so forth. This activity will enable you to integrate most of the issues you have learned about in organizational behavior.

Source: Written by Bruce Kemelgor, University of Louisville.

NOTES

1. L.E. Greiner, "Evolution and Revolution as Organizations Grow," *Harvard Business Review* 50 (1972): 37–46.

2. D.A. Whetten, "Organizational Decline: A Neglected Topic in Organizational Science," *Academy of Management Review* 5 (1980): 557; E. Stark, "Surviving Organizational Death," *Psychology Today*, June 1989, 17; R. D'Aveni, "The Aftermath of Organizational Decline," *Academy of Management Journal* 32 (1989): 577–605; P.C. Nystrom and W.H. Starbuck, "To Avoid Organizational Crises, Unlearn," *Organizational Dynamics* (Spring 1984): 54.

3. J. Basaszewski, "Thirteen Ways to Get a Company in Trouble," *Inc.*, September 1981, 97–100; R.L. Daft, *Organization Theory and Design* (St. Paul, Minn.: West, 1983); T.J. Peters, "Putting Excellence into Management," *Business Week*, July 21, 1980, 196–205.

4. W.L. French and C.H. Bell, *Organization Development: Behavioral Science Interventions for Organization Improvement*, 2d ed. (Englewood Cliffs, N.J.: Prentice-Hall, 1978), 14; J.I. Porras, *Steam Analysis* (Reading, Mass.: Addison-Wesley, 1987).

5. K. Lewin, *Field Theory in Social Science* (New York: Harper and Row, 1951).

6. L.Coch and J.R.P. French, "Overcoming Resistance to Change," *Human Relations* 1 (1948): 512–532.

7. P.R. Lawrence, "How to Deal with Resistance to Change," *Harvard Business Review* 47 (1969): 115–122.

8. M. Beer, *Organization Change and Development: A Systems View* (Glenview, Ill.: Scott, Foresman, 1980); A. Armenakis, M. Harris, and K. Mossholder, "Creating Readiness for Large-Scale Change," *Human Relations* 46 (1993): 681–703.

9. French and Bell, *Organization Development.*

10. R.R. Blake, H.A. Shepard, and J.S. Mouton, *Managing Intergroup Conflict in Industry* (Houston: Gulf, 1965).

11. S.E. Seashore, "Defining and Measuring the Quality of Work Life," in *The Quality of Working Life,* vol. 1, eds. L.E. David and A. Cherns (New York: Free Press, 1975), 105–118; M. Fields and J. Thacker, "Influence of Quality of Work Life on Company and Union Commitment," *Academy of Management Journal* 35 (1992): 439–450.

12. J.M. Rosow, "Quality of Work Life Issues for the 1980s," in *Work in America,* eds. C. Kerr and J. Rosow (New York: Van Nostrand, 1979), 157–187; R. Golembiewski and B. Sun, "Positive-Findings Bias in QWL Studies: Rigor and Outcomes in a Large Sample," *Journal of Management* 16 (1990): 665–674.

13. French and Bell, *Organization Development.*

14. T.D. Cook and D.T. Campbell, *Quasi-experimentation: Design and Analysis Issues for Field Settings* (Chicago: Rand McNally, 1979).

15. R.L. Solomon, "An Extension of Control Group Design," *Psychological Bulletin* 46 (1949): 137–150.

16. J.R. Terborg, G.S. Howard, and S.E. Maxwell, "Evaluating Planned Organizational Change: A Method for Assessing Alpha, Beta, and Gamma Change," *Academy of Management Review* 5 (1980): 109–121.

17. R.T. Golembiewski and K.R. Billingsley, "Measuring Change in OD Panel Designs: A Response to Critics," *Academy of Management Review* 5 (1980): 97–103.

18. Terborg, Howard, and Maxwell, "Evaluating Planned Organizational Change."

19. N.C. Roberts and J. I. Porras, "Progress in Organization Development Research," *Group and Organization Studies* 7 (1982): 91–116.

20. J.I. Porras and P.O. Berg, "The Impact of Organization Development," *Academy of Management Review* 3 (1978): 249–266; J.I. Porras, P.J. Robertson, and L. Goldman, "Organization Development: Theory, Practice, and Research," in *Handbook of Industrial/Organizational Psychology,* ed. M.D. Dunnette (Palo Alto, Calif.: Consulting Psychologists Press, 1992); G.A. Neuman, J. Edwards, and N. Raja, "Organizational Development Interventions: A Meta-analysis of Their Effects on Satisfaction and Other Attitudes," *Personnel Psychology* 42 (1989): 461–483.

21. D. Terpstra, "Relationship between Methodological Rigor and Reported Outcomes in Organizational Development Evaluation Research," *Journal of Applied Psychology* (1981): 541–542.

22. A.J. DuBrin, *Foundations of Organizational Behavior* (Englewood Cliffs, N.J.: Prentice-Hall, 1984); P.J. Robertson, D.R. Roberts, and J.I. Porras, "Dynamics of Planned Organizational Change: Assessing Empirical Support for a Theoretical Model," *Academy of Management Journal* 36 (1993): 619–634.

23. Ibid., 471.

24. W.G. Bennis, *Organization Development: Its Nature, Origins, and Prospects* (Reading, Mass.: Addison-Wesley, 1969).

VIDEO CASE   STRUCTURE, CHANGE, AND QUALITY

Continuous economic and technological changes have forced many organizations to change the way they do business. This can mean redefining the organization's mission, changing the organization's culture, and creating new relationships with customers and employees. Organizational restructuring due to downsizing, redefinition of core competencies, and quality initiatives have resulted in an unprecedented rate of organizational change.

Structure, Change, and Quality illustrates the process of change in two organizations, one undergoing strategic reorganization and the other implementing Total Quality Management. In both instances, change is imposed on employees by management. Employees at both organizations are uncertain about what the future holds and are reluctant to let go of the past.

Change is never smooth. Organizational change requires upsetting the established way of doing things, and threatens familiar work methods and procedures. Hal, head of systems maintenance in the factory scenario, reacts defensively to the change effort at his plant. He misinterprets his organization's adoption of Total Quality Management as an insinuation that he has not been producing quality. Hal initially ignores that his coworkers are also undergoing the change, beseeching the foreman to end the process. Likewise, employees in the office vignette are concerned that the strategic reorganization will eventually cost them their jobs. It is important for all employees affected by the change to understand the stages of planned change.

Change proceeds through several phases. The first stage involves a period of grieving, as employees slowly give up familiar work activities. Employees need time to break the emotional investment they have in habitual work habits and methods. In the next stage, employees learn to live with and accept ambiguity. Employees should share experiences with coworkers to reinforce that they are not alone in this turbulent change process. In the final stage, employees refocus their negative energy toward productive outcomes. Thus, the change process consists of envisioning a future organizational state, stumbling through an ambiguous middle state, and then steering toward a new beginning. Whether change is perceived as an exciting opportunity or a stressful occurrence depends on employees' attitudes and on whether the change is self-initiated or imposed on employees unwillingly.

Managers need to accurately read employees' behaviors. A manager who misreads employees' demeanor may inappropriately respond in a way that further disengages people rather than involves them in the process. In the office scenario, the manager was insensitive to signs of survival syndrome in his employees. Managers must help employees make sense of the confusion. Similarly, employees need to maintain their sense of identity and belonging in the organization. Management's failure to acknowledge Hal's past contributions to systems maintenance left him feeling dejected and disengaged from his work.

Managers can use a number of techniques to facilitate change. Among them are:

- *Education and communication.* Individual meetings, group presentations, memos, discussions, and demonstrations can introduce the notion of change to individuals and help them prepare for the change process. Managers can also use these methods to clarify perceived inaccuracies about the effects of the change.

- *Participation and involvement.* Encouraging participation from all members affected by the change process can facilitate the introduction and implementation phases of change.

Employees can offer opinions and ideas about the design and implementation of the change effort, either voluntarily or through their participation in task forces and committees. Individuals who participate in designing a change are more committed to making the change work.

- *Facilitation and support.* Employees often have difficulties adjusting to the constraints imposed by the change. Managers can help employees cope with change by listening to employees' concerns and complaints, training employees in new techniques required by the change, and helping employees understand and deal with performance requirements.

- *Negotiation and agreement.* Some employees may feel that the proposed change will force them to lose something of value. Resistors to change may be offered incentives or benefits through negotiated agreements.

- *Manipulation and co-optation.* Influencing others and manipulating their perception of change can lessen resistance. Scaring employees into thinking a crisis is looming that can be avoided only by changing is an example of covert manipulation of information.

- *Explicit and implicit coercion.* Use of explicit or implicit force or threats, such as threaten-

ing to fire or transfer employees, can induce change. Although employees will resist forced change, coercion may be the most effective strategy if the change must be done swiftly.

Effective change efforts use a combination of these techniques. Managers who embrace only one technique will face more difficulty in implementing the change. Situational variables, such as anticipated resistance, distributions of power, and the stakes involved in the change effort, must also be considered in selecting the appropriate strategies. Finally, for change to be successfully implemented, change strategies must be carefully planned and incorporated into the organization's overall business strategy.

QUESTIONS

1. What could have been done differently in these organizations to make the change process smoother?

2. Which change facilitation techniques were used by managers in the video?

3. What are the advantages and disadvantages of the various change techniques?

4. What is survival syndrome? What can managers do to ameliorate its effects?

Source: John P. Kotter and Leonard A. Schlesinger, "Choosing Strategies for Change," *Harvard Business Review,* March/April, 1979, 109–112. "Video Case: Structure, Change and Quality," written by Melissa Waite, State University of New York, University at Buffalo; and Susan Stites-Doe, State University of New York, College at Brockport.

The Academy of Management Code of Ethical Conduct*

CREDO

We believe in discovering, sharing, and applying managerial knowledge.

PREAMBLE

Our professional goals are to enhance the learning of students, colleagues, and others and to improve the effectiveness of organizations through our teaching, research, and practice of management. We have five major responsibilities:

- To our students—Relationships with students require respect, fairness, and caring, along with recognition of our commitment to the subject matter and to teaching excellence.
- To managerial knowledge—Prudence in research design, human subject use, confidentiality, result reporting, and proper attribution of work is a necessity.
- To the Academy of Management and the larger professional environment—Support of the Academy's mission and objectives, service to the Academy and our institutions, and the recognition of the dignity and personal worth of colleagues is required.
- To both managers and the practice of management—Exchange of ideas and information between the academic and organizational communities is essential.
- To all people with whom we live and work in the world community—Sensitivity to other people, to diverse cultures, to the needs of the poor and disadvantaged, to ethical issues, and to newly emerging ethical dilemmas is required.

STUDENT RELATIONSHIPS

In our roles as educators, the central principles that underlie appropriate student-educator relationships are professionalism, respect, fairness, and concern.

STRIVING FOR TEACHING EXCELLENCE.   It is the duty of Academy members who are educators to prepare themselves carefully. Maintenance of *current knowledge* in the field requires a broad understanding of management theories, research and practice, and use of current classroom materials. Educators should have or develop expertise in the areas in which they teach. *Effective teaching* requires sufficient time allocated to preparation, clear classroom communication, timely grading, and a willingness to provide an explanation of a student's grade. Educators should act as role models in their relationships. They should also sensitize students to the ethical dimensions of management. In addition, educators have an obligation to present material without conscious

*Source: © *Academy of Management Journal* 1993, Vol. 36, No. 6, 1694–1698.

bias and to make their own relevant biases known to their students. Educators should attempt to evaluate their teaching through some appropriate *outcome assessment* method which goes beyond concept retention.

SHOWING RESPECT FOR STUDENTS.   It is the duty of Academy members who are educators to show appropriate respect for student feelings, interests, needs, contributions, and intellectual freedom. Students' *right to privacy* requires maintaining the confidentiality of academic records and private communications, unless disclosure is mandated by law, institutional policy, or morally compelling purpose. Educators must *avoid manipulation, coercion, or exploitation* of students (especially acts directed at securing monetary, ego, or sexual gratification) and should demonstrate a sensitivity to cultural and personal diversity by avoiding racial, sexual, religious, and ethnic discrimination.

MAINTENANCE OF OBJECTIVITY AND FAIRNESS.   It is the duty of Academy members who are educators to treat students equitably. *Fair treatment* of students requires explaining and adhering to academic requirements and standards. Any subsequent change in these requirements or standards, either of the institution or in an individual course, should appropriately recognize the impact on students. *Impartiality, objectivity, and fairness* are required in all dealings with students. Examinations should be carefully prepared and written work graded in an impartial manner. Educators should scrupulously avoid entering any overly personal relationship or accepting any gift or favor which might influence, or appear to influence, an objective evaluation of a student's work. *Appropriate evaluation* of student performance requires test design, assignments, and testing conditions which minimize the possibility of academic misconduct. It is the educator's responsibility to pursue appropriate disciplinary action.

COUNSELING OF STUDENTS.   It is the duty of Academy members to be helpful and sensitive in counseling students. When serving as *academic advisors,* members must be knowledgeable about academic requirements and should communicate these clearly and fully to advisees. Educators may play critical roles in a variety of *counseling situations*. This requires careful analysis of the student and situation and calls for special expertise and competence. Counseling advice should be identified as an expression of the member's own opinion. *Letters of recommendation* require candor and fairness. Members should not make insupportable statements nor fail to disclose material facts.

ADVANCEMENT OF MANAGERIAL KNOWLEDGE

Academy member research should be done honestly, have a clear purpose, show respect for the rights of all individuals and organizations, efficiently use resources, and advance knowledge in the field.

CONDUCTING AND REPORTING.   It is the duty of Academy members conducting research to design, implement, analyze, report, and present their findings rigorously. *Research rigor* includes careful design, execution, analysis, interpretation of results, and retention of data. *Presentation* of research should fairly represent the relevant literature and should include a treatment of the data that is honest and that reveals both strengths and weaknesses of findings. When important alternate hypotheses or explanations exist, they should be noted and data that disconfirm hypotheses should be acknowledged. *Authorship and credit* should be shared in correct proportion to the various parties' contributions. Whether published or not, ideas or concepts derived from others should be acknowledged, as should advice and assistance received. Many management-related journals have policies prohibiting or restricting potential articles from being reviewed concurrently in other outlets. These policies should be closely observed or there should be explicit discussion with the relevant journal editors concerning the intended *multiple submissions*. More than one report of essentially the same data and results should not be published unless the reports are explicitly directed to different audiences through different types of outlets. When several separate but *related reports* result from a single study, the existence of the different reports should be made known to the relevant journal editors and the reports should reference each other. *Reviewer comments* should be considered thoughtfully before a manuscript is submitted to a different journal.

PARTICIPANTS.   It is the duty of Academy members to preserve and protect the privacy, dignity, well-being, and freedom of research participants. This requires both careful research design and informed consent from all participants. *Risks and the possibility of harm* to research participants must be carefully considered and, to the extent possible, be minimized. When there is a degree of risk or potential harm inherent in the research, potential participants—organizations as well as individuals—must be informed. *Informed consent* means explaining to potential participants the purposes and nature of the research so they can freely choose whether or not to become involved. Such explanations include warning of possible harm and providing explicit opportunities to refuse to participate and to terminate participation at any time. Because students and employees are particularly subject to possible coercion, even when unintended, special care must be taken in obtaining their informed consent. *Third-party review* is one means of protecting the interests of research participants. Research plans involving human participants should be reviewed by an appropriate third party, such as a university human subjects committee or a focus group of potential participants. *Confidentiality and/or anonymity* questions must be resolved between researcher and potential research participants, both individuals and organizations, and when requested must be honored. *Deception* should be minimized and, when necessary, the degree and effects must be mitigated as much as possible. Researchers should carefully weigh the gains achieved against the cost in human dignity. To the extent that concealment and/or deception is necessary, the researcher must provide a full and accurate explanation to participants at the conclusion of the study, including counseling, if appropriate.

DISSEMINATION.   It is the duty of journal editors and reviewers to exercise their position of privilege in a confidential, unbiased, prompt, constructive, and sensitive manner. They have a duty to judge manuscripts only on their scholarly merits. *Conflicts of interest* may arise when a reviewer is in basic disagreement with the research approach or the line of research represented by a manuscript. In such cases, a reviewer should consult with the journal editor to decide whether to accept or decline to review the manuscript. *Protecting intellectual property* is a responsibility of the reviewer and the editor. The content of a manuscript is the property of its author(s). It is therefore inappropriate to use ideas or show another person a manuscript one has been asked to review, without the explicit permission of its author, obtained through the journal editor. Advice regarding specific, limited aspects of the manuscript may be sought from qualified colleagues so long as the author's intellectual property remains secure. *Sharing of reviewing responsibilities* is inappropriate. The review is the sole responsibility of the person to whom it was assigned by the journal editor. In particular, students and colleagues should not be asked to prepare reviews unless the journal's editor has given explicit approval. Anyone contributing to a review should receive formal recognition. *Constructive review* means providing critiques and comments in a spirit of collegiality with thoroughness, timeliness, compassion, and respect, and in ways intended to improve the quality of the manuscript.

GRANTS AND CONTRACTS.   It is the duty of Academy members to accurately represent themselves and their proposed projects and to manage those projects as promised. *Representation* means accurate disclosure of one's level of expertise and expected actual involvement, the outcomes that can be reasonably expected, the realistic funding level needed, and potential conflicts of interest. *Grant and contract management* requires independence and objectivity such that one does not compromise one's responsibilities or create conflicts of interest. One must also manage time and budget responsibly and use the funds as promised unless permission is explicitly granted to do otherwise.

THE ACADEMY OF MANAGEMENT AND THE LARGER PROFESSIONAL ENVIRONMENT

The Mission Statement of the Academy describes member benefits and professional opportunities which impose corresponding duties and service responsibilities.

SHARING AND DISSEMINATION OF INFORMATION. To encourage meaningful exchange, Academy members should foster a climate of free interchange and constructive criticism within the Academy and be willing to share research findings and insights fully with other members.

ACADEMY PARTICIPATION. The Academy is a voluntary association whose existence and operations are dependent on cooperation, involvement, and leadership from its members. Members should abide by the Constitution, By Laws, policies, and codes of the Academy. Members should consider offering their time and talent to carry out activities necessary to maintain the Academy and its functions. Officers and members should fulfill their Academy *obligations and responsibilities* in a timely, diligent, and sensitive manner, without regard to friendships or personal gain. Members should honor all *professional meeting commitments* including presentation of accepted papers and participation in scheduled roles as chair, discussant, or panel members. Where absence from scheduled meeting responsibilities is unavoidable, members must contact appropriate individuals and pursue suitable alternative arrangements. One should consider the *impact* one's projects or activities may have on the integrity of the reputation of the Academy and not engage in those which may have possible negative implications. Members should not imply that their work is sanctioned by the Academy unless an appropriate Academy body has specifically done so.

COMMITMENT TO PROFESSIONAL STANDARDS OF CONDUCT. By this Code, the Academy provides ongoing ethical guidance for its members. Members should work to *raise membership consciousness* concerning ethical responsibilities and encourage acceptance of these responsibilities. Members should *notify* appropriate Academy officers or committees of the practices or actions of members which they feel may violate Academy regulations or general standards of ethical conduct. In this manner, the aspirational and educational goals of this code are served through discussion of the ethical dilemmas and values of our profession.

STRENGTHENING AND RENEWAL OF THE ACADEMY. The Academy of Management must have continuous infusions of people and new points of view to remain viable and relevant as a professional association. Members may contribute to this infusion by encouraging participation in the Academy by all eligible individuals, and by assisting new and prospective members to develop their skills and knowledge, and their understanding of their professional obligations.

The professional environment for many Academy members includes the university community. The central values which underlie appropriate university participation are understanding, involvement, respect, fairness, and the pursuit of knowledge.

PARTICIPATION IN UNIVERSITY LEADERSHIP. Professors should take an active interest in university governance. Professors should be *aware* of university policies that affect the dissemination of knowledge and be involved in the development of such policies. Professors should endeavor to positively *influence* policies relating to the quality of education and service to students. Active *organizational involvement* requires exercise of personal voting rights and respect for such rights of others, without regard to rank or tenure. Professors should *evaluate colleagues* for purposes of promotion and/or tenure on the basis of appropriate Academic criteria fairly weighted in accordance with standards understood by the faculty and communicated to the subject of the evaluation. It is the duty of Academy members to treat their colleagues with respect and fairness. Members should safeguard confidential *personal matters* and avoid disclosing opinions expressed, attribution of statements, voting behavior, and outcomes. Members should *address misunderstandings* and conflicts with those directly involved and avoid speculative criticism that might damage the reputations of individuals or groups. When speaking or *acting outside their university role,* professors should avoid creating the impression that they are speaking or acting for their university and/or its administration. Professors should dispose of *complimentary books* requested from publishers by a manner other than sale.

All Academy members, whether affiliated with a university, business, governmental, service, or consulting organization have an obligation to interact with others in a professional manner.

MEMBERSHIP IN THE PROFESSIONAL COMMUNITY. It is the duty of Academy members to interact with others in our community in a manner that recognizes individual dignity and merit. The responsible professional promotes and protects *the rights of individuals* without regard to race, color, religion, national origin, handicap, sex, sexual orientation, age, political beliefs, or academic ideology, and refrains from sexual harassment. In the spirit of intellectual inquiry, the professional should *welcome suggestions* and complaints openly without reprisal. Members should ensure that *outside activities* do not significantly diminish their availability and energy to meet their institutional obligations.

MANAGERS AND THE PRACTICE OF MANAGEMENT

Consulting with client organizations ("clients") has the potential for enriching the teaching and practice of management, for translating theory into practice, and for furthering research and community service. To maximize such potential benefits, it is essential that members who consult be guided by the ideals of competence, integrity, and objectivity.

CREDENTIALS AND CAPABILITIES. It is the duty of consultants to represent their credentials and capabilities in an accurate and objective manner. Consultants shall accept only those assignments for which they have *appropriate expertise.* Consultants shall refrain from exaggerating their professional qualifications to secure prospective assignments. Consultants shall examine any factors (e.g., prior experience, capabilities, other commitments) that might limit their judgment or objectivity in carrying out an assignment. *University endorsement* of the consulting activities of Academy members employed by academic institutions should not be represented or implied to potential clients unless the assignment is formally under university sponsorship or is so approved.

OBLIGATIONS TO CLIENTS. Consultants have a duty to fulfill their obligations to their present and prospective clients in a professionally responsible and timely manner. Consultants shall place the highest possible priority on their *clients' interests.* Consultants shall avoid or withdraw from situations in which their clients' interests come into serious conflict with their own. Consultants shall not serve two or more *competing clients* without the consent of all parties. Consultants shall *fully inform* their clients. This means presenting results and/or advice in an unbiased manner, and discussing fully with the client the values, risks, and limitations of the recommendations.

CLIENT RELATIONS.   Consultants must fulfill duties of confidentiality and efficiency as part of the relationship with their clients. Consultants shall maintain *confidentiality* with respect to their clients' identities and the assignments undertaken unless granted permission by the client. Consultants should exercise concern for the protection of client employees and other stakeholders by maintaining, in particular, appropriate confidentiality. Consultants shall not take *personal or financial advantage* of confidential information acquired as a result of their professional relationships, nor shall they provide the basis upon which others may take such advantage. Consultants should meet their time *commitments* and conserve the resources utilized.

REMUNERATION.   It is the duty of consultants to negotiate clear and mutually accepted remuneration agreements for their services. Consultants shall provide a *realistic estimate* of the fees to be charged in advance of assignments. Fees charged shall be commensurate with the services performed.

SOCIETAL RESPONSIBILITIES.   Consultants have a duty to uphold the legal and moral obligations of the society in which they function. Consultants should report to the appropriate authorities any *unlawful activities* that may have been uncovered during the course of engagements (except where one's functional professional code directs otherwise).

STUDENTS AND EMPLOYEES.   It is the duty of the consultant to safeguard student and employee rights when they are involved in consulting assignments. Consultants may *involve students* in work generated by engagements, especially if such work possesses learning potential, but students must not be coerced into participation. When they are so involved, students, as well as employees, should be fairly compensated and be made aware of the nature of the work they are doing.

THE WORLD COMMUNITY

As citizens of the world community, Academy members may have much to contribute in shaping global consciousness by their teaching, research, and service.

WORLD VIEW.   Academy members have a duty to consider their responsibilities to the world community. In their role as *educators,* members of the Academy can play a vital role in encouraging a broader horizon for decision making, viewing issues from a multiplicity of perspectives, including those of the least advantaged. As *researchers,* members of the Academy should consider, where appropriate, increasing their exposure to other cultures via travel, study, and research. Where appropriate, research might highlight the responsible stewardship of the Earth's resources. In addition, members should take as a challenge the ongoing task of identifying evolving ethical issues by listening to those whose welfare is affected and by exploring the interaction of people and technology. In fulfilling their *service* responsibilities, members of the Academy should consider how they might lend their time and talent to enhance the world community through involvement in uncompensated public service.

Glossary*

Accommodating A style of conflict management involving giving in to another's wishes. (14)

Achievement-oriented leadership In path–goal theory, a leader behavior that entails setting challenging goals while simultaneously showing confidence in the subordinates' abilities. (11)

Administrative model A decision-making model recognizing that bounded rationality limits the making of optimally rational-economic decisions. (12)

Adverse impact A primary issue in legal cases charging companies with discriminatory practices: Does an employment practice have a disparate negative effect on the opportunities of a protected class of employees? (8)

Affective component The emotional aspect of an attitude. (4)

Alienative involvement Organizational involvement typified by members' hostile and extremely negative attitudes. (9)

Alpha change A shift in response that is produced by a program itself. (20)

Alternating ranking technique A ranking of employees that entails writing down the name of the best performer, followed by that of the poorest performer, followed by that of the next-best performer, and so on. (8)

Approach–approach conflict A type of intrapersonal conflict arising when an individual must choose between two attractive alternatives. (14)

Approach–avoidance conflict A type of intrapersonal conflict arising when an individual must choose whether to approach or avoid a goal that has both attractive and unattractive qualities. (14)

Archival research A type of OB research using existing information found, for example, in scholarly books and journals, newspapers, and government documents. (2)

Assessment center An evaluation technique using situational exercises conducted over a period of several days in order to identify promotable, high-potential employees. (8)

Attitude An idea charged with emotion that predisposes a set of actions to a specific set of stimuli. (4)

Attribution theory A theory that suggests that we observe the behavior of others and then attribute internal or external causes to it. (3)

Audience factor A factor involved in attitude change that deals with the influence of individual characteristics of the target person. (4)

Authoritarianism The extent to which a person believes that power and status should be concentrated in a leader or class. The stronger the belief, the more the person is said to be authoritarian. (3)

Authority Power based on the legitimate right to try to change others' behavior or tell them what to do. (9)

Availability heuristic A process used when an individual estimates the frequency or probability of an event or class of objects by the ease with which instances can be brought to mind. (12)

Avoidance–avoidance conflict A type of intrapersonal conflict arising when an individual must choose between two equally unattractive alternatives. (14)

Avoiding A style of conflict management in which a person attempts to adopt a neutral stance. (14)

Balance theory The idea that individuals try to maintain consistency among their beliefs. (4)

Bank Wiring Room study One of the Hawthorne studies, revealing ways in which peer pressure can affect individual productivity. (1)

Barnum effect The tendency to accept vague, ambiguous, and general statements of one's personality as descriptively accurate. (3)

Behavior modification An approach to motivation that uses the principles of operant conditioning. (6)

---

* The chapter in which a glossary term is initially discussed is given in parentheses.

Behavioral component The aspect of an attitude predisposing a set of actions. (4)

Behavioral observation scales (BOS) Rating scales similar to BARS that measure the frequency with which a ratee engages in specific behaviors. (8)

Behavioral theory of decision making An approach to decision making that recognizes that bounded rationality limits the making of optimal decisions. (12)

Behaviorally anchored rating scales (BARS) Rating scales developed by raters and/or ratees in which specific behavioral incidents serve as anchors. (8)

Beta change A shift in response that reflects a change in the way an employee responds to the survey. (20)

Boundary-spanning position A position within an organization that represents the organization to various constituencies in the external environment. (14) (18)

Bounded discretion Limitations imposed on the decision-making process that result from moral and ethical constraints. (12)

Bounded rationality The assumption that organizational, social, and human limitations lead decision makers to settle on decisions that are "good enough" rather than optimal. (12)

Brainstorming A technique designed to generate creative solutions to problems by encouraging group members to express their ideas freely in a noncritical atmosphere. (12)

Bureaucracy An organizational structure proposed by Weber emphasizing rationality and including such features as adherence to

formal rules, a hierarchy of authority, specialization, hiring based on qualifications, and promotion based on merit. (17)

Burnout Physical, emotional, and mental exhaustion resulting from prolonged exposure to stressful situations. (15)

Calculative involvement Organizational involvement in which members' relationship to the organization is rational and oriented toward maximizing personal gain. (9)

Case study A type of OB research consisting of an in-depth examination of an organization, usually conducted over an extended period. (2)

Cautious shift A tendency for groups to make more conservative decisions than individuals. (12)

Central tendency error The tendency to rate all ratees around the middle range of a scale. (8)

Central traits Specific traits of individuals that are more responsible than others in influencing the formation of impressions. (3)

Centralized network A communication network in which members have unequal opportunities to obtain and pass on information. Information flows through a pivotal or central person. (16)

Chain of command A concept maintaining that information and authority proceed from level to level in a strict hierarchical fashion. (17)

Changing The second phase of Lewin's model of change, in which a new plan or system is implemented. (20)

Charismatic leadership Leadership based on referent power and characterized by self-confidence, sense of purpose, and an articulated vision. (10)

Classical conditioning An approach to learning in which an unconditioned stimulus is repeatedly paired with a neutral stimulus until the neutral stimulus alone can elicit the same response that was evoked by the unconditioned stimulus. When this occurs, the neutral stimulus is termed a conditioned stimulus and the response, a conditioned response. (5)

Classical decision theory An approach to decision making that assumes that decision makers are objective, have complete information, and consider all possible alternatives and their consequences before selecting the optimal solution. *See also* Rational–economic model (12)

Closed group A group in which the membership remains fairly stable. (13)

Closed system A system that does not interact with its external environment. (18)

Coercive power Power based on the extent to which an individual or organization has control over punishments. The opposite of reward power. (9)

Cognitive component The knowing aspect of an attitude. (4)

Cognitive dissonance Occurs when a person exhibits behavior that is inconsistent with his or her attitudes. (4)

Cognitive resource theory The view that directive leaders who are intelligent and possess relevant job experience will be more effective if they are in stress-free settings with subordinates who are supportive. (10)

Cognitive style Mode of gathering and evaluating information. Jung identified four types: sensing, intuiting, thinking, and feeling. (3)

Cohesiveness The sum of all forces acting on group members to remain a part of the group. (13)

Collaborating A style of conflict management that attempts to satisfy the concerns of both sides through honest discussion. (14)

Communication The creation of a mental image in the mind of a receiver in exactly the same detail as intended by the sender. (16)

Communication role The specific functions an individual serves in an organization's communication network. (16)

Comparison level The standard by which people evaluate the rewards and costs of a relationship. The average value of all outcomes of past relationships of a particular type. (13)

Comparison level of alternatives The standard an individual uses in deciding whether to maintain or terminate a relationship. (13)

Complementary transaction In transactional analysis, a relationship between two people that is predictable. (16)

Compliance An individual's acceptance of an influence attempt in the belief that rewards will follow or punishment will be avoided. (9)

Compromising A style of conflict management that strives for partial satisfaction of both sides' desires. (14)

Conditioned response In classical conditioning, a reflexive response evoked by a conditioned stimulus. (5)

Conditioned stimulus In classical conditioning, a neutral stimulus that has attained the capacity to evoke a conditioned response. (5)

Conflict A form of interaction between individuals or groups in situations that occurs when one or both sides perceive that the other has thwarted or is about to thwart an important concern. (14)

Conformity An individual's change of attitudes or behavior in response to real or imagined pressure from others. (9)

Confrontation meetings An organizational development technique in which conflicting groups are brought together in a structured situation designed to enhance cooperation. (20)

Conglomerate An organizational firm that includes a broad range of diverse business units. (18)

Consideration A factor referring to the extent to which a leader exhibits concern for the welfare of the group members. (10)

Content theories Theories that focus on the specific factors that motivate people to perform. Examples are the theories of Maslow, Herzberg, and McClelland. (6)

Contextual dimensions Characteristics of the entire organization and its external environment, such as size, technology, and external constituents (e.g., customers, suppliers, and competitors). (18)

Contingency approach An approach to organizational behavior stating that there is no one best way to manage every situation, but that management must find different ways to deal with different situations. (1)

Contingency model of leadership effectiveness A theory suggesting that leadership effectiveness is determined both by the characteristics of the leader and by the level of situational favorableness that exists. (11)

Continuous reinforcement A schedule designed to reinforce correct behavior every time it is exhibited. (5)

Correlational method A method employed by OB research that examines the relationship between two variables, particularly whether changes in one variable produce changes in the other. (2)

Cosmopolite An individual whose communication network extends into the organization's external environment. (16)

Culture Assimilator A culture-specific, programmed learning exercise designed to provide the learner with feedback on his or her responses to hypothetical situations. (19)

Culture-quality movement A perspective emerging in the early 1980s that emphasized the importance of such organizational value issues as employee involvement and commitment in influencing the quality of production output. (1)

Decentralization The degree to which decision making occurs lower down in an organization. (17)

Decentralized network A communication network in which

each member has an equal opportunity to obtain and pass on information. (16)

Deduction To infer something about a particular case from a general principle that holds for all such cases. (2)

Deficiency needs The lower-order needs (physiological, safety, and social) in Maslow's hierarchy that must be satisfied to ensure a person's existence. (6)

Delphi technique A technique for improving group decision making in which the opinions of experts are solicited by a mailed questionnaire and then compiled. The consensus is used to make a decision. (12)

Demand characteristics In laboratory experiments, the cues and signals of an experimental setting that indicate to the subject how to respond to the experimenter's wishes. (2)

Dependent variable An outcome or consequence that is attributable to the independent variable. (2)

Differentiation A concept that refers to the degree of difference in orientations and perspectives among an organization's subunits. (18)

Diffusion of responsibility A concept, often used to explain the risky shift, that holds that individual responsibility is shared among a group's members. (12)

Directive leadership In path–goal theory, a leader behavior that involves giving specific guidance to subordinates and asking that they follow standard rules and regulations. (11)

Distributive justice The fairness of the amount of a reward as perceived by the reward's recipient,

and as compared against the amount of a reward given to another. (6)

Dogmatism A system of beliefs insisting upon the existence of certain truths and opposed to skepticism. (3)

Dominant culture A set of core values that is shared by most employees. (19)

Downward communication Communication that flows from higher to lower levels within an organization. (16)

Emotional labor The active self-management of behaviors, affective tone, and moods by employees in order to maintain a positive self-presentation. (15)

Employee empowerment A set of motivational techniques designed to improve employee performance through increased levels of employee participation and self-determination. (7)

Employee envy A pattern of thoughts, emotions, and behaviors that results when an employee feels a loss of self-esteem in response to another obtaining personally desired outcomes. (15)

Employee growth-need strength The strength of an employee's desire for personal growth experiences in the work setting. (7)

Employee jealousy A pattern of thoughts, emotions, and behaviors that results from an employee's felt loss of self-esteem and the loss of outcomes associated with a working relationship. (15)

Employee orientation A style of leadership referring to the extent a leader shows concern for the welfare of the group members. (10)

Enacted role The actual set of behaviors exhibited by an individual in a position. (13)

Equity theory A theory that suggests that a person will strive to maintain a ratio of input to outcome that is equal to the ratio of a comparison other. (6)

Evaluation research Techniques of research design used to evaluate a program's success. The three major designs are pre-experimental, experimental, and quasi-experimental. (20)

Expectancy theory A theory suggesting that behavior is a function of a person's expectancies about the future and the value of future outcomes. (6)

Expected role The formal set of behaviors conveyed both by a job description and by members of the work unit. (13)

Experimental method A method employed by OB research that manipulates one variable (the independent variable) in the hope of observing resulting changes in another variable (the dependent variable). (2)

Expert power Individual power based on the possession of expert, job-relevant knowledge. (9)

Expert systems The procedure of analyzing an individual's or a group's decision-making process and using the resultant model as an aid in subsequent decisions. The expert systems approach is sometimes termed *bootstrapping*. (12)

External validity The extent to which a study's results can be generalized beyond the immediate situation. (2)

Extinction The decline in response rate that occurs when reinforcement is removed from behaviors that were previously rewarded. (5)

Extrinsic reward A reward external to the job, such as pay or promotion. (7)

Faceted approach An approach to studying job satisfaction that breaks down an employee's reaction to a job into several facets (e.g., one's supervisor, pay, or working conditions). (4)

Feedback interview A meeting between manager and employee in which the results of a performance appraisal are conveyed to the employee. (8)

Field experiment A type of OB research in which an investigator attempts to manipulate and control variables in a natural setting rather than in a laboratory. (2)

Fixed interval schedule A schedule in which a reward is applied only after a fixed amount of time has passed since the last reward was given. (5)

Fixed ratio schedule A schedule in which a set number of responses must be performed before a reward is applied. (5)

Fixed schedule A reinforcement schedule in which the amount of time or number of behaviors performed is specified. (5)

Flat structure Describes an organization with fewer levels of authority and larger spans of control. (17)

Flextime A work schedule that gives employees some discretion in arranging their working hours, specifically their starting and ending times. (7)

Flow A totally absorbing experience in which one senses joy, fulfillment, and creativity. (6)

Foot-in-the-door principle The tendency to comply with a request for a sizable favor following a request for a small favor. (9)

Forced distribution An evaluating technique in which the rater assigns employees to categories on the basis of performance, but limits the percentage of employees placed in any one category. (8)

Forcing A form of conflict management that attempts to overwhelm an opposing side with formal authority, threats, or the use of power. (14)

Formal group A group formed within an organization to accomplish the goals of the organization. (13)

Forming The earliest stage of group development, in which members determine behaviors that are acceptable and unacceptable. (13)

Four-fifths rule In discrimination cases, adverse impact is said to exist if a protected group's selection rate for employment decisions is less than four-fifths (80 percent) of the rate for the nonprotected group. (8)

Functional form A basic type of organization design that groups personnel and activities according to resources that are essential to the production process. (17)

Functional turnover The assumption that high turnover among poor performers can benefit an organization. (4)

Fundamental attribution error The tendency to attribute the behavior of others to internal forces. (3)

Gain sharing An incentive scheme that ties an individual's bonuses to the performance of a business unit. (7)

Game playing Forms of patterned social interaction based on giving and getting "strokes" in the transactional analysis view. (16)

Gamma change A shift in response that reflects a change in the way an employee conceptualizes the construct being measured. (20)

Gatekeeper An individual in an organization who controls the flow of information to others. (16)

General Adaptation Syndrome Refers to the three stages of stress identified by Selye: alarm, resistance, and exhaustion. (15)

Global approach An approach to studying job satisfaction taking into account an employee's overall reaction to a job. (4)

Goal acceptance The degree of a person's acceptance of the goal. (7)

Goal difficulty The degree of proficiency or level of job performance that is being sought by the goal. (7)

Goal specificity The degree of precision of the goal. (7)

Grapevine Informal channels of communication that exist within an organization and short-circuit the formal channels. (16)

Graphic rating scale An evaluation technique in which the rater checks the point on the scale that best represents the performance level of the employee. (8)

Graphic scale A method of measuring attitudes in which an individual checks the point on a scale that best represents his or her degree of agreement with a statement. (4)

Greenfield site A new facility with a new work force, often established as part of an effort to introduce self-directed work teams. (7)

Grid analysis A technique for improving creativity in which ideas are listed on the sides of a two-dimensional grid and all possible combinations of ideas are examined. (12)

Group A collection of two or more individuals who interact with each other, share common beliefs, and perceive themselves as being in a group. (13)

Group polarization The tendency for members of a group to move to extreme positions (in the direction they originally favored) following group discussion. (12)

Groupthink The tendency for members of a highly cohesive group to seek consensus so strongly that they fail to explore alternative, possibly correcting, courses of action. (12)

Growth needs The higher-order needs (esteem and self-actualization) in Maslow's hierarchy that are concerned with the realization of one's potential. (6)

Halo effect An overall favorable or unfavorable impression of a person that is used as a basis for performance evaluation, regardless of the actual performance level. (3)

Halo error Occurs when a rater assigns the same rating to all aspects of an employee's performance, regardless of the actual level, because of an overall favorable or unfavorable impression of the employee. (8)

Harshness error The tendency to rate all ratees unfavorably. (8)

Hawthorne effect A phenomenon seen in test situations, in which enhanced employee performance largely results from the employees' awareness that they are being observed. (1)

Hawthorne studies A series of studies of worker behavior conducted at the Hawthorne plant of Western Electric near Chicago from 1924 to 1934. The studies, which demonstrated the effect of social processes on job performance, provided the impetus for the human relations approach to organizations. (1)

Hedonism One of the earliest views on motivation, hedonism argues that people will seek pleasure and comfort, and try to avoid pain and discomfort. (6)

Hersey–Blanchard situational theory A theory proposing that optimal leader behavior is related to the maturity of subordinates. (11)

Heuristics Simplified decision rules (rules of thumb) that are used to make quick decisions. (12)

Hierarchy of needs Maslow's theory that there are five sets of needs arranged in such a way that lower-level, more basic needs must be satisfied before higher-level needs can be fulfilled. The needs are physiological, safety, social, esteem, and self-actualization. (6)

Hindsight bias The claim that one would have foreseen the relative inevitability of a known outcome. (1)

Horizontal communication Communication between individuals at the same level in an organization. (16)

Human relations approach An approach recognizing the importance of social factors and processes in explaining worker behavior. (1)

Human resources management A field of study that applies principles of behavioral sciences to design and implement ways of attracting, developing, and motivating individuals in an organization. (1)

Hybrid form A type of organization design that combines the functional and product forms. (17)

Hygiene factors In two-factor theory, the group of variables that pertains to the context in which a job is performed (e.g., job security, company policies, and working conditions). (6)

Hypothesis A proposition of how the independent and dependent variables are related that is assumed in order to test its logical consequences. (2)

Identification An individual's acceptance of an influence attempt out of a desire to establish or maintain a satisfying relationship with the source of influence. (9)

Illumination experiments One of the Hawthorne studies, showing that psychological aspects of the job setting external to the job itself can influence worker behavior. (1)

Immediacy A concept used in interpreting nonverbal communication based on the fact that people physically approach people whom they evaluate positively and withdraw from those whom they evaluate negatively. (16)

Implicit favorite bias The tendency to have a preferred alternative in a decision-making exercise, and to engage in the review of alternatives so as to confirm the initial prejudice. (12)

Implicit personality theory The tendency to perceive a trait in a person because he or she exhibits a linked trait. (3)

Impressionistic prediction An approach in which we combine intuitive or subjective information about others when attempting to predict behavior. (3)

Independent variable A factor or event believed to influence or cause a change in another variable (the dependent variable). (2)

Induction A process in which a principle is inferred from observing many cases. (2)

Influence Efforts by individuals to change the behavior of others in situations in which they do not possess formal power or authority over their targets. (9)

Informal group A group in which membership is voluntary and based on interpersonal attraction. (13)

Informal leader An individual who lacks formal authority but possesses substantial influence in a group. (10)

Information overload A situation occurring when the information-processing capacities of a member of a communication network are saturated. (16)

Initiating structure A factor referring to the extent to which a leader initiates activity in a group, organizes it, and defines the way that work is to be done. (10)

Instincts Predispositions that are inborn or innate. (6)

Institutionalized arrangements An organization's "way of doing business," exemplified by formal policies, reward systems, and lines of authority and communication. (19)

Integrating department A formal and permanent mechanism with a goal of integrating the efforts of other departments. (14)

Integration A concept that refers to the degree of unity of effort among an organization's subunits. (18)

Intensive technology Operations that use skills or services to transform an object; a hospital exemplifies intensive technology. (18)

Intergroup conflict Conflict that exists between groups. (14)

Interlocking directorates A situation created when a company places board members of another corporation on its own board. (18)

Internal validity The extent to which the independent variable had the intended effect in a study. (2)

Internalization An individual's acceptance of an influence attempt in the belief that the resulting behavior is correct and appropriate. (9)

Interpersonal conflict Conflict that exists between two individuals. (14)

Interval schedule A schedule that reinforces behavior on the basis of time elapsed. (5)

Intervening variable An unobservable state or process that helps explain the link between the independent variable and the dependent variable. (2)

Intrapersonal conflict Conflict that exists within an individual. (14)

Intrinsic reward A reward that is a part of the job itself, such as degree of challenge or responsibility. (7)

Isolate An individual in an organization who has very little or no contact with other members of the organization. (16)

Japanese management A management approach incorporating informal control of employees, an emphasis on quality and productivity, intensive socialization, slow evaluation and promotion, commitment to the worker, and consensus seeking. (19)

Job characteristics theory A model of job enrichment in which the presence of five job characteristics—skill variety, task identity, task significance, autonomy, and feedback—leads to three critical psychological states that in turn result in positive work-related outcomes. (7)

Job description A concise summary description of the duties performed by an employee. (8)

Job diagnostic survey A series of questions designed to determine the extent to which workers view their jobs as possessing the five characteristics of job characteristics theory. (7)

Job enlargement Expansion of a worker's job to include more and varied tasks at the same level; the horizontal expansion of a job. (7)

Job enrichment Efforts to make jobs more satisfying by providing the workers that perform them with greater autonomy and decision-making responsibility; the vertical expansion of a job. (7)

Job involvement   The extent to which an employee identifies with his or her job and relies on personal job performance as evidence of self-worth. (4)

Job maturity   The component of subordinate maturity that is defined in terms of subordinates' technical knowledge and job-related skills. (11)

Job rotation   Systematically shifting workers from one job to another with the goal of increasing motivation and interest. (7)

Job satisfaction   An individual's attitude toward his or her job. One of the more widely studied aspects of the field of organizational behavior. (4)

Laboratory experiment   A type of OB research in which the investigator creates an artificial setting in which variables can be tightly controlled and manipulated. (2)

Last-chance meeting   A technique for countering groupthink in which a meeting is held where members are encouraged to voice any nagging doubts or hesitations about a decision. (12)

Law of attraction   A finding that the greater the proportion of similar attitudes that two people share, the greater the degree of interpersonal attraction. (13)

Law of Effect   A law that proposes that behavior that produces pleasant outcomes is more likely to recur, whereas behavior that produces unpleasant outcomes is less likely to recur. (5)

Leader–member relations   A factor in the contingency model referring to the degree of confidence, trust, and respect that the leader obtains from the group members. (11)

Leadership   The process through which leaders influence the attitudes, behavior, and values of others. (10)

Leadership neutralizer   Individual, task, or organizational characteristic that may prevent the leader from being effective. (11)

Leadership substitute   Individual, task, or organizational characteristic that may make leadership superfluous. (11)

Learning   A fairly permanent change in behavior that occurs as a result of experience. (5)

Least preferred coworker (LPC)   A questionnaire that measures how respondents characterize their feelings about a person with whom they work least effectively. A high LPC score (favoring the least preferred coworker) is considered to indicate a relationship-oriented individual, while a low LPC score is considered to indicate a task-oriented individual. (11)

Legitimate power   Individual power based on the belief that the individual has a legitimate right to exert control over others. (9)

Leniency error   The tendency to rate all ratees favorably. (8)

Liaison   An individual in an organization who serves as a communication link between groups but is not a member of either group. (16)

Locus of control   The extent to which a person believes that his or her behavior has a direct impact on the consequences of that behavior. People with an internal locus of control believe they control their lives themselves. People with an external locus of control view their lives as guided by external factors. (3)

Long-linked technology   Sequential, or serially linked, operations. (18)

Long-run process production   A technology in which the entire manufacturing process is continuous and mechanized. (18)

Loss-aversion bias   A decision-making tendency wherein losses are treated as more important than gains, though their objective value is equal. (12)

Mach Scale   An attitude scale that measures the extent to which individuals agree with Machiavelli's views (and are thus assumed to be domineering and manipulative). (9)

Management by objectives (MBO)   A process in which superiors and their subordinates set goals for a specified time period, at the end of which they meet again to assess the subordinate's performance in terms of the previously designated goals. (7)

Mass production   A technology based on long runs of standardized parts or products. (18)

Mass psychogenic illness   Group outbreaks of physical illness that are psychological in origin and are suspected to be triggered by work-related stress. (15)

Matrix design   A form of organization design in which a product form is superimposed on a functional form, creating a dual system of authority. (17)

Maximize   The attempt to find the best or optimal solution to a problem. (12)

Mechanistic or statistical prediction   An approach to predicting behavior that employs the mathematical manipulation of data. (3)

Mechanistic organization An organization characterized by a high degree of formalization and centralization. (18)

Mediating technology Operations that join otherwise effective, independent units of an organization or different types of customers. (18)

Medium factor A factor in attitude change attempts that involves the effects of the channel employed. (4)

Message factor The specific content and structure of what is transmitted in an attitude change attempt. (4)

Method-bound A term describing a theory that can be supported only by a particular method. (6)

Moderating variable A factor influencing the nature of the relationship between the independent and the dependent variables. (2)

Modified workweek A shortened workweek. The most common form involves working 4 days a week, 10 hours each day (called a 4-40). (7)

Moral involvement Organizational involvement in which members are committed to the socially beneficial features of the organization. (9)

Moral maturity refers to one's stage of ethical judgment. Kohlberg identifies six stages of moral development, grouped into three categories: preconventional level, conventional level, and principled level. (3)

Motivation to manage The desire to attain managerial responsibility. (10)

Motivator factors In two-factor theory, the group of variables that pertains to the content of the job

(e.g., career advancement, degree of responsibility, and feelings of achievement). (6)

Need for achievement The need to excel or to accomplish a goal or task more efficiently than others. (6)

Need for affiliation The need for human companionship. (6)

Need for power The need to control or have an impact on others. (6)

Negative affectivity The stable predisposition to feel dissatisfied with one's job or life in general in the absence of any objective source of stress. (4)

Negative reinforcement The use of stimuli to weaken undesired responses, leading to their elimination. (5)

Negotiation An interactive process, wherein two or more groups discuss the allocation of resources. (14)

Networks Patterns of relationships. (16)

Nominal group technique (NGT) A technique for improving group decision making in which a small group of individuals presents and discusses its ideas before privately voting on its preferred course of action. The group's decision is derived by pooling the votes into a single preferred alternative. (12)

Noncomplementary transaction In transactional analysis, a relationship between two people that is unexpected or unpredictable. (16)

Nonprogrammed decision A decision made about a unique, complex situation for which there is no preestablished course of action. (12)

Nonverbal communication The transmission of information through facial expressions, eye contact, body language, and the use of physical objects and space. (16)

Nonverbal cues Messages sent with facial expressions, posture, shifts of tone or pitch of voice, and eye and head movements. (3)

Normative power Organizational power that relies on its members' sense of affiliation with the organization and its values. (9)

Norming The third stage of group development, in which group cohesiveness develops. (13)

Norms Written or unwritten rules of conduct that guide group members' behavior. (13, 19)

OB Mod The application of operant conditioning principles to individuals in organizational settings, usually aimed at increasing desired behaviors through the use of positive reinforcement. (5)

Observational learning The learning that occurs when an individual witnesses the behavior of another and vicariously experiences the outcomes of the other person's actions. (5)

One-group pretest–post-test design A pre-experimental evaluation design that provides a baseline comparison measurement by testing before and after a program, but does not control many confounding variables, i.e., other change-producing events or the testing process itself. (20)

Open group A group that frequently changes its membership. (13)

Open system A system that has some degree of interaction with its external environment. All organizations are open systems, though they vary in degree of environmental interaction. (18)

Operant conditioning A form of learning in which behaviors that produce positive outcomes or eliminate negative ones are acquired or strengthened. (5)

Organic organization An organization characterized by a relatively low degree of formalization and centralization. (18)

Organizational behavior (OB) The study of human behavior within an organizational setting. OB borrows many concepts and methods from such fields as psychology, sociology, and cultural anthropology to explore (1) individual perceptions and values, (2) interpersonal and work-group processes, and (3) organizational and environmental forces. (1)

Organizational Citizenship Behaviors Voluntary, on-the-job, behaviors that reflect altruism, courtesy, sportsmanship, conscientiousness, and civic virtue, and that promote the smooth operation of an organization. (8)

Organizational commitment The degree to which an employee identifies with an organization and its goals, as well as the employee's desire to maintain membership. (4)

Organizational culture The system of values, beliefs, and norms that exists in an organization and that is transmitted to new employees. (19)

Organizational decision making Decisions that pertain to the problems and practices of organizations. (12)

Organizational decline Cutbacks in the size of an organization's

profits, budget, work force, or clients. (20)

Organizational development (OD) The process of introducing and managing changes in organizational settings. (1, 20)

Organizational form In the population ecology perspective, a configuration of an organization's goals, human resources, products, and technology that will be acceptable to the environment. (18)

Organizational politics Activities used to acquire, develop, and use power to attain one's preferred (and usually selfish) outcome in situations in which there is uncertainty or disagreement. (9)

Organizational theory A field of study focusing on the organization (and such attributes as goals, technology, and culture) as a unit of analysis. (1)

Paired comparison A technique for evaluating performance that entails comparing employees two at a time. (8)

Paradigm An implicit or underlying framework that identifies specific variables and suggests how these variables are arranged in a causal sequence. (10)

Partial reinforcement A situation in which a response is rewarded in a noncontinuous or variable manner. Behavior acquired under partial reinforcement is usually more resistant to extinction than that acquired under continuous reinforcement. (5)

Participative leadership In path-goal theory, a leader behavior in which the leader shares authority and responsibility with subordinates, encouraging their participation in decision making and on matters affecting their jobs. (11)

Path–goal theory A theory based on the expectancy model of motivation suggesting that leaders can affect the satisfaction and performance of subordinates by basing rewards on the accomplishment of performance goals and by clarifying the path to these goals. (11)

Peak experience An intense, mystical experience in which a person exists in a state of joy, fulfillment, and wonderment. (6)

Perceived role The set of behaviors that an individual believes he or she is expected to perform. (13)

Perception The process by which the individual receives and interprets information about the environment. (3)

Perceptual distortion The act of altering perception to avoid an unpleasant reality. Forms include denying events, modifying or distorting reality, seeing only what we want to see, and accepting illusions. (3)

Performing The fourth and final stage of group development, in which the group directs its energies toward performance of valued goals. (13)

Personal decision making Decisions that directly affect an individual rather than others. (12)

Personal experience bias The tendency to be influenced by vivid, personal experiences rather than by valid and relevant objective information when making a decision. (12)

Personal space zones Culturally defined distances that exist between people. (16)

Personality The set of traits and characteristics that form a pattern distinguishing one person from all others. (3)

Personality inventories A widely used method of assessing personality characteristics that asks respondents to indicate whether statements are applicable to themselves. (3)

Personality ratings A device for assessing personality in which respondents rate themselves on scales either with adjectives as endpoints or with specific definitions for each point in the scale. (3)

Population ecology perspective A view of how organizations relate to their environment contending that the success of an organization depends on its finding a niche in a highly competitive surrounding. (18)

Porter–Lawler model A conceptual framework that attempts to integrate the various approaches to motivation. (6)

Position power A factor in the contingency model referring to the power inherent in a position. (11)

Positive reinforcement The use of stimuli to strengthen desired responses, leading to their recurrence. (5)

Power The ability of a person or group to change the attitudes or behavior of others. (9, 16)

Pre-experimental design A form of evaluation research in which observations are taken after the occurrence of a program. This design omits any baseline comparison measurement and does not control variables. (20)

Prepotency In Maslow's hierarchy of needs, the capacity of lower-order needs to assert themselves over higher-order needs. (6)

Pretest–post-test control group design An experimental evaluation design that adds a control group to the one-group pretest–post-test design and assigns subjects to either group by a random procedure. (20)

Procedural justice The fairness of the manner (or method) by which rewards are allocated, as perceived by the recipient of a reward. (6)

Process theories Theories that focus on the process by which rewards control behavior. Examples are expectancy, equity, and reinforcement theories. (6)

Product form A basic type of organization design that groups personnel and activities according to a product line. (17)

Programmed decision A fairly routine decision that can be made according to preestablished procedures. (12)

Progressive discipline The use of a sequence of penalties for infractions of rules, in which each penalty is more severe than the preceding one. (5)

Projection The tendency to ascribe our emotions and attributes to others; a defense mechanism. (3)

Projective techniques Tests that are based on the idea that people will provide highly individualistic responses to ambiguous stimuli. Projective techniques include the Rorschach test, storytelling, and sentence completions. (3)

Proxemics The study of physical space as a form of nonverbal communication. (16)

Psychological maturity A component of subordinate maturity that is defined in terms of the subordinate's self-confidence, and willingness and ability to take on responsibility. (11)

Punishment The presentation of an unpleasant event that follows an undesirable behavior. It is a negative reinforcer that attempts to eliminate the undesired behavior. (5)

Qualitative approach The attempt to study organizational behavior by relying on relatively more subjective techniques for gathering information, in order to obtain new insights. (2)

Quality circle A small group of workers who volunteer to meet regularly to identify, analyze, and solve quality and related problems pertaining to their work. (7)

Quality of work life (QWL) An organizational development approach that seeks to enhance the work climate of an organization. QWL programs are assumed to improve both productivity and employees' psychological experiences at work. (20)

Quasi-experimental design A form of evaluation research in which a control group does not exist, but inferences are cautiously drawn from patterns in available data. (20)

Random assignment A situation afforded by laboratory experiments, in which individuals have an equal likelihood of being placed in an experimental group or a comparison group. (2)

Ratio schedule A schedule that reinforces behavior on the basis of the number of times a behavior is performed. (5)

Rational–economic model A model that assumes that decision making is and should be a rational process consisting of a sequence of steps that enhance the probability of attaining a desired goal. *See also* Classical decision theory. (12)

Reactivity In evaluation research, a problem occurring when the employees respond to the testing process itself. (20)

Referent power Individual power based on a high level of admiration or respect for the power holder. (9)

Refreezing The third phase of Lewin's model of change, in which newly created systems or behaviors become part of ongoing organizational processes. (20)

Reinforcement theory A theory using operant conditioning principles that views present behavior as a function of the consequences of past behavior. (6)

Relay Assembly Room study One of the Hawthorne studies, which first suggested that increased productivity could be partially attributed to the employees' awareness that they are being observed (the Hawthorne effect). (1)

Representativeness heuristic An assessment made on the basis of the similarity between the specific attributes of a given event or object and the attributes of a class of such events or objects. (12)

Resistance to extinction The persistence of a behavior in the absence of reinforcement. (5)

Resource dependence model A view of how organizations relate to their environment contending that the success of an organization is a function of how well it manages its environment. (18)

Retention A stage in the population ecology perspective in which certain successful organizational forms are institutionalized. (18)

Retrofit To introduce self-directed work teams to an existing work force. (7)

Reward power Individual power based on the extent to which one person controls rewards valued by another. The opposite of coercive power. (9)

Risky shift The tendency for groups to make riskier decisions than individuals. (12)

Role The set of expected behaviors associated with an individual's position in a group. (13)

Role ambiguity A situation occurring when an individual is uncertain about how he or she is expected to behave in a role. (13, 15)

Role conflict A situation occurring when an individual receives conflicting messages regarding appropriate role behavior. (13, 15)

Role episode The process by which individuals receive information about their role and adjust their behavior accordingly. (13)

Role overload A situation occurring when too many activities are expected of an employee given the time available and ability level of the employee. (15)

Rorschach test A projective technique for assessing personality consisting of inkblots that the respondent describes in terms of what they look like to him or her. (3)

Rumors Unverified beliefs transmitted through informal channels within an organization. (16)

Sandwich approach A method of conducting feedback interviews in which positive points of the employee's performance are followed by discussion of negative aspects, and ending on a positive note. (8)

Satisfice A situation in which a decision maker considers alternatives only until one arises that is minimally acceptable and then looks no farther. (12)

Scientific management One of the first approaches to managing worker behavior, developed by Frederick W. Taylor, an engineer. Scientific management sought to improve job performance by (1) measuring productivity, (2) emphasizing efficiency in job procedures, and (3) instituting incentive pay schemes. (1)

Selection A stage in the population ecology perspective in which only organizations that possess the needed form survive, and those that do not, fail. (18)

Selective perception The tendency to be influenced by our own interests. (3)

Selective perception bias The tendency to attend only to specific information because of strong prior expectations. (12)

Self-directed work team A highly trained group of employees, responsible for creating a product, sharing decision making, and rotating jobs, with pay based on skill proficiency. (7)

Self-efficacy Feelings of competency that are derived from a sense of being able to master a task. (5)

Self-fulfilling prophecy (SFP) A phenomenon in which ratees perform in accordance with a rater's prophecy, or expectations, for them. (7)

Self-serving bias The tendency to attribute success to internal factors and to attribute failure to external factors. (3)

Semantic differential scale A method of measuring attitudes that asks for ratings on a scale anchored by a pair of adjectives opposite in meaning. (4)

Sensitivity training An organizational development technique that seeks to enhance employees' understanding of their own behavior and its impact on others. Such enhanced sensitivity is assumed to reduce interpersonal conflict in the organization. (20)

Sentence completion A projective technique for assessing personality in which respondents are asked to supply the endings for a series of incomplete sentences. (3)

Shaping A behavior modification technique in which the individual receives reinforcement for small successive approximations of the desired behavior. (5)

Situational favorableness In the contingency model, the notion of how easy or difficult a situation might be for a leader. Three factors—leader–member relations, task structure, and position power—combine to represent a range of possible situations. (11)

Situational tests A technique involving the direct observation of an individual's behavior in a test situation designed to provide information about personality. (3)

Social exchange theory A theory suggesting that in relationships people continually monitor the difference between rewards and costs, and judge the outcomes against two standards: a comparison level and a comparison level of alternatives. (13)

Social facilitation effect The tendency for the presence of others to enhance an individual's performance. (13)

Social inhibition effect The tendency for the presence of others to impair an individual's performance. (13)

Socialization Deliberate efforts by employers to increase employee identification and commitment through training programs and rules for conduct and appearance. (19)

Social learning theory An approach to motivation emphasizing the importance of modeling and self-regulatory processes in learning. (6)

Social loafing The tendency for group members to exert less individual effort on a task the larger the group size. (12)

Sociofugal areas Arrangements of physical space that drive people away from each other. (16)

Sociopetal areas Arrangements of physical space that bring people together. (16)

Sociotechnical system The view that every organization is simultaneously a technical and a social system and that attempts to change either system must take into account their interrelatedness. (17)

Solomon four-group design An experimental evaluation design that attempts to eliminate reactivity to being pretested by adding to the pretest–post-test control group design two groups, one of which is a control group, that are only post-tested. (20)

Source factor A factor involved in attitude change that refers to the individual characteristics of the presenter of an attitude change attempt. (4)

Span of control The number of people who report to a given supervisor. (17)

Status The social ranking or worth accorded to an individual because of the position he or she occupies in a group. (13)

Status incongruence A situation in which all dimensions of an individual's status are not congruent. (13)

Stepladder technique A decision-making structure for groups that begins with a small, core group and, through adding members one at a time, actively involves all members in making the final decision. (12)

Stereotypes Beliefs that all members of a group (e.g., a racial, ethnic, religious, or occupational group) share the same traits and behaviors. (3)

Storming The second stage of group development, in which members wrestle with the division of power and status. (13)

Storytelling A projective technique for assessing personality in which respondents supply stories about pictures they are shown. *See also* Thematic Apperception Test (3)

Strategic alliance A cooperative venture involving two or more firms within technically related areas. (18)

Strategy A plan of action formulated by top-level management to deal with the future. (18)

Stress Physical and psychological reactions experienced by an individual when confronted with a threatening or excessively demanding situation (such as extreme conflict). (15)

Strokes Positive reactions from others, including praise and recognition. In transactional analysis, the giving and getting of strokes is seen as motivating much of the social interplay of people in organizations. (16)

Strong culture A set of values and norms that is widely endorsed and intensely held. (19)

Structural dimensions An organization's internal characteristics, such as degree of specialization, hierarchy, and decentralization. (18)

Subculture A set of values and norms that is unique to a given organizational unit. (19)

Subjective probabilities Estimates of the likelihood that one event will follow another (e.g., that performance will lead to a given outcome). (6)

Subliminal influences Factors influencing perceptions that occur below the threshold of awareness. (3)

Subordinate maturity The critical situational attribute in the Hersey–Blanchard model. It consists of the job maturity and psychological maturity of the subordinate for a given task. (11)

Supportive leadership In path–goal theory, a leader behavior that entails being sensitive to and supportive of group members' needs. (11)

Survey A type of OB research in which a set of written or oral questions is designed to collect personal responses about a topic of interest to the investigator. (2)

Survey feedback An organizational development technique in which questionnaires are used to obtain information on issues of concern, and the results are summarized and returned to employees for consideration and interpretation. (20)

Symbolism Includes rituals and ceremonies. Symbols communicate values, legitimize practices, and help to socialize members and build loyalty. (19)

Tall structure Describes an organization with more levels of authority and smaller spans of control. (17)

Task orientation A style of leadership referring to the extent to which a leader shows concern for getting a job done and helps steer the group to meet its goals. (10)

Task structure A factor in the contingency model referring to the degree to which a job can be clearly specified. (11)

Team building An organizational development program designed to help existing work groups or newly formed special groups improve performance by tackling obstacles and problems. (20)

Technology The knowledge, tools, and techniques used by organizations in performing their work. (18)

Telecommuting The use of a computer link to complete all or part of one's job at home. (7)

Territory A specific physical location toward which an individual has a proprietary attitude. (16)

Thematic Apperception Test A storytelling device for assessing personality composed of 20 pictures portraying situations of ambiguous meaning. The respondent constructs stories that are analyzed for recurrent themes. (3)

Theory X A philosophy of human nature that holds that people are passive, self-interested, lacking in ambition, and desirous of being led. (10)

Theory Y A philosophy of human nature that holds that people are active, supportive of their employees, ambitious, and seeking self-control in the workplace. (10)

Theory Z A management approach developed by William Ouchi that incorporates Japanese management principles. (19)

360-degree feedback An evaluative process in which information is obtained from a full range of sources (supervisors, peers, subordinates, customers, the employee, and consultants). (8)

Time management A strategy for coping with job-related stress through effective self-management. (15)

Time-series design A quasi-experimental research design that allows repeated testing before and after a program. (20)

Total Quality Management A set of principles that emphasizes establishing and maintaining high-quality output. (7)

Transactional analysis Originally a psychotherapeutic device, a set of concepts used in organizations to teach people how to communicate more effectively. In each two-person interaction, the participants are viewed as acting out of three ego states: Parent, Adult, or Child, and such transactions are termed either complementary or noncomplementary. (16)

Transactional leadership A leadership style based on exchanges of rewards for performance. (10)

Transformational leadership A leadership style that implies reshaping the entire strategy of an organization. (10)

Triarchic model of intelligence A view of general intelligence that argues for the notion of three fundamental components: analytical reasoning, social intelligence, and creativity. (10)

Two-factor theory Herzberg's theory of job satisfaction contending that satisfaction and dissatisfaction stem from different groups of variables, termed motivator and hygiene factors. (6)

Type A personality A personality type characterized by impatience, competitiveness, and the drive to succeed. (15)

Type B personality A personality type characterized by a relaxed, easygoing, noncompetitive attitude toward work and life. (15)

Unconditioned response In classical conditioning, a reflexive response evoked by the occurrence of an unconditioned stimulus. (5)

Unconditioned stimulus In classical conditioning, a stimulus that has the ability to evoke a natural reflexive response (an unconditioned response). (5)

Unfreezing The first phase in Lewin's model of change, in which people become aware of the need for change. (20)

Unit production A technology in which products are custom-made in response to specific customer orders. (18)

Unity of command A concept maintaining that employees are accountable to and take orders from only one superior. (17)

Unobtrusive measure A research approach that does not disturb or interfere with the subject's usual behavior. (2)

Upward communication Communication that flows from lower to higher levels within an organization. (16)

Utilitarian power Organizational power that relies on contingent incentives to extract compliance from members. (9)

Valence The value a person places on rewards that he or she expects to receive. (6)

Values Preferences of an organization's members from among activities and outcomes. (19)

Variable interval schedule A schedule in which a reward is applied after a variable amount of time has passed since the last reward was given. (5)

Variable ratio schedule A schedule in which a reward is applied after a variable number of responses are performed. (5)

Variable schedule A schedule for reinforcement in which the amount of time or number of responses performed varies. (5)

Variation A stage in the population ecology perspective referring to the development of organizations with unique attributes. (18)

Verification Determining the truth or falsehood of a hypothesis by gathering data to test whether the prediction holds. (2)

Vertical dyad linkage model A model stressing the importance of individual relationships between leader and subordinates. Each relationship is termed a vertical dyad. (11)

Vertical integration A situation that occurs when one organization acquires another with the goal of controlling forces that affect its production process. (18)

Vroom–Yetton model A model that focuses on selecting the appropriate leadership style for decision making, based on situational considerations. The model proposes five styles: two are autocratic (AI and AII), two are consultative (CI and CII), and one is oriented to a group decision. (G). (11)

Wellness program A proactive approach to health management that focuses on prevention of illness. (15)

Work ethic A belief in the dignity of all work, especially the belief that hard work brings success. (3)

Name Index

Organization Index

Subject Index